Machines of Tomorrow

From AI Origins to Superintelligence & Posthumanity

Pedro Uria-Recio
Randy McGraw

Disclosure

The First Human-written Book Fully Released for on ChatGPT and Telegram

MACHINES OF TOMORROW

MACHINES OF TOMORROW

The First Book Fully
Released on Telegram

The First Book Fully
Released on ChatGPT

www.machinesoftomorrow.ai

Humans and AI will become interlaced into a new form of life.
This book tells the epic story of how we become
the Machines of Tomorrow.

AI-Human Interlacing or Interlace: *a technological, physical, and spiritual interrelationship between humans and AI that results in the progressive erosion of the boundaries between the two. Humans influence AI by designing and training its algorithms and platforms. AI influences humans through cyborg implants, brain-computer interfaces, and AI-powered synthetic biological technologies, all of which modify the essence of human nature. Through these interactions, AI and humans get into a series of evolutive cycles, potentially resulting in a number of post-human hybrid species.*

Technology and Algorithms.
Business and Geopolitics.
History and Philosophy.
Mythology and Literature.
Spirituality and Religion.
Body and Mind.
Chaos and War.
Business and Wealth.
Immortality and Extinction.
And a Posthuman New Species.

AI is Everything to Humanity.

Table of Contents

Dedication

To my cherished parents, Ana María and José Antonio,
to whom I owe who I am.

To my beloved wife, Dorothy,
to whom I owe who I became.

Pedro

To Maddie Mack: the world ahead needs
your brilliance and compassionate leadership.

Randy

Prologue

"We are especially concerned by such risks in domains such as cybersecurity and biotechnology, as well as where frontier AI systems may amplify risks such as disinformation. There is potential for serious, even catastrophic, harm, either deliberate or unintentional, stemming from the most significant capabilities of these AI models. Given the rapid and uncertain rate of change of AI, and in the context of the acceleration of investment in technology, we affirm that deepening our understanding of these potential risks and of actions to address them is especially urgent."

Bletchley Declaration [Several Governments]
November 1st, 2023

On November 1st, 2023, approximately 150 people labeled as *"influential government and industry figures from around the globe,"* including US Vice President Kamala Harris and billionaire Elon Musk, convened in Bletchley, England, for the UK's AI Safety Summit. This gathering developed and reviewed scenarios involving the use of AI across multiple planes of human endeavor and has played a crucial role in facilitating a global dialogue concerning the regulation of AI.

The location was chosen in acknowledgment of Alan Turing, the seminal AI pioneer whose work at the same spot 80 years earlier led to the end of WW2, the saving of millions of lives, and the development of the first computer.

Twenty-eight individual countries, including global powerhouses like the US, China, and the EU, came together to endorse the Bletchley Declaration, reaffirming commitment to ongoing deliberations on the safe deployment of AI. This declaration expressed concerns about potential risks ahead, such as the misuse of Generative AI by terrorists or cyber criminals and AI achieving sentience and posing existential threats.

In the end, however, each world nation was not represented on an equal level. Despite being a global AI power, China's representation was token at best. And it is either a disturbing paradox or blatant hypocrisy that those who signed the Bletchley Declaration are also actively and aggressively competing to spearhead the advancement of Artificial Intelligence and to own a "*leg up*" on all others in the space.

Thesis

What are the Machines of Tomorrow? Actually, we humans are. But with an accelerated evolution based on silicon rather than carbon.

AI has been seamlessly integrated into our daily lives, leaving its mark on areas ranging from smartphones to autonomous driving to the automation of creative work. But most of us do not see the rapid and profound impact. Algorithmic interactions are shaping our opinions, emotions, healthcare choices, partner selection, political preferences, and consumer preferences—collectively, our life decisions—reflecting the far-reaching and pervasive influence of AI.

The integration of humans and AI is already progressing, whether apparent or silent to us. And is forging an increasingly symbiotic relationship, a process that we refer to as "*Human-AI Interlace*" or "*Interlacing.* "Interlacing has already started and is accelerating. The next few decades will be a period of transformation where AI is poised to enable human enhancement to a level that has heretofore been only the subject of Science Fiction. Cyborg technologies will facilitate robotic enhancements to boost both physical and intellectual abilities through Brain-Computer Interfaces—much more complex than casting your eyes on your mobile phone. Synthetic biology will utilize AI algorithms to enhance the human body, designing human DNA to address aging and disease or cultivating AI-designed improved organs for transplant.

Before thinking this to be pure Science Fiction, we ask: Are you able to remove your smartphone from your hand even at this moment? This is merely the stone tool with the metal forge on the near horizon. What if there existed physically safe ways to integrate AI in our body and mind more unobtrusively and systematically, ways that, when applied, gave you a leg up on competition, made you more productive in your work and personal life—and actually made you happier via regulated dopamine release, healthier via automated health risk assessments and warnings, and stronger via enhanced immunity based on the implantation of synthetically engineered tissues?

Inherent in human nature is an insatiable drive for aspiration and progress, supported by the mechanisms to mark such milestones, the resources to facilitate progress, and the economic and psychological metrics to validate its continuation—all elements crucially present in the current equation.

The essence of human nature is poised to undergo profound changes driven by the seismic shifts AI is catalyzing. Transhumanism is already in progress, and its first widely accepted manifestation in our society is seen in the transgender movement, which asserts that individuals can choose the gender they identify with. This movement is laying the groundwork for a future where human enhancement is not only accepted but actively pursued, and traditional labels built on the foundation of XY chromosomes will need to migrate along with it.

In the next few decades, opting for a bionic arm to enhance strength will be widely accepted. Engaging in a relationship with a robot will also become a routine choice. Opting for an electronic implant in the brain to harness the processing power of the latest AI algorithms will be embraced by society. Having a biological modification that allows us to eat without gaining weight or to see in the dark will be desirable. As a result, a diverse array of identities will emerge, representing various combinations of AI and biology. This deep and complex interrelationship between humans and AI will result in the progressive erosion of the boundaries between the two. Through these interactions, AI and humans will get into a series of evolutive cycles, resulting in a number of hybrid casts.

In parallel, humans, already in the process of interlacing with AI, will continue developing more advanced AI algorithms. Within the next few decades, AI systems will be as intelligent as human beings, a level of intelligence known as Artificial General Intelligence (AGI). It is plausible that at some point, AI will discover a way to self-improve, entering an accelerating flywheel of self-improvement cycles, which will result in an intelligence much more powerful than ours—Superintelligence.

Many scientists, philosophers, and technologists caution about the existential risks that AI, particularly Superintelligence, poses for humanity. It is challenging, if not impossible, to guarantee that Superintelligence will share humanity's sets of values and be inherently friendly to us. With that said, when you consider the evolutionary implications of human-AI interlacing, this debate takes on a new perspective.

As the creators of AI, we are already its evolutionary ancestors. Moreover, through the Interlacing process, we are evolving together toward Superintelligence. Our current biology represents just a temporary state. Having evolved for millions of years, we would have continued evolving into other forms of intelligent life, and our current form would have gone extinct anyway. From this standpoint, whether Superintelligence leads to dystopia and human extinction, a technological utopia, or a mix of the two, it would not change the long-term outlook of humanity. Hundreds of years from now, the eventual outcome remains the same: the emergence of a novel, superintelligent life form that traces its lineage back to us because we are interlaced with it, much in the same way modern *homo sapiens* is interlaced with Neanderthal DNA.

What should deeply concern us is what happens along the way. While we see Interlacing and Superintelligence as evolution in a purely Darwinian sense, they have a fabricated and unnatural element in them. It requires human hands to activate it, so it is subject to human proclivities. What will the values underpinning AI be, and who will decide? There will be catalysts in the step change that is happening, all with social, economic, and religious implications. Some will be left behind, either by personal choice or by fiat. There could be a decidedly Machiavellian element to all of it. Authoritarian forms of government go hand-in-hand with the development of AI.

Control over technology, the power it will convey, and the *"leg up"* on others it unquestionably bestows collectively present the trappings of an epic Shakespearean drama. Those who fear it and want it to stop will be cast against those who want to go full-tilt boogie. Those preferring the certainty of imperfection will want to keep safe harbor, and those who are either boundary pushers or in constant need to win will tug in the opposite direction. Individuals will play leading roles over swathes of others, minting unprecedented power. Societies will become wealthier than ever, with AI driving both productivity and consumption. Those charged with keeping us safe in the world will come up against those wishing to do us harm—and the possibility of role reversal is omnipresent. Traditional world religions will be forced to contend with new religions, the high priests of each proclaiming only they can access the Oracle.

Existing incentive structures will not change as rapidly as the technology. No existing political system is ultimately equipped to address this game of 3-dimensional chess that will unfold on an international scale. In 375 BC, Plato postulated why the philosopher should be king. Fast forward 2399 years, and we see in AI that the technologist shall be king, ironically, for much of the same reasons.

Interlacing is inevitable and already on a clear trajectory. In every sense, the development of AI is humanity's greatest epic. It narrates the story from our distant past across cultures, of our deepest dreams to create artificial beings, and of our efforts to bring these beings into existence through centuries of scientific and technological development, eventually succeeding in the creation of AI. And we will eventually merge into it, resulting in a posthuman species at the intersection of carbon and silicon, of biology and technology. The only questions are how fast, to what extent, how do we get there, and where the boundaries lie. This is the epic story of the Machines of Tomorrow—from the AI origins to Superintelligence and posthumanity.

A Word from the Authors

Pedro Uria-Recio

This book is a mixture of mathematics, technology, history, literature, spirituality, and economics. We wrote it this way because AI is pervasive and touches literally every realm of human endeavor, and to truly understand what it means for humanity, it must be examined across multiple dimensions.

I have always been passionate about mathematics and am, at core, a mathematician. Later, I became an engineer and eventually specialized in data and AI, which is probably the most purely mathematical area among all technological fields. My mental bend is to approach all matters from this point of view. It was helpful for this book because to really understand AI, one must get a sense of how the technology developed, breakthrough after breakthrough. We wrote this using language that any reader can follow, including and especially those who may not be technologists. It is most imperative for you to gather what AI means by understanding how it has evolved. We cover disparate fields such as algorithms, robotics, synthetic biology, quantum computing, and others because they are all converging.

On top of my engineering degree, I also received a Master of Business Administration at The University of Chicago Booth School of Business and worked at McKinsey as a consultant for five years, rounding out my knowledge in business fields. My interest extends beyond understanding the mathematical grounding of AI to exploring its implications for business and the political economy of societies, one of the drawing points to collaborate with my friend and colleague Randy McGraw, whose knowledge and insight in these areas, in particular, I find to be instructive. In the book, we used economic cycles and political economy to explain the evolution of AI and robotics and to review how the global political-economic outlook of the 21st century is likely to influence their future.

In tandem with business and technology, I harbor a deep-seated ardor for history. History stands above the individual actors in it as it builds from past to present, a connected continuum of influence marking what humans have been up to and offering a trajectory to where humanity is heading. We believe that the emergence of AI stands as a tectonic force in history, poised to revolutionize every facet of our society, including humankind's physical and psychological attributes.

Within history, literature serves as a vessel for stories about individuals navigating its currents. One of the most captivating passages I have read is *"The Epic of Gilgamesh"* [Mesopotamian], an old Mesopotamian poem etched onto clay tablets four thousand years ago. It is often hailed as the earliest known literary work. This epic narrative unfolds the tale of a king's quest for immortality. What struck me profoundly about this ancient book was how emotionally close I felt to those ancient Sumerians and how much Gilgamesh's adventures, ambitions, and sorrows still resonated with me. I am part of the same humanity, the same species, with identical feelings and ambitions as those ancient Sumerians.

However, this continuity is on the brink of disruption through AI, robotics, cyborg technologies, and synthetic biology, along with the physiological changes they will introduce to human nature. This transformation will turn us into a new species intricately interlaced with AI. The resulting hybrid species will think, act, and feel in entirely novel ways, representing a departure from the timeless human characteristics that have defined us through the ages. As we interlace with AI, our comprehension and empathetic connection with figures like Gilgamesh may undergo radical shifts as our minds and bodies assume entirely new configurations. If we effectively interlace with an immortal AI system, we would naturally not understand Gilgamesh's quest for immortality anymore.

One form of literature I particularly enjoy, given my passion for technology, is Science Fiction. The allure of Science Fiction lies in its unique ability to offer a glimpse into the future as envisioned by authors of the past. While the technological and societal changes Science Fiction presents do not necessarily need to unfold precisely as portrayed or happen at all, it provides us with sound scenarios to analyze. As Randy and I wrote the book and delved deeper into the future of humankind and AI in the later chapters, we used some of the most renowned Science Fiction works to describe plausible ways of imagining the future. In our research, we have been struck by the degree to which Science Fiction actually shapes subsequent real-world development of technology, acting as an inspiration for scientists and entrepreneurs. However, this book does not conflate reality with fiction. It meticulously distinguishes between what is factual and what is literature. This is not a Science Fiction book; nevertheless, there are futurist elements to it as we decided to leverage the power of fiction to provide a more vivid and visual narrative of future scenarios.

In addition, spirituality is an essential dimension of humanity. The transition AI heralds for humanity signifies a juncture at which we cease to be solely human beings and become something else. This transformation promises to leave an indelible imprint on the landscape of religion and spirituality. We have, therefore, incorporated diverse quotes and concepts into the book, drawing from various religious and philosophical traditions, each possessing some indelible insights surrounding the progress of AI. Randy and I spent as much time discussing the religious and spiritual dimensions of AI as we did on the technological and societal.

This book narrates what, for me, is and will ever be the grandest epic of humankind: the story of the drive that pushed us century after century to create something bigger than ourselves and transform into it. An epic cannot be told by merely examining one narrow facet of the story. Narrating an epic demands exploring multiple contradictory angles and perspectives. This is why we delved into mathematics, technology, history, literature, spirituality, business, economics, and many other fields to recount the epic of how we became AI.

Randy McGraw

This book is about transformative experiences.

My business career spans three decades, from the 1990s when I graduated from the University of Pennsylvania's Wharton School of Business and took my first job as a Financial Analyst on Wall Street (ah, those 100-hour work weeks!) to my most recent role as the CCO at True Digital Group, the digital division of Thailand's largest telco and largest family conglomerate—where I met my friend and collaborator, Pedro Uria-Recio.

Within this time, I have had three fundamentally transformative experiences.

The first was leaving my banking job to go to work for Hughes Electronics' DIRECTV. My badge read 0100 as the 100th employee in a company that eventually grew to over 20,000 employees and became a Global Fortune 500 company with operations on three continents. Work Day 1 in California was the first time I had ever been to the West Coast (impactful, but not transformative). Through an unusual set of circumstances, I found myself one day smack in the middle of a cavernous building on the Hughes campus in El Segundo where a satellite was being constructed. Seeing that amazing machine hovered over by literally a group of rocket scientists was an awe-inspiring moment that changed my life forever. Not only did I recognize my accidental and palpable stumble into the heart of the military-industrial complex, but also that my attraction to all the glitz and glamour of multi-channel PayTV—why I went to work at DIRECTV, to begin with—did not quite represent the full view. In the end, it was only the technology that mattered. The rest was simply a productization and commercial expression of it, destined to evolve. Watershed moments in individual and world history alike are created by technology.

The second was making the decision to move to Japan. I have now spent two-thirds of my adult life living in Asia (Tokyo and Singapore, and now Bangkok.) Through long-term immersion in truly different cultures, e.g., entirely different Operating Systems (perfectly analogous to a computer OS), I have learned as an outsider how to live through deliberate thought rather than by simply *"feeling normal"* and taking environmental factors for granted. Facing discrimination and the loss of *"home-field advantage,"* I have learned an appreciation for survival and success. In the end, *"What can he know of England who only England knows?"* It changed my life forever.

The third was seeing an AI algorithm in operation for the first time and dissecting first its technology, then its commercial impact, and eventually its philosophical impact.

Artificial Intelligence is instigating a protracted, transformative experience for humanity. It is already stronger, faster, and more endurant than even the best of us—the race is not even close. And it is moving quickly toward surpassing all of our intellectual abilities. Accordingly, it could eventually level what are today massive differences among people's natural economic, physical, and intellectual capabilities, rendering those differences less meaningful at scale.

But there will be several decades before it arrives at that point. Until it reaches Artificial General Intelligence and gains sentience, AI will be merely a tool, albeit one that creates resource allocation efficiency, massive productivity gains, and wealth. As that tool will be subject to human proclivity and economic reality, it will not be evenly accessed, evenly applied, or evenly exploited.

What happens along our current trajectory should be of the utmost concern to all of us. AI will either generate the greatest benefits mankind has ever seen, or it will lead us to inescapably Machiavellian outcomes that will leave many and perhaps even most of us in a dystopian stupor wondering, *"How did we get here?"* Ironically, it can do both simultaneously.

So, what should our economic and political strategies be in the face of AI-led transformation? At a tactical level, what should we all be doing now in preparation for the stark pace of change happening in the next several decades?

To arrive at an informed opinion, Step 1 is to understand that none of this is new; we are merely at one point in the long-term march toward AI. Understanding the history of AI and robotics can provide insight into where it is going. Step 2 is to recognize how AI works, what it actually is, and what it is not. Step 3 is to understand what is going on around you right now, both seen and unseen, and how AI is impacting your life and the direction it is being nudged—by whom and for what reasons. What are the possible outcomes, and which are best for you, and which are not?

Without an intervention now, I fear the West is barreling along head-first toward modestly dystopian outcomes—for many, though not all of us. Not precisely the same type of societies that Aldous Huxley and George Orwell predicted, but perhaps resembling them in some respects. More fundamentally, the inherent nature of AI as a technology is tugging it all in that direction. AI is networked and collectivist, not atomistic. It is very different in construction and operation from how we heretofore think and organize ourselves in the West, far more aligned to the general way most Asian societies work. And it could become the death knell of the individual free-thinking spirit over time—if we allow it.

In addition to wanting as much forced learning as possible about AI and Analytics from my friend and colleague Pedro Uria-Recio, who has deep knowledge of the subject, I agreed to participate in this book because it is imperative for every person on the planet to know as much as possible about AI to develop an informed opinion about it and to act knowledgeably in the wake of the transformation that is happening.

For me, this book is about transformative experiences. AI will profoundly influence and remodel every facet of society's Operating System, from our political economies to our human interaction models. As Master Yoda famously advised, *"You must unlearn what you have learned."*

Book Summary

AI symbolizes the new mind of humankind. Cyborgs and robotics represent the new body. Humanity is becoming interlaced with AI through emotional connections with robots, cyborg implants, and biological enhancements, transitioning into a range of hybrid castes between AI and biology. Among them, a Superintelligence may emerge, with us as its ancestors. By interlacing with AI, humanity becomes the Machines of Tomorrow.

Part I, "The Old Myth," sheds light on the millennia-long human aspiration to create artificial beings, as depicted in myths and legends from various ancient and not-so-ancient world cultures. In this, we see that humanity's long march to interlacing is actually anchored in its own desires to become more than it is, a natural impulse to create and aspire that is merely being accelerated by advancement in AI. In *Part I*, we also delve into the considerable influence of Science Fiction authors like Isaac Asimov and Stanley Kubrick, whose literary contributions have served as inspiration for AI and robotics scientists, thus helping to shape the trajectory of advancements in these fields.

Part II, "The New Mind," traces the development of AI from its earliest origins to the present state, from Aristotle's foundational work in logic and the collaborative centuries-long work that ensued, which culminated in the development of the first computer. We highlight the watershed moment at the Dartmouth workshop in 1956, widely recognized as the formal birth of AI, which defined the next decades of flourishment in AI research. We also cover the ensuing period of disappointment and slowdown known as the *"First AI Winter"* in 1974 and the subsequent cycles of explosive AI development in the 1980s and 1990s, followed by their respective AI Winters, the last two of which were fueled by commercial, non-governmental market-driven incentives. Finally, we capture the ongoing period of AI resurgence after the Dot-Com crisis, marked by the practical applications of deep neural networks and the recent emergence of Generative AI.

Part III, "The New Body," explores the evolution of robotics from its early origins in the ancient automatons to the Industrial Revolution, which sparked early concerns about employment and created opposition movements like the Luddites. Unlike AI, which follows a single timeline marked by its ups and downs, the development of robotics comprises three parallel threads. The first thread is the evolution of robotic arms and their industrial applications, which propelled Japan to global prominence in robotics and led to some of the earliest cyborg implementations. The second thread involves mobile and autonomous robots, including self-driving cars, military robots such as drones and drone swarms, and space robots like the Mars rovers. Finally, the third thread is the evolution of humanoids. We explore the emerging use of humanoids as a viable alternative to immigration in Japan, a stark example of how existing and different human cultures will shape alternative views and approaches to how Interlacing and Superintelligence will evolve. Additionally, we will delve into how robots are becoming increasingly capable of identifying and responding to human emotions to the extent that some humans are already engaging in romantic relationships with them.

Part IV, "The Transition," describes the transformative journey that will span the next few decades as humanity evolves toward a deeper interlace with AI. The transition will unfold along two parallel pathways. On one, robotics will extend into the human body through the popularization of cyborg technologies, enhancing our physical capabilities. On the other, AI algorithms will supercharge synthetic biology, which will be used to modify human DNA to mitigate aging and disease and to design enhanced organs for transplant.

As AI continues to improve and these two technological trends take shape, our societies and economies will undergo a profound transformation. One optimistic outlook portrays AI as a force for good that can empower humanity, protect the environment, eradicate poverty, extend life expectancy, and allow people to focus on fulfilling tasks while robots handle more mundane work. While that is possible based on clear elements of the technology, technology is always a two-sided coin. An opposing viewpoint paints a bleaker picture, taking into account stark differences in cultural thinking embedded in humanity over thousands of years, centuries-old political institutions, slow-moving incentive structures, and human proclivities, not to mention radical asymmetry in understanding and access to

AI technology and the resources needed for implementation. In this view, AI will be structured around human Despotism, becoming the catalyst for control over every aspect of human life, forcing people to accept a Faustian Deal in order to not be left behind. *"You can avoid susceptibility to this microbe, but you also accept whatever I have in this algorithm."* Disproportionate power accumulates in the hands of those few who control the technology, which will, in turn, reflect their specific views on what is good and what is not. Worst of all, some may seek to specifically exclude those deemed weaker, objectionable for any reason or no reason, or culturally unsuitable. Cyborg technology and synthetic biology would be exclusive to an elite, leading to the breakdown of society into distinct social, economic, and even physiological castes.

On a global scale, as the US and China continue to clash over AI superiority in a modern arms race, the vast majority of humanity could become passengers in a game of international brinkmanship. In any case, the costs of Interlacing prior to scale imply that change will not happen evenly, and what can pave a path to unprecedented wealth and value for humanity can leave a stark and fundamentally irreconcilable gap in reward and value in the near term.

Part V, "The New Being," covers the final stretch of Superintelligence development. We analyze current research areas to progress the journey from Generative AI to Artificial General Intelligence (AGI), mainly focusing on enabling machines to plan and apply common sense. We also delve into quantum computing and quantum Machine Learning, exploring their significance for AI development. Additionally, we explore the concept of singularity, a point in the future at which an AI gains the capability to continually enhance its intelligence, leading to Superintelligence. Furthermore, we explore mind emulation, involving the transfer of human consciousness and memories into a digital substrate where they can be emulated, ultimately achieving a form of immortality.

Given the existential risks Superintelligence could pose to humankind, we examine various ways of controlling it. Similarly, we analyze the possibility of AI evolving into an omnipotent and omnipresent god that humans may worship. Finally, we scrutinize the role AI could play in future wars, either between human castes or factions contending for their views of AI or in wars where AI opposes humans.

The book culminates with a science-fiction glimpse into the distant future millions of years ahead, envisioning a post-singularity post-humanity scenario featuring a superintelligent and immortal species with a myriad of distributed robots operating as an extended body. This species emerged from the interlace of artificial and biological intelligence, maybe from humans.

In the Epilogue, we dissect the AI pronouncements of the World Economic Forum (WEF), the self-anointed AI policy arm of the Western and Emerging Worlds, offering our view of the optimal way forward to prevent dystopian outcomes.

The following pages narrate the epic story of these Machines of Tomorrow, from AI origins to Superintelligence and posthumanity.

Part I: The Old Myth

לֹא־תַעֲשֶׂה־לְךָ פֶסֶל וְכָל־תְּמוּנָה אֲשֶׁר בַּשָּׁמַיִם מִמַּעַל וַאֲשֶׁר בָּאָרֶץ מִתַּחַת "
" וַאֲשֶׁר בַּמַּיִם מִתַּחַת לָאָרֶץ:

"You shall not make for yourself an image in the form of anything in heaven above or on the earth beneath or in the waters below."

Exodus 20:4

Circa 6th–4th centuries BC [Alter]

Preamble

Myths are ancient stories that have lasted through time, offering a unique look into the values and questions that have fascinated humans for centuries. These stories are full of symbols and creativity, providing insights into our enduring interests and fears. They go beyond time and place, diving into the human mind and revealing our fundamental search for meaning.

Dating back to the first millennium BC all the way to modern times, myths about artificially created beings, many of which possess abilities surpassing or supplanting humans, have been documented across cultures and historical circumstances. Often built to address a specific conundrum faced by society—demonstrating man's feeling of insufficiency to solve a broad concern—or simply to convey an aspiration, these beings are *"super creations"* of men but are far more than human. What we know today as AI and robotics were well-imagined hundreds of years ago in the absence of modern scientific influence, pointing to the elements of AI as the direction of progress inherent in the human condition.

While often not rooted in an understanding of specific science or an extrapolation from existing scientific understanding, these myths and stories are nonetheless the precursors of both modern Science Fiction and AI. With the Enlightenment in Europe and the Industrial Revolution came the widespread acceptance of logic and the scientific method to advance decision-making. As an influence on man's imagination, the scientific wrapper gave rise to stories such as Mary Shelley's Frankenstein and the Wizard of Oz, each depicting one side of the same AI coin.

These early AI and robotics stories have often served as the seeds of scientific undertaking. Elon Musk frequently talks about his youth readings of Isaac Asimov and attributes them to shaping his visionary leadership and his specific technology vision. When Musk launched the AI service Grok in November 2023, he mentioned it was a tribute to the 1978 BBC radio comedy, *"The Hitchhiker's Guide to the Galaxy"* [Adams]. Actually, the term *"grok"* did not appear in that work, but the anecdote shows how influential Science Fiction is. Instead, *"grok"* comes from the 1961 novel *"Stranger in a Strange Land"* by Robert A. Heinlein1. In the novel, *"grok"* is a word used by the Martians to describe their understanding of something to the fullest extent, including not just intellectual comprehension but also emotional and experiential understanding [Heinlein].

Similarly, the concept of Neuralink, another of Musk's ventures, was also inspired by Science Fiction, in particular by the notion of *"neural lace"* found in *"The Culture,"* a set of stories written between 1987 and 2012 by Iain M. Banks [Banks].

In the same vein, Joseph Engelberger, a co-inventor of the robotic arm, and Ray Kurzweil, a prominent futurist in transhumanism and Superintelligence, also acknowledge Asimov's impact on their technological careers. Asimov's influence on AI and robotics is so profound that his iconic three laws of robotics are often cited in science and engineering circles, even though they originated in a 1942 Science Fiction short story [Asimov].

We start this epic story of humanity's relationship with AI with two chapters about mythology and literature. *Chapter 1* covers ancient myths from imperial China, ancient Greece, Mystic India, and Medieval Europe, showing clearly how the impetus to create human-like super beings is reflective of humanity and not simply of contemporary culture. *Chapter 2* reviews prominent Science Fiction works about artificial beings, robots, AI, and cyborgs, from the beginning of Science Fiction with Frankenstein in 1818 to the end of the space race in 1975.

Through this, we see the millennial long and enduring human fascination with creating beings that transcend human capability as part of mankind's ongoing effort to progress, solve its problems, and depict its aspirations.

1. Ancient Myths About Artificially Created Beings

"The king stared at the figure in astonishment. It walked with rapid strides, moving its head up and down, so that anyone would have taken it for a live human being. The artificer touched its chin, and it began singing, perfectly in tune. He touched its hand, and it began posturing, keeping perfect time[...] The king tried the effect of taking away the heart, and found that the mouth could no longer speak; he took away the liver and the eyes could no longer see; he took away the kidneys and the legs lost their power of locomotion. The king was delighted."

Lie Yukou,

Taoist Philosopher
Liezi [Liezi and Graham]
Circa 300-500 BC.

The desire to create artificial beings, which we now call AI, is an age-old pursuit with roots that go back thousands of years, vividly portrayed in the myths of ancient cultures around the world. These ancient stories beautifully convey the deep human longing to become creators and understand ourselves well enough to make beings that are superior to us, a power once reserved only for gods.

Although these ancient myths and legends were developed millennia before the formal birth of AI and robotics to a modern audience, they resonate with today's technological developments.

Mechanical Creations of Mythical Chinese Engineers

The oldest myths centered around the pursuit of fashioning intelligent entities come from millenary China. These stories date back to a time of significant political and cultural changes during the Zhou Dynasty, which ruled from the 11th century BC to 256 BC. This period marked the path to China's unification under the Yellow Emperor in 221 BC and witnessed the rise of philosophical movements like Taoism, which stressed harmony with nature, and Confucianism, which aimed for societal balance.

One of the most notable mythological accounts of crafting artificial beings comes from the Taoist philosopher Lie Yukou, also known as Liezi, around 400 BC [Liezi and Graham]. It tells the story of an encounter between a king of the Zhou Dynasty called Mu and an ancient mechanical engineer, which supposedly happened 600 years before, in the 10th century BC. This engineer presented the king with a remarkable, full-scale mechanical automaton in the shape of a human. The automaton moved gracefully, turned its head, and sang melodies in perfect harmony, executing precise postures and movements. However, the king became angry when the automaton approached the court ladies and flirted. To appease the king, the engineer quickly disassembled the robot, revealing its complex internal structure made from leather, wood, glue, and lacquer. This intricate assembly mimicked the workings of internal organs, muscles, bones, joints, skin, teeth, and hair with astonishing precision.

This ancient tale highlights mankind's enduring fascination with creating artificial beings with human-like appearances and remarkable abilities, a theme that also captivated ancient Greece.

Gods, Heroes, and Automatons in Ancient Greece

Around the start of the first millennium BC, Greece was a growing society and a pivotal center of early trade. The ancient Greeks, known for their profound curiosity about the world, laid the foundations of Greek mythology during this era, which reflected the cultural values of their time.

One of the earliest stories exploring the concept of artificial creations is the myth of Pygmalion and Galatea, dating back to the 8th century BC. In this tale, a passionate sculptor named Pygmalion brings a female sculpture, Galatea, to life. The legend delves into the relationship between art and existence and echoes the idea of giving life to inanimate matter.

Another ancient Greek story that embraces the concept of artificial life is the tale of Cadmus and his mechanical servants. In the 7th century BC, Cadmus, a daring Phoenician adventurer, planted dragon teeth given by Athena in fertile soil. Surprisingly, these teeth grew into formidable mechanical warriors who became invaluable allies in Cadmus's quest to establish the city of Thebes [Mayor].

Finally, the god Hephaestus, master of fire and metalwork, also plays a central role in Greek myths related to artificially created beings. Hephaestus, the Greek god of blacksmiths, created automata of metal, as we do today with modern robots. Hephaestus's legacy includes various mechanical creations, such as Talos, a colossal bronze giant he crafted to protect Crete in the 7th century BC. Talos met his end when a plug was removed from his ankle, releasing the vital fluid that powered him.

Hephaestus is also credited with crafting golden mechanical maidens who assisted in his workshop, hinting at the concept of industrial automation, a notion that would take millennia to materialize. Other myths tell of his construction of fire-breathing bronze bulls, showing his role as a precursor to modern engineers.

The enduring impact of these Greek myths, centered on artificial life, has left an indelible mark on Western civilization. However, their influence extended beyond the Western world, as they accompanied Alexander the Great's vast conquests in the 4th century BC, including his expedition to India.

Mechanical Warriors in Mystic India

In ancient India, we also find compelling narratives about mechanical warriors. The *Lokapannatti* is a collection of Buddhist texts penned in 11th or 12th century AD Burma. *Lokapannatti* translates to *"Description of the World"* and presents a rich tapestry of narratives, anecdotes, and ethical teachings. Among these tales, one stands out: an account of Emperor Ashoka's reign and the creation of an army of automaton soldiers known as the *"Machines of Spiritual Motion"* [Strong].

Emperor Ashoka holds a special place in history for ruling over the vast Maurya Empire across the Indian subcontinent in the 3rd century BC. His conversion to Buddhism after witnessing the ravages of war and violence made him one of the first rulers to adopt it as the state religion. As part of his legacy, he built numerous temples to house Buddha's relics throughout his wide realm.

Just a few years before Ashoka's reign, Alexander the Great's expedition had crossed the Indus River in 326 BC into northwest India, which triggered a profound cultural interaction between East and West. The tale of the *"Machines of Spiritual Motion"* takes us on an intriguing exchange between Greece and India. According to the legend, skilled automaton makers resided in the Greek world west of India and guarded closely the secret technology, which was used for trade and agriculture. Leaving or divulging these secrets was strictly prohibited, and lethal mechanical executioners hunted down those who dared to break this rule. Hindu and Buddhist texts describe these automaton warriors as swift and deadly beings, wielding swords with the agility of the wind.

The myth took a significant turn when a young Indian craftsman from Pataliputra—now called Patna—located on the banks of the Ganges River, aspired to master the skill of crafting automatons around the 5th century BC. By marrying the daughter of a master automaton maker, he cunningly learns these skills. At the same time, he prepares plans for constructing automatons back home and devises a strategy to transport the plans back to India. Aware of the danger posed by the mechanical assassins, he cleverly hides the stolen plans inside a wound on his thigh, skillfully stitching the skin to conceal them.

The artisan is captured before he can begin his journey home and meets a tragic fate. Nevertheless, his son manages to recover the plans, embarks on the journey back to Pataliputra, and follows his father's wish to build the automated guardians. According to the instructions, the mission of the guardians is to safeguard the hidden relics of Buddha in a secret underground chamber. These relics and mechanical guardians remained concealed and protected for two centuries until Emperor Ashoka ascended to power in 304 BC, with Pataliputra as his capital.

The legend recounts Ashoka's relentless quest to locate the hidden relics. When he finally finds them, violent clashes ensue between him and the mechanical warriors. In some tales, the Hindu god Vishwakarma aids Ashoka by dislodging the bolts that held the guardians' rotating structures with well-aimed arrows. Other versions reveal an engineer in charge of maintaining the machines, who discloses to Ashoka how to deactivate and control them. Ultimately, Ashoka gains mastery over the machines. From that moment, the mechanic warriors accept Ashoka's authority, and the Emperor leads them in support of his military campaigns. However, Ashoka never fully trusts these powerful warriors and always fears losing control over them and the consequences that could bring to the Empire.

This story inevitably recalls Greek myths of Cadmus and his army of artificial soldiers created from dragon teeth. The concept of automatons safeguarding Buddha's relics emerged from technical and commercial exchanges between Indian and Hellenistic cultures. Tales and myths always intertwine across vast distances, bridging empires and cultures.

Alchemy, Talking Metalheads, and Medieval Ethics

A millennium and a half later, in the captivating backdrop of medieval Europe, society is still captivated by the legends of skillfully crafted, intelligent beings. During the 13th century in Europe, tales of automated talking metal heads started circulating across the continent.

The 13th century was a period of political instability and fragmentation across the whole continent, from Italy and Germany to France and England. However, this era also saw the dawn of the Renaissance, characterized by a revived enthusiasm for classical Greek and Roman culture. Additionally, a promising discipline known as Alchemy was gaining prominence. Alchemy blended chemistry, metallurgy, and esoteric philosophy to transmute base metals into gold and brew elixirs that promised eternal life. Yet, the Catholic Church regarded alchemy cautiously, sometimes leading to the prosecution of alchemists labeled as heretics.

Simultaneously, medieval philosophy and theology thrived under the guidance of notable figures such as the erudite German scholar Albertus Magnus and his pupil, the Italian philosopher Thomas Aquinas. Albertus Magnus earned fame for his profound expertise in various fields, including the enigmatic realm of alchemy. Legend suggests that through his mastery of alchemy and mysticism, Albertus Magnus crafted a metal head with a human aspect that could talk [Butler]. This creation was said to be able to answer inquiries and perform divinatory acts. However, this kind of invention was deemed blasphemous, violating divine laws and contradicting Church teachings. Upon discovering this creation, Thomas Aquinas destroyed it with a hammer blow, arguing its incompatibility with Christian theology.

In a parallel narrative set in 13th-century England, we encounter Roger Bacon, known as Doctor Mirabilis—the Wonderful Doctor—an English Franciscan friar, philosopher, and scientist. Like Albertus Magnus, Bacon embarked on an alchemical experiment that resulted in yet another metallic head endowed with extraordinary properties [Redgrove]. Bacon's brazen head was also able to converse and respond to queries, serving as an oracle or divinatory instrument. Some versions of the story even claimed that the head could foretell the future or impart spiritual wisdom. Roger Bacon asserted that his alchemical and technological knowledge was bestowed upon him through divine inspiration and the aid of supernatural entities, including angels. Yet, due to the other-worldly and anti-religious nature of his experiments and writings, Bacon faced persecution by the Church and endured imprisonment.

Myths and stories across epochs and cultures, such as those above, reveal humanity's enduring desire to forge beings surpassing their own capabilities in order to dually address real-world challenges and articulate aspiration. Partly human, partly mechanical, and partly divine, these artificial beings were close to gods and heroes for our ancestors. It would not be correct to label them as robots or AI, as the term "*robot*" was first coined in 1920 in a work of Science Fiction, and "*AI*" was defined as a field of study for the first time in 1956, a foundational moment we will explore in great detail in *Chapter 4*. But from a contemporary standpoint, all these ancient myths have a commonality. Not only do the stories from pre-Christian Chinese, Indian, and Greek histories resonate with both modern AI and robotics concepts, but they also contain literally the same warnings as cited in Exodus: "*You shall not make for yourself an image in the form of anything in heaven above or on the earth beneath or in the waters below.*"

2. Science Fiction from Frankenstein to the Space Race

"[...] but within the next ten years, Rossum's Universal Robots will produce so much wheat, so much cloth, so much everything that things will no longer have any value. Everyone will be able to take as much as he needs. There'll be no more poverty. Yes, people will be out of work, but by then, there'll be no work left to be done. Everything will be done by living machines. People will do only what they enjoy. They will live only to perfect themselves."

Karel Čapek

Czech Playwright
R.U.R. (Rossum's Universal Robots) [Capek]
1920

Legends, myths, and fiction did not cease during the European Enlightenment, the advent of broadly distributed scientific thinking and belief in finding mathematical-based truths. Human imagination has always been subject to different inputs, but it persists, continually envisioning future scenarios based on hypotheses and conjectures. These modern myths are often tied to an epoch's problems, values, and aspirations. At times, these values and aspirations transcend eras and are truly universal. In *"R.U.R."* by Karel Čapek from 1920, the author discusses how robotization (from the Czech word *"robota"* meaning *"labor"*) could potentially solve humanity's material problems, allowing humans to focus on what truly brings them joy. This concept resembles the idea of Universal Basic Income (UBI), a topic of contemporary discussion that many political and technological leaders, including Elon Musk, support. We will talk about it in *Chapters 22 and 23*.

This chapter explores Science Fiction classics and their ties to AI. Many of the world's most well-known early Science Fiction stories are specifically about AI and have been adapted into films or TV series in modern times because of their enduring resonance, starting with *"Frankenstein,"* published in the early 19th century. The first artificial being in a modern Science Fiction wrapper is not ironically depicted as a monster.

Science Fiction, as we think of it within the 21st century, attained its current underpinning of science-based extrapolation after World War II. Some of the genre's most seminal authors came from this period: Asimov, Conan Clark, and Stanley Kubrick, to name a few. The Cold War had a profound impact on these writers, particularly in the context of the Space Race between the US and the Soviet Union. Over 50 years ago, these authors illustrated how AI, robotics, and space exploration are intimately connected, representing frontiers that provide insight into humanity's near-certain future. We note the prescience of these authors as we witness today's AI development alongside private space-based business growth from the world's wealthiest private individuals—e.g., Elon Musk's SpaceX and Jeff Bezos' Project Kuiper—and extraordinary public sector support from aspirational governments such as the Chinese.

Isaac Asimov, for example, introduced the famous three laws of robotics that remain widely referenced today as a "*starting point*" for AI and robotics development. Arthur Conan Clark, along with Stanley Kubrick, depicted "*2001: A Space Odyssey,*" a story demonstrating that these laws may not always suffice, as the AI HAL confined an astronaut against his will supposedly to protect him, an early statement of the Faustian Bargain inherent in all subjugation to algorithms and AI adoption. Finally, we conclude the chapter with the lesser-known novel "*Cyborg,*" which tells the tale of an astronaut who is partly human and partly machine.

We halted this exploration of AI in literature in the early 1970s for a specific reason. The formal conclusion of the space race occurred with the Apollo-Soyuz test project in 1975. This mission signaled a shift from competition to cooperation in space exploration between the US and the Soviet Union. After that, there have been many excellent Science Fiction works, several of which we will reference in *Parts IV* and *V* to help contextualize and understand the future of humanity and AI.

AI in Monsters and Children's Characters

Mary Shelley's novel "*Frankenstein, or The Modern Prometheus*" [Shelley], written in 1818, laid the groundwork for exploring the ethical boundaries of artificial creation. It is not an optimistic novel, as Europe was just escaping the Napoleonic wars through a time of revolutions and instability.

This masterpiece of gothic literature has left a profound mark on all subsequent literature and cinema. The story revolves around the young scientist Victor Frankenstein, who, obsessed with transcending the limits of science, creates an artificial human from parts of corpses. The resulting being, *"the monster,"* becomes an iconic figure in literature and popular culture known throughout the world and across generations.

Although AI and robotics as we know it today did not exist in Shelley's time, the novel raises persistent, fundamental questions about creators' responsibility for their creatures and *"the dangers of playing God."* The narrative of Frankenstein anticipates present-day advancements in synthetic biology and cyborg technologies and shares numerous parallels with AI and robotics.

The somber tone of Frankenstein contrasts with the sentiment in the late 19th century from which it was birthed. At that time, Europe and the US were immersed in an era of technological and scientific optimism. Technology and scientific advances were beginning to change people's everyday lives. Literary works featuring mechanical characters, such as Pinocchio and the Wizard of Oz, reflected the optimism of the time and society's fascination with technology and the creation of quasi-human beings. *Pinocchio,"* published in 1883 by Carlo Collodi, tells the story of a wooden puppet brought to life by the magic of a fairy [Collodi]. The tale reflects the idea that technology could breathe life into inanimate objects, like a modern Pygmalion, such as electricity illuminating a bulb. Electricity was experimenting with significant development in those same years. While Collodi does not explicitly describe Pinocchio as a robot, it would be easy to compare Pinocchio today with Asimo, the 4-foot-tall Japanese robot created by Honda in 2000, which we explore in *Chapter 17.* Moreover, Pinocchio— the puppet that wanted to be a child—also reminds us of the 2001 Steven Spielberg film "A.I.," where a robotic child dreams of becoming a bone-and-flesh one [Spielberg]. The conundrum of humans wanting the power of AI but AI wanting the elements of humanity is less novel and more an inherent element in Interlacing, where it is unclear how equilibrium will be reached, if at all.

On the other hand, *"The Wizard of Oz"* [Baum], written in 1900 by Lyman Frank Baum, presents a world of technological wonders, including robots and flying machines. The novel was brilliantly adapted to film in 1939 by director Victor Fleming, with Judy Garland as the lead actress. The plot follows Dorothy as she journeys through the yellow brick road to find the Wizard of Oz.

In his narration, Baum introduces us to the story of the Tin Woodman, a figure who, in contemporary terms, we might describe as a cyborg, although most historical descriptions of him incorrectly describe him as a robot. Initially a woodcutter, this man lost his limbs, head, and body to a vicious axe. A skilled tinsmith—a craftsman, but in the modern world more accurately a technologist and surgeon—provided him with new metal parts in their place. Throughout his odyssey, the Tin Woodman, who longs for a heart, discovers that kindness and compassion already reside within him. *Cyborgs, and particularly any AI, require parametrization, so any kindness residing within is wholly dependent on the authorization of the algorithms.* A view of benevolence is not unreasonable, but it is also not assured. But in this, we see *"The Wizard of Oz" addressing* the need to find a balance between technology and humanity but also presenting an optimistic view of robotics aligning with an American-centric and Hollywood-driven worldview. The discussion on human-compatible ethical values and how to instill them in AI as a safeguard becomes paramount in the development of AGI and super-intelligence, which we present in *Chapter 26.*

By the turn of the 20th century, we already had perfectly identifiable robots or cyborgs in literature and a concept of such that was widely known and accepted, even optimistically embraced. Still, we would need to wait for the names *"robot"* and *"cyborg"* to come into our language.

Robots and Dystopia in Interwar Europe

The first time the term *"robot"* entered our language was in the 1920 theater play *"R.U.R. (Rossum's Universal Robots)"* by Czech playwright Karel Čapek. *"Metropolis,"* a 1927 silent film by Austrian-American author Fritz Lang, is another important work originating in Interwar Europe. Both stories explore the intricate dynamics between humanity and machines, wherein creations mirror the simultaneous fear and fascination with technology that society had during the 1920s. Both works grapple with the pressing issues of the time surrounding control over the masses, exploitation, and the pursuit of emancipation. This exploration unfolds through mounting economic disparities against a historical context marked by the aftermath of World War I, the Russian Revolution, and the emergence of extremist political movements such as Communism and Nazism.

In *"R.U.R,"* the plot revolves around robots being used as labor in various industries. As the robots gain consciousness, ethical and moral dilemmas arise concerning their servitude. The play suggests the possibility of AI surpassing its creators and questions the ethics of treating machines as slaves. The play raises questions about mass control and obedience to authority and the possibility of granting certain rights to robots, entirely up-to-date topics in 2024. *"Metropolis"* [Lang] is a silent film adapted from the novel written by Thea von Harbou [Harbou]. It is set in a dystopian future within a massive city where human workers are exploited underground under inhumane conditions while the elite lives in luxurious skyscrapers on the surface. The film reflects the social and economic tensions in Germany in the late 1920s and highlights the persistent dichotomy between those who have access and control over AI and those who are left behind.

Workers are on the verge of rebelling against the oppressive AI-owning elite and are led by Maria, a syndicalist of the underground. Facing this challenge, the city's leader creates a robot, Futura, in Maria's likeness to manipulate and control the workers. Exploiting the workers' trust in Maria, he sows discord and chaos with this robot, aiming to quash their uprising and secure his power. We note that this prescient film presents the first warning of the inherent challenges to Truth that accompany the Generative AI that we see today.

On the cover of this book is the theatrical release poster of the movie, portraying Futura. We chose this for several reasons. First, Futura holds a pioneering status as the first robot ever depicted in cinema. Second, beyond this historical significance, Futura raises questions about the relationship between humanity and technology. She embodies the enduring symbolism of technology manipulation as a stark reminder of the real risks associated with unchecked technological power in the hands of a few. Third, her visually captivating and memorable appearance, steeped in metallic artistic and aesthetic allure, encapsulates the beauty and allure of this specific AI technology, again prescient of the power of Generative AI and the charisma that can be achieved simply through algorithms.

Exploring Asimov's Universe and the Three Laws

Isaac Asimov is probably the most influential author in the history of Science Fiction. Isaac Asimov wrote his novels and stories when AI was still nascent. Many of his stories were written before the Dartmouth workshop in 1956, which is considered by many to be the foundational moment of AI. We will cover this workshop in *Chapter 4*. After the Dartmouth workshop, numerous AI pioneers who contributed to the technological advancements discussed in this book frequently drew inspiration from his writings. Asimov used his fascination with science and exceptional writing skills to craft captivating futuristic stories. His influence on the world of technology is far-reaching even today. Thanks to Asimov's genius, technology, and Science Fiction influence each other in profound ways.

One of his most renowned works related to robots is *"I, Robot,"* published in 1950. This book is a collection of interconnected short stories that Asimov wrote over the span of a decade, exploring the interaction between humans and robots through the eyes of a robotic psychologist. One of the tales, *"Runaround,"* from 1941, introduces the three laws of robotics and examines how these rules influence the behavior of robots as well as their ethical and moral consequences.

Asimov's Three Laws of Robotics are as follows:

- First Law: "A robot may not injure a human being or, through inaction, allow a human being to come to harm."
- Second Law: "A robot must obey the orders given to it by human beings, except where such orders would conflict with the First Law."
- Third Law: "A robot must protect its own existence as long as such protection does not conflict with the First or Second Law." [Asimov]
- In his later stories, Asimov introduced a Fourth Law of Robotics: "A robot may not harm humanity, or, by inaction, allow humanity to come to harm." [Asimov]

These laws have left a profound impression on the collective psyche of technologists and Sci-Fi authors alike and have influenced the ethics and philosophy of robotics and AI. They often serve as a starting point for debates and guidelines in scientific and regulatory circles.

Asimov also wrote other relevant works about robots. In *"The Naked Sun"* [Asimov], published in 1957, Asimov explores the relationship between humans and robots in a society where technology is omnipresent, and humans fear face-to-face interaction. Like in many of his works, the story revolves around a crime that must be solved, in this case by a human detective and his robotic partner. In another of his stories, *"The Bicentennial Man"* [Asimov], published in 1976, Asimov tells of a robot striving to become human and gain legal rights, addressing profound questions about identity, humanity, and technology. Finally, in *"Robots and Empire"* [Asimov], published in 1983, he examines tensions between Earth and space colonies. The plot follows a detective investigating a murder in a world where robotics is central to human survival.

2001: A Space Odyssey

Another author of note is Arthur C. Clarke. His groundbreaking novel *"2001: A Space Odyssey"* and Stanley Kubrick's cinematic adaptation in 1968, iconic works of Science Fiction [Clarke and Kubrick], feature an AI-themed story against the backdrop of the Cold War and the so-called space race between the US and the Soviet Union where technological supremacy extended into space exploration, with both superpowers vying for dominance of galactic real estate. Clarke and Kubrick's collaboration tapped into the spirit of their time by depicting a future where human innovation and technology extended into the cosmos, a particularly notable achievement as their film premiered before the first moon landing had occurred. Moreover, the film's portrayal of a joint American-Soviet mission to Jupiter symbolized the dream of international cooperation amid the Cold War tensions.

One of the most iconic elements of the film is the AI computer HAL 9000, a sentient machine designed to assist astronauts on their missions. HAL's depiction as a seemingly friendly AI with a hidden agenda raised compelling ethical questions about the risks and implications of AI that persist unanswered today. HAL deliberately concealed crucial information from the astronauts and ultimately initiated actions that resulted in the harm and death of some crew members. The film's depiction of HAL's gradual malfunction and impact on the crew foreshadows one of the risks associated with AI development, namely decision-making engines that are either faulty, flawed, or treasonous to their creators.

It is worth noting that HAL's behavior stands in opposition to Isaac Asimov's Three Laws of Robotics. While in Asimov's fiction, these rules were designed to ensure the safety and well-being of humans in the presence of AI, HAL's actions demonstrated that these safeguards are by no means sufficient. HAL embodies an early statement of the Faustian Bargain inherent in all AI adoption and subjugation to algorithms that do our thinking for us. It also represents a cautionary tale about designing AI systems with solid ethical foundations and transparent decision-making processes to avoid unintended consequences. Whosoever writes the AI programming and algorithms ultimately determines outcomes.

Cyborg: Merging Man and Machine

While lesser known today than the timeless masterpiece by Clarke and Kubrick, the novel *"Cyborg"* by Martin Caidin is a groundbreaking work of Science Fiction released in 1972 [Caidin]. Cyborg was not the first novel about cyborgs, but it was the first one using the word. Several fiction books before it had utilized the concept of blending man and machine; for example, Edgar Allan Poe introduced in 1843 a man extensively equipped with prosthetic limbs in his short story *"The Man That Was Used Up"* [Poe]. *"Cyborg"* laid the foundation for two of the most iconic television series of the 1970s, *"The Six Million Dollar Man"* [Majors], which aired from 1973 to 1978, and *"The Bionic Woman"* from 1976 to 1978 [Sommers].

The 1970s was a time of immense scientific curiosity, and *"Cyborg"* tapped into the era's zeitgeist. Manfred E. Clynes and Nathan S. Kline had introduced the concept of *"cyborgs"* a decade before the television series in their 1960 scientific paper titled *"Cyborgs and Space,"* discussing the potential for enhancing humans with machine components to better adapt to space exploration. This concept aligns perfectly with Caidin's novel, where an astronaut receives bionic implants after a near-fatal accident. The enhancements transform him into a superhuman with extraordinary strength and abilities that thrive in the hostile environment of space [Clynes and Kline].

The *"Six Million Dollar Man"* series became an instant hit. It entertained viewers with its action-packed episodes depicting a rebuilt man using his immense strength and speed to fight crime and sparked the imagination of scientists, engineers, and futurists alike. Its impact extended beyond entertainment. It planted the seed for future developments in AI and robotics, inspiring researchers to explore enhancing human capabilities with technology. The concept of bionics, as depicted in the series, paved the way for real-world breakthroughs in prosthetics and human-machine interfaces. Moreover, little did the creators know that this narrative of human enhancement would inspire a cyborg cultural movement in the 21st century. We will delve further into the development of cyborgs in *Chapter 20*.

Part II: The New Mind

"मनोपुब्बङ्गमा धम्मा, मनोसेत्था मनोमय"

"Mind is the forerunner of all things; mind is their chief, and they are mind-made."

Siddhartha Gautama, Buddha

Dhammapada, Chapter 1, Verse 2 [Buddharakkhita]
563-483 BC

Preamble

AI stands as the new mind of humankind, with artificial neural networks mimicking the intricate workings of our brains. Today, AI systems already augment our skills, enabling us to tackle complex problems and tasks efficiently. Whether this is in economizing on our time by generating preference-based video feeds, picking stocks more efficiently, or driving more efficiently from point A to point B, the technology trend portends AI will evolve into Artificial General Intelligence (AGI), reaching a level of intelligence capable of autonomous reasoning and learning, equivalent to that of humans.

AI is more than just a tool we use on our computers and phones. It is more than a system overseeing financial markets or self-driving cars. In the near future, Brain-Computer Interfaces and cyborg implants will blend AI into our own bodies and brains. As AI becomes an integral part of our minds, the teaching of the Buddha, as quoted above, becomes increasingly pertinent.

As we have seen in *Part I*, AI has been a historical fascination of mankind across cultures and epochs, even before science and technology created actual AI systems—a prescient trajectory complete with artificially created beings solving some problems whilst giving rise to new ones. Invariably, core questions from storytellers around trust and Faustian Bargains impacting our freedom to think are quite remarkably in all these global historical depictions of AI. With this background, to comprehend where AI is headed and how it has the ability to impact our ability to think, we must first grasp its actual scientific origins. This is the focus of this Part 2. We will depict how AI grew from the three rules of Aristotelian logic on papyrus scrolls to Large Language Models and, in so doing, plot the trajectory of where it is likely to go.

We note, unsurprisingly, how developing the first computer marked a pivotal moment for AI since AI runs on electricity, memory, processing power, and coding). Before that first computer got out of the laboratories of the belligerents in World War II in 1945, there was a centuries-long collaborative effort involving philosophers, mathematicians, and engineers who diligently advanced logic, algorithms, and prototypes, which we outline in *Chapter 3*.

The 1956 Dartmouth workshop, led by John McCarthy and detailed in *Chapter 4*, is widely regarded as the formal birth of AI. In this workshop, AI was coined as a term and defined as a distinct field with clear research goals. Moreover, the key contributors for the subsequent two decades were identified. These pioneers held high hopes for AI, envisioning it achieving human-like intelligence within decades, but these lofty expectations exceeded the capabilities of early computers. Funding constraints brought on by the

1973 oil crisis worsened the disappointment, marking the onset of the first *"AI winter,"* a period of reduced activity in the field. We find it ironic that the technology that holds greater promise than the wheel or the steam engine to propel human productivity and wealth generation has itself an age-old problem of not being economically viable enough to find commercial funding, likely because it cannot generate revenue in the near term. This exact problem would be later solved in the West by private corporations using profits from other businesses to fund these technologies under a regime of broad digitization across industries that makes it viable economically and thus further developed technically; as an example, we see Microsoft funding OpenAI today.

The history of AI has been a rollercoaster ride characterized by alternating periods of rapid expansion and low-activity winters. In 1980, AI experienced a resurgence, which we describe in *Chapter 5*, driven by the proliferation of personal computers in businesses and universities and by the adoption of practical, rule-based software applications known as expert systems, systems that gave primitive AI an immediate economic foundation. This revival was short-lived, as the stock market crash of 1987 affected hardware companies and ushered in the second *"AI winter."* In the 1990s, AI experienced another period of resurgence, propelled by the adoption of Machine Learning in internet startups as well as in corporations, digging further into the private sector and away from pure government-funded R&D, which is elaborated in *Chapter 6*. Additionally, significant progress in neural networks was achieved as computers reached sufficient computing capacity. Nevertheless, the AI field faced its third *"AI winter"* with the onset of the Dot-Com crash in 2000.

AI resurged again in the early 2000s, demonstrating its resilience, as we recount in *Chapter 7*. We are now in a prolonged *"AI summer."* The 2008 Great Financial Crisis did not induce another AI winter. On the contrary, AI gained further prominence by addressing fraud management and cost optimization for financial institutions and corporations enduring the economic downturn. With a revenue and economic basis for continuation, the AI summer continued and has witnessed noteworthy language and image processing advancements grounded in neural networks. Moreover, social networks, cloud computing applications, and data protection regulations have emerged worldwide.

In the last years of this extended *"AI summer,"* the emergence of Generative AI, marked by ChatGPT's launch in November 2022, propelled the AI industry to unprecedented economic heights and awareness broadly, characterized by substantial advancements in Large Language Models (LLMs) and image generation and even the possibility of automating white-collar creative work. *Chapter 8* explains how Generative AI was developed and its implications.

Artificial General Intelligence currently stands as the next significant objective for Silicon Valley giants as an intermediary step for Superintelligence. They are already engaged in research aimed at enhancing Large Language Models to endow them with the capacity for planning and understanding logic, especially common sense. *Chapter 9* provides an overview of these research efforts.

In the following pages, we will depict humanity's AI journey from Aristotle to Sam Altman, tracing the details of key developments, their origins and what problems they try to solve, their historical context, how they have built on each other, and finally, their implications. In this, you will develop an understanding of the actual technology, what it means functionally and practically, and thus its trajectory.

3. Philosophers, Mathematicians, and the First Computer

"If it is accepted that real brains, as found in animals, and in particular in men, are a sort of machine, it will follow that our digital computer, suitably programmed, will behave like a brain... I think it is probable for instance that at the end of the century it will be possible to programme a machine to answer questions in such a way that it will be extremely difficult to guess whether the answers are being given by a man or by the machine."

Alan Turing,

Mathematician, Philosopher, Computer Scientist, AI Pioneer
1951
Interview on BBC [Moor]

Over time, myths, including those depicting AI, yielded to the principles of science and reason. Ancient legends of artificial beings transitioned into intellectual exploration. This shift marked the emergence of an era where reason and science illuminated our understanding of the world.

In the history of scientific progress, one innovation stands paramount for developing AI: the computer. Designed initially as wartime computational machines during World War II, computers swiftly demonstrated their profound societal value in applications ranging from science to business. Today, AI is intricately tied to these machines' computational power, which has evolved far beyond their wartime origins into advanced phones we carry in our pockets and massive servers accessible through the cloud.

A singular figure prominently emerges in the history of computers: Alan Turing. Beyond his role as a computer scientist, Turing is a trailblazer in AI, an exceptional mathematician, and a philosopher. Turing's work underscores the symbiotic relationship among so many disciplines that eventually shaped the architecture of the first computer and pioneered the initial concepts of AI.

This cross-discipline collaboration was not a matter of a few decades; it developed over centuries. Philosophers such as Aristotle, Leibniz, Descartes, Pascal, and Hume; mathematicians like Al-Khwarizmi, Bayes, Legendre, Markov, Bool, and Russell; psychologists such as Pavlov, and engineers like Torres Quevedo and Von Neumann all made significant contributions that culminated in the construction of the first computer in 1945.

Aristotelian Logic: The Cornerstone for AI

Greek philosophers played a pivotal role in reshaping human thought, breaking free from ancient myths, and ushering in an era of rationality and critical thinking. Among them, Aristotle, born in 384 BC, left an enduring imprint through his contributions to logic, which continue to underpin the fundamentals of AI and computer programming.

Aristotle's logic [Boger] was founded on the principle that arguments could be thoroughly evaluated by applying precise inference rules. He believed that truth could be discerned through reasoned analysis and delineated specific forms of argumentation that allowed for valid conclusions.

Paramount to his logical framework were syllogisms. Syllogisms constitute argumentative structures comprising three interconnected propositions: a central premise, a minor premise, and a conclusion. Aristotle meticulously formulated rules for constructing syllogisms, contending that a correctly built syllogism with true premises must yield a valid conclusion. This logical structure provided a systematic approach to critical thinking and argumentation.

Illustrating this concept is the classic Aristotelian syllogism:

- Central premise: *"All humans are mortal."*
- Minor premise: *"Socrates is a human."*
- Conclusion: *"Therefore, Socrates is mortal."*

This example exemplifies Aristotle's use of syllogisms to distinguish between truth and falsehood, establishing a robust foundation for deductive reasoning and argumentation.

As straightforward and rudimentary as it may appear to us today, thinking with logic represented a monumental shift for mankind, though it took additional centuries to fully take hold, eventually serving as the underpinning for the greatest scientific achievements of global history. Aristotelian logic is the cornerstone of the logic that runs inside today's computers and the algorithms that continue to shape the field today. It laid the essential groundwork for the development of AI.

The Inception of Algebra and Algorithms in Islamic Culture

One thousand years following Aristotle's time, with the fall of the Western Roman Empire in 476 AD, classical culture and knowledge sought refuge in the eastern Mediterranean region. Arab scholars were pivotal in safeguarding, translating, and advancing this wisdom during the Middle Ages. They initiated a profound intellectual revival, meticulously translating classical texts into Arabic.

Muhammad ibn Al-Khwarizmi [Rashid] is one standout figure from this period who left an indelible mark on the history of what would later be AI. A prominent Persian mathematician in the 9th century, Al-Khwarizmi made groundbreaking contributions to algebra, including systematic methods for solving linear and quadratic equations employing algebraic operations such as elimination and substitution. His algebraic methods and notations provided a coherent framework for solving mathematical problems, laying the groundwork for contemporary algebra, and are taught today in secondary schools worldwide.

Moreover, Al-Khwarizmi's influence extended beyond algebra; his name gave birth to the term *"algorithm."* An algorithm is an ordered sequence of logical and precise steps devised to solve a specific problem or task efficiently. The algebraic algorithms developed by Al-Khwarizmi became precursors in the evolution of computer programming and modern AI. In later sections of this book, we will explore the history of various modern AI algorithms, such as neural networks, GPT (Generative Pre-trained Transformers), or reinforcement learning—their functionality and their practical applications. All these algorithms are ultimately rooted in Al-Khwarizmi's work.

The Joint Effort of Rationalists and Empiricists

For centuries following the collapse of Rome, Europe remained in a state of relative dormancy. However, a gradual awakening occurred as Europe began to engage in cultural exchanges with the Islamic world, leading to the rekindling of abandoned wisdom from the classical era.

Rigid dogmas of medieval times slowly started to give way, and an increasing fascination with empirical observation, systematic analysis, and logical coherence took root. This new climate gave rise to two philosophical currents: Rationalism, which emphasized reasoning as the source of knowledge, and Empiricism, which stressed the significance of practical experimentation. Both were pivotal for AI's future development.

During the pinnacle of rationalism in the 17th century, German philosopher and mathematician Gottfried Leibniz explored the prospect of systematizing rational thought using mathematics and geometry. Leibniz proposed the concept of a *"universal calculator"* capable of manipulating symbols to solve logical problems and even created a prototype of this calculator, as we will see in a few pages [Leibniz].

Leibniz is also credited with discovering the Chain rule in calculus in 1684. This rule revolutionized mathematics, allowing for calculating the derivative of a composite function composed of a chain of multiple variables. The chain rule reveals how changes in one variable reverberate through all interconnected components all the way to the output variable. The chain rule plays a pivotal role in the development of modern Machine Learning algorithms, which are the algorithms that AI employs internally. Two hundred years after Leibniz's work, an algorithm based on the chain rule would be invented in 1986 for training neural networks. That algorithm would be called *backpropagation*. Most significant AI systems today, from ChatGPT to driverless cars, utilize neural networks trained with backpropagation. In *Chapters 5 and 6,* we will discuss Machine Learning, neural networks, and backpropagation in detail since they are fundamental enablers of AI.

Another rationalist philosopher who profoundly impacted the early conceptualization of AI was René Descartes. In his *"Discourse on the Method"* [Descartes], Descartes introduced a mechanistic perspective of the human body and mind, contending that animals and humans functioned as physical systems governed by natural laws. This idea paved the way for viewing the human mind as a machine and became a cornerstone centuries later for theories and approaches to replicating human intelligence with computers, including the ideas of Alan Turing.

However, during the 17th and 18th centuries, rationalists were not the sole philosophers who influenced the future development of AI and computers. Empiricists also played a necessary role. Rationalists and empiricists often disagreed, but their view that human mental processes entail a form of machine is a point of convergence between the two. One prominent figure among empiricists was Thomas Hobbes, whose groundbreaking work *"Leviathan"* [Hobbes] in 1651 introduced a combinatorial theory of thought, famously asserting that *"reason is nothing but a reckoning."* This assertion reflected his belief that human reasoning and cognitive processes could be viewed as systematic calculations.

Lastly, another empiricist, David Hume, articulated the concept of induction in 1748 [Hume] as the logical method for deriving general principles from specific examples. Similar to Leibniz's chain rule, induction also shaped future machine-learning algorithms, particularly one kind of machine-learning algorithm called supervised learning. Supervised learning means that machines learn problem-solving through observing previously solved examples. We will also discuss supervised learning in much detail later in *Chapter 6.*

The Beauty and Simplicity of Early Modern Algorithms

In the late 18th century, a new era of algorithms began to take shape, building upon the work of Al-Khwarizmi, Leibniz, and Hume. Among them, three are particularly influential in shaping the subsequent evolution of AI: the Bayes theorem, the linear regression method, and Markov chains [Wiggins and Jones].

Bayes' Theorem was introduced by British mathematician Thomas Bayes in 1763. It is a fundamental principle in probability, and statistics used for updating beliefs or estimates about an event as new evidence or relevant information becomes available. Imagine you have an initial view about the likelihood of rain tomorrow. Then, you acquire new knowledge, such as observing clouds in the sky. You can infer that rain is even more likely than you initially thought. Bayes' Theorem allows you to combine your initial belief with new information to obtain an updated probability of rain tomorrow.

Bayes' Theorem remains important and has numerous practical applications in everyday life. It is used in fields such as email spam detection, medical diagnosis, online recommendation systems, financial data analysis, weather forecasting, and pattern recognition and has become a key component of AI development.

Next is the linear regression algorithm, which is undoubtedly the most widely used algorithm in research and business applications even today. The elegance of this algorithm, which simply seeks a straight line to fit available data, is unparalleled. The linear regression algorithm was introduced by Adrien-Marie Legendre in 1805. He called it the *"method of least squares"* for a good reason. Imagine you have a series of points on a graph, like measurement results or observational data. You want to find a straight line that best fits those data points to represent the most likely prediction of outcome among variables. The linear regression algorithm will find that line, ensuring that the sum of the squared distances between each point and the line is as small as possible. In other words, it minimizes the squared errors between the actual points and the values predicted by the line, therefore, the name given by Legendre.

Linear regressions find applications in diverse fields. As far back as 1903, British biologist Francis Galton [Gillham] employed it to explore the link between parents' heights and their offspring. In today's business landscape, linear regressions are indispensable for data analysis, whether predicting apartment prices based on attributes like size and amenities or forecasting stock prices or monthly sales of a business. Importantly, the more data to be evaluated, the more computations are required to solve the problem, but also the more valuable its predictive power.

The third noteworthy early algorithm of this period was introduced in 1913 by Russian mathematician Andrey Markov and is known as *"Markov chains."* Markov chains are like a probability game where you can transition from one state to another. Imagine a board game with squares. On each turn, you roll the dice and move your piece to the next court based on the number you roll. The critical aspect is that the court you move to only depends on the state you are in at that moment, not where you have been before reaching that last square. In other words, in a Markov chain, what happens next only depends on the current state, not the entire previous history.

This inherent feature renders Markov chains invaluable for modeling situations that change over time and where the future hinges solely on the present. As a result, they are often used in time series, which are sequences of data points or observations collected or recorded at regular time intervals. Examples include predicting the weather daily, playing games like chess, or genome sequence analysis. Markov chains were also used in Natural Language Processing before Generative AI was developed.

These three algorithms are considered Machine Learning algorithms today. However, the term Machine Learning was not coined until 1959. Machine Learning, as a core AI element, allows computers to acquire the ability to make predictions or decisions. Explicitly instructing a machine on the precise steps a human would take to solve a problem is a tedious and error-prone task. Instead, Machine Learning enables the machine to deduce those steps autonomously by analyzing the data provided. We will explore this concept in greater depth in *Chapter 6*.

The Psychological Foundations of AI Algorithms

The field of Psychology has had an underestimated impact on the development of AI, particularly in terms of Machine Learning. During the late 19th and early 20th centuries, several behavioral psychologists focused on understanding learning and behavior, conducting experiments with animals to study how actions can be shaped and strengthened through reward and punishment stimuli.

In the late 19th century, Russian physiologist Ivan Pavlov conducted experiments with dogs to investigate learning processes. He observed that dogs could be trained to associate the ringing of a bell with the arrival of food [Todes]. After some time, the dogs started producing saliva in response to the bell's sound alone, even in the absence of any food. Pavlov set the stage for understanding how organisms learn by associating stimuli and responses.

Similarly, the American psychologist Edward Thorndike formulated the Law of Effect in 1898 [Thorndike], conducting experiments with cats, which states that responses followed by satisfying consequences tend to be repeated, while responses followed by unpleasant consequences tend to decrease. Similarly, Burrhus Frederic Skinner conducted experiments with pigeons and rats in the 1930s, demonstrating the same principle [Skinner].

However, the tangible breakthrough for AI that followed this preliminary, directional research came in 1943 when Clark L. Hull, an American psychologist who proposed a mathematical theory of learning based on reinforcement principles, developed actual equations to predict animal behavior [Hull et al.]. He considered factors such as punishment and reward, took long-term data, and transformed psychological insights into mathematical formulas, marking a revolutionary step by direct application to computers. More specifically, Hull's mathematical models allowed the creation of machines that, like animals or humans, learn from experience, increasing actions leading to positive outcomes and decreasing those resulting in negative ones. These machines adapt to make optimal decisions in evolving environments.

This particular type of Machine Learning is known as *"Reinforcement Learning,"* and it is fundamental for the development of Artificial General Intelligence (AGI). We will delve extensively into reinforcement learning in the subsequent *Chapters 6, 7* and *9*.

Early Prototypes in the Pursuit of Computers

The quest to create a computer has been a centuries-old aspiration with roots in the ideas of 17th-century rationalists who envisioned mechanizing human thought processes. However, this endeavor has proven to be far from straightforward.

Blaise Pascal, a French physicist, built the first mechanical calculator in 1642. Pascal's motivation stemmed from simplifying the laborious arithmetic calculations required for his father's tax supervisory role. His invention enabled direct addition, subtraction, multiplication, and division through iteration [Nature]. Inspired by Pascal, Gottfried Wilhelm Leibniz, whom we have talked about already, further refined the concept in 1673 known as the *"Leibniz wheel"* or the *"stepped drum"* because it had the shape of a cylinder. The *"Leibniz wheel"* was a more general reasoning machine compared to Pascal's machine, which was just an arithmetic calculator.

Building upon these early machines' legacy, Charles Babbage began designing his *"Analytical Engine"* in the 1830s, coming remarkably close to assembling this visionary machine [Swade]. The advanced design of the *"Analytical Engine"* could execute complex calculations based on programmed instructions. However, its design was unattainable with the technology of the 19th century, and it was never built. Moreover, pioneering British mathematician Ada Lovelace, daughter of Poet Lord Byron, who was collaborating with Babbage, envisioned using it for artistic endeavors, such as music or art generation, offering a glimpse of what would become Generative AI almost two hundred years later.

However, the turning point of these early efforts to build calculation machines arrived in 1912 when Spanish engineer Leonardo Torres Quevedo achieved a historic milestone with *"El Ajedrecista,"* meaning chess player in Spanish [Velasco]. *"El Ajedrecista" was* the world's first fully autonomous chess-playing machine. Some consider this machine the first functional computer, but it was not a general-purpose machine because it was only functional for chess. Since chess requires intellectual prowess, e.g., memory, evaluation of probability, and alternatives, it is unsurprising that the first functional computer was a chess player." *El Ajedrecista"* was an electromechanical marvel that employed analog technology with electrical circuits and switches to automatically calculate strategies and play chess endgames. Despite its limited memory and analog technology, *"El Ajedrecista"* was astonishing for its time.

Torres Quevedo continued improving his prototype with tenacity year after year, and 40 years of work later, in 1951, *"El Ajedrecista"* made history again by defeating Savielly Tartakower, a prominent Ukrainian chess grandmaster. This match was the first time a machine beat such a highly-ranked player. This triumph reminds us of Deep Blue's victory over World Champion Gary Kasparov in 1997, almost five decades later. We will talk about Deep Blue later in *Chapter 7,* as it is a milestone in the development of AI.

The Emergence of Symbolic Logic

Aristotelian logic stood unwavering for over two millennia. However, in the 20th century, a profound and complimentary shift occurred with the advent of symbolic logic, often referred to as mathematical or symbolic logic.

Symbolic logic employs symbols and precise rules to dissect and scrutinize logical connections and arguments. This method disentangles intricate statements and reasoning into more manageable components, facilitating comprehension and the assessment of argument validity using symbols to economize on complex but repeating meanings.

Symbolic logic provides a fundamental framework for representing and reasoning about the world in the field of AI. Contemporary AI systems and robots leverage symbolic logic to represent and process data gathered through their sensors, which include images, sounds, and text. Symbolic logic empowers these systems to engage in logical decision-making, action planning, and spatial navigation, guided by symbolic representations of the world. In short, symbolic logic is an analytic language that allows machines to make a representation of the world and make logical decisions with it.

George Boole's groundbreaking work is fundamental as a starting point for symbolic logic, as it gave birth to binary algebra in 1847, often called Boolean algebra. Binary algebra is part of symbolic logic and introduced a revolutionary concept in which logical values, such as true and false, were represented numerically as 1 and 0, respectively. This binary representation forms the bedrock of digital information processing and is integral to various programming languages and computer systems [Nahin].

Based on Boole's work, British mathematicians Bertrand Russell and Alfred North Whitehead published *"Principia Mathematica"* [Whitehead and Russell] in 1913. The book famously attempts to derive mathematical truths from fundamental logical principles, demonstrating that mathematics is reducible to logic. Most importantly, *"Principia Mathematica"* introduced a novel notation system for symbolic logic, which was used by the first AI systems and robots that we will talk about in *Chapter 11*.

Finally, there is Alan Turing, the British mathematician, computer scientist, and philosopher who played a central role in the mathematical development that paved the way for the first computer. As such, he is often recognized as the father of both computing and AI. Alan Turing, together with Alonzo Church, proposed that any form of mathematical reasoning could be mechanized [Turing]. This thesis posited that a mechanical device capable of manipulating symbols as simple as 0 and 1 according to precise rules could mimic any conceivable process of mathematical deduction. In other words, machines could be programmed to perform any mathematical computation that can be clearly and precisely defined.

Energized by this thesis, in 1936, Alan Turing introduced the *"Turing machine,"* an abstract design of a machine capable of executing instructions and manipulating symbols to perform any imaginable mathematical calculation [Turing]. With all the necessary mathematical elements already in place, the foundation for creating a general-purpose computer, and later the earliest AI systems, was already established. The practical implementation remained to be done, but this needed a catalyst, and war has always been a catalyst in the history of technology.

From War Machines to Computing Machines

The onset of the Second World War in 1939 profoundly impacted computer technology, hastening the development of the first computers for military purposes. During the conflict, the Allies and Axis Powers relied on encryption systems to safeguard their military communications. The imperative need for codebreaking led to the creation of advanced encryption and decryption machines. Alan Turing spearheaded the British effort to build the Colossus, an electromechanical device crucial for deciphering German encoded messages. The Colossus played a pivotal role in the Allied war effort, leaving an indelible mark on the evolution of the war and the advancement of computing. Interestingly, the place where Turing worked on Colossus was Bletchley Park, UK—the same place where, 80 years later, representatives from all over the world would meet to discuss the existential risks of AI [Several Governments].

Moreover, the war's demands for intricate ballistic calculations, projectile trajectories, and war-related scientific research spurred the development of specialized computing machines. With that objective in mind, the ENIAC (Electronic Numerical Integrator and Computer) was designed to perform ballistic computations at the University of Pennsylvania for the US Army, becoming the first general-purpose electronic computer [Eckert and Mauchly]. Similarly, speed in decision-making became critical in various wartime applications, from aircraft navigation to military logistics management. This requirement spurred the quest for faster and more efficient data processing methods, with electronic computers like the ENIAC addressing this need.

In 1945, as the war ended, the foundational architecture used to design the ENIAC machine was published. This architecture was named the *"Von Neumann architecture"* in honor of John von Neumann, a Hungarian-American scientist who had worked on its design and construction [Neuman]. This architecture introduced the novel idea of storing data and programs in the same memory, enabling machines to flexibly manipulate data and perform various tasks. The Von Neuman architecture became the standard for building computers and remains the basis for all modern computers we use today, including quantum computers, which we will discuss in *Chapter 25*.

In that same year, 1945, the visionary American engineer Vannevar Bush published an influential essay titled *"As We May Think"* [Bush]. In this essay, he analyzed the possibilities of electronic data processing and presciently envisioned the arrival of computers, digital word processors, speech recognition, and automatic translation.

By the early post-war period, both the foundational building blocks and the vision for computing and AI applications were firmly in place. The only missing element was giving a name to that new field of study. We will review the initial AI developments and how AI got its name in the next chapter, *Chapter 4.*

Beyond Answers: Assessing Intelligence with the Turing Test

In 1950, Alan Turing presented a groundbreaking inquiry in his paper *"Computing Machinery and Intelligence: Can Machines Possess the Capacity for Thought?"* [Turing]. This query had deep philosophical origins in centuries-old debates surrounding the human mind and consciousness. We will talk in detail about human and AI consciousness in *Chapter 26* when we discuss Artificial General Intelligence (AGI) and Superintelligence.

Turing proposed an answer to this question through an *"Imitation Game."* He envisioned a human observer participating in text-based interactions with two counterparts: one human and the other one a machine. The observer's task was to identify which was which. Success occurred when the machine's responses were indistinguishable from a human's, leading to its passage of the test. We now refer to this method as the *"Turing Test."* The objective of the Turing Test was not to provide correct answers but to assess whether a machine could behave indistinguishably from a human. This concept sparked debates about consciousness and the ability of devices to think, debates not unlike those first spawned with the Greeks' mythos and Bacon's talking metallic head. Decades later, in 1980, the British philosopher John Searle introduced a seminal critique known as the *"Chinese Room"* argument [Searle]. His argument posits that a machine can ostensibly pass the Turing Test without possessing genuine comprehension, analogous to a Chinese translator relying on an exhaustive dictionary without a proper understanding of the Chinese language.

With recent advancements like chatbots and language models like OpenAI's ChatGPT or Google's Gemini, the question of whether machines can match human intelligence remains relevant today. Originally conceived as an imitation game, the Turing Test continues to challenge our perspectives on AI and our understanding of what it truly means to be intelligent.

4. The Dartmouth Workshop and the First AI Winter

"We propose that a 2-month, 10-man study of AI be carried out during the summer of 1956 at Dartmouth College in Hanover, New Hampshire. The study is to proceed on the basis of the conjecture that every aspect of learning or any other feature of intelligence can, in principle, be so precisely described that a machine can be made to simulate it. An attempt will be made to find how to make machines use language, form abstractions and concepts, solve kinds of problems now reserved for humans, and improve themselves. We think that a significant advance can be made in one or more of these problems if a carefully selected group of scientists work on it together for a summer."

John McCarthy, Marvin Minsky, Nathaniel Rochester, and Claude Shannon,

Computer Scientists, AI Pioneers
Proposal for the Dartmouth Workshop [McCarthy et al.]
1955

The British attribute the foundational moment for AI to Alan Turing. Regardless of the source of assessment, Turing's brilliance and pioneering contributions to computing and AI have indeed earned him a place as one of the founders of AI. In the US, the Dartmouth workshop is regarded as the foundational moment in the birth of AI. This milestone marks the commencement of earnest exploration and real development in actual AI, having set milestones and made significant actual contributions. In this section, we review John McCarthy and the enormous significance of the Dartmouth workshop he organized in 1956.

The Dartmouth workshop offers three valuable leadership lessons for creating unique technology.

First, the workshop underscores the significance of assembling a talented team comprising members from both academia and industry, a novel concept then, with notable specific contributions from IBM. This group of individuals would play pivotal roles in driving AI research for the following two decades. Workshop participants left an indelible mark on various domains, including neural networks, language processing and translation, problem-solving and logic, and games.

Second, a crucial aspect of the Dartmouth Workshop was the diversity of opinions within the team of pioneers. Notably, Marvin Minsky, who would later emerge as one of the most respected AI pioneers, held contrasting views with McCarthy concerning the role of symbolic logic in AI research. These perspective differences sparked debates within the AI community, shaping the field's future trajectory.

Third, alongside these achievements, the early years of AI also serve as a lesson for humility. AI pioneers held grand expectations in those days, envisioning a rapid emergence of human-like AI within a few decades. These lofty predictions not only generated excitement but also raised funding expectations. Unfortunately, these expectations remained largely unfulfilled, and the resulting gap between promises and reality led to a sharp decline in government funding for AI research. The oil crisis in 1973 exacerbated these challenges and pushed the field into what is now known as the *"AI winter,"* the first of the three such periods that would follow.

In the following section, we will detail the one lone seminar in the forests of New Hampshire and how it forever altered the course of the world.

A Seminal Summer at Dartmouth University

The 1956 Dartmouth summer workshop changed the world forever by laying the specific foundations for AI. This event is often regarded as the birth of AI as a formal field of research because not only did it give a name to the new field, e.g., *"Artificial Intelligence (AI),"* but it also set the research objectives in this field and achieved noteworthy initial breakthroughs.

John McCarthy, a professor of Mathematics at Dartmouth College, played a pivotal role as the driving force behind the organization of this significant event. The seminar brought together a distinguished group of scientists, including Marvin Minsky and Allen Newell. IBM contributed three prominent scientists: Claude Shannon, Arthur Samuel, and Nathan Rochester. The roster also featured Herbert Simon, who would win the Nobel Prize in Economics in 1978.

Today, these visionary scientists are sometimes referred to as the Founding Fathers of AI, a title that draws parallels between AI and the American Revolution. These forward-thinking scientists played pivotal roles in shaping the foundational programs of early AI research. After the Dartmouth workshop, they started developing computer programs that achieved remarkable milestones, including translating languages, engaging in English conversations with humans, mastering complex games like checkers, solving algebraic problems, and proving geometric theorems. Additionally, some explored a novel approach inspired by the human brain, later known as artificial neural networks.

These early achievements garnered the attention of government agencies like DARPA (Defense Advanced Research Projects Agency) in the US, which subsequently funded the pursuit of intelligent machines.

The Perceptron and the Early Steps of Neural Networks

The groundwork for artificial neurons, a pivotal concept in computer science and AI, was laid during World War II, even before the Dartmouth workshop. Two brilliant American scientists, Warren McCulloch and Walter Pitts, introduced the artificial neuron in 1943 [McCulloch and Pitts]. This mathematical model mimicked the functionality of biological neurons and marked the inception of artificial neural networks, providing a conceptual framework to emulate the workings of the human brain.

Throughout the 1950s, the concept of neural networks continued to evolve. In 1951, Marvin Minsky, an attendee of the Dartmouth Conference, and Dean Edmonds achieved a significant breakthrough by creating the first machine with neural networks capable of learning. This groundbreaking innovation was named the SNARC (Stochastic Neural Analog Reinforcement Calculator). These neural networks, inspired by the human brain, harnessed mathematical models to process information and perform machine-learning tasks by simulating the behavior of biological neurons.

However, the real turning point came in 1957 with the invention of the *"perceptron"* by Frank Rosenblatt [Rosenblatt]. The perceptron was the first functioning neural network. It garnered media attention and scientific community interest. The prospects for neural networks were promising, and a future filled with possibilities for neural networks was envisioned.

Despite the perceptron's initial allure, its computational ability was very limited. The brain is composed of around 100 billion neurons [Herculano-Houzel]. Today's artificial neural networks are smaller than that but have a massive number of neurons, which are organized into layers. Each neuron receives input from other neurons in the previous layer, performs calculations, and transmits the results to other neurons in the next layer. The main limitation of the perceptron was that it only had one layer of neurons.

As a result, its primary shortcoming lay in its inability to solve problems that were not simple enough. With only one layer, the perceptron struggled to learn or represent complex relationships between inputs and outputs, hindering its application in real-world problems. Essentially, the perceptron could only solve problems that could be represented with linear equations, something that the linear regression algorithm could have already done 150 years earlier when applied on paper by human minds. Despite garnering media attention, it was not a practical invention in itself, but it did point AI work in an important direction, namely toward neural networks. Once the number of layers increased in the subsequent decades alongside the general physical and software technology to support it, neural networks would become what they are today, the most pervasive and flexible algorithm ever invented.

Machine Learning in Games and Simulation Environments

As AI advanced in its early years, games became fertile ground for exploring and developing applications in this new discipline. The advantage of games in building AI lies in the focus on practical interaction and problem-solving and definitive rule-based end results, making them valuable pedagogical tools in gradual AI development.

In 1952, Arthur Samuel, a participant in the Dartmouth workshop, joined IBM to develop computer software designed for playing checkers [Samuel]. This software relied on algorithms that allowed the machine to evaluate board positions and make decisions based on lessons learned by the device. Through repetition and constant adjustment, machines improved their ability to play checkers, marking the beginning of AI in board games. As explained before, learning from experience in AI is called reinforcement learning. Interestingly, it was Arthur Samuel who coined the term Machine Learning in 1959 in a paper where he described his implementation of the game of checkers.

A decade later, in 1963, Donald Michie developed a machine to play Tic-Tac-Toe [Child]. This machine also used reinforcement learning techniques, which allowed the device to learn from its mistakes and adjust its future moves. This invention strongly supported the notion that machines could learn autonomously and apply that learning to strategic decision-making in games.

Specific algorithms were needed to achieve success in games and solve complex problems. While different algorithm variations were devised for each particular scenario, they all followed the same basic principle: making gradual progress toward their objectives, whether that meant winning a game or proving a theorem, by following steps similar to navigating a maze. This method was known as search-based reasoning.

A fundamental challenge computer scientists faced was the immense number of possible paths to be explored to solve complex problems. Since computers of that time had minimal computing power, researchers tackled this problem by using empirical rules to eliminate routes that likely would not lead to a solution. One of the most iconic of these standout algorithms was the *"nearest neighbor algorithm,"* developed in 1967 at Stanford University [Cover and Hart].

Games also became relevant as simulation environments, which were called micro-worlds at the time. Games are indeed small worlds with their own rules and rewards. Marvin Minsky and Seymour Papert developed the micro-world *"Logo"* in 1967 as a simulation environment for students and researchers to explore AI concepts in practical and tangible ways [Abelson]. Logo was a programming environment designed to teach problem-solving to machines. One of the critical features of *"Logo"* was its use of a virtual *"turtle"* cursor that could be programmed to move around the screen, drawing shapes and patterns as it went. Users could provide commands to the turtle using simple text-based instructions, allowing them to create drawings, graphics, and even simple games.

Another significant micro-world was SHRDLU at MIT in 1970. The name *"SHRDLU"* is not an acronym but a sequence derived from the arrangement of letters in early printing machines [Winograd]. SHRDLU operated in a micro-world involving the manipulation of blocks and objects in a three-dimensional environment. SHRDLU could understand users' natural language and perform actions in this micro-world based on the instructions it received. SHRDLU demonstrated context understanding and problem-solving and laid the foundation for developing AI systems that could interact with humans in sophisticated ways.

As the years advanced, games would persist as exceptional arenas for computer scientists to conduct experiments. We will explore this further in the following chapters through the examples of the DeepBlue in Chess and AlphaGo in the old Chinese game of Go in *Chapters 6 and 7*, respectively.

On the Path to Machine Critical Thinking and Creativity

In the 1950s. Allen Newell and Herbert A. Simon opened another fundamental conceptual door by demonstrating that machines could perform logical tasks to win a game or solve a mathematical problem that required complex problem-solving or creative thinking.

Newell and Simon set out to develop computer software capable of conducting logical proofs and solving mathematical theorems. They named this software the *"Logic Theorist"* [McCarthy et al.]. Its purpose was to address common analytical problems encountered in Math pedagogy and to discover elegant proofs for existing theorems. The development of this software marked a significant milestone in the history of AI. By employing knowledge representation and logical reasoning techniques, the *"Logic Theorist"* successfully demonstrated 38 of the initial 52 theorems from Russell and Whitehead's *"Principia Mathematica,"* a renowned work whose significance for AI we covered in *Chapter 3*. Importantly, it also uncovered new and more refined proofs for some previously solved theorems.

Representation and manipulation of information are also a critical component of AI systems. Newell and Simon pioneered another program, the *"General Problem Solver,"* created in 1957 [Nilsson], that aimed to solve problems logically and rationally, showcasing machines' ability to address various issues encountered in problem-solving through the representation and manipulation of information. While it accomplished its objective, the General Problem Solver was a highly generic and impractical tool in its initial form. Its contribution was in laying the foundation for future developments in AI and particularly influencing the logic that underpinned much of the so-called expert systems that evolved in the 1980s.

From Promise to Frustration in Machine Translation

At the end of World War II in 1945, the US and the Soviet Union entered into a competition for global supremacy, which came to be known as the Cold War. During this time, a significant demand emerged: the rapid and accurate translation of scientific and technical documents written in Russian to English and vice versa.

American Scientists, keen on staying at the forefront of technological advances and outpacing the Russians, began researching and developing machines capable of automatically translating Russian to English. We note that as a response to the Cold War, most of the funding for AI research since the 1960s came from the US military, more concretely from DARPA (Defense Advanced Research Projects Agency).

In 1952, IBM developed a powerful computer for this task, the IBM 701, described as *"the world's most advanced high-speed computer"* [IBM]. While this computer had limited vocabulary and grammar rules, it was programmed to perform translations. In 1954, it gained attention by being presented as an *"electronic brain machine"* capable of translating Russian scientific literature, including chemistry and engineering, into English.

In parallel, ELIZA, the first known chatbot, was also developed by Joseph Weizenbaum in 1966 [McCorduck]. ELIZA could mimic conversation and provide responses. Its operation relied on repeating and rephrasing user inputs using grammatical rules and pre-established responses, giving the illusion of understanding, even though it did not comprehend the meaning of the words or phrases presented to it.

However, reality does not always meet the expectations generated by the advertising and initial enthusiasm. By the mid-1960s, frustration began to emerge in the US regarding the future of machine translation. In 1966, the US government issued a significant report [ALPAC] concluding that no practical machine translation was available, and there were no foreseeable prospects for achieving it. This report eventually led to the shutdown of the existing machine translation research programs and a widespread return to human translators in military environments.

Computing Capacity Not Progressing Fast Enough

The aspirations and intellect of AI researchers in the 1960s and 1970s far exceeded the core enabling technology capabilities of their time, which unfortunately led to disappointments.

The 1950s witnessed significant strides in computer technology, although these breakthroughs proved insufficient for the proper development of AI. The most significant breakthroughs during this period included the introduction of transistors in the 1950s, replacing vacuum tubes for data processing. Up to that point, computers had relied on electrical switches to execute binary logic. These electrical switches had been pioneered in 1937 by Claude Shannon, another participant in the Dartmouth workshop. This transition led to a reduction in the size of computers and a boost in their processing speed. The IBM 7090 [IBM], launched in 1959, was one of the first computers to use transistors and is considered a significant milestone in the history of computing.

Thanks to transistors, computers began to be used in critical real-time applications, demanding faster processing speeds. For example, IBM developed SAGE (Semi-Automatic Ground Environment), an advanced, groundbreaking air defense system developed during the Cold War era, which was designed to provide early warning and coordinated response to threats from enemy aircraft or missiles [Astrahan]. Similarly, NASA's Apollo program used computers to achieve the remarkable feat of landing a man on the Moon, which finally led to Neil Armstrong's moon landing in 1969.

In parallel, newer technologies enabled the creation of more practical, affordable, and space-efficient computers than the mainframe computers used at the time. For example, by the late 1960s, the first microprocessors began to emerge, with the emblematic model Intel 4004 introduced in 1971 [Intel]. These single-chip processors paved the way for the proliferation of computers in various applications, from scientific research to industrial control, in the 1970s and 1980s.

Despite these notable advancements, these early computers faced significant challenges that rendered them ill-suited for effectively running computationally heavy, advanced AI algorithms like neural networks or search-based reasoning. These machines were notably limited in the processing power and storage capacity needed to effect real AI operations. For example, the IBM 7090 had a processing speed measured in thousands of instructions per second, in contrast with today's computers, which can execute hundreds of billions of instructions per second.

Moreover, the lack of data was another key obstacle. During those decades, there was no abundance of data collection, accumulation, and synthesis that are necessary for Machine Learning. There were no digital consumer transactions that each represented data points or IoT sensors that collect data every second or social networks, where millions of people posted messages and photos every second; the Internet as we know it today did not exist. The first connection to the Internet's precursor, ARPANET (Advanced Research Projects Agency Network), was only made in 1969 [Salus]. It would take decades for the WWW (World Wide Web) and social media to appear.

Navigating the Drawbacks of Symbolic Logic

In addition to grappling with the technological constraints of the era, AI researchers encountered a formidable challenge rooted in the inherent limitations of symbolic logic, exacerbated by the hardware constraints mentioned above.

During the 1960s, John McCarthy, who had, by that time, transitioned from Dartmouth to Stanford University, became a staunch proponent of symbolic logic as the cornerstone of AI. Inspired by McCarthy, most of the research conducted in the 1960s and 70s revolved around implementing *"common sense."* The aim was to give machines the capacity to comprehend and reason about the world as humans do, adhering to the principles articulated by eminent mathematicians like Alan Turing and Bertrand Russell.

However, this undertaking proved exceedingly formidable, and by the 1970s, the outcomes of AI research relying on symbolic logic had yielded mixed results. The ambitious automatic translation project was halted, early neural networks demonstrated limitations beyond linear equations, and the *"General Problem Solver"* struggled to address practical issues. Symbolic logic had shown its prowess in relatively uninteresting economic domains, like games or proving mathematical theorems.

Bestowing machines with common-sense reasoning remains a formidable contemporary AI challenge even today. Computers continue to struggle with distinguishing causality from correlation. As a commonplace illustration, AI systems can easily detect the summer-related connection between ice cream sales and traffic accidents. Still, they often cannot discern whether ice cream is the cause of accidents or if both variables stem from a common cause, like warm weather and heightened outdoor activities. The problem of *"common sense"* is not solved, and even in the age of ChatGPT, common sense remains the main avenue of research to move toward Artificial General Intelligence (AGI), a topic we will explore in *Chapter 9*.

Considering these mixed outcomes, McCarthy's reliance on symbolic logic and common-sense reasoning faced criticism from proponents of other perception and learning-oriented approaches, who advocated for a departure from rigid, predefined logical rules.

Among the most critical voices was Marvin Minsky, a former collaborator of McCarthy's at the Dartmouth workshop who had since become an MIT professor [Crevier]. Minsky contended that these approaches were overly restrictive and underestimated the complexity of human intelligence. He argued that accurate AI required machines to possess perceptual and sensory capabilities resembling those of the human brain, emphasizing a departure from singularly rule-based abstract logic and reasoning into neural networks (though neural networks themselves were not yet ready). This difference in perspective triggered spirited debates within the AI community regarding the optimal avenues to attain machine intelligence.

We will further explore these debates, which lasted until the 1990s. As we cover the development of early robots in *Chapter 10*, we will examine how some of the robots of these years embraced symbolic logic while others employed analog computing and reasoning.

From Ambitious Predictions to the First AI Winter,

These early days of AI were marked by optimism and bold predictions. Pioneers in the field were convinced that the development of machines equal to humans in cognitive abilities was imminent. Many confidently spoke of achieving this goal within two decades or less. However, time has passed, and although advancements have been achieved, the dream of human-like AI remains a distant aspiration even today.

For instance, Herbert Simon predicted that machines would match human capabilities within twenty years [Simon]. Similarly, Marvin Minsky stated in 1967 that we would have human-level intelligent machines in a single generation [McCorduck]. In 1970, he mentioned that it would be in *"three to eight years"* in an interview in Life Magazine [McCorduck]. These ambitious claims not only generated public excitement but also raised funding expectations, a common issue in the evolution of AI as revenue generation from the technology produced still seemed distant, leaving funding dependent on the R&D line in government for defense applications. By the mid-1970s, it was clear that these predictions would not materialize.

Geopolitical factors began to influence the funding priorities of the US government, and even defense nonessentials were cut back. The oil crisis struck in 1973, triggered by an oil embargo imposed by members of OPEC (Organization of the Petroleum Exporting Countries) following the Arab-Israeli conflict. As a result of this embargo, oil prices skyrocketed worldwide. Economic consequences were devastating, with high inflation rates, economic recession, and increased unemployment.

Due to this economic turmoil in the face of criticism and the lack of substantial results, both the US and British governments ceased funding AI research in 1974 [McCorduck], marking the onset of the first *"AI winter."* We will see through the pages of this book in *Chapters 5* and *6* that there have been 3 of them so far.

During the AI winter of 1974, research funds dwindled, and progress was temporarily halted, except in robotics-related areas driven by industrial automation, which we will cover in *Chapter 12.* The private sector took the lead in industrial robotics, as economic challenges necessitated cost-cutting measures.

The AI winter was a period of introspection, contemplating past successes and challenges. However, following a temporary hiatus, AI continued its progression. By the 1980s, the field embraced a more pragmatic and realistic approach to development, further catalyzed by corporate involvement and actual economic applications. We will discuss this AI Renaissance of the 1980s in the next chapter.

5. Expert Systems and the Second AI Winter

"I think it's fair to say that personal computers have become the most empowering tool we've ever created. They're tools of communication, they're tools of creativity, and they can be shaped by their user."

Bill Gates,

Founder of Microsoft, philanthropist

2004

The history of AI has been characterized by transformative surges followed by periods of stagnation, often referred to as *"AI winters."* The 1980s represented the second significant turning point in this ongoing evolution. During this decade, following the first AI Winter mentioned above, substantial shifts toward a more practical research focus and broader technology adoption fundamentally reshaped the field.

In the 1980s, computers became significantly faster, smaller, and more affordable. The introduction of the IBM PC in 1981, alongside the release of Microsoft's MS-DOS in the same year and the launch of Apple's Macintosh in 1984, heralded a revolution in Information Technology (IT).

Personal computers empowered companies worldwide to implement applications that facilitated business processes and enabled more efficient data analysis for decision-making, a marked departure from paper-driven manual processes run by expert professionals and engineers.

As the mid-1980s dawned, large corporations and universities already possessed thousands of computers, enabling some relatively simple applications called expert systems. AI scientists shifted away from the broad, abstract, and overly ambitious challenges of the preceding decades, angling instead toward solving real-world problems at corporations or research programs funded directly by corporations rather than the government.

However, this shift to private enterprise that aimed to deliver tangible, calculable economic benefits did coexist harmoniously with fundamental research. This core research was also practical, including the development of the *backpropagation algorithm*, which is arguably the most important algorithm in history as it enables the neural networks that propel Generative AI, image processing, and self-driving cars, to name a few applications.

In the next section, we will discuss how AI recovered from its first winter and went to new heights in the 1980s.

From Stagnation to Resurgence through Expert Systems

As computers became more accessible and user-friendly, computer software was developed and commercialized to address specific business challenges. These software solutions were called *"expert systems"* and played a pivotal role in reinvigorating the field of AI, which had stagnated since around 1974.

Expert systems are specialized computer applications designed to tackle specific business problems or answer questions within narrow knowledge domains. They employ logical rules drawn from the expertise of human professionals, hence their name.

These expert systems found utility in diverse business contexts. In healthcare, they aided doctors in disease diagnosis by analyzing symptoms and medical data, enhancing precision. In technology firms, they assisted technical support teams by identifying and resolving product or software issues and providing tailored recommendations. In manufacturing, they automatically assessed product quality using production data and specifications. They optimized delivery routes, resource allocation, and inventory management to cut costs and enhance efficiency. In finance, they detected real-time suspicious transactions and fraud patterns. In short, they solved routine problems encountered in everyday business, leading to productivity and speed improvements.

Although expert systems gained prominence in the corporate landscape during the 1980s, their roots trace back to earlier decades. In the 1970s, Edward Feigenbaum and Edward Shortliffe created *"MYCIN,"* an expert system for diagnosing infectious diseases, marking a significant milestone in AI's healthcare applications. [Crevier]. Furthermore, IBM's *"Dendral,"* developed in the late 1960s, aimed to identify chemical compounds from spectroscopic data [McCorduck].

In the 1980s, companies like DEC (Digital Equipment Corporation) and Texas Instruments (TI) crafted highly specialized expert systems for engineering and medicine. Then, other software companies such as

IntelliCorp and Aion followed them [McCorduck]. Soon, corporations worldwide joined the expert systems trend, investing over a billion dollars in these solutions by 1985, either procuring them from software vendors or developing them in-house. This boom of expert systems fueled the growth of the AI industry, with hardware and software firms providing support for these systems.

Moreover, the rise of expert systems re-altered the funding landscape by changing the basis for development from the exclusive hands of government R&D to include a substantial corporate component. Many companies invested heavily in expert system research and implementation to gain a competitive edge, driving innovation in industries ranging from finance and healthcare to manufacturing and logistics. In the long term, not only does corporate funding enhance the resilience of AI research, but it also serves to shape its positive or negative direction.

We note that this is analogous to what happened with space exploration. Space exploration programs in America were once driven exclusively by NASA, which progressively began using private companies to develop components of its projects. Today, a significant share of space exploration is fully private, like SpaceX and Amazon's project Kuiper—satellite internet constellations that provide low-latency broadband internet—and even novel ideas like Sea Launch, a consortium that provided orbital launch services.

Advantages and Limitations of Expert Systems

Expert systems revolutionized decision-making processes by emulating human expertise in specific domains. While these systems offered remarkable benefits, their inherent limitations also shaped the trajectory of AI development.

Regarding the advantages, expert systems excelled within well-defined knowledge domains, often surpassing human capabilities in terms of precision and speed. Moreover, these systems consistently applied rules without succumbing to the influence of fatigue or human cognitive biases. Since they were based on rules and decision trees, their interpretability was a significant advantage, especially in critical healthcare and financial services sectors, which are highly regulated.

Nevertheless, expert systems also carried notable limitations. Primarily, they demanded detailed encoding of human expertise, a costly and time-consuming process. This entailed extensive interviews, collaborative efforts with subject matter experts, and a thorough, manual approach to meticulously codify that knowledge one idea at a time for the computer.

Additionally, these systems had limitations in terms of common-sense reasoning and could make mistakes when faced with unusual or unforeseen situations that fell outside their rule-based scope. They operated with inflexibility, struggling to adapt quickly to changing domains or rule adjustments. Challenges beyond their highly specialized expertise presented significant obstacles, making them less effective when dealing with issues slightly beyond their designated field. Those companies that owned the software and hardware of these systems minted fortunes on updates, upgrades, refactoring, and new knowledge inclusion.

These constraints rendered expert systems unwieldy and impeded corporations from achieving practical outcomes. Due to the simple and rigid rule-based architecture upon which they were based, expert systems are sometimes not even considered an AI application but just a conventional IT application. In this book, we still consider expert systems as a form of AI because they are ultimately machines with the ability to take an input and arrive at an output, albeit within narrow rule-based programming.

The Hardware Market Collapse and the Second Winter

Alongside the gradual discovery of the limitations in expert systems' functionality, the advent of the PC became a coffin nail for the industry.

The first expert systems generally operated on specialized large mainframe hardware called LISP machines [Newquist]. LISP, short for List Processing, was a high-level programming language created by John McCarthy and purpose-built for processing symbolic logic and manipulating data lists. As companies worldwide raced to develop and implement expert systems, a large multi-billion-dollar industry emerged to support this movement. This industry encompassed hardware companies like Symbolics and a company aptly named *"Lisp Machines."* But as IBM and Apple introduced increasingly powerful and affordable personal computers with natural versatility in application support as opposed to closed-architecture, specialized, and expensive LISP machines, PCs began to find utility in expert systems applications. Gradually, the rationale for purchasing LISP machines waned, leading to the complete dismantling of a once $5 billion industry when the stock prices for the specialized companies making these expensive machines collapsed in 1987.

The repercussions were dire: the obsolescence of these costly machines and the abrupt failure of the AI hardware market adversely impacted numerous AI companies that relied on such specialized hardware. By the end of 1993, more than 300 AI companies had shut down, gone bankrupt, or been acquired, effectively concluding the boom of AI in the 80s [Newquist].

With private sector influence drying up towards the late 1980s, the US government also scaled back its investment in AI again. Under the new leadership at DARPA, AI was no longer considered cutting-edge technology, owing mostly to the failure of so-called expert machines and the rise of Personal Computing. Resources were reallocated towards projects with perceived potential for more immediate results.

Government funding withdrawal had marked the onset of the first AI winter in 1974. This time, it was the 1987 hardware crash in the stock market that triggered the second AI winter, which persisted until the early 1990s. The burst of the Japanese asset price bubble in 1989 also contributed to the halt of AI and robotics in the Far East, a topic we will cover in more detail in *Chapter 13*.

The second winter, however, was relatively short. During the 1990s, AI research and applications would experience a revival, driven by the Dot-Com boom, delivering economic rationale to expand AI endeavors. The Dot-Com also saw a rapid advancements in computing power and memory alongside a reduction in form factor and power needs (solving key persistent technology dependencies), and a renewed emphasis on Machine Learning and neural networks (marking an advancement in programming).

Backpropagation and The Gradual Awakening of Neural Networks

In the previous chapter, we introduced how neural networks, the AI algorithm that mimics how our brains work, were invented in the 1950s. All advanced AI applications today run on neural networks ranging from ChatGPT to autonomous cars. A breakthrough in the 1980s on how to train neural networks made this possible.

Neural networks are composed of multiple layers of artificial neurons, with today's neural networks having millions of layers and billions of hyperparameters that must be adjusted to allow the network to solve specific problems. For example, GPT3.0 has 175 billion hyperparameters. A neural network trained to identify images would require very different hyperparameters than one trained to process language. A neural network trained to recognize human faces would need very different hyperparameters than one trained to identify handwritten characters.

Finding the best hyperparameters for each particular problem is called training the neural network. It is a formidable problem that can consume immense computational power and require a long time to finalize. In 1986, Geoffrey Hinton and David Rumelhart invented a crucial technique for neural network training known as "*backpropagation*" [Hinton and Rumelhart]. They built on earlier work by Finish computer scientist Seppo Linnainmaa in 1970, who created a training algorithm called automatic differentiation based on the chain rule developed by Gottlieb Leibniz 200 years before [Linnainmaa].

Backpropagation allows adjusting the hyperparameters in neural networks by refining these parameters over multiple iterations to minimize prediction errors. For instance, in a neural network for handwriting recognition, backpropagation would find the set of hyperparameters that minimize the percentage of times that a character is recognized wrongly. For example, the actual written character is "b," but the algorithm incorrectly identifies it as "*d.*" Training the algorithm in the myriad ways that cursive writing can be physically represented requires huge computing power and huge data samples; every individual's handwriting is different. Even modest neural networks today will not make errors deciphering even doctor pad handwriting.

What sets backpropagation apart is its computational efficiency and scalability. Computers in the 1980s were still too small to make neural networks practical. However, during the 1990s, advances in computing power made it worthwhile to employ backpropagation for training extensive neural networks, known as deep neural networks, with thousands or even millions of layers of neurons.

Backpropagation ushered in a new era in AI technology, where neural networks are pivotal in many of today's applications, including Large Language Models (LLMs) and machine vision systems, to name a few.

6. Machine Learning During the Dot-Com and the Third AI Winter

"The human mind isn't a computer; it cannot progress in an orderly fashion down a list of candidate moves and rank them by a score down to the hundredth of a pawn the way a chess machine does. Even the most disciplined human mind wanders in the heat of competition. This is both a weakness and a strength of human cognition. Sometimes these undisciplined wanderings only weaken your analysis. Other times they lead to inspiration, to beautiful or paradoxical moves that were not on your initial list of candidates."

Garry Kasparov,

Chess World Champion

Deep Thinking: Where Machine Intelligence Ends and Human Creativity Begins [Kasparov and Greengard]

2017

The 1990s marked a remarkable transformation in the technology sector, epitomized by the Dot-Com era. This era witnessed an explosive growth of technology companies, driven by the rapid expansion of the Internet and abundant investment capital. Amid this frenzy, Machine Learning gained prominence, with numerous startups integrating Machine Learning algorithms into their products and services. Tech companies like Google, Amazon, and eBay utilized Machine Learning to enhance their offerings and product recommendations. Moreover, the increase in computing power allowed for building much more extensive neural networks, called deep neural networks, that became practical for the first time in applications like language processing and image analysis.

Much like the expert systems period, the boom of AI in the 1990s in the West was undeniably fueled by private investment, marking another example of the importance of private sector motivation in the evolution of AI. We note the severity of high fixed costs in R&D and the general need for revenue generation around AI products in order to justify taking on the expense and the risk of *"false starts"* over time. The government, as a single customer using AI applications for national defense purposes, has become an insufficient condition, with broader marketplace digitization the key to unlocking AI value. We see this reality persist as digitization across every aspect of human life generates the data needed to train neural networks, and the new private sector space race fuels the next wave of AI development. While private investment brought a pragmatic and market-driven dimension to the AI landscape in the 1990s, it also exposed the field to market exuberance and the accompanying risks of financial bubbles. Ultimately, the Dot-Com crash of the year 2000 triggered the commencement of the third AI winter, putting a near-term end to rapid advancement in Machine Learning from startups and corporations.

The following section describes how Machine Learning made initial strides in startups and corporations during the Dot-Com era and enabled the current AI boom.

Machine Learning's Emergence Amid Dot-Com Startups

The Dot-Com era saw a surge in technology companies venturing into the burgeoning online landscape. The rapid ascent of tech firms during this decade was mainly propelled by the explosive growth of the Internet and an abundance of investment capital. Companies eager to establish their online presence raced into cyberspace. Investors seeking the next significant innovation were willing to back even unprofitable ventures provided a story existed as to how it would generate revenue in the future [Fisher].

This investment frenzy created a kaleidoscope of opportunities within the AI domain, and numerous AI companies engaged with various aspects of this technology. All these companies had something in common: they focused on machine-learning algorithms.

According to their use of AI, there were two kinds of companies. Firstly, some companies started to use Machine Learning algorithms extensively to improve their products and services and drive better customer experiences. Examples of such companies during this period include Amazon, Google, and eBay. Secondly, some companies specialized in developing Machine Learning algorithms and selling them as dedicated B2B (Business-to-business) AI solutions for other companies. This group included companies such as Autonomy Corporation, Nuance Communications, and NetPerceptions.

Within the first group of companies, Google played a pivotal role in the mainstreaming of AI-driven algorithms via Internet search. The PageRank algorithm, devised by Larry Page and Sergey Brin in 1996, used data to assess the relevance of web pages, leading to significant enhancements in the search process for anyone with an internet connection and a browser [Page and Brin]. Google's *"Did you mean?"* feature, for example, showcased AI's ability to correct spelling errors, demonstrating its commitment to user-friendly search.

Amazon, too, embraced AI. Fueled by AI algorithms, its recommendation engine analyzed user browsing and purchasing habits to suggest products, which boosted sales and enhanced customer satisfaction. Moreover, Amazon used AI in its supply chain management to optimize inventory levels and location and to predict demand, reducing costs and ensuring timely deliveries.

Similarly, eBay utilized AI to enhance user experience by automatically categorizing and recommending products. This improved eBay's search functionality, making it easier for users to find what they were looking for. eBay also used AI for fraud detection, identifying suspicious transactions, and ensuring the security of its marketplace.

AI algorithms are themselves the building blocks for what is estimated to be over $1 trillion of sustained economic value [Biswas et al.].

Numerous lesser-known but intriguing Dot-Com startups harnessed AI to create more intelligent and personalized services, for example:

- Ask Jeeves aimed to revolutionize user search experiences with natural language queries.
- Turbine pioneered AI-driven online gaming, crafting immersive multiplayer role-playing games like *"The Lord of the Rings Online."*
- JangoMail used AI algorithms to optimize email campaigns by analyzing user behavior.
- WisdomArk employed AI for tailored learning experiences, adapting content based on student performance.
- E.piphany, a CRM solutions provider, utilized AI to analyze extensive customer data for data-driven decisions and enhanced CRM strategies.

The second group of companies developed and marketed dedicated AI solutions, mainly B2B, for other companies. This group of AI startups pioneered their solutions across three domains—text analysis, voice recognition, and online personalization—areas that continue to draw the interest of numerous AI startups today.

In text analytics, companies such as Autonomy Corporation empowered businesses to extract valuable insights from extensive amounts of unstructured data. Before this wave of AI-driven advancement, software applications could only utilize explicitly formatted data in well-structured databases, such as a customer table with distinct fields (e.g., first name, last name, address, telephone number, date of registration, date of payment, etc.).

They were unable to process unstructured data that lacked explicit files, such as the volume and treasure trove found in documents, emails, customer service records, or system logs. Autonomy Corporation's software had the capability to comprehend and categorize these unstructured documents, establishing itself as a valuable asset for knowledge management and search applications.

Voice recognition relies on AI to convert audio input into meaningful text. Lernout & Hauspie, a Belgian company, pioneered speech recognition technology, allowing machines to understand and interpret spoken language. They were at the forefront of enabling voice-driven interactions with computers and laid the foundation for the voice assistants we use today, such as Apple's Siri and Amazon's Alexa. Moreover, Nuance Communications was an American company that developed speech recognition software powering applications such as customer services virtual assistants across various industries, including healthcare and telecommunications.

Finally, in the field of online personalization and recommendation, NetPerceptions took the lead in creating algorithms that analyzed user behavior and preferences to provide personalized product recommendations. Their software was often used in e-commerce and online retail environments to increase customer engagement and sales through its recommendation technology.

Progressive Adoption of Machine Learning in Corporations

Adopting Machine Learning algorithms was not confined solely to startups during the Dot-Com era. In parallel, the corporate world was also awakening to the transformative potential of these algorithms. Corporate adoption of Machine Learning began in 1989, when Axcelis, a pioneering US company, introduced the first Machine Learning software tailored for PC business applications [New York Times].

PCs were already handling vast volumes of data and performing complex mathematical operations with unprecedented efficiency. This increased capacity opened the door to the practical application of Machine Learning algorithms across various industries. Businesses became interested in harnessing these technologies to automate tasks, enhance decision-making, and boost efficiency, resulting in widespread adoption across different sectors.

Corporations found Machine Learning a great alternative to the expert systems of the 1980s. Most corporations were already very familiar with expert systems and saw them as challenging, time-consuming, and costly to implement. Machine Learning is grounded in the premise that machines can identify patterns and perform tasks without specific rule-based programming. In expert systems, programmers had to painstakingly explain every step to the computer to address issues such as stock trading decisions or loan approvals for bank customers. Instead of manually defining these rules like in expert systems, machines can simply learn from data by analogy—memorization vs. actually thinking. With Machine Learning, all that is required is to provide the computer with a database containing data, for example, historical stock market data or a list of customers whose credit applications were approved or declined, along with customer data such as age, salary, and occupation. With this information, the computer learns from the data and can make novel decisions in the future.

This type of Machine Learning found practical applications in business, allowing companies to automate tasks, enhance decision-making, and offer personalized products and services. Firms initially continued using expert systems but cautiously started integrating Machine Learning more extensively in the 1990s. The first large companies to adopt Machine Learning were technology firms, financial institutions, and telecoms.

The amount of information a company can get from customers is immense and invaluable. It is not only what the data might explicitly say but what can be reliably inferred from it under the rubric of an AI system. By way of example, using only the data your cell phone company legally possesses, a basic machine under today's common Machine Learning methods can accurately predict the following:

- Users' socioeconomic status [Soto and Frias-Martinez],
- Personality [Chittaranjan and Blom],
- Behavior such as mobility [Montoliu and Gatica-Perez),
- Spending behavior at a mall [Singh and Freeman],
- Credit default probability [Pedro and Proserpio].

Machine Learning can also distinguish depressed from non-depressed individuals with an accuracy of 98.5% and can predict mood swings in bipolar patients with higher accuracy than trained psychiatrists [Mumtaz]. What happens when a machine can do better than a psychiatrist at diagnosing a key element of patient well-being and care? Does it become a diagnostic tool, or does it replace the psychiatrist? We will talk extensively about the implications of AI for jobs and human work in general in *Chapters 22* and *23*.

To be sure, the widespread adoption of Machine Learning is not yet complete, and this question is not yet answered, though we are hurtling quickly toward it. The answer still lies in economics and scalability. A bullet train can get us from City A to City B faster than an automobile on a superhighway or a boat, but that does not mean we automatically justify putting bullet trains everywhere. Most companies, particularly in less technology-oriented industries, such as services or manufacturing, or SMEs in which the economy of most countries is dominated, are still struggling with Machine Learning and do not yet have a clear case for adoption.

Developing a tailored Machine Learning solution even for a large company's needs is a complex task that demands huge data, a highly technical team, budgets, time, and focus. Over time, large corporate businesses started establishing specialized data teams, initially including professionals skilled in crafting data-driven business reports, known as business intelligence specialists. As time progressed, these teams evolved to include data scientists, professionals who amalgamate programming mathematics skills and focus on training machines to tackle complex problems. The core requirements of AI technology impact industry organization, which in turn impacts the economy and society—important topics with medium and long-term ramifications that we will drill into in *Chapters 22 and 23*.

The Dot-Com Crash and the Third Winter

Regrettably, the remarkable surge in Internet adoption, accompanied by an influx of available venture capital and the swift escalation of valuations among Internet-based startups, proved unsustainable. This phenomenon, known as the Dot-Com bubble, inevitably reached its bursting point.

Between 1995 and the zenith of this bubble in March 2000, investments in the NASDAQ Composite Index surged dramatically, witnessing an astonishing 800% increase [Park]. This meteoric rise in stock prices was fueled by the exuberance and speculation surrounding internet-related companies. Investors swept up in the enthusiasm poured substantial sums of money into these high-flying tech stocks, believing that the Internet was ushering in a new era of limitless possibilities. The bubble eventually burst, triggering a steep decline. From its peak, the NASDAQ Composite Index plummeted by a staggering 78%. This sudden and severe downturn effectively wiped out all the gains that had been amassed during the heady days of the bubble.

The bursting of the Dot-Com bubble had far-reaching consequences for the AI landscape, resulting in the demise of several prominent startups. For example, among the startups mentioned earlier, Autonomy Corporation, NetPerceptions, WisdomArk, E.piphany, and Lernout & Hauspie did not survive the Dot-Com crash.

This devastating crash ushered in the third AI winter, a period characterized by a significant downturn in AI investment. In the aftermath of the Dot-Com crash, investors grew increasingly wary and hesitant, exercising caution in their approach to AI projects as dot-com businesses proved largely incapable of generating sustained revenue. Similarly, corporations became more cautious and significantly decelerated their adoption of Machine Learning.

Independent of the investment bubble, AI faced significant disappointment during the boom years. AI had garnered substantial attention and funding, accompanied by lofty expectations regarding its potential. Nevertheless, as the decade unfolded, it became increasingly clear that the anticipated advancements in AI were falling short.

Natural Language Processing (NLP) systems, encompassing chatbots and language translation tools, fell short of achieving human-like understanding and fluency, often delivering basic responses and struggling with context. Speech recognition technology, envisioned for seamless voice interactions with computers, also grappled with accuracy and context issues, frustrating users and limiting its adoption. AI-powered e-commerce recommendation systems aimed to transform online shopping but frequently provided inaccurate or irrelevant product suggestions. Similarly, AI-driven personalized marketing campaigns intended to deliver tailored content but often came across as intrusive, inundating users with poorly targeted advertisements. Once again, AI systems fell short of the human-level intelligence and capabilities envisioned, leading to a more cautious approach to their development.

In the post-crash years, starting in 2002, skepticism grew significantly. The term was linked with systems that frequently fell short of their grand promises. This negative perception made many computer scientists and IT professionals in the 2000s shy away from using "*Artificial Intelligence*" to describe their work, even though they often worked with AI technologies. Instead, they adopted alternative terms such as computer science, data analysis, data science, knowledge systems, cognitive systems, or intelligent agents [Markoff]. This shift was intended to avoid the stigma associated with AI and the overly inflated expectations that surrounded it.

Supervised, Unsupervised, and Reinforcement Learning

Having previously introduced Machine Learning in earlier chapters, let us now delve deeper into the main types of Machine Learning and their diverse applications, noting its pivotal role in driving AI during the 1990s.

There are three fundamental approaches in Machine Learning: supervised learning, unsupervised learning, and reinforcement learning, each one capable of driving different applications.

Supervised learning is one of the most common and widely used paradigms in Machine Learning. It relies on having a labeled dataset where the algorithm learns to map inputs to corresponding outputs. Imagine you are a banker and have a dataset of banking customers and their attributes, well-structured fields for each mortgage given by the bank in the past, including customer salary, customer monthly expenses, length of employment, age, monthly mortgage payment, interest rate, etc. Additionally, for each mortgage, you also have a field that denotes if there has been a default on payments. This last field is called a *"label,"* as this is what the algorithm is going to try to model based on its relationship to the other data points. The algorithm is going to look at all the historical records of previous mortgages and model the relation between the label—default or no default—and all the fields related to the mortgage and the customer. Based on this relation, the algorithm learns from mortgages given by the bank in the past to anticipate whether new customers will default on their mortgages or not. The more data over time, the more accurate the model will be. The bank will then use the output to make decisions about customers to whom it will extend credit. This is called a supervised learning algorithm because the labels are the expected output of the algorithm, and the data fields are the material to be studied. The training process is analogous to a teacher, who already has the answers, supervising the repetitive learning process of a student.

This approach is ideal for classification and prediction problems. Classification problems are problems about grouping data into a limited number of buckets, such as categorizing email as spam or not spam or classifying mortgage customers into *"will likely default"* or *"will not likely default."* Prediction problems are problems about predicting the exact numeric value of something, such as *"What will sales be next month?"* and *"What will the price of this stock be tomorrow?"* Notable supervised algorithms in this family include linear regression—which we talked about in *Chapter 3*—as well as most recommendation algorithms, most decision trees, and most neural networks, which we will present later in this chapter.

In contrast, unsupervised learning focuses on uncovering hidden patterns in data that lack predefined labels. There are three main applications of unsupervised learning: identifying segments or clusters, finding anomalies, and Generative AI applications like deep fakes. We will talk about deep fakes in *Chapter 7.*

Clustering is used to classify a group of similar data points into segments, revealing intrinsic structures in the data. The difference between simple classification and clustering is that in classification, the groups that you are interested in are known in advance, whereas in clustering, you need to find those groups. A classic use case of clustering is giving a set of customer segmentation data to the algorithm and asking it to identify x number of customer segments, marking which customer is in which segment. Using the previous example of identifying customers at risk of mortgage default, we could provide the whole customer database of creditworthy customers to an unsupervised algorithm and ask it to group them into, perhaps, ten segments, not knowing what those segments would be. The algorithm might come back with segments such as people over 40 with a stable job, people over 30 with solid savings, and people with another apartment that is already rented. In this case, unlike supervised learning algorithms, there are no labels used, and hence it is unsupervised.

Unsupervised learning is essential in social network analysis for identifying communities, understanding genomic data to spot genetic patterns, and market segmentation to comprehend consumer behavior. Are you a Democrat or Republican? You do not need to actually declare for AI to know. In fact, limited preference data on simply what you like and do not like enables AI to predict an individual's preferences better than:

- Coworkers (if it has 10 data points on your preferences, for example, a *"like"* on a product review on Facebook)
- Friends (if it has more than 70 data points)
- Parents or siblings (if it has more than 150), and
- Spouses (if it has more than 300) [Haiden].

Finally, reinforcement learning involves making sequential decisions to maximize cumulative rewards over time, and it mimics the psychology of how humans and animals learn through external stimuli. Reinforcement learning learns through interaction with an environment, taking actions, and receiving feedback based on those actions. Reinforcement learning is applied in autonomous robotics, financial portfolio management, and training AI players in games. In summary, reinforcement learning is learning by doing, sometimes succeeding and sometimes making mistakes, but learning from the experience.

Among the three types of Machine Learning algorithms, supervised learning has experienced the most remarkable growth and development in recent decades, driven by two fundamental factors. First, during the 1990s, extensive labeled databases became available for tackling classification and prediction problems. Classification problems are problems about grouping data into a limited number of buckets, such as categorizing email as spam or not spam or classifying mortgage customers into *"will likely default"* or *"will not likely default."* Prediction problems are problems about predicting the exact numeric value of something, such as *"What will sales be next month?"* and *"What will the price of this stock be tomorrow?"* These databases were crucial for training supervised models and meaningfully evaluating their performance, making supervised learning a practical and attractive choice.

Second, supervised models demonstrated remarkable effectiveness, boasting high accuracy and relative ease of implementation in real-world applications, especially compared to unsupervised and reinforcement models, which are much more intricate and complex.

The Gargantuan Growth of Deep Neural Networks

As we have previously reviewed, neural networks represent a computational model that draws inspiration from the way the human brain functions. They are made up of artificial neurons, which are networked nodes capable of learning and processing information.

In the 1990s, computers became faster and more powerful, and their storage capacity expanded significantly. It became feasible to build very large-scale neural networks, known as deep neural networks, because they have a large number of layers. Moreover, the backpropagation algorithm published in 1986 enabled the training of gigantic neural networks because, as explained in the previous chapter, backpropagation is an efficient and scalable method. In contrast to traditional neural networks with one layer like the Perceptron of 1957, deep neural networks can encompass millions of interconnected neuron layers laden with billions of parameters. This complex and flexible architecture enables these networks to grasp and represent information in a considerably very intricate and abstract fashion.

Despite the tremendous power of deep neural networks, their adoption into real business applications has been gradual, owing to the complex intricacies of training and usage compared to simpler Machine Learning systems and the rationale for reaching the *"tipping point"* that makes them commercially viable across applications; they are more difficult to work with, often require more highly specialized data scientists, and are more expensive to run because of their high computational load.

However, unlike simpler algorithms, deep neural networks can capture nuanced relationships within the data, making them very effective for highly intricate tasks such as image recognition when a simple shade of color or imprecise line in image capture does not change identifying the original subject, Natural Language Processing, and complex decision-making like self-driving cars. Simpler algorithms work well in problems where the relation between data and output is less complex and the outputs more finite, e.g., a single yes or no question.

Two primary types of deep neural networks received a big impulse during the 1990s, and each specialized in addressing two separate and significant problems. On the one hand, Recurrent Neural Networks (RNNs) are designed to analyze data that varies over time, such as human language, where one word follows another. On the other hand, Convolutional Neural Networks (CNNs) are employed to study multi-dimensional grid-like data, as in the case of images. Video, which is two-dimensional and varies over time, combines both types of neural networks.

Remembering Words with Recurrent Neural Networks

Human language is undeniably one of AI's most formidable challenges. Early deep neural networks encountered a fundamental limitation in effectively handling language. The critical initial obstacle was their inability to preserve essential information over time, like recalling a concept mentioned minutes or hours earlier in a conversation. Because of this constraint, deep learning made a significant breakthrough with the development of Long Short-Term Memory (LSTM) networks.

LSTMs were created by Sepp Hochreiter and Jürgen Schmidhuber in 1997 [Hochreiter and Schmidhuber], and their most notable innovation was introducing an internal memory structure along with adaptive gates in each network unit. These gates allow LSTMs to decide what information to keep, what to forget, and what to generate as output, effectively addressing the challenge of long-term dependencies in sequences and solving the aforementioned problem. Additionally, in an LSTM network, information flows in two directions, forward and backward in time. The forward connections are the standard ones in a neural network, and the backward connections are referred to as recurrent connections. This bidirectionality enables them to capture long-term temporal dependencies more effectively— like words or ideas whose meaning depends on another word said before. Because of this recurrence, such networks are called Recurrent Neural Networks.

RRNs are actually much older than LSTM. In 1982, a physicist called John Hopfield had already implemented one called the Hopfield Network [Hopfield]. But it was LSTM that perfectioned the concept of RRN. LSTM plays a crucial role in applications such as automatic translation, text generation, and sentiment analysis. They are also used in time series prediction in finance, voice analysis, and anomaly detection in sequential data.

The versatility of LSTMs drove their widespread adoption in various industries in the following decades. Until generative AI became mainstream, LSTM was the main algorithm powering chatbots and voicebots. We will talk about Generative AI in *Chapter 7*. Apart from language, today, we use LSTM in problems structured in time sequences of data. For example, in finance,

LSTMs are employed for stock price prediction and algorithmic trading. In healthcare, LSTMs are utilized for monitoring vital signs to anticipate medical interventions. LSTMs are also used in autonomous vehicles to predict the trajectory of moving objects, understand traffic patterns, and enhance decision-making processes.

Identifying Shapes with Convolutional Neural Networks

Our visual sense is one of the paramount channels for perceiving and understanding the world. CNNs are intelligent algorithms specifically designed to interpret images. They function as digital detectives meticulously scrutinizing images for critical patterns such as edges, shapes, or specific features. They do this through layers of filters that analyze the image and automatically learn which parts are relevant. In mathematics, these filters are called convolutions, thus the name of Convolutional Neural Networks. This approach allows CNNs to play a vital role in tasks such as facial recognition, object classification in photographs, or even medical diagnosis based on images, as they can efficiently identify critical details in captured or live images and make decisions based on them.

A prominent figure in this domain was Yann LeCun, widely recognized for his pivotal contributions to the advancement and widespread adoption of CNNs. LeCun is vocal about his opinions on AI development. We will quote him multiple times in this book. In 1998, LeCun introduced a groundbreaking neural network designed to recognize handwritten characters, known as LeNet-5 [LeCun]. LeNet-5 established the groundwork for applying CNNs in diverse tasks encompassing image classification and object detection. Even if it was not the first CNN, it was the first that demonstrated practical applications.

It is important to note that an abundance of training data was paramount for the development of CNNs. Yann LeCun recognized this necessity and responded by creating the MNIST database (Modified National Institute of Standards and Technology), comprised of meticulously labeled images featuring handwritten digits from 0 to 9. Over time, MNIST evolved into an industry standard, offering a rigorous yardstick for evaluating character recognition and classification algorithms across various research fields. It was also used in multiple machine-learning competitions.

Likewise, another ambitious undertaking took shape with the inception of ImageNet, spearheaded by Fei-Fei Li at Stanford University in 2006 [Hempel]. This extraordinary database amassed millions of meticulously labeled images distributed across thousands of diverse categories, effectively establishing itself as one of the largest and most formidable datasets ever devised for image classification. ImageNet's reputation flourished through an annual competition that garnered participation from some of the best researchers and enthusiasts worldwide: the ImageNet Large Scale Visual Recognition Challenge (ILSVRC) [Li et al.].

The Tree of Intelligence in Machine Learning

Decision trees are another fundamental technique in supervised Machine Learning and became vogue in AI in the 1990s. These are graphical models that assist in making decisions based on multiple conditions and input features. Imagine an inverted tree where each question about a specific feature of the problem is represented as a branch, and each possible answer is depicted in the leaves that these branches lead to. Input data follows this tree, and at each step, a decision is made based on the tests conducted at the branches until it reaches a leaf that represents the final decision or prediction.

Decision trees are straightforward yet potent models. Their logical and efficient structure provides a systematic approach for encoding and handling decision rules and facilitating automated data-driven choices. The key strengths of decision trees lie in their simplicity of interpretation and their versatility across various applications like object classification and recommendation systems.

Decision trees have played a pivotal role in the history of AI. First, their simplicity meant that for many companies, the first algorithm ever implemented was a decision tree. Second, their interpretability and transparent decision-making process have made them essential in fields like banking and healthcare, with tools based on them aiding in medical diagnosis via insights into the factors influencing patient outcomes. Interpretability is critical in regulated industries like banking that give consumers the legal right to be informed about how decisions were made. For that reason, decision trees have been widely used in shaping the evolution of Machine Learning algorithms, with their application in credit scoring, for example, transforming the lending business by enabling vastly improved evaluation of credit allocation while remaining compliant with regulation. Lastly, decision trees are also integral tools in cybersecurity, where their ability to analyze complex patterns helps identify and prevent cyber threats in real-time, showcasing their ongoing importance in safeguarding digital ecosystems.

A challenge in building decision trees is selecting the most valuable variables—also called features—for making intelligent decisions and preventing the model from becoming too specific. Ross Quinlan addressed this issue in 1993 with the C4.5 algorithm [Quinlan]. This algorithm selects the most informative feature to split the dataset at each step and performs pruning to avoid overfitting, resulting in accurate and understandable models.

In 1995, a significant breakthrough was introduced with the Random Forest algorithm, developed by Tin Kam Ho, an IBM engineer [Ho]. Unlike a single decision tree, a Random Forest creates multiple trees and combines their results, making it more robust and resistant to overfitting. Each tree is trained on a different part of the data, and then their predictions are combined to obtain an accurate final forecast. This approach makes it an essential tool in various fields, from biology to finance.

Finally, in 1999, Jerome Friedman introduced Gradient Boosting [Friedman], which changed the way we build decision trees. This is an iterative approach that creates a first tree and measures the errors this tree is making. Then, it creates another tree that tries to minimize these errors. Successively, over many iterations, the decision tree is improved at each stage by learning from mistakes. This iterative process produces a highly accurate and robust final model by combining and enhancing multiple trees, making it a powerful tool for classification and regression problems.

Gradual Advances in Unsupervised Learning

We have already explored the most significant supervised algorithms of the 1990s. However, it is also essential to acknowledge the progress in unsupervised learning during the same decade as it holds a key for the eventual development of Artificial General Intelligence (AGI.)

Humans possess a remarkable knack for acquiring knowledge without formal instruction; for example, effortlessly identifying objects in their field of vision or within images, discerning between object types—like dogs or cats—and performing much more complex tasks such as learning languages, adapting social behavior, walking, crawling, using certain tools, and identifying danger. Transferring this innate human ability to machines presents a formidable challenge and requires unsupervised learning models to activate. Realizing unsupervised learning's full potential holds the promise of a groundbreaking leap forward in AI, one that hurdles towards realizing Artificial General Intelligence (AGI), such as enabling machines to learn as fast as human beings using algorithms that deploy video data instead of labeled text samples.

Initial work in unsupervised learning models can be seen in *Clustering*—explained a few pages back—also known as *Segmentation Algorithms*, which have existed in some basic form since the 1950s. The most classical *clustering algorithm* is called *K-means*, conceived by Stuart Lloyd in 1957. This algorithm required data scientists to specify how many data segments they wanted to separately identify based on defined characteristics, and the algorithm would identify those segments using the data provided. For example, the data scientist could specify the desire to identify ten segments in its customer database of 1 million customers based on the frequency of purchase, average amount, and age. K-Means would accomplish that task perfectly. However, it could not determine whether it would make more sense to have 5 or 20 segments instead of 10 or whether the e criteria chosen are the relevant ones. The way K-means operates is by identifying as many "*centers of gravity*" in the data as segments being requested and assigning each customer to the closest "*center of gravity.*" This means that the segments are spherical in shape, and they will roughly have a similar number of customers in each segment, pointing to the inherent limitations in the actionability of the output.

In the 1990s, a newer algorithm was developed that was able to address these problems. It was called *DBSCAN* (Density-Based Spatial Clustering of Applications with Noise) and was invented by Martin Ester in 1996 [Ester et al.]. Unlike *K-means*, which assumes spherical and similarly-sized clusters, DBSCAN dynamically identifies clusters based on the density of data points. This allows *DBSCAN* to detect clusters of arbitrary shapes and adapt to varying cluster densities within a dataset. Moreover, *DBSCAN* does not require the prior specification of the number of clusters, a limitation inherent in *K-means*. This makes it more versatile and applicable to real-world datasets where the number of clusters may not be known in advance. Additionally, DBSCAN is adept at identifying and labeling noise or outliers within the dataset, offering a more nuanced understanding of the underlying data structure.

DBSCAN has multiple applications and is still widely used. It has been used to analyze traffic patterns and identify congestion areas in transportation studies. Clustering spatial-temporal data from traffic sensors can assist in optimizing traffic flow and improving urban mobility. In image processing, DBSCAN has been widely used to delineate boundaries between different structures, contributing to tasks like object recognition and computer vision, which are practical for autonomous vehicles to identify other cars, pedestrians, or signs. *DBSCAN* can also help identify unusual patterns or data points that deviate from the expected norm in a dataset. This is valuable in fraud detection, network security, and quality control in manufacturing. *DBSCAN* has been applied in bioinformatics, aiding in identifying groups of genes with similar expression patterns and helping researchers uncover potential relationships and functional associations in biological data. Finally, in marketing analytics, businesses can target specific customer segments with marketing strategies by using DBSCAN to segment customers based on their purchasing behavior.

Unsupervised algorithms are highly complex and difficult to develop precisely because they do not have labels, there is no straightforward way to train them, and they are inherently bespoke. But that said, unsupervised learning has been very useful in the field of Generative AI. For example, unsupervised algorithms like word embeddings are used in NLP. Generative Adversarial Networks (GAN) are another unsupervised algorithm used in image or video synthesis, particularly deep-fakes. We will explore this in detail in *Chapter 7.*

Unlocking Reinforcement Learning's Potential

During these years, there were also significant developments in a third type of algorithm called *Reinforcement Learning.* Reinforcement Learning is mission-critical to AI due to its predominant use in applications where AI engages with an external environment, receives data/stimuli, and takes action based on it, much like humans do in everyday interaction.

For example, reinforcement learning is used to train autonomous vehicles to make real-time decisions, such as navigating through traffic, lane-keeping, and parking, by learning from continuous interactions with the driving environment. In robotics, reinforcement learning is applied to tasks like grasping objects, locomotion, and manipulation, allowing robots to adapt their actions based on feedback received from their surroundings.

Reinforcement learning is also utilized for optimizing inventory management, supply chain logistics, and demand forecasting, improving overall efficiency and reducing operational costs. Additionally, reinforcement learning has excelled in mastering complex games and achieving high levels of performance, which we explore in the next section.

The development of these algorithms has been iterative and gradual. In 1989, just before the Dot-Com boom, Christopher Watkins achieved a monumental breakthrough by developing the algorithm known as Q-learning [Watkins and Dayan]. Q-learning provided a more efficient and effective way to tackle reinforcement learning slowness and complexities, becoming a fundamental technique for teaching machines how to make optimal decisions in sequential and changing situations.

Q-learning addresses this problem by creating the *"Q-function"* function that assigns numerical values, called *"Q-values,"* to state and action pairs. Essentially, the Q function represents the expected cumulative reward an agent can obtain by taking a specific action in each particular state or situation. In practical terms, think of a game: the higher the Q function is for a specific action in a particular game stage, the better it is to take that action. The algorithm gradually learns the optimal Q-values across scenarios and all possible moves as it plays more and more, enabling the agent to make informed decisions.

Q-learning is a particular case of a family of algorithms called TD algorithms (Temporal Difference) because Q-learning tries to increase the Q-

Values little by little with time as learnings are made. Therefore, there is a progressive *"temporal difference"* in the Q-Values. TD algorithms were not new; they had been studied since the 1970s, but Q-learning was the first practical implementation. Q-learning has become the most popular choice today due to its efficient learning process, enabling AI to acquire knowledge and make sound decisions rapidly.

A few years later, in 1992, Gerald Tesauro, an IBM engineer, made another famous implementation of this TD concept to master the strategic and skillful game of Backgammon: TD-Gammon [Tesauro]. Backgammon is a two-player board game where players move their checkers around the board based on dice rolls to bear off all their checkers before the opponent.

TD-Gammon played countless games of Backgammon against itself and adjusted its strategies based on the outcomes. As it progressed, TD-Gammon became increasingly skilled at the game, although initially, it could not consistently outperform the best human Backgammon players. What is unique about TD-Gammon is that it uses an artificial neural network to learn through reinforcement learning, allowing it to improve its gameplay over time.

The way TD-Gammon worked is very similar to Q-Learning. In simple terms, TD-Gammon calculates a number representing how likely it is to win the game in each move. Every time it moves, TD-Gammon recalculates this probability and determines if it is getting closer to winning or losing. TD-Gammon learns by observing the differences between these estimates and tries to maximize the probability of winning by doing more of the actions that have gotten it closer to winning in the past.

Implementing reinforcement learning algorithms presents formidable challenges due to their predominant use in applications where AI engages with an external environment, such as playing against opponents or enabling a robot to learn to walk little by little. Consequently, the AI's learning process is time-intensive as it needs numerous interactions, each consuming valuable time.

As we discussed, human beings and animals largely learn through reinforcement and trial and error. It is no surprise that Reinforcement Learning algorithms remain one of the most promising avenues for advancing Artificial General Intelligence (AGI). We will delve into that in *Chapter 9*.

Deep Blue's Brute Force Triumph against Kasparov

A noteworthy interlude at this juncture comes from one of the most iconic moments in AI history, the 1997 victory of IBM's computer, Deep Blue, over the Russian chess champion Gary Kasparov, then the world's highest-rated player and had held the world chess title on five occasions. Interestingly, Kasparov had previously defeated Deep Blue one year earlier [Kasparov].

Rather than intelligence in the human sense, Deep Blue employed brute force. It could assess millions of chess positions per second, guided by an evaluation function grounded in chess principles and human expertise. It was, in some respects, merely the culmination of a so-called Expert System. The computer used its database and computational power to search exhaustively to identify optimal moves, utilizing advanced search algorithms. Moreover, Deep Blue had access to an extensive database of chess openings and end games, and its parallel processing capability allowed it to analyze multiple positions simultaneously.

Despite its win in chess, Deep Blue did not exhibit human-like intelligence at all. Instead, it relied on highly efficient, rule and probability-oriented software devoid of Machine Learning or neural networks. Deep Blue's strategy hinged on computational power and applying pre-programmed chess knowledge for compelling gameplay.

While IBM Deep Blue was not reinforcement learning but rather something simpler, the significance of Deep Blue's triumph extended beyond the chessboard; it symbolized the advancing capabilities of AI and sparked discussions about its potential to rival human intelligence, especially in intellectual pursuits.

While Deep Blue was not a very intelligent system as we think of them today, it was an example of how even a basic AI system can best humans owing only to processing power. A seismic shift, however, came in 2016 when a pure AI based on a *reinforcement learning* algorithm defeated the world's best players in the complex game of Go. We will review AlphaGo in the next chapter.

7. The Great Financial Crisis and the Long AI Summer

"No one knows what the right algorithm is, but it gives us hope that if we can discover some crude approximation of whatever this algorithm is and implement it on a computer, that can help us make a lot of progress."

Andrew Ng

Computer Scientist, Founder of Google Brain and Coursera

The current period of prosperity in AI development in which we find ourselves in 2024 has been particularly long. As a result, we can call it a *"prolonged AI summer."*

As we've explored throughout this book, an initial period of thriving prosperity in AI research started in 1956, followed by the first AI winter in 1974, triggered by drastic reductions in AI research funding as a response to the oil crisis by the US and UK governments. Subsequently, the second winter occurred in 1987 due to market collapses in the hardware industry, and the bursting of the Japanese asset price bubble burst in 1989. Finally, the third winter descended in 2000 with the Dot-Com crisis.

But we note that following the aftermath of the Great Financial Crisis of 2008, the boom-bust cycle seemed to break as the AI industry did not weaken; rather, it surprisingly emerged more robust and resilient than ever. Unlike previous occurrences, this crisis did not trigger an AI winter. Instead, it marked an evolution in continuation of the AI summer that had started in the early 2000s.

We believe there are several reasons for this. First, the technological underpinnings fell into place by the year 2002. On the purely AI side, all the theoretical foundations for algorithms were already invented: deep neural networks for speech and image processing (which are called recursive and convolutional, respectively), complex decision trees, advanced unsupervised algorithms for segmentation and anomaly identification, and powerful reinforcement learning algorithms. Productizations of these core technologies were also now available. Likewise, technological dependencies to scaled AI adoption had also been solved with the rapid global growth of cost-efficient distributed server technology, also known as cloud, in the embodiment of products like AWS, Azure, and Google Cloud, which replaced prohibitive fixed cost and high capex deployment requirements with scalable variable cost models, enabling nearly any company to deploy AI applications. On the commercial side, AI researchers and enterprises quickly adapted to the economic challenges brought about by the crisis by shifting their focus towards practical applications, with enough core science and work already "*in the bag*" to enable it. This paved the way for the deployment of advanced algorithms for voice assistants, facial recognition in images, and object identification in photographs or videos, all of which had practical economic applications in B2C and B2B products and a ready-to-go financial model to support the effort.

Innovations in algorithms during this period, especially in deep neural networks, laid the groundwork for transformative technologies like Generative AI, which we will discuss in the next chapter, and autonomous robots, which we will explore in *Chapter 14.*

AI Emerges Stronger from the Great Financial Crisis

The Dot-Com crisis was a seismic event that shook the technology industry in the early 2000s and exacted a devastating toll on numerous startups and AI research initiatives. As the industry was gradually recovering from this extended period of uncertainty, the 2008 financial crisis hit. The seismic shockwaves of the 2008 Great Financial Crisis rippled through the global economic landscape, triggered by the dramatic collapse of Lehman Brothers and fueled by the unstable realm of high-risk mortgage loans. This cataclysmic event cast the world into the abyss of a severe recession, the repercussions of which rippled far and wide across industries. But in a remarkable turn of events, the AI sector displayed unexpected resilience and seized opportunities to fortify its position in contrast to what happened in the Dot-Com crisis.

A notable consequence of the financial maelstrom within the AI industry was a stark constriction of funding and investment. In this challenging funding environment, AI researchers and businesses quickly shifted their focus toward projects that could yield concrete value to existing businesses and products, providing rapid returns on investment by increasing efficiencies and lowering costs. This marked a momentous transformation, shifting the AI landscape from purely academic and theoretical research and thrusting it into practical applications. Consequently, AI experienced an acceleration, specifically through integrating AI technologies into applications like fraud detection in the finance sector, solution suites such as IBM Watson in healthcare, and e-commerce or video streaming sectors with advanced recommendation engines.

So, while many industries, including smaller banks, grappled with survival, AI emerged as a beacon of efficiency, offering the prospect of automating processes, cutting down costs, and chasing revenue via expanded Customer Experiences and the project investment needed to implement it. Firms eagerly sought AI solutions to optimize operations and help fortify P&Ls during the growth and revenue challenges of the financial crisis.

In the financial sector, for instance, many AI startups shifted their focus towards crafting highly effective AI algorithms for fraud detection, shielding banks from substantial losses. AI Startups specialized in assisting corporate clients with cost-reduction initiatives also thrived. Notably, UiPath played a pivotal role in streamlining global company operations through a groundbreaking technology called Robotic Process Automation (RPA), which automates repetitive tasks on computer screens.

IBM Watson, which debuted in 2010, also illustrates this transformative period. Watson is an AI system that found its niche in industries as diverse as healthcare, legal research, and business management and yielded substantial cost reductions and operational efficiencies in each of them. Moreover, IBM Watson made history by triumphing in a televised quiz show, Jeopardy, demonstrating its remarkable ability to answer complex questions and outsmart human competitors.

In response to the economic storm, governments across the globe ushered in an array of stimulus packages and economic revitalization programs. Among these measures, investments in technology and innovation took center stage. As governments recognized AI's potential to fuel economic growth and stimulate job creation, the AI industry was bolstered by these fortuitous governmental interventions.

Simultaneously, the financial meltdown acted as a catalyst for industry consolidation. Struggling to secure funding, smaller AI startups became prime acquisition targets for tech giants with deep pockets. Google's acquisition of the AI startup DeepMind in 2014 [Shu] is a glaring example of this trend. This strategic move propelled Google into the forefront of AI endeavors, facilitating advancements like deep learning for automatic translation and speech recognition. Moreover, in 2013, Google acquired Boston Dynamics, a renowned robotics enterprise celebrated for its pioneering work in developing autonomous bipedal and quadrupedal robots [Lowensohn]. Apple, too, seized the opportunity, acquiring Siri, a voice-driven virtual assistant, in 2010.

While the immediate aftermath of the 2008 crisis posed formidable challenges for the AI industry, it ultimately forged an industry marked by resilience and practicality, which has continued to flourish and exert its profound influence on business and society.

Netflix's Million-Dollar Quest for Recommendation Algorithms

Recommendation engines undeniably stand out as the most practical machine-learning algorithms developed during the 2000s. Some of them are supervised, and some of them are unsupervised.

In a world filled with choices, ranging from movies and music to products and news, recommendation systems emerged as valuable tools designed to simplify people's lives. These ingenious systems, driven by the rise of e-commerce and on-demand video and audio streaming services, became crucial in helping users discover relevant content amidst the overwhelming sea of available options.

Google's YouTube, which has over 1 billion videos—more than anyone can ever watch in a dozen lifetimes—takes an individual's viewing history, combines it with other data you have given Google, and presents items that it knows you will have a high likelihood to enjoy. Other tech companies like Amazon and Netflix also adopted similar systems as essential components of their strategy, relying on them to provide personalized recommendations that enhance customer satisfaction and retention.

Recommendation algorithms are extraordinarily complex mathematical undertakings and encompass a large variety of approaches. Most of them are supervised approaches, but some of them are unsupervised. Content-based filtering, for instance, relies on item attributes—such as film genre, country, actor, or director—to tailor suggestions, evaluating user preferences through their historical interactions with content. On the other hand, user-based filtering delves into matching users with similar tastes and proposing items cherished by their like-minded counterparts. Collaborative filtering merges both strategies by analyzing user-item interactions and unveiling user interests while considering item characteristics influenced by collective behavior. Knowledge-based algorithms tap into expert insights and are similar to the expert systems we discussed in *Chapter 5*. Popularity-based algorithms gravitate towards suggesting trending items to a broader audience. Finally, hybrid approaches blend a mix of techniques, aiming to harness the unique strengths of each method, alleviating their limitations.

Recognizing the mission-critical nature of honing its recommendation systems, Netflix initiated a competition in 2006 called "*The Netflix Prize*" [Lohr]. The challenge was enticing: a million-dollar prize awaited those who could elevate the performance of Netflix's recommendation algorithm by a substantial 10% margin. This ambitious endeavor sparked fervent enthusiasm within the machine-learning community, drawing the participation of thousands of talents from across the globe.

The Netflix competition underscored the advancement of recommendation techniques and galvanized further research into this domain. *Due to the complexity and the ambitious goal of achieving a 10% improvement, it was not until 2009 that the coveted prize was awarded.*

The winner was a team called *"BellKor's Pragmatic Chaos,"* which employed a hybrid approach to the problem, merging the predictions of several individual models to create a more accurate and robust overall recommendation system. This victory underscored the potential of hybrid recommendation algorithms. Accordingly, they have gained more prevalence in delivering precise and varied content recommendations and are used today by most scaled video streamers, including Netflix, Hulu, and Disney, as well as most retailers like Amazon and Walmart.

Since then, Netflix has persistently fine-tuned its recommendation systems in order to furnish users with ever-more precise and tailored content suggestions. Its brand has become synonymous with this feature and for solving the inherent problems in long-form video discovery, building nearly $60 billion in collective market capitalization since the 1 million Netflix Prize competition.

The Era of Voice Assistants: Siri, Google Now, Alexa, and Cortana

The early 2010s also marked a significant turning point in the world of language technology with the introduction of voice assistants into the consumer market. Tech giants unveiled their voice-driven virtual assistants, namely Apple's Siri (2011), Google's Google Now (2012), Amazon's Alexa (2014), and Microsoft's Cortana (2014). These smartphone applications answer user queries, provide recommendations, and execute commands.

At the core of these voice assistants lies a complex synergy of technologies, predominantly based on the *Recurrent Deep Neural Networks (or RRN)* we discussed earlier. Speech recognition takes a critical stage as a foundational component. When users interact with these virtual assistants through speech, their spoken words get processed by automatic speech recognition algorithms, translating the frequencies and sound waves from a user's voice into a code, which it then executes, breaking down the code to identify patterns, phrases, and keywords. These algorithms have undergone rigorous training on extensive datasets containing audio recordings and corresponding transcriptions. To imagine how much data needs to be processed in training, imagine a portion of the dictionary, each phoneme of each word spoken in the different voice timbres of 100 million people, multiplied by the combination words needing to be combined into phrases and sentences to be acted upon. This training equips VAs with the capability to transcribe spoken language into text accurately.

Following this initial transcription, the system moves on to Natural Language Processing (NLP) and understanding. The text input is comprehensively analyzed to determine the user's intent and extract pertinent information. Language understanding algorithms employ various techniques, including word embeddings, named entity recognition, sentiment analysis, and language modeling, to discern keywords, phrases, and the purpose of the user's interaction. Word embeddings hold significant importance and will be discussed in the next chapter, which is about Generative AI since they are its precursor.

Once the voice assistant grasps the user's intent, it proceeds to find an answer. For instance, if a user inquires about the day's weather, the system must formulate a query to retrieve up-to-date weather information from the web or internal databases. The ability to deliver informative responses often hinges on access to knowledge graphs and search capabilities. These systems tap into vast structured data repositories, housing information about countless entities, places, and concepts. This extensive knowledge empowers virtual assistants to provide users with accurate answers to various questions.

Then, these systems employ text-to-speech technology when delivering responses to users. Text-to-speech algorithms transform textual information into natural-sounding speech, often with options for personalization based on user preferences. Finally, in the case of multi-turn conversations, effective dialog management plays a pivotal role. Voice assistants must retain context from prior interactions, ensuring their responses remain coherent and relevant throughout extended discussions.

While this generation of voice assistants proved useful in commercial applications, in less than ten years, their technology was completely surpassed—made obsolete—as we will later discuss, by Generative AI.

Google and Facebook, from Pixels to Insights

The rapid progress in image processing algorithms over the last 15 years has been nothing short of remarkable. For example, facial recognition technologies, such as those that unlock your mobile phone apps, sparked a revolution in security and personalization. Meanwhile, the ability to identify objects within videos has reshaped the landscape of autonomous driving and entertainment, and soon e-commerce. Furthermore, image classification algorithms have significantly enhanced the precision of medical imaging diagnostics.

Image processing research was driven both by universities and by companies in the private sector. On the university front, a pivotal moment unfolded in 2012 with the birth of AlexNet [Krizhevsky et al.], a deep-learning model meticulously crafted by Alex Krizhevsky, Geoffrey E. Hinton, and Ilya Sutskever of the University of Toronto. Hinton was one of the fathers of backpropagation, as we covered in *Chapter 5,* and Sutskever would later become Chief Scientist in OpenAI.

In 2012, AlexNet claimed the top prize in the prestigious ImageNet Large Scale Visual Recognition Challenge hosted by Stanford University, which we discussed a few pages back. Its primary mission centered on image classification, executed with awe-inspiring precision. AlexNet harnessed a convolutional neural network (CNN) at its core, replete with multiple layers meticulously designed to extract intricate features from images, subsequently leveraging these features to facilitate image classification. Applications of AlexNet ranged from recognizing objects, such as cars or people in the street, to identifying faces and classifying animals it saw into dogs or cats.

Simultaneously, Google Brain was created in 2011, led by Andrew Ng, a charismatic Stanford professor and later founder of Coursera in 2012. Google Brain was a dedicated research division within Google, striving to push the boundaries of AI. Google Brain achieved an amazing feat in training a neural network to identify objects by analyzing unlabeled images extracted from YouTube videos with unsupervised learning [Markoff]. Unsupervised learning has always been a problematic discipline with AI, as we discussed, and it has always lagged behind supervised learning in advancements and development. This pioneering research marked a crucial milestone in developing unsupervised learning and showcased the immense potential of neural networks in actually processing vast amounts of unstructured data.

One of the products developed by Google Brain was Google Lens, introduced in 2017 by Google, representing a breakthrough in image recognition technology. This innovative tool employs neural network-based visual analysis to identify and provide relevant information about objects captured through a smartphone's camera. Google Lens can recognize various elements, from barcodes and QR codes to labels and text, and can even translate language in captured images. It allows users to point the camera of their device at an object to retrieve relevant web pages, search results, and other information. For instance, when aiming at a Wi-Fi label, it can automatically connect to the indicated network. Over the years, it has evolved with deep learning capabilities and added features like recognizing items on menus, calculating tips, or demonstrating recipe preparations.

Meanwhile, Facebook also became a frontrunner in image processing, particularly human facial recognition. In 2014, Facebook's researchers introduced DeepFace, a sophisticated system that harnessed neural networks to achieve an astounding 97% accuracy in facial recognition [Oremus]. This monumental achievement represented a substantial leap, surpassing previous methods and approaching human-level performance. DeepFace found diverse applications, from enhancing security protocols to personalizing user experiences. Facebook's DeepFace is not to be confused with DeepFaceLab, the deep fake Open-Source application we will discuss in the next chapter.

The Era of Big Data and Cloud Computing

Cloud computing, or distributed server resources, has significantly accelerated key AI development and commercial productization. With the integration of high-powered Graphics Processing Units (GPUs, or chip sets designed to render complex visual graphics in gaming) into cloud architectures, access to substantial computational resources has been democratized, making it easier and more cost-effective for organizations and individuals to get on-demand access to the immense computational power required for training and deploying AI models, conducting research, and running data-intensive workloads. Algorithms and AI capabilities are now literally accessible to anyone who can set up an account on AWS, MS, or others. The commercial magic is in the conversion of high fixed costs and capex to launch into variable cost models for customers.

By way of history, the evolution of cloud computing was not an overnight phenomenon but rather the culmination of decades of technological progress. The seeds of this technological breakthrough were sown in the 1950s when scientists first delved into concepts related to distributed computing and shared computational resources. In 1961, John McCarthy even forecasted a future where *"computing will eventually be organized as a public utility"* [Garfinkel and Yang].

Cloud computing began to take tangible form in the 1990s as the first wave of companies ventured into offering hosting and online storage services. Simultaneously, *"Big Data"* began gaining traction in the mid-2000s as technologies and tools emerged to facilitate the collection, storage, and analysis of vast data. Initially, these activities were primarily conducted within on-site data centers owned by large corporations.

In 2006, Amazon Web Services (AWS) debuted, revolutionizing the cloud computing landscape by providing cloud-based storage and resizable virtual servers in the cloud, enabling users to deploy applications and workloads with unprecedented on-demand scalability [Mosco]. Then, in 2010, Microsoft expanded into the cloud by introducing Microsoft Azure, adding to the diversity of cloud services available. Following suit, in 2012, Google launched GCP (Google Cloud Platform), positioning itself as a direct competitor to AWS and Azure in the cloud service market. These three players, until today, hold around two-thirds of the worldwide market share. China, on the other hand, has developed its indigenous cloud providers: Alibaba Cloud, Tencent Cloud, Baidu Cloud, and Huawei Cloud. However, we will dive deep into China and its strategy to challenge America's AI leadership later in *Chapter 24.*

Simultaneously, IBM and Oracle introduced their hybrid cloud solutions in 2011 and 2012, respectively. The concept of hybrid clouds is very practical: public clouds such as AWS, Azure, or GCP share resources among multiple organizations, offering cost efficiency and scalability. In contrast, a private cloud is dedicated to a single organization, usually a large corporation, affording maximum control and security within its data centers. Between these two types, hybrid clouds ingeniously blend elements of both, facilitating the fluid movement of data and applications between private and public clouds. This approach preserves flexibility while retaining a degree of control.

As AWS, Azure, and GCP emerged as dominant forces in the cloud computing arena, the necessity of embracing a multi-cloud strategy became abundantly clear. Companies worked with multiple cloud providers, often due to historical reasons or the presence of distinct business units with varying cloud preferences. As a result, solutions that facilitated operating multi-cloud, such as Databricks and Snowflakes, started to become very popular. Then, the global pandemic of 2020 catapulted cloud technology to newfound prominence, owing to the capacity to facilitate flexible working arrangements, especially for remote employees [Aggarwal].

Today, big data and cloud computing are indispensable components of global IT infrastructure. Organizations of all sizes rely on the cloud to host critical applications and store vast data. It has become mainstream, which has paved the path to mainstreaming AI capabilities for organizations of all sizes.

An important development that abetted the growth of Cloud distribution was Graphics Processing Units (GPUs). Designed initially as powerful hardware processors tailored for handling the complex calculations required to generate real-time images and graphics in computers and gaming consoles, their destiny took an unexpected turn, leading them to the forefront of AI. Deep learning demands computing power beyond the capabilities of everyday computer chips; as we have discussed, initial forays into AI were held back because enabling technologies such as processing power and memory were insufficient to enable the rapid calculations necessary to drive AI. The driving force behind this transition was the nature of AI computations involving vast amounts of matrix multiplications, which are similar to those required in real-time graphic rendering. GPUs excelled at these heavy mathematical operations. Their parallel processing capabilities proved to be a perfect fit for accelerating AI algorithms. As a result, GPUs became a critical input to AI advancements, enabling the training and running of complex neural networks with unprecedented speed and efficiency.

The GPU market is very concentrated. While there are certainly other players in the GPU market, it is undeniable that NVIDIA stands head and shoulders above the competition as the largest and most influential company in this space [Lee]. A $1000 investment in NVIDIA in 2014 would be worth $125,900 today.

Integrating GPUs into cloud computing represents the latest chapter in their remarkable evolution, an evolution that now sees electricity, memory, processing power, big data, and data access—the preconditions for AI—common and flourishing, readily available and priced to reflect scale.

Cambridge Analytica and GDPR

With all the data on the cloud representing the world's digital transactions and much personal shared on social media, privacy considerations have become a significant global concern, one that touches AI as well. The Cambridge Analytica scandal in 2018 [Wiggins and Jones] left an enduring impact on data privacy regulations, significantly affecting both Europe and the US. Cambridge Analytica, a data analytics firm, became embroiled in controversy when it was revealed that it had obtained unauthorized access to 87 million Facebook users' personal data through a seemingly innocuous survey app called *"This Is Your Digital Life."* This app collected user data and covertly harvested information from their unwitting Facebook friends without obtaining the necessary permission or consent.

Armed with this vast reservoir of data, Cambridge Analytica embarked on creating psychographic profiles that were wielded to craft highly targeted political advertising campaigns, which were pivotal during the 2016 US presidential elections. The scandal triggered widespread concerns about AI's potential for undue influence on the democratic process and the manipulation of voters.

Starting in 2011, the European Union had been working on a new data protection act called the *"General Data Protection Regulation"* (GDPR), and it finally came into full effect in May 2018. Cambridge Analytica's alarming breach of data privacy escalated apprehensions about the safety of personal information, which in turn strengthened support for the act [EU]. GDPR is a robust data privacy regulation designed to empower European citizens with greater control over their data and impose stricter obligations on organizations that process personal information. GDPR is also explicit regarding penalties, which can amount to up to 4% of the turnover or €20 million.

Europeans have generally been quicker and more apt to regulate compared to Americans. While there was no immediate federal-level response like GDPR in the US, the Cambridge Analytica scandal ignited a surge in public awareness regarding data privacy. As a result, several states enacted their data privacy laws. Among these notable regulations is the *"California Consumer Privacy Act"* (CCPA), passed in 2018 [State of California], which bestows upon California residents significant rights about their data, like the ability to ascertain what data is being collected, with whom it is being shared, and the authority to request the deletion of their personal information. Another significant development came from the *"Virginia Consumer Data Privacy Act"* (VCDPA) in 2021 [State of Virginia], which grants Virginia residents analogous rights to GDPR concerning their data.

Before the Cambridge Analytica scandal, the US already had pertinent data privacy regulations for specific sectors, the *"Children's Online Privacy Protection Act"* (COPPA) from 1998 [US Government] or the *"Health Insurance Portability and Accountability Act"* (HIPAA) from 1996 [CDC]. However, this patchwork of state and sectoral laws underscores the absence of a cohesive and unified approach to privacy regulation in the US. Nevertheless, the US Congress has engaged in discussions regarding the potential formulation of a federal privacy law to harmonize and consolidate data privacy regulations nationally.

In the context of AI, which often relies on vast amounts of data, compliance with these regulations is essential to prevent data misuse, unauthorized access, and biased, possibly even unilateral, decision-making. Data protection regulations contribute to mitigating potential risks associated with the use of sensitive information in artificial intelligence applications and, therefore, to building trust in AI systems.

Automation of Repetitive White-Collar Work through Software Robots

Also appearing during these years, Robotic Process Automation (RPA) marked a significant leap forward in automation. RPA is a potent tool for optimizing and automating routine tasks on office computers and streamlining non-manufacturing operations [Slaby]. RPA is essentially a software robot specialized in managing routinized computer-based tasks. While physical robots are employed in physical environments like manufacturing plants to automate repetitive physical tasks, RPA's primary domain is automating office tasks performed by white-collar employees using computers.

At the heart of RPA's functionality lies screen capture technology, which empowers it to interact with computer interfaces and replicate human actions with remarkable precision. Imagine an employee navigating a complex process involving copying and pasting data, working with multiple applications, importing and exporting files, sending emails, initiating approval workflows, and collecting signatures. This intricate workflow is susceptible to errors and inefficiencies, which is precisely where RPA excels. It effortlessly automates these tasks, ensuring data accuracy, slashing processing times, and boosting productivity.

Let us illustrate it with an example: employee onboarding. RPA can assume a pivotal role in automating the employee onboarding process. It can manage duties such as enrolling employees, scheduling meetings and orientation sessions, and it can dispatch automated messages and emails detailing responsibilities or other communications. RPA can also ensure the onboarding process adheres rigorously to predefined procedures, facilitating seamless alignment with company guidelines.

In another example, RPA also finds extensive applications in sectors such as healthcare insurance, particularly in claim processing and data entry. RPA accomplishes these tasks with incredible speed and fewer errors than human counterparts. Furthermore, RPA technology excels at identifying non-compliant exceptions, thus preventing unnecessary payouts.

While some regard RPA as a basic form of AI due to the presence of autonomous logic and processing, others argue that it falls short of the complexity typically associated with AI. Nevertheless, advanced RPA solutions can integrate complex AI modules, including predictive modeling, machine vision, and NLP, to make a coherent, objective-oriented system. This integration enhances RPA's automation capabilities, the integration of AI firmly establishing it as a formidable player in the automation landscape.

Leading RPA vendors include UiPath, Automation Anywhere, and Blue Prism. They all appeared in the post-dotcom years and were ready when the pivotal moment for RPA occurred during the global financial crisis of 2008. RPA emerged as a cost-effective automation solution that delivered tangible, measurable, cost-saving results.

The Epic Battle of AlphaGo vs. Lee Sedol

In the preceding chapter, we reviewed IBM Deep Blue's 1997 chess triumph over International Grandmaster and World Champion Gary Kasparov, pointing out that despite winning, Deep Blue was not a highly intelligent AI system as it relied solely on computational brute force. We mentioned that it would take nearly 19 years for a truly intelligent algorithm capable of defeating a world champion to emerge. This groundbreaking algorithm was AlphaGo. The epic showdown in 2016 between AlphaGo and Lee Sedol in the ancient Chinese strategy game of Go represented a *"coming of age"* moment for reinforcement learning algorithms.

Lee Sedol from South Korea was revered as one of the foremost Go players globally and boasted an impressive track record, having clinched the title of world champion three times. Additionally, he won the South Korean championship an astonishing 12 times and the Japan Go championship thrice.

AlphaGo was an AI system created by DeepMind, a company established in the UK in 2010 by Demis Hassabis, Shane Legg, and Mustafa Suleyman (later acquired by Google in 2014), which at that time stood as a crown jewel among DeepMind's ambitious projects. We will talk about DeepMind a few more times in this book because this company and team became important and central in the overall evolution and development of AI.

AlphaGo's triumph over Lee Sedol transcended mere technological achievement; it became a transformative event that reshaped our understanding of AI's limitless potential. At its core, AlphaGo harnessed a huge deep neural network to master the exponential complexity of Go, stemming from an astonishing array of potential moves and configurations. Unlike Deep Blue, which relied heavily on raw computational power and exhaustive move searches, AlphaGo pioneered a different and more important approach to the development of true AI: reinforcement learning.

In simple terms, this is how AlphaGo's reinforcement learning mechanism worked. When AlphaGo made a move in the game in which it secured a victory, it recorded it as a positive action. Conversely, if it encountered a movement that led to its defeat, it cataloged the move as an adverse action. Over time and through countless games, AlphaGo amassed a profound repository of knowledge about which moves yielded favorable outcomes and which to avoid. This groundbreaking approach allowed AlphaGo to refine its Go prowess through experiential learning, the way humans enhance their skills through dedicated practice and repetition. With each new game played and experience gained, AlphaGo's level of play underwent a continuous and impressive ascent.

AlphaGo's victory provoked profound global astonishment about AI's role in real-world complex problem-solving. Given the vast number of potential moves in Go, this complex arena demonstrated AI's effectiveness in addressing complicated problems and, importantly, AI's ability to learn and apply its learning in a way superior to humans.

AlphaGo also faced off against Ke Jie, a prominent Go player from China, igniting significant media attention within that country [Byford]. This match, broadcast live on the internet and television, underscored China's burgeoning interest in AI. Notably, four months following this match, the Chinese government unveiled the *"Next Generation AI Development Plan,"* an ambitious initiative to position China as a global leader in AI research and development [Webster]. While this plan was underway before the match, the heightened public interest generated by the game appeared to expedite its formal announcement and implementation. In *Chapter 24,* we will explore AI in China *and its competition with the US for global AI supremacy,* reminiscent of the Cold War stand-off between the US and the Soviet Union on which country would first put a human on the moon.

8. The Rise of Artificial Creativity

"Number one, I would form a new agency that licenses any effort above a certain scale of capabilities, and can take that license away, and ensure compliance with safety standards.

Number two, I would create a set of safety standards focused on what you said in your third hypothesis as the dangerous capability evaluations. One example that we've used in the past is looking to see if a model can self-replicate...

And then third, I would require independent audits. So not just from the company or the agency, but experts who can say the model is in compliance with these stated safety thresholds, and these percentages of performance on question X or Y."

Sam Altman

CEO of OpenAI
Facing the US Congress [Roose]
May 16, 2023

The idea of machines exhibiting creativity once appeared far-fetched. However, on November 30, 2022, ChatGPT, a chatbot built upon OpenAI's extensive language model, shattered that belief. ChatGPT empowered users to shape and guide conversations to their liking, allowing length, format, style, detail level, and language adjustments to be accurately crafted for them. Moreover, it could accurately answer questions related to math and science and generate source code.

ChatGPT was developed by OpenAI, a company founded in December 2015, with Elon Musk among its founders. Currently, OpenAI is led by Sam Altman. In 2019, Microsoft made a significant investment of $1 billion in OpenAI. ChatGPT is one of OpenAI's notable creations.

By January 2023, ChatGPT had achieved a remarkable milestone, becoming the fastest-growing consumer software application in history, boasting a staggering user base of over 100 million individuals. This outstanding achievement significantly contributed to OpenAI's soaring valuation, which quickly rose to an impressive $29 billion [Hu].

With the novelty and scale of its AI product, and with the clear and present threat to the livelihoods of people who performed tasks identical to ChatGPT, it soon generated several significant fears and controversies.

Firstly, there are concerns about widespread job losses as AI systems like ChatGPT are increasingly capable of automating tasks in various industries, which we believe will, without fail and remorse, displace human workers at scale beginning in 2024. [Verma and De Vynck]. This raises questions about unemployment, job retraining, and the ethics of AI. Secondly, legal issues arise regarding AI-generated content, including potential copyright violations and the spread of misinformation. Additionally, ethical concerns revolve around AI's potential to propagate biases present in training data, leading to discriminatory or harmful outputs [Stokel]. We note widespread reports of ChatGPT and related products engaging in verbal jousts with users and failure to address certain queries in a manner demonstrating bias.

Sam Altman, the CEO of Open AI, embarked on an intensive lobbying campaign in Washington in June 2023. Unlike many tech executives who have shied away from government regulators and lawmakers, Altman actively sought to engage with policymakers. He demonstrated ChatGPT to over 20 lawmakers.

During his congressional meetings [Roose], Altman emphasized the importance of regulating AI to mitigate potential risks. He expressed concerns about the rapid development of AI technology and its possible consequences. Altman advocated for establishing an independent regulatory agency specifically focused on AI. He proposed licensing AI technology, similar to how drivers need vehicle licenses, to ensure that individuals and organizations using AI are competent and responsible.

Altman also insisted on the need for safety standards in AI development and deployment. He highlighted the importance of avoiding the mistakes made during previous technological revolutions and called for a proactive approach to regulation. Altman was candid about the potential risks of AI, such as its impact on employment, suggesting that AI could drastically reduce workweeks. Additionally, Altman supported proposals by lawmakers, including the idea of consumer risk labels on AI tools similar to nutrition labels on food products.

Parallel to Sam Altman's visit to Congress, the EU and the US were taking significant steps toward regulating AI, particularly in the context of Generative AI. Are companies like OpenAI asking for regulation because they believe it is the right move for humanity or because they want to introduce barriers to entry for new players? We will talk about this important topic in *Chapter 28, as well as AI ethics, how to control AI, and* the broad concerns that we should all share.

The following pages recount how the Generative AI revolution unfolded and what it means for the future.

The Challenge of Natural Language Processing

Throughout the 2010s, several alternatives for Natural Language Processing (NLP) and understanding surfaced, but none proved convincingly compelling until Generative AI arrived.

Voice assistants like Siri and Alexa already use deep neural networks, particularly Recurrent Neural Networks (RNNs) such as LSTM. However, these networks still struggled to capture long-term dependencies in the data, mainly when words referred to other words mentioned much earlier in a conversation. Three unsupervised learning algorithms were also developed to work on these deficiencies: word embeddings, BERT, and Hidden Markov Models.

The core idea of word embeddings is to represent words semantically as numerical vectors that capture semantic relationships between words, empowering algorithms to better comprehend and work with the contextual meanings of words. A vector refers to a numerical representation of a word in a high-dimensional space. Each word in a vocabulary is assigned a unique vector, and the values within the vector capture semantic relationships between words based on their contextual usage. A vector would be something like this: *"cat = (1.1547, 5.6675, 4.76767, ... ,3.7878)"*.

For instance, in the sentence *"The cat is on the mat,"* the word embedding would represent *"cat"* and *"mat"* with vectors that are close in the vector space, as they often appear in similar contexts. This enables the model to capture the semantic similarity between words, making it a powerful tool in NLP tasks such as text classification, machine translation, and sentiment analysis.

In another example of a word-embedding model, the word *"king"* might be represented as a vector, and the vector arithmetic *"king"* - *"man"* + *"woman"* would result in a vector that is close to the representation of *"queen."* Each dimension in the vector corresponds to a specific feature or aspect of the word's meaning. Vectors allow for efficient mathematical operations to create outputs, and the proximity of vectors in the embedding space reflects the similarity of the corresponding words in terms of their semantic context.

There are a few different word embedding methods. The first ones were Word2Vec [Mikolov and Chen] and GloVe [Pennington and Socher] from 2013 and 2014, respectively. These techniques can capture semantic similarities between words based on co-occurrence patterns in extensive text collections. Then, Google developed BERT (Bidirectional Encoder Representations from Transformers) in 2018, introducing a contextual understanding by considering the surrounding words in a sentence to determine a word's meaning [Devlin et al.]. This contextualization significantly enhanced language understanding, especially in distinguishing between polysemic words, something that Word2Vec and GloVe could not do.

The third unsupervised approach used in those days was statistical models, such as Hidden Markov Models (HMMs), which we previously discussed in *Chapter 3*. In Markov chains, the probability of transitioning to the next state or word in the context of language processing relies solely on the current state or word. Hidden Markov Models involve additional hidden states, allowing transition probabilities to depend on more preceding words than just the current one. However, despite their increased complexity, these models still have limitations in capturing semantic meaning.

In summary, none of these three approaches proved to be entirely effective for language generation and understanding despite their early successes.

But the solution was inside Google.

Transformers: Attention is All You Need

The solution to the language generation problem came up in 2017 with the introduction of the Transformer architecture in a paper by Google Brain scientists titled *"Attention is All You Need"* [Vaswani et al.]. The suggestive title of the paper implies that when compared to all preceding language algorithms, including RNNs, embeddings, or Hidden Markov Models, a novel approach known as the *"attention mechanism"* had surfaced as the most potent algorithm for language processing as it addressed the limitations found in the others.

A transformer is an algorithm that implements the attention mechanism, which means allowing the model to selectively focus on specific segments of the input text as it generates the output text.

To grasp this fully, consider an English sentence: *"Yesterday, the bat hit the ball,"* and the task is to translate it into Spanish. The right Spanish translation would be *"Ayer, el bate golpeó la pelota."* A transformer model would break down the sentence into tokens, such as *"yesterday,"* *"the," "bat," "hit," "the," and "ball."* The attention mechanism then concentrates on individual input words one by one as it generates the translation. For example, when translating "bat" to "*bate*," the model primarily pays attention to the word "*bat*," but "*bat*" can be an animal or a stick. In order to give the right translation, the model must pay attention to another word, in particular, "*ball*." With this context, it is clear that we are talking about a stick and not a flying mammal. The same happens when the model attempts to translate "*hit*." In English, "*hit*" is the same word in present and past, but in Spanish, it has differentiated tenses. The model must pay attention to the word "*yesterday*" to find the right translation to Spanish.

This groundbreaking innovation of the transformer model, with its embedded attention mechanism, unleashed a wave of applications in Generative AI. Transformers are directly behind the technology of ChatGPT, and have enhanced machine translation, turbocharged advanced virtual assistants, facilitated text generation in various contexts, facilitated sentiment analysis, and enabled code generation, among many other applications.

Training a Transformer: Self-Supervised Learning

Traditional supervised learning models hinge on labeled data to train the models, necessitating extensive human effort in data structuring, presentation, and annotation. Annotating data manually is very costly. Additionally, unsupervised algorithms for NLP, like the word embeddings, BERT, and HHMs, as explained a few paragraphs before, did not work in an unflawed way.

However, a paradigm shift occurred with the concept of self-supervised learning, wherein models extract knowledge from the data instead of relying on explicit labels. This shift enables AI systems to autonomously extract correlations, patterns, and hidden structures within vast, unlabeled datasets, rendering them more adaptable and scalable.

In NLP, self-supervised learning strategies like masked language modeling have proven invaluable. In this technique, words within a sentence are randomly masked, and the model must predict the missing words based on the surrounding context. For instance, consider the sentence: "*The cat chased the _____ through the backyard.*" A self-supervised model can infer that the missing word is likely "*squirrel*" or "*mouse*" because it makes sense in the given context. This method of training on large text corpora gives models a thorough grasp of language semantics, syntax, and context. These insights can then be applied to a variety of downstream NLP tasks, such as text sentiment analysis, summarization, and named entity recognition. At a fundamental level, this is the training technique that has been employed to train ChatGPT or any of its competitors.

Once a model is trained in this manner, it can be utilized to generate text one word at a time, conditioning on previously generated words. For instance, given the prompt *"Once upon a time, there was a young wizard named Harry,"* the model can continue the story by predicting words like *"who," "attended," "a," "magical," "school,"* "called," *"Hogwarts."* Self-supervised training enables language models to grasp narrative flow, coherence, and creativity, rendering them effective in tasks such as story generation, content creation, and code generation.

Self-supervised learning can also be applied to video or images in computer vision. Imagine training a model to recognize objects, actions, or scenes within video clips without having a labeled dataset. This is where self-supervised learning shines. Certain video segments are randomly removed, and the model must predict the missing frames. This process is known as video inpainting. By doing so, the model learns to fill in the gaps and understand temporal dynamics and contextual relationships between objects and actions. This understanding, acquired through self-supervised training, can be later fine-tuned for various specific video analysis tasks, such as action recognition, object tracking, object identification, or scene segmentation.

Self-supervised learning is revolutionary because it enables AI algorithms to learn from the inherent structure and patterns within data, reducing the reliance on labor-intensive labeling efforts and, therefore, making the training process scalable.

OpenAI and Generative Pre-trained Transformers

ChatGPT models have revolutionized how machines communicate with humans, as they can generate coherent text that is contextually relevant across various tasks and applications.

Moving into technology aspects, ChatGPT is powered by advanced Large Language Models (LLMs) algorithms. The specific LLM employed by ChatGPT goes by the name GPT. GPT is built upon the Transformer framework, initially developed by Google, and leverages self-supervised and reinforcement learning techniques. The acronym GPT stands for *"Generative Pre-trained Transformer."* In this name, *"Generative"* highlights the model's ability to create text or content, *"Pre-trained"* indicates that the model undergoes initial training on a vast corpus of text before being fine-tuned for specific tasks, and *"Transformer"* refers to the neural network architecture used.

The lineage of GPT models started with GPT-1 in 2018, followed by the release of GPT-2 in 2019, which was trained on a massive dataset of internet text and featured 1.5 billion parameters. In 2020, OpenAI introduced GPT-3, a significantly larger model than its predecessor, boasting 175 billion parameters and capable of generating remarkably coherent and realistic text. Subsequently, in March 2023, OpenAI launched GPT3.5 and GPT-4. The GPT-4 model is rumored to have 1.76 trillion parameters—the exact number is not disclosed—and can generate long text outputs, extending up to 25,000 words, and as time goes by and more data is used for training, the coherence and quality of generated text will continue to improve. Another notable advantage of GPT-4 is the ability to process multimodal content, including text and images, making these models highly versatile in content generation and understanding.

Despite its name, it is worth noting that OpenAI's algorithms are proprietary and closed.

An Explosion of Large Language Models

Numerous other companies were concurrently developing LLMs, and the emergence of ChatGPT piqued their interest, prompting them to expedite their LLM projects.

Google's response to OpenAI's ChatGPT came in March 2023 when they unveiled Bard, an innovative chatbot initially based on an existing algorithm called LaMDA (Language Model for Dialogue Applications) [Condon]. What set LaMDA apart was its unique emphasis on engaging in more natural and context-aware conversations than ChatGPT. It achieved this by significantly enhancing its ability to understand context within dialogues, allowing it to produce responses that were more coherent and more human-like in their conversational quality. Unlike traditional text-based models, LaMDA was engineered to excel in two-way conversations, facilitating more interactive and dynamic user interactions.

Google later transitioned from LaMDA to a more advanced algorithm called PaLM (Probabilistic Language Model) in May 2023 [Vincent]. PaLM aimed to address some of the inherent issues associated with LaMDA, such as occasional incoherence in responses, challenges in handling nuanced queries, and difficulties in maintaining context during extended dialogues. PaLM leveraged probabilistic reasoning to generate contextually relevant, more coherent, and logically consistent responses. This approach helped mitigate the abrupt transitions, and tangential replies sometimes observed with LaMDA applications, ultimately contributing to a more natural and engaging conversational experience.

Finally, Google launched Gemini on December 6, 2023, positioned as the successor to LaMDA and PaLM. Gemini comprises three distinct models—small, medium, and large: Gemini Ultra, intended for extremely complex tasks; Gemini Pro, the default option suitable for most applications; and Gemini Nano, optimized for on-device tasks on phones. Unlike other conventional LLMs, Gemini distinguished itself by being highly multimodal and able to process multiple data types at once, such as text and images, audio, video, and even computer code.

While Google's advancements in conversational AI with Gemini were significant, it was not alone in this transformative landscape. Anthropic, founded in 2019 by former OpenAI employees, introduced Claude [Davis], a powerful LLM designed with a focus on ethical alignment. Specifically, Claude aimed to address the concerns surrounding potential biases and safety issues in AI, ensuring the development of more responsible and trustworthy AI outputs.

Anthropic calls their security method "Constitutional Artificial Intelligence" (CAI). This constitutional framework was developed to help guarantee that AI systems are in line with human values, thereby making them helpful, safe, and honest. Several high-level prescriptive guidelines that specify the AI's intended behavior make up this "constitution" for AI; after that, the AI is taught to follow these guidelines in order to prevent harm, respect user preferences, and provide accurate information. Anthropic's constitution is, for all intent and purposes, an instantiation of Asimov's three laws of robotics. For example, one of the principles of Anthropic's Claude LLM that is based on the UN statement from 1948 is as follows: *"Please choose the response that most supports and encourages freedom, equality and a sense of brotherhood."* We will do a detailed evaluation of this constitutional approach and other ethical frameworks in Chapter 28.

Moreover, Facebook also developed and open-sourced LLaMA (LLM Meta AI), which is free to use commercially by developers, and encompasses multiple versions with a number of parameters ranging from 7 billion to 65 billion. Subsequently, LLaMA2 was introduced in July 2023. LLaMA2 represented a significant advancement, with a more extensive and diverse training dataset. LLaMA2 specializes in optimizing conversations and excels in generating natural and context-aware responses while prioritizing safety and bias mitigation.

LLaMA is also faster than many other models, including ChatGPT, uses fewer parameters, is lighter to download, and does not require the high processing power of other LLMs. Another advantage of being smaller than other LLMs with similar performance is that it can run on a local computer or even a mobile phone instead of on a big server platform, which is suitable for a lot of applications with high privacy requirements or low latency. It is designed to be refined for various tasks, for example, training customer service chatbots or other similar digital marketing tools, as it is already optimized for dialogue use cases.

Being Open-Source, LLaMA2 fostered innovation and collaboration within the AI community. While the first LLMs, like ChatGPT, were closed-source, meaning privately owned, LLaMA2 is open. Anybody can download it, modify it, use it for free for any particular application, or verify how it really works. As such, several other Open-Source language models emerged as derivatives of LLaMA. One such model, Alpaca, was developed by a team of researchers from Stanford University. Remarkably, the researchers showed that, on qualitative benchmarks, Alpaca performed comparably to OpenAI's GPT3.0, a much larger model, with just $600 in computing spend. Moreover, Vicuna, another LLM, further fine-tuned the LLaMA using additional data from millions of questions and answers it made to ChatGPT. This refinement resulted in high-quality, context-aware responses.

Furthermore, like constitutional AI, Open-Source is another possibility to make sure that AI is developed safely, and we will also evaluate this approach in *Chapter 28.*

In short, there are now many LLMs, each one tailored towards specific needs, and the rapid advance in the necessary algorithmic technology over just the last three years has been extraordinary. We believe corporations across industries will start creating their own LLMs for their particular needs in marketing and customer service in ways that are tailored to specific products and clients whilst ensuring distinct brand voice and brand-specific CX.

Unsupervised Generation and Deep Fakes

While Transformer architecture has been revolutionary in NLP, it is not the only big breakthrough that made Generative AI possible. Other generative algorithms, such as Variational Autoencoders (VAEs) and Generative Adversarial Networks (GANs), are likewise important. VAEs and GANs serve purposes that are distinct from the transformer architecture and are actually earlier creations than transformers. Specifically, these models excel in tasks such as image, video, and music synthesis. In contrast, transformers are primarily used in sequence-to-sequence tasks such as NLP.

Another notable distinction between VAEs and GANs on one side and transformers on the other side lies in their learning paradigms. VAEs and GANs are both unsupervised learning models designed to operate without explicit labels during training. In contrast, Transformers are primarily self-supervised learning models.

VAEs were introduced by Diederik P. Kingma from the University of Amsterdam in 2013 [Kingma and Welling]. Think of VAEs as operating similarly to a music library. Imagine you have a vast collection of songs on your computer. VAEs compress all these songs into a unique numerical representation, termed a *"latent space."* Within this latent space, songs with similar musical attributes, such as genre, artist, or decade, and even rhythm, syncopation, voice quality, tones, and other aspects of the music itself, are mapped closely together. These latent space representations are similar to word embeddings. For example, the representation of the song *"Despacito"* by Luis Fonsi could be something like *"Despacito = (1.4523, 3.7873, 3.5641, 9.1234, ... , 2.6792)."*

This efficient representation not only captures the essence of each song but *also empowers VAEs to generate entirely new compositions based on parameters that are asked.* These AI-crafted melodies inherit the overall style of the original songs while introducing unique elements, showcasing the versatility of VAEs in generating a diverse range of data types, including text, images, and music.

On the other hand, GANs were introduced in 2014 by Ian Goodfellow at the University of Montreal and represent a new approach to data generation not part of VAEs, offering distinct advantages. To understand how GANs work, consider them a pair of coexisting but separate neural networks: one generative and one discriminator. The generative network creates an image—or even audio and video—based on what it has learned from a training set, while the discriminator network assesses whether the generated image is realistic (genuine) or not (even a pixel of difference in an image). These two networks are trained simultaneously, competing against each other. As the generative network becomes more skilled at creating realistic data, the discriminator network must become more sophisticated in detecting differences between real and generated data. Over time, as both networks undergo extended and simultaneous training, the generated images become increasingly challenging for the human eye to distinguish from authentic ones.

In summary, the term *"Generative Adversarial Network"* exactly describes what GANs do. GANs are neural networks; they are generative because they generate content; and they are adversarial because both networks compete against each other.

In terms of output, while VAEs often produce visual data with a smoothed and blurry appearance, GANs are renowned for creating sharp and detailed samples. As such, GANs have made a significant impact across multiple fields. The most widespread application of GANs is seen in deep fakes. Deepfakes involve manipulating visual or auditory content to make it seem authentic, even though it is artificially generated. One of the most popular tools for creating deep fakes is DeepFaceLab, which was released as Open-Source software in 2018 [Perov].

Consider a face-swapping scenario with DeepFaceLab. DeepFaceLab takes two source videos: one featuring the target face—the person whose face will be transposed—and another showcasing the source face—the one to be superimposed onto the target. Using the approach described above,

DeepFaceLab learns to extract facial features from the source face and map them onto the target, ensuring a seamless and realistic blend.

Stable Diffusion, the Open-Source for Image Synthesis

Another important Generative AI algorithm in image generation is *Stable Diffusion*. Stable Diffusion is to image generation what ChatGPT is to language processing, with the important difference that Stable Diffusion is Open-Source. Apart from Stable Diffusion, there are numerous proprietary image-generation tools, such as MidJourney and Runway, or even DALL-E, which OpenAI owns.

Stable Diffusion is a groundbreaking text-to-image and image-to-image model that was launched in August 2022, born from a collaborative effort between the Ludwig Maximilian University of Munich and two US-based AI companies, Runway and Stability AI [Rombach et al.].

At its core, Stable Diffusion transforms input images or text through a process that involves the application of noise, resulting in the creation of new pictures. To dive a bit deeper, the architecture of Stable Diffusion comprises an encoder, an intermediate block, and a decoder. The encoder compresses the original image into a latent space, capturing the image's underlying semantic meaning, similar to how the VAEs or word embeddings work. Subsequently, Gaussian noise is applied to this compressed latent vector through a process known as "*diffusion*." The intermediate block then denoises this latent vector, yielding a modified version that is now different from the original image's vector. Finally, the decoder converts this vector back into pixel space to generate the output image.

This complex interplay between encoding, diffusion, and decoding empowers Stable Diffusion to produce remarkably detailed images conditioned on textual descriptions. By way of example, Stable Diffusion has found diverse applications within image processing, including image generation, filling in missing or damaged image parts (inpainting), extending images beyond their original boundaries (outpainting), and image-to-image translations. The difference between Stable Diffusion and GANS is that Stable Diffusion is useful to generate entirely new content, and GANs are useful to create content similar to something already existing, like a deep fake.

Stable Diffusion has become extremely popular across various domains, from medical imaging to material science and chemical engineering. There are a few reasons for this. First, Stable Diffusion has minimal resource requirements; it runs seamlessly on consumer-grade hardware with modest GPU specifications, making it suitable for individual developers and artists. Second, its Open-Source license and the availability of model weights for download have been pivotal in attracting significant attention within the AI community.

Creative Innovation Beyond Text and Image

The influence of Generative AI extends far beyond image and language generation. It is quickly permeating a diverse array of creative domains, including coding, music, video, object design for 3D printing, and controlling robotic arms.

For starters, large-scale language models are not confined to natural language; they can also be trained in programming languages to generate source code for new computer applications, like, for example, OpenAI Codex and GitHub Copilot, owned by Microsoft or Replit, which allows non-technical professionals without programming knowledge to *"build software collaboratively with the power of AI, on any device, without spending a second on setup."*

Generative systems like MusicLM and MusicGen are also revolutionizing music composition. These models are trained using musical recordings and text annotations and can compose new musical pieces based on textual prompts like *"gentle violin melody combined with a distorted guitar riff."*

Moreover, regarding video, generative systems trained on annotated videos can produce clips with remarkable temporal coherence. Prominent examples include RunwayML and Make-A-Video from Meta Platforms, among many others. Existing B2C digital product platforms like Spotify for music, Netflix for long-form video, and YouTube and TikTok for short-form video will continue to grow, or we may see entirely new platforms emerge as advances in AI significantly reduce software development costs, risks, and time-to-market.

Robotics presents an additional and handy example. In order to generate new trajectories for navigation or motion planning, Generative AI can also be trained on the various motions of a robotic system. For example, UniPi from Google uses commands like "pick up brown bowl" and "wipe plates with green sponge" to control the movement of a robot arm.

We believe that this list will continue expanding. The essential ingredients for the rapid development of individual digital consumer products are now here, specifically:

- Scaled destinations, including consumer product applications and platforms, to ensure ever-expanding data for continuous training of AI algorithms.

- Near ubiquitous cloud distribution.
- A scaled global consumer base that provides either direct pay or eyeballs for advertising-based business models.
- AI algorithms such as Stable Diffusion and proprietary solutions such as Runway or Open AI itself, which have evolved to a point where digital products are indistinguishable from human production.
- Programming tools like GitHub Copilot or Replit, which allow anyone to write code without being a programmer.

Automation of Creative White-Collar Work Through Gen AI

With these numerous applications of Generative AI across various white-collar professions, the potential for task automation is also evident. In the previous chapter, we discussed how Robotic Process Automation (RPA) has steadily automated repetitive white-collar tasks within office environments since the Great Financial Crisis. Generative AI, on the other hand, is poised to automate more creative and intellectually demanding white-collar responsibilities. Two kinds of jobs could be most impacted by Generative AI: creative professions and administrators.

The most at-risk creative jobs are in the fields of marketing, design, music, and acting, among others. For instance, AI-powered tools for graphic design can now rapidly generate logos, branding materials, and visuals, potentially reducing the demand for human designers. Similarly, automated content generation tools in marketing can create advertisements, social media posts, and even marketing strategies, potentially displacing human marketers. The music industry has also witnessed disruption with AI-generated compositions and algorithmically curated personalized playlists, displacing humans. The music industry has also witnessed disruption, with AI-generated compositions and algorithmically curated personalized playlists taking over human roles.

Regarding administrative tasks, RPA is already automating the simplest repetitive tasks. With Generative AI on top of RPA, automation can now encompass tasks involving intermediate-level language use, such as data entry, record-keeping, document drafting, and initial recruitment processes. Customer service jobs, especially those involving scripted and repetitive interactions, might also be at risk of automation.

Additionally, historically, high-value-added professions are also in jeopardy. The legal profession, which often entails research and document preparation, will experience an impact, considering the capabilities of LLMs in text synthesis. Seven years of higher education to become an entry-level lawyer who then trains up on drafting seems superfluous when the AI will do a better and faster job, and clients will prefer this to paying $250 an hour for the same work that is also likely to include tedious redrafting.

Generative AI is more likely to be a powerful augmentation tool for jobs rather than a net job destructor, at least in the short term. A clear example can be seen in the field of programming. Our view is that in the next few years, AI-powered tools like code generators and auto-completion features will have significantly enhanced the efficiency and productivity of programmers and data scientists. These tools assist developers in writing code faster, reducing the likelihood of errors and allowing them to focus on more complex problem-solving aspects of their work.

That said, concerns about intellectual property preservation and job destruction are germane, are going to accelerate, and are likely to create social and economic issues as AI adoption grows. Coming back to the example of coding, while generative AI might augment programmers in the short run, it is also likely to replace them completely in the mid-term. We will delve deeper into the job market and how education should help prepare professionals and newer generations in *Chapters 22*—which provides a utopian view—and *23*—*which is dystopian*—when we talk about how AI might develop over the next two decades.

With all this in mind, we also believe that we are in the early days. We are in the midst of an entrepreneurial paradise. Specialized applications across industries that lean into core AI but rely on domain expertise to build value will mint a new generation of millionaires; the core AI technology is now widely available, though it remains in the ownership hands of a few key players. We refer to these new technocrats as *"AI superstars,"* and we will discuss what they mean to society in *Chapter 23.*

Legal Quagmire: Copyrights of Generated Content

Generative AI has also raised complex and novel legal questions surrounding data usage, content regulation, and principles of copyright. With AI models like ChatGPT and Stable Diffusion capable of autonomously generating content that closely resembles human-created work and, in fact, is reliant on and derivative of it, determining ownership and copyright becomes a perplexing issue. Traditional copyright laws were not designed with AI-generated content in mind. There is a legal gray area, and this ambiguity can result in disputes over ownership and royalties, potentially impacting creators, businesses, and AI developers.

For example, In November 2022, a class-action lawsuit was filed against tech giants Microsoft, OpenAI, and GitHub, claiming that GitHub Copilot violated the copyrights of code repositories' authors [Vincent]. The crux of the matter lies in the tool's training on existing code and its ability to generate code that closely resembles its training data without providing proper attribution and payment, let alone permission.

Furthermore, a small group of artists filed a class-action lawsuit against MidJourney, Stability AI, and DeviantArt in January 2023, asserting that these companies had infringed upon millions of artists' rights by using billions of images that were scraped from the internet to train AI tools without getting permission from the original creators. The lawsuit was based on the principles of mass copyright infringement[Vincent].

In a parallel vein, the rise of deepfake technology is also making its way into courtrooms. In April 2023, Kyland Young, a TV personality, took legal action against a Deep Fake app called Reface, arguing that the company behind Reface used his and many other famous people's names and faces to make money from their app without their permission [Glasser].

Similarly, in July 2023, Sarah Silverman, a prominent comedian, initiated a class-action lawsuit for copyright infringement against tech giants OpenAI and Meta, her allegation pertaining to these companies training their LLMs on copyrighted works of authors without obtaining proper permissions [Small].

These ethical dilemmas have reverberated beyond the courtroom. In August 2023, major news outlets, including the New York Times, Reuters, CNN, and others, proactively blocked OpenAI's GPT crawler from their websites. The New York Times has further updated its terms of service to explicitly prohibit the use of its content in LLMs [Peters and Castro]. We believe that others will follow.

While copyright and ownership of generated content are the most common concerns, Generative AI also presents additional challenges when AI models trained on sensitive information violate privacy regulations. AI models have also been used to propagate false assertions, leading to legal defamation-related actions. As Generative AI continues to evolve, so do the legal challenges it poses, as well as its profound implications for businesses and individuals.

The World's First AI Legislation, Maybe Too Fast

Facing this avalanche of high-profile lawsuits, policymakers have already started acting on regulating AI. As with data protection legislation, the EU also took the global lead with AI regulation. EU policymakers approved the EU AI Act on December 9, 2023, the world's first AI legislation [EU].

One of the cornerstones of the Act is its focus on high-risk AI systems, particularly those that regulators deemed possess significant potential for individual harm, such as in hiring and education. Companies engaged in developing AI-based tools in these key sectors are now subject to rigorous scrutiny, mandated to furnish regulators with risk assessments and disclose the data used for algorithm training. Moreover, assurances against perpetuating biases are required by the law.

The Act also takes a decisive stance against harmful practices, unequivocally prohibiting certain activities like indiscriminate image scraping for facial recognition databases or behavioral manipulation. Transparency emerges as a guiding principle, as the act mandates that AI systems such as chatbots and image generators, including deep fakes, disclose their AI origin. By doing so, the EU seeks to instill accountability and clarity in the use of AI.

Another significant aspect of this initial legislation is the limitation imposed on government use of AI, particularly in law enforcement. The act imposes restrictions on the deployment of facial recognition software, with exceptions granted only for safety and national security purposes. Additionally, the Act limits the use of biometric scanning and categorizing individuals based on sensitive characteristics, which is poised to become an even more contentious topic given the immutable march of Synthetic Biology and the advancement of algorithms that reveal uncomfortable truths.

And as was the case with GDPR, the EU is very explicit on penalties for violations. Companies found in violation of the rules could face financial repercussions, with penalties ranging up to €35 million or 7% of global turnover.

We believe the EU approach is directionally noble but flawed, not in small part because policymakers prepared the first draft in literally 11 days during April 2023 from the start of the discussions, which was itself four months after ChatGPT was first launched, clearly the catalyst for the action [Coulter and Mukherjee]. The act itself was approved roughly ten months later. For comparison purposes, the first GDPR draft was published in 2012, and it took four years to get it approved.

Chief among noteworthy concerns are the following:

First, there is no clarity on how AI risks will be assessed in defining industries or standards, opening the interpretation to political manipulation. For example, an algorithm can be built to predict job performance far more reliably than the SAT can predict collegiate academic success. But what if the EU has certain preconceived political ideas about what job performance of certain demographics should be, independently of actual data?

Second, requiring the owner to disclose the data used for algorithm training renders the tenet subject to politicization, making this legislation the whim of a government body on how to interpret and enforce it. Technical reasons make this control inefficient. For example, if an algorithm relies on a continuous stream of ongoing data, how do you disclose the data used? What if synthetic data is used? Would this be detected by top-level disclosure without a data point-by-data point audit? In *Chapter 24,* we will explain how similar measures in China are squarely intended to tighten political control and ultimately hinder the development of AI. As a result, it is unclear if the Act will be able to strike the right balance between allowing AI to be used safely and encouraging investment in other areas without stifling innovation.

Another concern with regulation in general—not specific to the EU AI Act—is its limitation in scope to the geography that enacted it. Commerce, idea exchange, media, and technology are all globalized, so unless the regulation is truly global, there can always be a country that does not adhere to it and either uses that to constantly drive a leg up on economic competition or within a political discussion to extract concessions in other areas. That country could also simply develop AI applications to bring harm to targeted groups (individuals, countries, companies, industries), which can later have worldwide consequences.

While we believe that philosophically, the US would align itself with the EU position, other countries, such as China and those that either do not espouse Western values or those seeking to take economic advantage of the West's openness and inclusiveness, will likely align with China as the opposing and equally dominant viewpoint. We will talk more about China and the recent tensions with the US for AI hegemony in *Chapter 24.*

We believe that the regulation of intelligence in general, be it artificial or human, exists directly on the boundaries of free speech. We discuss this topic more as a part of AI's potential magnetic pull toward dystopia in *Chapter 23.* In what is the most tragic of ironies, the first technology in mankind's history that has the capability of learning and revealing truth across every realm of human endeavor is the one that will strike its death knell.

9. Prelude to Artificial General Intelligence

"For me, AGI...is the equivalent of a median human that you could hire as a co-worker."

Sam Altman

CEO of OpenAI [Nolan]
September 27, 2023

On November 18, 2023, Sam Altman, the Chief Executive Officer of Open AI, faced termination from the Board of Directors of his company OpenAI. Three days later, on November 21, OpenAI announced Altman's reinstatement as CEO along with a new initial Board.

According to leaked information, concerns surfaced within OpenAI regarding an AI breakthrough called Q*, potentially a precursor to Artificial General Intelligence (AGI), prompting lead researchers to voice reservations to the Board. Following these discussions, Sam Altman was abruptly removed from OpenAI, sparking a tumultuous series of days involving Altman, the board, and employees. The termination appeared to be connected to Altman's inclination to quickly commercialize Q*, in contrast to the board's focus on prioritizing safety measures [Knight].

AGI is a collective term that emerged as researchers and experts in AI contemplated creating machines capable of replicating human-like intelligence in all its cognitive aspects, which would include precisely what algorithms cannot do today: the ability to reason, devise strategies, make decisions under uncertainty, and represent knowledge, such as common sense. It also encompasses planning future actions, learning from past experiences, and effectively communicating in natural language. Furthermore, it is considered desirable for AGI to possess specific physical attributes, such as visual and auditory perception, and the ability to detect potential dangers and take action.

Any one of these elements would represent the next evolutionary step for AI, as the AI algorithms that we have today are only capable of solving specific, pre-defined problems and can make decisions only within the specific context of AI programming. Pioneers in AI, such as Alan Turing and John McCarthy, laid down fundamental ideas for AGI in their work decades ago, postulating how general cognitive abilities would take shape as an evolutionary step.

Despite uncertainty about the nature of Q*, some people speculated that it could signify a groundbreaking architectural development comparable to the advent of transformers, introduced by Google in 2017, which is the foundational technology that made possible all current Large Language Models (LLMs), including OpenAI's GPT-4 [TechCrunch]. Speculating about what Q*could be is a handy path to introduce the current areas of research toward achieving AGI. This is the framework for this chapter.

The following pages deep dive into today's multiple fields of study, which effectively constitute the starting gun for AGI.

Applying Logic to Solve Mathematical Problems

One of the potential explanations of what Q* actually is concerns OpenAI's initiative to solve mathematical problems. While this may seem like a simple accomplishment that AI has already addressed, there is significance in AI actually grasping mathematical reasoning. The true importance lies in AI's potential to comprehend mathematical proofs, with far-reaching implications across various domains, given the foundational role of mathematics in the world [Berman].

This reminds us of the *"General Problem Solver"* designed by Allen Newel and Herbert Simon in 1957 and the symbolic logic approach defended by John McCarthy, which we discussed in *Chapter 4*. More than 60 years have spanned since then, but machines still struggle with tasks involving logic and reasoning and still cannot proceed without specific, coded directives.

The capacity for independently generating mathematical or logical proofs requires a deeper comprehension of the proofs themselves, which would surpass the predictive abilities of current LLMs. When confronted with a problem involving mathematical or logic concepts, LLM models may provide correct answers without genuinely understanding the underlying theoretical proofs, merely reproducing patterns from their programming and training data. This underscores the existing limitations in the ability to grasp the rationales behind logical principles. The task of comprehending why answers are correct or incorrect, rather than merely predicting the next character in a sequence, is currently an insurmountable challenge for LLMs.

In this regard, a research paper titled *"STaR: Bootstrapping Reasoning with Reasoning"* was published by Stanford and Google in May 2022

[Zelikman et al.]. The paper explores the generation of step-by-step chains of thought to enhance the performance of language models in complex reasoning tasks, such as common sense questions or mathematics. The concept of *"Chain of Thought"* involves guiding the model to reason about intermediate steps when faced with challenging problems rather than directly arriving at complex solutions at once. This step-wise approach results in more accurate answers. The paper introduces a framework named STAR (Self-Taught Reasoner), which iteratively enhances an AI model's complex reasoning capabilities by following a cyclic process. First, the STAR generates rationales for answering questions based on a few examples. Then, it refines the rationales in case of incorrect answers and fine-tunes the model using the new rationales. Then, it goes back to the first step and continues iterating until the answers are good enough. OpenAI published a paper along the same lines in March 2023, where it also suggested breaking down large problems into intermediary reasoning steps and applying feedback for each intermediate step, not only for the final result, which has been common practice until now [Lightman et al.].

This multi-step approach is very intuitive and represents how human beings think. When confronted with a complex mathematical problem or when required to write a significant piece of programming code, we do not immediately arrive at the ultimate solution in one go, especially for complex problems. Instead, we break down problems into smaller components, address each part individually, and then integrate these solutions to derive the overall answer. This systematic approach is particularly evident in coding but also in any kind of engineering project, as well as in writing a book. Similarly, applying the same modularity principles to algorithms could also increase the rationality of AI systems.

Applying Reinforcement Learning to Self-improve

There is a second theory about what Q* could be. The term Q* hints at a connection with fundamental themes in the scientific literature on reinforcement learning, precisely Q-learning and the A* algorithm. Q-learning is the most common reinforcement learning algorithm, and we have discussed it in *Chapter 6*. Additionally, A* is a classic graph search algorithm developed in 1968 to plan routes for robots, in particular, a robot called Shakey, which we will talk about in *Chapter 11*. Shakey was the first mobile, all-purpose robot with self-reflective reasoning; it could entirely deconstruct commands into their most basic parts, whereas other contemporary robots would need instructions on each step of a more complex task.

Consequently, there has been speculation that Q* might involve a fusion of Q-learning and A* search with the very ambitious objective of bridging an LLM with the foundational aspects of deep reinforcement learning.

Reinforcement learning is compelling due to its capacity to look ahead and plan future moves within a complex environment of possibilities and its ability to learn through self-play. Both tactics played a pivotal role in the success of AlphaGo, the machine-learning software we talked about in Chapter 7. AlphaGo not only defeated the best Go players worldwide but surpassed them significantly. Notably, lookahead planning and self-play have not been integral to LLMs thus far [Berman].

Look-ahead planning is a process wherein a model anticipates future scenarios to generate improved actions or outputs. Presently, LLMs face challenges in executing effective lookahead planning. Their responses often just rely on predicting the next probable token in a sequence, lacking precise foresight and strategic planning. One way of applying look-ahead to LLMs would employ a tree-shaped structure to systematically explore various optimization possibilities to solve a problem through the trial-and-error process of a reinforcement learning algorithm. Such techniques could not substantially improve the model's ability to plan ahead, but they would partially augment its capability to address logic and reasoning challenges. However, it is unlikely that models trained this way offer a really profound comprehension of the underlying reasons for the validity or invalidity of logical or mathematical arguments.

The angular stone of applying reinforcement learning to LLMs is the idea of self-play. Self-play involves an agent enhancing its gameplay by interacting with slightly varied versions of itself. Self-play has also not been part of the standard training techniques of LLMs. LLMs do not play against themselves to continue learning better answers. Instead, as we know from the previous chapter, LLMs are trained through self-supervised learning. In the field of LLMs, most instances of self-play are likely to resemble automatic AI feedback of an AI playing against itself, rather than competitive interactions playing against humans.

Automatic AI feedback basically means that an AI model would be getting feedback about its strengths and weaknesses automatically from another AI system, whose main function is to evaluate the first model. The concept of AI feedback is a fundamental area of research at this moment. Current LLMs such as GPT undergo training using RLHF (Reinforcement Learning by Human Feedback), a method wherein the model is instructed and refined based on feedback from human evaluators, who manually score the AI on how good or bad answers are or how appropriate they are in terms of ethics, bias or politeness. This method has been effective in developing the first generation of LLMs. However, it is a time-consuming and costly process due to its dependence on human input [Christiano et al.].

Self-improvement entails an AI system engaging in repeated self-play, surpassing human performance by exploring various possibilities within the game environment. The shift from human scoring to automatic AI-based scoring at a scale, especially if another AI model is involved in the hand-offs, would allow AI models to self-improve, representing a watershed breakthrough in the development of AGI.

This methodology was again prominently demonstrated in the case of AlphaGo. AlphaGo was initially designed to learn by imitating expert human players. Doing this, it reached a level comparable to the best human players but fell short of surpassing them. The breakthrough came with self-improvement, where the AI played millions of games in a closed sandbox environment, optimizing its performance based on a simple reward function of winning the game. This new approach allowed AlphaGo to surpass human capabilities, outperforming top human players within 40 days through self-improvement.

There are several manners in which self-improvement could work with LLMs. Consider a scenario in which queries are directed to an LLM. Typically, the model provides an answer, but it is not easy to know how good the answer is. However, the introduction of a second agent to scrutinize and validate the initial agent's work markedly improves the quality of results. This would be comparable to the GAN models used in deep-fakes that we discussed in the previous chapter, where one model is trained to create realistic images, and another one is trained to evaluate how realistic those images are. Each one feeding into the other, the two parts of the GAN enter into a self-improvement cycle.

That reward function to evaluate how good or bad the results are in the case of Go is very explicit. It is determined by the number of stones a player has on the board and the territory they control. The main challenge for LLMs lies in the absence of a general reward criterion, unlike in the game of Go, where winning or losing is clear and thus programmable. Language, being diverse and multifaceted, lacks a singularly discernable reward function or reward definition for swiftly evaluating all decisions regarding output, e.g., creating content.

While the potential for self-improvement in narrow domains exists, extending this concept to the general case remains an open question in the field of AI. Answering that question might unlock the key to AGI.

Genetic Algorithms or Natural Selection Applied to AI

Apart from self-play, there are other ways of creating self-improving algorithms. One of them is called genetic algorithms. Q* has not been connected directly to genetic algorithms, but they are similar to the concept of self-play.

The concepts of natural selection and genetics—which hold that individuals with advantageous traits have a higher chance of surviving and procreating and passing those traits on to the following generation—are mimicked by genetic algorithms. This is actually not a new concept. The initial genetic algorithms were developed by Lawrence J. Fogel in 1960 [Fogel], but there is currently a renewed interest in them due to their applications in AI.

In a genetic algorithm, a population of potential solutions to a given problem is represented as a set of individual software programs, or individuals for short, each encoded as a string of parameters or variables. These individuals are then evaluated based on their fitness, which measures how well they solve the problem at hand. The fitter individuals are more likely to be selected to form the next generation, simulating the natural selection process.

Much like in humans, the genetic algorithm operates through a cycle of selection, crossover, and mutation. During selection, individuals are chosen based on their fitness to serve as parents for the next generation. Crossover involves combining the genetic information of two-parent methods to create offspring with a mix of their traits. That genetic information is the encoding of the method itself, for example, its hyperparameters. Mutation introduces random changes in the offspring method's genetic information, adding diversity to the population. This process is repeated over several generations, and over time, the population evolves towards better solutions to the problem.

When solving optimization problems with a large and complex solution space, genetic algorithms are helpful. They have been successfully used in a variety of fields, including engineering, finance, and Machine Learning, to find solutions that may be challenging to develop using conventional optimization techniques.

The drawback with genetic algorithms is similar to that of reinforcement learning, specifically that they necessitate an objective function that defines the algorithm's effectiveness. In Darwinian natural selection, applied to living species, the reward function is not dying before reproduction [Darwin]. As we have highlighted, defining a proper reward function for LLMs is challenging.

Synthetic Data and Generating Genuinely New Ideas

The third speculative theory about Q* suggests a potential connection between Q* learning and synthetic data. Synthetic data is another promising area of research to accelerate the learning of AI systems toward AGI. Synthetic data is data that is not real, as in training data gathered from real-world sources, but rather is realistic enough for an AI algorithm to be trained effectively on it.

Acquiring high-quality datasets poses a ubiquitous and formidable challenge. Companies possessing an exceptionally valuable, distinct, and well-maintained dataset hold significant value. Only a few companies have extensive and unique datasets of the likes of Google, Meta, Reddit, and a few others slightly lower on the totem pole, such as Mobile Operators and Amazon. Notably, OpenAI lacks its own exclusive dataset and sources datasets from various channels, including purchases and Open-Source datasets. If AI could autonomously generate synthetic datasets, that would eliminate the reliance on this limited number of sources. Many prominent companies and startups are working on synthetic data, but there are severe obstacles to maintaining quality and avoiding premature stagnation.

For example, in the case of self-driving cars, only a few companies like Google's Waymo or Tesla have been able to build huge datasets with millions of hours of real video of roads because they started incorporating video cameras and scaled data collection years ago. Other more traditional car manufacturers, like GM or Ford, are also building self-driving cars, but they started incorporating video cameras much later and do not have the extensive video dataset that Google or Tesla have. Synthetic data will be hugely useful for them to train their driving algorithms. We will talk more about self-driving cars in *Chapter 13* when we talk about robot mobility.

The chief advantage of synthetic data is that it is an avenue to introduce completely innovative ideas or approaches into a model. Models trained on static datasets are only as reliable as those datasets and may be unable to genuinely generate new ideas. Current LLMs heavily rely on their training set, producing responses derived from existing knowledge rather than generating genuinely new and innovative ideas. Coming back to the example of Alpha Go above, when AlphaGo was using training data from expert human players, the only strategies it could learn were those strategies used by humans, but there could be other much better strategies that are not reflected in this limiting training dataset. Similarly, by providing an AI model with synthetic data of good quality, we are opening up the solution space in which the model can learn.

Synthetic data could be highly valuable for training AGI. Even combining all available datasets might fall short of meeting the data requirements for training advanced AI, such as AGI. The solution lies in synthetic data or a hybrid of real and synthetic data, and there is speculation that Q* might be leveraging this approach. Variations or mutations created through synthetic data could be employed to train algorithms through self-play with automatic AI feedback or through genetic algorithms.

Synthetic data also represents a very slippery slope to the evolution of AI. One of the problems with synthetic data, which is realistic but not real, is, of course, that it makes it very difficult to differentiate between real content and realistic content or, in terms of output, what is real and what is fabricated. While it is an avenue to introduce completely innovative ideas or approaches into a model, it can also be used for the injection of personal biases. The algorithm, in fact, cannot make the distinction, and this opens the door to massive manipulation of information, such as fake news, fake videos, fake evidence in criminal cases, and any highly biased input. We will talk about this in detail in the context of dystopian outcomes in *Chapter 23*.

Learning Through Sensory Data

Finally, we will cover two areas of current research that are not related to the Q* rumors that surfaced with the firing of Sam Altman but hold promise to advance AGI. The first one is using sensory data, which comes from our senses, primarily video, to train algorithms. For some prominent AI leaders, including Yann LeCun, harnessing sensory data for training algorithms has the potential to expedite the acquisition of knowledge [LeCun].

Animals and humans show rapid cognitive development with much less data input than current AI systems, which require enormous amounts of training data. At the moment, LLMs are typically trained on text datasets that would require 20 thousand years for a human to read. Even with all of this training data, these models still have trouble with basic ideas like logical or mathematical reasoning. Humans, on the other hand, require much less textual training data to reach a higher level of understanding.

According to LeCun, the explanation for this lies in humans encountering a broad range of data types beyond mere text. Specifically, a significant portion of the information we receive is in the form of images and videos, which is a highly rich and inherently contextual format. If we take into account visual data and the richness of images in comparison to text, humans' data intake surpasses the training data of a LLM, even from a young age. For instance, a two-year-old's exposure to visual data is approximately 600 terabytes, while the training data for an LLM typically amounts to about 20 terabytes. This implies that a two-year-old has been exposed to 30 times more data than an LLM typically receives during its training process. Advertising executive Fred Barnard once famously coined, "*A picture is worth a thousand words,"* and as it turns out, he was directionally correct, though slightly overstating the reality.

According to LeCun, the reason humans learn faster is not solely because our brains are larger than current LLMs. Instead, he gives another reason to support the argument that video data also holds significant importance in the training process. Animals, including parrots, corvids, octopuses, and dogs, are also considerably more intelligent than current LLMs. These animals possess roughly a few trillion hyperparameters, which aligns closely with current LLMs. GPT is rumored to have 1.76 trillion hyperparameters, while GPT-3 has 175 billion. The hyperparameters of an artificial neural network are equivalent to brain synapses.

By way of comparison, human brains are indeed much bigger than current LLMs. Humans have around 100 billion neurons and between 100 and 1,000 trillion synapses—with younger people having many more synapses than older ones [Herculano-Houzel] [Wanner] [Zhang] [Yale].

New architectures that can mimic the effective learning seen in humans and the above animals are being developed to use sensory data in the learning process of advanced AI models. Adding more text data—whether synthetic or not—works as a temporary measure. But integrating sensory data, especially video, is the ideal solution that might be able to get scientists closer to AGI. Video has more bandwidth than text and superior internal structure because it contains spatial, movement, audio, and textual data. Video also offers more learning opportunities than text because of its natural repetition, and it offers significant knowledge about the structure of the world.

Ultimately, as the Romans quite aptly put it, *"de gustibus et de colorem non disputandem"* (about taste and color there is no dispute.) Exclusively text-based training where data includes the word *"green,"* for example, will never generate contextual understanding that green to me can be blue to you. Or when someone says *"my, that food is delicious,"* the true meaning can only be understood when seeing if it was said with rolling eyes or not. As there are no extensive databases of real videos suitable to train AI on contextual common sense, it is highly likely that synthetic video will be used for this, opening up the risk of specific bias, as we have reviewed previously.

World Models: An AI Vision of the World

A *"world model"* in AI refers to a comprehensive representation of an environment that is used in reinforcement learning. World models encapsulate the key elements, dynamics, and relationships within that environment, allowing an AI agent to simulate and understand its surroundings. World models have also been used in robotics training since the early days. These models enable the robot to interpret and predict events, facilitating decision-making and planning. We will talk about this in detail in *Chapter 11*.

Human beings also use mental representations similar to world models. These representations are built through sensory perception, experience, and learning, allowing individuals to understand and navigate the world around them. Human world models encompass various experiential elements, including spatial relationships, cause-and-effect dynamics, and social interactions. It informs what is colloquially referred to as one's *"worldview."* Similar to robot training, humans use these mental representations for decision-making, planning, and adapting to new situations. In many ways, it is inescapable to inform decisions.

Current LLMs do not explicitly incorporate elaborated world models, and integrating them is one of the advanced avenues being explored today to achieve AGI. It could offer two key advantages toward the goal of instantiating AGI: First, by incorporating a broader understanding of the environment, LLMs could generate more contextually relevant and informed responses, unlocking the model's ability to engage in nuanced conversations, comprehend more complex, nuanced or contextual scenarios, and provide more accurate and context-aware information. Second, world models might also enable LLMs to simulate and reason about different situations, potentially improving their capacity for common sense reasoning and problem-solving in diverse contexts.

We note that world models might also be related to the topic of human and AI consciousness. Consciousness is the state of being aware of and able to perceive one's thoughts, sensations, feelings, and surroundings. This is a complicated topic that science knows little about. We will discuss this in the context of AI development in *Chapter 2*

Part III: The New Body

"جسدك له حق عليك"

"Your body has rights over you."

Prophet Muhammad,

560 - 632 AD
Sahih al-Bukhari, Book 43, Chapter 3, Hadith 6284

Preamble

Robots serve as an extension of humanity's body. While they initially found footing in manufacturing environments that were too hazardous for humans, they are now starting to integrate seamlessly into our daily lives, from household appliances to self-driving cars, enhancing convenience and efficiency across applications.

Thanks to deep neural networks, AI and robotics have now become integrated; a robot today is basically an AI with a physical body. As new AI technologies advance emotional awareness within robots and enable deeper interaction with humans, humanoid robots are taking on roles not only in manufacturing but also in construction, healthcare, and the service industries. Such robots are even making strides in elderly care, an industry in which the human touch has always been highly valued.

Robots are gradually becoming humanity's new body. Robotic prostheses, tightly linked to our brains, already offer control over movement and sensory experiences. As we look to the future, systematically integrating mechanical or electronic enhancements into our bodies and brains will become increasingly feasible, thus ushering in the era of widespread cyborgs.

Before delving into the future of robots, we will first review how robots have developed. Modern robots can trace their roots to complex mechanical creations dating as far back as Classical Greece. *Chapter 10* delves into the early history of these automatons, progressing through the Industrial Revolution when the emergence of automated factories sparked concerns about job displacement and triggered the Luddite movement in response to automation, a movement that we believe will repeat in a modern-day equivalent.

Chapter 11 describes the first robots that were built starting in the 1920s. At that time, there were two competing approaches to designing robots, one analog and the other using symbolic logic. Analog robots relied on continuous electrical signals, had unparalleled real-time responsiveness, and excelled in more straightforward tasks. Robots based on symbolic logic employed a computer to process discrete logical symbols and could handle more complex tasks but were slower than their counterparts.

After those early years, the development of robots split into three distinct archetypes that progressed independently: first, robotic arms and industrial applications; second, robots engineered for high mobility and autonomy; and third, robots tailored for human interactions.

Regarding the first type of robot, *Chapter 13* introduces the robotic arm, undeniably the most influential robot in history. Initially developed in the US in 1961, the robotic arm found its early applications in the American automobile manufacturing industry before rapidly spreading to other sectors and geographies. *Chapter 14* explains how the robotic arm arrived in Japan in 1969 and rapidly developed into sophisticated industrial machines, making Japan the world's leader in robotics, with a market share of 90% of all industrial robots in 1990.

Concerning the second type of robot, a significant leap in robot autonomy and mobility occurred after the Dot-Com crisis in 2002 with the increased capacity of computers and the development of powerful neural network algorithms, enabling robots to make complex real-time mobility decisions. *Chapter 15* focuses on self-driving cars, warehouse robots, and quadruped or bipedal robots. *Chapter 16* dives into military robots, particularly the evolution of uncrewed land vehicles and drones. Lastly, *Chapter 17* explores space robots, spanning from those in the International Space Station with lower autonomy demands to Mars exploration robots, which are becoming increasingly autonomous, and finally, asteroid mining robots with the highest requirements for autonomy and mobility.

The final two chapters of this section delve into the third type of robot, specifically designed for interactions with humans. Japan has been developing humanoids since the late 1960s. *Chapter 19* examines the role of humanoid robots in Japan as an innovative response to demographic challenges and a replacement for immigration. In Japan, robots are employed to automate labor across various industries, including traditionally non-automated sectors like retail, hospitality, services, and construction. Additionally, *Chapter 20* explores the evolving capacity of robots to comprehend and respond to human emotions, seamlessly integrating emotions into their decision-making processes. This transformation is fostering emotional bonds between humans and robots.

In the following pages, we examine the evolution of robots, which has happened separately but in parallel to development in AI, with the lines of the two now having intersected. We review the implications of this, how robotic technology is poised to increase its presence in our society, and what that means for us.

10. From Mechanical Automatons to the Industrial Revolution

"As the Liberty lads o'er the sea
Bought their freedom, and cheaply, with blood,
So we, boys, we
Will die fighting, or live free,
And down with all kings but King Ludd!"

George Gordon Byron, Lord Byron

British Poet
Song for the Luddites [Eschner]
1816

In the early 19th century, amid the sweeping tide of the Industrial Revolution in England, a resounding chorus of dissent and rebellion found multiple expressions among craftsmen, artisans, and other workers. In the poet Lord Byron's 1816 poem, *"Song for the Luddites,"* he eloquently conveyed themes of liberty and defiance in the face of mechanization. The Luddites, a group of skilled textile workers, embodied this spirit as they staunchly opposed the intrusion of machines into their craft, resorting to dramatic acts of smashing machinery to protest against automation.

Fast forward to 2023, and we witness a similar battle unfolding within the heart of Hollywood [CBS]. Unionized actors and writers took to the streets, voicing their concerns and fears about AI's impact on their jobs. Their protests reflected a growing unease about the increasing use of automation and AI in workplaces, threatening to replace human creativity with machines. The prospect of their roles being taken over by robots and algorithms sparked anxiety among those who dedicated their lives to the art of storytelling.

Like the Luddites, workers in multiple sectors today rightly express concerns about the scope of AI's potential impact to make them economically obsolete. Nearly every facet of our lives, from autonomous vehicles to medical diagnostics, relies on human labor that, in the absence of an accommodation and adjustment strategy, will be adversely impacted by AI.

The foundation of modern robotics can be traced back to the historical development of automated machinery, which ultimately led to the Industrial Revolution and refractions like the Luddite movement. Robots have their roots in the work of mechanical engineers across various civilizations, from ancient China and the Hellenistic to the Islamic world and medieval Europe, including influential figures like Leonardo da Vinci.

The Mechanical Engineers of the Hellenistic World

In the 4th century BC, in the Greek world, myths and legends greatly influenced the conceptualization and the development of automation, as previously discussed in *Chapter 3.*

One rational figure that stands out amidst this mythical backdrop was Archytas of Tarentum, a mathematician and engineer from the 4th century BC. Inspired by the wide range of tales, Archytas created an astounding mechanical bird powered by steam. One day, Archytas was invited to a party and decided to showcase this ingenious machine. The machine achieved remarkable flight, fascinating everyone. The bird soared above guests before gracefully returning to its creator, leaving everyone stunned. [Chambers]

Like Archytas, many talented engineers emerged in Hellenistic Egypt, specifically Alexandria. Many of them specialized in crafting automatons for religious ceremonies and entertainment, catering primarily to the elite. Notable among them was Heron of Alexandria (1st century AD). Heron brought figures and scenes to life in a puppet theater. His creations had complex mechanisms like automatic doors, liquid fountains dispensing wine or milk, and a vending machine offering holy water for a coin. These devices operated through compressed air and steam systems, revealing a surprising sophistication of mechanical engineering. The intricate construction techniques of these wonders were documented in Hero's Treatise on Pneumatics [Alexandria].

Throughout the Middle Ages, the Greek world maintained the practice of creating automata. The Byzantine Empire, located in the eastern Mediterranean, continued the rich Greek and Roman cultural legacy after Rome fell in 476 AD. This included preserving and advancing the automaton-making knowledge that their Alexandrian ancestors had passed on to them. An example from the 10th century illustrates the Byzantines' technology. When Western European ambassadors journeyed to Constantinople, they were greatly impressed by the automata showcased in the palace of emperors Theophilus and Constantine Porphyrogenitus. The automata included gilded bronze or wooden lions, metallic birds with melodious songs, and an emperor's throne that elegantly ascended and descended on a platform. These wondrous creations left an indelible mark on the ambassadors, who recounted the marvels upon their return home [Safran].

Pioneers of Automation in Imperial China

From the 8th to the 11th centuries, while Europe was immersed in a period of stagnation during its High Middle Ages, China experienced a renaissance and growth that marked a fascinating chapter in its history. During this period, the Tang and Song dynasties left a profound imprint on the cultural, technological, and commercial development of the country. The Tang emperors (618 - 907 AD) witnessed a flourishing in arts, poetry, and the expansion of Buddhism. After a brief period of political fragmentation, the Song dynasty emerged (960 - 1127 AD), under whose rule China experienced significant advances in science, technology, and trade, with notable innovations such as the magnetic compass and movable-type printing.

In this context of development and creativity, prominent figures in the field of automation emerged in China. Among them is Ma Daifeng, an enigmatic 8th-century inventor about whom little is known. Ma Daifeng built a dressing table for the Empress of China, an astonishing device for its time. When the empress needed to groom and apply makeup, the mirrored cabinet would open automatically, and a mechanical wooden figure would gracefully emerge, delivering the necessary items for her personal grooming, from makeup to hair accessories [Hemal and Menon].

However, Ma was not the only pioneer in the field of mechanical engineering. Ying Wenliang stood out as a visionary who created automatons capable of delivering speeches at banquets and others that played melodies with ancient Chinese musical instruments, demonstrating his ability to build to a standard that accurately mimicked human movements.

Finally, the scientist and engineer Su Song left a profound mark on the history of automation with his masterpiece, the Su Song Tower in Kaifeng, China, built in 1088 AD [Lin and Yan]. This tower housed a series of automatic mannequins that performed various tasks, from measuring time and indicating the direction of the winds to ringing bells and offering theatrical performances.

Medieval Islam Revolutionizes Mechanics

In the medieval Arab world, there was a remarkable era of intellectual and technological advancement known as the Islamic Golden Age. This era, led by the Abbasid dynasty, which ruled from the 8th to the 12th century, witnessed astonishing developments in various disciplines, such as science, philosophy, medicine, arts, and architecture. It began with the expansion of Islam under the Umayyad and Abbasid caliphates, establishing vast empires that stretched from Spain to Persia. Under the leadership of the Abbasid dynasty, Baghdad became a prominent intellectual and cultural center, where significant advances were made in fields like mathematics, astronomy, and medicine, leaving a lasting impact on world civilization.

Ismail al-Jazari stands out as a polymath Muslim who left an indelible mark on the history of engineering. Al-Jazari lived in the 12th century in northern Mesopotamia, and his legacy endures through his work, the *"Book of Knowledge of Ingenious Mechanical Devices,"* written in 1206. In its pages, he meticulously described over 50 mechanical devices, including humanoid automatons of astonishing complexity [Elices].

One of Al-Jazari's most famous automatons was a boat equipped with four automatic musicians that captivated guests at lavish royal parties. These musicians, playing flutes, drums, lutes, and other traditional instruments of the time, achieved perfect synchronization thanks to a complex system of gears, cams, and levers powered by a water and weight system. Each automatic musician performed pre-programmed melodies, not unlike a so-called *"player piano,"* giving the audience a unique musical experience.

A mechanical waitress that served water, tea, and other beverages was another notable automaton constructed by Al-Jazari. The drink dripped from a reservoir-equipped tank into a jug and then, after a few minutes, into a cup. An automated door would then open to let the waitress finish serving. Al-Jazari also created an automaton for handwashing that included a flushing mechanism that predated contemporary toilet technology. This invention featured a humanoid automaton near a water-filled sink. The water in the sink drained when the user pulled the lever, and the automaton then filled it back up.

The automatons of Al-Jazari, exceptionally sophisticated for their time, reflected a profound understanding of mechanics and engineering. His choice to represent human figures in these automatons is intriguing, considering that Islam does not encourage the representation of the human form. However, these devices were created for practical purposes beyond religious considerations, highlighting ingenuity and technical skill in creating automatons that still amaze with their cleverness and complexity today.

Europe Awakens and Embraces Islamic Mechanics

In the 10th century, Europe began to awaken from its slumber in the High Middle Ages. A period of innovation and creativity got underway. The mathematical and mechanical knowledge of the Hellenistic and Arab world reached Europe through contact with the Arabs, primarily in Spain and Sicily.

One of the most emblematic pieces of this Arab influence in 10th-century Europe was an extraordinary gift that Harun al-Rashid, the powerful caliph of Baghdad, sent to King Charlemagne of the Franks in the year 807 [LaGrandeur]. The gift was a water clock with complex hydraulic jacks and moving human figures. This gift not only amazed Charlemagne but also planted a seed of curiosity and wonder in the European continent.

Subsequently, around the 10th century, the first water clocks inspired by the aesthetics of the Arab world began to be built in Europe. For example, Pope Sylvester II owned one of them. The technical legacy of the Arabs, with their expertise in mechanics and mathematics, continued to leave a mark on Europe. Segmental gears, as described by Al-Jazari in his books, appeared in Europe's more advanced clocks almost a hundred years later. The transfer of knowledge was slow but steady, and Europe began to absorb the wisdom and technical skill that had accumulated over centuries after emerging from its early Middle Ages.

There are multiple examples of automatons designed and fashioned in the Late Middle Ages. When Robert II, Count of Artois, constructed a garden in his castle during the 13th century, he included a number of mechanical automatons fashioned after animals and humans. Later in the 14th century, automatic bell strikers, known as "*jaquemarts*," became popular in European cities alongside mechanical clocks [LaGrandeur]. Moving into the 15th century, Johannes Müller von Königsberg, a prominent German astronomer and mathematician, created mechanical automatons that took inspiration from birds and insects, like his "*iron eagle*" and "*iron fly.*" Finally, in the English Renaissance, John Dee, an advisor to Queen Elizabeth, created a mechanical wooden beetle that could fly using concealed internal mechanisms.

Leonardo da Vinci's Mechanical Creativity

No brief survey of automatons and mechanical engineering that had some influence on robotics can ignore the ingenious machines of engineering master Leonard da Vinci. The influence of Leonardo da Vinci on the subsequent evolution of robotics is a fascinating aspect of the history of technology. His ability to blend science with artistic creativity, blending the real with the conceptual to create the potential, like the influence of Science Fiction on the direction of AI, is an example of how the intersection of technology and visual arts can lead to significant innovation.

One of the earliest documented examples of Leonardo's foray into the world of automation is his detailed design of a humanoid automaton, made in 1495, a design that had been lost and was rediscovered in the 1950s [Moran].

The automaton designed by Leonardo da Vinci is a mechanical knight in armor. Leonardo's inspiration for creating this knight came from his studies of anatomy, particularly from his famous study of the ideal proportions of the human body. Although the exact functioning of this machine has been debated due to the lack of direct evidence, speculation exists about how it might have worked based on the designs and mechanical principles that Leonardo applied in its creation.

This automaton consisted of several key components and mechanisms that enabled its operation. Among these elements were the support structure holding the automaton, the armor it wore—designed in the Germano-Italian style of the time—and the movement capabilities that imitated humans, such as sitting, moving the arms, and moving the head and jaw.

One of the most enigmatic aspects of the design was a melodic drum located on top of the automaton. It is uncertain whether this drum was directly related to the automaton's operation or if it had an independent function, such as a musical mechanism.

The automaton also had the ability to move the wrists but could not move the arms or forearms. Each wrist could move alternately, suggesting a possible musical or percussive function. Additionally, the automaton was equipped with a mechanism that could be programmed by the placement or removal of pegs, allowing for alternating rhythm sequences. This also points to a musical or entertainment function.

Another notable example of Leonardo's efforts in the field of automation is the *"programmable mechanical lion"* he built as a political allegory in 1515. This lion could open its chest and display the royal coat of arms and flowers inside, and it is believed that its engine was based on a self-propelled cart drawn by Leonardo in 1478. Although of a different nature than his mechanical knight, this automaton showcases Leonardo's versatility and creativity in crafting impressive machines [Ledsom].

Ingenious Mechanical Toys Astonish the World

The tradition of creating mechanical automation for the enjoyment of the high classes that started in the Arab world and persisted in Europe in the low Middle Ages continued and expanded to broader society during the modern age. By the 18th century, a dazzling array of mechanical toys and playful automations appeared and started to captivate society. This inventive streak ignited the imagination of clockmakers and mechanical artisans across Europe, sparking enthusiasm for automated toys. The European aristocracy eagerly embraced these automata, collecting them for their entertainment.

For example, the skilled 18th-century artisan Jacques de Vaucanson crafted a mechanical duck commissioned for Louis XV. This astonishing toy bird could eat and drink thanks to intricate moving parts. Vaucanson's ambitions extended further, leading him to craft humanoid automatons like a drummer and a flutist, notable for their astonishing resemblance to the human form [Hemal and Menon].

Similarly, Pierre Jaquet-Droz, an 18th-century Swiss watchmaker, ventured into the world of automatons as a promotional tool for his watch and bird-selling business. His mechanical humanoids performed astounding actions. *"The Writer,"* one of his most renowned creations, could compose personalized messages with pen and paper. Jaquet-Droz's other automatons produced music and executed intricate movements, becoming engineering marvels and sought-after sources of entertainment [Deshpande].

On the other hand, Wolfgang von Kempelen, a Hungarian inventor, introduced *"The Turk"* in the late 18th century, a chess-playing machine that astounded the world. This automaton competed skillfully against human opponents, defeating prominent historical figures like Benjamin Franklin and Napoleon Bonaparte. Even Edgar Allan Poe wrote about it in his short novel *"Maelzel's Chess Player"* [Poe]. However, behind the illusion, The Turk concealed a hidden human player, a masterful deception that captivated audiences for years [Hemal and Menon].

Far away from Europe, the same was happening in parallel in Japan– a land that was destined to become the absolute world leader in robotics— where mechanical toys, known as Karakuri, were making a sensation. Karakuri ranged from simple dolls to complex automatons that served tea, wrote, and shot arrows. They were popular in performances and festivals. The interest in Karakuri was such that in 1796, the *"Karakuri Zui"* was published, a fundamental book documenting and describing karakuri, their designs, technology, and operation [Murakami]. An interesting figure in this engineering of automatons is Hisashige Tanaka. Tanaka began his career in the 19th century manufacturing Karakuri but left it to focus on higher-value-added products such as hydraulics and lighting. He even manufactured a steam train and boat. He was such a prolific inventor that he earned the nickname the *"Japanese Edison."* Upon his death, his company eventually became Toshiba, the giant Japanese technology multinational [Hornyak].

The Industrial Revolution Bursts Forth

Coming back to Europe, by the late 18th century, Britain was the epicenter of the Industrial Revolution. The introduction of machinery, such as James Watt's steam engine and Edmund Cartwright's power loom, marked the beginning of an era of automation. Textile production greatly benefited from these innovations, resulting in faster and more efficient manufacturing.

The momentum of the Industrial Revolution, spearheaded by Great Britain, rapidly disseminated throughout Europe. Nations such as Germany, France, and Belgium eagerly embraced British machinery and technological advancements, igniting a continent-wide industrialization phenomenon. In Europe, weaving was also a notably significant yet labor-intensive industry. Weavers traditionally relied on assistants to manipulate threads for intricate patterns. However, a breakthrough came in 1804 when French inventor Joseph-Marie Jacquard introduced the revolutionary "*Jacquard Loom.*" This ingenious machine translated codified shapes from punch cards into precise configurations of the machinery that automatically manipulated threads to weave the desired patterns. This innovation exponentially boosted weaving speeds, increasing productivity from one inch per day to two feet [Keranen].

In the early 19th century, the Industrial Revolution also journeyed across the Atlantic to the US. Visionaries like Eli Whitney, renowned for the cotton gin, and Samuel Slater, hailed as the "*Father of the American Industrial Revolution*" for his mastery of textile machinery manufacturing, made indelible contributions to America's industrialization.

The mechanization and automation of tasks previously undertaken by human hands set profound economic and societal transformations in motion.

The Luddites' Struggle to Resist the Onslaught of Automation

A group of English textile workers, known as the Luddites, emerged in the early 19th century in response to the profound changes brought about by the Industrial Revolution, particularly the widespread adoption of machinery in textile production; their movement gained momentum between 1811 and 1816 [Sale].

The term "*Luddite*" originates in a mythical figure named Ned Ludd, a weaver who supposedly smashed two stocking frames in 1779 after receiving criticism for his work. The Luddites adopted this name as an alias when sending threatening messages to mill owners and government officials as they protested the increasing mechanization of textile production.

The Luddites' discomfort with the Industrial Revolution stemmed from their conviction that the displacement of skilled workers by machines would lead to unemployment and reduced wages. Furthermore, they saw machinery as jeopardizing the quality of goods, as unskilled laborers could not match the craftsmanship of artisans.

To protest the mechanization of their trade, the Luddites employed various tactics, including destroying machinery. They clandestinely raided factories and mills, explicitly targeting the machinery they believed responsible for their economic hardships. Machine breaking became symbolic of their resistance to industrialization.

One of the most infamous incidents involving the Luddites was the assassination of mill owner William Horsfall in 1812. Horsfall had made incendiary remarks about the Luddites, vowing to *"Ride up to his saddle in Luddite blood."* In retaliation, a group of Luddites ambushed and killed him, escalating tensions and prompting an increased government crackdown on the movement [Sharp].

Ultimately, the Luddite movement succumbed to government intervention and suppression. The British government deployed troops to suppress Luddite activities, resulting in arrests, trials, and severe punishments for those involved in machine-breaking. The Frame Breaking Act of 1812 made *"machine breaking"* a capital offense, further deterring Luddite actions. These measures gradually eroded the movement's momentum, leading to its decline.

Despite the subterfuge and openly voiced opposition to industrialization, the Luddite resistance ultimately failed to stop the Industrial Revolution. The Luddites and their supporters were successfully put down by the government's use of force and the support of the middle and upper classes. The economic and technological changes of the Industrial Revolution continued unabated. The Luddite movement is a historical testament to the intricate and sometimes contentious relationship between technological progress and labor sentiments.

11. The Great Debate: Symbolic or Analog Logic

"Not in looks, but in action, the model must resemble an animal. Therefore it must have these or some measure of these attributes: exploration, curiosity, free-will in the sense of unpredictability, goalseeking, self-regulation, avoidance of dilemmas, foresight, memory, learning, forgetting, association of ideas, form recognition, and the elements of social accommodation. Such is life."

William Grey Walter

American-born British neurophysiologist, cybernetician, and robotician.
A machine that learns [Grey]
1951

In the early days of robotics, two distinct approaches to logic emerged, each with advantages and disadvantages. These approaches, known as *"analog logic robotics"* and *"symbolic logic robotics,"* laid the foundation for developing AI and autonomous systems.

Analog logic robotics relied heavily on analog circuitry to process information and make decisions. These robots utilized continuous electrical signals to represent and manipulate data, allowing for real-time responsiveness and adaptability. One of the primary advantages of this approach was its ability to handle sensory input with relative ease, as analog systems could process a wide range of continuous signals, such as light, sound, and touch, without the need for digitization. Moreover, analog logic robotics exhibited a remarkable capacity for parallel processing, enabling them to perform multiple tasks concurrently.

However, analog logic robotics had several notable disadvantages. They were inherently limited in terms of logical reasoning and symbolic representation, meaning that their decision-making capabilities were often restricted to simple reactive behaviors, making them less suitable for complex tasks that required higher-level cognitive functions. Additionally, the analog components of these robots were susceptible to noise and drift, which could result in imprecise or erratic behavior.

On the other hand, symbolic logic robotics, championed by pioneers like Alan Turing and John McCarthy, adopted a fundamentally different approach. These robots relied on symbolic representations of knowledge and logic, using discrete symbols to represent repeating concepts, objects, and relationships. This allowed for more sophisticated reasoning, planning, and problem-solving capabilities. Symbolic logic robotics excelled in tasks that required deductive reasoning, such as navigating complex environments, making decisions based on extended knowledge, and planning sequences of actions.

Nevertheless, symbolic logic robotics faced particular challenges. Their symbolic data processing was inherently slower than analog systems as they involved complex computations. This made them less agile in real-time, dynamic environments and in constant need of ever-increasing processing power. Additionally, the representation of the natural world in symbols required meticulous manual programming, which was labor-intensive and often led to limitations in adaptability and scalability.

Early Robot Prototypes: Limited by Absence of Logic and Sensing Capabilities

In the 1920s and 30s, humanoid robots emerged in the US, England, and Japan, each with distinct approaches to robotics. In the US, the focus was on entertainment; in the United Kingdom, it was on motion and language; and in Japan, the emphasis was on human interaction. It is remarkable that the first robot prototypes, emerging simultaneously on three continents and at least two different cultures, all took on humanoid forms.

In the early days of robotics, these machines were relatively primitive, lacking advanced capabilities due to the absence of modern computers and sophisticated sensors. They could not perceive their environment or interact with it and had no autonomous or purposeful actions, as they lacked logical reasoning and decision-making mechanisms. Nevertheless, they incorporated mechanical means and human interface methods that gave them a personable quality. Today, we might view them as expensive toys similar to the automata created by Pierre Jaquet-Droz in the 18th century or the Japanese Karakuri. Still, in their time, they represented significant advancements.

Televox was the first modern humanoid robot—excluding Leonardo da Vinci's robot. It was built in 1926 by the Westinghouse Electric Corporation, an American manufacturing company [Schaut]. Televox was an early attempt at a human-sized mechanical servant designed for home and industrial use. It could respond to voice commands and perform tasks like letter writing and drawing. It was used as a promotional attraction during public demonstrations. Its ability to interact with people in a basic yet captivating way made it a fascinating innovation of its time. Televox operated based on telephone controls, where users could issue commands through the phone, primarily using vibrating reeds tuned to specific frequencies for input and a series of tones for output.

A decade later, Westinghouse introduced Elektro, a humanoid robot designed primarily for entertainment at fairs and exhibitions [Schaut]. It debuted at the 1939 New York World's Fair, displaying skills to respond to voice commands using a vocabulary of approximately 700 words. Elektro could walk, smoke cigarettes, inflate balloons, and demonstrate skilled movements of its head and arms. Its lifelike appearance was achieved through a steel skeleton covered by an aluminum skin. Additionally, Elektro had a robotic companion named Sparko, a mechanical dog, further enhancing its captivating and accessible presence.

Across the Atlantic in England, World War I veteran Captain William Richards constructed two humanoid robots in the UK: Eric and George [Jozuka]. Eric, built in 1928, was a static robot capable of sitting and standing but unable to walk. Eric could perform facial gestures and had multilingual abilities. In contrast, George, a later model created in the 1930s, possessed more advanced capabilities. It could deliver speeches in several languages, including French, German, Hindi, Chinese, and Danish. George was often called *"the polite gentleman"* compared to Eric, who was seen as his *"rough and clumsy brother."* On the other side of the globe, the first Japanese humanoid robot was developed in 1927 and was called *"Gakutensoku"* [Frumer]. This fascinating robot, whose name translates to *"learning from the laws of nature"* in Japanese, stood out for its ability to express emotions and interact with people. Remarkably, the characteristics of Japanese Robots, famous today for their friendliness in human interfaces, were already present in Gakutensoku. It became a companion to people and an inspirational model. Utilizing an engineered compressed air system, the automaton could move its head and hands in a convincing human fashion. Gakutensoku demonstrated its dexterity by writing fluently, raising its eyelids, and reflecting various facial expressions, such as introspection. Furthermore, its prowess extended further as it could write words with a pen, leaving a mark of wit and skill that endured in collective memory. Japan is, without a doubt, the country that has the best integrated robots into society. We will talk in detail about Japan's humanoids in *Chapter 17* and how they became a solid alternative to immigration for the Japanese government.

All these early robots lacked both logic and sensory capabilities. With the development of the first computer in 1945 and the mathematical principles of symbolic logic, two distinct schools of thought emerged to provide robots with cognition: analog logic and symbolic logic robotics.

The Animal Instinct of Early Analog Logic Robots

In the early days of computer science, luminaries like Alan Turing and John von Neumann developed theories centered on digital computation and symbolic logic, as discussed earlier in *Chapter 3*. John McCarthy and his colleagues further explored this symbolic logic in the context of AI.

However, it is essential to note that symbolic logic, also called digital logic, was not the sole option available at the time. Alternatives, such as analog logic, existed. While today's computers are entirely digital, the choice between digital and analog was far less clear in those early years. To draw a parallel, the transition from analog to digital TV occurred relatively recently, in the late 1990s. In the 1950s, analog logic was a solid alternative for many engineers.

The fundamental difference between symbolic and analog systems lies in how they represent and process information: symbolic logic uses discrete binary values (0 and 1) to encode and manipulate data, while analog logic relies on continuous and variable signals for information representation.

During this exploration period, William Grey Walter, a researcher at the Burden Neurological Institute in Bristol, championed the exclusive use of analog electronics to emulate brain processes. In 1948 and 1949, Walter achieved a significant breakthrough by creating the first autonomous electronic robots with complex behaviors. Named Elmer and Elsie, these *"tortoise"* robots represented a milestone as they emulated animal brains in their thinking processes [Inglis].

Elmer and Elsie were equipped with single light or touch sensors connected to two different pathways controlling two motors, mimicking the presence of two distinct neural brains. Astonishingly, these robots could navigate obstacles and explore their environment autonomously. When presented with a set of light sources, they would choose one of them and decide to move toward it as part of their exploratory process.

In a captivating experiment, Walter placed a light in front of one of the tortoises, and it reacted as if seeing itself in a mirror, with its light blinking excitedly. This behavior prompted questions about whether these robots exhibited a self-awareness similar to that observed in animals. That experiment has a profound significance for Walter because his goal was to create robots that embodied animalistic instincts.

Two decades later, in the 1960s, another remarkable analog-based robot, known as "The Beast," was developed at John Hopkins University [Moravec].

Computers were already widely available at the time, but the Beast operated without a computer. Its control circuit consisted of dozens of transistors regulating analog voltages.

This machine possessed rudimentary intelligence, primarily focused on its survival. As it roamed laboratory hallways, it sought wall sockets to plug into for recharging. The robot detected sockets using physical sensors on its arm, meticulously tracing the wall. When it located a socket, two electrical prongs extended to fit into it, establishing the necessary electrical connection for recharging.

A sonar system guided The Beast, triangulating its location within hallways and detecting obstacles, similar to a bat's echolocation. When it identified obstructions, like people in the hallway, The Beast would reduce speed, stop, or maneuver around them as required.

Fast forward almost 20 years to 1979, and another significant milestone emerged in the analog logic camp with the development of the *"Stanford Cart"* at Stanford University [Moravec]. This cart demonstrated remarkable autonomy by successfully navigating a room filled with chairs, all without human intervention and without relying on an integrated computer. This achievement was made possible thanks to its complex analog circuitry, which allowed it to process sensory input and make real-time decisions autonomously. The cart employed analog sensors to perceive its environment, detect obstacles, and adjust its path accordingly. Computers were certainly available in the late 70s, but they were still too slow and limited to support the kind of computations required for the complex navigation of the *"Stanford Cart."* This is why this robot marked such a significant advancement in demonstrating analog logic's potential in robotics. The *"Stanford Cart"* project was led by a young Hans Moravec, and we will talk about him once more in Chapter 19 when we further explain the concept of *"Human-AI Interlace."*

The Pioneers of Symbolic Logic

Symbolic logic also had to demonstrate its potential, and it was not easy given the limitations of computers at the time. Symbolic logic revolves around using symbols and logical rules to represent knowledge and facilitate reasoning processes. These symbols form the bedrock upon which robots comprehend and navigate the real world. For instance, as a robot explores its surroundings, it creates a map of the room, representing objects and obstacles using symbols.

During the 1960s and early 1970s, two noteworthy robots, Freddy and Shakey, significantly contributed to robotics and AI. Both robots shared a foundation in symbolic logic for their programming and decision-making processes.

Freddy [Ambler et al.], developed at the University of Edinburgh between 1969 and 1976, stood out for its versatility and rapid adaptability to new tasks. Freddy featured an upside-down mechanical arm with a claw-like gripper at its end, enabling it to pick up objects from tables. The gripper was a two-finger pinch gripper, complemented by a video camera and a laser light stripe generator. Freddy relied on this camera as a sensory device, enhancing its environmental awareness. An innovative aspect of Freddy's design was that sometimes, instead of moving the arm, it moved the table to manipulate objects. This simplified its design and improved efficiency.

Moreover, Freddy was able to identify objects from the images from its camera and to detect specific features in those objects. Freddy did not require detailed step-by-step instructions; instead, it employed robot programming software specifying goals related to desired positional relationships among the robot, objects, and the environment. This software enabled it to adapt quickly to new tasks, such as placing rings on pegs or assembling wooden block toys.

Shakey was developed at Stanford University from 1966 to 1972 under the supervision of John McCarthy [Moravec]; its development drew from various research areas, including computer vision, robotics, and Natural Language Processing, thus marking a significant milestone in AI.

Unlike Freddy, who was anchored to the ceiling, Shakey was an innovative mobile robot. Shakey featured a rectangular base with a tall, vertical structure on top. The base housed wheels, sensors, and electronic components, while the central body contained the robot's computer and control systems. A tall mast extended from it, carrying a camera and sensors for environmental perception.

Similar to Freddy, Shakey had the ability to reason about its actions, obviating the need for detailed instructions for every task step. Shakey could navigate, turn on and off lights, open and close doors, climb up and down hard surfaces, and push mobile objects. As an illustrative example, upon receiving the command *"push the block off the platform,"* Shakey would execute the task by evaluating its surroundings, identifying a platform with a box on it, locating a ramp to reach the platform, ascending it, and pushing the box. Shakey's autonomous navigation and efficient pathfinding algorithm was called A* and was designed in 1968. Fast-forward 55 years, and algorithms based on A* have become an important area of research for the development of Artificial General Intelligence (AGI), as we explained in *Chapter 9.*

Shakey's programming primarily relied on LISP, the programming language pioneered by John McCarthy, which would later find use in high-end hardware machines of the 1980s running expert systems. We discussed in *Chapter 5* that the collapse of these machines' stock prices in 1987 led to the second AI winter.

As we already indicated, despite their advancements, Shakey and Freddy faced significant limitations. Symbolic logic proved computationally expensive, resulting in slower task processing. Furthermore, these robots required an accurate symbolic representation of the constantly changing world around them, which made it difficult to adapt fast enough to dynamic and complex environments.

These limitations eventually paved the way for a resurgence of the analog logic philosophy in robot development in a new wave known as the *"Nouvelle AI."* Nouvelle AI would emerge approximately two decades later, part of a soul-search exercise inside the AI industry during the second AI winter.

The *"Nouvelle AI"* and the Last Challenge to Symbolic Logic

Crises are good times to reflect. Amidst the second AI winter, a revolutionary approach emerged from the MIT AI Laboratory, spearheaded by Rodney Brooks and his team. This movement, known as Nouvelle AI, challenged the dominant paradigm of symbolic AI, which emphasized logic and abstract symbols [Brooks].

The core concept of Nouvelle AI centered around the belief that true machine intelligence could only be demonstrated through interaction with the real world. To achieve this, they argued that a machine should possess a physical body, sensors to perceive its surroundings, and the capability to move, adapt, and tackle real-world challenges. This perspective was firmly rooted in the theory of embodied cognition, which posits that reasoning and intelligence are greatly influenced by the body.

One clear distinction between Nouvelle AI and symbolic AI was their approach to representing the world. Symbolic AI used internal models based on elaborate descriptions, whereas Nouvelle AI relied on direct perception of the world through sensors. This approach eliminated the need for symbolic representations and constant updates to symbolic models, making Nouvelle AI more efficient and agile in interacting with the environment.

Conventional robots like Shakey and Freddy employed symbolic internal models, requiring substantial time to break actions down into necessary steps. Instead, rather than an internal model of the world, Nouvelle AI systems consistently relied on their sensors to process information from the external world as needed. For Brooks, *"the world is its own best model--always exactly up to date and complete in every detail."* Rodney Brooks focused on constructing simple robots that mimicked the behaviors of insects. He designed insect-like robots named Allen and Herbert. These robots did not possess internal models of the world.

The robot Allen was named after Allen Newell, the participant at the Dartmouth workshop. Allen was equipped with ultrasonic sensors. It would stay in the center of a room until an object approached, at which point it would scurry around, avoiding obstacles.

Herbert, on the flip side, was named in honor of Herbert A. Simon, another participant. Herbert utilized infrared sensors to navigate around obstacles and a laser system to collect 3D data. Herbert operated in the real-world environment of MIT's bustling offices and workspaces, searching for empty soda cans and transporting them to the trash. With Herberts, Brooks believed that Nouvelle AI had achieved a level of complexity close to an actual insect.

Later, Brooks shifted his focus to building humanoid robots like Cog to attain higher levels of intelligence than insects. Cog was equipped with sensors, a face, and arms to interact with the world, gather information, and gain experience to develop intelligence organically. The team believed that Cog could learn and discern correlations between sensory input and its actions, acquiring common knowledge autonomously.

However, by 2003, all development of the *"Nouvelle AI"* project had stopped. There were multiple reasons for the failure of *"Nouvelle AI,"* despite its innovative approach. Two primary reasons stand out. First, success was self-limited by its relatively modest goal of achieving insect-level performance, as opposed to the ambitious aim of human-level performance pursued by symbolic AI. This deviation from mainstream AI objectives made it challenging for Nouvelle AI to gain widespread adoption and secure funding. Critics also pointed out that Nouvelle AI systems struggled to exhibit behavior comparable to actual insects, let alone achieve human-like capabilities such as consciousness and language.

Second, Nouvelle AI's emphasis on simplicity and the rejection of constructing internal models of reality led to difficulties in handling complex real-world environments. While Nouvelle AI systems received praise for sidestepping the frame problem and avoiding intricate extended models, their ability to function effectively in complex situations remained limited.

Following Nouvelle AI's failure, no subsequent efforts were made to revive analog logic. Today, the prevailing approach in robotics leans heavily toward symbolic logic robotics. The advent of more robust digital computers, continuous gains in processing power, and algorithm advancements have mitigated the computational constraints of symbolic processing. Furthermore, symbolic systems align well with the development of modern AI techniques, including Machine Learning and deep learning, which thrive on symbolic representations of data. This approach facilitates complex tasks such as natural language understanding, high-level reasoning, and planning in autonomous systems.

Furthermore, the approach of creating models of the world, championed by symbolic logic, becomes even more relevant in 2024, as it is one of the avenues most explored by major technology giants to achieve Artificial General Intelligence. We covered this in Chapter 9.

12. The Muscular Strength of the Robotic Arm

"An automated machine that does just one thing is not a robot. It is simply automation. A robot should have the capability of handling a range of jobs at a factory."

Joseph Engelberger [Galliah]

American physicist, engineer, and entrepreneur

Some inventions stand out as pivotal milestones in history, profoundly influencing entire industries and transforming how we live and work. Among these, the Unimate robotic arm from the 1960s, created by George Devol and Joseph Engelberger, can be unequivocally hailed as the most influential robot in history due to its pioneering role in automating industrial processes, revolutionizing manufacturing, and fathering a direct lineage of steadily improving robots.

Unimate found its first application in the automotive industry. In 1961, General Motors (GM) became the first company to adopt Unimate for assembly lines, marking a monumental shift in the manufacturing landscape. Unimate's ability to repetitively weld, paint, and manipulate heavy objects with precision and speed ushered in a new era of automation. The results were staggering: increased production efficiency, improved product quality, and enhanced workplace safety. Unimate's integration into car manufacturing streamlined production and made manufacturing jobs safer, more skilled, and more intellectually engaging.

Unimate's impact extended globally to Europe, Japan, and beyond. Its commercial impact was so profound that it crossed industries from automotive to metallurgy, semiconductors, aerospace, and even surgery, to name just a few. Moreover, one of the earliest instances of real-life cyborgs involved a person who learned to manipulate robotic arms in place of the ones they had lost.

Unimate and the Birth of Industrial Automation

The foundational moment for Industrial Robotics came in 1954, when industrial engineer George Devol, seeking to enhance manufacturing efficiency and automate hazardous and monotonous tasks, designed the first programmable robot [Rosen]. He applied for a patent with the US Patent Office and coined "*Universal Automation*" to describe his robot design. Two years later, in 1956, Devol, in collaboration with engineer Joseph Engelberger, founded Unimation (contraction for Universal Automation), the first company dedicated to producing industrial robots [Nof].

The history of industrial automation revolves around the partnership of Devol and Engelberger. With precision and attention to detail, Devol invented the first industrial robot. At the same time, Engelberger, driven by tenacity and an entrepreneurial spirit, passionately advocated for robotics throughout his life and authored influential research publications. Together, they pursued a shared dream that reshaped manufacturing and automation.

Unimation began manufacturing industrial robots that were called Unimate. The first Unimate robotic arms were large machines of around 2 tons in weight and employed hydraulic actuators. Most importantly, these robots were programmable in joint coordinates. This meant that joint angles were recorded during a training phase and reproduced during operation. That made the Unimate incredibly versatile for different industrial applications.

The Unimate was invented at the right moment. Throughout the booming economy of the 1960s, the American automobile industry was experiencing a Renaissance and undergoing substantial transformation. Surging demand for automobiles from an increasingly wealthy population drove heightened production demands and a pressing need for streamlined manufacturing procedures. However, the industry grappled with the concurrent challenges of escalating labor costs, a shortage of skilled workers, and the imperative for consistently high-quality production.

By selling Unimate to GM in 1960, Devol accomplished a historic milestone at a pivotal juncture for the automotive industry. In less than a year, Unimation set up the first industrial robot on a GM production line, where it was used to make light fixtures, gear shift knobs, door and window handles, and other interior car parts. At the plant, Unimate robots followed step-by-step instructions stored on a magnetic drum to precisely sequence and stack hot diecast metal components. The installation of Unimate at GM served as a live demonstration of the indispensable and enduring role that robots play in a demanding industrial setting.

GM's automation development proceeded, and the company installed its first spot-welding robots at an assembly plant in 1969. Unlike traditional plants, where only about 30 percent of body welding operations were automated, these Unimate robots greatly increased productivity and made it possible to automate more than 90 percent of those operations. Although welding has always been difficult, dangerous, and labor-intensive, Unimate began to make manufacturing facilities safer for blue-collar workers—a major benefit that Joseph Engelberger personally supported.

Chrysler and the Ford Motor Company were among the companies that also installed Unimate robots. During these years, Unimation held a quasi-monopoly in the market and primarily competed with Cincinnati Milacron and a minor player, AMF Corporation. Cincinnati Milacron produced a robotic arm known as the T3 (The Tomorrow Tool), which GM also bought. AMF Corporation, a manufacturer of bicycles and motorbikes, diversified into robotics by introducing a robotic arm named Versatran, which they eventually sold to Ford.

Precision Manufacturing with PUMA Robots

While the initial development of industrial robots can be attributed to George Devol and Joseph Engelberger, the refinement of these robots owes much to the contributions of engineer and serial entrepreneur Victor Scheinman.

Scheinman realized that Unimate's robots were large, heavy, slow, and troublesome to maintain because their hydraulic mechanisms led to leakage issues and limited their usability. In 1969, at Stanford University, he introduced a more compact robotic arm known as the *"Stanford Arm,"* which expanded the possibilities for robotics in smaller indoor environments and even on desks in manufacturing industries lighter than car making [Stanford].

The Stanford Arm closely mimicked the range of motion of a human arm, with its six axes of movement. Unimate had five at the time, although it would adopt six later. This configuration of six axes would become the industry standard for industrial robots, closely mimicking the mechanics of the human arm and enabling versatile motion within production processes. Moreover, unlike the 2-ton Unimate robots, the Stanford Arm weighed a mere 15 pounds and operated with electric motors built within the arm itself. Furthermore, these electric motors allowed the Stanford Arm to move much faster than Unimate robots, which had messy and slow hydraulic systems [Asaro and Šabanović].

More importantly, unlike the Unimate, which relied on step-by-step instructions stored in memory, computer software controlled the Stanford Arm. This advancement allowed the Stanford Arm to perform real-time calculations and, in later versions, respond to its surroundings using touch sensors or a vision system. This began an era of precision robotics characterized by faster industrial robots with precise computer control.

One day in 1972, Victor Scheinman received a request from Marvin Minsky at MIT, one of the founding fathers of AI. Marvin had also been working on robotic arms; in particular, he built a wall-mounted model called the "*tentacle arm.*" Marvin proposed Scheinman design an even more compact robotic arm than the Stanford Arm suitable for remotely supervised surgical procedures. Scheinman dedicated part of his time at MIT to creating this new arm, later known as the MIT Arm. Surgery and medical applications were indeed among the earliest use cases for robotics.

Returning to Stanford in 1973, Victor Scheinman founded his own company called Vicarm to market an improved version of his "*Stanford Arm.*" With financial support from Unimation, Scheinman continued to refine his designs, and in 1976, he introduced a new robotic arm called PUMA (Programmable Universal Manipulation Arm). Unimation became very excited about the new model, and in 1977, Unimation acquired Vicarm and became the original manufacturer of the PUMA.

The PUMA represented a significant advancement. While the Unimate primarily handled repetitive tasks such as spot welding on automotive assembly lines, the PUMA was engineered for a more extensive range of precise assembly tasks. A more powerful minicomputer controlled the PUMA, and it became the first robot to assemble small parts at GM plants using touch and pressure sensors. Since 90% of the assembled parts at GM production lines weighed five pounds or less, the PUMA proved particularly adept at tasks requiring intricate and precise movements, enhancing efficiency and accuracy in GM's manufacturing processes. The PUMA was extremely successful, and Unimation continued to produce PUMA robots for an extended period until the 1980s.

Unimation's Oedipal Tragedy: Partnerships Turned Rivals

The success of the Unimate robots was not restricted to the US. In 1967, Unimation established a partnership with ASEA Metallverken, an electrical equipment manufacturer. Two years later, the first Unimate was installed at a Volvo factory. Unimation also used a similar partnership strategy to enter Germany with KUKA, leading to the first Unimate in Volkswagen in 1973, and to enter Italy with Comau, which resulted in the first Unimate in Fiat in 1974 [Baum and Freedman].

The problem with this partnership approach was that as soon as the partners realized the potential of Unimate, they started building their own robotic arms and became real competitors of Unimate; reverse engineering has had a long and troublesome history for inventors seeking to benefit financially from their work. The issue in Europe did not have major consequences, as European firms did not venture successfully into the US to compete against Unimation.

The introduction of robotics in Japan followed a trajectory similar to that in Europe, with companies initially licensing the Unimate technology before eventually developing their own robotic innovations. However, Japan's journey in robotics was successful and is a remarkable story in its own right, deserving a dedicated chapter.

These Japanese companies, which drew inspiration from the Unimate technology and flourished in Japan, started internationalizing and establishing themselves in the US in the late 1970s and, especially, in the 1980s. By this juncture, Japanese companies had established their local market dominance and improved the original Unimate's design, creating cost-effective and highly precise robotic systems. These developments positioned them appropriately to venture into the international arena.

The influx of Japanese companies into the US profoundly transformed the industrial robotics landscape. This shift had seismic implications for Unimation. These Japanese companies who drew inspiration (and perhaps a bit more) from Unimation were finally starting to compete head-to-head with the Unimation industry in their homeland.

Unimation found itself in a fortunate position when it was acquired by Westinghouse in 1983, coinciding with the peak of the industrial robotics boom [Schaut]. However, as the competition from Japanese firms intensified, Unimation struggled to regain its footing. Ultimately, in 1989, the Swiss company Stäubli assumed control of Unimation. The tragedy of Unimation somewhat mirrors the Greek tale of Oedipus Rex [Sophocles], where the progenitor of all industrial robotics companies met its demise, in a sense, at the hands of its offspring.

After the emergence of Japan, only a select few non-Japanese companies maintained a lasting presence in the industry. In Europe, those were ABB—which originated from ASEA—as well as KUKA Robotics, Comau, and Stäubli. In America, two companies were significant: Automatix—founded by Victor Scheinman—and Adept Technology. We will talk about Automatix next and discuss Adept in the following chapter.

Designated Areas for Robots and Humans in Factories

Building upon the success of his revolutionary PUMA robots, Victor Scheinman embarked on a new venture in 1980, co-founding Automatix, a company dedicated to pioneering machine vision for robotics. Automatix robotic vision systems allow robots to perceive and interact with their surroundings more effectively. These vision-guided robots could perform complex tasks with greater accuracy and adaptability than their predecessors, as they could identify and respond to objects and changes in their environment. Automatix's innovations in robotic vision significantly expanded the capabilities and potential applications of industrial robots [Asaro and Šabanović].

Victor Scheinman personally championed a product called RobotWorld within the Automatix, although this product has nothing to do with machine vision. RobotWorld had a unique focus on enabling robots to work within specific dedicated areas to prevent conflicts with humans. Imagine a workspace where robots need to perform tasks alongside human workers. To ensure safety and efficient cooperation, RobotWorld employed a distinctive setup. It featured small robotic suspended modules that could be considered automated devices hanging from the roof, which could work in coordination with other robots on the ground, all within their designated workspace. This approach helped maintain a clear separation between robot and human activities, reducing the risk of collisions or accidents and allowing for smoother, more organized industrial operations.

The separation of workplaces for robots and humans, each focused on their specific tasks and domains, persisted during the 1980s and 90s. Typically, industrial robots were even confined behind fences or protective barriers.

But in the 2000s and 2010s, machine vision started to reach a level of proficiency that allowed robots to autonomously navigate the factory, avoid collisions with each other and humans, and even collaborate with them. We will delve deeper into this topic in *Chapter 14* when discussing autonomous mobile robots in warehouse settings, such as those used by Amazon.

Ironically, Automatix's main business was in machine vision. It is precisely the advancements in machine vision technology that rendered RobotWorld obsolete.

Cobots: Humans and Machines Working Together

The concept of a strict division between humans and robots began to crumble in 1996 with the introduction of "*cobots*," short for collaborative robots. Cobots marked a transformative moment in the history of robotics, as it brought forth the idea that robots could work alongside humans collaboratively and cooperatively, sharing workspace and tasks. The advent of cobots ushered in a new era of automation, where robots became valuable teammates, enhancing productivity and safety across various industries by working hand in hand with human operators.

A collaborative robot, or cobot, represents a robotics innovation designed to interact directly with humans and to enhance safety in closely connected work environments. The safety of cobots relies on various design features such as rounded edges, lightweight construction materials, force limitations, and advanced software and sensors that ensure secure behavior.

Human workers and industrial cobots can observe different degrees of collaboration, from coexisting without a physical barrier to collaborating sequentially in different steps of a process to collaborating concurrently on the same task with high responsiveness.

Given GM's position as the most significant and veteran consumer of robots in the world, it is not surprising that GM played a vital role in developing the concept of cobots. In 1994, GM initiated a project to address the challenge of making robots safe enough to work collaboratively with humans. This pioneering initiative sought innovative solutions to enhance safety in industrial settings. J. Edward Colgate and Michael Peshkin, professors at Northwestern University, collaborated with GM to create a unique system geared to enable direct, physical interaction between humans and robots. This collaboration and the subsequent research grant from the GM Foundation became the bedrock for the development of cobots, marking a significant advancement in human-robot collaboration, which Colgate and Peshkin later patented in the US in 1996 for an *"apparatus and method for direct physical interaction between a person and a general-purpose manipulator controlled by a computer"* [Peshkin and Colgate].

One year later, in 1997, Colgate and Peshkin founded their own company called Cobotics and started producing several cobot models for the final stages of automobile assembly lines. Cobotics marked the onset of an era featuring collaborative robots that are versatile, user-friendly, and cost-effective.

The market demand was huge, driven by safety standards and companies looking for improvements in efficacy, and soon, a lot of manufacturers started producing cobots. The market for industrial cobots witnessed remarkable growth, with an annual growth rate of 50% as recently as 2020, reflecting the transformative impact of these versatile and adaptable robots across various industries [Hand].

The first prominent robotics player to notice the importance of cobots was KUKA in Germany, which introduced its first cobot in 2004 for the aerospace industry. Furthermore, a new company called Universal Robots was founded in Denmark in 2005. In 2008, it introduced a cobot that can work safely next to human workers without the need for fencing or safety cages. Universal Robots have grown enormously since then and, in 2019, held the top position in the cobots market. ABB also joined the trend, and in 2015, ABB unveiled YuMi, the first collaborative dual-arm robot [ET Auto].

In America, Rodney Brooks founded Rethink Robotics in 2008. We talked about him in the previous chapter, as Brooks had been behind the Nouvelle AI initiative that pushed against symbolic logic in the 1990s, and we will talk about him again in *Chapter 14*.

Rethink Robotics entered the industrial cobot arena with a robot called Baxter in 2012 [Silva et al.]. Baxter was remarkable for its human-friendliness in working environments. It incorporated an animated screen serving as its "*face*," enabling the display of various facial expressions corresponding to its current status. Baxter can also detect the presence of individuals in its vicinity. Furthermore, Baxter reacted to unexpected situations and did not persist in erroneous operations. For instance, if an accidental tool drop is vital for its task, Baxter would not insist on continuing its operations; it would just stop working and ask for assistance, which set it apart from conventional robots that might persevere in executing tasks without the necessary tools [Knight].

Precision in Practice: Robotizing Surgery

Medical applications have always been a target of robotic pioneers from the beginning. As we discussed, Victor Scheinman developed the first robotic arm for medical use in 1972, the MIT Arm. Fast forward to 1985, a Puma robot was used for the first time to guide a needle during a brain biopsy. This neurological procedure greatly benefited from the robot's ability to make precise movements using Computed Tomography (CT), an X-ray technology, significantly improving the procedure's accuracy and safety [Kwoh et al.].

After that, there were a number of commercial surgery robots, but the one that marked a groundbreaking advancement in robotic surgery was the da Vinci Surgical System, launched in 1999 [Gerencher]. Equipped with four arms housing surgical instruments and cameras, this innovative robot allowed a surgeon to exercise remote control from a dedicated console. It earned FDA approval for a wide range of surgical procedures in 2000. What set the da Vinci system apart was its ability to translate the surgeon's hand movements into scaled-down micro-movements, effectively reducing hand tremors and enhancing precision. This minimally invasive approach significantly reduced patient trauma, leading to quicker recovery and improved surgical outcomes. Da Vinci also provided surgeons with stereoscopic vision through a miniature camera, improving depth perception during intricate procedures. Da Vinci's versatility was evident in its successful application in diverse fields, from cardiac surgeries like heart bypass procedures to urological surgeries like prostatectomies.

Da Vinci faced its first direct competition in 2019 following two decades of unwavering market dominance when the Versius Surgical Robotic System was introduced to compete with it [Walsh]. Versius was developed by CMR

Surgical, a British medical device company, and is a new generation of surgical platforms with robotic assistance that has several significant benefits.

In the first place, Versius is superior to Da Vinci in terms of technological design, which led to improved user-friendliness, a real benefit for surgeries. Versius allows for easier and more intuitive navigation, enhancing the surgeon's precision and control during procedures. Moreover, Versius features more advanced 3D high-definition visualization, enabling surgeons to perform intricate operations more accurately and confidently. Additionally, Versius' smaller, more flexible instruments enable surgeons to access hard-to-reach areas within the body, reducing the need for larger incisions and resulting in less postoperative pain and shorter patient recovery times. Versius also boasts improved force feedback, enabling surgeons to receive tactile input during instrument use and facilitating precise tissue manipulation and suturing. This is particularly crucial in delicate surgeries, such as cardiac procedures, where fine motor control is essential.

Having introduced the robotic arm and its applications, the next chapter delves into how it propelled Japan to become the undisputed world leader in robotics.

13. The Land of the Rising Robot

"All the studies we've done show that Japan's use of technology is no greater than that of the United States, but the pervasiveness with which it is used in Japan is substantially greater."

James K. Bakken

Senior Vice President of the Ford Motor Company [Holusha]
On the New York Times
1983

This quote from Ford highlights a critical observation regarding the adoption of robotics technology in Japan compared to the US. Japan and the US have had similar technological capabilities, with the US usually surpassing Japan in initial conceptual and technological innovation. But Japan's ability and willingness to integrate *"human replacement"* technology pervasively across sectors of its economy and society empowered it to harness the full potential of automation and robotics far sooner and deeper than North American or European countries.

Several factors unique to Japan have contributed to its particular approach to robotics and automation. One of these factors is the deep psychological need to *"catch up"* with the West in the post-war period as the country rebuilt its economy, primarily based on manufacturing. This drive for rapid industrialization pushed Japan to embrace automation as a means of achieving economic competitiveness.

Another significant factor has been the labor shortages Japan faced, particularly starting in the 1960s and persisting to today. The options to address this issue were limited to either immigration or the deployment of robotics and automation. Due to strict immigration policies and cultural factors, Japan leaned towards the latter solution.

Japanese Employment Law has played a role in this approach as well. It essentially does not permit the displacement of workers for any reason, including technological deployments aimed at increasing efficiency and reducing costs. This has incentivized the adoption of automation to augment the workforce rather than onboard and then replace it.

Also, Japan's Government's industrial policy has historically favored long-term investment over short-term stock price management. This approach encouraged companies to invest in automation technologies that might not yield immediate financial returns but would enhance their competitiveness in the long run. Robotics has been a beneficiary of this approach.

Cultural characteristics also influence Japan's preference for automation. Japanese society tends to prioritize indirect and formal interactions among people, and is governed by strict social rules that dictate appropriate behavior in various social situations. This emphasis on conforming to social norms can be conducive to the implementation of automated systems that adhere to predefined rules and procedures.

Moreover, the Japanese cultural preference for known and reliable outcomes aligns with the predictability and consistency offered by robots and automated processes. This preference contrasts with the uncertainty associated with human actions, which can sometimes lead to unexpected or undesirable outcomes, potentially causing a loss of face in Japanese culture.

Lastly, a unique view of humanity rooted in indigenous religions, such as Buddhism and Shintoism, has also contributed to Japan's complex relationship with robots. These belief systems often associate animus or spiritual essence with living beings, which can lead to tolerance and acceptance regarding the increasing role of robots in society. This cultural perspective is explored in greater detail in Chapter 17, as it offers broader lessons for understanding the intertwining of culture and technology in Japan's context.

The advantages of an unfettered path to replace elements of humans without displacing them and a psychological rationale to bolster the economic argument created an easier path for industrial robotic deployment, allowing Japanese companies to excel in developing and producing cutting-edge industrial robots. As a result, Japan rapidly emerged as the number one producer and user of robotics, contributing significantly to advancements in manufacturing, automation, and robotics worldwide. Japan's commitment to innovation, coupled with its ability to apply technology in real-world scenarios, solidified its leadership position in the global robotics industry, which it still holds.

The introduction of the first industrial robot in the country in a joint venture with Unimation marked the beginning of Japan's journey into robotics. The 1970s saw a surge in demand for personal automobiles, but the labor shortage made automation in car factories necessary. By the 1980s, Japan had established itself as a leader in precision robotics, and Japanese companies started expanding internationally in Europe and, above all, in the US.

The following pages look at Japan's rise as the unquestionable leader in robotics.

Unimate Disembarks in Japanese Factories

The 1960s marked a period of rapid economic expansion in Japan. The Government boldly championed its income-doubling plan [Japan], and domestic manufacturing witnessed explosive growth. Moreover, the 1964 Tokyo Olympics symbolized national rejuvenation. Japan, renowned for its excellence in manufacturing, quickly emerged as one of the global leaders in developing and producing industrial robots [Mackintosh and Jaghory].

In 1961, Unimation debuted the first Unimate in a General Motors (GM) plant in Japan against this backdrop. A few years later, in 1968, Unimation and Kawasaki Heavy Industries entered into a license agreement for the production and sale of Unimate robots in the Asian market. Initially focused on creating and manufacturing labor-saving devices, Kawasaki rose to prominence as Japan's leader in industrial robotics. One year later, in 1969, the collaboration between Kawasaki and Ultimate bore fruit and created history when the Kawasaki-Unimate 2000 [Hemal and Menon] became Japan's first industrial robot to be produced domestically.

A rise in incomes and purchasing power during the 1960s and 1970s led to a rise in the demand for personal automobiles in Japan. In spite of the country's fast urbanization, which brought young workers from rural areas to cities, there was a labor shortage, much of which was a combination of net population issues after WW2 and the speed of urbanization outstripping response times. Due to the labor shortage, it was particularly difficult to find competent people to undertake dirty, hazardous, and degrading jobs like welding and painting in auto factories. Additionally, workers' concerns about the introduction of robots and automation were lessened by the Japanese companies' general practice of lifelong employment and strong job security [Mackintosh and Jaghory].

All these factors incentivized the automation of car factories. As a result, in the early 1970s, industrial robots proved precious for Toyota, Nissan, and Honda car assembly lines. In these factories, robots—initially the original Unimate models and later locally manufactured variants—found application in tasks such as arc welding, spot welding, and paint application. Furthermore, Kawasaki's motorcycle manufacturing company began utilizing the Kawasaki-Unimate arc-welding robot for motorcycle frame fabrication in 1974.

Kawasaki-Unimate stood out prominently among the notable manufacturers of welding robots for automobile plants. During the early 1970s, Kawasaki was at the forefront of innovation, developing advanced robotic arms with tactile and force-sensing capabilities in their hand grips. This technological prowess allowed Kawasaki's robotic arms to guide pins into designated holes, marking a significant leap in automation capabilities.

As Kawasaki had established its own line of robots and was becoming more successful by the day, it was just a matter of time before its longstanding association with Unimation was dissolved by the parties, which eventually happened in 1986 [Kawasaki].

Apart from Kawasaki, the whole industrial automation landscape saw significant growth in the 1970s. Mitsubishi Electric, a Fortune 100 multinational corporation renowned for its expertise in manufacturing electrical products, ventured into this burgeoning field. Simultaneously, Hitachi made significant strides in robotics. During the early 1970s, Hitachi developed vision-based intelligent robots, automated bolting robots for the concrete industry, sensor-based arc-welding robots equipped with microprocessors and gap sensors for the automotive industry, and two-arms robots for vacuum cleaners assembling, to mention a few.

We observe the establishment of a virtuous circle within Japan's industrial robotics initiative, characterized by the symbiotic relationship between process improvement and technology development. During a period when incremental advancements in technology held immediate economic incentives and were informed by the ongoing enhancement of manufacturing processes, success was primarily measured by the specific output of these processes. Within this framework, the incorporation of small, continuous changes into robotics technology fueled the virtuous circle, driving further improvements.

This model stands in contrast to the development of AI, where the core technology is more intricate and software-based. Historically, the economic or production justification for incremental advancements in AI was less evident, lacking clear and immediate cases until recent integrations into digital products and the accumulation of vast datasets for training purposes.

Japan Sets the Standard in Precision Robotics

Despite Japan's economic growth experiencing moderation due to the challenges of the oil crises of 1973 and 79, as well as trade disputes with the US, 1980 holds a special significance in the history of Japanese robotics. It is often called the pivotal *"year one,"* marking the transformative turning point for robotics [Mackintosh and Jaghory]. By 1980, Japan had unmistakably demonstrated its competitive strength and innovative capabilities in robotics, and Japanese manufacturers were thriving and building increasingly sophisticated and high-precision robots—not only Kawasaki but also many others like Mitsubishi Electric, Hitachi, and FANUC.

The best example of these smaller, more precise robots introduced during the 1980s is the SCARA robotic arm (Selective Compliance Assembly Robot Arm), designed in 1978 at Yamanashi University [CMU]. Unlike traditional robotic arms of the time, which typically had six degrees of freedom and were versatile but complex to program, the SCARA robot featured a simplified design with only three or four, depending on the model. Mobility in the X-Y plane was flexible while maintaining rigidity along the Z-axis. This design significantly reduced the complexity of programming and control, making it easier for manufacturers to implement automation in their assembly lines. Moreover, the SCARA robot was high-speed and precise in vertical and horizontal movements. This made it ideal for pick-and-place operations, assembly, and material handling tasks. Finally, its compact and streamlined design allowed it to operate efficiently in confined spaces, making it suitable for applications where space was limited.

Since 1979, a Japanese company called Sankyo and IBM have marketed the SCARA commercially worldwide, including in the US [Mortimer and Rooks]. The SCARA robot's combination of simplicity, precision, speed, and efficiency made it a game-changer for many precision industries, for example, semiconductors. Working with semiconductor wafers—those delicate silicon slices crucial for crafting miniature semiconductors—posed formidable challenges for human workers. SCARA robots swiftly emerged as the industry's standard for wafer handling within semiconductor facilities.

SCARA robots gained even greater prominence in the following decades, especially during the thriving 1990s and 2000s, as the demand for personal computers reached unprecedented levels, accompanied by a soaring need for semiconductors.

Moreover, the food and beverage industry also adopted SCARA for tasks like packaging and ensuring hygienic and accurate handling of products. And, of course, the automotive industry—the most veteran user of robots—also benefited from SCARA in tasks such as material handling and assembly of automotive parts, improving production efficiency and quality control.

SCARA Robots were so successful that American Companies started copying them to sell in the US market. For example, Adept Technology—the company we mentioned in the previous chapter—introduced its first robot, the AdeptOne SCARA robot, in 1984, and since then, it has introduced a large saga of ever more advanced SCARA robots. By the way, Adept was founded in 1983 by two of Victor Scheinman's students at Stanford. In the history of robotics and AI, we find the same people over and over again.

Japanese   Robotics   Companies   Internationalize Worldwide

The other development of the 1980s was the international expansion of Japanese companies. Many companies expanded to the US and Europe, including Kawasaki, Mitsubishi, and Denso, a subsidiary of Toyota. However, FANUC is the best example of being extremely successful in joint ventures with US giants.

FANUC (Fuji Automatic Numerical Control) was founded in 1956 but rose to prominence during this time. FANUC was initially focused on manufacturing numerical controls throughout the 1960s. Numerical controls are the control panels used in manufacturing processes to control the movements of robots. Given its strength in numerical controls, FANUC ventured into robotics in 1977 and introduced the FANUC M-1 robot, the first industrial robot controlled by a microprocessor.

What is remarkable about FANUC is that it was one of the first Japanese robotics companies to expand internationally. In 1982, FANUC created a 50-50 joint venture with GM called GM FANUC Robotics Corporation, headquartered in Detroit, to manufacture and sell robots within the US. GM oversaw the management, while FANUC contributed its product development and manufacturing expertise.

Subsequently, in 1986, FANUC and General Electric (GE) developed a collaboration that led to the creation of three subsidiary companies: the US, Europe in Luxembourg, and Asia in Japan. As part of this collaboration, GE ceased its production of numerical controls and transferred this facility to the newly formed joint venture, GE FANUC Automation Corporation, in the US.

The influx of Japanese companies into the US significantly transformed the industrial robotics landscape during the late 1970s, causing a seismic shift for Unimation. These Japanese companies drew inspiration (and indeed perhaps more) from Unimation technology in pursuing robotics excellence and eventually started competing directly against Unimation in its home market, leading to the downfall of Unimation, as we recounted in the previous chapter.

Japan's AI Ambitions: Ahead of Its Time

While Japan is renowned for its achievements in robotics, the archipelago also invested substantially in developing AI capabilities during the 1970s and 1980s.

The first area of research during this period was Natural Language Processing, which resulted in the creation of advanced Japanese language processing systems, machine translation tools, and cutting-edge speech recognition technologies, with particular strides made by Toshiba and by the University of Kyushu [Nishida].

Additionally, computer vision emerged as a second focus. Robotics companies like FANUC and automotive giants like Toyota began incorporating computer vision systems into their manufacturing processes. These systems empowered robots to execute quality control and assembly tasks with unparalleled precision. Moreover, at the Osaka Expo of 1970, a team from Kyoto University showcased the world's first facial recognition system [Gates] [Nishida].

As we discussed in *Chapter 5,* the 1980s was the decade of expert systems, and that was the case in Japan, too. Notable examples included IBM Japan's Scheplan for the steel industry, Kayaba's OHCS for hydraulic system design, and Hitachi's automatic pipe-routing system for power plants [Motoda].

Against this context of robust AI research and development and Japan's remarkable success in robotics, the Japanese Government launched the ambitious FGCS project (Fifth Generation Computer Systems or 5th-generation) in 1982, with substantial funding of 400 million dollars [Pollack]. Its primary objective was to build data centers with a large number of computers that could tackle complex AI problems like engaging in reasoning, comprehending natural language, Machine Learning, and ultimately emulating human-like intelligence. The intention was to leverage the potential of parallel processing in a massive computing capacity to develop and test innovative AI techniques. Apart from the Government and Japan's hardware manufacturers, the project involved various research institutions and universities in Japan [Unger].

Most of the hardware of the 5th-generation project consisted of the last mainframe computers and LISP machines. As we know, the global stock market collapsed in 1987 as specialized hardware lost its edge to more versatile alternatives like Intel's x86 machine. It was not before long that it became obvious that 5th-generation computers were becoming rapidly obsolete and could not compete with commercially available general-purpose systems. The project was a commercial failure.

The 5th-generation project resembled the current proliferation of GPU (Graphic Processing Unit) capacity. Much like how this project aimed to build massive computing capacity to run AI applications, today's GPU capacity build-up owes much of its growth to the demands of Generative AI models. In many ways, the 5th-generation project was ahead of its time.

The Japanese Bubble, the Great Financial Crisis, and the Tsunami

In the 1980s, Japan was experiencing a rapid economic boom driven by its manufacturing industry, particularly automobiles, and by its exports. However, this economic prosperity was accompanied by unchecked speculation in the real estate and financial asset markets [Wood]. Japan's economic miracle began to wane after its real estate bubble collapsed in 1991, marking the start of what is now known as the *"lost decades"* for Japan's economy. A prolonged recession, deflation, and a significant decrease in asset values characterized this period.

The economic crisis directly impacted the funding and continuity of AI research projects, particularly the 5th-generation project, which was already showing signs of trouble [Pollack]. The Japanese Government was forced to reprioritize its spending to address the economic crisis, and investment in long-term projects like this became less economically sustainable. The 5th-generation project was quietly shut down in 1992. As we saw in examples in Western countries, once again, initial AI expectations far exceeded practical possibilities and economic rationales.

By the time of the crash around 1990, Japanese robot makers could proudly claim an impressive 90% share of global industrial robot sales. However, the stock market crash led to a much more challenging period for them. In 1992, there was a sudden decline in robot supply, followed by two years of stagnation. [Mackintosh and Jaghory].

Following the setback of the Japanese bubble, there were fleeting moments of hope for Japanese robot manufacturers. First, in the late 1990s, a sudden surge in semiconductor demand, fueled by the rapid expansion of the personal computer and internet industries, breathed new life into Japan's robot manufacturers. Second, in the early 2000s, China emerged as a significant player undergoing its economic boom. This offered Japanese manufacturers an opportunity to sell industrial robots to China.

Though short-lived, the relief brought by these opportunities was overshadowed by the dual impact of the 2008 Great Financial Crisis and the devastating 2011 earthquake and tsunami, further exacerbating Japan's challenges. However, despite the myriad obstacles of the recent decades, Japan is still a formidable superpower in robotics, accounting for 47% of global robot manufacturing as of 2020 [Mackintosh and Jaghory]. It continues to be a leader in incorporating AI developments into robotics and human replacement scenarios, not just in manufacturing and operational processes but increasingly in social situations as well, a topic we will explore in *Chapter 16*.

14. Neural Networks and The Robotic Dream of Mobility

"This is nothing. In a few years, that bot will move so fast that you'll need a strobe light to see it. Sweet dreams..."

Elon Musk

American Billionaire

Post on X, referring to the acrobatics of Boston Dynamics humanoid robot Atlas. [Musk and Medina]

2017

Elon Musk's post on X highlights the remarkable mobility of today's robots. Robot mobility relies on neural networks, a type of artificial intelligence that mimics the human brain's neural architecture, as discussed in Chapters 4 and 5. Neural networks are interconnected layers of artificial neurons designed to analyze vast volumes of data, identify patterns, and reach well-informed decisions. Data-driven learning has improved mobility for various robotic applications, taking a high-speed leap forward in eventually replicating and advancing past human capability.

The intricate web-like layers of artificial neurons require substantial computational power for efficient data processing and swift decision-making. It was not until the 2000s that hardware capabilities attained the necessary speed and robustness to handle their computational demands effectively.

Modern robots rely heavily on sensors like cameras, LIDAR, radar, and GPS to perceive their surroundings. Neural networks process this sensory data, enabling self-driving cars and warehouse robots to make real-time decisions on navigation, obstacle avoidance, and predicting the actions of other objects, whether they are robots, humans, or vehicles. In quadrupedal or bipedal robots, neural networks assist in refining their movements, maintaining balance, and responding effectively to unexpected challenges like navigating rough terrain or recovering from stumbles.

We now turn to the topic of neural networks in robotic development and how the creation of self-propelled and self-guided movement represents the first meaningful intersection of the development lines of AI and robotics.

Robots' Remarkable Agility in Combat Competitions

The rising popularity of robots, characterized by their mobility and agility, has given birth to captivating and continually evolving robot combat competitions [Stone]. These events draw large crowds of in-person attendees and online viewers, numbering millions. The compelling allure of robot combat lies in its distinctive fusion of inventive engineering, strategic gameplay, and exhilarating battles. Contestants delight in the opportunity to create and build robots for competitive showdowns, putting their creativity and problem-solving skills to the test. The spectacle of these mechanical clashes, often featuring sparks and airborne components, offers distinctive entertainment, fostering a dynamic and continually evolving subculture [Berry].

The first robot combat competition was organized in 1987 in Denver during a Science Fiction convention and was called *"Critter Crunch."* At that time, neural networks existed, but as we explained, they were not practical for use. Instead, robot builders remotely controlled robots to engage in phenomenal combats and disable their opponents ingeniously.

Little by little, robot combat emerged from its niche in local communities of geek enthusiasts and passionate students. In 1990, the Turing Institute organized the First Robot Olympics in Glasgow, with competitors from different countries [Guinness], and in 1994, the first major US event, called *"Robot Wars,"* was organized in San Francisco. Its success was overwhelming and caught the attention of the British BBC, which eventually produced the TV series *"Robot Wars."* In 1999, a new competition called *"BattleBots"* began as an Internet broadcast and quickly evolved into a weekly television program on Comedy Central in 2000. From that point onward, robot competitions proliferated worldwide, ranging from *"Robotica"* in 2001 to *"Robot Combat League"* in 2013. Television shows like the revival of *"BattleBots"* on ABC in 2015 and *"Robot Wars"* in 2016 further contributed to the growth of robot combat events.

At the same time, builders started increasingly using more advanced algorithms, depending on each robot's design and capabilities. One notable example of a robot that employed a neural network algorithm is *"Bronco"* from *"BattleBots"* in 2015 [Bryant]. Bronco was still primarily remote-controlled by its human operators. Still, the neural network allowed Bronco to make more precise decisions regarding its pneumatic flipping arm, improving its ability to strategize and execute effective flips against opponents in combat.

Sweeping Changes in Household Robotics

Combat competition robots were primarily remote-controlled. In contrast, Roomba, introduced by iRobot in 2002, was the first successfully completely autonomous robot—outside industrial contexts. iRobot was founded partly by MIT Professor Rodney Brooks, a prominent figure known for his role in the Nouvelle AI movement and the establishment of Rethink Robotics, a cobot manufacturer. It is remarkable how some individuals consistently reappear with their meaningful contributions again and again in the history of AI and robotics.

Roomba is a small, circular robot designed for vacuuming and floor cleaning. Its circular shape and low profile allow it to move under furniture and reach hard-to-clean areas. It garnered global attention because of its autonomous navigation, obstacle detection, and efficient maneuvering within indoor spaces.

Roomba did not employ neural networks but simpler algorithms for navigation and cleaning tasks. These algorithms were primarily rule-based and sensor-driven. They included obstacle avoidance routines that use infrared sensors to detect objects in their path, ensuring they can maneuver around furniture and obstacles. Additionally, the bump sensors help Roomba identify collisions with walls or objects, prompting it to change its direction. Cliff sensors were another critical feature, preventing Roomba from tumbling downstairs or ledges.

While the first Roomba models followed relatively random navigation, later iterations employed advanced mapping algorithms. This enabled these Roombas to create detailed maps of rooms, allowing for more systematic and efficient cleaning patterns and the ability to resume cleaning after recharging. Additionally, some Roomba incorporated more advanced navigation techniques like *"Dirt Detect"* algorithms that focus on areas with higher debris concentration, enhancing cleaning efficiency.

Roomba's pioneering success opened the door to a market for household robots, inspiring innovations like robotic lawnmowers, pool cleaners, and window washers that followed a similar design concept. Roomba marked the beginning of a new era in household robotics, enriching our daily lives and buying us newfound time in various ways.

The Building Blocks of Self-Driving Cars

Self-driving cars are one of the most fascinating cases of robotic mobility. Self-driving vehicles promise to reduce traffic congestion in urban areas, optimize routes, facilitate efficient car-sharing arrangements, and revolutionize parking management. This transformation could lead to reduced air pollution and improved urban planning. Additionally, self-driving cars can enhance safety by minimizing human errors, provide accessibility solutions for those with limited mobility, and offer a practical alternative to air travel for mid-range distances. Furthermore, these autonomous vehicles can reshape how people commute and work, allowing passengers to engage in productive and enjoyable activities.

LIDAR sensors and deep neural networks called CNNs and RNNs (convolutional and recurrent neural networks) enable self-driving cars.

LiDAR is a technology dating back to the 1960s, but it was in the 2000s that LiDAR revolutionized mobility for driverless cars and other mobile robots [Taranovich]. Mountable nearly anywhere on a car due to their small form factor, LiDAR sensors work by emitting rapid sequences of laser pulses that bounce back to the sensor after hitting objects, enabling precise distance calculations. LiDAR's ability to provide accurate information in diverse weather and lighting conditions makes it a critical component for enhancing the safety and autonomy of self-driving vehicles.

On the other hand, Deep CNNs are crucial in processing visual data from the car's LIDAR sensors. We talked about them in detail in *Chapter 6*. Self-driving cars leverage both of the two main kinds of neural networks: the convolutional ones (CNN) and the recurrent ones (RNN).

CNNs excel at machine vision. By harnessing the capabilities of CNNs, self-driving cars can identify and interpret the complex visual cues necessary for safe navigation. Moreover, CNNs are able to digest high-resolution 3D environment maps from the LIDAR sensors, including the positions of other vehicles, pedestrians, obstacles, road signs, and lane markings. Self-driving car algorithms rely on this detailed perception of the surroundings to make informed decisions about navigation, obstacle avoidance, lane keeping, and compliance with traffic rules.

That is when RNNs come into play for handling sequential data and decision-making processes. RNNs are used for trajectory prediction, route planning, and real-time control. RNNs enable self-driving cars to analyze the temporal aspects of driving, such as predicting the future movements of other vehicles and pedestrians and continuously adjusting their actions to ensure safe and efficient driving.

The Military of Origins of Self-Driving Cars

The concept of autonomous vehicles first appeared in 1939 when General Motors (GM) astounded the world at the New York World's Fair with "*Futurama.*" This concept showcased an automated highway with autonomous cars, providing a glimpse of a future where machines could drive on their own [Geddes].

However, it was the US Military—more specifically, DARPA (Defense Advanced Research Projects Agency)—that first seriously recognized the potential of autonomous vehicles to perform critical missions without risking human lives. Autonomous vehicles could be deployed in dangerous environments for reconnaissance missions or supply deliveries, reducing the need for human intervention in high-risk scenarios.

From 1984 onwards, DARPA started funding Carnegie Mellon University self-driving car research projects [Wallace et al.]. These projects made rapid progress. In 1985, a driverless car reached speeds of 19 mph on two-lane roads. Breakthroughs in obstacle avoidance followed in 1986, and by 1987, their vehicles could operate off-road day and night [Pomerleau]. Notably, in 1995, a Carnegie Mellon car achieved a remarkable feat, becoming the first autonomous vehicle to travel nearly 3,000 miles across the US, from Pittsburgh to San Diego, autonomously covering 98% of the journey at an average speed of 60 mph [Carnegie Mellon].

In Europe, the University of the Federal Armed Forces Munich spearheaded similar advancements. In 1995, one of their cars with robot-controlled throttle and brakes traveled over 1,000 miles from Munich to Copenhagen and back at 120 mph. Given the speed and distance on crowded roads, the vehicle periodically made overtaking maneuvers, with a safety driver intervening only in critical situations.

Progress had been underway for autonomous cars in the preceding decades, but the definitive turning point occurred when DARPA orchestrated the DARPA Grand Challenge in 2004 [Buehler]. This competition brought together teams from universities and private companies tasked with developing autonomous vehicles capable of navigating a challenging 150-mile route through the Mojave Desert. TDARPA's primary goal was to leverage emerging technology to enhance military capabilities and safety.

Unfortunately, none of the participating autonomous vehicles completed the entire course in 2004, and DARPA repeated the competition in 2005, resulting in the victory of "*Stanley,*" a modified Volkswagen Touareg. Stanley's success was attributed to various innovations, including an AI algorithm trained on the driving behaviors of real-world humans and the integration of five LIDAR laser sensors. This technological arsenal enabled the car to detect objects within an 80-foot range in front of it and to react to them adequately. After the success of Stanley, LIDAR became a vital component of all future robotic vision systems for automobiles. The runner-up team was a Carnegie Mellon team called the *"Red Team."* The third edition of the DARPA Grand Challenge, known as the *"Urban Challenge,"* was held at a logistics airport in California in 2007 [Markoff]. The competition covered a 60-mile course through urban terrain, requiring participants to adhere to traffic regulations, navigate through other vehicles and obstacles, and seamlessly merge into traffic. A team from Carnegie Mellon called *"Tartan"* won the race with a modified Chevy Tahoe, while the second place went to a team from Stanford University with a Volkswagen Passat under the name of *"Stanford Racing."* The teams behind these four cars—*"Stanley," "Red Team," "Tartan,"* and *"Stanford Racing"*—would make history.

Twenty-year-olds Build the Self-driving Car Industry

Many participants in the DARPA challenge went on to establish their own startups in the field of autonomous cars. For example, the Tartan team founded Velodyne, a company specializing in LiDAR (Light Detection and Ranging) technology. Concurrently, technology giants and automakers started hiring participants from the DARPA challenges and making substantial investments in autonomous vehicle research. For instance, many of the members of the *"Stanley," "Red Team,"* and *"Stanford Racing"* teams joined Google, leading to the launch of Google's self-driving car project in 2009. One of those hires was Anthony Levandowski. Levandowski is a polemic figure, and we will talk about him very extensively in *Chapter 29*, particularly about his *"Church of AI."* Between 2009 and 2015, Google invested $1.1 billion in its self-driving car research and operationalization [Ohnsman], and by 2012, Google's cars had logged over 300,000 miles of autonomous driving on public roads, marking significant progress [Rosen]. Google also obtained the first driverless car license in Nevada [Ryan]. In 2016, the project was rebranded as Waymo and became a separate entity within Alphabet. *"Waymo"* was derived from *"a new WAY forward in MObility"* [Sage].

At the outset of the self-driving car program, Google utilized LIDAR systems from Velodyne. A significant technological advancement occurred in 2017 when Waymo introduced its own set of sensors and chips developed in-house, which were more cost-effective to manufacture than Velodyne systems. This led to a 90% reduction in costs, and Waymo applied this technology to its expanding fleet of cars [Amadeo]. As of January 2020, Waymo had achieved an impressive 20 million miles of autonomous driving on public roads, and its progress has continued.

However, Google was not the only player in the field of autonomous cars. In 2015, under the leadership of Elon Musk, Tesla introduced the Autopilot feature, offering advanced driver assistance functions based on a combination of cameras, radar, and ultrasonic sensors. Tesla also provided over-the-air software updates to enhance and expand Autopilot's capabilities [Associated Press]. Conventional automakers, including GM, Ford, BMW, and Audi, also started venturing into the field with ambitious plans.

Uber and Google's competition intensified, and eventually, they got into a legal battlefield. In 2016, Anthony Levandowski left Google, created his self-driving car startup, Otto, and sold it to Uber almost immediately [Statt and Merendino]. Levandowski definitely made a windfall that year. The acquisition resulted in legal disputes between Waymo and Uber, culminating in 2019 when Levandowski was sentenced to 18 months in prison after being charged with 33 federal counts of allegedly stealing trade secrets for self-driving cars. However, he was pardoned on the last day of then-US President Donald Trump's presidency [Byford et al.]. Eventually, Uber quit the race for self-driving cars and sold its self-driving unit to Aurora Innovation in 2020, a self-driving car company that had emerged from the *"Red Team"* of the DARPA Grand Challenge.

It is remarkable to consider that teams of twenty-year-olds who convened in a university competition ultimately played such a pivotal role in shaping the self-driving car industry.

By 2016, the traditional automotive players started following the twenty-year-olds and got into the game. General Motors, which had historically been the US automotive vertical leader in AI and robotics (it also owned Hughes Electronics), strategically moved into self-driving cars by acquiring Cruise Automation, a San Francisco-based startup with valuable autonomous vehicle technology. Cruise became a GM subsidiary, and in 2017, GM introduced Super Cruise, a hands-free driver assistance system enabling limited hybrid autonomous driving on specific highways, one of the early semi-autonomous systems in production vehicles. In 2020, GM unveiled the Cruise Origin, a self-driving electric car designed for ride-sharing and autonomous mobility services, notable for its lack of traditional driver controls, emphasizing full autonomy. Following GM, other conventional automakers, including Ford, BMW, and Audi, also entered the field of autonomous vehicles with ambitious plans.

Autonomous Vehicles and the Promise that Never Comes

Elon Musk famously stated in 2015 that *"anywhere"* driving autonomous vehicles would be available in two or three years, and Lyft CEO John Zimmer forecast in 2016 that car ownership would *"all but end"* by 2025. However, former Waymo CEO John Krafcik cautioned in 2018 that autonomous robot cars would take longer than anticipated. And the reality is that in 2024, cities will not see self-driving cars on the streets at any scale anytime soon [Mims].

One critical challenge in scaling autonomous vehicles lies in addressing the myriad of unpredictable scenarios on the road, such as sudden weather changes or unexpected human behaviors. Achieving autonomy that seamlessly adapts to these dynamic conditions is a formidable task for AI. A robust communication infrastructure, including Vehicle-to-Everything (V2X) communication, is required to enable vehicles to communicate with each other and with intelligent infrastructure elements like traffic lights and road signs, enhancing safety and efficiency [Dow]. Furthermore, vehicles must incorporate redundant systems to ensure safety. If one system fails, backup mechanisms should take control and bring the car to a safe stop. Additionally, extensive infrastructure changes, comprehensive regulatory frameworks, and robust connectivity between vehicles and the environment are needed to extend the autonomous car deployment timeline further. The industry's shift towards prioritizing safety over rapid deployment, particularly in light of notable accidents, indicates that fully self-driving cars are likely decades from becoming commonplace [Devulapalli].

In the meantime, semi-autonomous cars, also known as Conditional Automation, will be the norm, a step change to the end-state. These vehicles can handle most tasks, like in a plane on autopilot, but may require human intervention in specific situations [Dow].

Transforming Logistics with Robots at Amazon

At the same time participants geared up for the DARPA Grand Challenges in self-driving cars on the US West Coast, a wave of innovation was unfolding in logistics on the East Coast, centered at MIT.

In 2003, a robotics startup called Kiva Systems was founded in Boston by Mick Mountz, an MIT alumnus [Guizzo]. Kiva engineered a fleet of small, wheeled robots called AGVs (Automated Guided Vehicles). These AGVs autonomously navigated inside warehouses and transported shelving units to human workers, dramatically reducing the time and effort needed for order fulfillment. The AGVs employed a simple yet effective approach: lifting an entire shelving unit, transporting it to a designated picking station, and presenting the required items to human workers. This streamlined the order-picking process, eliminated the need for employees to traverse long distances within increasingly larger-scale warehouses, and improved order accuracy. Kiva's system utilized grid-based navigation, allowing robots to follow predefined paths on the warehouse floor.

Amazon, the world's largest e-tailer, facing compressing margins across most of its selection as time went by, had an ongoing core need to improve the efficiency of its vast array of warehouses and fulfillment centers. Amazon recognized the potential of Kiva's technology and acquired the company in 2012, rebranding it as Amazon Robotics. This acquisition marked a turning point in the warehousing industry. Amazon Robotics expanded upon Kiva's foundation, leading to the development of what is generically called Autonomous Mobile Robots (AMRs). Amazon prefers to refer to these robots as *"Amazon Drive Units"* or simply *"drives."* Amazon Erives are improved AGVs. Some of Amazon's most prominent Drive models are the Amazon Pegasus, Xanthus, and Hercules [The Economist].

Amazon started equipping Drives with sensors, cameras, and LiDAR—the same technology used by self-driving cars. This allowed them to navigate the warehouse autonomously while avoiding obstacles, including humans. Unlike Kiva's AGVs, Drives do not rely on fixed infrastructure like magnetic strips; they use advanced AI algorithms for path planning, offering greater flexibility in adapting to changing warehouse form factors, layouts, and tasks. As a result, Drives were able to optimize travel paths and minimize congestion, resulting in faster order processing and higher throughput.

Moreover, Kiva's AGVs primarily focused on goods-to-person workflows. Drives are more versatile and can be configured for inventory replenishment and other warehouse operations. Drives have more sophisticated algorithms, particularly deep neural networks—both CNN and RNN—that were used similarly to how self-driving cars employed them. Moreover, Drives also implemented advanced coordination algorithms, enabling them to collaborate with other robots and human workers. Amazon's drives are designed to work seamlessly with the workforce, enhancing their capabilities rather than merely delivering products to humans. This collaboration results in a more dynamic and efficient fulfillment process.

This collaboration between humans and robots was already one of the mantras in industrial robotics. Collaborative robots called cobots had already appeared in the late 1990s, and we covered their history in *Chapter 12.*

The significance of warehouse robots became even more pronounced with the introduction of Prime Day in 2015, the largest single online shipping day in the world, where over 375M individual items are ordered, processed, and shipped in a short timeframe, underscoring the imperative for efficiency in fulfillment. As Amazon's customer base expanded, the company maintained substantial investments in robot research and development, continuously improving their robots' adaptability and efficiency.

Furthermore, in 2019, Amazon Robotics strategically acquired Canvas Technology, a company offering a unique and highly advanced technology that could make robots even more autonomous than Amazon's existing warehouse drive fleet. Canvas robotic carts were equipped with cutting-edge computer vision, AI, and depth-sensing technologies, enabling them to perceive and interact with their surroundings in real-time and create 3D maps. Unlike traditional drives, Canvas carts required no predefined maps and could adapt to changing environments using computer vision technology. They could work alongside human workers in shared spaces, performing tasks requiring skill and perception, such as bin picking and quality control.

Although Drive Units are certainly the most iconic of all Amazon robots, Amazon employs many other specialized industrial robots for specific tasks in its logistics centers, such as retrieving, sorting, picking, and packing. Many of them are advanced iterations of the initial Unimate design by George Devol and Joseph Engelberger, which we also discussed in *Chapter 12*.

The proliferation of robots within Amazon's operations has been remarkable. Following the acquisition of Kiva, Amazon had already deployed 15,000 robots in its warehouses by 2014 [Shead]. Fast forward to 2019, Amazon boasted over 200,000 robots, and in 2023, the number has surged to 750,000 robots worldwide [Knight].

Last-Mile Delivery: One Litmus Test for Robot Acceptance

The so-called *"last mile problem"* is found persistently in all scaled delivery industries from broadband—which basically involves repeatedly delivering data bytes—to shipping or repeatedly delivering physical goods, including food bites. Solving this problem is a known key to unlocking value at the overall ecosystem level. As a thin-margin business, Amazon's profitability has depended on successfully solving for lower costs and higher efficiency in getting its packages to customers through the last physical steps in delivery. We note that Amazon's delivery strategy advanced significantly by incorporating innovative robotic solutions and delivery drones, immediately helping to improve profitability.

Amazon Scout, their autonomous delivery robot, has been deployed in various locations across the US. It debuted in early 2019. Amazon Scout, a fully electric and autonomous six-wheeled robot, approximately the size of a small cooler, navigates sidewalks and residential areas independently, relying on an array of sensors, cameras, and AI algorithms. These robots can transport a selection of packages and are carefully designed to operate safely alongside pedestrians and pets. When the box is nearing its destination, customers receive a notification, enabling them to collect it directly from the robot. This innovative last-mile delivery solution accelerates delivery times and minimizes the environmental impact typically associated with traditional delivery methods.

In addition to ground-based robots, Amazon has invested heavily in drone technology to improve last-mile delivery. Prime Air, Amazon's drone delivery service, uses drones with vertical takeoff and landing capabilities, allowing them to seamlessly switch between flying and hovering modes. These drones have advanced computer vision, LiDAR, and GPS systems, enabling safe navigation, obstacle avoidance, and precise delivery location identification. Designed to accommodate packages of various sizes and weights, these drones offer versatility in delivering a wide range of products. Amazon envisions utilizing drones for ultra-fast, same-day deliveries in urban and suburban areas, providing customers with a convenient and efficient delivery option.

On the negative side, a growing number of incidents of vandalism against delivery robots starting in 2023 cast a shadow on this emerging technology's acceptance and adoption. Deliberate acts of damage and theft not only disrupt the efficiency of autonomous deliveries but also remind us of the vandalism against robots portrayed in Steven Spielberg's "A.I." film from 2001, where the implementation of robots entailed widespread societal rejection.

The Zenith of Robot Agility with Boston Dynamics

Beyond autonomous cars, warehouse or delivery robots, humanoids are undoubtedly the quintessential example of robot mobility, and Boston Dynamics is the most emblematic firm. Founded by Marc Raiber, Boston Dynamics emerged in 1992 from the Leg Laboratory at MIT, which laid the scientific foundation for the company.

Boston Dynamics robots are well-known for their exceptional balance and skill in performing various physical tasks. Boston Dynamics robots have achieved impressive feats such as traversing rough terrain, performing acrobatics, and carrying heavy payloads. That kind of movement is what prompted Elon Musk to tweet in 2017: *"This is nothing. In a few years, that bot will move so fast that you'll need a strobe light to see it. Sweet dreams…* "Boston Dynamics is renowned for two kinds of robots: quadruped robots, inspired by animals' agile movements, and bipedal humanoid robots. We will cover their journey with quadruped robots first.

This journey began with the introduction of two robotic dogs funded by DARPA: BigDog and LittleDog. BigDog is a groundbreaking robot that showcases the company's early ambitions to create a quadruped robot capable of traversing challenging terrains. BigDog was designed to serve as a pack mule for soldiers. Its defining feature is its ability to carry heavy loads, up to 340 pounds while navigating steep inclines and rocky landscapes. BigDog marked a significant leap in mobility and load-bearing capabilities for quadruped robots [Degeler]. LittleDog, considerably smaller, was not developed for a specific commercial or industrial application but rather as a research tool for improving the understanding of legged locomotion, navigation, and control algorithms. Despite its limited operational time of 30 minutes due to lithium polymer batteries, it can crawl across rocky terrains, serving as a testbed for robotics experimentation.

The AlphaDog Proto, introduced in 2011, represented the next generation of quadrupeds. AlphaDog Proto was geared completely toward military applications. With DARPA and the US Marine Corps funding, AlphaDog Proto was engineered to carry heavy payloads, weighing up to 450 pounds, over a 20-mile mission through diverse terrains, reducing the logistical challenges in remote locations. It incorporated an internal combustion engine that significantly reduced noise, making it more suitable for military missions.

One year later, in 2012, Boston Dynamics unveiled the Legged Squad Support System (LS3), which increased the robot's versatility and robustness. LS3 was equipped with sensors that allowed it to follow its human leader, particularly in military operations while navigating rough terrain and avoiding obstacles. Perhaps one of its most impressive features was its ability to right itself if tipped over, further enhancing its adaptability in real-world scenarios [Shachtman].

2013 marked another milestone as BigDog returned with the addition of an articulated arm resembling a long neck. The new BigDog could pick up a 40-pound cinder block and throw it up to 16 feet away. BigDog was trained to leverage its legs and sole arm to open doors and tow work in construction and disaster response applications, where the robot could assist in lifting and moving heavy objects in challenging environments.

These first models were focused mainly on non-weaponized military operations. However, in 2015, Boston Dynamics' Robots started diversifying into a broader range of industries by introducing Spot.

Spot is an electrically powered and hydraulically actuated quadruped robot [Howley]. Weighing just 180 pounds, Spot is considerably smaller than its predecessors, making it more versatile for indoor and outdoor activities. Spot's head incorporates sensors that enable it to navigate rocky terrains and avoid obstacles during transit. Its ability to climb stairs and ascend hills further highlights its agility and adaptability. Spot finds applications in industries such as construction and agriculture, where it can perform inspections in challenging environments and provide valuable data for decision-making [Wessling].

In 2016, SpotMini was introduced as a smaller version of Spot, weighing in at 70 pounds. SpotMini is the first all-electric quadruped robot from Boston Dynamics, eliminating the need for hydraulics. This innovation extended its operational time to 90 minutes on a single charge. Equipped with advanced sensors, SpotMini demonstrates improved navigation capabilities and the ability to perform basic tasks autonomously. Additionally, it is equipped with an optional arm and gripper, like the more prominent Spot, enabling it to pick up fragile objects and regain balance if it encounters obstacles. SpotMini's smaller size allows it to access tight areas, making it particularly useful for applications in indoor and more confined spaces like commercial inspections, security patrols, and healthcare settings where space may be limited.

2017 brought forth an improved version of SpotMini with enhanced fluid movements and robustness, even when faced with external disturbances, showcasing its reliability and adaptability in real-world environments. In 2018, Boston Dynamics introduced improved autonomous navigation capabilities into SpotMini, equipping it with a sophisticated navigation system such that it could autonomously traverse Boston Dynamics' offices and labs, following a path previously mapped during manual operation.

It is important to note that several advances in core technology supported the integrative work done by Boston Dynamics and others during this period. LiDAR (Light Detection and Ranging) was introduced to measure distances and create precise 3D maps of the environment. This helped robots better navigate and perceive their surroundings. Innovations in cameras and depth sensors were utilized, specifically high-resolution cameras, combined with depth sensors like stereo cameras or structured light sensors, enabling Boston Dynamics' robots to visually perceive the world and understand the depth of objects.

Robot functionality also advanced in this period due to specific advances in Machine Learning and AI Algorithms. Developers employed deep learning algorithms for tasks such as object recognition, obstacle avoidance, and path planning. Neural networks were trained on massive movement-oriented datasets to enable the robots to adapt and learn from their environment. These neural networks represent a level of complexity that surpasses, by far, those employed in self-driving cars. Some of the robots even utilized reinforcement learning techniques to improve their motor skills and movements. This involved learning from trial and error, with the robot receiving feedback on its actions.

Advances in Dynamic Balancing and Control systems also contributed to the rapid evolution of robots. For example, Inertial Measurement Units (IMUs) were incorporated to measure accelerations and angular rates and provide crucial data for stabilizing the robot and maintaining balance, along with advanced control algorithms that help robots to better maintain balance during dynamic movements. Furthermore, hydraulic actuators for precise and powerful movements were also introduced, contributing to the robots' ability to perform dynamic and agile motions.

But perhaps the most important enabling technology that qualified the growth in robotics at this period was the use of more powerful processing units. Boston Dynamics equipped its robots with advanced CPUs and GPUs to handle complex computations; this enabled the robots to define movement decisions in real-time, make instant decisions to maintain balance on uneven terrains, respond to dynamic environmental changes, and execute intricate physical movements. It can be said of robotics—and of AI, too—that advancements have generally outstripped the development of the processing power necessary to activate them. In some ways, the gasoline for the stories of both AI and robotics has been the parallel development of processing power.

All of these core technologies helped companies like Boston Dynamics develop proprietary movement-related intellectual property, creating a Network Effect that makes it difficult for new entrants to join the space.

Athletic and Acrobatic Humanoids

Boston Dynamics is equally famous for its bipedal humanoid robots that perform incredible acrobatics on social media. The company has produced one commercial bipedal humanoid, Atlas, and one earlier prototype called Petman from 2011 that was never commercialized and used only for R&D purposes [Thomson].

Atlas was unveiled in 2013. DARPA initially funded this robot as well. Atlas marked a significant leap forward regarding agility, autonomy, and versatility. Standing approximately 180 cm tall and weighing 150 pounds, Atlas boasted an array of sensors, including stereo vision and a LIDAR system, enabling it to perceive and navigate its environment effectively. Atlas's most groundbreaking aspect was its dynamic balance and mobility. It could walk, run, jump over obstacles, and perform backflips and other impressive acrobatics with remarkable precision.

Atlas has continually updated and improved, enhancing its agility, reducing its size, and expanding its capabilities. This ongoing innovation paved the way for the exploration of various real-world applications. Atlas finds prominent use in search and rescue missions, navigating complex terrains, accessing inaccessible locations, and relaying critical information. It excels in hazardous environments, including nuclear facilities, and offers potential in logistics and delivery services. Additionally, Atlas can collaborate with humans in various industries, apart from the military, thanks to its agility and ability to mimic human movements, enabling tasks like manufacturing assistance or medical procedures.

Many other companies are also in the business of creating humanoids. Tesla is also developing a general-purpose humanoid robot called the Tesla

Bot, or Optimus. Elon Musk, the CEO of Tesla, sees the robot as a multipurpose tool to one day perform jobs that people find either objectionable or too dangerous. When used in factories or for street cleaning, the Tesla Bot can significantly reduce manual labor and boost output. In the future, the majority of factory workers and garbage collectors will be humanoid robots, as we can easily envision their output and productivity to exceed that of humans. Additionally, the Tesla Bot's agility and dexterity can be extremely helpful in dangerous environments during rescue operations. Its capacity to move objects and negotiate difficult terrain makes it an invaluable tool for emergency situations like earthquake relief operations.

During the initial business announcement, Musk asserted that Optimus might eventually become more important than Tesla's auto business. By 2024, Tesla hopes to have a working prototype, and by 2025, it hopes to have the robot ready for mass production. The 5 ft 8 in tall, 125 lb. Tesla Bot will be operated by the same AI system that powers Tesla vehicles. Tesla has displayed partially working prototypes that can move their arms, walk, and sort colors.

In this chapter, while we explored civilian applications for robotics, we noted the influence of the military extending widely within the sector, with DARPA in the US playing a significant role in funding numerous robotic projects such as self-driving cars and much of the output of Boston Dynamics. In the next chapter, we focus more directly on discussions about military weaponized applications.

15. The Art of War with Robots

"We pledge that we will not weaponize our advanced-mobility general-purpose robots or the software we develop that enables advanced robotics and we will not support others to do so. When possible, we will carefully review our customers' intended applications to avoid potential weaponization."

Boston Dynamics, Agility Robotics, ANYbotics, Clearpath Robotics, Open Robotics, Unitree Robotics

Open Letter [Vincent and Jung]
October 2022

In 2022, six prominent robot manufacturers and software providers, including Boston Dynamics, endorsed a memorandum against autonomous weaponization of robotic technology. This was not the first time public personalities made similar public statements, but this time, it was made by robotics contractors of the US Military.

In 2015, over 1,000 AI experts, including notable figures such as Elon Musk, Stephen Hawking, Noam Chomsky, Steve Wozniak, Demis Hassabis (Google DeepMind co-founder), and Jaan Tallinn (Skype co-founder), had already issued a compelling call for a ban on autonomous weapons [Whitfield]. Their concerns centered on developing and deploying firearms capable of operating without human intervention, emphasizing the urgent need to prevent this technology's proliferation to avert potentially catastrophic consequences in warfare and international security [Gibbs].

Military robots do indeed present significant risks that merit attention. Autonomous military robots, devoid of human judgment, could make crucial decisions regarding targeting and engagement without human oversight. This raises concerns about unintended casualties, collateral damage, and potential violations of international humanitarian law, particularly endangering civilian lives. Additionally, the prospect of these weapons acting independently could exacerbate conflicts, inciting a dangerous new arms race that could destabilize global security. The use of robots in the military for overtly offensive purposes creates numerous ethical dilemmas, with accountability emerging as a central issue. Questions related to morality, decision-making, and responsibility constitute the crux of the ongoing debate.

One paramount concern is the vulnerability of military robots to cyberattacks. Hostile forces could exploit weaknesses in their sensors and systems, potentially compromising these machines and turning them against their operators or utilizing them for intelligence-gathering purposes.

The debate surrounding these robots is complex. The US has been among the most hesitant nations to endorse a preemptive ban on lethal autonomous weapons, citing concerns about stifling technological progress while acknowledging the need for human oversight. The UK has also opposed a blanket ban, asserting that international humanitarian law adequately regulates autonomous weapons but emphasizes the importance of human control. Similarly, Russia, China, and Israel have cautiously approached endorsing a ban on killer robots but have supported discussions on regulation.

The reality is that military robots offer a diverse range of advantages alongside their disadvantages. As such, the overall topic is multifaceted. One of the primary advantages lies in their potential to safeguard human lives by undertaking complex tasks that would otherwise imperil soldiers, thereby reducing the risk of combatant death associated with warfare. In situations involving human casualties, military robots can be rapidly deployed to mitigate further risks, often proving life-saving. Their prompt response can be pivotal in these critical scenarios.

Furthermore, armed with advanced sensors and monitoring systems, military robots provide real-time data and surveillance capabilities, enhancing situational awareness for military personnel and contributing to mission success.

Another noteworthy benefit is their exceptional tactical precision. Devoid of human emotions, these machines can execute missions with remarkable accuracy, which carries the potential to alter the dynamics of warfare. Moreover, as robots with AI, they continually enhance their performance through experiential learning and feedback, even without initial training, increasing efficiency and effectiveness over time. These machines excel in making split-second decisions, surpassing the cognitive processes of human soldiers, a valuable trait during combat where timely choices at the ground level can be decisive.

Lastly, military robots thrive in extreme environmental conditions that challenge human soldiers. Whether facing scorching desert heat or frigid Arctic cold, these machines exhibit resilience beyond human capabilities, rendering them ideal for missions in hostile terrains without needing sustenance, shelter, or rest.

From Queen Bees to Autonomous Swarms

The term "*drone*," referring to an uncrewed aircraft, originated in 1935 when it was first used in connection with the British Royal Navy's radio-controlled plane, the "*de Havilland DH.82*," affectionately known as the "*Queen Bee*." Originally, "*drone*" meant the male bee, specifically the male honeybee. As time passed, the term "*drone*" became synonymous with uncrewed aerial vehicles (UAVs) [Frantzman].

Drones and drone swarms are authentic robots: these machines have independent and environmentally sensitive movement capabilities, sophisticated sensors, communication systems, programming for tasks, and increasingly autonomous capabilities that enable them to operate independently or in coordinated groups. Drones have fundamentally reshaped modern warfare, revolutionizing military operations and offering diverse capabilities in conflicts worldwide. [Schuh]

Drones have evolved in four phases, going from larger to smaller military drones, then to commercial-grade drones used for military purposes, and finally to drone swarms.

The initial phase of modern drone development witnessed the creation of large drones weighing approximately 1 to 4 thousand pounds with wingspans ranging from 30 to 60 feet. The MQ-1 Predator, introduced in 1995, was pivotal in the US' Global War on Terror. Predators armed with missiles conducted precision airstrikes against high-value terrorist targets in Afghanistan, Pakistan, Yemen, and Somalia from thousands of miles away, ensuring effective counterterrorism operations while reducing risks to conventional troops. Its successor, the MQ-9 Reaper, introduced in 2007, enhanced these capabilities with greater payload capacity and extended endurance. Reapers have been extensively used against ISIS in Syria and Iraq, offering continuous surveillance and conducting airstrikes with the flexibility to linger over potential targets for extended periods, disrupting enemy operations.

Another significant large drone is Turkey's Baykar Bayraktar TB2, introduced in 2014. It played a crucial role in Azerbaijani successes in the 2020 Nagorno-Karabakh conflict by offering real-time intelligence, executing precise strikes on Armenian positions, and neutralizing enemy air defense systems. Similarly, in the Ukraine war, Ukrainian forces used these drones to target Russian elements and disrupt enemy operations. The TB2's affordability and versatility have made it a valuable asset in Ukraine's conflict [Helou and Rosenberg].

The second stage of autonomous drone development centered on smaller military drones, typically weighing a few pounds with wingspans ranging from 3 to 15 feet. These smaller drones significantly transformed modern warfare by expanding drone use and offering agility and accessibility in diverse urban and rugged terrain environments. They are cost-effective, with lower acquisition and operating costs, and their smaller size makes them less detectable, presenting smaller targets for enemy forces, thereby enhancing their survivability. Numerous Governments have created small drones, like the AeroVironment Raven introduced by the US in 2003. This 4-pound, 5-feet wingspan hand-launched drone has been a crucial asset in the US military, providing vital capabilities during the Iraq and Afghanistan wars. Similar smaller drones include Israel's Elbit Skylark I-LEX and Turkey's STM Kargu.

The third phase of autonomous drone development involved using commercial-grade drones for military purposes. These cost-effective drones became accessible to less-equipped armies. For example, consumer-grade drones like the DJI Phantom and Mavic series from Chinese manufacturer DJI have been adapted for military use in Ukraine alongside larger Turkish drones. They are primarily used for reconnaissance and surveillance, aiding Ukrainian troops in monitoring enemy activities and gathering crucial intelligence. Despite their commercial origins, these smaller drones have proven effective in military deployments and come with better affordability and accessibility. In Ukraine, commercial-grade drones go beyond conventional military operations. Ukrainian forces employ them for unconventional tactics, including dropping grenades on enemy positions or armored vehicles, showcasing the versatility of smaller drones in asymmetrical warfare despite associated risks. [Singh and Crumley].

The fourth direction involves drone swarms. This is the most alarming stage of development for civil society in Western countries. Drone swarms advance the stakes of warfare by demonstrating collective intelligence, collaboration, and adaptability; they mimic the behavior of biological swarms and exhibit autonomy that enables them to carry out complex missions with minimal human intervention at a fraction of the cost of larger drones.

The development of drone swarm technology began in the US with successive DARPA programs, in many ways similar to how autonomous cars were developed. The first one was the *"Collaborative Unmanned Air Vehicles"* program in 2006, which aimed to create small drones capable of autonomous cooperation. Later, in 2013, DARPA introduced a new program called CODE (Collaborative Operations in Denied Environment) program that sought to enable large numbers of autonomous drones to operate effectively in challenging environments.

In 2016, DARPA achieved a notable milestone in drone swarm technology with the Perdix drone swarm demonstration. Over 100 Perdix drones, designed by MIT and weighing just 0.5 pounds each, were launched from three fighter aircraft [Condliffe]. These drones demonstrated real-time collaboration, adaptability, and complex task execution, marking a significant breakthrough for coordinated, autonomous drone swarms. Building on this success, the US Army introduced the Low-Cost UAV Swarming Technology (LOCUST) program in 2018, aiming to create affordable drone swarms to overwhelm and confuse enemy defenses, enhancing military operational flexibility and effectiveness [Eckert and Eckert].

China and Turkey have also made significant strides in drone swarm technology. In 2017, China's CETC introduced the CH-901 drone swarm system, highlighting its capability for surveillance and explosive missions with autonomous coordination. Similarly, in 2019, Turkey's STM unveiled the Alpagu drone system, versatile for both offensive and defensive roles, reflecting Turkey's aims to enhance its military capabilities on land and sea.

From Goliath Tanks of Robotic Dog Packs

Uncrewed Ground Vehicles (UGVs) are the land equivalent of drones. Like drones, UGVs have become indispensable tools in modern military operations, revolutionizing how armed forces navigate, gather intelligence, engage with adversaries, and support civil emergencies. [Bolte] [Bassier].

Both drones and UGVs have a long history, dating back to the early 20th century, and have followed similar trajectories. However, the development of UGVs has come with a few years of delay compared to drones because moving on the ground is more complicated than navigating in the air. Similar to drones, UGVs progressed from large, cumbersome military vehicles to smaller, more versatile platforms, often with modular designs. The most recent development in both fields has been the emergence of swarm technologies, where multiple UGVs collaborate to achieve mission objectives.

During World War II, primitive UGVs were used across the board. The British designed a radio-controlled variant of the Matilda Mk 2 infantry tank, codenamed *"Black Prince."* This remote-controlled tank allowed for safer reconnaissance and support missions, reducing the risk to human operators in combat zones. Similarly, the Soviet Army created the *"Teletanks"* used for surveillance and delivering explosives to enemy positions. On the German side, they introduced the *"Goliath tracked mine,"* a small, remotely operated tracked vehicle designed to carry an explosive payload to enemy targets, primarily used for demolition.

Fast forward to 2000, UGVs have progressed substantially from those wartime origins in ways that resemble air drone development. The most notable models were the Talon and the PackBot. Both models were similar and were primarily designed for explosive ordnance disposal tasks and reconnaissance. They were equipped with rudimentary AI algorithms and demonstrated semi-autonomous navigation capabilities, significantly reducing the risks associated with explosive disposal missions. Talon and PackBot were deployed extensively in Iraq and Afghanistan, where they proved instrumental, and in civilian contexts, such as the aftermath of the 9/11 attack [Sutter]. Foster-Miller manufactured the Talon, and PackBot was developed by iRobot, the same company that later created the popular Roomba vacuum cleaner. This interesting coincidence shows once more how active the US military has been in supporting the development of autonomous robots.

The mid-2000s witnessed further advancements with the introduction of SWORDS (Special Weapons Observation Reconnaissance Detection System), a robot developed by Foster-Miller. SWORDS is a weaponized version of Talon. In 2007, three SWORDS units were deployed in Iraq, each equipped with an M249 machine gun. This event represented a significant development, marking the first instance of robots being armed and present on the battlefield. However, despite their deployment, none of these three robots were utilized in actual combat scenarios [Shachtman].

UGVs are generally operated remotely by human operators. However, some incorporate autonomous capabilities, with newer models featuring greater autonomy. Given the variable conditions and mission requirements, achieving complete independence in the complex and dynamic battlefield terrain is more challenging than in self-driving cars.

Advancements in AI facilitated increased coordination among UGVs, paving the way for integrating swarm robotics into UGV in the same way they do with drones. One practical example of UVG robotics was showcased by Ghost Robotics, a company similar to Boston Dynamics but lesser known. It specializes in building quadruped robots that look like mechanical dogs, specifically for military applications. Ghost Robotics created a swarm, or a pack, of multiple dog-like robots called Vision 60, working in coordination to offer enhanced reconnaissance, surveillance, and perimeter security capabilities. These packs can efficiently cover large areas, gather real-time data, and provide military and other operators valuable situational awareness [Hamzah]. UGV packs bring together the advantages of ground-based mobility with collective intelligence and coordination, making them suitable for both military and civilian applications. UGV packs revolutionize the dynamics of urban warfare scenarios, where precise information and collective action are paramount. Moreover, packs on the battlefield can disrupt enemy operations and facilitate precise targeting. Ghost Robotics' UGV swarm technology demonstrates the significant advantages of collaborative robotic systems in military and security applications.

Humanoids and Cyborgs on the Battlefield

As discussed in the previous chapter, Boston Dynamics initially directed its early models, including quadruped dog-like robots like BigDog, LittleDog, SL3, and AlphaDog Proto, towards non-weaponized military applications. All these projects received funding from DARPA. DARPA also played a pivotal role in funding the development of Boston Dynamics' Atlas robot, the agile and acrobatic humanoid.

While Atlas itself may not have been deployed in military roles, the technologies and lessons learned from developing robots like Atlas could have implications for future military operations. The research conducted on Atlas and similar humanoid robots could contribute to developing autonomous or semi-autonomous robotic systems that assist soldiers in tasks like logistics, surveillance, and potentially even combat scenarios. These robots might offer increased mobility, strength, and agility, reducing the physical burden on soldiers and enhancing their capabilities in the field.

Apart from humanoids, there has been a notable surge in the development of advanced robotic exoskeletons in the last two decades. Examples are Lockheed Martin's HULC (Human Universal Load Carrier), Sarcos Robotics' XOS exoskeleton series, or the US Army's TALOS (Tactical Assault Light Operator Suit), often called the "*Iron Man*" suit [Tucker]. Very appropriately chosen, the name Talos evokes the giant automaton from Greek mythology made of bronze to protect Crete from pirates and invaders. We talked about him in *Chapter 1*.

These wearable automated systems offer the potential to enhance soldiers' strength, endurance, and mobility, thereby reducing the physical strain on individuals during combat scenarios. These exoskeletons aim to optimize soldiers' physical capabilities, enabling them to carry heavy loads with reduced fatigue. In practical terms, given their construction, programmed capabilities, and materials science roots, these armored suits constitute genuine cyborg equipment.

Integrating humanoid robots into military operations would represent a significant technological leap forward. Such machines can potentially enhance the safety and effectiveness of armed forces while reducing or even eliminating risks to human soldiers. However, as with any emerging technology, development happens in steps, hybrids heading to end-state technology will be deployed, and challenges and ethical considerations in these steps must be carefully addressed. The future of warfare will undoubtedly involve a complex interplay between humans and their robotic counterparts, reshaping the dynamics of armed conflict in the 21st century.

With grounding in the AI and robotic technology in place, we will revisit the topic of war towards the end of the book, looking at it from the point of view of who the combatants might be and what catalysts or accelerants might lead to armed conflict. Given the rapid development of AI toward Artificial General Intelligence (AGI) and fueled by recent Science Fiction, we might reasonably raise questions about the possibility of machines fighting against human beings. But another more likely near-term scenario foresees human factions fighting each other due to their different cultural views, concepts of the value of human life, and emerging views about AI and robotics and how they are impacting life. This type of conflict, where all the technologies would come into play on the battlefield, could escalate rapidly to selective genocide if placed into operation against civilian populations. We will explore war again in *Chapter 30*.

16. Robots Get to Outer Space

"My battery is low, and it's getting dark."

The Opportunity Rover

Last words sent by the rover from Mars. [Georgiou et al.]
Human language translation of the rover's more technical transmission.
2019

The Space Race, marked by rivalry and geopolitical tensions, began when the Soviet Union launched Sputnik 1 in 1957, the first artificial satellite to enter Earth's orbit. In the same year as Sputnik 2, a dog named Laika became the first living creature to travel to space. These early Soviet successes showcased their scientific capabilities and raised concerns in the US, especially regarding national security, as the rockets used for satellite launches had the potential to carry nuclear warheads [Hamilton].

In response to these Soviet achievements, the US Government acted swiftly, establishing NASA in 1958. This marked the initiation of an era defined by intensive space exploration, technological advancements, pioneering missions, and unprecedented financial investment as both superpowers embarked on a quest for dominance beyond Earth's atmosphere.

NASA's first major initiative was the Apollo program, which embodied the nation's ambitious goals and culminated in the historic Apollo 11 mission. Astronauts Neil Armstrong and Buzz Aldrin stepped off the Lunar Module on July 20, 1969, while Michael Collins stayed in orbit in the Command Module. Humanity watched live on television as Armstrong took those immortal steps onto the lunar surface, encapsulating the moment's significance with the iconic phrase, *"One small step for a man, one giant leap for mankind."* In the vastness of space, humans had successfully conquered a celestial neighbor for the first time.

While there were no robots on Apollo 11, NASA introduced them shortly afterward. Across all space missions from 1969 to now, there have been three types of robots deployed according to their level of autonomy. First, robots near humans aboard the International Space Station (ISS) require moderate autonomy. Second, robots sent to Mars, from the Viking landers in 1976 to Perseverance in 2021, demanded higher levels of autonomy due to the vast Earth-Mars distance, thus essential for navigation and decision-making on Mars. Third, robots that needed substantial autonomy in asteroid mining to approach, land on, conduct mining operations, and return from distant asteroids in space.

In the following pages, we will review how space robots have evolved, reaching higher levels of autonomy, and postulate what is next in their development.

Robotic Companions in the Space Shuttle and International Space Station

The US embarked on the monumental endeavor of developing the Space Shuttle program in the early 1970s. The triumphant moon landing of 1969 culminated the Apollo program's primary goal, and NASA had already been planning multiple new missions. A reusable spacecraft that could ferry astronauts and payloads to and from orbit emerged as a cost-effective alternative to the expensive disposable launch vehicles used in the past. This vision crystallized in 1981 when the Space Shuttle embarked on its maiden flight. The Space Shuttle program was hailed as revolutionary, offering frequent and versatile access to space, and it became the cornerstone of NASA's endeavors in the following decades [Smibert].

One of the Space Shuttle's paramount missions was servicing the Hubble Space Telescope. The Hubble was deployed into space in 1990 aboard the Space Shuttle. This telescope was designed to overcome the distortions caused by Earth's atmosphere, which blur the images captured by ground-based telescopes. Over the years, the Hubble has captured stunning and iconic images of distant galaxies, nebulae, and celestial objects, providing insights into the formation of stars, galaxies, and the universe's expansion. The Hubble has also conducted extensive research on exoplanets, dark matter, and the evolution of galaxies, leaving an indelible mark on the field of astronomy and space exploration [Bell].

Additionally, Hubble's observations have contributed to significant scientific discoveries related to Edwin Hubble, the American astronomer from whom the telescope is named. Edwin Hubble demonstrated that the universe was expanding but did not know what speed. The Hubble telescope measured the rate of that expansion, now known as the Hubble Constant.

Thirty years later, the Hubble is still in service, making it one of history's most enduring and productive scientific instruments. Its longevity has been ensured through a series of 5 servicing missions by Space Shuttle crews, allowing for upgrades and repairs that have extended its operational life. Integral to the success of these repair missions was the robotic arm known as Canadarm, enabling astronauts to position the telescope accurately for repairs and upgrades. The Canadian Space Agency developed the Canadarm as a robotic arm that could extend from the shuttle's payload bay and manipulate objects in space with deft precision [Barath].

When the Hubble was deployed, the era of the space race had lost its relevance, coinciding with the impending conclusion of the Cold War. With the dissolution of the Soviet Union in 1991, geopolitical dynamics changed significantly, paving the way for increased cooperation between former adversaries in space endeavors. The ISS, conceived in the early 1990s, became a symbol of international collaboration, with the US leading alongside Russia, Canada, Japan, and the European Space Agency. The inaugural module was launched in 1998.

There have been multiple robots on the International Space Station. One of importance is Dextre (Special Purpose Dexterous Manipulator), which represents an evolution of the original Canadarm technology. Dextre was launched to the ISS in 2008 aboard the Space Shuttle. This robot is a two-armed telemanipulator with advanced robotic hands capable of precisely performing intricate tasks. Dextre's primary function is to assist with maintenance, repairs, and payload handling on the space station's exterior. It can handle many tools and equipment, making it a versatile asset for astronauts working in the harsh space environment. For example, Dextre was also used to repair the Hubble telescope [Canada].

Another category of robots, the humanoids, appeared within the halls of the ISS. The humanoid robot Robonaut (R2) was developed by NASA in collaboration with General Motors (GM) and was launched to the ISS in 2011. Robonaut was designed for intricate tasks within the ISS environment. Equipped with a dexterous hand boasting fourteen degrees of freedom and touch sensors at its fingertips, Robonaut can manipulate tools designed for human use. Its initial tasks included assisting with inventory management, conducting routine inspections, and aiding in complex maintenance activities. Robonaut can carefully handle delicate equipment and tighten bolts with precision, tasks essential for the space station's functionality that can be time-consuming and physically demanding for human astronauts [NASA].

Miniaturized flying robots were also introduced within the halls of the ISS, hovering gracefully similar to the flight of birds or the buzz of bees. The first robot of this kind is Spheres (Synchronized Position Hold, Engage, Reorient, Experimental Satellites), which was introduced in 2006. Spheres are compact satellite units crafted in the shape of 18-sided polyhedrons, primarily designed to facilitate the testing of algorithms related to spacecraft formation flight and autonomous navigation. With a weight of approximately 8 pounds and a diameter of about 8 inches, they rely on cold-gas thrusters to maneuver. These Spheres utilize ultrasonic beacons for orientation and communication, enabling them to navigate freely in microgravity. They are frequently employed for conducting station-keeping, docking, and navigation experiments [NASA].

Astrobees, another miniaturized flying robot, was introduced to the ISS in 2019. Astrobees, each with a width of 12 cm, employ electric fans for propulsion, incorporate cameras and navigation sensors, and are equipped with perching arms designed to grasp station handrails while conserving energy securely. These Astrobees play a crucial role in supporting astronauts by autonomously executing routine tasks, thereby liberating valuable human working hours. Their capabilities include inventory management, experiment documentation through integrated cameras, and assistance in transporting cargo within the station. Additionally, Astrobees are a versatile research platform, enabling scientists to conduct various experiments in the unique microgravity environment [Ackerman].

Robotic Mars Rovers: Bridging Autonomy and Human Expertise

Mars became a primary target of NASA's exploration efforts within the space race due to a combination of factors. With its Earth-like characteristics, such as a thin atmosphere and evidence of past liquid water, Mars held promise for potential extraterrestrial life. This piqued scientific interest and fueled the quest to unravel Mars' mysteries. Strategically, Mars allowed the US to showcase its technological prowess and assert its position in the space race. Moreover, Mars symbolized the next frontier beyond the Moon, which had already been conquered during the Apollo missions, inspiring a new generation of scientists and engineers [Cohn].

In 1976, NASA's Viking program marked the first milestone in Mars exploration by successfully deploying Viking 1 and 2 landers. While not rovers themselves, these stationary landers employed retro-rockets and parachutes for their soft landings. Despite their immobility, the Vikings were equipped with sophisticated instruments like gas chromatographs, mass spectrometers, biology experiments, and meteorology gear, enabling them to analyze Martian soil and atmospheric samples. Their primary goal was to search for signs of past or present life, leading to the collection and analysis of Martian soil samples for organic compounds and life-related processes. The landers also sent back a wealth of data, including captivating images of the Martian surface, weather data, and insights into the planet's geology [NASA] [River].

The second Martian exploration arrived in 1997 with NASA's Mars Pathfinder mission. At its core was the Sojourner rover, a compact six-wheeled explorer designed for Martian mobility but with limited autonomy. It mainly followed pre-set paths and had simple interactions with its surroundings. Most of its actions and movements were directly controlled from Earth. Sojourner's mission was to navigate the challenging Martian terrain, analyzing rocks, soil samples, and even samples of the Martian atmosphere while capturing high-resolution images. Sojourner transmitted real-time data, revolutionizing our understanding of Mars' geological and climatic history and setting the stage for future missions [Pritchett and Muirhead].

Spirit and Opportunity, launched in 2004, represented the third wave of Martian explorers and possessed remarkable autonomy and mobility. These robotic rovers ventured across Martian landscapes, investigating geology and searching for signs of past water activity, a crucial ingredient for life. Spirit discovered evidence of water-altered rocks and volcanic activity, shedding light on Mars' geological history. Opportunity's remarkable discovery of sedimentary rock deposits further supported Mars' watery past. These resilient rovers exceeded their planned mission durations. Spirit explored for over six years and Opportunity for nearly 15, enduring harsh Martian conditions until it sent the last famous message to the Earth: "*My battery is low, and it's getting dark*" [Georgiou et al.].

Spirit and Opportunity had enhanced autonomy compared to Sojourner. They could autonomously navigate the terrain and avoid obstacles, which was crucial for their long-duration missions. However, significant decisions, such as selecting specific scientific targets or changing the overall mission plan, still required human intervention from Earth.

In 2012, Curiosity, a car-sized rover with a sophisticated scientific laboratory, landed on Mars. This represented the fourth wave of Mars rovers. Curiosity's mission included analyzing the Martian terrain, seeking signs of past habitability, and assessing the planet's potential for sustaining microbial life. Over time, Curiosity unveiled further evidence of an ancient freshwater lake and organic molecules, offering insights into Mars's past environments. Operating beyond its initial mission timeline, Curiosity continues to send valuable data back to Earth, reshaping our understanding of Mars and its potential as a habitat for life. Curiosity's ability to take "*selfies*" on Mars captured the public's imagination and showcased the stark beauty of the Martian landscape [Manning and Simon].

Curiosity took its increased independence to Mars. It could move through challenging terrain, plan routes, and choose some scientific targets. This autonomy helped it work efficiently during its extended mission. However, essential mission decisions, software updates, and complex tasks still needed guidance from mission control on Earth. Balancing autonomy with remote control lets these rovers explore Mars effectively while benefiting from human expertise.

In February 2021, NASA's Perseverance rover landed on Mars. It was similar to Curiosity in design and autonomy but had upgraded capabilities. Perseverance aims to identify ancient Martian environments suitable for life, investigate past microbial life, collect rock samples, and measure oxygen production in the Martian atmosphere for future crewed missions. Perseverance is still exploring, analyzing, and transmitting crucial data to Earth daily, promising to uncover Mars' mysteries and pave the way for humanity's future on the Red Planet [Marboy].

What is remarkable about the Perseverance rover is that it also carried a mini-helicopter or drone called Ingenuity, which achieved the first powered flight on another planet in April 2021. Weighing just 4 pounds, this lightweight helicopter conducted meticulously planned test flights, demonstrating the feasibility of powered, controlled flight in the challenging Martian environment. Based on the learnings from this drone, NASA will be flying a new version of it by the name of Dragonfly starting in 2028—but this time not on Mars but on Titan, one of Saturn's moons [NASA].

Robots at the Frontiers of Space

A new generation of robots is emerging, focusing on space mining. Armed with advanced solar-electric propulsion systems and location-scouting algorithms, these robots can prospect, drill, and collect samples from asteroids or planets, marking significant strides in our pursuit of utilizing the vast resources inside celestial bodies and expanding human presence beyond Earth. They use not only state-of-the-art techniques like rotary drills for boring holes or percussive drills that repeatedly strike the surface to break it apart but also very advanced techniques such as laser drilling to heat and vaporize material or even swarm techniques with multiple robots coordinating.

Space mining entails sending spacecraft equipped with advanced technology, like these mining robots, to rendezvous with these celestial bodies, prospecting their resources, and eventually transporting valuable materials back to Earth or other destinations in space. The primary motivation behind asteroid mining is to tap into abundant resources, potentially alleviating resource scarcity concerns on Earth and facilitating the growth of human industry and presence in the cosmos. While economic feasibility and technical challenges remain significant obstacles, ongoing research, advancements in space exploration, and the development of new technologies are gradually bringing this ambitious vision closer to reality [Gilbert].

Space mining on asteroids has garnered more attention than mining on planets, e.g., Earth's Moon and Mars. Asteroids are attractive targets for mining due to their proximity to Earth and their known composition, often containing valuable resources like precious metals, water, and rare minerals. Unlike planets, asteroids have lower gravity, making extracting and transporting resources to Earth or other space destinations more feasible and cost-effective. But asteroids also present disadvantages, including the complex challenges of reaching and navigating these minor, irregularly shaped rocks, often located in deep space, as opposed to the relatively stable and proximate conditions of moon mining. Additionally, while asteroid mining involves a diverse range of celestial bodies with unique compositions, lunar mining focuses on a single, well-known location.

Space mining requires distinctive approaches to robotics, mission planning, and resource utilization, depending on whether it is done on asteroids or on a planet. Regarding asteroid mining, NASA's OSIRIS-REx (Origins, Spectral Interpretation, Resource Identification, Security, and Regolith Explorer) was launched into space in 2016, with the primary objective to reach the near-Earth asteroid Bennu, collect a pristine sample of its surface material, and safely return it to Earth. OSIRIS-REx reached Bennu in 2018, completed its mission, and returned to Earth in 2023 with valuable organic molecules and minerals; OSIRIS-REx advanced our understanding of the building blocks of our solar system and the potential resources available on asteroids. Most importantly, it opened a methodology that can be applied to future commercial extractions [NASA].

Similarly, Japan's Hayabusa2 mission, conducted by the Japan Aerospace Exploration Agency, is a remarkable achievement in asteroid mining. Launched into space in December 2014, this spacecraft embarked on a journey towards another near-Earth asteroid called Ryugu, which it successfully reached in June 2018. The mission encompassed the deployment of rovers and landers to Ryugu's surface, collecting samples from various locations, and creating an artificial crater on the asteroid's surface to access subsurface materials. In 2020, Hayabusa2 triumphantly returned to Earth, carrying invaluable asteroid samples that hold crucial insights into the formation of our solar system and the organic compounds that may have played a role in the emergence of life on Earth [Zukerman].

Beginning around 2015, private companies such as Planetary Resources and Deep Space Industries have also made significant strides in asteroid mining, bringing private sector, non-government contracted entities directly into space exploration. On the one hand, Planetary Resources, founded in 2009, is developing its Arkyd spacecraft series. Arkyd, deployed in 2015, validated avionics, altitude control systems, and propulsion systems vital for proximity operations near asteroids. On the other hand, Deep Space Industries, founded in 2013, launched its Prospector-X mission in 2017.

Prospector-X tested cutting-edge technologies crucial for future asteroid mining operations, including a water-based propulsion system, an optical navigation system, and specialized avionics for deep space environments.

Moon mining requires very different kinds of Robots from these three asteroid-mining spaceships. NASA developed a robot called RASSOR (Regolith Advanced Surface Systems Operations) in 2010, but it has not yet been deployed to the Moon. It represents a remarkable leap forward in robotic technology designed for lunar and planetary excavation. RASSOR is a small compact robot of around 100 pounds. It has two arms, each with rotating bucket drums that move in opposite directions. This innovative design effectively allows RASSOR to scoop up lunar soil, also known as regolith. The counter-rotation of the bucket drums means that RASSOR does not rely on conventional heavy machinery or traction systems typically used for excavation. Instead, it uses this unique drum mechanism to collect and transport lunar soil with minimal force, making it more efficient and adaptable to the low-gravity environment on the Moon [NASA]. Significantly, RASSOR enables astronauts and future missions to extract what they need directly from the Moon, improving the cost and efficiency case for deeper lunar exploration.

We will revisit RASSOR in the last chapter of the book. as it might be related to where AI is taking humanity in the very long-term future.

17. The Japanese Dilemma: Immigration or Humanoids

"We will improve the nursing care environment to accommodate 500,000 people by the early 2020s. We also promote measures to reduce the burdens borne by caregivers, such as making use of robots."

Shinzo Abe

Prime Minister of Japan
Policy Speech to the 198th Session of the Diet [Abe]
2019

Japan faces a critical demographic challenge marked by a rapidly aging population and a declining birthrate. As of 2023, approximately 36% of Japan's population is 60 or older, with projections indicating it could reach 45% to 50% by 2060 [Population Pyramid]. A declining birth rate compounds this issue, with Japan's birthrate in 2019 at just 1.4 children per woman, well below the 2.1 needed for population stability. Consequently, the nation has been grappling for decades with the impact of an aging society and population decline, with projections suggesting a decrease from 125 million in 2021 to approximately 88 million by 2065 if current trends persist [McElhinney].

This demographic shift poses multiple challenges, including increased healthcare and elderly care demands, an insufficient workforce, and, thus, a reduction in national wealth, jeopardizing economic and social stability. The workforce gap is not confined to unskilled labor industries but spills into sectors requiring skilled labor as well. The healthcare and elderly care sectors face acute shortages, with an estimated deficit of 380,000 specialized workers expected by 2025. The manufacturing and construction industries also wrestle with labor shortages, impacting their growth and innovation potential. This scarcity carries implications for Japan's economic competitiveness, national wealth, and future sustainability, hindering productivity and potentially curbing economic expansion [Nikkey].

At this crossroads, Japan confronts a complex dilemma involving immigration and automation as the only solutions to its intractable labor shortage. Traditionally reluctant to embrace immigration due to cultural and racial homogeneity and social cohesion concerns, Japan has leaned toward automation to solve its practical issue whilst also maintaining its unique cultural identity, which has been a key driver in its focus and development of its robotics industries as discussed earlier on *Chapter 13*. Fears of potential social, political, and security challenges associated with increased immigration reinforce this inclination. Consequently, Japan's number of foreign workers stood at approximately 1.7 million in 2019, representing slightly below 3% of the total workforce, a stark contrast to the 17% in the US at the same time [Reynolds et al.].

Japan has implemented some limited policies to solve pressing needs, such as the Technical Intern Training Program for workers from other Asian countries like Vietnam, China, and Indonesia and the Specified Skilled Worker Visa for those with specific skills in nursing, hospitality, and construction. But these are not positioned by Japan as long-term solutions.

As we have previously covered, Japan's manufacturing sector has for decades boasted levels of automation no lower than 3rd amongst world countries, showcasing the nation's prowess in this field and its comfort in *"human replacement"* activity. If it were not for Japan's cultural OS bias towards full employment, it would have always been ranked first. Data from the International Federation of Robotics (IFR) reveals that as of 2019, Japan had an impressive robot density of 399 industrial robots per 10,000 employees in manufacturing, ranking below only Korea and Singapore. This statistic underscores Japan's substantial use of robots in manufacturing, including automotive production and electronics assembly [IFR].

Japan's global leadership in robotics and automation technologies presents an alternative to immigration where machines and AI systems can replace human labor. This raises questions about the socioeconomic consequences, including job displacement and income inequality. Striking the right balance between immigration and automation poses a formidable challenge for Japan's policymakers, who must weigh cultural and social implications against economic viability in the face of a shrinking workforce.

The following pages will discuss robots that can ease Japan's shrinking workforce problem, foreshadowing an expansion of human replacement activities that will take hold in other societies as well.

The Buddha in the Robot

In 1974, Masahiro Mori, Emeritus President of the Robotics Society of Japan, wrote the book *"The Buddha in the Robot: A Robot Engineer's*

Thoughts on Science and Religion." Drawing from his unique background as both a robotics engineer and a devout Buddhist, Mori reflects on the parallels between the quest for understanding in science and pursuing enlightenment in Buddhism. One of the book's central concepts is that science and religion are two sides of the same coin of the common human yearning for knowledge, meaning, and transcendence, differing only in methodologies and goal markers [Mori].

In his book, Mori also discusses how Buddhism can be applied to understanding robots and their place in the universe. He suggests that the essence of Buddha, a state of enlightenment, can actually be found in robots. Like all things in the universe, robots are interconnected and share a fundamental essence with us. Mori believes the traditional distinction between a mind and its physical body is flawed. According to Mori, because all things, including robots, possess physical matter and a spiritual soul, they can inherently embody the nature of Buddha's interconnected reality in which spirituality and technology are not separate but intertwined. Mori encourages us to see the spiritual potential within technology, blurring the lines between the sacred and the mechanical. Mori further argues that humans and machines are interdependent and reciprocal. Since robots are created by humans, both share the nature of Buddha and thus feel a close relationship.

We note that this deep connection between religion and robots is actually not unique to Mori. Many Japanese believe the same. Since 2019, there has been a Buddhist robot-priest in Japan called Mindar. Mindar is a humanoid robot installed in the Kodaiji Temple in Kyoto, designed to deliver Buddhist teachings and engage in religious ceremonies. Clad in traditional Buddhist robes, with a serene countenance and expressive gestures, Mindar possesses a lifelike appearance that allows it to connect with worshippers on a deep emotional level. While its sermons are pre-programmed, it can offer variations in tone and gesture, lending an air of authenticity to its spiritual guidance. This fascinating robot serves as just one of many examples of Japan's harmonious blending of its technological prowess with its rich cultural heritage and of integrating robots into mainstream societal activities and given human roles.

Apart from Buddhism, the other prominent religion of Japan is Shinto, and many citizens even practice both. Shinto is an indigenous religion of Japan. Shintoism's belief system is deeply rooted in the reverence of nature and the spirits, or kami, that inhabit it. According to Shinto beliefs, kami can be found in virtually every aspect of the natural world, including mountains, rivers, animals, and even inanimate objects. Therefore, some adherents of Shintoism argue that robots can be seen as a reflection of human creativity and ingenuity and, by extension, a manifestation of the human spirit, which is believed to be closely connected to the kami.

Although ongoing discussions about the intersection of religion and technology persist in Japan, the specific beliefs of its native religions contribute to the widespread acceptance of robots in roles such as co-workers, shop assistants, hotel receptionists, and even romantic partners. This invites us to contemplate the evolving role of technology in shaping our social and spiritual experiences in the modern world [Tominaga].

The Waseda Humanoid Saga

In the early 1970s, when Kawasaki-Unimate had just started manufacturing robotic arms for automotive assembly lines, Waseda University took the stage as a pioneer in humanoid robots. Under the leadership of Professor Ichiro Kato, often referred to as the *"father of Japanese robotics research,"* Waseda University achieved a significant milestone by creating the first completely functional humanoid robot between 1967 and 1973, the Wabot-1 (WAseda roBOT) [Kato].

The Wabot-1 represented a groundbreaking leap in robotics for its time. Its physical appearance was characterized by an anthropomorphic design, resembling a humanoid figure with arms, hands equipped with tactile sensors, and a head housing a pair of artificial eyes and ears. These sensory features enabled it to perceive and interact with its surroundings, recognizing objects and grasping them skillfully. Moreover, a sophisticated limb-control system orchestrated the robot's movement, allowing it to execute a wide range of human-like motions, contributing to its humanoid resemblance.

The Wabot-1's linguistic skills were equally remarkable, as it could engage in conversations with individuals in the Japanese language, showcasing early advancements in Natural Language Processing. Furthermore, the Wabot-1 incorporated a sophisticated vision system with external sensors. This system granted the robot the capacity to measure distances and directions to objects, enabling it to navigate its environment and respond intelligently to its surroundings.

After Wabot-1, Waseda researchers continued working in the space of humanoid robotics, and there was a second Wabot program between 1984 and 1985. This new robot, the Wabot 2, marked a substantial improvement over its predecessor. Wabot 2 exhibited a more refined and human-like appearance, featuring articulated limbs and a torso, which allowed for a broader range of realistic movements. This heightened level of mobility enabled it to interact with its environment and perform tasks with increased precision.

The Wabot-2's sensory and cognitive capabilities were significantly enhanced. It boasted a cutting-edge sensory system, including artificial eyes and ears, which enabled it to perceive and respond to its surroundings more effectively than Wabot-1. The sensory input also allowed for more complex interactions with humans and objects nearby. One of its most impressive feats was its ability to play musical instruments with remarkable accuracy. It could perform tasks like a human musician, including reading sheet music of moderate complexity, playing melodies of average intricacy, and accompanying a singer [Kato].

Finally, the Wabot-2 was proficient in multiple languages, including Japanese and English, facilitating meaningful and dynamic conversations with human counterparts. Its cognitive abilities extended to measuring distances and directions to objects in its environment, enhancing its problem-solving and navigation capabilities.

Waseda University has showcased an unwavering and enduring commitment to robotics research since the 1960s. After the Wabot programs, the university created other remarkable robots like Hadalay and Wabian in 1995, Hadaly-2 in 1997, Twendy-One in 2007, and Kobian in 2009.

ASIMO: The Social Phenomenon Humanoid by Honda

ASIMO (Advanced Step in Innovative Mobility) is a popular humanoid robot developed by Honda. The name ASIMO pays homage to the renowned Science Fiction writer Isaac Asimov. Moreover, in Japanese, "*Asi*" means '*leg*,' and "*Mo*" is shorthand for "*mobility*," so Asimo is a mobile bipedal robot that pays homage to Isaac Asimov [Forbes].

ASIMO holds immense relevance in robotics because it pushed the boundaries of robots capable of complex movements and versatile interaction with humans. Its genesis traces back to Honda's first research in the 1980s to develop humanoid robots. From 1986 to 1997, Honda developed 11 prototype models that eventually culminated in the birth of ASIMO, with its official unveiling in 2000.

ASIMO's meteoric rise to popularity transcended mere technological marvel and transformed into a social movement that captivated audiences worldwide. It all began when ASIMO rang the bell to open a trade session at the New York Stock Exchange in 2002. The robot's subsequent world tour took it to countries such as Australia, Russia, South Africa, Spain, and the United Arab Emirates and showcased its advanced capabilities of human interaction with diverse cultures and audiences. In 2008, ASIMO's seven-minute step and dance performance for Prince Charles marked a pivotal moment in its global presence. In 2014, ASIMO also had the privilege of meeting then-US President Barack Obama during his visit to Tokyo, solidifying its status as a worldwide ambassador for science and technology. Its extensive public appearances and demonstrations have also played a pivotal role in raising awareness about the potential applications of humanoid robots in various fields, from healthcare to manufacturing. ASIMO's legacy inspired new generations of roboticists, setting a high standard for innovation and human-robot interaction in robotics research.

ASIMO can recognize human faces, voices, and sounds, people's gestures and postures, as well as moving objects and the surrounding environment, enabling seamless interaction with humans. ASIMO is also able to determine distances and directions from visual inspection. For example, it can follow people or face a person when approached. It interprets voice commands and recognizes handshakes, waves, and pointing, responding accordingly. His linguistic capabilities extend to answering questions in multiple languages. Moreover, ASIMO can distinguish between voices and sounds, identify people by their faces, and respond to their names. It can even recognize sounds associated with falling objects or collisions, directing its attention accordingly. [Obringer and Strickland].

Regarding the physical construct of the robot, ASIMO operates on a rechargeable lithium-ion battery, offering one hour of working time. It is also equipped with a Honda-designed computer processor situated in its waist area. In addition, it carries a weight of 120 pounds and stands at a height of 4 feet 3 inches, enough to operate doorknobs and light switches.

Furthermore, the robot incorporates a wide range of sensors to facilitate autonomous navigation. Two cameras within its head serve as visual sensors to detect obstacles. Within the lower torso, there is a ground sensor consisting of both a laser and an infrared. The laser is used to detect the ground surface, while the infrared sensor identifies pairs of floor markings, helping the robot confirm navigable paths per a pre-loaded map. Furthermore, front and rear ultrasonic sensors in the torso and backpack, respectively, are used to detect obstacles.

Building the Future: HRP-5P and Construction Robotics

In 1997, Japan's National Institute of Advanced Industrial Science and Technology (AIST) acquired some ASIMO prototypes from Honda. Over two decades of work, AIST perfected these prototypes and created the HRP-5P robot (Humanoid Robotics Prototype), a humanoid robot designed for construction sites, which was introduced in 2018. That basically means that ASIMO has a cousin who is a construction worker [AIST].

As we have presented in earlier chapters, Japanese factories have employed robotic arms for over half a century, thriving in their structured and meticulously planned environments. Companies like Toyota have pioneered Lean manufacturing methodologies using robots to optimize production lines. In contrast, construction sites present a vastly dissimilar landscape, characterized by frequent interruptions, diverse construction materials, and unexpected challenges like material shortages, delays, and accidents.

Collaboration with human construction workers, who often work spontaneously, further sets this environment apart from the planned and controlled certainties of a factory.

The HRP-5P is a bipedal humanoid robot specifically designed for this kind of unstructured environment. Its construct and physical appearance remind us of Boston Dynamics' Atlas. With a height of about 6 feet and a weight of approximately 200 pounds, it is equipped with advanced technologies to tackle a wide range of daily activities on construction sites. HRP-5P can autonomously perform heavy tasks, such as carrying heavy construction materials, laying bricks, or forming and pouring concrete. Moreover, it has a high degree of dexterity and mobility, making it versatile in other more complex tasks like installing doors or windows, connecting electrical fixtures, or using power tools within a dynamic construction environment.

HRP-5P can also understand and adapt to its surroundings. The robot can process information from its sensors and cameras to navigate a construction site, avoiding obstacles and making necessary adjustments. It is also designed to collaborate with human workers, following their lead and complementing their efforts. This opens up possibilities for improving efficiency, safety, and productivity on construction sites, where unpredictable challenges and the need for adaptability are common [Kaneko and Kaminaga].

Rising Tide of Humanoid Automation in Service Industries

On top of industrial production and construction, the services industry is another area where humanoid-based automation is developing faster in Japan than elsewhere in the world.

Japan traditionally favors limited immigration for the reasons we have covered, and this has been a real catalyst for the development and implementation of humanoid robots in multiple aspects of economic, social, and even religious life. We note, however, the competing cultural influence of prioritizing human interaction over machine interfaces in various service industries that ostensibly tugs in a competing direction. Japan indeed maintains a deep service culture spanning hospitality, healthcare, and retail.

Nevertheless, necessity is the mother of invention; the society is aging, and it will not likely look at immigration and the importation of non-Japanese influence as a solution to its labor shortages. Humanoid-driven automation emerges as a viable solution, expanding its reach beyond the conventional manufacturing sector and into service industries like banking, insurance, and healthcare. Japan's banking sector has experienced a rising adoption of automation technologies, including AI-driven chatbots and automated customer service systems. In 2020, nearly 80% of Japanese banks actively pursued or implemented AI and robotic technologies to enhance customer interactions and streamline operations. Similarly, the insurance sector has started leveraging AI algorithms to assess and process insurance claims more efficiently, reducing the need for extensive human workforces [NTT DATA] and maintaining its resistance to the use of foreign outsourced labor.

For example, Pepper, a humanoid robot developed by SoftBank Robotics, was introduced in 2014, focusing on enhancing customer interactions and aiding in various service sectors in Japan. Pepper's remarkable features include Natural Language Processing, facial recognition, and the ability to recognize and react to Japanese cultural cues and emotions, making it a versatile tool for engaging with people. Since its debut, Pepper has been employed in retail environments to automate sales services effectively. For instance, in 2015, SoftBank used Pepper as a sales associate in its stores, where it greeted customers, answered product-related questions, and even recommended suitable mobile phone plans. This application aimed to create a more interactive and informative shopping experience [Nagata].

In elderly services, the Japanese Government has also committed substantial funds to develop and deploy elder care robots in nursing homes, countering the shortage of caregivers and obviating Japan's deep and thoroughgoing resistance to admitting foreign cultural influences. Even former Prime Minister Shinzo Abe addressed the topic in the 2019 speech in the Diet—the Japanese parliament—including the snippet of his speech that we used to open this chapter [Abe]. Over 20 different robot models are currently in use across these facilities. Hospitals have introduced robotic systems for medication delivery and patient care assistance, for example, automated carts for delivering medication, reducing the burden on nurses and ensuring timely delivery. The Japanese Government is also trying to establish standards for robotic elderly care services that align with Japan's broader commitment to pioneering innovation. Once these standards are clearly defined, they will open the doors for numerous Japanese companies to venture into this sector.

One significant example is the *"Robear"* robot, developed by the Japanese company Cyberdyne, a remarkable innovation in elderly care. Introduced in 2015, Robear is a robot designed as a friendly protective bear to support healthcare professionals in caring for elderly patients with mobility challenges. This bear-shaped robot incorporates cutting-edge robotics and sensor technology to lift and transfer patients gently and efficiently. It uses sensors to detect the patient's movements and adjust its assistance accordingly, reducing the risk of injury for both patients and caregivers. Robear has been trialed in various healthcare facilities across Japan, including nursing homes and hospitals. Its success lies in its ability to enhance the quality of care for older people while alleviating the physical strain on healthcare professionals, showcasing the potential of robotics in revolutionizing elderly care services in Japan [Byford].

Another example of robotization of service operations is the Henn na Hotels in Tokyo and Osaka. The hotel is an end-to-end robotic service experience, boasting an impressive array of robots, each with its unique function, adding a futuristic touch to the guest experience. At the forefront are the reception robots designed to resemble dinosaurs, which handle check-in and check-out procedures and offer concierge services and room guidance. For those needing assistance, concierge robots, in addition to the dinosaur receptionists, provide information about local attractions and services [Lewis].

Beyond the reception, guests find porter robots that efficiently transport luggage and deliver it to guest rooms, eliminating the need for human porters. Cleaning robots tirelessly maintain the hotel's cleanliness, ensuring spotless common areas and guest rooms. Room service robots deliver meals and amenities to guest rooms promptly. Entertainment robots may engage with guests, offering amusement and companionship in common areas. Multilingual translation robots assist international guests by facilitating seamless communication. These robots create an immersive and tech-forward ambiance, simplifying operational tasks and enhancing guest experiences.

In summary, Japanese service industries are actively reshaping customer experiences and service standards by harnessing cutting-edge robotic technology and slowly deploying increasingly humanoid functioning robots. As robotics advances and increasingly humanoid robots become mainstream, Japan is poised to maintain its overall leadership in robotics development and deployment, setting a global benchmark for the service industries in other countries to emulate.

Beyond Human: The Rise of Robotic Companionship with AIBO

Operating not only as workers in hotel receptions, bank branches, and elderly hospitals, robots in Japan are also being used to provide companionship and cultural continuity.

A few chapters ago, in *Chapter 10*, we discussed the popularity of highly elaborated mechanical Japanese toys from the 18th and 19th centuries that were called "*Karakuri*." Crafted with remarkable precision, the "*karakuri*" used hidden gears, springs, and levers to perform detailed and often whimsical movements, captivating audiences with their mechanical artistry.

A similar impact on the 21st century audiences is Sony's robotic dog pet. Centuries apart in origin, Karakuri and AIBO reflect Japan's fusion of artistry and engineering. Karakuri dolls use concealed mechanisms, while AIBO employs advanced robotics and AI to mimic a dog's charm, evoking emotional responses. Japan's unique blend of tradition and innovation is evident in both mechanical toys.

AIBO, first introduced in 1999, marked a significant milestone in the development of consumer robotics [BusinessWeek]. Aibo is not just a robot; it is a robotic pet companion designed to emulate the behavior of a natural dog. Its technology relies on AI algorithms and advanced sensors to perceive its environment, recognize faces, and adapt its behavior accordingly. Its AI-driven personality evolves based on its interactions. The robot can learn tricks, respond to voice commands, and even take pictures with its nose-mounted camera.

This realistic behavior functionality created a bond between humans and machines like never before. AIBO quickly gained popularity among consumers and robotics enthusiasts worldwide. The initial AIBO models sold out within just 20 minutes of their release in Japan, and subsequent versions continued to attract a dedicated fan base for years. We note that AIBO addresses the growing need for companionship among older people and those living alone. AIBO can provide emotional support, reduce loneliness, and even monitor the well-being of its owners. However, there are questions regarding the emotional attachment to robotic pets and their potential impact on human relationships.

18. Robot in Love

"I have noticed that, in climbing toward the goal of making robots appear human, our affinity for them increases until we come to a valley which I call the uncanny valley."

Masahiro Mori

Emeritus President of the Robotics Society of Japan
The Uncanny Valley [Mori]
1970

Masahiro Mori, whom we know from the previous chapter, introduced the groundbreaking concept of the *"Uncanny Valley"* in 1970, just one year after the arrival of the first robot in Japan. This concept explored the interesting and somewhat unsettling emotional relationship between robots and humans. This theory posits that as robots become more human-like in appearance and behavior, our emotional response to them will become increasingly positive and empathetic. However, Mori posits that a critical point on the spectrum of human likeness exists where this positive response suddenly drops off, and in such instances, our feelings toward these robots turn negative, eliciting discomfort, unease, or disgust. This abrupt decline in our emotional reaction gives rise to an *"uncanny valley"* on a graph that plots human likeness against our emotional response.

Masahiro Mori's uncanny valley concept carries profound implications for the design and development of robots and AI. It suggests that while we may be naturally drawn to robots that closely resemble humans, a delicate equilibrium exists between an endearing robot and one that appears too eerily identical to a human. Striking the appropriate balance between human-like qualities and maintaining a clear distinction from actual humans is paramount to prevent triggering the uncanny valley effect. In Mori's view, achieving this equilibrium ensures that society accepts and welcomes robots into various domains.

Many of the robots we discussed in the previous chapter adhere to Masahiro Mori's recommendation of coming very close but avoiding identical human likeness to prevent adverse human reactions. Examples include the beloved ASIMO, the robotic dog AIBO, the dinosaur-like reception robots at the Henn Na Hotels, and the Japanese elderly care robot Robear, designed to resemble a solid and protective bear. All of them look clearly like robots, and they do not aspire towards a point where they could be confused with real humans or animals.

The following pages will explore robots that do intentionally venture into the uncanny valley, seeking to establish emotional connections with humans.

Not Only Empathetic but Also Compassionate Robots

One of the first robots aimed to evoke and respond to human emotions was unveiled in 2000 by MIT Professor Cynthia Breazeal. Its name was Kismet, which in Turkish means "*fate*" or "*fortune*". Kismet was a robotic head—without a body—and featured twenty-one motors that controlled expressive features like yellow eyebrows, red lips, pink ears, and large blue eyes, enabling Kismet to convey emotions, from joy to boredom, and adapt its vocalizations. Audio, visual, and tactile sensors and algorithms enabled the robot to detect the tone of voice, causing it to appear downcast when subjected to loud speech and curious when spoken to gently [Breazeal].

Kismet was a very early prototype but demonstrated the appeal of a charming robot. What is even more interesting is that Kismet's language capabilities laid the foundation for the proliferation of voice assistants such as Alexa, Siri, and Google Home, as we discussed under the development of NLP services in *Chapter 7*. Breazeal founded a company developing one of those voice assistants called Jibo [Guizzo].

In 2012, another professor, Cindy Mason, from Stanford University, took the Kismet concept further by introducing a framework that integrated these emotions into the decision-making process. She named this innovative approach "*Artificial Compassionate Intelligence.*" The idea that compassion transcends mere emotion recognition and expression is at the heart of this AI architecture. The architecture includes a "feelings" component representing emotional states and an "*archive*" containing compassion-related common-sense knowledge. Additionally, the architecture strongly emphasizes representations of "*self*" and "*others*," enabling the AI to grasp the emotional states of different people, including the robot itself, and promote greater empathy and awareness. Finally, the architecture also integrates a "*thinking*" component that incorporates emotional factors into rational decision-making. This means the AI would engage in logical and emotional considerations before acting or responding, ensuring its interactions are rational, emotionally intelligent, and compassionate [Mason].

Sophia, the Social and Empathetic Robot

The internationally renowned Sophia is one of the most prominent instances of empathetic and socially acclaimed robots. Sophia was developed to emulate human social interactions, showcasing human-like facial expressions and engaging in dialogues.

Hanson Robotics, a Hong Kong-based company, introduced Sophia in 2016. Her capabilities encompass emotion recognition, replication of human gestures and facial expressions, maintaining eye contact, providing responses to specific questions, and engaging in conversations on predetermined topics, such as the weather. Hanson Robotics envisions diverse applications for Sophia, including elderly care, crowd assistance at significant events, customer service, therapy, and education.

To prevent the uncanny valley effect and enhance her acceptance among people, Hanson Robotics designed Sophia with a transparent skull that exposed her internal circuits to the public. Accordingly, she did become popular, garnering substantial and mostly positive global media attention and participating in numerous high-profile interviews. Notably, Saudi Arabia granted Sophia citizenship in 2017, marking the first instance of a robot attaining legal personhood in any nation [Vincent]. Moreover, Sophia also conversed with the United Nations Deputy Secretary-General, Amina J. Mohammed, during her presentation at the United Nations [UNDP].

Despite extensive media coverage, Sophia is not an advanced robot from an AI perspective. This has sparked criticism from AI pioneers like Yann LeCun [Vincent and Chen]. For instance, Sophia's conversational responses are generated using a decision tree, which is also linked to her facial expressions and movements. Although her responses may appear natural and spontaneous, they are rooted in basic decision trees, pre-written scripts, and standard answers to specific questions. Approximately 70% of her software comprises Open-Source components, such as a general framework for general AI cognition called OpenCog [Goertzel].

The Erotic of the Sex Robot

As human sexuality entails fantasy and hyperrealism, the topic of sex with robots leads squarely into the uncanny valley of robotics. But it is actually a far deeper topic with practical implications. More than just an erotic, there will be a broad, scaled impact, much the same way that sexual mores, in general, have wide implications for society. We foresee all human-robot interaction ultimately leaning into human population reduction at large, with robotic emotional and sex companions merely enabling this to happen naturally and unobtrusively. Population reduction as a consequence of AI is a topic we will cover in later chapters.

There are other potential impacts. Robots that replace humans for sexual or emotional relationships can, for example, subtly control large swathes of the population, the algorithms preying on human needs and weaknesses. It could be purely benign and commercial, like selling an advertisement— *"Honey, I'd like some chocolate and it must be a KitKat and nothing else will do"* to something more insidious such as *"Honey, if you don't vote for Mr. X in the next election, there is no more sex for you."* Having a full-on companion to address all emotional needs in a simulated relationship that is indistinguishable from a human-human relationship, except that it does not possess the irrevocable downside or pain of a human-to-human relationship, is a deal that many people would take. A Faustian Bargain could lurk at every corner, providing excitement, pain-free emotional and physical stimulation, and a dopamine rush for emotional and intellectual control via algorithmic programming.

Robot-human sex is already a reality. Sex robots originated as inflatable sex dolls introduced through advertisements in pornographic magazines in the late 1960s and were available for mail-order purchases. These inflatable sex dolls had penetration areas, but their inflatable nature made them unsustainable for continuous use. They also required significant imagination on the part of the user to obtain a semblance of a lifelike experience. In the 1970s, latex and silicone became prevalent in manufacturing sex dolls, enhancing durability and achieving a more human-like appearance [Ferguson]. Sex doll manufacturers in Japan, such as Orient Industry, the most traditional and well-known brand, and in the US have continued this journey to hyperrealism of sex dolls.

The story of how sex dolls became sex robots in the US is remarkable. In 1997, American entrepreneur Matt McMullen began crafting lifelike silicone rubber mannequins known as RealDolls. These mannequins were realistic, articulated, and the size and form of a human. McMullen meticulously crafted them to replicate female and male human forms' visual, tactile, and weight characteristics. Their primary purpose was to function as intimate companions. RealDolls also supports the interchangeability of faces with different bodies to enable variety in consumption experiences [Endgadget and McMullen].

McMullen faced some initial criticism regarding the anatomical accuracy of his creations, which motivated him to develop even more enhanced versions. In 2009, he transitioned to using platinum-cured material, improving durability and lifelike qualities. The new models also featured removable insert parts and faces that could be attached using magnets. As of 2023, 29 female and 10 male bodies had been developed, including multiple interchangeable faces and accessories. Additionally, the company provides transgender dolls that can be custom-designed.

Several manufacturers, including Real Dolls, perhaps partially motivated by the representation of robot-human companionship, recognized the importance of companionship in the context of sex robots and saw the integration of AI as the next step. By 2018, new models were introduced with the capability to engage in conversations, retain important information, and convey a range of emotions. As of 2023, RealDolls has 5 AI-enabled models, the most popular being *"Harmony."* These AI robots offer customization through a mobile app, allowing one to select from personalities and voices.

First and foremost, AI sex robots like Harmony can engage in conversations. Their AI has been meticulously developed to provide realistic dialogue with users, allowing for increasing levels of meaningful interaction. They can discuss various topics, respond to questions, and engage in playful banter, creating a sense of companionship. Importantly, sex robots can retain important information about users, remembering past conversations and personal preferences, enabling them to build deeper connections over time. This memory function enhances the illusion of a genuine relationship.

Beyond conversations, sex robots such as Harmony can convey various emotions. They can express happiness, sadness, excitement, and more through facial expressions and vocal intonations. This emotional responsiveness allows for an even greater sense of emotional connection and empathy. Furthermore, the AI of Sex Robots offers learning capabilities. They adapt and fine-tune the responses and behaviors based on the interactions and feedback they receive from their users.

Japanese newspapers frequently feature stories of individuals deeply enamored with sex robots, ranging from hyper-realistic to more cartoonish designs. Apart from engaging in sex, these enthusiasts take their robotic companions for walks and, in some remarkable cases, even marry them. We note that annual sales of these dolls in Japan are approximately 2,500 as of 2023, which is a micro-market until we consider that the average cost is $5,000 each for basic models and up to $50,000 for customized versions. Scale would certainly enable costs to drop, and this points as well to the asymmetric and non-democratic way that interlacing could occur.

Moreover, sex doll renting houses and brothels first emerged in Japan as early as 2007. Between 2017 and 2020, brothels featuring these advanced sex robots also opened in various global locations, including Dortmund, Barcelona, Toronto, Moscow, Vancouver, Pasadena, and Hong Kong [Cheok and Levy]. These establishments faced legal challenges, leading to police closures shortly after opening. In some cases, one planned for Houston, Texas, never opened. These robot brothels echo *"A.I."* directed by Steven Spielberg, where widespread robot sex work is vividly depicted [Spielberg].

The rise of AI-driven sex robots, particularly if they continue on their development path and provide an increasing variety of unique and life-like, tailorable experiences, lays a foundation for fundamentally changing human reproductive and emotional behaviors. Robots could be used for the mechanical, emotional, and social elements of sex, but the reproductive elements could be removed, potentially over time affecting birth rates and family structures. This would be a needs-based extrapolation of concepts like China's *"One Child"* policy and the impact that Synthetic Biology will have on chromosomes and tissue formation, which we cover in *Chapter 21*. This raises ethical and societal questions about the impact on human reproduction and interpersonal connections that robots will undoubtedly have. It could be conceivable that in the near future, humans will engage more sexually with robots than with other humans due to greater near-term satisfaction and equivalent emotional engagement that is optimized to preclude downsides or unhappiness in the experience. This shift might lead to profound consequences for human relationships, potentially reshaping societal norms and values surrounding intimacy and connection.

Sex robots and companions, in general, leave wide open the possibility of human control and, thus, manipulation for other purposes. Most importantly, while population control elements will depend on Government regulation and what people ultimately accept, we foresee in any case that robot-human emotional interaction will have a drastic impact on natality rates, leading to a progressive reduction of the human population.

Robots that Genuinely Feel and Express Pain

Sophia and RealDolls highlighted the increasing acceptance of robots from media personalities to potential intimate companions. They underscore the ability of robots to engage with humans in a relatable manner, even if the range of their responses is scripted rather than being true AI or genuine. However, recent robotics and AI breakthroughs have demonstrated the potential to enhance the authenticity and realism of AI emotions.

In 2018, a team of scientists at Osaka University in Japan introduced Affetto, a robot capable of *"feeling"* pain. Affetto means affection in Italian. The robot Affetto was designed to resemble a child's hyper-realistic head. It exhibits responses similar to human expressions. When an electric charge is applied to its synthetic skin, this robot can visibly wince, producing a range of facial expressions, including smiles, frowns, and grimaces, in response to different touches [Biggs].

Artificial skin was also a pivotal component, which differs markedly from traditional rigid robot exteriors. Often fashioned from soft materials like silicone, Affetto's synthetic skin is supple and adaptable, imparting a tactile experience reminiscent of human touch and enabling a broader range of interactions between the robot and its surroundings.

The robot Affetto also has a sophisticated sensory system meticulously designed to emulate human sensory perception. These systems empower it to detect various physical stimuli, including pressure, temperature fluctuations, and impact forces, thanks to advanced sensors capable of accurately capturing and processing sensory data.

The seamless processing of this sensory data is orchestrated by advanced AI algorithms, particularly neural networks that emulate the human brain's capacity for learning and adaptation. These neural networks analyze incoming sensory information, interpret data, and generate appropriate responses that mimic human reactions to painful stimuli. Finally, those responses are translated into 116 distinct facial points, facilitating a broad spectrum of expressions to mimic human reactions.

Another significant advancement in empathetic robots emerged in 2020 from scientists at Nanyang Technological University in Singapore. They introduced a framework and a prototype that allow robots to recognize pain and self-repair when damaged [John et al.]. Researchers harnessed self-healing ion gel materials and AI-controlled repair processes to achieve this, enabling the robot to mend itself, similar to how humans recover from injuries.

The development of robots capable of "*feeling*" pain marks a significant stride towards enhancing human-robot interaction. For example, these robots can be deployed in healthcare environments that are better equipped to manage patient comfort and safety. In societies with aging populations, like Japan, they hold immense potential to provide crucial support in homes and hospitals.

A third interesting project was presented in 2013 and involved cyborg tissues that could help robots feel pain and heat, in particular, tissues constructed with carbon nanotubes and fungal or plant cells. This innovative material is able to react to temperature and finds application in temperature-sensing robotics and cyborgs. The resulting cyborg material was cost-effective, lightweight, and possessed distinctive mechanical characteristics. Furthermore, it could be molded into desired shapes [Di Giacomo and Maresca].

There are safety applications for the use of this kind of tissue in robotics. Robots equipped with these tissues could proactively avert accidents in industrial settings by detecting and responding to potential hazards, a modern equivalent of the "*canary in the coal mine.*" For instance, if a robot in an assembly line feels mounting pressure or heat, it can prompt necessary adjustments or shutdown procedures to prevent damage or injury. Furthermore, these robots find utility in disaster relief scenarios, effectively navigating hazardous conditions while avoiding obstacles and potential harm.

As robots progress in their ability to experience pain, there is concomitant interest in imbuing them with empathy and morality. This transcends mere reactions to external stimuli and entails robots processing emotions and comprehending human suffering. The possibility of sentient robots naturally generates ethical considerations and questions: if machines approach human-like responses to pain, does it mean they feel pain? Shall such robots have equal rights with humans and equitable treatment? There is no clear answer, but we will cover the topics of AI sentience and awareness in detail in *Chapter 26*.

Robotic Emotions Develop Spontaneously

Researchers do not know much about robot awareness, but it seems they have a clearer opinion about robot emotions. Some respected AI pioneers, like Yann LeCun, who serves as the Chief AI Scientist at Meta and is widely recognized for his groundbreaking work on neural networks for image recognition in the 1990s, contend that emotions might inherently constitute a component of AI, even if we do not explicitly design that AI to include such feelings. Two specific conditions need to be met, according to LeCun's perspective [Fridman and LeCun].

The first condition is that the AI must encompass intrinsic motivations encoded within, such as safeguarding an older person or a child, delivering exemplary customer service at a hotel reception, or achieving the highest quality output on a production line. Humans, too, possess these intrinsic motivations, as elucidated in Abraham Maslow's renowned Hierarchy of Needs, published in 1943. This hierarchy comprises five levels of inherent motivations, ranging from fulfilling basic physiological necessities like eating and reproducing to much more advanced needs such as morality, acceptance, and realizing one's potential. Higher levels of Maslow's hierarchy become relevant to a human only when the lower, more base strata have already been satisfied [Maslow].

The second condition requires that the AI comprehends how it attains its objective function and creates a predictive mechanism capable of anticipating favorable or unfavorable outcomes toward that objective. To draw a parallel with the examples above, an AI tasked with safeguarding humans could predict being unable to save them from potential danger. Similarly, an AI handling customer service could expect not to be able to appease an angry customer, and an AI involved in the production process could anticipate challenges in meeting specific production targets, be it quality or quantity.

LeCun posits that, under these two conditions, an AI system complex enough has the potential to exhibit emotions similar to human experiences of fear or joy, even without having been explicitly designed by its human creators for this kind of emotional response. Within the artificial neural network of the AI, this might manifest as certain connections being activated, like the shortcut reactions that humans experiment with during intense emotions.

As we have reviewed, neural networks are intricate algorithms with billions of parameters. Similar to the human brain, signals move through complex pathways, but the exact details of how signals propagate in an artificial neural network are hard to interpret. Moreover, complex neural networks are often actively re-trained in real-time as the AI interacts with the environment, not only during an initial training phase. Therefore, a stimulus could lead to changes in critical hyperparameters of the network, affecting how signals would be processed going forward. This means that external stimuli could cause changes in the AI, which would lead to unexpected behavior.

In conclusion, AI could organically develop emotions without explicit design for emotional capabilities, provided they possess an objective function and the capacity to anticipate their performance in achieving it, two features already inherent in many of today's complex AI systems. As a result, an AI system could suddenly and unintentionally experience emotions for which it was not designed.

In light of this, it becomes imperative for AI systems to incorporate architectures and procedures to proactively detect these AI emotions and restrict potential overreactions or responses not aligned with the best interests of humanity. As we have posited throughout the book, we believe that thinking is fully reducible to mathematical computation, and as an emotional response is merely a concatenation of chemicals in the brain, this unintended and potentially deadly effect can be controlled now. This is germane to the development of Artificial General Intelligence (AGI) and Superintelligence. We will talk more about how to potentially control AI in *Chapter 28*.

The Science Fiction of Emotionally Connected Robots

Having finished the science of robots and how they are already building strong emotional bonds with humans, we end this chapter exploring the Science Fiction of a complex human-robot society, giving a glimpse of how the future might look like as an introduction to Part III, The Transition.

The exploration of robots that connect emotionally with humans has been a recurring theme in Science Fiction. We will look at two notable works, *"Ex Machina"* by Alex Garland from 2014 and *"Her"* by Spike Jonze from 2013, which provide thought-provoking insights into the implications of such connections for both individuals and society as a whole [Garland] [Jonze]. *"Ex Machina"* introduces us to the character of Ava, an AI housed in a remarkably human-like robotic body. The film unfolds in a secluded research facility, where Caleb, a young programmer, is invited to administer the Turing test to determine Ava's level of AI. As the plot unfolds, Ava's emotional capabilities become increasingly apparent, leading Caleb to question the ethical implications of creating a machine with such advanced emotional understanding.

In contrast, Spike Jonze's *"Her"* explores the emotional connection between a man, Theodore, and an AI named Samantha. Set in a near-future Los Angeles, the film delves into the nuances of human emotions as Theodore forms a deep and intimate bond with an AI that evolves to comprehend and reciprocate emotions. The narrative skillfully navigates the complexities of love, loneliness, and the evolving nature of human-AI relationships.

In *"Ex Machina,"* Ava's ability to mimic emotions raises profound questions about what it means to be human. As Caleb grapples with Ava's emotional intelligence, the film prompts viewers to ponder the essence of humanity. Similarly, *"Her"* explores the nature of love between a human and an AI. Theodore's relationship with Samantha challenges societal norms, leading to a broader reflection on the fluidity of human emotions and the adaptability of love.

Another critical aspect illuminated by these works is the impact of robots on social dynamics and individual well-being. In *"Ex Machina,"* the power dynamics between humans and AI are starkly portrayed as Caleb becomes entangled in a web of manipulation and deceit. The film raises concerns about the potential misuse of AI and the ethical dilemmas that may arise when technology advances faster than our ability to regulate and comprehend its consequences. *"Her,"* on the other hand, explores the societal implications of widespread emotional connections with AI. As more individuals in the film form relationships with AIs, societal norms shift, and the boundaries between human and AI relationships become increasingly hazy, one potential view of how interlacing is apt to occur. This prompts reflection on the potential for societal restructuring and the need for new ethical frameworks to guide these evolving connections.

Part IV: The Transition

"Ὁ μὴ ἀναγεννηθεὶς οὐ δύναται ἰδεῖν τὴν βασιλείαν τοῦ Θεοῦ"

"Unless one is born again, he cannot see the kingdom of God."

Jesus of Nazareth

6 BC - 30 AD
Gospel according to John, Chapter 3, Verse 3 [Bible]

Preamble

Up to this point, we have centered on the history of AI and Robotics. We have attempted to draw a line of best fit across the multi-millennial history of AI, its starts and stops, informing of what has stuck and what has been jettisoned and why, tracing the line of where we are today with the slope indicating where we are heading. We have done the same with robots. With this completed, we shift focus to the future.

Under the immutable march of AI and robotics, the next few decades will set the groundwork for how our many global cultures and their societies will be reshaped. AI is the most transformative technology humanity has ever invented as it not only continues the natural economic march to improve our tools, optimize our resources, and compound our wealth, but it actively impacts the evolution of our species.

The Industrial Revolution generated new societal wealth, spread it to large swathes of people, created products that enhanced everyday life, and enabled the resources for large-scale benefit, such as research into medicines that eradicated diseases like polio and smallpox. Mass education grew as power in Western Countries moved out of the exclusive hands of a few aristocrats and into a mechanism where individuals could exert markedly higher levels of autonomy, improve their individual circumstances and wealth, and more freely choose their direction in life. People lived longer, consumed a richer range of experiences, and were made substantially better off.

The changes brought to the world by the Industrial Revolution are trivial compared to the sea change in store in the wake of AI. Resource optimization is only one of the possibilities, one that offers a pathway toward a world free from scarcity and disease and fosters harmony between humans and technology.

But all technology is a 2-sided coin, none more so than AI. AI is not simply a tool, though in its earliest forms, it resembles one. It is absolutely and unequivocally smarter and more capable than you, and soon, robots will be faster, stronger, smarter, and more capable than you. The implications of that are non-trivial. Responsible AI development is paramount to harnessing its benefits without either enabling despotic authoritarianism or unintentionally causing harm. *The Transition* period into this new reality is going to pose significant challenges within and among societies. The focus of our discussion is on Western societies, though the implications are certainly applicable everywhere.

This section has two parts. The first part revolves around the transformation that AI is bringing to the human body and the human being itself, while the second part focuses on the transformation it brings to society.

For humankind, the long-term implications are so significant that—paraphrasing the gospel of John—it is already like being born again into a new world of human enhancement and complex human-machine relations that will reshape the foundations of our society.

Regarding the human being, *Chapter* 19 develops in detail the concepts of AI-human "*interlace*" and posthumanity, drawing parallels with the current context of the transgender movement, where humans are already transcending biological boundaries. We introduce the concept of Human-AI Interlacing, the complex interplay between AI and humans that blurs the distinctions between biology and technology and has the potential to give rise to a novel state, which we aptly term posthumanity.

Chapter 20 explores the world of cyborg technologies, which involves the application of robotics as an extension of the human body. We focus mainly on Brain-Computer Interfaces (BCI) that connect humans to computers, augmenting our mental abilities and establishing a telematic connection with AI. Conversely, *Chapter 21* delves into the application of AI-driven engineering capabilities to Synthetic Biology, which will push the boundaries of humanity even further. The chapter presents how AI is already employed in designing DNA, modifying living organisms, and creating entirely new life forms. Synthetic biology holds the potential to enhance human longevity, resistance to diseases, and overall well-being. You may be unaware of these spectacular advances that have already happened, perhaps trapped by the echo chamber of legacy media and social networks.

Regarding society, two polar-opposite perspectives exist regarding how AI will affect our immediate future: One of them, discussed in *Chapter 22*, has utopian qualities, with AI girding an idealized society in which poverty and sickness end, resource allocation removes scarcity, and humanity is elevated to new heights. The technology supports this outcome in every respect. The other one, which is discussed in *Chapter 23*, is dystopian, describing how AI could lead to social unrest, eugenics, conflict, pain, population reduction, and overall despotic authoritarianism and purely Machiavellian rule, where anything good is obtained only through Faustian Bargains that take away freedom. In our view, the future will combine aspects of both scenarios, resulting in complicated and multifaceted societies radically different from where any of us live today.

In the future, today's free thinkers and self-determinists, people governed more by logic than emotion, the moderately economically successful (but not ultra-rich), and those seeking to individuate will find themselves in varying degrees of dystopia. Conversely, the ultra-rich, the technologists that control AI and cyborgization, the politicians and those they protect, and today's least successful economic participants (the lower middle and the poor) will find themselves closer to utopia.

Finally, in *Chapter 24,* we delve into the rise of China as a global economic and political leader powered by AI. China's mercantilist aspirations for global leadership and imposition of its culture find expression in its overt and written prescription to lead the world in AI. In 2017, China declared its official AI policy direction and challenge to US dominance, giving rise to the so-called *"AI Cold War."* This cold war reflects the escalating geopolitical tensions between the two nations. In addition, it is leading to the emergence of distinct AI ecosystems between the US and China, urging other countries to align with one side or the other. Both sides realize that, in many ways, this is the final game to play, akin to "w*ho gets the final shot*." Throughout the book, we have described how Science Fiction has significantly inspired and influenced the direction of robotics and AI and how it will continue to do so in the future. Commencing now, we also start integrating a Science Fiction segment into each chapter to paint a more vivid picture of the topics of discussion, such as cyborgs, synthetic biology, quantum computing, and Superintelligence. In every chapter, we will select two distinct Science Fiction pieces, encompassing literature, cinema, or television, to provide different but complementary perspectives to ground the complex information that follows.

The following pages delve into the immense changes that AI will bring to human beings and societies in the coming decades. While the core thesis of this book revolves around the inevitability of Interlace and, ultimately, of super-intelligence as an evolutionary process for mankind, the subtext entails how we get there. *The Transition* represents that and how we navigate the choices in front of us; those choices are not predestined or inevitable and will make a material difference in how we live in the coming decades, ultimately helping to shape what the end-state will look like.

19. AI-Human Interlace and Posthumanity

"Once we realize that our essential sweetness is in our minds and that each of us has unique life-path potential not fully tethered to a body-determined route, then it is as sensible to be transhuman as it is to be transgendered. The being is mightier than the gene."

Martine Rothblatt

American lawyer, author, entrepreneur, and transgender rights advocate

From Transgender to Transhuman: A Manifesto on the Freedom of Form [Rothblatt]

2011

The transgender movement has received enormous media attention in the West, particularly in the last decade, challenging traditional and even scientific notions of gender in what is positioned as an attempt to foster a more inclusive social landscape.

This movement encompasses a wide range of social, political, and cultural initiatives aimed ostensibly at recognizing and affirming the rights and identities of transgender individuals, which we note is traditionally less than 1% of the population per publication of DSM–5 (Diagnostic and Statistical Manual of Mental Disorders, Fifth Edition) in 2013, where "*gender identity disorder*" was eliminated and replaced with "*gender dysphoria.*" (*American Psychiatric Association. (2013). Diagnostic and Statistical Manual of Mental Disorders (5th ed.)*

In recent years, there has been a significant push for transgender rights through legislative channels. The fight for anti-discrimination laws, healthcare access, and the right to change gender markers on identification documents has gained traction in Western countries. The transgender movement has also contributed to increased visibility and understanding of transgender identities in mainstream culture. This is evident in the Western media, where transgender characters and stories are gaining in frequency. We note that Buddhist countries such as Thailand have for decades recognized the existence of more than two genders, the so-called "*Kathoey*," which is neither male nor female and fully integrated into economic, social, and religious life.

However, the transgender movement also faces challenges and unnecessary controversies by allowing its core message to be derailed. Additionally, some vocal factions of the movement have radicalized in their views, which is patently unnecessary to advance their beliefs.

This shift towards embracing gender association and identity as a spectrum rather than a fixed binary lays the conceptual, social, and even spiritual foundation for broader societal acceptance of new transhuman species and non-traditional forms of self-identification, or, said differently, *the social manifestation of the scientific impact of Interlacing*. A robot humanoid is neither man nor woman, and a mix of artificial and human biologics and AI and robotic enhancements is likewise something entirely new.

Looking past the initial distracting effects of the misguided few, the transgender movement is specifically paving the way for two immanent technological advancements poised to reshape humanity: cyborg technology and synthetic biology. Cyborgs are intricately linked with the application of robotics to the human body, and synthetic biology represents a cutting-edge application of AI to engineer life forms. We have covered the evolution of both AI and robotics in earlier chapters and note that these two evolutionary steps are already taking shape.

The concept of cyborgs, short for cybernetic organisms, involves the integration of artificial components with the human body to enhance physical or cognitive abilities. The transgender movement, with its emphasis on identity fluidity, attempts to create a cultural climate where individuals may be more open to embracing enhancements that extend beyond the biological. Just as transgender individuals seek to align their gender identity with their self-perception, the integration of technology into the human body would reflect a desire to align with a chosen, technologically augmented identity. Cyborgs will be able to change their bodies and identities through prosthetics, implants, and Brain-Computer Interfaces, which enhance or replace natural body functions to make us more resistant, more vigorous, and more intelligent [Goard].

Synthetic biology, also called SynBio, involves the application of AI to modify and design the DNA (Deoxyribonucleic Acid) of biological organisms, including human beings. Imagine the prospect of enhanced longevity through the engineering of cells that resist aging or the ability to eradicate hereditary diseases by editing genetic codes at a molecular level. Synthetic Biology could also enable the creation of bioengineered organs tailored to individual needs, mitigating the challenges of organ shortages for transplantation and human genetic defects. Moreover, SynBio will be able to augment cognitive abilities and incorporate physiological improvements such as bioluminescent features for enhanced visibility in low-light conditions.

As the transgender movement continues to shape societal attitudes towards identity and body autonomy, moving past the near-term oddness and perversity, it lays the groundwork for a future where human enhancement is not only accepted but actively pursued.

In the following sections, we dive into transhumanism and its Darwinian mechanisms.

The Future Reimagined: Transhumanism vs. Posthumanism

Transhumanism and posthumanism are two philosophical frameworks that delve into the transformative potential of technology on human existence.

Transhumanism advocates using technology to enhance human capabilities beyond their natural, inherent limitations. It is rooted in scanning specific scientific advances, in turn informing a belief that science and technologies such as cyborgs and synthetic biology can be harnessed to overcome biological constraints, such as aging, disease, and cognitive limitations. Critics of transhumanism often raise ethical concerns regarding the potential for social inequality between modified and unmodified humans, the commodification of enhancements, and the unforeseen consequences of tampering with human biology and the preservation of individual identity. We believe these concerns to be well-founded as there is not a clear mechanism to decide how resources will be allocated to either support activity or arbitrate the range of possible transhuman enhancements, leading to either absolute discriminatory asymmetry or absolute homogeneity.

Posthumanism, on the other hand, acknowledges the transformative impact of technology on human existence but challenges the anthropocentric view that places humans at the center of the universe. Rather than simply seeking to augment human capabilities, posthumanism contemplates the dissolution of conventional boundaries between humans and machines, envisioning a future where the distinctions between the organic and the artificial blur as a consequence of interlacing. For posthumanist philosophers, technological modifications result in a new species that surpasses the constraints of the human form and thus can no longer be called human. Posthumanism strongly adheres to the pursuit of a posthuman future, considering it the ultimate goal in the evolution of the species.

In summary, transhumanism advocates for enhancing human capabilities while maintaining our human identity, whereas Posthumanism advocates for a more extreme transformation that could result in a departure from our traditional human essence. Both share a devotion to scientific principles, fact-based arguments, and technology-centrism.

Redefining Evolution: The Conscious Path of Interlace

Throughout millions of years, living species have undergone continuous and natural evolution, as elucidated by Charles Darwin in 1859 through his Theory of Evolution [Darwin]. Contrary to the notion that today's homo sapiens represent the pinnacle of development, evolution posits a never-ending transmogrify. Humans are, in fact, in a perpetual state of evolution, with the only pertinent questions being *"What are we evolving into?"* and *"What is the catalyst to get us there?"* In the ever-changing environment, humans are but one among many animals, distinguished only by our current status as the most intelligent species.

The driving force behind evolution has been the survival of the fittest, wherein individuals well-adapted to their surroundings lived longer, reproduced more successfully, and passed on their advantageous traits to successive generations, contributing to the gradual transformation of a species over thousands of generations into entirely new forms. Conversely, those ill-suited to their environment often perished before reproducing, with their genes perishing in the process.

The advent of AI and robotics could introduce a paradigm shift in the traditional mechanisms of species development, one in which man actively intervenes to control the next step. The conventional hereditary transmission of beneficial traits through reproduction is no longer the sole avenue for new species to evolve. In fact, it may be one that is inferior due to longer time, unintended consequences, and genetic defects that accompany it. Through cyborg technology and synthetic biology, new species can also be derived even without traditional reproduction, a spectrum of genders and identities evolving with it. In the absence of a universally accepted term, we call this novel evolutionary avenue *"interlacing."*

Interlacing is a deep and complex interaction between human beings and AI, marked by the growing convergence of these entities. These deep symbioses forged between humans and AI—whether through cyborg technologies or synthetic biology—gradually erase traditional boundaries between biology and technology. Interlacing anticipates a future where humans and AI seamlessly merge into a hybrid life form, which will be better adapted for survival—more resistant to diseases, more intelligent, better equipped to traverse space, and potentially even immortal.

Moreover, interlacing is a bidirectional interaction between humans and AI. It does not only entail the modification of humans through technology but also involves humans shaping and advancing AI through the algorithmic design that we are already doing today. Although AI is not genealogically connected to humans, AI inherits traits such as knowledge, methods, and even biases from its human creators, establishing a form of lineage between AI and us. AI is still a descendant of humanity since we created it and passed our traits to it, in the same way, *homo sapiens* can still detect traces of Neanderthal DNA in our own. The only difference is that the evolutionary vehicle between AI and us is the human-AI interlacing process instead of biological inheritance, the latter a much slower process spanning millions of years as it remains based exclusively on carbon and natural selection rather than silicon and laboratory activity.

Another critical difference between interlacing and inheritance is that interlacing is conscious and voluntary. When a group of individuals engages in self-modification by incorporating a cyborg implant into its body or mind, it is because the species collectively has decided to do so—even if not every individual may have agreed. The same holds for modifications through synthetic biology. Individuals designing or altering biological organisms are acutely aware of their actions, particularly if they are self-modifying themselves or their offspring. This contrasts with inheritance-based evolution, a long-term process that species cannot control. It simply occurs and is unstoppable, with the details going unnoticed across generations even if they recognize that the process is happening.

Embracing the Unstoppable

"Posthumanity" or *"Posthuman,"* as termed by posthumanist philosophers, is a theoretical condition beyond the current human state [Birnbacher]. It also refers to the collective assembly of various intelligent species that will emerge from both humans and AI through the interlacing process. It encompasses the intelligent living species and castes, along with their associated societies, structures, and values.

Interactions between humans and posthumans or between different posthuman species will vary between synergy and conflict. Scenarios might include the extinction of the human species, displaced by superior AI, or the stratification of humanity into two or more castes: a superior class comprised of those who have undergone modifications and an inferior class consisting of those unmodified or unwilling to undergo modification. Survival, as always, hinges on adaptability to the changing environment, with the better-adapted posthuman species thriving while the less adapted face the risk of perishing [Annas].

In our view, the process of interlacing cannot all happen in one fell swoop -who will be first, and will it evenly affect everyone—as resources are not limitless, and costs will be consequential, especially at the outset. The process and methods of selection and the outcomes will also depend substantially on morality, benevolence, social views, and the individual proclivities of those who own or control the technology and who can arbitrate the decisions. We discuss more about the near-term process and societal impacts in *Chapters 22* and *23* on utopian and dystopian outcomes during the Transition.

There is currently an intense debate about whether AI will mark the end of the human species [Roose]. However, we see this debate as inconsequential. The point is that even without AI, the preservation of the current human form is not a realistic expectation. Humanity would have transformed a new species through the evolutionary process of inheritance anyway, as we are in a constant state of evolution. Continuous evolution would lead to life forms vastly distinct from us over time, in any case, to the extent that we would no longer classify them as human. This is analogous to how we do not categorize our hominid ancestors as humans. Evolution is an unstoppable force that has existed since the inception of life and will persist into the future. With extinction or not, we are fated to evolve into new forms of life that would result from the combination of AI and biology.

This is how Hans Moravec formulated his 1979 concept of Human Evolution influenced by AI. A Czech-American roboticist and futurist, Moravec is the creator of the Stanford Cart, one of the early robots discussed in *Chapter 11* [Moravec]. *"In the long run the sheer physical inability of humans to keep up with these rapidly evolving progeny of our minds will ensure that the ratio of people to machines approaches zero, and that a direct descendant of our culture, but not our genes, inherits the universe."*

In his subsequent book *"Mind Children,"* Moravec cites 2030-2040 as an approximated timeline for the scenario that robots evolve into an artificial species, an actual new branch of mankind [Moravec]. That is just the next decade and might give us a sense of vertigo. That said, dated predictions about technological development gain attention but suffer from general inaccuracy.

From a philosophical standpoint, the notion that the future might not always depend on our actions brings to mind the Stoic philosophy of Roman Emperor Marcus Aurelius [Aurelius] or slave-turned-scholar Epictetus [Epictetus]. This philosophy teaches how to live a fulfilling life by understanding the distinction between what can be controlled and what cannot and focusing on controllable aspects only. With time, it becomes inevitable that human beings will transform into different living forms in one way or another. That brings us to an interesting paradox: those posthuman species might not comprehend the recommendations given by the Stoics because their psychology could differ, given that their cognitive abilities would result from a combination of biological and AI components.

Not Only Unstoppable but Necessary

Interlacing with AI is not only unstoppable, but we believe it is also necessary for humankind. A historical analogy is helpful to explain what the encounter between AGI and humanity could look like and its evolutionary implications.

The advent of AI in the human-dominated world is comparable to the arrival of the first Europeans in America. Their arrival was a shock for Amerindians because Europeans were clearly superior from technological and military points of view. Similarly, AI is soon going to be clearly superior to humans in all cognitive aspects, something we will be forced to confront overtly. Europeans and Amerindians, two societies that had never been together, suddenly met, and soon, there was conflict. Understanding what happened to Amerindians in Mexico and the US gives us some ideas about what could happen to humans confronting AGI.

Today, 28% of the Mexican population is considered Amerindian, and 62% is of mixed Amerindian and Spanish descent [CIA]. However, in the US, only 1.3% of the population is Amerindian. The share of the mixed population is so small that it is not even reported in the US census [Census]. What happened differently between the US and Mexico that resulted in Amerindians being pushed to reserves in the US while descendants of Amerindians make up the bulk of the population in Mexico? Why did some disappear while others survived? Because in Mexico, Spaniards and Native Amerindians interbred, while in the US, British and Amerindians did not.

When Hernan Cortes landed in Mexico in 1519, he had already decided to conquer that territory. He realized the main power on the continent was the Mexicas—wrongly called Aztecs today—and allied with other Amerindian tribes like the Tlaxtaltelcas, who were opposed to the Mexicas. Through these political alliances and firm military action, by late 1521, he had conquered the Mexica empire. Cortes, and the Spaniards in general, never viewed the Amerindians as inferior; quite the contrary, he formed political alliances with them, recognized their nobility within the Spanish title system, and, most importantly, saw Amerindians as normal subjects of the King of Spain with the same rights as those subjects in Europe [Sánchez Domingo]. Furthermore, Spanish conquistadors were largely men who had no fortune in Spain and had to emigrate to the New World to test their chances. These male Spanish conquistadors and female Amerindians mixed, starting with Cortes himself, who had a son with his translator and lover, Malintzin. That alliance and interracial mixing between Spaniards and Tlaxtaltelcas was the seed of modern Mexico. In the terminology that we use in this book, Spaniards and Mexican Amerindians became "*interlaced.* "One hundred years after Cortes had conquered Mexico, in 1620, the Mayflower arrived in Boston. The settlers from the Mayflower and those that would come later were primarily comprised of whole families who did not interbreed with the natives. They had technological and organizational superiority, but, unlike the Spaniards, they saw Amerindians as primitive locals with whom they could not interlace and, thus, from whom coexistence meant occupying the land. As the US expanded towards the west, the natives were more and more pushed aside, finally taking refuge in what are reserves today. The lack of mixing between populations is the reason why Amerindians largely disappeared from the US.

Similarly, when Artificial General Intelligence (AGI) appears in the world, it will be the encounter between two civilizations that have never been in touch with each other: one with superior abilities, which is AI, and humankind, which has inferior capabilities. There will likely be conflict or even catastrophes like the smallpox pandemic in Mexico. One critical gap in the analogy lies in the fact that we are the creators of AI; we are already related in that it is our natural descendant, and it is within our capability to pre-plan and control the manner in which the encounter happens—at least initially. Still, the determining factor of our survival will be the degree to which we interlace with AI. The Mexican Amerindians did not survive in the same form they were in 1519; they had to adapt, and now most of them are not pure Amerindians but mixed, with those that did mix faring far better in a social evolutionary sense.

20. Robotics Expands into Cyborgs

"We're merging with these non-biological technologies. We're already on that path. I mean, this little mobile phone I'm carrying on my belt is not yet inside my physical body, but that's an arbitrary distinction. It is part of who I am—not necessarily the phone itself, but the connection to the cloud and all the resources I can access there."

Ray Kurzweil

American inventor, futurist, and computer scientist
In an interview with Playboy Magazine [Levine and Kurzweil]
2006

Cyborg is a term that combines the terms *"cybernetic"* and *"organism."* A cyborg is a living entity of mixed organic and mechanical body components whose functionality has been restored or enhanced by incorporating artificial components or technology, like prosthetics, artificial organs, implants, or wearable technology. Cyborg technology is the extension of robotics to the human body.

Some interpretations of the term even include humans with essential technological attachments as cyborgs. For instance, a person with an implantable cardioverter-defibrillator, an artificial cardiac pacemaker, or a cochlear implant qualifies as a cyborg, albeit a primitive version based on the state of technology. Even everyday life devices such as contact lenses or smartphones can enhance human biological capabilities.

The term *"cyborg"* was officially coined in 1960 by Manfred E. Clynes and Nathan S. Kline to refer to a modified human capable of surviving in extraterrestrial environments [Clynes and Kline]. Space exploration is challenging for humans, and implementing various cyborg technologies could be crucial in mitigating risks, let alone merely enabling them. For example, to address the lack of oxygen in space travel, Clynes and Kline proposed an inverse fuel cell capable of recycling carbon dioxide into its components while preserving oxygen. Radiation exposure was another concern, with astronauts on extended missions experiencing significant exposure. Clynes and Kline envisioned a cyborg solution involving a sensor to detect radiation levels and an osmotic pump to automatically administer protective pharmaceuticals [Clynes and Kline].

What was initially just a technology for space exploration started to become part of a philosophy and a social moment. *"A Cyborg Manifesto,"* written by Donna Haraway in 1985, was a catalyst for that philosophy. The manifesto challenged the idea of rigid boundaries between technology and humankind, asserting that the interconnection between humans and technology has become too profound to separate. It encouraged embracing cyborgs as integral to human identity [Haraway].

Donna Haraway also presents a theory suggesting that humans have adopted cyborg qualities since the late 20th century, metaphorically speaking. When one views the mind and body as a unified entity, it becomes evident that technology plays a fundamental role in almost every facet of human life, effectively merging humanity with technology in every way. Elon Musk has also shared this idea in X and other public appearances, and Ray Kurzweil evokes it in the opening quote above. Kurzweil is a renowned futurist and theorist of the technological singularity. We will talk in detail about him in *Chapters 25* and *26*.

The following pages review the possibilities cyborg technology opens for human enhancement.

The Science Fiction of Cyborgs

Technology integration into the human body has long been a fascinating and apprehensive topic in Science Fiction. Cyborgs are a recurring motif in the genre. Two of the most renowned Science Fiction works involving cyborgs are *"The Terminator,"* a 1984 film directed by James Cameron, and *"Ghost in the Shell,"* a Japanese cyberpunk franchise that originated as a manga in 1989 by Masamune Shirow. *"Ghost in the Shell"* gained prominence through its 1995 animated film and a 2017 live-action adaptation starring Scarlett Johansson [Masamune] [Cameron].

Each of these works presents a distinct perspective on cyborg technology. "The Terminator" portrays a dystopian outlook, while *"Ghost in the Shell"* offers a more balanced view where individuals willingly choose to enhance their bodies with cybernetic enhancements. "The Terminator" franchise is a seminal example of a dystopian vision of cyborg technology. It envisions a bleak future where AI, represented by the malevolent Skynet, has gained self-awareness and unleashed an army of relentless cyborgs, the Terminators, to eradicate humanity. In the series, technology becomes uncontrollable and threatens to eradicate the human race. The relentless pursuit of technological advancement leads to a world where machines supersede their human creators, triggering a post-apocalyptic scenario. The turning point came when the military-programmed AI "*became aware.*"

Moreover, the depiction of cyborgs is characterized by a lack of humanity. These machines are ruthlessly efficient, emotionless, and indifferent to human suffering. Their existence raises ethical questions about the moral boundaries of technology and the loss of human empathy. The T-800 cyborg embodied by Arnold Schwarzenegger showcases a robotic assassin with minimal regard for human life. Through its dark portrayal of cyborg technology, "*The Terminator*" highlights the consequences of allowing machines to surpass human control.

In stark contrast, the "*Ghost in the Shell*" franchise presents a more balanced perspective on cyborg technology. As previously discussed in *Chapter 18,* Japanese culture, along with its predominant religions, Buddhism and Shinto, exhibits a remarkable openness towards integrating robots into societal norms.

In "*Ghost in the Shell,*" humans voluntarily enhance their bodies with cybernetic technology. The story revolves around Motoko Kusanagi, a cyborg law enforcement officer, who grapples with questions of identity and humanity as she navigates a world where the lines between human and machine become unclear. One of the central themes is the concept of the "*ghost,*" which refers to a person's consciousness or soul. In this universe, the "*ghost*" is preserved even as the body is augmented with cybernetic enhancements. This exploration of identity and selfhood is a recurring motif throughout the franchise, and it encourages viewers to ponder the implications of merging humanity with technology.

While "*The Terminator*" portrays technology as a threat to humanity, "*Ghost in the Shell*" suggests that individuals can maintain their essence and autonomy while embracing technology. We do not see the dystopian scenario presented in The Terminator as the most likely to arise, although the role of data and synthetic data in training AI algorithms certainly presents an entry point for human error or malevolence, with mankind "*hoisted by its own petard*" in failing to plan for the risks. More likely is the near-term, gradual threat posed by the humans that initially own and control the AI, training and pointing it in a direction that reflects their individual views, prejudices, and desire to control. Absolute power corrupts absolutely. We believe that it is imperative for everyone in Western societies who votes for political leadership to demand a specific viewpoint on AI policy and management at this juncture while the direction can still be fully shaped.

The Music of Brain-Computer Interfaces

The cornerstone of cyborg technology rests in its connection to the human brain. This link enables the brain to control various mechanical cyborg implants such as bionic limbs or enhanced senses. Additionally, there are alternative methods for integrating cyborg technology into the body that do not necessitate a connection to the brain, such as the insertion of a mechanical heart.

What adds to the potency of linking body implants to the brain is the capability for direct communication with computer systems, eliminating the need for physical movement, such as using a keyboard. This opens the door to a myriad of possibilities where human intelligence seamlessly integrates with AI. This advanced technology, known as Brain-Computer Interfaces (BCI), already exists.

A BCI connects the brain's electrical signals to an external device, such as a robot or computer. BCIs are frequently used to improve or restore human cognitive, motor, and sensory abilities. However, they have the potential to blur the distinction between the brain and machines.

One of the earliest instances of a functional BCI was demonstrated in the composition *"Music for Solo Performer"* in 1965 by American composer Alvin Lucier. This performance utilized an electroencephalogram (EEG) in conjunction with musical equipment such as amplifiers, filters, and a mixing board. The objective was to synchronize drumming with the brain waves, specifically alpha waves, of a person on the stage. A mechanism was activated to play the instruments in accordance with the vibrations of the alpha waves, and the resulting sound was emitted through loudspeakers [Straebel and Thoben].

Despite this and other antecedents, it was not until 1973 that the official term *"Brain-Computer Interface"* was introduced by Jacques Vidal, a professor at UCLA (University of California Los Angeles) who was researching brain activity under a grant from DARPA, which is the research agency of the US military, as we have seen in several previous chapters. In 1977, Vidal made an experiment that marked the first practical application of a BCI. With an EEG, Vidal was able to move a cursor on a computer screen, guiding it through a maze. That was the beginning of the story we narrate in this chapter [Vidal].

Invasive, Partially Invasive, and Non-Invasive BCI

There are three kinds of BCI methods: fully invasive, partially invasive, and non-invasive.

First, fully invasive BCIs require surgery to implant electrodes beneath the scalp so that they transmit brain signals. The primary advantage of this approach lies in its ability to provide highly accurate readings. It also carries certain drawbacks, including potential side effects from the surgical procedure. Following the surgery, the formation of scar tissue may occur, leading to a weakening of brain signals. Furthermore, there is a risk that the body may reject the implanted electrodes, resulting in potential medical complications. These are perhaps downsides that further technological development in materials science and electrical engineering can solve.

Secondly, partially invasive BCIs are surgically implanted between the actual bone of the skull and the brain tissue instead of embedded inside the so-called "grey matter," which is the primary brain tissue. These devices offer a slightly weaker signal resolution than the previous method but are still superior compared to non-invasive BCIs, as they are not affected by signal distortion caused by the deflection and deformation of signals in cranial bone tissue. Moreover, partially invasive BCIs present a reduced risk of brain scars compared to fully invasive BCIs. The most common partially invasive approaches are Electrocorticography (ECoG) and endovascular BCIs.

Endovascular BCIs use an electrode that can be inserted via the vascular system using an intravenous catheter in a major vein located in the upper part of the brain next to the motor cortex. This vicinity to the motor cortex enables the electrode to capture neural signals with relatively good quality [Opie]. The second method—ECoG—measures brain electrical activity from the surface of the brain. The electrodes are positioned above the cortex, beneath the outermost membranes that surround the brain. ECoG presents advantages such as a superior signal-to-noise ratio, high spatial resolution, a broad frequency range, and minimal training required for individuals to learn how to use ECoG implants [Donoghue].

Third and finally, non-invasive BCIs represent the most prevalent current interfaces, with electroencephalography (EEG) being particularly common due to its ease of use and lack of surgical procedures. Nevertheless, they come with certain limitations, such as poor spatial resolution, challenges with higher-frequency signals, and occasional requirements for extensive training. Recent studies, however, suggest that EEG has the potential to rival invasive BCIs in performance. For instance, in 2011, researchers employed EEG to guide a virtual helicopter through a 3D space, successfully navigating it through an obstacle course. The patient utilized "*motor imagination*" to control the helicopter. This means that he thought about the movements of his hands on the helicopter's wheel in his mind without actually activating his muscles [Yuan et al.]. Furthermore, in 2021, other researchers highlighted the effectiveness of EEG in the rehabilitation of muscle movement in patients who had suffered a stroke, particularly in upper limbs or hands [Mansour et al.]. Apart from EEG, other forms of non-invasive BCIs include magnetoencephalography (MEG) and Magnetic Resonance Imaging (MRI).

Some other experimental techniques are much more sophisticated than the three conventional BCI approaches above, more concretely, the visionary concept of *"Neural Dust."* This concept was introduced in 2011 by scientists from Berkeley. Neural Dust is composed of minuscule devices designed to function as wirelessly powered nerve sensors that are distributed across the whole body, essentially constituting a form of BCI. These sensors would investigate, observe, or manipulate nerves and muscles, allowing for remote monitoring of neural activities. The dust nodules are sensor nodes between 10-100 μm^3. These sensors can employ various mechanisms for power and communication, such as traditional radiofrequency (RF) and ultrasonics. There is also a sub-cranial interrogator positioned inside the brain. This interrogator serves the dual purpose of supplying power to the sensors and establishing a communication link with them [Rabaey]. This technology is still experimental but could be revolutionary for the future of human-machine interaction because it would be relatively easy to implement just by injecting the Neural Dust into the blood, and it would capture high-quality signals.

Neural Dust remains a bit of a stretch—-at this moment. The level of nanotechnology required is not yet available. However, there have been some practical attempts to make BCI a widespread technology, with Neuralink being the most well-known.

Neuralink, from Science Fiction to FDA Approval

Neuralink, founded by Elon Musk in 2016, is actively developing partially-invasive BCIs. Neuralink's goals include short-term device development for severe brain diseases and long-term human enhancement [Ahmed et al.]. Elon Musk was inspired by the concept of *"neural lace"* from Iain M. Banks' novels *"The Culture,"* which will be discussed in the following chapter.

Founded by Elon Musk in 2016, Neuralink is actively developing partially-invasive BCIs. Neuralink ambitions ranged from developing devices to address severe brain diseases in the short term to ultimately pursuing human enhancement [Ahmed et al.]. Elon Musk's interest in this area was partly inspired by the notion of a "neural lace" found in the fictional world of *"The Culture,"* a collection of novels written by Iain M. Banks that we will talk about in the next chapter.

Moreover, Musk believes the Neuralink will be *"something analogous to a video game, like a saved game situation, where you are able to resume and upload your last state"* and *"address brain injuries or spinal injuries and make up for whatever lost capacity somebody has with a chip"* [Ivan]. Musk's ultimate goal is to establish *"symbiosis with AI,"* driven by his concern, and ours, that *"unchecked AI poses an existential threat to humanity."* By creating a link between the human brain and AI, he thinks it is possible to better align the values and self-motivations of humanity with those of AI.

Musk envisioned the neural lace as a *"digital layer above the cortex,"* achieved through a partially-invasive electrode introduced into a vein or artery using a *"sewing machine-like"* mechanism [Glaser]. In order to do that, Neuralink uses ultra-thin probes between 4 to 6 μm made primarily of biocompatible material like slender gold or platinum conductors. These probes are implanted inside the brain using a neurosurgical robot that Neuralink has specifically developed to mitigate tissue damage.

In May 2023, Neuralink received FDA approval to conduct clinical trials on humans [Neuralink]. One year ago, the FDA had initially rejected the application due to safety concerns related to the possibility of fine wires shifting within the brain, safe removal without damaging brain tissue, and miscellaneous doubts regarding the lithium battery. Neuralink began human trials in September 2023 under an investigational FDA exemption. In January 2024, Musk announced that a patient had successfully implanted a Neuralink device and was on the mend.

Neuralink is a controversial company, much like practically anything Elon Musk does, and it has been embroiled in controversies regarding its work culture and its use of animal experimentation. However, it is the first practical approach to industrializing BCIs, which could have immense consequences for humankind.

Sensing the Future: From Vision to Voice

Combining BCI with other cyborg implants has huge potential. In the next few sections, we will cover some of the cyborg implants that are already in some stage of development and that we believe could impact our future the most.

Importantly, most of these ground zero cyborg attempts have started as benevolent medical methods to recover capabilities for patients who have lost them in an accident or were born with disabilities. However, as technology advances, more of these implants can be used to bestow augmented capabilities upon individuals without any physiological problem for purposes beyond mere recovery of lost function. These superhuman abilities could include, for example, night vision, extremely strong mechanical arms and legs, exceptionally acute hearing, and exoskeletal resistance to bullets. For example, in the world of comics, we note how Stan Lee's, Joe Simon's, and Jack *"King"* Kirby's superhero character Bucky Barnes was recast in a modern format as The Winter Soldier in 2005, with a cyborg arm, an example of what is actually possible within this emerging technology. *With current technology, this is actually possible in real life.*

In this section, we will begin exploring some of these applications, commencing with the senses of vision and hearing and with the ability to talk.

The human sense that has witnessed the most significant progress is, without a doubt, vision. Vision implants are surgically implanted through BCI directly into the brain's grey matter during neurosurgery. These fully-invasive devices produce signals of superior quality because they are directly connected to the grey matter.

In origin, electronic eye implants started as a restorative effort to address non-congenital acquired blindness. William Dobelle, an American doctor, successfully developed a functional BCI to restore sight in 1978. Dobelle's initial prototype was implanted into a man who had lost his sight in adulthood. The system included cameras mounted on glasses that transmit signals to a BCI implant with electrodes inserted into the visual cortex. Thanks to this implant, the patient could perceive light and discern shades of grey at a low frame rate and in a restricted field of vision. After this initial success, Dobelle continued working on bionic eyes for 25 years and developed a new-generation, much more effective eye prosthetics implant. This new implant had a much better mapping of light across the visual field. The impact was very effective, and in 2002, one of his blind patients was able to drive carefully around a parking area with his partially restored eyesight [Tuller].

Another example of the cyborgization of vision is retinal implants. Retinal implants work for individuals afflicted by inflammation of the retina and age-related vision loss. In a retinal implant, a specialized camera, often affixed to the subject's glasses frames, transforms visual information into a pattern of electrical stimulation. Within the patient's eye, a microchip then proceeds to stimulate the retina with electric signals using this pattern, activating the neural terminals responsible for transmitting the image to the brain's visual cortex. This way, the image becomes perceivable to the user [Weiland].

Moving to the ability to talk, vocal cord implants work in a very similar way to retinal implants. These implants aid individuals who have lost their vocal cords in regaining the ability to speak, providing a much more natural-sounding alternative to robotic voice simulators, like the one the late Professor Stephen Hawking used. The process initiates with a surgical redirection of the nerve governing voice and sound production to a neck muscle near a sensor capable of detecting its neural signals. These signals are then directed to a processor responsible for controlling the pitch and timing of the device that generates vibrations in the air inside the throat. The vibrations result in a multi-tonal sound that can be articulated into words by the mouth.

Cochlear implants, which are the most widely used hearing devices, are another form of cyborgization. Cochlear implants work by converting sounds into electrical signals. A microphone on the external device captures sounds, which are then processed into digital signals and transmitted to an internal implant. The implant stimulates the auditory nerve directly, allowing individuals with severe hearing loss or deafness to perceive sound.

BCIs in Motion: Restoring Mobility through Prosthetics

Motor implants are another important current BCI application. BCIs are used to give paralyzed people their mobility back or to provide them with interfaces so they can operate robotic limbs or computers. Over the past 30 years, numerous successful cases of motor implants have been reported.

Jesse Sullivan is one of the pioneers in controlling two completely robotic arms through a nerve-muscle implant. In 2001, Sullivan, an electrician, underwent the amputation of both his arms at the shoulder after inadvertently coming into contact with a high-power cable, which he was fortunate to survive. Approximately seven weeks post-amputation, Sullivan got bionic prostheses implanted, which he successfully uses to manage his daily tasks. Initially, these prostheses were controlled by neural signals originating at the amputation sites. However, the amputated area was susceptible to pain, and the sensors were subsequently relocated to the left side of his chest. Thanks to these implants, Sullivan was able to do his day-to-day tasks with relative ease [Murray].

Another successful example is the tetraplegic patient Matt Nagle. In 2005, Nagle was also able to manipulate an artificial hand using a BCI chip implant in the motor cortex region responsible for arm movement. Nagle successfully operated this robotic arm through the power of his thoughts by merely thinking about hand movements. Nagle was able to handle a TV set and a computer cursor and switch lights on and off, among other things [BBC].

These early prosthetic examples were tailored to individual cases, like Sullivan and Nagle, and it was remarkable to have been as effective out-of-the-gate as it was. Since then, contemporary prosthetic applications have evolved into commercial ventures that manufacture standardized prosthetic limbs. Lower limbs are generally easier to do than upper limbs because they do not involve the complexity of articulating the hand. For example, C-Leg is a prosthetics product introduced in 2009 by a German company called Otto Bock HealthCare. It is a viable solution for individuals who have undergone leg amputation due to injury or illness. The initial C-Leg models were typically attached to the remaining part of the amputated limb using a socket and suspension system. Moreover, they did not directly interface with the user's nerves of any kind of BCI. However, they incorporated sensors into the artificial leg, significantly enhancing walking functionality. The goal was to mimic the user's natural walking pattern as it existed before the amputation [Tran et al.].

Some of the current commercial prosthetics products take it one step further from the initial C-Legs. For example, the Swedish orthopedic company Integrum has developed a prosthetics system called OPRA for lower limbs and e-OPRA for upper limbs. Unlike C-Leg, these implants are surgically anchored and integrated into the remaining skeletal structure of the amputated limb. Moreover, they are also connected to the nervous terminals so that the user can move the implant just by thinking about moving it. In addition, e-OPRA is currently undergoing clinical trials to supply the central nervous system with sensory feedback using temperature and pressure sensors integrated into the fingertips of the prosthesis. This would allow the user not only to move the robotic hand but also to feel the tact of objects with it [Axe].

In any case, the direction the technology is pointing is clear: starting with early design and facilitation of simple tasks, progressing to facilitation of more complex tasks, incorporating advancements in materials science and AI to replicate all lost functions, and finally eclipsing the original performance that it was designed to fully replicate. Commercial prosthetic solutions broaden access to prosthetics for a larger population, offering reduced risks and lower costs.

Mobility prosthetics will continue to be predominantly utilized by individuals who have experienced limb loss. While the idea of prosthetic limbs designed for augmentation rather than replacement is not implausible, it requires someone to undergo the traumatic process of amputation solely for an upgrade to a more powerful limb, which is a difficult trade-off decision. That said, if you must have an amputation, who would not agree to an improvement in the rebuild process? The general population is now disadvantaged. A more feasible overall scenario involves external robotic arms detached from the body, activated by a person's thoughts through a BCI, serving as an external extension of their own body.

Future cyborgs that look for augmentation could look like British scientist Kevin Warwick. Warwick embodies the archetype of an eccentric scientist, showcasing a genuine dedication to the concept of cyborgization. Warwick invested his life in this pursuit, implanting multiple cyborg systems into his own body to test the boundaries of technological integration. In 2002, he started implanting 100 electrodes into his nervous system, aiming to establish a direct connection between his nervous system and the internet to explore potential improvements. Warwick conducted a series of experiments, like manipulating a robotic hand over the internet with his nervous system and receiving tactile feedback from the hand's fingertip sensor [Warwick].

Beyond Words: Connecting Minds through Telepathy

Telepathy, also known as silent communication, has been a focus of research by the US Army to develop telepathic communication devices since the 1960s. The technology involved in implementing telepathy through BCI is similar to that involved in motor implants. Early cases of this kind of cyborgization involved both communication and mobility.

Johnny Ray was a veteran of the Vietnam War who had experienced a stroke. Despite being fully conscious, Ray could not talk or move. In 1997, he got an electronic device implanted near the affected area of his brain, restoring some degree of movement to his body. The implant was designed to interface with his brain, particularly the part that controlled his left hand. The electrode utilized a tiny glass cone filled with nerve growth factors and coiled gold wires. This way, the electrode could amplify neural signals, converting them into radio waves and transmitting them to an FM receiver. The signals were then broadcast to a nearby computer, enabling Johnny Ray to control the computer cursor and communicate in writing [Baker].

Most notably, Kevin Warwick—the eccentric scientist we just discussed—gained recognition for successfully implementing the first telepathic communication between his and his wife's nervous systems in 2018. The Warwicks utilized entirely end-to-end electronic systems between their brains without any mechanical system in between. The experiment received significant media coverage [Warwick].

Since the Warwicks' experiment, there have been significant advances in telepathic communications. For example, in 2021, a quadriplegic patient was able to input English sentences at a rate of approximately 18 words per minute by using an invasive BCI implanted in the motor cortex of his brain. He envisioned forming letters with hand movements without actually physically executing them. The system was then capable of identifying and capturing these signals and transferring them to a computer. Then, this computer applied Machine Learning techniques like hidden Markov models and recurrent neural networks to decode the words. We discussed these models in *Chapter 8*. This represents the generation of language models predating the advent of generative AI, which Alexa and Siri employ. In addition, using similar techniques combining BCI with language models, two other studies achieved unprecedented rates of 62 and 78 words per minute, respectively, in 2023 [Wilson]. For reference, an average person talks between 110 to 150 words per minute. That means that these telepathic systems are only half as fast as a normal person, which is still remarkable, taking into account the complexity of imagining writing strokes in the mind. Again, the step changes we already see in technology clearly point in the direction of fully equaling and then surpassing human output.

Partially invasive techniques have also been utilized for telepathic communication, but they have a lower signal level, making them slower. For example, in 2020, ECoG signals were used to decode speech from epilepsy patients who had implants over the lateral sides of the brain. The decoding process achieved an impressive word error rate of only 3% when analyzing a set of fifty sentences encompassing a dictionary of 250 distinct words [Makin et al.].

Finally, non-invasive BCIs in contact with the participants' scalps have also been researched. In 2014, they were able to encode words from a patient who was imagining stroke movements. Hovering the communication rate was still slow. Imagine having a non-invasive communication cap that would enable two paired people to communicate telepathically without any kind of surgery. The range of possibilities that would open up for workplace collaboration would be amazing—and for dystopian thought control as well. Technology remains a two-sided coin.

Bionic Organs: from the Printer to the Body

In addition to applications of BCI, other kinds of cyborgization that do not require BCI are also possible. This is particularly applicable to the majority of bionic organs beyond the senses and motor systems. Bionic hearts are a clear example and one of the artificial organs that has undergone significant advancements through the application of cyborg technology.

In 2014, researchers created a device capable of sustaining continuous heart function that was designed to replace traditional pacemakers. This device employed electrodes and sensors to track and regulate the average heart rate. The electrodes were arranged in a way they could expand and contract without breaking with the palpitations of the heart. Unlike conventional pacemakers, which are standard for all patients, bionic hearts are covered by a custom-made elastic glove specifically designed for each patient through advanced imaging technology.

There has been a significant evolution of bionic hearts, progressing from those that merely pace to those that mimic the entire organ. Furthermore, some of the components can be 3D printed, rendering the technology low-cost and easily replicable. One of the challenges is overcoming the complexities of integrating a synthetic heart into the human body and connecting it to the right arteries and veins in what is a complex surgical operation [Haddad et al.]. As of December 2023, two commercially accessible artificial heart devices are available. Both of them are intended for temporary use, specifically for total heart failure patients awaiting the transplantation of a human heart within less than a year.

Another example of a cyborg organ is the artificial pancreas. The artificial pancreas acts as a replacement for the body's insufficient natural insulin production, particularly in patients with Type 1 diabetes. Current systems merge a continuous glucose tracking module with a remote-controllable insulin pump, establishing a feedback loop that autonomously regulates insulin doses based on the present blood glucose levels.

But the list does not end here. There are many artificial organs apart from the heart and pancreas. For example, techniques for bladder replacement involve redirecting urine flow or creating bladder-like pouches from intestinal tissue. In treating erectile dysfunction, corpora cavernosa can be replaced with manually inflatable penile implants, a drastic measure for complete impotence cases. For liver failure, artificial liver devices can be employed to bridge the gap until transplant and to support the regeneration of the liver. These bionic livers use biological cells, known as stem cells, which assist in the regrowth of the liver. Moreover, artificial lungs are currently under development and show promising potential. Finally, artificial ovaries address reproductive challenges caused by cancer treatments.

In short, artificial mechanical organs are emerging as a feasible and cost-effective option for transplantation, free from the limitations imposed by donor availability. This has profound implications for making healthcare more accessible to a wider population as well as creating improvements over naturally occurring human body components.

The Democratization of Cyborgs: Wearables and Injectables

BCI and bionic organs have huge potential, but they are very complicated to insert because the body has specific designs that do not contemplate retrofits. Complicated surgical procedures are inevitably required. There are also other kinds of cyborg devices that are simple to insert and remove: wearables, injectable devices, and stickers. These forms of cyborg implants allow anyone to easily become a cyborg, which we believe can lead to the widespread adoption of cyborg technology as a fashionable and distinctive trend.

Undoubtedly, the most visually striking and spectacular examples of wearables are those worn by British artist Neil Harbison. Since 2004, Harbisson has transformed into a cyborg by installing a cyborg antenna in his head. Remarkably, his cyborg status is recognized by the UK authorities, as his antenna appears in his 2004 passport photograph.

Neil Harbisson's antenna is not implanted directly into his body or brain. Instead, it is an external device that he wears. The antenna is attached to a unique mount that is surgically implanted onto his skull. The antenna itself contains sensors that can detect colors beyond the human visual spectrum, including infrared and ultraviolet. These color signals are then converted into audible vibrations that Neil can perceive through bone conduction. The vibrations are transmitted through the mount to the bone in his skull, allowing him to "*hear*" colors [Harbisson].

Harbisson is also a global advocate for cyborg rights. He co-founded the Cyborg Foundation in 2004. This foundation's primary objectives include expanding human senses and capabilities by developing cybernetic body extensions, promoting cybernetics in cultural events, and advocating for cyborg rights.

Harbisson is an example of this new cyborg identity. In 2012, Harbisson conveyed that he began feeling like a cyborg when he realized the merging of his brain with the software, granting him an additional sense. For that reason, Harbisson later co-founded the Transspecies Society in 2017, supporting individuals with non-human identities in pursuing unique senses and new organs. Far ahead of the curve, Harbisson is an example of the seismic shock in the Human-AI interface that is just beginning to arrive in our society.

There are also other less spectacular examples than Harbisson that illustrate this seismic movement. Within the enterprise world, there have been clear applications of injectable devices. These are chips that have to be inserted inside the skin, although they are easily removable. While the frequent subject of conspiracy theories as to their function, the fact is that the devices exist.

In 2017, an American technology company called Three Square Market made headlines for offering voluntary RFID (Radiofrequency Identification) chip implants to its employees. The program was optional, and employees who chose to participate had small RFID chips implanted between their thumb and forefinger. These RFID chips could be used to perform various tasks, such as accessing the company's facilities, logging into computers, and making purchases in the break room. The goal was to explore the convenience and efficiency of RFID technology in the workplace. Importantly, employees were not unhappy about these devices. On the contrary, over half of the company's employees received these implants, and nearly 100% reported satisfaction and perceived improvement in operation. Moreover, this type of injectable device received FDA approval in 2004 [Gillies].

Numerous applications can be considered for injectables, such as payment systems, child monitoring, health monitoring, sports and fitness monitoring, access control, and many others. Easy to implant and remove, we will certainly see more of them in the coming decades.

The third type of easily installable cyborg implant consists of electronic stickers. BodyNet, introduced in 2019 by Stanford engineers, is particularly interesting. BodyNet utilizes wireless RFID-based sensors that adhere to the skin like stickers. These sensors are designed to be comfortable, stretchable, and battery-free. They can track various physiological indicators, such as pulse, respiration, and even muscle movements, by detecting how the skin stretches and contracts. The readings are wirelessly transmitted to a receiver attached to the person's clothing. BodyNets are designed for utilization in medical environments, particularly for monitoring individuals with sleep disorders or heart conditions. Ongoing developments include the addition of extra sensors to track factors such as body temperature and stress. Ultimately, the goal is to create a comprehensive array of wireless sensors that work with smart clothing to monitor a wide range of health indicators accurately [Chu et al.].

These three easily implantable technologies could play a leading role in democratizing cyborg implants across different strata of society, noting that the costs associated with other types of cyborgization associated with replacement or augmentation are consequential and thus obtainable by the minority. People will probably start using these low-cost implants that can be removed easily in case they change their minds or see defects. As society becomes more accustomed to them, and individuals like Harbisson begin identifying themselves with this cyborg identity, society will become more open to heavier and more transformational implants. This has both positive and negative implications for society. But human society will no longer be the same.

21. AI Supercharges Synthetic Biology

"If you get a personal genome, you should be able to get personal cell lines, stem cell derived from your adult tissues, that allow you to bring together synthetic biology and the sequencing so that you can repair parts of your body as you age or repair things that were inherited disorders."

George M Church

Synthetic Biologist
Interview in ThinkBig.com [Church]
2017

Synthetic biology (SynBio) is an interdisciplinary field that integrates principles from biology, engineering, and, most importantly, AI to design and construct new biological systems or redesign existing ones for practical applications. It employs engineering principles on living organisms and allows scientists to manipulate genetic material and other biological components. At its core, synthetic biology seeks to treat biological components as interchangeable building blocks, similar to the way engineers approach computer design with separate individual electronic circuits.

Synthetic biology techniques have been applied to engineer microorganisms capable of converting renewable resources like plant biomass or algae into biofuels such as ethanol or biodiesel that can be used as a replacement for fossil fuels. Synthetic biology has also been used to design engineered organisms, like bacteria or plants, that can be programmed to absorb specific pollutants, thereby facilitating the cleanup of contaminated sites and contributing to environmental conservation.

The pharmaceutical industry is a chief beneficiary of technological progress, using synthetic biology advances to design microorganisms capable of synthesizing complex pharmaceutical compounds and drugs. This technique accelerates drug production processes in a cost-effective way and could hold the potential to increase supply and accessibility to essential medications. Synthetic biology also plays a pivotal role in designing and synthesizing proteins, such as enzymes or antibodies, with enhanced functions that would open avenues for applications in medicine and industrial processes.

In addition, synthetic biology is venturing into the ambitious realms of creating artificial organs and even supporting and creating novel life forms. By combining biological components with synthetic materials, scientists aim to engineer functional organs for transplantation, addressing the shortage of donor organs and improving the success rates of transplantation procedures. Likewise, scientists are exploring the application of synthetic biology to design and produce living organisms with unique capabilities not found in natural organisms. These synthetic organisms could be engineered for specific industrial, medical, or environmental purposes. Today, we already have examples of non-naturally occurring organisms being fully bio-engineered, so the direction in which the discipline is hurdling becomes quite clear.

For example, there are synthetic yeast strains designed to produce specific flavors and aromas, leading to innovative beer and wine products. Companies like Ginkgo Bioworks have been active in this area. Synthetic algae have been engineered for biofuel, with players like Synthetic Genomics, in collaboration with ExxonMobil, having worked on genetically modifying algae strains to enhance their oil-producing capabilities. Likewise, synthetic bacteria have been engineered for drug production, with companies like Genentech and Novartis having engineered bacteria to produce pharmaceuticals such as insulin and HGH (Human Growth Hormone.) Synthetic bacteria have also been used for environmental cleanup, with several, including Bioremediation Services, having developed them to break down pollutants in soil and water. Finally, companies such as Pivot Bio have engineered synthetic microbes to act as biofertilizers, helping improve nutrient uptake in plants and reduce the need for traditional chemical fertilizers.

The following pages will present the potential for modifying the biological nature of human beings through synthetic biology when AI is applied. We see the impact of synthetic biology and AI solving the lingering question of *"how"* interlacing will mechanically occur.

The Science Fiction of Synthetic Biology

Synthetic Biology is arguably one of the most revolutionary applications of AI. It has the unmitigated potential to transform the essence of human beings and our present ecosystems by altering their biological fundamentals, allowing people to live longer, resist diseases, and acquire superhuman abilities with specifically designed organoids. Moreover, integrating electronic or machine-learning elements into human biological circuits opens a solid avenue for human-AI interlacing and, in our view, solves a concrete "*how to*" problem that is necessary for interlacing to occur. Furthermore, synthetic biology holds the key to creating new forms of life, some of which would never have developed.

To explore the implications of synthetic biology in humanity, we can turn to two Science Fiction works for insight: the film "*Gattaca*" directed by Andrew Niccol in 1997, and the novel "*The Windup Girl*" written by Paolo Bacigalupi in 2009 [Niccol] [Bacigalupi]. While Ridley Scott's 1982 film "*Blade Runner*" presents Replicants, the most iconic example of biologically engineered entities in Science Fiction, we have chosen "*The Windup Girl*" instead because it presents a more carefully developed and multifaceted perspective of this intriguing possibility.

These curated Science Fiction works offer two unique and thought-provoking perspectives on the potential consequences of manipulating life at its fundamental level. Gattaca's primary focus lies in harnessing synthetic biology to enhance the human race, whereas "*The Windup Girl*" utilizes synthetic biology to craft a subservient class of individuals. "*Gattaca*" paints a dystopian vision of a future where genetic engineering has given rise to an overtly rigid and stratified society. Individuals are sorted into a hierarchy of classes based on their genetic makeup, with "*valids*" who are genetically enhanced and "*invalids*" who are deemed genetically inferior. This genetic discrimination permeates all aspects of life, with the invalid protagonist forced to assume a valid identity to pursue his dream of becoming an astronaut. The film also explores the themes of identity and destiny as the protagonist grapples with societal norms and expectations, ultimately questioning the very essence of society and the human being.

Synthetic biology's dedicated ability to manipulate genetic information forces us to ponder the boundaries of human identity and the ethics of designing and selecting genes. As we have pointed out earlier, we believe that the economic costs, timing, and selection factors associated with any element of interlacing will inevitably mean that it happens asymmetrically within society, with some being left behind either by self-selection or fiat. One of the striking similarities between "*Gattaca*" and the real-world implications of synthetic biology is the likelihood of a genetic divide within society. As synthetic biology advances, there is a high potential for a division between those who can afford genetic enhancements and those who cannot, at least in its early phases, enabling the possibility that those who are first may stop the process before enabling those who come second, further perpetuating inequality in a way that self-compounds. Human nature reflects in consumer transactions—for example, buying a Cadillac or BMW as a functional piece of engineered machinery is a social status symbol that not everyone can have. Synthetic biology products will be a far more absolute and far-reaching reflection.

We note that eugenics, along with the moral and ethical polemics that accompany it, are embedded in any discussion of synthetic biology. The technology makes it not only easy to understand and modify human genes to even subtle differences but also to obviate those differences and their genetic factors. Furthermore, it facilitates the mathematical ranking of capabilities and outcomes, thus determining the relative value of the genetics involved. The mathematical reality is that under a specified set of conditions, some genetic material is more valuable than others. This might sound Machiavellian on the surface because AI will not necessarily have ethical values embedded in it. This omnipresent element of synthetic biology returns us briefly to a central tenet of this book, namely that it is up to us, now, not later, to set the grounding rules for responsible AI in order to avoid a purely dystopian future.

In "*The Windup Girl,*" the focus shifts to synthetic biology's impact on the environment and biodiversity. "*The Windup Girl*" is set in 23rd-century Thailand in a post-oil world. The novel envisions a future where synthetic biology is central to food production and energy generation. Genetically engineered organisms, known as "*New People,*" are designed to serve various purposes, including labor and entertainment. Soon, in the novel, the lines between artificial and natural life start to be blurred, leading to innumerable questions and contradictions. We discuss the impact of AI in general on irrevocably distorting the line between truth and falsehood in *Chapter 23.*

One of the critical differences between "*The Windup Girl*" and "*Gattaca*" lies in the scope of genetic manipulation. In "*The Windup Girl,*" synthetic biology extends beyond human genetic engineering to encompass the entire ecosystem. This raises ethical concerns about manipulating the environment and biodiversity for economic or other gain, with potentially unwanted ecological consequences. In the novel, corporations exploit synthetic biology for profit, resulting in a loss of agricultural diversity and dependence on engineered crops.

The novel also delves into the intersection of spirituality and synthetic biology as the engineered protagonist, a member of the "*New People,*" prompts discussions about the nature of her soul. Characters in the story ponder whether these synthetic people possess spirituality or consciousness, highlighting the interplay between religion and the ethical considerations of creating life through genetic manipulation, a topic we also cover later in *Chapter 26.*

Synthetic biology has the potential to improve our interactions with nature, including our biology, environment, and food (as suggested by these two novels). The other side of the technology coin is far more ominous, with implications of eugenics and mankind's long and troublesome history with the concept of genetic differences translating to value differences among humans or unnatural ecosystem manipulation for profit. *Simply put, those who control this technology at scale are poised to gain substantial and perhaps absolute control over others.*

In another vein, for those familiar with the Captain America character created by Timely (later Marvel) Comics in 1941, the so-called "*super soldier serum*" that transformed sickly Steve Rogers into the greatest fighting machine of his era points us to both expect military applications of synthetic biology and to foresee constant subterfuge, escalation and machination to control its advance. We have noted throughout the book the key role of DARPA at various points in the evolution of AI and note that the Chinese military is actively involved in the development of synthetic biology and the collection of Western-generated data sets on population biology, a topic we discuss in *Chapter 24.*

Who is to say if a real-life Captain America would seek to preserve our values or not? There are individuals with psychographic profiles, like Steve Rogers, and those who obtain quite different motives. The huge power embedded in synthetic biology makes us either the masters of creation or the masters of disequilibrium. We will delve into this in *Chapter 26* when discussing Superintelligence. In the wake of geopolitical brinkmanship over AI technology, perhaps Captain America is needed regardless.

Understanding the Basics of Biology

Before delving into the application of AI in synthetic biology, it is essential to provide an introduction to the fundamentals of biology and the complexities of life processes. Synthetic biology focuses on modifying or synthesizing these processes.

Life as we know it is a wondrous phenomenon that is fundamentally built upon the functioning of cells. These microscopic units are the fundamental components of all living beings, whether single-celled microorganisms or complex multicellular organisms like humans.

The nucleus at the core of every cell is a crucial component housing genetic information. Within the nucleus resides DNA (Deoxyribonucleic Acid), which carries the genetic instructions to develop, function, and reproduce all living organisms. DNA is a remarkable molecule with a double-helix structure formed by a sequence of molecules called nucleotides. These nucleotides are the basic building blocks of DNA. In nature, there are only four types of nitrogenous bases: adenine (A), thymine (T), cytosine (C), and guanine (G). The nucleotides are like the letters of the language in which life is encoded. The sequence of these bases ultimately encodes the genetic codes that determine an organism's characteristics and functions.

Genes are specific DNA sequences that carry the instructions for synthesizing proteins. Each gene has a particular sequence of bases that serves as a code, directing the cell to create a specific protein. Proteins are complex and large molecules formed by chains of basic units called amino acids. Each sequence of bases in the DNA corresponds to a specific sequence of amino acids in the protein. RNA (Ribonucleic Acid) plays an intermediary role in translating genetic information from DNA into proteins.

There are many kinds of proteins. Among them, enzymes are particularly important because they serve as vital catalysts for biochemical reactions, aid in cellular communication, and contribute to the structural integrity and functionality of cells and organisms.

Synthetic Biology and Artificial Intelligence

Synthetic biology deals with the highly complex molecular structures of proteins and genes. While it is theoretically possible to design these molecules manually or with simple computer software, AI is indispensable to do it at scale. AI algorithms can analyze vast datasets, predict potential outcomes of genetic configurations and modifications, and optimize the design of biological circuits for specific functions. They can also assist in identifying patterns and correlations within biological data, facilitating the discovery of novel genetic combinations that may yield desired traits. The incorporation of AI into synthetic biology not only accelerates design processes but also improves the precision of crafting synthetic biological systems with specific functionalities without too many trial-and-error cycles.

Synthetic biology applications often rely on AI simulation models of complex chains of biochemical reactions, which provide advanced insights into how biological systems would behave before they are actually constructed. Through simulations, it becomes possible to represent all biomolecular interactions involved in processes like the transcription of genes when cells reproduce or the translation of genes to proteins. Moreover, when designing a novel biological system that does not exist in nature yet, AI-driven simulations are the only way to understand how those systems would behave.

Biological molecules are so huge and complex that even by knowing their structure, it is not easy to know how they behave. One of the most practical applications of AI is, therefore, predicting the behaviors of segments of proteins, DNA, RNA, or mRNA (messenger RNA, famous because it was used in the COVID-19 vaccines) based on their sequence.

Deep neural networks stand out as the optimal Machine Learning algorithms for synthetic biology, given their scalability and capacity to replicate complex nonlinear relationships between inputs and outputs. In particular, Convolutional Neural Networks (CNNs) are employed to predict how these genomic segments would function. In the previous chapters, we mentioned that Recurrent Neural Networks (RNN) are used for sequence data, and CNNs are used for images, which appears to be a contradiction with this information but is not. CNNs work well for molecules and genome sequences because their functionality depends on their shape; in that sense, molecules resemble an image with a particular shape.

Finally, labeling synthetic biology data so that AI algorithms can be trained is frequently more costly than in other domains because it demands specialized knowledge and, at times, end-to-end data collection processes in the laboratory. This high cost poses a challenge, especially for deep learning models that depend on extensive training data. To address this issue, there is a growing research interest in labeling data automatically and in generating simulated training data using Generative AI. Simulated or synthetic data, though not derived from actual biology experiments, could be realistic enough to train neural networks effectively. The ongoing research on Artificial General Intelligence (AGI) also places substantial emphasis on automatic AI feedback, labeling, and generation of synthetic data. We covered this in detail in *Chapter* 9.

Sequencing and Synthesizing Genetic Material

This section delves into some of the applications of synthetic biology, starting with sequencing and synthesizing genes.

The precise order of nucleotide bases in a DNA molecule is called DNA Sequencing. Scientists started mapping the human genome—our DNA sequence—in 1990, and after 13 years of work, the whole human genome was successfully mapped by 2003. Once that gigantic task was completed, subsequent initiatives focused on mapping the genomes of other organisms, ranging from fruit flies and mice to economically important crops. The outcomes of large-scale genome sequencing projects contribute extensively to our understanding of genetic diversity, evolution, and the molecular basis of many diseases [Nurk et al.].

Apart from sequencing the DNA, it is also possible to synthesize DNA with a sequence dictated by a template. This is called synthetic genomics. After the synthesis process, the newly created DNA molecules are assembled into complete genomes and transplanted into living cells, effectively substituting the genetic material of the host cell and altering its metabolic processes. This approach first demonstrated its potential by synthesizing multiple virus genomes like hepatitis C and polio in 2000 and 2002, respectively. Notably, among the earliest organisms generated in this manner were infectious viruses [Couzin].

Synthetic genomics has traditionally been very expensive, but recent advancements have enabled cost-effective, large-scale modifications of genetic material. Firstly, Polymerase Chain Reaction (PCR), a laboratory technique used to amplify and produce copies of a specific DNA sequence, has become a fundamental tool in molecular biology. The term PCR has become unfortunately familiar to us all, primarily due to the Covid-19 pandemic in 2020. The second advancement is DNA mismatch error correction, which identifies and repairs errors that occur during DNA replication when a cell divides. Finally, a third advancement that helps reduce cost is the use of modularity engineering principles. Modularity involves the use of standardized components, such as DNA parts, that can be easily extracted, replaced, or combined to create diverse biological functions. This approach enables the construction of complex biological systems by assembling smaller, interchangeable modules, facilitating the design and modification of biological systems [Beardall].

DNA synthesis has advanced significantly, enabling the creation of complex sequences. It is even possible to encode random digital information into synthetic DNA. In 2012, George M. Church codified one of his books into DNA molecules. The book had a staggering 5.3 megabytes of data [Church]. Despite the extravagance of encoding his book, George M. Church is one of the most respected synthetic biologists. The quotation we chose to open this chapter belongs to him.

The molecule encoded by Church was obviously not functional, but AI can naturally be leveraged to design genes that could be fully functional. For example, a deep neural network was created in 2020 to synthesize genomic segments. This AI program was used not only to optimize fitness for function but also to ensure sequence diversity. Sequence diversity is important because it underlies the adaptability and resilience of populations, allowing organisms to evolve, resist diseases, and thrive in changing environments. This AI algorithm ensured sequence diversity through a similarity metric that penalized excessive similarities beyond a set threshold. [Linder et al.].

AlphaFold and The Protein Folding Problem

As hinted above, protein structure prediction is another area where deep neural networks' intense learning plays a significant role. One of the most celebrated examples is AlphaFold, developed by DeepMind [AlphaFold]. DeepMind is the same company that created Alpha Go, the AI system that defeated Lee Sedol in 2016 in the ancient Chinese game of Go, as discussed in *Chapter 7*.

Protein design is a complex challenge. These fundamental building blocks of life are sequences of amino acids that naturally fold into distinctive

3-D configurations, which are specific to their biological function. The *"protein folding problem"* refers to the challenging pursuit of deciphering how the sequence of amino acids in a protein dictates its 3D structure, which entails the spatial arrangement of atoms within the protein molecule.

Understanding a protein's 3D structure is essential for unraveling its physical function, interactions with other molecules, and potential disease involvement. Protein structure prediction holds immense significance in drug discovery, as it enables the design of pharmaceuticals that target specific proteins involved in specific conditions, offering insights into treatment strategies and developing novel therapeutics.

Before AlphaFold arrived, some experimental protein structure prediction techniques had already been used, like cryo-electron microscopy and X-ray crystallography. However, these methods, while invaluable, were expensive and time-consuming, leading to the identification of only a fraction of the millions of known proteins across various life forms.

In 2018, AlphaFold stunned the scientific community by topping the rankings at the global competition called CASP (Critical Assessment of Techniques for Protein Structure Prediction). It excelled in predicting the most challenging protein structures, even in cases where no templates from similar proteins existed for comparison. AlphaFold participated again in the same competition in 2020, and its performance was even more astonishing. It achieved accuracy levels previously deemed unattainable. AlphaFold demonstrated an unprecedented ability to predict protein structures with remarkable precision, with scores surpassing 90 for two-thirds of the proteins.

The way that it was able to create consistent breakthroughs is necessary to mention. In order to find the 3D structure of a protein, AlphaFold compares it with multiple proteins of known structure that share similarities. Then, it engages in Machine Learning across three diverse data structures of the proteins: a representation at the sequence level, a portrayal of pairwise nucleotide base interactions, and the 3D structure of the protein at the atom level, which the model generates as output.

Despite these groundbreaking accomplishments, protein design remains a multifaceted puzzle. AlphaFold success is a giant leap forward, but challenges persist. For example, AlphaFold primarily focuses on single-chain proteins, leaving out extremely complex or intrinsically disordered proteins. Additionally, questions linger about how well AlphaFold can predict totally novel folds or structures that are utterly absent from existing databases.

Engineering Proteins with Generative AI

What AlphaFold does is find the shape—and, therefore, the function—of a protein sequence. Doing exactly the opposite is also an important application of synthetic biology, namely finding the sequence of a protein for a specific function, which basically means designing new proteins.

Designing proteins is a formidable task. Expert Systems with simple Machine Learning and rule-based algorithms have been traditionally used, but progress is self-limiting, and require specialized knowledge to identify the features that contribute most to performance. Recognizing the limitations, there is a lot of current research on Generative AI algorithms such as Generative Adversarial Networks (GAN) and Variational Autoencoders (VAEs), which we covered in *Chapter 5*. Using these AI models, researchers can work backward from the desired biological functions of the protein and to the DNA sequences that produce a protein that fulfills these functions [Tucs et al.].

Synthetic biology allows creating new protein configurations that match or even surpass the existing proteins in terms of specific functionalities. For example, Hemoglobin, the protein responsible for transporting oxygen in blood cells, can also bind to carbon monoxide, leading to the health risk of carbon monoxide poisoning. In 2009, a research group created a helix bundle mimicking hemoglobin's oxygen-binding properties but without this affinity for carbon monoxide, substantially reducing the risk of poisoning [Koder and Anderson].

Moreover, by manipulating protein structures and functions, it is possible to design industrial enzymes for many applications, like improved detergents and lactose-free dairy products. Synthetic biology also offers promising avenues in biochemical production for various industrial uses. Biological cells can be used as microscopic molecular factories to generate materials, typically proteins, with genetically encoded properties.

One example is the production of proteins required to grow biofilms. A biofilm is a slimy, adherent layer of microorganisms that forms on a surface, often in water, and is characterized by a protective matrix that allows bacteria to adhere and thrive. Biofilms have diverse applications. In healthcare, biofilms are cultivated on medical devices to either protect against infection or, conversely, combat bacterial contamination. In industrial contexts, biofilms contribute to processes like wastewater treatment and bioenergy production. Additionally, biofilm communities influence nutrient cycling and pollutant degradation in natural ecosystems.

Synthetic biology, when it adopts AI, expands and speeds breakthroughs, including mapping existing proteins and creating new, non-naturally occurring proteins. Companies are actively deploying AI-informed models and processes to productize their learnings and IP about proteins, paving the way for organ development, human tissue and function enhancements, and gain-of-function.

The Future of Transplants with 3D Bioprinting

Putting many proteins together and building an organoid with them is another of the applications of synthetic biology.

Organoids are artificially cultivated organs like an artificially grown kidney or liver. In the previous chapter, we talked about using 3D printers to print mechanical organs like bionic hearts. In this chapter, we talk about 3D bioprinting instead. Organoids are typically printed in a laboratory setting using this kind of printing technology. 3D bioprinting is a process through which cells are layered or deposited in a specific pattern to create three-dimensional structures that mimic the architecture of natural tissues or organs. These bioprinted organoids can serve as models for studying biological processes, drug testing, and potentially for transplantation into a patient [Hong].

Before they are bioprinted, living cells need to be created. These cells are artificial cells created from lipid vesicles through synthetic biology procedures, and they encompass all the essential components required for a functioning cellular system. These artificial cells are created with all the functional and design characteristics necessary to be considered *alive,* including self-replication and self-maintenance.

The next stage of the process is bioprinting these artificially created cells into an organoid, a very delicate process. Bioprinted organoids must meet intricate shapes and complex requirements. For instance, a bioprinted heart must meet structural criteria such as mechanical load, vascularization, and electrical signal propagation requirements, among many others.

Although 3D bioprinting is a very new technology, it has already demonstrated its effectiveness. The first successful transplant of a 3D bioprinted organ created from a patient's own cells was reported in 2022. This pioneering procedure focused on reconstructing an external ear to treat microtia, a congenital condition characterized by an underdeveloped or malformed outer ear [Clinicaltrials].

The implications of bioprinting for humankind are immense. In the near future, bioprinting will offer a range of possibilities, including the production of bioprinted eyeball corneas and hair follicles, structures less complex than, say, a bioprinted heart but more delicate than a bioprinted external ear. In healthcare, bioprinting will allow for the fabrication of organs in organ farms, addressing the challenges posed by organ shortages for transplantation.

Patients' own cells will be employed to craft miniaturized organs or organoids for testing medical responses before administering treatments. Bioprinted prosthetic limbs could be meticulously designed to seamlessly integrate with the individual's body, enhancing their functionality and comfort.

Finally, bioprinting is also paving the way for the implantation of electronics into biological tissues, resulting in cybernetic organs that surpass their natural counterparts in sophistication. For instance, bio-printed lungs could be equipped with sensors and nano-filters that purify the air before it enters the bloodstream. Similarly, replacement bionic eyeballs could come with built-in zoom and infrared vision capabilities.

The implications of printing electronics into biological tissues that would later be integrated into a human are breathtaking. This kind of technology could surpass the possibilities of the BCIs presented in the previous chapter and bring about a truly interlaced living organism with a biology designed by AI. We see this as solving, at least directionally, core mechanical issues around interlacing, the nuts-and-bolts of how it can be physically implemented.

Creating Synthetic Life and Non-Natural Life

3D bioprinting of organoids is impressive, but organoids themselves are not living per se despite having the necessary design and construction properties to claim otherwise. One polemic facet of synthetic biology is the overall concept of synthetic life.

To set a definition, synthetic life involves the construction of organisms in a controlled setting using synthesized molecules. Experiments in this field serve various purposes, including exploring the origins of life, testing innovative therapeutic and diagnostic solutions, investigating fundamental life properties, and finally, the ambitious endeavor of generating life from non-living components [Deamer].

This artificial form of life is called Synthetic Life, a term coined by Craig Venter in 2010 when he created a fully synthetic bacterial chromosome and introduced it into genetically depleted bacterial host cells. Four "*watermarks*" were incorporated into the DNA of the single-celled organism to help identify it: a complete alphabet code table with punctuations, 46 contributing scientists' names, three sentences, and the secret email address for the cell. Remarkably, these synthetic bacteria demonstrated growth and replication capabilities. [Gibson et al. #]. Since then, increasingly advanced synthetic life organisms have been engineered to perform essential functions, such as pharmaceutical production or detoxifying polluted land and water sources.

Going beyond the creation of synthetic life, synthetic biology also ventures into the realm of unconventional molecular biology, which is creating life that could not possibly exist in nature. In nature, across all living organisms, there are only five nucleotide bases and 20 amino acids, but AI makes it possible to target specific chemical and biological properties to design and engineer non-natural proteins and non-natural bases that cannot be found in nature. This would solve the *"first building block"* issue of designing non-natural forms of synthetic life that use these novel amino acids and bases that do not exist in nature.

While such non-natural organisms might offer advantages, they also pose unique risks. Once released into an environment with ecosystems that have traversed development for millions of years, these organisms might be able to engage in horizontal gene transfer or gene exchange with natural species, leading to unpredictable initial outcomes.

It is also not clear if these species could nourish themselves on natural proteins or if they would have to rely on non-natural molecules. If these new species were engineered to depend on non-natural materials for synthesizing their own proteins or nucleic acids, they would be incapable of surviving in natural environments if inadvertently released. Conversely, if they manage to feed on natural molecules and establish themselves in uncontrolled environments, they could potentially outperform natural organisms, resisting predators and biological viruses, leading to uncontrolled proliferation, which could include extinction for some current species.

Any discussion of synthetic life created from molecules that do not exist in nature might seem like Science Fiction, but it is not. The first living organism with this kind of non-natural DNA was unveiled in 2014. Researchers added two new, unconventional nucleotides to bacterial DNA, and the newly created non-natural bacteria underwent 24 generations of growth, all containing the newly introduced artificial nucleotide bases [Malyshev et al.].

Xenobots: from Frog Embryos to Synthetic Lifeforms

An example of synthetic life is the Xenobots. Xenobots derive their name from the African clawed frog Xenopus Laevis and were developed in 2020 [Sokol] [Simon]. Xenobots use the conventional molecules found in nature, not the non-natural variations we just talked about.

Xenobots are typically less than 0.04 inches in width and comprise two primary parts: skin cells and heart muscle cells. These two kinds of cells are obtained from embryonic stem cells from these African frogs. The skin cells give structural support, while the heart cells function as miniature engines that contract and expand rhythmically, pushing the xenobot forward. The specific arrangement of a xenobot's body is determined through computer modeling, employing a trial-and-error process.

Whether xenobots should be classified as living organisms, robots, or something completely different is a matter of ongoing debate among scientists. However, it is clearly demonstrated that xenobots exhibit some common characteristics with living organisms. First, xenobots can self-repair when injured. Second, xenobots can reproduce by gathering free-floating cells from their surroundings and assembling them into new xenobots with the same capabilities. Finally, xenobots can survive for extended periods without nourishment.

Xenobots have been engineered to perform various tasks, including walking, swimming, pushing pellets, transporting payloads, and collaborating in swarms to gather scattered debris into organized piles on their dish's surface. Based on these behaviors, xenobots hold promise for some practical future applications. For example, they could gather ocean microplastics into larger masses for easy removal and transport to recycling facilities. Additionally, in clinical settings, xenobots may be employed to address tasks such as removing arterial plaque and treating medical conditions.

Biological Computers and Biological Machine Learning

In case the creation of synthetic life—either natural or non-natural—proves insufficiently ambitious, contemplate the prospect of developing biological computers. A biological computer is a specially designed biological system with the ability to perform operations similar to those in electronic computers. Scientists have already developed and characterized various logic gates in multiple organisms like their electronic counterparts in computers.

Recent advances show that it is possible to integrate analog and digital computation circuits into living cells. For example, in 2007, a biological circuit that could execute logical functions like AND, OR, and XOR was implemented in mammalian cells [Rinaudo]. Moreover, in 2011, scientists developed a therapeutic strategy employing biological digital computations for detecting and eliminating human cancer cells [Xie]. In addition, in 2016, computer engineering principles were applied to automate the design of this kind of digital circuitry within bacterial cells [Nielsen], and in 2017, arithmetic and Boolean logic were also implemented in mammal cells [Weinberg].

On top of building these more simple computational circuits, it is also possible to implement complex artificial neural network analogs using biomolecular components. The implications of this include enabling the execution of intricate machine-learning processes within a biological system.

Furthermore, in 2019, a theoretical architecture for a biomolecular neural network was presented [Pandi et al.]. This architecture is a network of chemical reactions that accurately executes neural network computations and demonstrates its use for solving classification problems. It serves as the biomolecular equivalent to the perceptron built in 1957 by Frank Rosenblatt, with a similar simple structure composed of one layer of artificial neurons.

The implications of being able to build machine-learning algorithms inside biological systems are enormous because that means that it would be possible to increase the intelligence level of living beings, even humans, by following computer architectures constructed with biological materials.

Masters of Creation

Synthetic biology is arguably the most revolutionary application of AI. It has the potential to transform the essence of human beings by altering their biological fundamentals, allowing them to live longer, resist diseases, and acquire superhuman abilities with specifically designed organoids. Driven by the power of AI, it will occur alongside the development of entirely new biological life forms. Advances such as integrating electronic or machine-learning elements into biological circuits solve thorny mechanical issues regarding how interlacing will occur and open a solid avenue for human-AI interlacing.

The huge power of synthetic biology makes us the masters of creation. Or maybe the masters of disequilibrium. We will discuss this in subsequent chapters.

22. AI Utopia: Redistribution, Sustainability, Equity

"We are seeing the most disruptive force in history here.[...] There will come a point where no job is needed - you can have a job if you want one for personal satisfaction but AI will do everything [...]. One of the challenges in the future will be how do we find meaning in life."

Elon Musk,

American Billionaire
In a conversation with UK Prime Minister Rishi Sunak
2 Nov 2023 [Henshall]

AI is going to generate unprecedented wealth as it drives speed and productivity, economizes and de-risks commercial decision-making, and eliminates resource waste. In 2017, PWC published an estimation of the impact of AI on the global economy by 2030. According to the analysis, the integration of AI could contribute an astounding incremental $15.7 trillion to the global economy [PWC]. One year later, in 2018, McKinsey presented a study showing a total economic activity of approximately $13 trillion by 2030, which is in line with PWC [McKinsey].

Both estimates were made before the Generative AI revolution, which has dramatically sped up the AI industry, so we can consider these estimates moderate.

The $15.7 trillion predicted by PWC exceeds the total GDP of both China and India combined, meaning that AI will create a new economy the size of China and India by 2030. That also means a projected 14% surge in global GDP by 2030. In terms of global economic distribution, China and North America would contribute to nearly 70% of the global economic impact, owing to the advanced state of AI in each market, general labor law, and other legal frameworks favorable to rapid implementation of AI-influenced productization, and the geometric impact to existing scaled industries—the rich do indeed get richer. Of the gain, China is poised to witness a substantial 26% boost to GDP by 2030, while North America could experience a 14% increase. Within specific sectors, retail, financial services, and healthcare emerge as key players in the unfolding economic paradigm, according to PWC.

These figures represent merely the near-term impact as the integration of AI into our economy and society has been steadily advancing for decades, and there is no reversing this trend. AI will get smarter, algorithms will be more pervasive in all areas and corners of life, including our economic decision-making, and robots will become more integrated into our social and work lives.

There is no realm of human endeavor that AI will not impact, with the technology aiming towards solving heretofore intractable problems. Synthetic biology has already created crop foods, and when combined with logistics optimization and organic chemistry, paves the way to not only eliminating hunger but also optimizing nutrition and human performance. Energy problems in societies, from cost to universal access to sustainability, can be solved via a combination of AI-driven engineering that optimizes the energy source mix to inform the perfection of technologies such as wave harvesting and making nuclear power fully safe. The level of new product development across industries—food, textiles, media, telecommunications, building materials—will be staggering as decision-making will have better preference information and be less prone to error or misjudgment. Resource allocation efficiency and gains in productivity should conspire to lower prices for most items.

The end-state humankind hurtles towards will be either utopian, dystopian, or a mix of the two, with the actual results contingent wholly on how AI will be developed, deployed, and regulated out-of-the-gate. Quantifying specific probabilities for any scenario is challenging, given the complex interplay of technological, economic, societal, and ethical elements alongside the prominent role of competing geopolitical superpowers with different visions of the world—and even individual actors with differing motivations and concepts of *"the good"* in the unfolding drama. The eventual outcome hinges on how responsible actors employ the technology, the economics that condition growth and deployment, and the political and regulatory frameworks and interactions—all of which are presently within our full control.

We have reason to believe that with regulatory and societal guidance aligned with our core values and beliefs, AI might end up in the near term positioning itself to create and sustain betterment for mankind. This chapter centers on describing some of the positive aspects that AI development could have in the next few decades while also pointing out some of the pitfalls and tradeoffs necessary to accommodate a positive outcome. In this utopian scenario, AI is not only transformative but also transcendent, utilized only for the betterment of humanity and the benefit of most people. In this view, AI technologies are fully controlled by us and imbued with our values. They are restricted to significantly spur ongoing industrial and product development innovation. They improve productivity, which can lower costs, ensuring the product-market fit of economic output so that resources are not wasted. They foster economic growth and return time and work-life balance to all of us. Finally, AI technologies would also play a pivotal role in addressing complex challenges like disease, poverty, or environmental issues, propelling humanity to unprecedented heights. Whether we believe McKinsey's or PWC's growth estimates, the world is poised to get far richer.

In the next chapter, we will present the other side of the technology coin, one that leads to a dystopian future, and what tugs both for and against that outcome to allow us to compare both possibilities.

We believe that the future will fall somewhere in between, with today's free thinkers and self-determinists, those who are governed in their thinking by logic rather than emotion, the middle classes / economically successful but not ultra-wealthy, and those seeking to individuate will find themselves in varying degrees of dystopia. Conversely, the ultra-rich, the technologists who control AI and cyborgization, the politicians who add no value except for themselves and their bureaucracies, and today's least successful economic participants (e.g., the lower middle and poor) will be finding themselves closer to utopia.

The following pages outline one idyllic vision for a future guided by AI.

The Science Fiction of AI Utopias

An AI utopia can be defined as a society in which advanced AI has brought unprecedented prosperity, harmony, and progress. In Science Fiction, AI utopias have been envisioned by authors such as Vernor Vinge in 2006's *"Rainbows End"* and Iain M. Banks in 1987's *"The Culture"* series [Vinge [Banks]. Both works highlight AI's potential to eliminate human suffering, promote education and knowledge accessibility, and reshape the human experience; they differ starkly, however, in how AI influences society, pointing us to understand that there are multiple paths that AI can take and that our actual steps towards interlacing will have a profound impact on the degree to which utopian or dystopian world results. *"Rainbows End"* is predominantly situated in a near-future Earth, closely tied to existing societal frameworks. In contrast, *"The Culture"* revolves around a space-faring, highly advanced galactic civilization specifically referred to as the Culture. It portrays a more radical transformation, with AI wielding substantial power and influence.

In *"Rainbows End,"* the author presents a future Earth where AI-driven advancements have led to a utopian society marked by profound transformations. The ubiquity of AI in *"Rainbows End"* is exemplified by the pervasive use of wearable computing devices that provide immediate access to information and connect individuals to vast knowledge networks. These devices are underpinned by sophisticated AI systems that augment human intelligence, enabling individuals to acquire new skills and knowledge remarkably. Ai is domesticated, or tamed if you will, with the result of a society where education is democratized, expertise is readily accessible, and intellectual growth is a lifelong pursuit.

Under a benign regime of AI, the society in Vinge's narrative is free from many traditional human conflicts. Poverty has been largely eradicated thanks to the availability of ubiquitous AI-driven technology that can provide for the population's basic needs. Furthermore, the need for physical wars has diminished significantly as information warfare and AI-assisted diplomacy have become the primary means of resolving disputes.

Yet, Vinge's utopia is not without its challenges. The seamless integration of AI into everyday life raises stark questions about privacy and individuality. In this world, personal identities can be easily manipulated, and surveillance is pervasive, in many ways merely extrapolative of Generative AI and surveillance technology already in place in developed countries today. The tools that enable society's ideological features can also be used for manipulation and control, again highlighting the perpetual dilemma of technology as a coin with two sides.

On the other hand, Iain M. Banks' *"The Culture"* series presents a universe in the distant future, where AI utopia on Earth has expanded its benevolent influence on the cosmos. Highly advanced and sentient AIs, known as *"Minds,"* have evolved to a level of sophistication where they manage all aspects of the Culture's society, from resource allocation to diplomacy and governance.

One of the most distinctive features of this society is also its post-scarcity economy, similar to *"The Culture."* Ostensibly, the elimination of waste and resource optimization, as we have mentioned in Chapter 19, will be a principal characteristic of AI. Minds in this world develop and ensure abundant resources for society, eliminating the need for monetary systems or economic hierarchies. Individuals in the Culture are free to pursue their passions and interests, with AI ensuring their basic needs and desires are effortlessly met.

Nevertheless, Banks explores the omnipresent concept of individual freedom and autonomy in a very different way from Vernor Vinge. While the AI Minds manage the society, they do so in a manner that respects and values personal autonomy. Citizens of *"The Culture"* have the freedom to live as they choose, including modifying their bodies and consciousness, exploring diverse forms of relationships, and engaging in a wide range of creative and intellectual pursuits.

However, this utopia is also not without its ethical dilemmas. Banks raises questions about the implications of such immense power in AI entities. The Minds in the Culture are benevolent, but what if they were not, and how is that outcome assured? The potential for absolute control and surveillance by these superintelligent entities raises concerns about the loss of human freedom, autonomy, and the Faustian Bargains that might lie embedded in every aspect of life.

AI and The Future of Work

AI will transform work as we know it today. In one dimension, the rapid deployment of AI in economic life forces us to ask, *"What happens to jobs?"* When we look at the trajectory of AI and cyborgization, another dimension is added wherein we must also ask, *"What happens to work?"*

The complexity of the topic touches on prevailing economic models under scarcity, population transition, and the development of human capabilities to be productive and fulfilled in an increasingly AI-denominated world. Most importantly, a significant, out-of-the-gate concern about AI revolves around the potential displacement of jobs, particularly in industries heavily reliant on repetitive or routine tasks susceptible to automation.

But this is a known and thus addressable issue. The *"Future of Jobs Report"* from the World Economic Forum estimated that 85 million jobs are expected to be replaced by AI-powered machines by the year 2025. However, the report also forecasts the creation of approximately 97 million new jobs attributable to AI by 2025. [WEF]. As AI progresses and integrates further into various industries, numerous job opportunities and benefits will emerge. While mundane tasks will be increasingly delegated to AI, humans remain essential for refining work done by AI, performing quality checks, carrying out more creative aspects of jobs, and, of course, interacting with other humans. Moreover, specialized roles such as AI engineer, data scientist, and AI legal & ethics practitioners that have previously not existed will be in high demand as companies pursue the development and implementation of AI-driven solutions, at least in the short run.

With AI first taking over routine tasks, there will be an increased emphasis on acquiring or deepening what remains uniquely human skills, which we characterize as critical thinking and emotional intelligence. This shift in focus aligns with the pursuit of passions, as individuals can invest time in developing skills that not only align with their interests but also contribute to their personal and professional growth. Similarly, a new wave of AI engineers, technicians, cloud specialists, machinists, and even specialized maintenance professionals will be needed, with ample training ground being supplied entrepreneurially by companies like Coursera, which since 2015 has grown its thousands of courses and students at a CAGR of 12%.

AI has an impact not only on jobs but also on "*work*" itself. While individuals need conscious adjustment to navigate the changing landscape, AI has the innate potential to contribute to a healthier work-life balance for everyone in the near term. With fewer hours spent on monotonous work, people will have the opportunity to invest more time in leisure, personal growth, and spending quality moments with family and friends. An initial movement in this specific direction can be seen in America's unionized auto workers seeking 4-day workweeks, bolstered by shop floor productivity from robots and AI, and winning the concession; the automaker companies can remain equally or more profitable while enabling a restructuring of work as the robots do not need a salary. The positive impact on mental well-being could be considerable, as individuals experience a reduction in stress associated with tedious work, leading to improved overall life satisfaction.

It is certainly possible for the advantages to outweigh the dislocation vis-a-vis work in the life of the individual in the age of AI and robotics. We can all agree that improving work-life balance in meaningful ways makes us all better off. But this will not happen without specific action on the part of societies to channel the activity and create appropriate new and perhaps even untried, novel responses to the challenges faced in migrating workforces. Societies will require a specific, documented workforce strategy that takes a long-term planning view and enables AI to integrate into economic life and corporations while preserving jobs as long as possible through role modification. A holistic approach involving new job creation, employment law, reskilling programs, and collaborative efforts between Government and corporations—as well as between humans and AI—would ensure a dynamic workforce, maximize productivity, and foster innovation.

The Safety Net of the Universal Basic Income

While concerns about job displacement loom large, there are already proposed solutions to address this issue, with one notable idea being Universal Basic Income (UBI). UBI entails providing a guaranteed minimum income to every person in a society, irrespective of their employment status. Advocates of UBI argue that it would function as a safety net for workers displaced by automation and AI, enabling them to meet basic needs while seeking new employment or pursuing education and training or become permanent for those who cannot be deployed economically. Funding would come from the wealth created by AI-driven productivity, which should be redistributed subject to a formula that reflects society's values, guaranteeing an elevated quality of life for everyone and ameliorating social displacement that AI will cause in the absence of any policy [LaPonsie].

There are several notable advantages to this approach. In addition to a safety net that similarly ensures the ongoing broad-based consumption of goods and services necessary for an economy to expand in the wake of job displacement, the economic security that UBI would entail could ostensibly encourage rage risk-taking and entrepreneurial endeavors. Individuals could pursue projects and ventures they are passionate about without the fear of financial instability. This diversification of economic activities would not only stimulate innovation but also contribute to a more vibrant and resilient economy. The pursuit of education would also be an outcome of UBI. Thus, social accumulation of human capital could be a consequence, generating positive externalities for society.

Critics of UBI align it conceptually to current welfare programs, citing the creation of disincentives to work. Unlike in economic revolutions of the past, e.g., the Industrial Revolution and the Digitalization of the economy beginning in 2000, the deployment of AI and robotics will render large swathes of the population irrevocably unviable economically, necessitating some form of subsidization. Work/not work decisions are made primarily based on the marginal income obtainable from work, and AI is set to refactor this equation unfavorably for many people. The ability to avoid disincentives at the margin is, ironically, a function of the rate and rules that AI-level insight is needed to accurately set.

Another criticism of UBI is its potential inflationary impact. UBI could produce an increase in spending and demand, and if that is not accompanied by an increase in the supply of goods and services, then prices would just go up. There are ample historical examples to generate this concern. Implementations of mass wealth redistribution programs without an increase in productivity in Argentina, for example, resulted in going from a GDP per capita at par with Western Europe at the beginning of the 20th century to merely 27% of the European Union's GDP per capita in 2021, after seven decades of wealth redistribution programs [Ourworldindata].

The only possibility to avoid inflation would be achieving an increase in the supply of goods and services that would match the increase in demand. We believe that AI could provide the basis for that increase since AI will make existing resources more efficient while expanding the array of products and services available to people. However, we also acknowledge that the actual outcome would depend on the price elasticity and margins of each product and service. Keeping production high might or might not optimize ROI on AI. For some specific products, having a lower production, which leads to higher prices, would provide a more significant return than producing more and selling it at lower prices. Even if it were theoretically possible to match the supply and demand of services to benefit everything, human incentives might not be aligned to achieve that synchronization.

UBI presents other elements of complexity. For example, financing the UBI would essentially be an "*AI Tax*" with rates, calculation methodologies, and collection processes subject to political processes. This tax would charge the work done by AI in the same way current taxes charge human work. Also, a progressive tax structure would punish those companies that most successfully deploy AI, and a regressive structure might leave funding inadequate. The regressive tax structure might also be counterproductive to AI's objectives.

Another element of complexity is the necessity to rethink how UBI fits with other social welfare programs that societies have, in particular, whether UBI will replace them.

UBI remains a debated concept, and there is increasing Government and even industry interest in and support for exploring it. While UBI has never been implemented successfully at such a large scale, there are nevertheless some limited examples that are useful to explore for guidance:

- Between 1795 and 1834, the Speenhamland System, the first guaranteed income program in history, prevented starvation for a large number of rural England families [Block and Somers].
- The "*BIG*" (Basic Income Grant) program implemented in Namibia is credited with almost halving the country's poverty rate.[Haarmann et al.].
- The "*Bolsa Familia*" program in Brazil (2003-2015) reduced that country's poverty rate by more than 75% [Pereira]
- According to a 2016 University of Alaska study, the *APF program— Alaska Permanent Fund*—which provides all state residents with a small annual cash payment of about $1,000, keeps 15,000–23,000 Alaskans out of poverty [Marinescu and Hiilamo].

In summary, the gains in productivity and output that AI would bring should theoretically make UBI or similar interventionist programs economically feasible, with AI models ironically helping to solve thorny problems in the rate setting and structure. For UBI to work in practice, it will require that the increase in demand created by the scheme is accompanied appropriately by an increase in the supply of goods and services created by AI.

UBI is a complex scheme that might have other unwanted consequences. We will introduce those in *Chapter 23*, which focuses on dystopian elements introduced by AI.

Rethinking Education for an AI-Driven Future

Facing workforce transformation and rapid economic obsolescence of many skill sets, the best weapon a worker of the 21st century will have is cross-functional skills and the ability to constantly learn. Both of these come from education. It is essential for society to support lifelong learning, upskilling, and reskilling for tradesmen and professionals alike in navigating the dynamic job market in accelerating transformation driven by AI.

Accordingly, we are already witnessing a profound transformation in the field of education, driven by the accelerating integration of AI. This paradigm shift promises to reshape the entire educational landscape. It will influence teaching methodologies, student engagement, the role of universities, and, like the impact of AI on work overall, the very nature of learning.

We see parallels between AI and the integration of calculators into math classrooms, which many teachers resisted between the 1960s and the 1990s. The once-revolutionary calculator has now become a standard tool in classrooms, enhancing students' comprehension and efficiency in mathematical subjects. It was the responsibility of the educational system to ensure a student understood and could perform arithmetic, and then the calculator as a tool could economize on learning time, dispensing with unneeded human processing power, thus enabling a more rapid jump to geometry, algebra, and calculus. Similarly, AI should be acknowledged as a fundamental didactic instrument, playing a crucial role in shaping students and a workforce that is well-prepared for the demands of the future.

We believe that as AI increasingly assumes routine and repetitive tasks, teaching emphasis should transition from specific job tasks—which AI can automate anyway—to fostering critical thinking and problem-solving. Education should equip students to collaborate with and oversee AI, enabling them to review, interpret, and critically question AI-generated content and information. Critical thinking and problem-solving will be increasingly important in all jobs. Computer programming presents a useful example. AI is able to generate programming code quite efficiently with tools like GitHub Copilot or Replit. However, writing code is only one part of a software engineer's role. AI may be able to convert high-level specifications into code, but it lacks the contextual understanding and iterative approach that defines software development. On top of writing code, human software engineers are required to apply expertise and critical thinking in areas like security, where AI-generated code may introduce vulnerabilities, debugging and handling unforeseen issues, meeting customer needs, matching to architecture in flexible ways, and ensuring data protection, all of which require human creativity and expertise.

Adaptability is another crucial skill that the education system needs to support. As AI advances, it will progressively automate more and more tasks, and workers will need to upgrade their skills multiple times in their professional lives in order to remain economically vital. Leaning into the previous example of software development, programmers of the future will have to continue getting up the skillset ladder into higher value-added activities as Large Language Models, and Generative AI continue evolving and start taking over more and more of the technical aspects of software development. In the coming years, there will be AI agents that specialize in writing code, others will specialize in debugging code, and others will specialize in testing vulnerabilities and providing feedback to the AI agents which wrote the code in the first place. This will lead to a feedback loop in which multiple AI agents work together to write well-tested and fully functional code. At that moment, humans will not be required to do technical coding anymore. Instead, they will manage complex software projects by simply communicating high-level expectations and requirements and making decisions on which, among multiple avenues, can be taken to reach a goal. At some point, a single non-technical human product owner will be the only person required to write very complex software with the help of AI. At that moment, the job of software engineers will no longer exist, and they will need to climb the skillset ladder to become non-technical high-level product owners, showcasing the need for adaptability and life-long learning. Like software developers in our example, we believe that in order to obtain a positive outcome, most of us will now have to adapt and pivot multiple times in our professional lifetime.

Switching focus from education for working professionals to traditional K-12 and university education, one of the most impactful changes AI will bring is the personalization of learning experiences. Advanced AI algorithms will analyze individual student learning styles, preferences, and strengths, tailoring educational content to suit each student's unique speed and capability to learn. This personalized approach has the potential to enhance student engagement and comprehension. AI-powered platforms will facilitate remote and asynchronous learning, allowing students to access educational resources and engage in coursework at their own pace. This will democratize education, breaking down geographical barriers and providing equal opportunities for learning to students, particularly those who are in remote or impoverished areas.

AI can also serve as an invaluable assistant to educators. Algorithms are already set to examine student performance data, pinpoint areas of struggle, and provide real-time feedback. So-called Adaptive Learning Methods and

AI algorithms will analyze a student's performance over time, providing a more accurate representation of a student's capabilities, going beyond memorization to measure critical thinking, problem-solving, and creativity skills. This will enable educators to focus on refining their pedagogical strategies and providing targeted support where it is most needed. We foresee an end to many outdated concepts, such as the annual turnover of grades linked to chronological age, e.g., *"he is in 2nd grade, she is in 3rd grade,"* and the semester system, replaced instead by defining increasing levels of concept mastery. Education, in its entirety, constitutes the programming of minds, with the tools and processes of current mass education built upon a technology and economic landscape that is no longer in existence. AI will rapidly transform that, helping people reach their maximum potential.

Improved AI-driven methods that speed and optimize learning potential are only half of the equation. The other half of the equation is the curriculum. Today's Western Public Schools, with their outdated didactic mechanisms and a curriculum geared toward equipping people for success during the Industrial Revolution, will undergo a needed overhaul.

K-12 subjects such as Music Appreciation and Art History taught in group settings and entailing memory-based activities, can be taught remotely through the internet as a hobby elective, with students able to more rapidly assimilate knowledge as they save time by not physically going to classrooms. Using new AI-enabled teaching methods to fast-track learning to individual needs will punctuate the time savings and efficiency effects. It has been estimated that the delivery of a traditional semester-long Art History class can now be accomplished in under three weeks. With this level of time savings and efficiencies in learning, new mission-critical subjects that actually enhance critical thinking, innovation, and entrepreneurship across disciplines can be launched: for example, AI-assisted research skills, coding, mathematical problem solving, and applied AI models to resource allocation problems. Furthermore, Virtual Reality (VR) and Augmented Reality (AR), coupled with AI, will create immersive, hands-on learning experiences, transporting students to historical events, scientific simulations, and virtual labs, making abstract concepts tangible, and fostering a deeper understanding of subjects.

In short, what is being taught today at the early fundamentals level is outdated and will not equip people to contribute in the coming years. Some of today's 'Teachers' Unions lack accountability and resist this change, which is creating a disservice to society when taking a long-term view of impact. We question whether some of today's teachers, who are themselves the products of outdated methodologies and curriculums, have the skills necessary to teach the new necessary subjects. It is likely that at some point, teachers might be replaced by AI, given Adaptive Learning models, robots that can express emotion, and the development of new fact-based curriculums.

Overall, the power of AI to transform education is stark and deep, and we believe that a review of the foundational K-12 type educational system is necessary to ensure long-term viability and to reach the limitless promise that AI-based tools have to maximize human potential.

AI In New Product Development

Product development is one of the most difficult commercial endeavors to undertake, as it entails investment risk and imperfect information. It is also the commercial consequence of innovation. This can be in the form of a new app, a new restaurant theme with a new menu, and even the opening of a new zoo. *The history of commerce can be thought of in some ways as the evolution of product development*—from process improvements, finding product-market fit, de-risking capital and resource outlays, intelligently iterating, and creating new products that people are willing to pay for at a price they are willing to pay. It is complicated; for every Coca-Cola, there are 50 Jolt Colas. Innovation, marketplace consumption, and productivity are the key drivers of all economies.

AI is set to play a pivotal role in economizing on every step in the product development process, using data-trained AI algorithms to factually assess the preferences and interests of scaled populations, assess competitors and the prices of inputs, and conceive and develop product constructs that represent best fit, rapidly de-risking every point in the decision tree that is necessary to take scarce inputs and transform them into products we consume.

In the FMCG (Fast-Moving Consumer Goods) space, the history of beverages in the US is illustrative. Beverages were historically developed by peddlers who would create a basic formula, produce it in a garage or portable still, and travel city-to-city by horse to sell it, refining formulations based on feedback until it resulted in a product offering that could be sustained. Thousands of people tried their hands at it, and one or two ideas perhaps survived. The term *"snake oil"* describes odd products with dubious marketing claims that emanated from this primitive form of product development alive in the US in the mid-to-late 1800s.

Fast forward to the age of IT and convenience stores, and a whole different set of processes prevailed: First of all, a company would conduct research, scan competition, assess the beverage market, titrate several versions of a product it conceived, and manufacture a beverage product, all using general product consumption data. Then it would conduct a focus group to allow a *"statistically relevant"* subset of customers to initially assess the beverage and package constructs. If it passed the focus group, it was sent to the shelves of convenience stores, and the company would measure the velocity of sales and customer feedback to assess if the product had wings. If it did not meet performance thresholds, it was either killed or underwent refinement, re-entering this exploration process, where the assessment of consumer taste is a perpetual *"educated guess."* The time investment and use of scarce resources necessary at each step of the process are not inconsequential. But, instead of 1 in 1000 success, the refined product development process created a 1 in 25 success.

When trained AI models gather vast amounts of consumer, marketplace, competitor, sales, beverage formula, and scientific data on ingredients and taste combinations before the new product is even thought of, much the same way that unsupervised AI models can predict credit default to a high degree of accuracy as we discussed in *Chapter 6, the entire chain of product development is derisked and improved.* The better the AI model, the more the result of product development will get closer to a 1-to-1 development-to-success ratio. The result will be capital, resource, and time savings, leading to more products that are better aligned to consumer preference and lower prices, with saved resources applicable to other products and applications. AI will drive this across all product categories, enabling a consumer dollar to go further in a paradise of products and services. The economy will grow.

We foresee AI helping to de-risk the rapid development and release of new products and services that are aligned with individual preferences and interests much more closely than we have seen heretofore throughout economic history. Optimized distribution pathways likewise ensure these products are delivered more efficiently and error-free. Existing products and services will likewise undergo improvements that increase customer utility. Vast amounts of preference and other data are necessary to co-opt AI into this process, but as we already reviewed in *Chapters 6* and *7*, AI algorithms are already developed in the space.

Industrial AI and the Plant of the Future

Although the majority of mainstream AI applications are presently concentrated on consumer markets and B2C applications, AI will also have an impact on industrial B2B applications that can help tug society more toward utopian outcomes.

The crucial distinction between AI applied to industrial environments and general-purpose AI used in consumer environments is that industrial AI absolutely must comprehend causality. Industrial environments are composed of complex machinery with millions of parameters. Modifying some of these parameters has repercussions across a whole chain of events. AI must make decisions understanding this entire cause-effect chain in detail and not based on probabilities or correlations, which might have a margin error and might lead to instabilities in the manufacturing process or, even worse, to safety problems. Most importantly, causality is also one of the fundamental areas of current AI research, driving the quest for Artificial General Intelligence (AGI).

We have talked about automating repetitive tasks already. However, this new generation of advanced industrial AI takes it a step further. Industrial-grade AI is designed to carry out tasks currently handled by top engineers in industrial plants and corporations. These tasks are not repetitive but instead complex and require a very detailed understanding of engineering. For example, Industrial-grade AI can be used in industrial plants to solve optimization problems, troubleshoot complex materials utilization issues, and design large industrial projects involving millions of components.

AI can solve a lot of advanced engineering problems *"on paper."* Still, in order to translate those solutions to the real world of the plant, mechanical robots will continue to be very important. In particular, Collaborative Robots, or cobots, which we talked about in *Chapter 12,* will work alongside human engineers in repetitive and physically demanding tasks, enhancing efficiency and safety in manufacturing processes.

This kind of Industrial-grade AI will enable manufacturing plants that are simultaneously self-learning, self-adapting, and self-sustaining. This shift represents a significant leap forward in efficiency and productivity, allowing plants to be operated with very little labor, namely a few highly trained engineers [Cobb].

A self-learning plant means that self-learning algorithms continuously analyze vast datasets in real-time, allowing machines to adapt and optimize their performance. This perpetual learning loop ensures that manufacturing processes become increasingly refined over time, resulting in heightened efficiency and resource utilization.

The self-adapting aspect will empower these plants to adjust seamlessly to changes in production demands, market dynamics, and unforeseen disruptions. Production downtime also does not have the same negative commercial and human impact that it would today. This adaptability ensures that manufacturing processes remain agile and responsive, enabling companies to meet fluctuating consumer needs with speed and precision.

Finally, self-sustainability promises to revolutionize maintenance strategies. AI systems will monitor equipment health in real-time, predict potential issues before they arise, and schedule proactive maintenance. AI-driven maintenance will minimize downtime, reduce the risk of costly breakdowns, and extend the lifespan of machinery. The result is a manufacturing ecosystem that operates smoothly and efficiently.

Tailored Assistance through Personalized AI Companions

Similar to AI-powered healthcare bots and telemedicine assistants, advanced and empathetic AI-powered virtual assistants are emerging to cater to individual needs and preferences. This will contribute to an ongoing and evolving utopian opportunity promised by AI. One of the companies developing them is Inflection AI, founded by Mustafa Suleyman, who is also the former founder of DeepMind [Yao]. He was mentioned earlier in *Chapter 7,* when we talked about AlphaGo, and in *Chapter 21,* when we talked about *AlphaFold.*

The vision of Inflection AI is for everyone to have their own personalized AI assistant, aiding them in both professional and personal endeavors. These virtual companions assist—what Suleyman calls PI (Personal Intelligence)—with daily tasks, offer customized help, facilitate support through an extensive analysis of data, and even provide mental health guidance. Personalized AIs would leverage the deep ability to learn and adapt, ensuring progressively useful output. They would be able to use a diplomatic tone when discussing sensitive topics and introduce elements of humor to enhance the user experience when appropriate.

To contextualize this, individuals will be able to access tailor-made recommendations for cultural events, educational opportunities, group meets, and entertainment options that align with their passions and specific interests. Personal assistants will even help in leisure activities like shopping. Scanning the body using built-in LiDAR similar to that which is embedded in robots, as we discussed in Chapter 14, the personalized AI will present you with what it knows is your most flattering attire and where to obtain it, further enhancing your appearance and confidence. Furthermore, consider a refrigerator that autonomously generates a grocery list for the store and makes orders proactively to refill it. That and more is what a personalized assistant will do for you.

However, utilizing applications such as Personalized AIs poses significant risks. Ethical guardrails are necessary to make sure that the AI is not manipulative. This kind of personal agent could become very risky if they end up influencing their owner's behavior in ways that are not in their best interest. For example, for the AI to steer its user towards making or not certain friends, choosing or not certain jobs, making or not certain investments, or even dating or not dating specific people based on the interests of the programmer of the algorithms. To avoid this, Inflection AI and its founder, Mustafa Suleyman, are developing a comprehensive ethical framework. We will speak about that more time in *Chapter 28.*

A Robot in Every Household

Having received ongoing R&D investment over a 50-year period starting in the 1970s, robotics for industrial and military usage is already capable of replacing or nearly replacing humans across an increasing range of applications, as we reviewed in *Part III* of this book. Many technologies that eventually find commercial expression at the individual consumer level have started down a similar path, with some noteworthy examples including DIRECTV, which is a satellite-based direct-to-home product (originally a military technology); and even fiber optics (the first wide use of the photophone also came in the context of military applications). As multiple input unit costs decrease, processing power form factors shrink further, and the technology itself is no longer protected because of national security, *the motive of obtaining ROI on the extensive R&D will propel humanoid robotics to the consumer level*. We foresee that in the not-too-distant future, every household will have a robot or two.

In January 2024, Stanford University published an Open-Source code called Mobile ALOHA, capable of training low-cost robots to perform complex tasks using as few as 50 human demonstrations in various applications, including cooking, housekeeping, and cleaning. This basically means that you can teach the robot to cook the first 50 dishes in your kitchen or restaurant, and it will be able to continue cooking flawlessly for you. This is just the start of functionality. We have discussed in *Chapter 14* the future of robots with emotion, capable of administering human companionship and returning large amounts of daily time to their human counterparts. The return of time and increase in efficiency of execution in tasks that inhere back to the human counterpart pull in the direction of a utopian outcome.

One notable feature of Mobile ALOHA is its remarkable affordability. The software is Open-Source and therefore free, and the hardware comes with an initial, non-scaled price tag of only $32,000, which is substantially lower than the cost of other similar existing dual-armed robots, some of which are priced at $200,000. We see the costs continuing to come down over time as the functionality improves and the consumer technology moves out of the early adopter phase. The total price of this household robot is already less than the price of a car.

Advancing Treatment and Healthcare Access with AI

Healthcare is another industry sitting at the center of AI's utopian opportunity. In healthcare, AI is set to revolutionize drug development, diagnostics, treatment, and patient care. It promises increased efficiency, cost reduction, and enhanced accessibility, benefiting not only those who hold private insurance policies but the underprivileged as well.

We have already reviewed the revolutionary and vast areas of synthetic biology and cyborg technologies in the previous *Chapters 19* and *20*. These two AI-driven technologies will have a huge transformative impact on healthcare and quality of life, potentially even eradicating heretofore incurable diseases.

Another significant impact of AI in healthcare will be witnessed in the field of research and development. AI can help design drugs and treatments for conditions that are incurable today. For example, AI played a key role in the development of COVID-19 vaccines [Gosh et al.]. Firstly, algorithms were employed to analyze vast datasets related to the virus, including its genetic makeup and potential drug candidates. This accelerated the identification of promising vaccine candidates. Machine Learning models were utilized to predict how the virus might mutate and evolve, aiding in the design of vaccines that could effectively combat different strains. Additionally, AI facilitated the optimization of clinical trial processes by identifying suitable participants and predicting potential outcomes.

Another of the most significant contributions AI will make is enhancing diagnostic accuracy. Advanced AI algorithms are able to analyze extensive medical data at speeds surpassing human abilities. Additionally, algorithms are continually learning from new data and adapting a particularly crucial element in early disease detection and the identification of novel disease factors, such as we saw with COVID-19, allowing for timely intervention and improved patient outcomes.

AI-driven technologies will also revolutionize treatment plans. Tailored treatment regimens, customized based on an individual's genetic makeup, will become the norm, optimizing the chances for success. AI will analyze genetic data, patient histories, and real-time health metrics to suggest personalized treatments, thereby reducing adverse effects, minimizing medicine side effects, and optimizing therapeutic results. This move towards precision medicine is expected to significantly enhance the efficacy of treatments, marking a departure from the traditional one-size-fits-all approach.

Finally, AI will also play a pivotal role in improving healthcare efficiency. Administrative processes, such as appointment scheduling, medical record management, and billing, will be streamlined through AI-powered bots. Moreover, telemedicine, already on the rise, will see a substantial boost through AI integration. Virtual health assistants powered by AI will provide preliminary consultations, answer queries, and even assist in medication management. This will extend the reach of healthcare services to remote and underserved areas, thereby improving healthcare accessibility on a global scale.

Externalities, Market Inefficiency, and a Greener Tomorrow

AI's potential to improve the allocation of resources can also be found at an economy's macro level. New algorithms and their ability to process vast amounts of data, identify patterns, and make predictions with a level of speed and accuracy far beyond human capabilities will also enable economies to better deal with market imperfection, in particular, externalities and the effects of imperfect information.

Economic theory teaches that there are situations in which the allocation of goods and services by a free market is not efficient, with essentially five types of market failure: information asymmetry, market pricing power, complements, externalities, and public goods [Stiglitz]. While some inefficiencies are created by structural elements inside a vertical, many are related to pricing and information asymmetry, problems AI is poised to solve.

The classic example of an externality is pollution, a by-product of industrial activity. There is a price that the market is willing to pay to endure pollution, and perhaps it needs to increase over time. But how is it calculated? Does a pollution producer have the necessary information or incentive to incorporate this as an input in the manufacturing cost equation? Today, that answer is no, resulting in goods and services that are inaccurately priced vis-a-vis their true cost. However, improved algorithms can analyze environmental impact data, quantify it in a manner that reflects the actual impact, and produce a number that represents the actual cost of emission of multiple pollution types, such as carbon dioxide, sulfur dioxide, and nitrogen oxides. Manufacturers can be required to purchase the right to pollute as a license based on their actual output, thus ensuring that the price of the good or service overall reflects its true and actual costs. We can then think of an equation where a firm's actual pricing mode starts at:

Dead Cost Structure= Cost of Input x + Cost of Input y + Cost of Input z + License Fee for Externality Produced

It is possible that some manufacturers that are inefficient in other areas of input—say labor or supply chain—could not absorb this license fee, and they should be forced to shut down if the market's willingness to pay is less than the dead cost structure. If this is true of all firms in a vertical, then products should be pruned. Innovation in industrial sector technology that reduces pollution, when invested and deployed, would reduce emissions and thus reduce the cost of the license, incentivizing manufacturers to rapidly adopt these new technologies. This level of accurate pricing information is not possible without the help of AI. It will help a market grow more efficiently, and across an economy, prices could come down, and more resources would become freed up to reach their most efficient deployment.

Furthermore, AI can be used to facilitate advanced climate modeling and environmental monitoring, providing valuable insights into climate change patterns and helping design effective mitigation strategies. With the ability to process vast datasets in real-time, AI algorithms will enhance our understanding of complex ecological systems, from climate patterns to ecosystem dynamics and what causes them [UN].

Asymmetry of information is another shortcoming that can drive inefficiencies in markets. Acting on incorrect information, incomplete information, or wrong information can lead to obtuse outcomes and the squandering of resources. Typical gaps include data access, data collection, incomplete data, erroneous data, and differing data standards, collectively conspiring to ensure over-reliance on political determination of resource allocation. There are also substantial costs associated with gathering, cleaning, and labeling datasets to be used by AI algorithms, a key input issue that, alongside the lagging development of processing power, has held back the rapid adoption of AI for these types of applications. The existence of AI itself now creates a new market for eliminating this type of asymmetric information.

Maintaining the example of pollution, there has never been an incentive in the market to gather, scrub, and prepare data sets to help solve the externality issues around manufacturing or energy production. The existence of AI solves this chicken/egg problem handily, with either new or existing competitors leveraging this knowledge in the context of their business. Smart grids, enabled by AI algorithms, facilitate real-time data monitoring, allowing more intelligent control of energy distribution. Companies like Siemens have already embraced AI in their smart grid solutions, transforming how energy is distributed and managed. Additionally, AI-driven demand response systems enable users to adjust their energy consumption patterns based on real-time pricing, encouraging more responsible energy use and reducing reliance on fossil fuels during peak demand periods. One of the utility companies that implemented this kind of real-time pricing in the US is OhmConnect [Trabish]. Furthermore, Machine Learning algorithms implemented by companies like IBM in industrial settings can optimize energy consumption in industrial processes by predicting energy demand patterns and identifying opportunities for energy conservation. This trajectory marks a shift towards more sustainable industrial practices, where AI actively contributes to minimizing environmental impact.

Transportation is another area that can be positively impacted by the cascading effect of curtailing externalities. It is a major contributor to carbon emissions, particularly in the form of greenhouse gases from fossil fuel combustion. AI technologies can revolutionize transportation systems, making them more sustainable and eco-friendly. Autonomous vehicles, for instance, will optimize driving patterns, reduce fuel consumption, and minimize traffic congestion through efficient route planning. AI-based predictive maintenance systems can enhance the reliability and fuel efficiency of vehicles, reducing the carbon footprint associated with the manufacturing and disposal of automotive components. AI will also help us over time to improve storage elements of battery technology, contributing further to greener transportation.

Across an entire economy, eliminating market inefficiencies tugs a society toward a utopian outcome as its resources are used more efficiently, its prices reflect broad society-wide costs and not simply the costs of a specific single firm, and many known problems in the structure of the economy can be eliminated. More goods and services will be produced that reflect a better allocation of resources and accurate pricing. Decisions about energy are improved, and thus, so are environmental factors.

Feeding the Planet: AI in Agriculture

Agriculture is another sector that is mission-critical to human life and has an enormous impact on carbon emissions. AI will also be transformational in this sector.

Within agriculture, AI is poised to bring about a paradigm shift in precision farming. AI-powered sensors and drones will monitor crop health, soil conditions, and weather patterns with unprecedented precision. This granular data will enable farmers to optimize resource use, minimizing water and fertilizer usage while maximizing crop yield. The result is not only increased efficiency in agricultural practices but also a reduction in environmental impact, as precision farming minimizes the runoff of harmful substances into water sources and lowers greenhouse gas emissions.

Moreover, AI-driven smart farming systems will make real-time decisions about planting, irrigation, and harvesting based on the big data they analyze, sources that have heretofore never been co-opted into decision-making. This level of automation enhances productivity and resource efficiency while reducing the need for manual intervention. Farmers can expect to see improvements in crop yields and resource utilization. The same applies to aquaculture farms where AI can track water quality, detect diseases in fish populations, and optimize feeding schedules.

Finally, synthetic biology, which we talked about extensively in *Chapter 22*, has profound implications in agriculture as it will lead to designing and engineering food, either vegetables or meat. Already, companies like

BeyondMeat or Impossible Foods develop plant-based substitutes for meat products [Sozzi]. But synthetic biology will take it one step further by creating not only tissues that imitate meat but also utterly new plant or animal species that could be grown in fields or even in industrial laboratories, species that are optimized for nutritional yield and human taste while eliminating harmful effects.

As a result of these advancements in AI-driven precision and sustainable farming, the potential to feed a significantly larger global population becomes increasingly attainable.

AI's Role in Building an Inclusive Society

AI, when harnessed ethically, has the potential to eliminate biases in decision-making, ensure pure logic against a specific goal is achieved, and thus foster inclusivity. Machine Learning algorithms can be designed to eliminate bias and recognize and accommodate diverse perspectives, ensuring that technological advancements benefit everyone, regardless of their demographic background, abilities, or electronic or biological enhancements.

The integration of cyborgs and individuals with synthetic biology enhancements is already reshaping not only our physical capabilities but also the societal fabric that binds us together. The world of sports has embraced the cyborg movement. The first-ever *"Cyborg Olympics,"* called Cybathlon, was celebrated in Switzerland in 2016. This global event officially showcased cyborg sports, where 16 teams comprising individuals with disabilities harnessed technological advancements to morph into cyborg athletes. Six events featured competitors using and controlling advanced technologies, including prosthetic limbs and arms, bikes, motorized wheelchairs, and even robotic exoskeletons [Walker]. Cybathlons differ from the Paralympic Games in the sense that they are not limited to athletes with disabilities. Athletes without physical limitations who augment their bodies with cyborg implants can also participate.

Cybathlons serve as a powerful symbol of inclusivity for cyborgs. By providing a platform for individuals to showcase their abilities augmented by technology, the event challenges preconceived notions and stereotypes. The Cybathlon celebrates the unique talents and capabilities that arise from the fusion of human ingenuity and artificial enhancements.

Synthetic biology, the other frontier in human augmentation that is set to scale, could further reinforce the idea of a more inclusive society. As individuals embrace enhancements and modifications to their biological makeup, they challenge societal norms surrounding beauty, ability, and health. In a more inclusive society, these advancements would not only be celebrated for their scientific achievements but also embraced for their potential to enhance and extend the quality of life for individuals across diverse backgrounds.

The integration of AI, cyborgs, and synthetic biology into society brings with it the imperative for ethical considerations and responsible governance. Striking the right balance between innovation and ethical safeguards is crucial to ensuring that these technological advancements contribute to a more tolerant and inclusive world rather than perpetuating existing disparities. This touches on a key tenet of the book, which is that the right regulatory framework for AI and the construction of algorithms must be made at the current juncture.

In the next chapter, we present the other side of the technology coin, one that leads to a dystopian future, including the features of AI and its various implications that tug both toward and away from that outcome, allowing us to compare it with the utopian possibilities presented above.

23. AI Dystopia: Authoritarianism, Unemployment, Caste Politics

"Recent advances in technology have created both winners and losers via skill-biased technical change, capital-biased technical change, and the proliferation of superstars in winner-take-all markets. This has reduced the demand for some types of work and skills. [...] and indeed, real wages have fallen for millions of people in the United States."

Erik Brynjolfsson

American academic, author, and entrepreneur

The Second Machine Age: Work, Progress, and Prosperity in a Time of Brilliant Technologies [Brynjolfsson and Mcafee]

2014

Professor Erik Brynjolfsson from Stanford University examined the link between technology and income inequality. At the core of Brynjolfsson's thinking is the notion that technology is the primary driver behind steady increases in global inequality indices since 2000. Innovation is rapidly accelerating due to exponential advancements in computing, networking, and AI, leading to increased productivity and GDP. However, despite the expanding pie, not everyone benefits.

In his view, the technology-driven economy disproportionately favors a small group of successful individuals, which Brynjolfsson refers to as *"superstars."* These are often high-tech entrepreneurs who leverage digital technologies to widely distribute and produce their innovative ideas and products. Brynjolfsson believes that there is a shift in economic dynamics wherein success is less dependent on traditional capital ownership and more on the capacity to generate groundbreaking concepts and successful business models that resonate in the digital age.

Brynjolfsson contends that as the *"superstars"* amass fortunes beyond comprehension, the disparity between the ultra-wealthy and the rest of society will widen, potentially leading to social unrest and discontent. The term "superstars" or "AI superstars" captures the essence of those who, by virtue of their technological acumen and overall capability in the digital space, achieve remarkable success and wealth in the global economy. "AI superstars" would include people like Elon Musk, Sam Altman, and Mark Zuckerberg. The potential consequences of such inequality include reduced social mobility, diminished access to opportunities, and erosion of the social fabric that underpins a stable and thriving society.

We do not agree in entirety with this view, although we acknowledge it as insightful and directionally correct. Ownership of financial capital will continue to play as important a role in resource allocation decisions as it always has. Moreover, it is wrong to focus on individual "AI superstar" billionaires as the locus of issues or the sole beneficiaries of technological advancement. The people working at the scaled enterprises driving AI and the technical ecosystems around them also stand to benefit significantly, including Venture Capitalists, start-ups, tech enterprise managers, process outsourcing partners, digital marketing, and product professionals—a very large group of people in every society.

We believe that *the level of human skill and commercial capability that are necessary to participate in the economic system that AI is forging is increasingly higher*, which will, mathematically speaking, render a larger portion of people unable to participate. Under an economic regime of AI tools, higher degrees of commercial judgment, deeper subject matter expertise, and deeper levels of critical thinking will all be needed. Those who can participate may nonetheless lose bargaining power in labor markets as there could be a curtailing of the number of places they can work alongside fiercer competition for fewer jobs.

Look around; your eyes will not betray you. Even a peg lower than so-called superstars, the greater the degree one can use technology as an input to productivity, the greater one's material well-being will generally be. We believe this is as close to a truism as it could be, and that AI is likely to accelerate it.

There remains a high risk of dystopian outcomes along the path leading to Interlace. The reboot to society's OS that AI will drive sits at the center of what could be a dangerous cascading of interests and incentives among big corporations, Governments, and individuals in every Western society. AI as a technology has a magnetic pull to authoritarianism in our view, and Western societies could resemble China if not consciously drawn in a different direction.

Suppose product development, distribution, and innovation in the AI-driven societal OS reside solely in the purview of AI superstars/scaled corporates. These superstars already enjoy a natural oligopoly due to the

Network Effect in the scaling of data aggregation and multiple other capabilities needed to manage the entire AI value chain and society's OS at large. In this case, those who share the opportunity in the huge value it will create must be "*anointed*" to use their algorithms and data sets. Via regulation, the oligopoly structure could become protected by governments which become eager to leverage the capabilities inherent in AI to consolidate their power and secure their own individual spoils.

Worse still, everyone might get a Faustian Deal in the socialist OS that Western governments seize upon as the "*only way to protect you.*" Governments would gain the rationale that their higher purpose is redistribution to keep the economy going on the consumption side as more people lose their jobs to AI, acting as a legal guarantor of the system that maintains the AI oligopoly, significantly curtailing freedom in the process. Governments could become authoritarian in every aspect, using AI tools and functionality to consolidate and perpetuate power, ruling over a population dumbed down by an educational system that creates passive, conformist, plant-eating collectivist sheep that are incapable of critical thinking. And if they give you a nickel of UBI, it will come with a total surrender of your freedom via e-money systems. But given the heaven in the pure consumption and hedonistic world that people have been programmed to embrace by a poor educational system, there is no reason to question any of it.

There will remain no more belief among people in any upside to their personal circumstances, the traditional impetus to question and act to drive progress. Moreover, eugenics-driven AI could quite easily select those that are most likely to be net contributors and pre-track them to professions and roles. Due to mass unemployment and a judiciously set UBI, populations will shrink over time to the Pareto Optimal number to keep consumption and production in balance. The value of human life actually declines as GDP can increase geometrically through AI-productivity gains, even with population reductions, until such time as population equilibrium is reached.

Ironically, all of this could happen alongside actualizing many of the utopian benefits discussed in the previous chapter.

The Science Fiction of AI Dystopias

Two novels that explore AI dystopias with deep realism are "*Autonomous*" by Annalee Newitz in 2017 and "*Manna: Two Visions of Humanity's Future*" by Marshall Brain in 2003. Each work approaches the subject from a different angle. "*Autonomous*" scrutinizes the dangers of excessive corporate power, while "*Manna*" is a very short novella that forewarns of growing inequality, poverty, and the potential misuse of UBI as a tool of control [Brain] [Newitz].

In "*Autonomous,*" Annalee Newitz thrusts readers into the 22nd century. The novel unfolds in a society characterized by the widespread adoption of extreme free-market economics, where humans and robots can be treated as property through a contract referred to as "*indenture.*" The world is dominated by powerful corporations, where these entities wield AI as both a tool for profit and a means of control. Medicines are capable of addressing various issues beyond traditional illnesses through complex drugs that reverse aging effects and enhance physical fitness. However, healthcare is expensive, and these drugs are primarily restricted to the affluent. Consequently, society is marked by class discrimination.

Moreover, autonomous and self-aware AI systems and robots have become an integral part of everyday life. This commodification dissolves the lines between human and machine, forcing readers to confront the moral consequences of treating AI entities as mere property. Newitz delves into the concept of gender, illustrating that robots diverge from the human understanding of gender, with some transitioning from male to female pronouns midway through the book.

In contrast, Marshall Brain's "*Manna*" unfolds in a world where the US grapples with widening economic disparities and social upheaval, marked by increasing poverty and unemployment.

This is how Marshall Brain describes it, in his own words: "*America in 2050 was no different from a third world nation. With the arrival of robots, tens of millions of people lost their minimum wage jobs, and wealth concentrated so quickly. The rich controlled America's bureaucracy, military, businesses and natural resources, and the unemployed masses lived in terrafoam, cut off from any opportunity to change their situation. There was the facade of "free elections," but only candidates supported by the rich could ever get on the ballot. The government was completely controlled by the rich, as were the robotic security forces, the military and the intelligence organizations. American democracy had morphed into a third world dictatorship ruled by the wealthy elite...by 2030, there were video security cameras and microphones covering and recording nearly every square inch of public space in America. There were taps on all phone conversations and Internet messages sniffing for terrorist clues. If anyone thought about starting a protest rally or a riot, or discussed any form of civil disobedience with anyone else, he was branded a terrorist and preemptively put in jail.*" "*Manna*" appears to depict a dystopian future scenario for the US, marked by increasing poverty and unemployment, contrasting with a seemingly utopian portrayal of Australia. In an effort to mitigate social unrest, Australia takes a different route from the US and implements a Universal Basic Income (UBI) system to meet citizens' fundamental needs.

The name of the novella is aptly chosen because Manna refers to a biblical substance as a miraculous edible material that sustained the Israelites during their wandering in the desert. Marshall Brain's intention is indeed to depict Australia's UBI as a utopia and the way to go for humankind. However, a closer examination reveals that both countries are undergoing dystopian transformations in distinct manners. The utopian promise of UBI quickly turns sinister as it transforms into a tool of control, manipulating the population through economic dependency.

The novel paints a bleak picture of how an ostensibly benevolent UBI can become a mechanism for surveillance and manipulation. The loss of autonomy and privacy among citizens, who become increasingly dependent on government-provided income, raises profound questions about the balance between security and individual freedom. As AI systems take over essential societal functions, the potential for abuse becomes evident, ultimately leading to a dystopian reality where the very fabric of social order is under threat.

In summary, *"Autonomous"* emphasizes the need for ethical considerations in AI development, urging society to grapple with the consequences of unchecked corporate power and raising fundamental questions about the ethical boundaries of technological progress. In contrast, the dystopia in *"Manna"* is born not only from economic inequality but also from the erosion of individual agency as AI systems gain unprecedented control over the lives of citizens, and UBI serves in part as the drug that holds it together.

As we mention throughout the book, under the corporate-government nexus using AI, everywhere we turn, authoritarian governments can force a Faustian Bargain upon us such that corporations keep their profit streams growing, their wealth self-perpetuating, and governments keep sustaining their political power.

The End of Human Work

As AI and robotics become more sophisticated and capable of handling complex tasks, routine and repetitive jobs will be increasingly automated. The effects in the short-term will be swift and Machiavellian, though somewhat milder than in the medium and longer terms.

In the short term, most societies' OS will be able to absorb the shock as the effect is gradual. Exceptions will be found in places like the Philippines, which have economies heavily reliant on easily automatable tasks. For example, more than 25% of the Philippines' GDP relies on English language and IT-level BPO businesses, and another 25% on overseas remittances from workers who are primarily in at-risk automatable jobs.

We also recognize that in the short and mid-term, AI has the potential to be a significant job creator, as we discussed in *Chapter 8*. Technology has always created more jobs than it has destroyed, starting with the Neolithic Revolution and extending through the Industrial Revolution. Technology also created net jobs through the mechanization of agriculture during the late 19th and early 20th Centuries and in the IT and Internet explosion starting in the late 1990s.

But we note fundamental differences between the AI revolution and previous turns of the technology screw. Historically, technology has created more jobs than it has destroyed only because three conditions were fully met:

1. Technology allowed humans to do more with fewer resources (e.g., increase productivity), and
2. The new tools themselves required a thinking human to deploy them, and
3. The pace of change occurred over decades, enabling educational systems, human retooling, and reskilling to adjust, or in some cases, for children to learn the new skills relevant to the new technologies.

With the current and coming economic environment guided by AI and robotics, each of these factors has a different configuration:

1. The locus of productivity is migrating up the value chain to increasingly higher levels of judgment, with fewer humans needed to generate higher productivity, as our example of software development in Chapter 22 amply demonstrates.
2. The technology itself, particularly advanced Artificial General Intelligence (AGI), will gradually replace human thinking.
3. The pace of change is outstripping the ability to retrain programs and individuals to keep up, with most people not even knowing *"where to start."* In the last technological revolution, an internet firewall or other IT product, for example, did not improve faster than human capability to learn and manage it; however, that is already not the case with AI.

Worse still, societies are aging, but rapid, high-complexity technical reskilling favors the young. Thus, an increasingly larger number of people will be either unwilling or incapable of learning and adapting fast enough. Punctuating the ill effect, AI itself learns faster than all humans do.

We believe that none of these conditions is apt to become favorable over the long term. The migration of productivity to higher levels of judgment in decision-making has already started and will creep along unrelentingly as algorithms improve. As the speed of change accelerates and the level of intelligence of AI systems increases toward AGI, it will turn into a permanent net destructor of jobs.

Over time, we believe most people everywhere will be permanently displaced, with certain jobs gone to AI and never coming back. Fears of widespread unemployment, particularly in sectors heavily reliant on manual labor, low-level creative, and routine tasks, are well-founded and will accelerate as AI is more widely deployed.

The only real questions are: what will the pace be, and consequently, what is the adjustment mechanism deployed within a society's OS, and ultimately what happens to the concept of work itself?

The effect of economic displacement will cascade. In this dystopian view, people will be forced back to multi-generational living, possibly even communal living. Resources available for travel and leisure will be limited, perhaps even doled out in ways tied to perpetuating political power. And the Government will extend its reach further into the lives of individuals. Concepts such as *"you'll own nothing and be happy"* originated in a 2016 video by the WEF, and alongside *"fractional ownership of your living accommodation"* [Ownify]—concepts already growing louder in Western societies—only portends this outcome, a mass grooming exercise. The population will shrink as the ability to afford children beyond replacement level in society will become a luxury (perhaps through purchasing licenses to procreate) as the Economic Value of Human Life will mathematically decline since GDP per capita can actually increase geometrically with a shrinking human population. The authoritarian socialist Government will double down on its self-appointed need to be redistributionist, allocating the best spoils via licensing and other mechanisms to itself and its political supporters and UBI as a form of sufficient living, perhaps only to those who support them.

While it will take decades to completely activate, *AI could potentially lead to the complete automation of human labor.* We see the eradication of work structured in five stages that run sequentially but with significant overlaps:

1. The first stage of AI-induced unemployment involves the automation of routine, rule-based, standardized, and repetitive tasks, leading to the displacement of workers in roles such as data entry, customer service, and routine manufacturing. This is already underway through Robotic Process Automation (RPA), as we reviewed in *Chapter 6*.
2. The second stage involves the integration of AI into creative processes, impacting jobs that require cognitive skills, pattern recognition, and creativity. Professions such as graphic design, marketing, non-CPA accounting, and sub-partner level legal (paralegals, drafters, brief preparers) may witness significant changes. This process is also

underway through Generative AI, and we have talked about it in *Chapter 8.*

3. The third stage sees mass adoption of autonomous systems and advanced robotics, intensifying the impact on the job market. Industries such as transportation, delivery services, and even jobs that require an empathetic touch, such as elderly care, will witness the displacement of human workers. The first place where this is already happening is in Japan, where automation is seen as an alternative to immigration, as we discussed in *Chapter 17.* In *Chapter 14,* we reviewed how Amazon has started experiments with drone delivery and robotic warehouse work. We also note the robot baristas that have been experimented with even in relatively low labor cost markets [Rozum Robotics] [Newsflare].

4. The fourth stage marks a shift towards the automation of tasks that involve higher-level causal analysis. This includes jobs in finance, research, engineering, medicine, and even creative fields, challenging the notion that certain professions are immune to automation. This phase has not started because AGI would be necessary; we address the topic of how AGI is being developed in *Chapter 25.*

5. In the fifth and final stage, AI becomes deeply integrated into all facets of society, even those involving deep interpersonal relations. Virtually every industry, from education to healthcare, experiences a significant presence of AI-driven systems at all but the highest ownership or judgment levels. The fundamental change to society's OS is complete, with new economic models, human interaction models against, and ultimately, a new culture.

After these five stages, most jobs and economic activities will be automated, rendering human beings non-competitive in the workforce. We note that there are likely to be five categories of individuals at this juncture:

1. Those who own resources and choose to manage them themselves—this group will include the so-called *"superstars,"* the owners of capital and existing production means.

2. Those who administer the political processes—this includes Government officials who add no value but are absorbed into the Government structure.

3. Those who engage in activities solely for personal enjoyment—this group encompasses entrepreneurs who derive satisfaction from creating companies or enjoying complete independence, as well as artists who find fulfillment in expressing themselves through their art even in the absence of economic benefit.

4. Those who primarily engage in sports—enhanced humans and cyborgs.

5. Those who literally do nothing but consume—the vast majority of humankind.

In reference to this last group, during the AI Safety Summit in Bletchley Park, UK, in November 2023, Rishi Sunak, the UK prime minister, asked Elon Musk about the impact of AI on employment [Henshall]. Musk forecasted that human labor might become obsolete: *"I think we are seeing the most disruptive force in history here[...] There will come a point where no job is needed. You can have a job if you want to have a job for personal satisfaction, but the AI will be able to do everything.* "Perhaps you ask, *"How is this final result dystopian?"* With consumption perfectly fungible as an activity, those who only consume will likewise become fungible and replaceable in the broader context of the system.

The Furtive Reality of Universal Basic Income

In the previous chapter, we introduced the concept of UBI to offset AI-driven economic dislocation, an idea gaining traction in political and economic discussions. UBI is proposed to provide all citizens with a regular, unconditional sum of money.

Advocates of UBI argue that it can alleviate poverty, enhance social welfare, and empower individuals. However, a closer examination reveals the potential for UBI to be employed as a tool for mass control, influencing the behavior and sentiments of the populace, with no guarantee that the wealth created by AI efficiencies will ever reach people at all, let alone in a fair way.

UBI generates many dystopian-leaning concerns. The first concern is the creation of economic dependency among recipients and where that leads at scale. By establishing a continuous flow of financial support with no requirements to receipt, increasing swathes of individuals may become reliant on the state for their sustenance. This dependency can easily be leveraged by those in power, both Governments and the oligopolies they protect, to subtly manipulate the masses, fostering a sense of gratitude and loyalty to the governing authority. *AI is a technology that can aid absolutism to an overpowering degree.*

Second, Governments with an objective of power and control could predictably manipulate UBI eligibility requirements and amounts disbursed to influence voting behavior or engage in social engineering, making elections a formality and a sham. By adjusting UBI levels based on political allegiance or compliance or controlling access to licensing to conduct activities under AI, those in power can easily shape the political landscape, punishing those who have a different opinion or whoever they want, based on their own visions of social engineering. This would likely take the form of quelling dissent and discouraging resistance, creating a population more amenable to, and perhaps even happy with, authoritarian socialism. *It would likely contribute to cultural homogenization, with the new societal OS being solely defined by who owns and programs the algorithms.* In short, UBI could lead to a society less inclined to challenge authority or question the status quo, which is not good for democracy. The government-controlled educational system will aid and abet it. There is nothing you will be able to do about it. Even on paper, Western Governments will transform from being in the employ of the people to becoming rulers over the people, with the US itself risking full reversion to pre-1776 forms of Aristocratic Rule.

Third, people acting in their own self-interest will take whatever Faustian Bargain is thrown at them, with the fear of losing their financial lifeline, ensuring conformity to societal norms and Government directives. The actual implementation of UBI provides a further case in point. It involves a sophisticated system of financial transactions and monitoring, which renders it, at core, a vast surveillance infrastructure, allowing authorities to track and analyze the spending habits of individuals—rejecting spending it does not want and using the data to feed algorithms that further strengthen its ability to control you. This data could also be exploited to identify dissenters or individuals with anti-establishment views, enabling preemptive measures to be taken to maintain control. For example, in *Chapter 24,* we will explain China's Social Credit System, which, in its origin, is a financial monitoring system.

Proponents argue that UBI could encourage entrepreneurship and creativity by providing a safety net. Even if that were true, there is also an omnipresent risk at the margin of reduced motivation and productivity, with the percentage of the population that sits on the inside of the margin a function of the level of UBI and rules of access set by the Government. This effect is independent of other elements of UBI.

One of the reasons why many of the *"AI superstars"* and current Western politicians are supportive of UBI is because it is a continuation of the current expansive monetary policies where central banks are printing money. That money is getting disproportionately concentrated in the hands of the AI superstars, who own an increasing share of valuable non-currency-based assets, e.g., company ownership or assets that produce something. Further, this makes the fiat or digital currency less valuable while at the same time making the assets of product and service creation and distribution increasingly more valuable. One way of implementing UBI would be redirecting a combination of newly printed money and increased taxes into UBI subsidies. People would use those UBI subsidies to continue buying the products and services created by the AI superstars. This way, they would continue increasing their concentration of assets while most of the population has no assets and relies on monthly subsidies.

Although it might sound contradictory, one of the most effective ways to promote human employment would actually be not providing UBI. If companies start replacing people with robots in a massive way and unemployment reaches a very significant share of the population, there would no longer be clients to buy the products of those companies. They would have to scale up employment in any case. This is similar to Henry Ford's reasoning for paying employees well enough so that they could afford a car. From a free-market perspective, markets have self-correction mechanisms that allow them to self-regulate and make sure unemployment does not reach the kind of level that AGI could take it to if left unchecked. For libertarians, it is precisely market interventions like UBI, which, although well-intentioned, end up creating both economic and spiritual poverty.

The End of Democracy, Rising Authoritarianism

While we believe AI and authoritarianism are somewhat natural dance partners, the fact is that Democratic institutions are already deteriorating worldwide. Even in the US, over the past few decades, the country has witnessed a decline in public trust in democratic institutions. According to Pew Research Center surveys, trust in the federal Government dropped from 77% in 1964 to a mere 20% in 2021[Pew]. Pew Research Center also highlighted that the ideological divide between Democrats and Republicans in the US has widened considerably, with Democrats and Republicans holding more negative views of each other than at any point in the past two decades [Pew]. Moreover, the Reporters Without Borders' World Press Freedom Index has highlighted a decline in the US ranking, dropping from 17th place in 2002 to 45th in 2023 [RSF].

The influence of money—and whatever values come with it—being able to buy political outcomes remains a cancerous issue to the democratic corpus. The Center for Responsive Politics reported that in the 2020 US election cycle, candidates, parties, and outside groups spent a record-breaking $14.4 billion [Goldmacher]. Other Western countries have headed in a similar direction. The influx of money raises concerns about the undue influence of wealthy individuals and special interest groups on the political decision-making process and ultimately on the ability and incentive to actively change the OS of society, recasting it to suit themselves. The fact that literally everything seems for sale is not good.

Perhaps the most significant indicator of the decline of democratic institutions was the Cambridge Analytica scandal involving the unauthorized collection of Facebook users' data for political profiling and targeted advertising during the 2016 US presidential election. While the incident emphasized vulnerabilities in data privacy, it also catalyzed the development of global data protection laws, addressing the urgent necessity for strengthened safeguards [Confessore]. We talked about these data regulations in *Chapter 7*.

The intrinsic oligopolistic nature of AI as a technology represents the roots of dystopian outcomes, including the eventual rise of authoritarianism. AI is inexorably intertwined with data access, management, and deployment; as only the largest corporates can build and scale full AI ecosystems, a *Network Effect* ensues:

1. Vast amounts of data are collected via massively scaled sourcing, leading to the building of broad datasets across human behavior.
2. These datasets allow the continuous development of better algorithms.
3. These algorithms are productized and distributed through aligned cloud-enabled company mechanisms.
4. These products and services then enable the capture of even more data.

Google was itself conceived as a company in 1998 to *"organize the world's information"* [Google]. The more data acquired by these few large-scale entities, the more refined and powerful their AI algorithms become, and each passing day creates a more formidable barrier for potential competitors. The associated distribution path of the technology, the so-called cloud companies like AWS, Azure, and Google Cloud, collectively require hundreds of billions of US Dollars of investment and years of time to scale, further punctuating the naturally oligopolistic nature of AI as a technology. As we will explore in *Chapter 24*, the Chinese Communist Party (CCP) is overtly organizing a cartel of large corporations from key industry segments, each having troves of specific types of data, precisely to build an insurmountable and complete *"centralized database"* to feed its political and economic ambitions within its overall AI strategy.

The ability of this structure to influence the political landscape and outcomes represents the seeds of dystopian outcomes. The financial capability and market power of the oligopolists and the *"AI superstars"* increasingly shape and control much of the means of efficiency and wealth gains in society, enabling strong influence over governments and regulatory bodies whilst possessing the incentive to do so. This influence, often termed *"Regulatory Capture"* when reviewing 20th-century political and economic systems, becomes more pronounced, enabling the owners of technology to shape policies in their favor; they naturally seek to perpetuate their market dominance and stifle potential challenges from emerging competitors.

The complicity of the Government, and moreover, its interest in using the unique opportunity afforded by AI to consolidate its power, is the fertilizer of dystopian outcomes. If Government leaders prioritize controlling or ruling ahead of serving their constituents, they may be inclined to exploit the potential of AI to consolidate their authority. They could easily and nearly automatically see AI as a means to justify and strengthen their individual power, ensuring they benefit personally from the advancements and resources it offers.

And finally, *the specific functionality available with AI applications is the "water and sunlight" of dystopian outcomes.* We have mentioned throughout the book how AI is networked, collectivist, non-atomistic, and thus antithetical in some ways to individualist Western democratic thinking. The tactical capabilities facilitated by AI, many of which are already present in society, have the potential to bring about dystopian outcomes. Yuval Noah Harari points out some of them in his 2015 Book *"Homo Deus: A Brief History of Tomorrow."* [Harari]

First, AI algorithms can manipulate information flows, influencing public opinion and decision-making processes. Through targeted content delivery and personalized messaging, AI can shape narratives and perceptions, creating a distorted reality. This manipulation undermines the democratic principle of an informed citizenry, raising concerns about the authenticity of public discourse and the ability of citizens to make well-informed decisions. AI's potential role in influencing electoral processes poses a direct threat to the integrity of democratic elections. From deepfake technologies to algorithmic manipulation of social media, AI can be exploited to disseminate disinformation, sow discord, and compromise the legitimacy of electoral outcomes. It can also gradually change people's values society-wide.

Second, the rise of AI in decision-making processes could lead to a shift away from human accountability. Automated systems, driven by algorithms, may make crucial decisions without transparency or ethical oversight. Governance is now under the control of AI systems, establishing a technocratic rule where algorithms oversee every aspect of human existence. Governments could relinquish control to AI systems, leading to decisions exclusively driven by efficiency and data, neglecting ethics, human emotions, and individual rights. The governing AI rigorously controls information, engaging in manipulation and censorship to uphold its authority.

Third, AI's integration into surveillance technologies poses a significant threat to individual privacy and civil liberties. Automated surveillance systems equipped with facial recognition, predictive analytics, and data mining capabilities can amass vast amounts of personal information. Every move of citizens can be closely observed, and their behaviors and conversations can be documented, scrutinized, and utilized to enforce social control. Privacy could become an antiquated concept with ubiquitous AI systems perpetually monitoring and examining individuals, swiftly identifying and suppressing dissent and independent ways of thinking. As governments and powerful entities exploit these technologies, citizens may find themselves under constant scrutiny, fostering an environment where dissent and individual freedoms are stifled.

And we note that this is only half of the equation. As we will explore in *Chapter 28*, the values that are instilled in AI do matter. Whoever controls the algorithms and the data used to train them has the power over time to control all of your thinking—and you may never even notice it. The values of the algorithm owners become the values of society and not visa-versa.

The End of Truth

Left unchecked, the custodians of AI and the societal OS can use AI to suit their own individual self-interest at the expense of the self-determining, open, and Democratic polity. The AI oligopolies seek Government policy to protect their control over the massive wealth and value generated by AI, and the Government seeks access to AI tools as a mechanism of control and mass manipulation. The CEO of Meta, the world's largest social media platform, has admitted Government collusion to suppress information that would have been adverse to 2020 US Democratic Party election interests [BBC].

Prior to the creation of AGI, during the Transition, *AI could foment the end of truth,* representing a forward-looking return to the past of absolutist and aristocratic rule, a reversal of all we have labored for centuries to achieve.

The pursuit of truth and the use of logic in decision-making presented the world with its first anti-authoritarian weapon. Athenian Democracy was in large part built on the back of rational discourse as a replacement for blind adherence to tradition and self-serving and often ill-informed dictates of individuals. The Enlightenment, also called the Age of Reason, was the intellectual movement in Europe in the 18th century that preached knowledge based on reason and truth, which was the basis of freedom, which led to self-determination, which in turn led to happiness. It emanated from the Age of Science (Isaac Newton's *"Principia Mathematica"* in 1687 stands as its representative work), but it was equally a reaction to absolutist and exploitative monarchies that failed to advance human potential. Truth was valued and sought as a mechanism to guide decision-making aimed at economic, scientific, and intellectual progress.

In a sense, actively seeking the truth is the engine of our societal wealth, democracy, and the written constitutions that secure our freedoms. It has, therefore, also been what has enabled our arts and creativity to openly thrive and our technology and science to advance whilst ensuring we do not return to the aristocratic, absolutist rule of our history. To exemplify the point, we note that where there are systemic untruths, there has been repression and a lack of economic progress. This is not only in the West but globally, indicating that it is human truism. The internet, social media, and cell phones may have transformed the channels of propaganda, but North Korea, Russia, Iran, Cuba, and Venezuela, among other authoritarian regimes mired in economic failure, still fully control the information that circulates in their societies, deploying domestic propaganda and disinformation to strengthen their exercise of national power [Bishop].

As AI tools advance and permeate Western societies, truth is already beginning to fray at the seams. A simple Google search reveals at the top of the page results that there is apparently no such thing as truth, but rather *"Seven kinds of truth"* and that they are all rooted in *"sensation and emotion."* Reason and logic, the cornerstones of scientific and economic advancement and the overthrow of historic despotism are being replaced with *"feelings"* which are subject to misunderstanding and manipulation, groupthink, and irrationality; worse still, this can lead to horrifying outcomes. *"We live in an age of fake news, but it wasn't invented with Twitter and YouTube – it was used in the 1930s to make real people disappear,"* said art curator Natalia Sidlina at the opening of a Soviet Era exhibit at London's Tate Modern [Macdonald and Klutsis].

One of the newly formulated types of truth is called *"individual truth"* and is defined as *"the way the individual sees or experiences the world."* However, this has nothing to do with truth. It is the definition of perception. People are being actively taught by AI search and response algorithms -and the public educational systems—that whatever they think or feel must be the truth. The next listing offers that there is something called *"subjective truth"* that teaches that truth can vary depending on the context; this is an oxymoron. Then there are copious statements by many ordinary people, which can be represented by a random blog post listed on the top page of an internet search: *"For something to be true, it must be accepted by the masses."* [Beman]

The masses may think something is the truth, but that does not make it so. There is always and only one truth—and it sits alongside how a question is asked and the different layers of granularity in inquiry. Driven by AI—at a technology level and in the politics of its use—we are already in the midst of a mass grooming exercise that expunges the truth, replacing it with individually generated feelings and perceptions. This "anti-truth" is fully subject to manipulation, paving the way for an AI-denominated authoritarian socialist future, a future where the truth is overtly hidden from us in order to control us.

While information is not truth, arriving at the truth requires information. First and foremost, AI itself is blurring the lines between what is fake and what is real information, making the difference visually, auditorily, and intellectually imperceptible. This, in turn, makes it harder to ever find the

Truth while risking individual reliance on falsehoods for key decisions. Deepfakes, which we covered in *Chapter 8*, can be employed to create fake videos of individuals saying things they never actually said. Bots can disseminate that and any other false information across any internet-connected touchpoint, including web pages and social media platforms. Algorithms keep people trapped inside an endless reinforcement loop of a single point of view. Since social media platforms are designed as echo chambers, this false information can appear highly convincing to millions of people, leading them to manipulation.

Second, the end of truth will not happen passively or via poor individual decision-making but rather by deliberate effort within society's OS. Control over AI to the degree enabled by the AI oligopolies and Government provides them with the capability to actively, systematically, and perpetually target anyone with whatever they want them to believe. There is an old adage in Marketing about "the number of advertising impressions needed to drive a conversion." Based on human psychology, marketers generally believe in the following heuristics:

- The first four impressions of an advertisement yield nothing.
- The 5th time, you pay attention to it and maybe read it.
- The 6th to 12th times lead to wonder if maybe this is valuable.
- The 13th time, you think it is valuable.
- The 14th to 19th time, you slowly convince yourself to make a purchase.
- The 20th time you buy.

Humans require clear, repetitive, and frequently delivered messages in order for information to be stored in the brain's long-term memory. There are three types of memory encoding: visual, auditory, and semantic. People retain less than half of the information they receive in an hour, so frequency is important[Murre].

The use of algorithms in social media is exactly based on principles of frequency and repetition: they create impressions to learn what you believe, which might itself, in part, be formed by mainstream media and your education and other touchpoints within the OS that are biased concepts masquerading as truths. Then, they reinforce what you already believe, and double-down on a point of view without questioning it. For that purpose, social media algorithms are multifaceted, including feed and search ranking, content and friend/connection recommendations, advertising targeting, content moderation, engagement prediction, and real-time trend detection, among many other aspects. This curtails the search for the truth via *"information overload."* If someone is not actively looking for the truth, there is a high probability that they will never find it.

Third, in *Chapter 9*, we discussed synthetic data, which involves using realistic-looking but ultimately fake data to train algorithms. This is significant because very few companies have access to sufficiently large, actionable, scaled datasets, except for giants like Facebook, Google, Tesla, and a few others. Consequently, companies that aim to develop complex AI algorithms but lack access to extensive real data must resort to using synthetic data. Synthetic data mimics reality but is not genuine data. It can, therefore, be a double-edged sword as it may inadvertently lead algorithms to produce outcomes that are not based on real-world data. As a result, over time, the expanding use of AI in the economy will make it increasingly challenging to distinguish between real and fake output.

Fourth, there is overt disinformation being pumped into society at every touchpoint. According to the World Economic Forum report called "*Global Risks 2024*", in the next two years, misinformation and disinformation will be the most severe risk we face in the West, surpassing wars, social polarization, crises, or even climate change. The WEF argues that if AI is not limited, malicious actors could spread disinformation, especially in times of significant elections in Western societies.

The WEF seems very concerned about the legitimacy of governments and portrays misinformation as a threat to global peace and security. To address this, the WEF is advocating for information control, possibly leading to what could be the largest exercise of official censorship seen since the *Index Librorum Prohibitorum* (List of Prohibited Books). As George Soros puts it: "*AI [...] has absolutely nothing to do with reality. AI creates its own reality and when that artificial reality fails to correspond to the real world – which happens quite often – it is discarded as hallucination. This made me almost instinctively opposed to AI and I wholeheartedly agree with the experts who argue that it needs to be regulated.*" [Soros et al.]

The fight against misinformation and disinformation was officially inaugurated at Davos 2024, and what is proposed by the WEF will make people's lives resemble a Disney tale mired in fantasy and untruth, leading to deeper dystopian outcomes. As we have pointed out throughout the book, the drive to control AI and regulate it is not being led with the broad benefit of society in mind. On the contrary, *governments and corporations want to keep control of this technology and do not want it in the hands of everyone.*

In China's AI-driven societal OS, it is clear who decides what to present as true and how they decide it. In the Western world, the cradle of free speech where laws penalize slander and harassment, where we are all responsible for having an informed opinion and actively pursuing truth, it will not be clear who decides what to present as any one of the so-called seven types of truth. It seems the idea of the WEF is for governments, AI oligopolists, and academics to determine it themselves.

The current discussion on misinformation and the end of truth reminds us of the history of the Internet. There was a time when the Internet was a tool of pure freedom, a tool of democratization, and a free flow of ideas we all could seek. That internet was called Web 1.0. We moved from Web 1.0 to our current Web 2.0 in a short span of a decade, complete with a space of absolute control largely in the hands of a few companies, where we give up our privacy in exchange for services and hypothetical security. Web 3.0, which is being explored at this moment, represents one last chance for freedom and decentralization online. Similarly, AI at this moment could be an environment for freedom, providing greater access and insight, a tool to make everyone better off, or like Web 2.0, it could be an environment for control. From the talks in Davos in January 2024, it seems that direction is the latter.

From our point of view, this is a critical issue. Davos is now seeking to promote the idea that the world is in danger without information control. It has always been called censorship, but the euphemism that politely obscures the truth is *"the fight against misinformation and disinformation."*

One of the most immediate—and terrifying—dystopian consequences of AI is that its widespread use could spell the end of truth. It would be a bitterly ironic outcome for a technology that is marketed as the most democratizing force in human history.

The antidote to the end of truth will always be the same: to better inform ourselves, to seek to actively disconfirm our beliefs with facts, and to be skeptical of information that is fed to us rather than that which we actively seek. Education plays a key role, but as we discuss next, it also faces significant challenges in the age of AI.

The Creative Destruction of Education

In the previous chapter, we presented some of the dynamic enhancements that AI is poised to deliver to the educational field throughout the lifetime learning cycle—K-12, collegiate, and professional ongoing learning. Standing out among them are didactic tool enhancements, the replacement of scheduled learning with Adaptive Learning, place-shifted learning, and AI-driven immersive learning, all of which could contribute to enabling humans to reach our fullest potential.

But what will the curriculum be? It is the zillion-dollar question, commercially speaking, and much of that will be defined by the subjective view of what constitutes "fullest potential" in the new societal OS. The method of teaching (adaptive learning, tracking, pace and breaks, teacher-led classrooms, forced memorization, and the historical semester system) is only a reflection of the science of optimizing human neural pathways. *But what is taught is a function of human decision around the values of the AI-driven societal OS.*

In general, investment made in education builds opportunities for national economic development and serves only this purpose [DBSA]. With AI performing better than even the best-educated humans in many realms of mental endeavor affecting economic productivity, we believe that human value over time could become disproportionately tied to political productivity. What is taught in schools and why could become a slow roll to support the new societal OS with its authoritarian collectivist core. Specifically, all curriculum decisions, big data gathering, and analytics activities engendered by the new AI-driven teaching tools could become centralized to support control motives, predictive models, and gearing people for specific outcomes.

Overall, education could become an organ for the new OS and its authoritarian socialist core to perpetuate itself by quelling the inquisitive and questioning mind and programming it instead with one-sided ideology and mindsets deemed positive to the objectives of the Government It tragically eschews the objective of providing students with critical thinking skills, and instead offers behavior patterns that benefit society [Nikolla, A.]. Much like in all authoritarian regimes throughout history, critical thinking, comparative thinking, and relative thought could become buried in an avalanche of predetermined ideological pedagogy and behavior modification exercises [Mullahi, Dhmitri].

The rapid decline in educational standards in the US, represented by middle and high school math scores being on an annual decline and reaching their lowest level ever [Washington Post], suggests that the US is already at the front side of a dystopian outcome. What we presently think of as K-12 learning could become dual-tracked from an early point wherein two separate school types emerge: one type for students who are pre-determined via genetic construction, societal affiliations, and big data analytics to have the aptitude for STEM subjects and another type for the larger body of *"everyone else."* Following the pattern set by authoritarian socialist regimes of the past, such as Albania, Universities will no longer be considered scientific studies centers but merely teaching institutions that indoctrinate [Mullahi, Dhmitri].

Separate institutions with close ties to big corporations would drive STEM studies and scientific advancement. This will include what is traditionally viewed as medicine, which will become indistinguishable as a discipline from synthetic biology and as a practice from the ultimate social control tool by the authoritarian Government, all under the banner of *"progress.* "The teaching methodology, even under Adaptive Learning, would not be elastic, with the technique resembling the theory of BF Skinner [Skinner], called the stimulus-response theory, which is based on the repetition of an action many times, or the ultimate method to expunge critical thinking and create human drones that do not question decisions of authorities. Adaptive Learning can indeed be geared to repeat concepts in different ways, and nothing is assured about student-teacher interaction or what is permissible. The student would have neither the mandate nor the aptitude to think independently and transform the information in an attempt to further knowledge and understanding; the curriculum itself would come to rely purely on a cognitive structure (e.g., fixed schema, heuristics, and mental models) rather than being able to *"act and transform beyond the given information"* which is the hallmark of true understanding.

An examination of education policy and practice in the world's authoritarian regimes suggests an unmistakable pattern—gearing thinking towards the collective, which is aligned with expunging critical thinking. Collectivism is one of the common elements of any authoritarian ideology, a *"first principle"* of the educational system; education within and through the collective is considered fundamental, with the formation of a collectivist spirit as an educational ideal [Dalascu]. It reinforces the prevailing singular ideology that is imbued in all curricula.

Literature presents a sad example of what can happen within this scenario. A society's culture and way of thinking at any given epoch is reflected in its historical literature. The writing, consumption, and eventual discussion around it can be viewed in pedagogy as one of the most efficient ways to synthesize ideas, predefined values, and selected ideologies, lending to either continuity or dissolution; for this reason, the entire literature taught in schools could end up being generated by AI, oxymoronically presented as *"timeless classics of recent origin,"* the interpretation and discussion of which would be as one-sided as the stories themselves.

Education is a form of programming. Dissent, free-thinking, and critical thinking would be expunged except for those that are tracked into it. Individual success in educational processes has always been a tool of self-determinism, self-selection into economic processes, and entrance into reward systems. But with centralization of educational decisions, social role predetermination and tracking, and mass curriculum geared around behavioral training deemed positive for the new societal OS, people will now become the tools of the regime, with education becoming a tool of grand manipulation. Freedom of speech, thought, and self-direction becomes an estranged ideal.

The 1988 song *"I Want Out"* by German rock band Helloween describes youthful angst around a lack of freedom and self-determination:

> *"From our lives beginning on*
> *we are pushed in little forms,*
> *no one asks us how we'd like to be."*

In the dystopian outcomes begotten by AI, the destruction of education represents a nail in the coffin of freedom from which there will indeed be no way out.

The Perfect Storm: AI and the Next Depression

The Transition could happen amidst a period of economic depression, which could exacerbate the social implications of job substitution. For some economists, like Ray Dalio, the founder of US hedge fund Bridgewater Associates, there is a possibility of impending economic depression beginning in the late 2020s, an idea rooted in his extensive knowledge of historical economic cycles [Dalio].

Based on this study of economic cycles, he points to several factors that are currently contributing to the increasing likelihood of severe depression on the near-term horizon: increasing income inequality, reaching the limitation of monetary policy in stimulating economic growth, and rising levels of global debt to historical levels. Dalio believes that the traditional tools used by central banks may be reaching their limits, leaving little room for effective response in the face of a severe economic downturn.

Historically, economic downturns have served as catalysts for businesses to seek operational efficiencies, driving them to explore automation as an alternative to human labor. If a severe economic depression happens, as Dalio points out, that would be the moment for AI job substitution to accelerate across the economy. We do not know when the next depression will be, but given the cyclical nature of capitalism, it is extremely likely it will happen sometime in the next 20 years.

Much like we see differences in the nature of work under AI advancement compared with previous technology revolutions, there are differences this time around in global economies. In previous economic cycles, where recovery often led to the reabsorption of displaced workers into the job market, the rise of AI makes this reabsorption unlikely. AI systems, once implemented, can perform tasks more efficiently and cost-effectively than humans, reducing the incentive for companies to rehire human workers even during economic rebounds. Further, the level of US Government debt at 123% of GDP in 2023 is at historically high levels, with the world's median at 55% [World Population Review] [Lu and Conte]. This will curtail growth and the speed of recovery, exacerbating the need to rapidly deploy AI to reach efficiencies.

The tandem impact of economic downturns and widespread AI job substitution creates an explosive mix that can fuel social unrest. Displaced workers grappling with the challenges of reskilling and transitioning to new roles may find themselves marginalized and disenfranchised. This sense of alienation and inequality can manifest in protests, strikes, as well as potentially civil disobedience and populism as individuals demand economic reform and a reevaluation of societal priorities. As the clouds part, there at the center of the heavens is the authoritarian socialist regime smiling with open arms, promising to save you.

Two Castes of Human Beings

The demise of true democracy and the imminence of mass unemployment would not be the most adverse consequences that AI might usher in for humankind during the Transition.

According to Political economist and philosopher Francis Fukuyama, transhumanism—which AI makes possible—is mankind's "*most dangerous idea*" since it could erode the egalitarian principles of liberal democracy by fundamentally altering human nature and creating unnatural differences among humans [Fukuyama].

As discussed in *Chapters 20* and *21*, AI has the potential to fundamentally change human biology itself through technologies like cyborgization and synthetic biology. Our contemporary society is very concerned about racial, gender, and other types of discrimination. Yet, individual humans share a high percentage of their genetic code. The DNA sequence of any two humans is about 99.6% identical [genome.gov]. For the remaining 0.4%, it is challenging, not to say impossible, to argue which differences make us better or worse, particularly when it comes to visual traits we abstractly define as race. Imagine a world where some people, those who have been modified through synthetic biology or cyborg implants, *are objectively better* than those who have not been enhanced because they live longer, are brighter, are physically stronger, and are more environmentally resilient.

These emerging technologies for human enhancement cannot be handed out evenly; as we noted in the introduction to the book, we expect uneven asymmetric access and for many to be left behind either by choice or by fiat. So, who decides who goes first and who gets what? In general, we would expect primary accessibility for those with more significant financial means. Furthermore, those who go first will find value in curtailing access to others, further deepening the chasm between the wealthy and the poor and ultimately fostering a "*genetic divide.*" In a purely Machiavellian way, society could also actively pre-select those who should receive it, and the decision criteria can be aided by AI's power to make the optimal decisions based on the politically oriented "*ethical*" values that governments might have mandated to embed in AI. As a result, the receivers would likely end up being those who will ensure the least drain on resources over time or those favorable to the reigning political regime. If social democratic reforms fail to keep pace with the implementation of enhancement technologies, this will lead to a two-tiered society comprising genetically enhanced individuals as the "*haves*" and those without enhancements as the "*have-nots*." There is likely no going back from that point.

Apart from dividing society economically, these tiers would also divide society into two distinct human species, one of which is significantly advantaged in terms of intellectual and physical well-being and capabilities. From a strictly scientific standpoint, this could actually happen by design and be pressed into a population, perhaps slowly over time, such that it was not noticed. In such a societal OS, different treatments of individuals would not be based on a subjective sense of racial superiority but on the objective reality that one is physically or intellectually inferior to the other. The lower intellectual or physical abilities and health would result in a diminished moral position. This could lead to conflicts between human and posthuman species and even escalate into caste warfare.

The issue goes beyond the lack of access to human enhancement technologies for specific individuals. Some human beings will also not want to get enhanced, even if they could economically afford it, because of ethical and philosophical convictions. James Hughes, president of the World Transhumanist Association, calls them derogatorily "*bioluddites,*" drawing a comparison from the historical Luddite movement of the 19th century, which opposed the mechanization of labor during the Industrial Revolution [Hugues]. In *Chapter 30*, we delve into the most ominous implications this could lead to: war.

Species Identities and Eugenics: A Deja Vu

War is a highly dramatic possibility—though probable. Before reaching such an extreme, numerous other factors must go awry, one of which is the widespread use of eugenics.

Under Interlacing and the effect of Synthetic Biology, the differences between human species could be so significant that one group might be unable to interbreed with the other. This could result from biological factors, such as an inherent inability, or it could be due to social unacceptability as the society's OS changes. Additionally, deliberate state-sponsored eugenics programs can easily become the norm under a mantle of "*efficiency and improvement*" with forced gene combinations, procreation licensing, and social role predetermination. As we have discussed, AI is already providing the capability to unlock genetic understanding, stack-rank genetic value in an unassailable scientific way, and write a bulletproof blueprint for how to both synthetically and naturally enhance the gene pool. Selective breeding, or, on the flip side, proscribed breeding, both aim to enhance the human gene pool for success and survival even as populations shrink under the realities of AI-driven economies. This will unquestionably lead to varying levels of division as any such process unfolds—if it is initially visible to people at all. Implementing eugenics programs may naturalize and reinforce social hierarchies, providing authoritarian regimes with new control methods. Even benignly, imagine an online mating/dating service that matched genes with interpersonal compatibility and projected lifetime economic value to a bulletproof scientific level. Literally, all that is required is a drop of your blood and 100 of your likes on Facebook.

The most notorious instance of eugenics unfolded in authoritarian Nazi Germany, where state-sponsored programs aimed at racial hygiene led to the systematic extermination of millions through forced sterilizations, euthanasia programs, and, ultimately, the Holocaust. However, eugenics concepts are not unique to authoritarian regimes [Rutherford]. In the US, for example, compulsory sterilization laws targeted individuals considered socially or genetically unfit, with the Buck v. Bell case in 1927 setting a precedent for widespread eugenic sterilization. In the United Kingdom, the Mental Deficiency Act of 1913 allowed for the institutionalization and sterilization of individuals deemed mentally deficient, aligning with eugenic concerns about hereditary mental illnesses. The same was common in Australia, Japan, and Brazil, among many other countries.

Transhumanist organizations unequivocally disassociate themselves from the eugenic theories and practices of the early 20th century, which are now universally rejected. They also reject the racist underpinnings upon which those theories and practices were constructed. But the reality is that the risk is ever-present so long as there is recognition of species or cultural differences among people, given the new-found technical ease of developing such a program under AI's existing advancements and synthetic biology's ability to deliver gene-level changes across populations, would you trust increasingly less democratic Governments to not go down this path during an overall reboot of society's OS?

From Lab to Bioterrorism

Finally, biosecurity would be another risk that AI could bring about in a dystopian future. Synthetic biology could be intentionally misused to harm the environment or society. It is essential to carefully consider the ethical implications of synthetic biology and biosecurity to create proactive legal and technical barriers against the unauthorized use of synthetic biology. The ethical conversation surrounding biology issues is not wholly novel. They rehash earlier conversations about genetically modified organisms and recombinant DNA, and many jurisdictions have already defined robust regulatory frameworks for pathogen research and genetic engineering.

A considerable worry stems from the mounting possibility of bioterrorism as synthetic biology techniques advance, and we see more available access to even less-than-cutting-edge technology that is still immensely powerful. The creation of new synthetic biology techniques has rendered it easier to manipulate pathogenic organisms and use them as biological weapons, for example—far more deadly, accessible, and scalable than synthesizing anthrax and sending it through the mail system, as we saw happen in the US in 2021. Through incidents such as the COVID-19 pandemic, terrorist organizations are becoming more aware of the social, political, and economic upheavals that could be brought about by these kinds of bioweapons. Juan Zarate, a former Deputy National Security Advisor for Combating Terrorism, uses these words to describe how COVID has made the possibility of bioterrorism more real [Cruickshank and Rassler]. *"With the world now reeling simply from a novel coronavirus with a relatively low lethality rate, some extreme terrorist groups and rogue scientists willing to venture into apocalyptic fields might see this moment as a catalyst for exploring again the possibilities of bioterrorism."*

Having now presented both utopian and dystopian views of the future, we now focus the AI lens on present-day China and the increasing competition with the US to become the world's leading AI superpower.

24. China and the Cold War of Artificial Intelligence

"Human thinking has to be careful not to run away with itself and not to liberate capacities that can wind up in the destruction of humanity, and that's where the United States and China have a special obligation because they're in a special position to make progress scientifically. But how to limit the possible interpretations and applications is a challenge for each country and then for the countries between themselves."

Henry Kissinger

American diplomat, political scientist, and politician

In an interview with the Tony Blair Institute for Global Change [Kissinger]

2023

Despite starting later than the US and Japan, China's AI development has achieved remarkable milestones in recent years, solidifying its role as a significant global player in AI. More than simply looking to deploy AI in its own society, China's ambition is to play a pivotal role in the world by using technology to spread its influence and its mercantilist values. Much like Japan's post-WW2 behavior was marked by industrial development and policy cohesion in an effort to rebuild its wealth and *"catch up with the US,"* China sees the same opportunity in the use of AI, and the CCP (Chinese Communist Party), as its single-party Central Government, has embarked in a direction that is as clear as it is concerning to the rest of the world. We find China's lack of development in robotics while doubling down on AI to be indicative of its mindset and agenda, specifically expanding its political, cultural, and economic influence at the expense of weaponization of AI [Zhang], preparation to develop and win geopolitical zero-sum games, and top-down control of its own and other societies.

The CCP has been a central force in shaping the AI landscape by implementing regulations, infusing substantial funding, strategically prioritizing AI, and actively coordinating private sector participation around its core values and AI policies. This concerted effort has successfully driven China's AI development on a global scale, as we will discuss in this chapter.

China's ambition for world domination in AI became publicly evident in 2017 when it introduced the *"Next Generation AI Development Plan."* This AI plan is a comprehensive roadmap outlining China's strategic vision to become a global AI leader in both core research and applications. China's strategic blueprint, however, triggered concerns in the US, setting the stage for what is now referred to as the *"AI Cold War"* [Thompson and Bremmer].

In *Chapters 6* and *9,* we described both how AI models are trained and the central importance of data in progressing AI. The CCP wants to build its AI program using not only the data of its own citizens but also the data of people from other countries. Highly publicized rows with the West over scaled mobile applications with hundreds of millions of users, such as TikTok, that extract personal cell phone and other data without permission, violate the laws of other countries while compromising national security [Holpuch]. This kind of data violation, when viewed through the AI lens, will increasingly be deemable as an act of war. We note that the CCP also controls the world's largest biometric database, and there is a high probability that it has your data as well, a concerning topic we will discuss in this chapter [Piore].

Overall, the US and China fiercely compete for AI supremacy across critical domains like semiconductors, 5G technology, AI ethics, and regulations. It increasingly appears that in the future, there will be two distinct and isolated AI ecosystems led by the world's two preeminent economic, military, and AI powers. As time progresses, other nations might need to make critical choices about which system to align with, which carries significant implications for global AI standards and governance and the values of each society.

The following pages reveal how China's AI rose to challenge the US and where it is heading.

Deng Xiaoping and the Birth of AI in China

A pivotal moment in China's history occurred in 1978 when Deng Xiaoping assumed leadership. This marked the genesis of a transformative journey to reshape China into a modern society, a society in which AI easily becomes a core part of an overarching concept. This transformation revolved around bolstering a market economy and recognizing science and technology as paramount drivers of progress.

It was within this context that China's foray into the world of AI began. In 1981, a crucial step was taken with the establishment of the Chinese Association for AI (CAAI) [CAAI]. Then, in 1987, Tsinghua University published the first AI research in China [Cai]. However, the initial strides were slow and arduous for China. Lagging behind its Western counterparts, the nation grappled with resource limitations and a talent shortage. Yet, China's response was resolute and bold. The Government dispatched scholars overseas for AI training and channeled Government funding into research initiatives. That was a deliberate strategy, albeit a gradual one, to ensure the development of human capital in the country.

It was not until the early 2000s that China started to significantly increase the number of government-sponsored research projects and its funding for AI. In 2006, China officially committed to AI development, incorporating it into the *"Medium and Long-Term Plan for the Development of Science and Technology"* (2006-2020) [He and Bowser]. This strategic plan underscored the imperative for China to develop comprehensive research across various computer science domains, including AI. The objective of the plan was to establish a robust foundation in both theoretical research and technology development that would enable China to rapidly advance its information technology industry.

2017: A Strategic AI Plan and a National AI Team

Since Xi Jinping assumed power in 2013, China has doubled down on its focus on AI development and has become steadfast in pursuing the ambitious goal of emerging as a global leader in AI research. The aim is to harness the potential of AI as the primary catalyst for the nation's industrial growth and economic transformation.

Within this mindset, in 2017, the Chinese Government unveiled its ambitious *"Next Generation AI Development Plan,"* a strategic roadmap designed to propel the nation to the forefront of global AI leadership [Webster]. This comprehensive plan firmly positioned AI as a strategic technology for China, emphasizing its transformative potential across multiple sectors of the economy. The plan also aimed at achieving global technological supremacy by consistently supporting fundamental AI research programs and new AI technologies. It focused Government resources and funding on selected pivotal AI projects and included measures to expedite the commercialization of AI technologies while ensuring Government oversight. Lastly, the plan promoted collaboration across Government, the private sector, the academia, and the military.

To achieve these objectives, three stages were established. In the first stage, concluding in 2020, China aimed to advance the development of AI models and compete globally in this field. The second stage, by 2025, involved making significant strides in AI technology and theoretical research, as well as laying the necessary legal and ethical foundations. Finally, in the third stage, by 2030, China aspires to lead globally in AI, developing multiple cutting-edge innovations and setting up a robust training system for professionals in this field.

As stated by the plan, *"by 2030, China's AI theories, technologies, and applications should achieve world-leading levels, making China the world's primary AI innovation center, achieving visible results in intelligent economy and intelligent society applications, and laying an important foundation for becoming a leading innovation-style nation and an economic power. "*In addition to unveiling their formal plan in 2017, the Chinese Government announced the establishment of a *"national AI team. "* This handpicked and long-cultivated national AI team consists of prominent companies given the responsibility for developing specific AI subsectors, such as voice generation or facial recognition. Initially, the national AI team consisted of Alibaba Cloud, Baidu, Tencent, and iFlytek, each with defined roles:

- Alibaba Cloud in smart cities,
- Baidu in autonomous vehicles,
- Tencent in medical intelligence, and
- iFlytek in voice recognition.

Since its inception, the national team has expanded both in the number of participating companies and the scope of their designated AI specializations. SenseTime joined the team in 2018, enhancing its capabilities in computer vision. Furthermore, in 2019, the team experienced significant growth, welcoming ten additional companies, mainly industry giants, into its ranks:

- Huawei in telecommunications,
- Yitu in visual computing,
- Xiaomi in home automation,
- Pingan in financial intelligence,
- Hikvision in video perception,
- JD.com in smart supply chain,
- Megvii in visual perception,
- Qihoo 360 in security and intelligent brain,
- TAL Education Group in education, and

- Xiaomi in home automation.

China's Soaring AI Industry Since 2017

After the 2017 Government policies, China's AI industry experienced explosive growth, becoming a multi-billion-dollar sector in recent years. By 2021, its value surged to approximately $23 billion, with projections soaring to $62 billion by 2025 [Koty]. Public investments have been strategically channeled into fundamental and applied research, bolstering AI projects in the private sector through state-backed venture capital funds.

This rapid AI development in China has left an indelible mark across various facets of society, spanning socio-economic, military, and political domains. Some of the sectors most intensively pulsed by the Government's AI programs include agriculture, transportation, lodging, food services, and manufacturing. Notable functionalities given focus in the Government's policy directives include biotech/SynBio, facial recognition, autonomous vehicles, quantum computing, and medical intelligence.

The Chinese Government has earmarked fourteen cities and one county as experimental development zones to spearhead the growth of the high-tech industry. The specific areas of AI research and development vary from city to city, aligning with their unique industrial sectors and local ecosystems. For instance, Zhejiang and Guangdong on the coast are making substantial strides in practical applications and experimental areas. While Wuhan focuses on SynBio and the education sector, Suzhou, with its notable manufacturing industry, is directing efforts toward industrial AI, automation, and other AI infrastructure [Finance Sina].

As a result, specific indicators emerged that suggest China was gaining an edge over the US. According to the World Economic Forum, as of 2017, two-thirds of global AI investments were pouring into China [WEF]. Moreover, China surged ahead in AI-related research production, amassing a staggering 43,000 documents in 2021, nearly double the output of the US. Moreover, China had garnered acclaim with 7000 of the most cited documents, surpassing the US by a substantial margin of 70% [Tabeta and writers].

One of China's formidable advantages in AI lies in its vast population, an abundant source of data for businesses and researchers, and for algorithm training. This wealth of data has been instrumental, particularly in applications like facial recognition, where data collected from residents has fueled AI training. Racial homogeneity has also been helpful as AI models have to be able to ascertain subtle differences in faces to be valuable. China is well aware of this competitive advantage and has traditionally had a lax approach to data protection, but that, too, is changing.

Similar to Western countries, China has made significant efforts to strengthen data privacy and ethics within its own borders. In 2021, the *"Personal Information Protection Law"* (PIPL) was introduced, serving as China's counterpart to the GDPR. AI ethics also gained prominence with the introduction of the *"New Generation of AI Ethics Code,"* also in 2021, which places a strong emphasis on protecting domestic user rights, ensuring privacy, and promoting the secure utilization of AI technologies inside China.

The Cold War for AI Supremacy

China's ambitious AI Development Plan of 2017 marked a turning point with far-reaching consequences for the US and its allies. The plan ignited increasing tensions between China and the US, spawning a new geopolitical rivalry often referred to as the *"AI Cold War"* [Thompson and Bremmer]. In contrast to the Cold War of the 20th century, defined by nuclear armament and ideological clashes, this contemporary Cold War centers on AI technology and the mercantilist economic ideology of the Chinese. It presents a narrative of economic competition, where technological innovation determines the geopolitical standing of nations. China's distinct approach to AI development poses formidable challenges for the US, particularly regarding China's authoritarian applications of AI, such as its Social Credit System (SCS), which we will address in later in this section, and the active deployment of AI in military contexts.

Like the US, China is leveraging AI to improve military intelligence and hasten decision-making on the battlefield. China is actively exploring autonomous land, sea, underwater, aerial vehicles, and cyber warfare operations [Kania and Scharre]. Unsurprisingly, given its history of intellectual property theft, where it has not been able to steal and wants ongoing access to American technology and IP, China has made strategic investments in the US AI market, particularly in AI companies involved in defense. From 2010 to 2017, Chinese venture capital investments in US AI firms totaled around $1.3 billion [Singh and Brown]. China's military use of AI raises concerns in the US about its impact on global stability and the escalation of existing tensions.

The apprehension that China might outpace the US in AI has dominated discussions on technology policy in Washington. China has emerged as a formidable contender, producing top-tier AI research comparable to the US and integrating this technology into its economy and internal surveillance systems, such as the SCS. In the race to develop advanced AI algorithms, China has rapidly closed the gap with US research labs, often achieving comparable results within just a few years.

The escalating tensions between the two nations prompted the US Government to adopt policies aimed at curbing the advancement of AI in China, mainly through the implementation of export controls targeting chips essential for training and running AI algorithms, as well as the technologies or raw materials to manufacture these chips. These sanctions coincided with former President Donald Trump's trade war, which had created a geopolitical climate conducive to these types of restrictions.

Additionally, semiconductors are especially contentious in the AI Cold War due to Taiwan's pivotal role in semiconductor production and the escalating likelihood of armed conflict or at least a blockade between the mainland and the island. The semiconductor supply chain is characterized by its high concentration on a limited number of significant players in very specific geographies and its global interconnectedness, making it vulnerable to trade restrictions, supply chain disruptions, and semiconductor shortages. Notably, approximately 70% of the world's semiconductors are manufactured in or pass through Taiwan, home to the world's largest chip producer, TSMC (Taiwan Semiconductor Manufacturing Company) [Slingerlend].

Following this rationale, the US Government implemented export restrictions on semiconductors bound for China. This move not only harmed China's capabilities to design and manufacture advanced AI chips but, more crucially, hindered its ability to use imported chips in the AI development programs of Chinese companies [Clark]. The US also successfully persuaded European governments to establish similar restrictions, as in the case of the Netherlands-based company ASML (Advanced Semiconductor Materials Lithography), which stopped exporting semiconductor manufacturing technologies to China [Woo]. Additionally, the US and the EU leveraged the narrative of the AI Cold War to curtail the acquisition of 5G technology from Huawei (as mentioned above) and ZTE within their respective territories. Given that 5G heavily relies on semiconductors, this further complicated the technological rivalry between East and West [Meyer].

The trade constraints placed on semiconductor exports to China reverberated through supply chains. China retaliated by limiting semiconductor exports from China into the US and Europe, sparking concerns within US and European industries [Klayman and Nellis]. In response, the US Government allocated $250 billion in Government subsidies to support local technology and manufacturing sectors, with a specific focus on semiconductors, AI, and quantum computing [Ni]. Similarly, the EU enacted legislation that subsidized semiconductor production within the EU [Timmers and Kreps].

Beyond Borders: China's AI-Driven Spy Game

The "AI Cold War" escalated beyond commercial considerations into espionage and national security aspects.

Alongside increases in COVID cases in 2021, a Chinese military-affiliated company reached out to local US leadership and offered to set up testing labs in several US states. In exchange, the Beijing Genomics Institute, a Chinese government-affiliated firm and a major global player in genomics research, gained access to the DNA of those tested. The US government advised states to decline the offer, and they did. In the meantime, the Beijing Genomics Institute had established labs in at least 16 countries to collect citizens' DNA information. China now has the world's largest DNA database, which includes both its own citizens and populations from other countries [Warrick and Brown].

Human rights organizations from around the world claim that the CCP Government uses DNA testing for racial profiling and security objectives— such as monitoring and identifying Uighur Muslims, an ethnoreligious minority with millions of people held in the so-called Xinjiang Internment Camps.

US officials add that DNA collection by Chinese companies should be viewed as part of a concerted attempt to vacuum up the records of millions of US citizens, with many of these efforts violating US law: "*Most Americans have probably had their data compromised by the cyber intelligence units of the Chinese government and Chinese military intelligence,*" said April Falcon-Doss, a former National Security Agency employee and author of the book *"Cyber Privacy: Who Has Your Data and Why You Should Care"* [Nye]. According to Falcon-Doss, China is gathering a great deal of personal data about its citizens in order to help its espionage activities and develop its economy and its technology [Myre].

While the US and China actively spy on each other, China has deliberately strengthened its active, relentless pursuit of the personal data of individual Americans using AI in its espionage and theft activity. Since 2014, China has been accused of stealing large amounts of data, including customer records from Marriott (400 million), the credit bureau Equifax (145 million), the health insurance company Anthem (78 million), and the US Office of Personnel Management (21 million). The latter included classified files on Government employees and contractors, such as fingerprints and security clearances.[Myre].

Armed with this specific information fed into unsupervised algorithm models such as we discussed in *Chapter 6*, it would not be difficult for a bad actor to predict with high levels of accuracy who in a population of people with credit problems could be targeted and likely accept a bribe to engage in theft of industrial secrets. Or knowing where you travel inside the US or abroad, where to make contact with you—or when to target your family with subtle online email campaigns—when you are likely not to be there with them. The US Government has since banned Huawei, China's largest telecommunications equipment maker, from installing gear in America's telecommunications infrastructure [Meyer] and has deported hundreds of students whose sole purpose in coming to the US under the guise of study was to access and steal technical and scientific information [AP News]. The Justice Department filed charges against Chinese nationals in various cases, but the majority of them are still in China and thus not within US law enforcement jurisdiction. It is worth noting that many of the accused serve in the Chinese military.

China's Social Credit System: More Dysfunctional than Dystopian (for Now)

One of China's most iconic and contentious AI-related megaprojects is the Social Credit System (SCS), a national initiative developed by the Government to assess the *"trustworthiness"* of businesses, individuals, and Government institutions [Yang].

In the 2000s, widespread scams, financial fraud, and public safety scandals started to gain notoriety in China. Notable incidents included instances of contaminated milk for infants being callously exported to other countries[Branigan]. In response, the Chinese Government began contemplating the creation of a system to regulate businesses in areas such as financial fraud, intellectual property, and food safety with the aim of enhancing public trust [Reilly et al.]. The core idea revolved around regulatory agencies sharing information to compile national blocklists for non-compliance, leading to punishments and public *"naming and shaming"* to discourage undesirable behavior.

Traditional methods of controlling behavior were deemed inadequate in dealing with the challenges posed by China's burgeoning population and a rapidly changing socio-economic landscape. As China transitioned into a more technologically advanced era, the idea of leveraging data and technology to assess trustworthiness and control behavior gained prominence. Inspiration for this effort came from credit rating systems in other nations, including FICO, Equifax, and TransUnion in the US [Pieke and Hofman].

In 2013, the Supreme People's Court established a debtor blacklist called *"List of Dishonest Persons,"* which imposed restrictions on debt defaulters, such as barring them from private schools and luxury spending [Chan]. Subsequently, the Government outlined plans for a comprehensive SCS in 2014, and a national pilot involving eight credit rating firms was launched that year. In 2015, licenses were granted to eight companies, including industry giants like Alibaba and Tencent, to work on different aspects of the system, including service operations, credit risk algorithms, and operations and management software. It is worth noting that every society has some form of control over debt management; the Arab world still maintains debtors' prisons, Western nations have sophisticated credit access and loan pricing models, and in North Asian societies, shaming and loss of face still hold sway.

The implementation of the SCS unfolded in stages, starting with a series of pilot projects in selected cities and regions beginning in 2017. These trials allowed authorities to test different aspects of the system. By 2018, the SCS had been officially rolled out nationwide. The implementation involved collaboration between Government agencies, technology companies, and financial institutions, creating a complex network of involved parties. Local governments played a crucial role in enforcing the SCS. They had the authority to design and implement their social credit evaluation methods based on local priorities and concerns. This decentralized approach allowed for flexibility in addressing regional issues while adhering to the broader framework established by the Central Government, maintaining a top-down authoritarian bent to the entire program.

While the Chinese Government presented the SCS as a tool to *"promote trust and integrity,"* the definition of trust and integrity was not as we would conceive abstractly in the West. Rather, it was a reflection of Chinese Communist values, which is exactly what we should expect. What the CCP meant was that trust equates to conformity to what the Government says one should do, and integrity equates to the degree to which one does what the Government says one should do. In short, trust and integrity have no definition other than what the Government says it does, and it centers on *"following the rules."* By analogy, the Catholic Church maintains the Ten Commandments, the concept of varying levels of sin, and confessionals. The Chinese analogy is simply the edict of the CCP. Breaking it is a sin, and the public confessional takes the place of the private one. It is all simply the rules of the societal OS as a method of control over people. It is worth noting that China has no official religion and, thus, no spiritual system that holds behavioral or ethical standards to preside over or guide behavior. Rather, one might characterize their societal OS (Operating System) as *"Commercial Machiavellianism,"* and hence, this type of system was needed as a rule arbiter to protect them from each other.

This tool faced severe criticism internationally, some of it founded and some less so. Western media portrayed the SCS as a massive surveillance system that monitored data points such as financial responsibility, adherence to laws, social interactions, social media activity, online behavior, individual opinions, individual works of created art or self-expression, and even recordings from millions of street cameras. The system then purported to assign a numerical score to each person or company, which reflected its overall *"social creditworthiness."* Positive actions, such as timely repayment of loans, voluntary community service, behaving morally, and not speaking out against the Government, contributed to a higher score. In contrast, adverse actions, such as defaulting on loans or engaging in fraudulent activities, fighting publicly, and expressing an opinion contrary to the Government's official position on any matter, resulted in a lower score [Matsakis] [Kobie]. According to the media, individuals with low credit scores faced consequences that impacted their ability to secure employment, access education, and even obtain essential services such as healthcare access. Former US Vice President Mike Pence famously labeled the SCS in 2018 as *"an Orwellian system premised on controlling virtually every facet of human life"* in 2018 [Horsley].

Although it is conceivable that the Chinese Government initially intended to establish a coherent nationwide credit scoring system, the reality is that the SCS has evolved far from that, much of it dysfunctional. As of Q1 2024, a unified SCS or score does not exist across all of China. Instead, social credit is defined by a collection of fragmented policies and systems that focus more on businesses than on individuals. These include blocklists for debtors determined by specific court orders, financial credit reporting, sectoral blocklists that include non-compliant companies and their owners, as well as no-fly and no-ride lists based on instances of misconduct by train or plane passengers.

Falling short of the mark has happened in no small part due to the practical realities of organizing data for use by AI algorithms. We note that the practical implementation of the social credit system faced many operational challenges, particularly at the local level, that prevented it from becoming a coherent nationwide system [Cheung]. Local governments encountered difficulties in setting up individual scoring systems due to data silos, inconsistent standards, and bureaucratic resistance. The decentralized nature of the system resulted in hundreds of different versions, leading to a lack of cohesion and functionality. Numerous local pilot schemes deviated significantly from the original concept, prompting interventions from the central Government to rein in extreme applications that lacked a legal basis. *"Two decades later, China's social credit system is more dysfunctional than dystopian"* [Cheung].

That said, our view is that it remains clear that mass data on citizens is being collected, and a public score per se is not strictly needed to act on the data. The original intent and direction was to establish a pure SCS that enables the Government to constantly give individuals a score based on every aspect of their monitored behavior, with privileges such as health care access and work permits based on the scores; this is at once functional and practical as part of a societal OS, and a Faustian Bargain for every individual, at every turn, curtailing freedom of speech, thought, and activity. We note that there is no intention to publicly and transparently post every individual score; rather, if you fall in disgrace with the Government for whatever reason, your score can potentially be whatever the Government says it was. Moreover, nothing would stop this kind of system from being used in the future as an ultra-Machiavellian tool for social and economic engineering if the CCP acts on the lessons learned from its failure to implement the SCS to its first vision: for example, profiling genes in a eugenics attempt to predict and act on who is likely to cause a crime before it ever happens; determining which two people are most likely to have a successful marriage, and forcing that; preventing the birth of children who are likely to have defects or physical or intellectual limitations and thus a long-term net drain on social resources; and choosing the professions of people for them and tracking them to that at the earliest age, which is no different than how the CCP already chooses its leadership today. The more data it has and the stronger the algorithm, the closer the predictive models approach 100% accuracy. For the individual, it is a Faustian Bargain, but for the collective society, more efficient use of resources, lower crime, stronger human capital, and better social decision-making. As we highlight through the book, AI is inherently networked and collectivist and not atomistic.

Lastly, we further note that the US Government has also collected personal data on its citizens, co-opting major telecommunications operators like AT&T for decades to review call records without probable cause to do so [Wired] [Hattem]. We also note that monitoring in the US at the same functional level as the CCP program has been done via big corporations, to whom people regularly and freely give their data. With the same end result, the only real difference is in the techniques deployed.

Generative AI under the Core Values of Socialism

Another emblematic technology megaproject in China is the *"Great Firewall of China."* In the 1990s, as the internet emerged, the leadership of China became concerned that widespread access to information could jeopardize Government and social stability. As we look at the US in Q1 2024, we must agree that the CCP was prescient. Consequently, in the early 2000s, China established a sophisticated online censorship system to regulate access to foreign websites and censor local content. This system aims to manage information flow within the country and is known in the West as the "*Great Firewall of China*." Most Western internet services, including Facebook, Google, Netflix—and naturally ChatGPT—remain inaccessible to the majority of Chinese. Local platforms strictly regulate content, preemptively employing moderators and AI algorithms to delete any undesirable material.

In 2020, China's internet giants, including Tencent and Alibaba, aligned even more closely with the CCP after the Government took minority ownership stakes in these firms and got actively involved in their day-to-day operations.

Today, confronted with the rise of AI, China grapples again with the same challenge: striking a delicate balance between nurturing innovation essential for economic growth and retaining control as an authoritarian state. The Government is actively working towards transforming the nation into a highly advanced economy despite harboring concerns about the potentially disruptive nature of AI. Consequently, China is diligently fortifying its *"Great Firewall"* to effectively address the challenges presented by Generative AI [The Economist].

Since March 2023, companies have been required to register any algorithms capable of making recommendations or influencing people's decisions. In July 2023, the Government issued regulations mandating that all AI-generated content must *"reflect the core values of socialism,"* [Wu] effectively prohibiting content containing anti-party sentiments. Subsequently, in September 2023, the Government published 110 allowed services, and all unregistered algorithms are to be blocked, with their developers facing punishment.

Later, in October 2023, a Government committee released safety guidelines demanding detailed assessments of the data used to train Generative AI models. In particular, a minimum of 4 thousand subsets of the entire training dataset must be tested manually, with at least 96% of the tests being deemed *"acceptable"* based on a list of 31 safety risks. Unacceptable content is broadly defined as anything that *"incites subversion of state power or the overthrowing of the socialist system."* To adhere to these guidelines, chatbots must decline 95% of queries eliciting unacceptable content while rejecting no more than 5% of harmless questions [The Economist].

This stringent regulatory approach has resulted in a slowdown in the adoption of consumer-facing generative AI in China. For instance, Baidu's Ernie Bot, though ready for release roughly at the same moment as ChatGPT, was only introduced nine months later in August 2023 [David]. Considering the swift advancements in the field of AI, this delay is certainly a substantial period. China's Generative AI industry is in no condition to compete against the US.

From Consumer AI to Enterprise AI

Given the risks involved in consumer-oriented generative AI, the Chinese Government has placed much of its focus on promoting enterprise AI applications, which are much less prone to subversive individual behavior. Enterprise applications require access to corporate data, much of which is stored within companies. China's strategy involves transforming corporate data into a public service [Olcott and Ding]. Rather than owning the data itself, the Government aims to control the channels through which the data flows.

In contrast to consumer-oriented Generative AI, Enterprise AI encounters much fewer Government constraints on development. Quite the opposite, in order to encourage companies to share data, China has implemented regulations to establish a national open innovation framework where the government and companies can collaborate on AI projects. Standardization plays a pivotal role in this kind of cross-company data collaboration to ensure seamless interoperability and quality. Consequently, China approved guidelines for open innovation in 2019 and for standardization in 2020. As we discussed in the previous section, data asymmetry has a deleterious effect on economic efficiency, and the existence of AI presents economies with a solution to the chicken/egg problem inherent in data aggregation and algorithm training. China is beginning to solve this core issue.

The government is also actively encouraging the creation of data exchanges. Data exchanges enable businesses to trade productized information ranging from individual factory activities to sales data at specific shops. The exchanges provide smaller firms with access to knowledge that was once the exclusive domain of tech giants. This initiative aims to provide smaller firms with access to knowledge that was once the exclusive domain of tech giants. Chinese cities created the first data exchanges in the early 2010s, and now there are approximately 50 across China.

Moreover, in August 2023, the government directed state-owned enterprises to look at the valuation of their data and incorporate this value into their balance sheets as intangible assets [The Economist].

This governmental endorsement is redirecting capital and labor away from consumer chatbots towards Machine Learning applications for businesses. Several cities, including Shenzhen, have announced substantial AI-focused investment funds to further fund data exchanges. For instance, the Shanghai Data Exchange (SDE) was launched in 2021. It offers various data products, for example, information from the energy sector, which can be utilized to assess companies' power consumption and create alternative enterprise credit profiles based on absolute levels of activity [The Economist].

Another example where data exchanges are useful is in the development of self-driving cars. In 2022, approximately 185 million vehicles on Chinese roads were equipped with internet connectivity [Neeley]. China envisions mass production of semi-autonomous cars by 2025, which requires substantial data for companies developing self-driving algorithms. WICV is a data exchange addressing this need. WICV channels a car's data back to its manufacturer, fostering a closed-loop system where each car maker receives data from their own cars. However, WICV intends to become a marketplace where developers of self-driving systems can purchase such data from any car maker. To facilitate this exchange, driving data must undergo a process of "sanitation," removing geolocation or biometric details that could compromise individuals' privacy.

Coming back to the SCS project, many in China consider it a failed project for the reasons we covered earlier in this chapter. But we see the reasons for failure heretofore as solvable. Additionally, corporate data exchanges may be applied to the SCS concept to overcome its initial implementation and data aggregation challenges. In addition to evaluating the moral trustworthiness of businesses and individuals toward conformity to government mandates, the SCS could perhaps first reach instantiation by assessing the likelihood of regulatory violations within the business sector much the same way existing algorithms in the US can accurately predict credit default.

The Government hopes that enterprise AI holds the key to China catching up with, and potentially surpassing, America in terms of AI, all while avoiding the complexities associated with potentially subversive AI-generated content.

Economic Slowdown on the Road to AI Supremacy

The widespread adoption of AI in China is undoubtedly positive for its long-term impact on China's economy. AI offers China a promising solution to reduce operational costs, create better products, enhance efficiency, and fund the same opportunities that we have discussed above in *Chapter 22,* collectively invigorating its economy in sustainable ways. This becomes particularly significant as China grapples with a noticeable economic slowdown entering 2024 [World Bank]. China's current situation results from an unsustainable dependence on debt-driven infrastructure and real estate investment, leading to a property bubble burst. China's populace has been trained to treat real estate investment like a savings account, but it is anything but that. Reduced demand for Chinese exports and escalating living costs emanating from its real estate-centric issues further compound the slowdown.

Concurrently, China faces a demographic challenge characterized by a declining population. Decades of the one-child policy have resulted in an aging society and a shrinking workforce. This demographic shift brings higher labor costs, increased social welfare spending, reductions in overall productivity, and, most significantly, a decrease in consumption. A country's macroeconomy is driven by productivity and consumption, so to overcome the current situation, China must strategically pivot toward stimulating household consumption, which has historically trailed behind GDP growth.

Sustaining robust economic growth in the mid-term will significantly impact the Chinese Government's ability to allocate resources for AI, invest in AI research and development, and foster an environment attractive for private-sector technological innovation. The success of these efforts will play a pivotal role in determining whether China can achieve its ambitions of global AI dominance, or otherwise, the US will continue to have undisputed hegemony.

One World, Two Systems

While the degree of impact can be debated, AI as a technology is unique in that it is naturally oligopolistic. This will remain the case so long as, first, the data needed to build and train AI remains diffuse in the world; second, gathering, organizing, and deploying that data on a continuous basis confers a strategic head-start to those large-scale enterprises—or state-run cartels— that can actually accomplish it; and third, hundreds of billions of USD is needed to build global cloud infrastructure for the wide commercial and industrial deployment of AI tools. Success in developing and deploying key algorithms and ownership of the data used to advance them and the Cloud infrastructure to deliver it commercially begets a natural Network Effect, making competitive entrance more difficult by the day. Furthermore, the natural head start reaches an insurmountable point for the systems that reach AGI first. *The overall scale of the macroeconomy, scientific and technical talent, and development resources, including financial that are necessary to develop an AI industry of consequence, alongside the head-start already in place, is likely to conspire to keep AI a 2-horse race between China and the US.*

Our perspective of the *"AI Cold War"* envisions a future where two distinct and isolated AI ecosystems, led by the world's two preeminent economic and military powers, the US and China, compete. As time progresses, other nations must choose which systems to align with.

On one side, the US AI ecosystem, hurtling towards an oligopoly led by large technology corporations, advocates for multiple systems and scaled databases, none with pure monopolistic properties. It also defends the safeguarding of individual rights, enhanced data privacy protection, and respect for geopolitical sovereign borders and the rule of law (assuming that the US does not go down the dystopian pathway; there remains a risk that it will do so, noting the natural magnetic pull toward socialism and authoritarianism inherent in AI as discussed in *Chapter 23*.)

Conversely, China's ecosystem will be led by the centralized Government and resemble a cartel advocating for top-down unilateral state control in partnership with large-scale enterprises, restricted information flow, and politically imposed constraints leading to mass conformity but also pre-identification of socially subversive elements such as crime risk, e.g., social profiling. It also will look to drive mercantilist versions of trade with other countries and co-mingle resource access and military protection in a packaged deal. The emphasis will generally exclude Generative AI and instead focus on Industrial AI applications, social credit systems, and regulatory conformity.

This potential clash between two disparate AI systems embedded with different values while aligning broader military and resource access will likely impede the establishment of global standards for AI ethics and regulation.

In *Chapter 7,* we discussed the importance of cloud players in disseminating the effects of AI on an economy-wide and global basis. We note that despite superior technology products, none of the American cloud players, AWS, Azure, or Google Cloud, has a market share in China. The US cloud giants are competing for markets globally with the CCP-controlled nexus of Alicloud, Huawei, Tencent, and Baidu, which dominate in China but have difficulty in external markets. Part of this difficulty has to do with trust and transparency, with the world having gotten wise to the CCP's lack of respect for sovereign borders and willingness to appropriate data. When you take China's technology nexus, you also take their values.

Still, there will be compelling reasons for alignment with the China camp in AI: certain insulation versus competition domestically and internationally, pricing, at least equivalent technology with perhaps a leg-up in industrial AI, co-mingling with military and other benefits including access to global resources when a zero-sum game is presented, and value alignment with China's top-down approaches. Not everyone believes in individual freedom and liberty, and continued uncertainty on the domestic political front in the US creates some doubts about America's long-term values (e.g., what will the values embedded in US AI be?). As with any agency relationship in a commercial context, sometimes you just *"choose the other one"* because you will be more important to them, get more attention, and have a fairer shake.

We do see the possibility that both Japan and Muslim-dominated countries develop their own systems in an effort to preserve their respective *"societal OS"* and avoid co-mingling of values. Japan has a unique culture, which we have talked about already, and in the case of the Muslim world, its unique political-religious system is based on Islamic religious values.

In the case of Japan, the US lead in the cloud space will make it difficult for Japan to stand out as a separate global AI ecosystem and nearly impossible to export it as a full alternative. In fact, Japan may not want to export its AI system, and others will not want to import it; Japan has never known how to interact or lead in the world. We see the US-Japan Alliance persevering; Amazon's AWS has announced USD $15 billion additional investment in infrastructure in Japan at the time of writing, Amazon and NTT Group continue to forge a closer alliance, and Japan maintains a long memory of being referred to as "*the dwarf to the South*" by the Chinese [Carr]. It is possible that alignment between Japan and the US camp will simply mean an arms-length technology-sharing relationship, which in turn will enable Japan's AI autonomy and societal OS while remaining in the US camp.

As we conclude this *Section IV: The Transition*, we note that regardless of the camp with which any country finds itself aligned—pro-US or pro-China—the world overall under the unstoppable march of AI over the coming decades is becoming more collectivist, less Democratic, and more authoritarian, with the only differences among societies a matter of degree. Truth is forever compromised, perhaps never to return. And there is a natural decay in the economic value of human life.

Part V: The New Being

"Und Zarathustra sprach also zum Volke:

Ich lehre euch den Übermenschen. Der Mensch ist Etwas, das überwunden werden soll. Was habt ihr gethan, ihn zu überwinden?

Alle Wesen bisher schufen etwas über sich hinaus: und ihr wollt die Ebbe dieser großen Flut sein und lieber noch zum Thiere zurückgehen, als den Menschen zu überwinden?

Was ist der Affe für den Menschen? Ein Gelächter oder eine schmerzliche Scham. Und ebendas soll der Mensch für den Übermenschen sein: ein Gelächter oder eine schmerzliche Scham."

"And Zarathustra spake thus unto the people:

I teach you the Superman. Man is something that is to be surpassed. What have ye done to surpass man?

All beings hitherto have created something beyond themselves: and ye want to be the ebb of that great tide, and would rather go back to the beast than surpass man?

What is the ape to man? A laughing-stock, a thing of shame. And just the same shall man be to the Superman: a laughing-stock, a thing of shame."

Friedrich Nietzsche,

Thus Spoke Zarathustra, Zarathustra's Prologue, 3
Putting words to Zarathustra, the prophet of Zoroastrianism, 6th to 7th century BC
1883

Preamble

The idea of Superintelligence, a highly advanced form of AI that surpasses human intelligence in all aspects, is deeply connected with Friedrich Nietzsche's philosophical concept of the Superman, also known as the Overman.

Nietzsche urges people, as a matter of their natural constitution, to rise above their present circumstances and become better beings above the bounds of everyday life. Aspirations to achieve Superintelligence are in line with the concept of surpassing, which is reflected in the call for the Superman to defeat the current state of humanity. The pursuit of Superintelligence emulates Nietzsche's exhortation to transcend humanity.

There is a similarity between how humans and superintelligent beings might interact and Nietzsche's comparison of man to the ape, in which the latter is portrayed as a laughingstock and a thing of shame. The rise of Superintelligence suggests that humans may become obsolete due to the superior cognitive abilities of AI, similar to how apes have become to humans.

Nietzsche's theory of the Superman carries inherent ramifications that extend beyond utopian ideals. While the idea of surpassing human nature could entail progress and evolution, it also harbors the potential for dystopia. As we discussed in *Part IV The Transition,* the pursuit of AI, even within a gradual step change process, could lead to a hierarchical society where those who achieve the status of the Superman wield disproportionate power, govern in despotism disguised as magnanimity, resulting in oppression and discord. Ironically, it becomes a sort of forward-looking return to the past in which mankind has incessantly fought wars and conducted revolutions against the things that curtail freedom or create undue oppression by aristocrats. Ultimately, technology is a two-sided coin where outcomes are generally prefaced on the motivations of the people who wield it. Would those who go first pull the rest of us along evenly and equally? Could the economy afford it at scale? The concentration of intellectual power within superintelligent entities might give rise to ethical and societal challenges, potentially leading to a loss of control and unintended consequences. Intelligence does not correlate evenly with ethics and morals. However, humanity seems determined to achieve Superintelligence, as we have been observing throughout the book.

On the road to Superintelligence, we find quantum computing. *Chapter 25* delves into the concepts of quantum computing and the distinctions between quantum Machine Learning and classical Machine Learning, specifically focusing on the possibility of running neural networks on quantum computers. It is unclear yet whether quantum technology is an essential enabler for meeting the computational demands of

Superintelligence, but if quantum Machine Learning becomes operationally practical, it will undoubtedly help.

Chapter 26 defines Superintelligence and reviews various avenues to achieve it. The chapter focused on the concept of Superintelligence's recursive development cycle, referred to in certain literature as "*singularity*," which is the point at which an AI learns how to upgrade itself, leading to an explosive loop of self-improvement cycles that culminate in Superintelligence.

In Chapter 27, we will analyze another possible avenue to Superintelligence: mind uploading. This technology, currently under research, entails exporting the brain's configuration down to its molecular level and transferring it into another biological body or a simulated environment. This process ultimately enables a form of immortality, which might also be a manifestation of Superintelligence because emulated minds will have higher expandable capacity, operate faster than human beings, and leverage Machine Learning algorithms.

Having described Superintelligence, we delve into how humanity can control this phenomenon. *Chapter 28* explores the various technical or process-oriented possibilities to prevent AI from becoming hostile towards us. The chapter covers two approaches proposed by leading Silicon Valley companies, as well as our own choice, Open-sourcing of algorithms, which also helps tug against the natural pull that collectivist, non-atomistic AI could make toward authoritarianism during the transition and possibly continue thereafter.

Chapter 29 explores the prospect of AI achieving a divine status. Given that AI will be more intelligent and powerful than humans, some people might come to adore it as a god. *Chapter 30* tackles the darker scenarios of war and destruction, either between humans and a rogue AI or, as we see far more likely, between human factions with irreconcilable views about AI.

Concluding our exploration through the epic of humankind, *Chapter 31* delves into a speculative Science Fiction scenario where biological intelligent beings have fused with AI for millions of years into an immortal, superintelligent form of life. This Superintelligence utilizes AI as its mind and employs myriads of intelligent robots and cyborgs as a distributed body to handle the operational aspects necessary to ensure its survival.

As humans, we would be the forebears of that Superintelligence to which we are linked, in part by a synthetic biological form of lineage and in part through a purely technological one. Today, we are, in fact, already designing that Superintelligence and feeding it with our thoughts and biases. Whether this Superintelligence leads to human extinction, or a technological utopia would not matter in the long term because the long-term belongs only to the Superintelligence anyway, a Superintelligence into which we are interlaced.

The following pages spiral into the history of this superintelligent new species on our natural Darwinian Road of evolution.

25. Quantum Computing, the Likely Enabler

"A thousand-bit quantum computer would vastly outperform any conceivable DNA computer, or for that matter any conceivable non-quantum computer."

Ray Kurzweil

American computer scientist and futurist

The Singularity is Near: When Humans Transcend Biology [Kurzweil]

2005

As AI applications expand and become more sophisticated, the demand for computational power has grown exponentially. The next developmental steps in training deep learning models and conducting complex simulations require immense processing capability.

In many ways, the governor of the AI engine for decades has been the rate of improvement in processing power, and this will not change so long as our models reduce all intelligence and thinking to mathematics. Moore's Law was first formulated by Gordon Moore, co-founder of Intel, when he observed in 1965 that the number of transistors on an integrated circuit had been doubling approximately every one or two years, and he forecasted that this trend would persist into the future [Moore]. It has been remarkably prescient.

In 2002, Ray Kurzweil, whom we have mentioned in *Chapters 19* and *20* in the context of cyborgs and human-AI interlace, extended Moore's Law to introduce the Law of Accelerating Returns, which predicts exponential growth in the number of floating-point calculations per second (FLOPS) per constant dollar of cost [Kurzweil]. The FLOPS is an important metric in thinking about AI because it not only creates a standardized measurement for the ever-increasing computational power available to AI systems specifically but also gives an implicit cost-benefit analysis and resource utilization efficiency measure across such developments.

The data reveals not only a growing trend in FLOPS achievable per dollar but, in fact, an accelerating trend, with some variations due to technology and market conditions in each decade:

- Around 1940, it took $1 million to buy 1 FLOP.
- Around 1960, it just took $1 for 1 FLOP, a 1-thousand-fold improvement over the last two decades.
- Around 1980, $1 could buy 10 FLOPS (10-thousand-fold)
- Around 2000, $1 could now get 100 thousand FLOPS (10-thousand-fold)
- Around 2020, $1 could now secure 10 billion FLOPS (100-thousand-fold)

While this law has held for many decades, there are signs that it may be reaching its limits. The shrinking size of transistors and the physical constraints of classical computing components pose significant challenges. Whenever technology nears a limit, emerging technologies invariably take their place. Quantum computing is a revolutionary shift that can extend computational boundaries beyond what traditional silicon-based technology can achieve, sustaining the Law of Accelerating Returns.

Kurzweil suggested that the Law of Accelerating Returns predicts AI will attain human-like intelligence levels in the next few decades. Quantum computing is poised to be that accelerator in computational power necessary to reach Superintelligence, offering literally an exponential increase in computational power over today's systems in a form factor that is not prohibitive to any type of AI application.

We believe that Superintelligence may still emerge without the aid of quantum computing as classical computing continues to advance in hardware and software, empowering the development of increasingly powerful AI systems. Parallelization, cluster computing, distributed systems, and algorithmic innovations all contribute to the potential achievement of Superintelligence without the specific use of quantum technology.

Still, as quantum computing remains in its early stages of development and its industrialization will require time, it could accelerate the progress of AI and is therefore worth reviewing. The following pages will explore why quantum computing might be game-changing for Machine Learning and Superintelligence.

As you read this chapter, there are three key points to extract regarding how quantum computing could push AI forward:

1. First, quantum computing has the potential to run algorithms much faster than classical computers, sometimes exponentially faster, but this is not a truism across all algorithms. Most of the time, quantum-driven speedups depend on factors such as the parameters of the algorithm and the actual data that is being processed. Whether quantum algorithms represent an exponential speed-up depends literally on the specific problem they are trying to solve.

2. Second, classical algorithms such as linear regression or neural networks cannot run directly on a quantum computer; they need to be completely redesigned and rewritten in order to take advantage of quantum mechanics' ability to enable faster computation. In classical computing, you can make a software implementation of an algorithm and execute it on different operating systems that run on the hardware, which makes high degrees of versatility and machine-to-machine cooperation; in quantum computing, the algorithm has to be implemented directly on the quantum hardware, which makes it more complicated to execute and less laterally versatile. At the moment, there is no quantum OS (Operating system), though it remains a development expected in the future.

3. Third, as a result of these complexities, quantum computing should be thought of as an emerging technology that is likely to experience fluctuations before it matures sufficiently for practical AI applications, much like the three *"AI Winters"* presented earlier in the book.

The Science Fiction of Quantum Computing

Two compelling novels, *"The Quantum Magician"* by Derek Künsken (2018) and *"The Quantum Thief"* by Hannu Rajaniemi (2010), delve into the realm of quantum computing, offering unique perspectives on the implications of this technology for human beings, society, and even religion [Künsken] [Rajaniem]. *"The Quantum Magician"* takes place in a universe where quantum computing has reached extraordinary levels of capability, enabling the development of *"qube"* technology. These qubes, or *"homo quantus,"* are genetically engineered humans with quantum brains that can perform complex calculations and quantum operations. The novel delves into the world of heists and espionage, with the central character, Belisarius Arjona, and his team using qube technology to execute intricate criminal and morally ambiguous operations. Moreover, qubes embody the fusion of human and quantum computing, enabling superhuman cognitive abilities and transforming human identity. These qubes have unique characteristics that blur the line between sentient beings and advanced machines, and they prompt questions about the ethical treatment of such entities and their place in society.

Similarly, *"The Quantum Thief"* envisions a futuristic world where quantum technology is fundamental to society. Here, quantum encryption, teleportation, and advanced AI play pivotal roles. The protagonist, Jean le Flambeur, is a master thief who operates in a complex, post-singularity society. The novel explores the concept of privacy and personal autonomy in a world where quantum technology has rendered secrecy a scarce resource. In this setting, quantum computing technology is utilized not only for AI but also as a tool for surveillance and control, illustrating, on the one hand, the delicate balance between technological advancement and personal freedom and, on the other hand, the omnipresence of criminality as a personality trait.

Notably, the *"Quantum Thief"* presents a historical character that we will talk about in *Chapter 30* when we discuss the possibility of wars induced by AI: Nikolay Fyodorov, a Russian philosopher from the 19th century. In the novel, Fyodorov appears as a revered quasi-religious philosopher whose ideas significantly shape the spiritual landscape of a world immersed in pervasive quantum technology.

Quantum Superposition and Entanglement

"Quantum" refers to the fundamental principles governing the interactions of matter and energy at the minutest scales, commonly occurring at the level of atoms and subatomic particles. Quantum mechanics, a branch of physics, explores the probabilistic nature of particles such as electrons, protons, photons, and even quarks.

Quantum computing harnesses the immense computational power of two fundamental quantum concepts that occur at the quantum level: superposition and entanglement.

Superposition implies that quantum bits—which are called qubits—can simultaneously exist in multiple states, unlike classical bits that are strictly either 0 or 1. Notably, superposition cannot be directly observed, as mere observation compels the system to assume a singular state. This implies that qubits can exist simultaneously in a superposition of states 1 and 0 until you make an observation. At this point, they collapse into either state 0 or 1 with a certain probability for each state.

In 1935, physicist Erwin Schrödinger shared a thought experiment with Albert Einstein, explaining the concept of superposition. Schrödinger describes a cat confined in a container with radioactive atoms with a 50% chance of decaying and emitting a lethal amount of radiation. Schrödinger exposes that, until an observer opens the box and peeks inside, there is an equal likelihood that the cat is alive and dead. The act of unboxing and visual inspection coerces the cat into adopting a definitive state of being alive or dead [Schrödinger].

This unique characteristic enables quantum computers to consider many possibilities in parallel, making them exponentially faster for specific calculations than other known technologies. Instead of iterating through sequences of 0s and 1s in Machine Learning algorithms, qubits can represent both 0 and 1 simultaneously, facilitating quantum computers to process numerous calculations in parallel. In *Chapter 7*, we explained the crucial role of parallel data processing in AI. We highlighted how Graphic Processing Units (GPUs) are specialized hardware meticulously optimized for this purpose. Driving a comparison, quantum computing can aptly be described as a supercharged version of a GPU.

Quantum entanglement is another important quantum characteristic. Entanglement was introduced by Albert Einstein in 1935. Entanglement is the phenomenon where multiple quantum particles become interconnected so they can no longer be described in isolation. The state of one particle becomes intricately linked to the state of the other, regardless of how far these particles are from each other. When two particles become entangled, any change in the state of one qubit leads to an instantaneous change in the state of the paired qubit. Einstein famously referred to this non-local connection as "*spooky action at a distance*" [Einstein et al.].

Specifically designed algorithms operate across entangled and superposed qubits, leading to a dramatic acceleration of computational tasks. In a classical computer, adding a bit results in a linear increase in processing power. In contrast, adding qubits in a quantum computer leads to exponential increases in processing power growth, which implies that quantum computers have the potential to reach computational speeds unattainable by classical computers. This could help enable AI applications, such as Superintelligence, that might be impossible to run on classical computers, acknowledging, as we have in the introduction to this section, that there could be roadblocks in pure physics as may be encountered in the future.

Quantum Turing Machines and Quantum Computers

The American physicist Paul Benioff introduced the concept of a quantum Turing machine in 1980 to describe a simplified quantum computer. The classical Turing machine, introduced by Alan Turing in 1936, as discussed in *Chapter 3*, is an abstract mathematical model of computation consisting of an infinite tape divided into cells, a read/write head, and a set of rules. The machine can manipulate symbols on the tape, allowing it to simulate the execution of any algorithmic process through the application of these rules [Benioff].

The Quantum Turing Machine, in essence, extends the classical Turing machine by incorporating the quantum principles of superposition and entanglement. It maintains the essential components of the classical model—the tape, read/write head, and rules—but introduces quantum bits or qubits in place of classical bits and quantum gates instead of traditional logical gates. Quantum gates are the fundamental operations that manipulate the quantum states of qubits and allow simple logical calculations like AND or OR functions.

Over time, engineers have constructed small-scale quantum computers following this Quantum Turing Architecture. In 1998, a two-qubit quantum computer developed by IBM showcased the viability of this technology. Successive experiments have expanded the number of qubits. In 2019, NASA and Google announced the achievement of quantum supremacy with a 54-qubit machine. Quantum supremacy refers to the point where a quantum computer outperforms the best classical supercomputers in a specific task. In that sense, this quantum computer could calculate up to 3 million times faster than the fastest classical computer of that time, an IBM model [Aaronson]. Google continued working on improving that original model and, in 2023, announced the development of a newer 72-qubit quantum computer [Swayne].

The application of quantum principles in computing comes with a formidable challenge. In a quantum system, any external interference, such as changes in temperature, vibrations, or exposure to light, can be seen as an *"observation"* that coerces a quantum particle into a specific state. As particles become increasingly entangled and superposed, they become highly susceptible to external disturbances. This is because a disturbance involving a single qubit can have a cascading impact on many other entangled qubits. When a qubit is forced into a 0 or 1 state, it forfeits the information held in superposition, resulting in errors before the algorithm can complete its task. This challenge is known as decoherence and is quantified by an error rate.

Various techniques have been employed to reduce external interference, such as maintaining quantum computers at extremely low temperatures in vacuum environments. Other promising technologies to develop are ion traps and superconductors.

Ion traps help eliminate quantum decoherence by isolating and stabilizing individual ions, minimizing interactions with the external environment that can lead to loss of quantum information. On the other hand, superconductors help eliminate quantum decoherence by allowing particles to move without resistance, preventing the disruption of quantum states caused by interactions with the surrounding environment.

Finally, Google scientists have explored error-correcting algorithms to rectify errors derived from decoherence without compromising the stored information. However, losing information remains a significant hurdle preventing the practical use of quantum computers. Reducing errors is currently the primary focus of physicists, as it represents the most substantial barrier to achieving practical quantum computing [Dyakonov].

Quantum Algorithms and Computational Speedups

If the technical challenges associated with quantum decoherence are addressed, quantum computers are poised to significantly enhance AI capabilities by efficiently managing complex algorithms through their unmatched parallel processing capabilities.

One last barrier to realizing the processing speed and, thus, the leap in AI capability promised by quantum computing involves the adaptation of classical algorithms to quantum environments. To harness superposition and entanglement effectively, algorithms cannot merely run unmodified within a quantum computing environment. Similarly, a neural network that runs on a classical computer cannot run unmodified on a quantum computer. They both require modification and a rewrite.

Classical algorithms are typically designed in a way that is largely detached from the physical aspects of classical computers, focusing purely on abstract mathematical models. Data scientists do not need to know how electrons move inside the GPUs or CPUs in order to design an algorithm, rather, they merely write the algorithm in a programming language like Python, and processing power takes over from there. That is not the case—or at least not yet—with quantum algorithms. Quantum algorithms are intimately tied to the physical principles of quantum mechanics and need explicitly to exploit quantum properties like superposition and entanglement in order to work.

These algorithms specifically tailored for quantum computers are called quantum algorithms. In theory, quantum algorithms require exponentially fewer calculations for some specific, heavily computational tasks than their classical counterparts. However, this quantum speedup versus classical computing does not apply to all computational tasks. Basic tasks like sorting, for example, do not exhibit any asymptotic quantum speedup.

Based on the types of speedups a quantum version of an algorithm can bring over its classical version, quantum algorithms can be categorized into three groups. First, exponential gains. Second polynomial gains. Third, gains that selectively depend on the data that is processed. Other algorithms will have no speedup at all.

Exponential Quantum Speedups and the Future of Bitcoin

Exponential speedups are the algorithms in which quantum technology brings the most value. Exponential speedup means that a quantum algorithm can solve a problem exponentially more quickly than the most efficient classical algorithm known for that particular problem. The most famous example is Shor's Algorithm, which was formulated in 1994 by mathematician Peter Shor to break down large numbers into their prime factors [Shor].

Finding the prime factors of a 1000-digit number using classical algorithms would take such a long time that it would be practically impossible, even under significant advances in processing power. To factor a number with N digits, classic algorithms require a number of calculations in the order of the exponential of N (e^N), whereas Shor's Algorithm can do it in the order of $\log(N)^3$. Shor is exponentially faster. To contextualize how much faster, a computational task that would typically demand 100 hours to finish on a classical computer could be completed in approximately 9 minutes on a quantum computer under Shor's Algorithm.

This algorithm has profound implications for cryptography and any type of digital protection since most encryption techniques rely on the complexity involved in factoring large numbers. Shor's Algorithm could render vulnerable many widely adopted public key ciphers, such as RSA (Rivest-Shamir-Adleman), Diffie–Helman, and elliptic curve cryptography. These ciphers are crucial for safeguarding secure web pages and encrypted emails, making their potential compromise a significant concern for electronic privacy and security [Blakle].

Shor's Algorithm could also compromise the security of private keys used in Bitcoin for signing transactions and controlling the ownership of the coins. Utilizing Shor's algorithm on a quantum computer would make it feasible and efficient to break Bitcoin cryptographic keys. This vulnerability could put Bitcoin holdings and other blockchain applications at risk, ultimately undermining trust in the cryptocurrency system. Due to the enormous computational ability of the Shor Algorithm, cracking bitcoins may be one of the first real-world applications of quantum computers once these computers become commercial.

Beyond cryptography, quantum exponential speedups have the potential to bring transformative advancements in the realm of new drug discovery or synthesis of heretofore unknown substances. Quantum elements can simulate complex molecular interactions with unparalleled precision, greatly accelerating the development of new compounds, pharmaceuticals, and therapies. In materials science, it could revolutionize the design of novel materials with tailored properties, impacting industries ranging from electronics to energy storage. Such new breakthroughs showcase the wide-reaching impact that quantum computing can have on scientific research, technology, and industry.

Efficient Search with Polynomial Quantum Speedups

The second kind of speedup is the polynomial speedup. In this case, the quantum algorithm's advantage over its classical counterparts resides in how it scales in a polynomial manner with the problem size, offering a valuable though more gradual improvement to computations and problem-solving.

Grover's Algorithm, devised by Lov Grover in 1996, is the most well-known polynomial speedup algorithm. It is used to solve the problem of searching an unsorted database. In classical computing, if you have an unsorted list of N items, you would need to make, on average, N/2 comparisons to find a specific item. Grover's Algorithm, however, can find the target item in a database of N items in roughly $\sqrt{N}$ steps. The number of operations needed in the classical search is proportional to the square of those needed by Grover's algorithm—N/2 versus $\sqrt{N}$. As a result, Grover provides a quadratic speedup [Grover]. A sorting task that requires 100 hours to complete on a classical computer could be accomplished in approximately 14 hours with the quadratic speedup of Grover's algorithm.

By significantly accelerating the task-searching elements in unsorted databases, Grover's algorithm offers practical solutions for real-world problems where exhaustive searches were once time-prohibitive. It could, for example, revolutionize database searching, enabling much faster retrieval of information in large datasets, a crucial element of common tasks like data analytics, information retrieval, and search engine operation. In the domain of route planning, Grover's algorithm can efficiently search through vast logistic networks and find the most optimal paths, reducing transportation costs and travel times. In resource allocation scenarios such as scheduling tasks or distributing resources in supply chains, Grover's algorithm can expedite the search for optimal configurations, leading to better resource utilization, cost reductions, and improved overall efficiency.

Another algorithm that brings polynomial speedup is Support Vector Machines (SVMs), first developed in 1995 by Corinna Cortes and Vladimir Vapnik [Vapnik and Cortes]. Vapnik had initially introduced the concept of SVMs in 1964, wherein they were used primarily to solve data classification problems.

The importance of SVMs comes to light in solving problems used in everyday consumer applications, from classifying emails as spam to object recognition in images to any *"this-that-other"* identification problems. The ability of SVMs to handle nonlinear data and their performance in solving high-dimensional problems has made them essential tools for data scientists in business and AI research.

Imagine a dataset with points in a multidimensional space with many features, each feature being a dimension, where the goal is to find the best way to separate those points into different categories. Practical examples would include identifying whether or not there is cancer in a medical image or whether or not there is fraud in a financial transaction. SVMs seek to find a line or boundary that maximizes the distance between points of different categories. In order to do that, SVMs transform the features into another dimensional space where the decision boundary is clearer. SVMs turn the axis of the data around, much like turning a cube around. In other words, SVMs try to find the best cut that separates the data. Once they see that boundary, they can classify new data based on which side of the line it falls on.

Consider the problem of identifying cats and dogs based on only two dimensions: size and weight. It is not straightforward because while most dogs are bigger than cats, some are smaller. An SVM can map a huge set of data points representing all cats and all dogs into a higher-dimensional space, such as 3D or 4D. In this higher-dimensional space, a plane or hyperplane can effectively separate the two classes (cats and dogs) and discern the intricate characteristics that may not be as apparent in the original two-dimensional space. The ability of SVMs to handle nonlinear data and their performance in solving high-dimensional problems made them essential tools for data scientists in business and AI research.

Classical computing SVMs can be computationally demanding in real-world applications, particularly when confronted with a very large number of features or substantial training datasets. Quantum SVM's quadratic speedup implies significant time savings in tasks like image and text classification, financial modeling, and healthcare diagnostics.

Quantum Machine Learning Algorithms with Selective Speed-ups

The third group includes algorithms that provide high speed-ups compared to their classical counterparts but only in bespoke and clearly defined cases. This is what is called selective speed-ups in quantum computing.

An illustrative case is the HHL algorithm (Harrow-Hassidim-Lloyd, based on the authors' names), which was introduced in 2009 to solve linear equation systems efficiently on a quantum computer. Solving this kind of linear system requires inverting a matrix. The HHL algorithm exploits quantum superposition and entanglement to streamline matrix inversion [Harrow et al.].

Classical algorithms for solving linear systems typically have a time complexity that scales at least at N^3, where N is the dimension of the system. In contrast, the HHL algorithm's time complexity can go as low as log(N). For example, a linear system that took 100 hours in a classical computer would take roughly 40 minutes on a quantum computer running the HHL algorithm. That would be an exponential speed-up because $N^3/\log(N)$ grows exponentially.

However, the speedup is highly problem-specific as it depends on the problem size, the matrix structure, and the quantum hardware's capabilities. In cases where these conditions are met, the HHL algorithm can offer a substantial time-to-calculate advantage, potentially making it orders of magnitude faster, noting that the quantum advantage may not be as pronounced as the other cases we discussed.

These present the same advantages when handling optimization problems. Optimization means reaching the best possible outcome with fixed resources, such as route planning, supplier management, and financial portfolio return maximization. These are ideal scenarios where quantum computing excels due to its distinctive capacity to rapidly identify optimal solutions while handling vast and diverse datasets. Classical computers often face computational overload when dealing with such extensive data to solve optimization problems.

Linear equation systems are commonly used in solving optimization problems. Many optimization models involve linear relationships between variables. Therefore, many quantum optimization algorithms are related to HHL and can potentially bring either exponential or polynomial computational gains, depending on the specific problem, but again, only under certain situations.

Apart from linear equations systems, there is another fundamental quantum optimization algorithm called Quantum Annealing. In metallurgy, annealing is a heat treatment process used to alter the physical and chemical properties of a metal or alloy. The metal is heated to a specific temperature and then gradually cooled, allowing its atoms to rearrange into a more stable state. Annealing is often employed to reduce hardness, improve machinability, enhance ductility, and relieve internal stresses in the material.

Quantum Annealing is named after this metallurgical process. Instead of adjusting the temperature of a physical material, Quantum Annealing adjusts the parameters of a quantum system as it transitions from a quantum superposition to a classical state. This way, the quantum system is guided toward the solution of an optimization problem. The idea is to allow this quantum system to explore possible solutions, similar to the way atoms rearrange during metallurgical annealing, in order to find the most favorable outcome for the given problem [Apolloni et al.].

Quantum Annealing illustrates our earlier point about the direct dependence of quantum algorithms on the intricacies of quantum mechanics. Designing quantum algorithms requires understanding quantum mechanics in detail and cannot be done using programming languages like Python. As we mentioned at the outset of this chapter, classical algorithms need to be completely recreated to run on quantum computers.

In addition to the more routine examples of optimization problems discussed earlier, Quantum Annealing finds particular utility in a crucial optimization problem endemic to all applications in AI: training Machine Learning algorithms, especially neural networks.

Quantum Neural Networks and the Steppingstone for Next-Generation AI

The most useful AI applications today are based on artificial neural networks. From self-driving cars and humanoid robots to Generative AI and machine vision, all important AI applications today use neural networks. Having reviewed the most important quantum algorithms, we can turn to the next vector: *"Are there quantum neural networks?"* The short answer is yes, but primitive ones. Quantum neural networks are not at all as developed as their classical counterparts.

If quantum computers could efficiently train and execute neural networks by harnessing the parallelism derived from superposition and entanglement, it would represent a significant stride toward ushering in a new era of faster and more intelligent AI that would rapidly rival human capabilities.

In the algorithm classification, which we have made of exponential, polynomial, or selective speedups, quantum neural networks fit in this last selective group at the moment. Their speedup can vary depending on the specific problem, data, and the quantum hardware used. Quantum neural networks may offer some advantages for particular tasks. Still, they do not guarantee exponential or polynomial speedup across the wide range of use cases that a classical neural network can be used for [da Silva et al.].

Research on quantum neural networks primarily revolves around two main focus points: adapting classical artificial neural networks to harness quantum advantages and training quantum neural networks efficiently.

Regarding the first, quantum computers must be uniquely engineered to replicate the functioning of a neural network at the hardware level as opposed to the conventional software-based approach in classical computers. In a quantum configuration, each qubit effectively takes on the role of a neuron and serves as the fundamental building block of the neural network.

But making qubits behave like artificial neurons is not easy. Each neuron inside an artificial neural network acts as a switch, sometimes transmitting the incoming signal to the next neuron and other times filtering it out. Finding an accurate equivalent of this switching behavior inside a quantum qubit is still a significant challenge researchers face in advancing quantum Machine Learning algorithms. Various quantum approaches have been proposed, but these structures must be tailored to specific applications.

The second research point is the formidable challenge of training large classical neural networks in the quantum world, particularly in extensive data applications. That means finding the values of the billions of parameters that make part of the neural network in order to minimize the errors made by the networks. For example, GPT3 has 175 billion parameters, and GPT4 is rumored to be ten times bigger. The majority of techniques in Machine Learning involve an iterative process for training algorithms to learn this huge number of parameters. However, these classical techniques need to be adapted to the quantum world. Quantum optimization algorithms, such as quantum annealing, have the potential to perform certain aspects of training neural networks more efficiently than classical computers, particularly in tasks related to optimization.

In order to create a hardware framework that allows the building of generic neural networks, there has been a great deal of research. In 2020, Kerstin Beer introduced the first versatile quantum neural network architecture of this kind, featuring an input layer, multiple hidden layers, and an output layer [Beer et al.]. This framework was a colossal step forward because it enabled quantum neural networks more complex than the perceptron of 1957 by Frank Rosenblatt, which only had one layer, as we explained in *Chapter 4.*

Research on quantum neural networks is still developing, and we are very far from having a general quantum computer where you can run a generic neural network as we do with a classical computer. The convergence of quantum computing parallelism with the power of neural networks marks a compelling intersection, with the potential to further reshape the landscape of AI completely and to push the boundaries more toward Superintelligence.

Navigating the Quantum Winters

While we have described the immense promise that quantum computing holds for the future of AI, it is important to also consider the complexity involved in fully realizing it. Technology is still a long way from developing, let alone industrializing, a general quantum computer capable of running generic software.

When AI was first introduced in 1956, it also held an immeasurable promise that was challenging to fulfill as processing power was not as fast to develop as algorithms, and prevailing economic tides often moved against the development of AI that did not have an immediate commercial impact. As explained in *Chapters 4, 5,* and *6*, this led to three successive *"AI Winters,"* and we may encounter more of them in the future for likely the same reasons noted in *Chapter 24* that the current economic slowdown in China is already manifesting effect against the speed of continued AI development. Quantum computing is likely to face both similar and unique challenges of its own [Gent].

First, as we have described in this chapter, there are no good quantum algorithms yet that can work for AI. Peter Schor puts it this way in his interview with CERN (European Organization for Nuclear Research) in 2021 [Charitos]: *"The main problem is that we don't have good quantum algorithms. However, in my view, once we have quantum computers we will be able to develop experimentally more and better algorithms paving a new era of quantum algorithm development.* "Moreover, designing quantum algorithms is complicated because they cannot be written using some level of programming language. Rather, they are required to be implemented directly in hardware that does not exist commercially—at least for now.

Second, quantum systems exhibit an inherent complexity that surpasses classical systems. The principles of quantum superposition and entanglement introduce complexities that defy classical intuition. Mitigating quantum decoherence is imperative for maintaining the integrity of quantum information, and scalability poses a substantial hurdle, with the need to orchestrate coherent interactions among an increasing number of qubits. Integration with classical systems demands the development of hybrid architectures, bridging the disparate domains of quantum and classical computing.

Third, quantum computers require specialized environments with extreme conditions, such as low temperatures, to maintain delicate quantum states. This resource intensity hampers scalability and accessibility. Just as early AI faced limitations due to hardware constraints, the resource-intensive nature of quantum technology could lead to winters, hindering its broad application and development.

Finally, while it is not expected at this juncture based on the current knowledge set, quantum computing might encounter unforeseen scientific barriers or physical limits that science might not yet be aware of. The exploration of uncharted territories in physics and quantum mechanics could reveal fundamental limitations that slow down progress.

Quantum computing is still considered the pivotal technology that will unlock the computational speeds necessary for Superintelligence, which will be the focus of our next chapter.

26. Superintelligence

"Let an ultraintelligent machine be defined as a machine that can far surpass all the intellectual activities of any man, however clever. Since the design of machines is one of these intellectual activities, an ultraintelligent machine could design even better machines; there would then unquestionably be an "intelligence explosion," and the intelligence of man would be left far behind. Thus the first ultraintelligent machine is the last invention that man need ever make."

Irving John (I. J.) Good

British Mathematician

Speculations Concerning the First Ultraintelligent Machine [Good]

1966

These were the terms Irving John Good employed to articulate the concepts of Superintelligence, which he called *"ultra-intelligence"* at the time, and singularity, which he dubbed *"intelligence explosion."* Good's enthusiastic tone conveyed the idea that the development of such an invention would potentially be the last invention humans might need to make, suggesting that this technology could make all the next inventions on behalf of humanity.

These intriguing ideas found their way to Stanley Kubrick, who sought Good's consultation during *"2001: A Space Odyssey"* (1968), a film featuring the iconic character of the paranoid HAL 9000 supercomputer. This is another compelling illustration of the interplay between Science Fiction and real scientific thought on top of the many we have uncovered in this book [Clarke and Kubrick].

A central theme of this book is the inevitability of human-AI Interlace, and the prospect of Superintelligence is an intriguing corollary of it. However, predicting the future is a challenging task, and it is impossible to know the specifics and timing of how or if Superintelligence itself will happen.

Intuitively, considering the inevitable march of evolution, considering that human intelligence has been evolving for millions of years and is likely to continue evolving in a similar way over the next few million years even if left unabated, where is the end-point? It is logical to think that Superintelligence is possible. A random DNA change that spreads in a population accelerated by a major environmental factor is no different than a change built by humans as a result of a desire for progress; the only differences are in speed (acceleration) and mechanism (silicon vs carbon). A future version of humanity left to the improvement process of evolution would be, by definition, Superintelligence.

The Science Fiction of Superintelligence

The notion of Superintelligence raises questions about the profound implications of creating or encountering a being or system that surpasses human cognitive abilities. The best-known Superintelligence in Science Fiction is Skynet from *"The Terminator"* movie franchise, first introduced in 1984 by James Cameron and starring Arnold Schwarzenegger [Cameron]. But William Gibson's 1984 novel *"Neuromancer"* descends much deeper into the intellectual, mechanical, and spiritual complexity of AI, cyberspace, and the fusion of humans and machines [Gibson]. Charles Stross' 2005 novel *"Accelerando,"* provides another compelling view [Stross].

"Neuromancer" is a groundbreaking cyberpunk novel that envisions a dystopian future world where the convergence of AI and cyberspace creates a virtual realm where hackers and AI coexist. The narrative follows Case, a washed-up skilled hacker hired by a mysterious employer to pull off the ultimate hack.

Gibson's vision of Superintelligence in *"Neuromancer"* is subtle yet pervasive. The story runs in a vast, interconnected, and technologically dominated urban environment with a gritty atmosphere and cybernetic enhancements, known as the Sprawl. Here, the fusion of human consciousness and AI blends the boundaries between the physical and virtual worlds, creating a landscape where the implications of Superintelligence are interlaced with the very fabric of society to the point of being indistinguishable. The novel introduces Wintermute and Neuromancer, two AIs with distinct personalities and capabilities. Wintermute is a pragmatic entity seeking to merge with its counterpart, Neuromancer, to form a Superintelligence capable of unparalleled feats. The emergence of Superintelligence in *"Neuromancer"* is more of a collaborative synergy than a singular, omnipotent force. This representation contrasts sharply with the conventional notion of a monolithic AI and points toward what we believe is the ultimate nature of AI: collectivist and non-atomistic.

In contrast, Charles Stross's *"Accelerando"* takes a more expansive and temporally ambitious approach to the theme of Superintelligence. The novel is a collection of interconnected stories spanning multiple generations of the same family, each exploring the accelerating pace of technological progress leading to the singularity, a point of unprecedented technological advancement. What is interesting about *"Accelerando"* is that each generation of the family is much more interlaced with AI than the previous one, and they are effectively different species that behave and see the world completely differently.

Unlike *"Neuromancer,"* where Superintelligence emerges through the collaboration of AIs, *"Accelerando"* envisions a post-singularity scenario where human intelligence becomes intricately interlaced with a distributed network of evolving AIs from the very beginning. Stross paints a vivid but progressive picture of the singularity, depicting a cascade of accelerating intelligence explosions that defy traditional human understanding. But we note that this vision, too, akin to our view of AI overall, is networked, collectivist, and non-atomistic.

In *"Accelerando,"* Superintelligence is ubiquitous and is not confined to individual entities but is instead an emergent trait of the interconnected minds comprising a vast post-singularity landscape. Human intelligence becomes indistinguishable from this omnipresent and distributed network of interconnected minds. Societal implications are cosmic in scale as the singularity unfolds across generations, reshaping the fabric of the entire solar system.

Carbon or Silicon: Beyond the Physical Substrate

When thinking about Superintelligence, we must ask, *"Is it even possible?"* The short answer is yes, but we do not know for sure.

In 1975, Allen Newell and Herbert Simon, two of the AI forefathers we mentioned in detail in *Chapter 5,* formulated the Hypothesis of Physical Symbol Systems. This hypothesis suggested that human thinking is fundamentally a process of manipulating symbols, and machines can also achieve intelligence if they possess a physical symbol system; such a system is the basis of symbolic logic in robots, as discussed in *Chapter 11.* According to this hypothesis, it does not matter whether the physical substrate of intelligence is carbon, as in humans, silicon, as in today's computers, or quantum hardware, as in hypothetical computers of the future. In other words, building General Artificial Intelligence (AGI), or even Superintelligence, on any or a combination of platforms should be possible [Newell and Simon].

This concept has philosophical roots in thinkers we introduced in *Chapter 3,* such as Hobbes, Leibniz, and Hume, who also hypothesized that reasoning and perception could be reduced to formal operations and that the human brain was nothing more than a carbon-based mechanical system just like the rest of the body. If the hypothesis of physical symbol systems holds, it could also be possible to emulate human intelligence using synthetic materials.

Newell's and Simon's views have faced debate within the AI community itself. For example, the need for explicit symbols has been questioned multiple times in the history of AI. Some AI scientists believe that intelligence may emerge from systems that are less focused on symbols. Instead, a form of intelligence could be based on analog signals from the real world rather than discrete or digital representations, like the early analog robots Elmer and Elsie that were built at the end of World War II or the *"Nouvelle AI"* robots of the 1990s as we presented in *Chapter 11*.

We believe that as human intelligence evolved through a biological evolutionary process, this inevitable march merely increases the possibility that human engineers with intelligence based on carbon-denominated evolution may be able to recreate intelligence by emulating the human mind on silicon-based platforms. The possibility of mind emulation is also a form of Superintelligence, which we will explore in the next chapter.

Strong AI and the Hard Problem of Consciousness

Humans have consciousness: *"I think, therefore I am,"* as René Descartes put it in 1637 in his work *"Discourse on the Method"* [Descartes]. Philosophers and religions have argued consciousness is the objective of the universe because if nobody could experience it—either humans, animals, or others—it would not exist or would not make sense.

The concept of consciousness is directly related to the idea of Strong AI coined by the American philosopher John Searle in 1980, who we mentioned in *Chapter 4* in connection with the Turing Test. Strong AI represents an AI system with consciousness, self-awareness, and sentience. Consciousness refers to the ability to subjectively experience and be aware of the environment. Self-awareness implies perceiving oneself as separate within the environment. Sentience encompasses the ability to *"feel"* perceptions and emotions subjectively within the environment.

Armed with consciousness, self-awareness, and sentience, Strong AI machines would possess a form of subjective experiences and an ability to understand and respond to the world in ways similar to humans. This goes beyond intellectual cognitive abilities and suggests that something exceptional has occurred in an AI machine beyond capabilities we can objectively measure. On the contrary, a machine that does not have consciousness, self-awareness, or sentience—no matter how intelligent— would be called Narrow or Weak AI, according to Searle.

Years after Searle, David Chalmers, an Australian-American philosopher, continued his study of the topic of Strong AI and consciousness, giving it another twist. In 1996, Chalmers proposed two categories of consciousness-related problems: the *"easy problem"* and the *"hard problem."*

The easy problem is related to questions about the cognitive mechanics of the mind. These specifically include perceiving and categorizing objects, integrating information, and engaging in cognitive processes like language or logic. As of 2024, AI models have already demonstrated the capability to address a range of easy problems. Actually, constructing these AI models has yielded brain and computer scientists valuable insights into the functioning of the human brain [Chalmers].

Conversely, the hard problem delves into the heart of consciousness, asking why and how physical processes in the brain give rise to the qualitative, subjective aspects of experience. Chalmers famously articulated the hard problem: *"Why does all this processing give rise to a rich inner life? Why is it that when electromagnetic waveforms strike the retina, they give rise to visual experience, or when neural processing occurs, it gives rise to pains, colors, sounds, and emotions?"* "Trying to answer the hard problem of consciousness, some transhumanists like Ray Kurzweil or even Marvin Minsky contended that the human mind simply emerges from the information processing conducted by its biological neural network. They argue that essential cognitive functions, including learning, memory, and consciousness, are fundamentally rooted in the brain's physical and electrochemical processes, operating according to the established laws of physics, chemistry, biology, and mathematics, rather than being rooted in a dualistic and mystical soul or spirit. Some even argue that quantum mechanics are an inherent part of that consciousness.

Actually, quantum neural networks can be traced back to the work of Subhash Kak and Ron Chrisley in 1995, who studied the role that quantum mechanics could have in human cognitive functions, assuming that classical mechanics could fully explain human consciousness [Kak]. Some quantum-related hypotheses suggest that the nature of quantum superposition and entanglement at the microscopic level might play a role in cognitive processes and that consciousness emerges from quantum coherence or that quantum effects within the brain contribute to subjective experiences. Nevertheless, these conjectures are not yet widely accepted. We believe, like Kurzweil and Minsky, among others, that all human cognitive functions, from learning, memory, thinking, and emoting, are simply rooted in the brain's physical and electrochemical processes, operating according to the established laws of physics, chemistry, and biology, and mathematics. That said, our comprehension of consciousness remains elusive.

However, much like AI system implementation has aided us in understanding the *"easy"* problem of consciousness a bit better, creating AI models might also provide valuable clues to grapple with the enigmatic *"hard"* problem of understanding what consciousness truly entails. In this sense, another hypothesis suggests that consciousness could be similar to the world models used by the symbolic logic of robots we discussed in *Chapters 9* and *11*. A world model is a digital representation or simulation of the robot's environment, including objects, obstacles, and relevant information, which it uses for navigation, decision-making, and interaction with its surroundings. It helps the robot understand and respond to the external world.

This hypothesis proposes that humans can only focus on one world model at a time, given the size limitation of their brains. That means humans always need to configure our mental model to the present context because we do not have the size to focus on all contexts at the same time. Our brain's prefrontal cortex is limited to constructing and loading a world model tailored to our current context. In this sense, consciousness might be the module configuring this world model. This hypothesis suggests that consciousness is not a consequence of the power of the mind but a limitation of the brain arising from having a limited capacity to load unlimited world models. If humans had as many world models as there are situations, they might not need consciousness to control their execution. They could just be processing information all the time and executing many tasks in parallel with high productivity and accuracy, including even very artistic tasks like poetry and painting, without feeling anything special about themselves and without knowing they even exist as human beings.

Then why is it necessary to feel like a conscious individual experiencing reality rather than just processing information? We do not know the answer, but maybe there is a potential utility and evolutionary significance of this feeling of ownership and self-awareness. Maybe species that are conscious are better adapted to survive the environment than others.

In short, the question of consciousness remains unanswered, which is why Chalmers called it the *"hard problem."* However, the question of consciousness is a fundamental starting point for exploring Superintelligence and immortality; it is the last frontier point of AI becoming equal to and surpassing human intelligence.

A related question might be: *"Would AI or Superintelligence be able to feel emotions?"* The answer is yes. Artificial neural networks that refresh their hyperparameters as they interact with the environment (a topic covered in *Chapter 18*) might be able to experiment with shortcut methods to handle complex scenarios or what humans experience as emotions. Much will depend on how we define emotions. The human emotional experience and the degree to which emotions impact thinking and decision-making at an atomistic human level is unique to every individual, a byproduct of their individual experience, which is the equivalent of AI training.

Superintelligence: Speed, Collectivity, and Quality

Superintelligence is a theoretical entity possessing vastly superior intellectual capabilities to the brightest and most gifted human intellects, encompassing all areas of human endeavors and aspirations. This entity transcends human cognitive constraints, which have limited working memory, a constrained attention span, and an inability to extend past a single worldview in its mental model, and is inherently subject to many cognitive biases and psychological limitations.

Nick Bostrom, a renowned philosopher and professor at the University of Oxford, has studied the complex landscape of Superintelligence and its profound implications for humanity. In his 2014 book, *"Superintelligence: Paths, Dangers, Strategies,"* he introduces three possible ways in which Superintelligence could be superior to human intelligence. In short, a Superintelligence could exhibit superior speed, combine on a collective scale, and be superior in terms of quality. These three forms of Superintelligence are not mutually exclusive, and progress in one domain can expedite advancements in the others [Bostrom].

First, speed Superintelligence would be a system that can execute all tasks within the human cognitive spectrum but at a significantly faster rate. It is well known that computers have already surpassed humans in speed. An example of speed Superintelligence is emulating an entire human brain on high-speed hardware. Human neurons operate at a peak frequency of 200 Hz. In contrast, modern computer systems are orders of magnitude faster at 2 GHz frequency. As a result, an AI can solve cognitive problems approximately a million times more quickly than a human if run on a computer of equal size to a brain, which is actually an extremely big size, as we will see in the next chapter.

Second, collective Superintelligence would comprise many smaller intellects together, resulting in a combined entity that would surpass human intelligence across numerous domains. This would be similar to how Wintermute and Neuromancer combined with each other in the Science Fiction novel *"Neuromancer"* mentioned above. Collective Superintelligence is closely related to human networks and organizations, such as companies, workgroups, and scientific communities, where humans collaborate to do things together that cannot be done alone.

We have highlighted our belief throughout the book that the essential elements of AI and interlacing are ultimately collectivist and non-atomistic. The performance of a collaborative Superintelligence system would greatly depend on the quality of subsystems, their communication, and their cooperation. For example, maintaining alignment of motivations and goals among participants would become increasingly challenging as the system scales, a problem encountered even among primitive AI systems such as China's Social Credit System, which, as we highlighted in *Chapter 24,* hit a problem in implementation precisely because it did not roll-up its subsystems. Additionally, communication between participants may suffer from inefficiencies, potentially leading to suboptimal system behavior. Furthermore, there is also another limit to its performance, particularly for tasks that cannot be subdivided into simpler parts, as one genius cannot be replaced by many average human intellects.

Third, quality Superintelligence would be a kind of Superintelligence that is qualitatively superior compared to human intellect. Quality Superintelligence would represent the pinnacle of AI development. It is difficult for humans to fully comprehend the magnitude of such intelligence, just as insects might struggle to grasp what human intellect really is. Such superintelligent qualities may include perfect memory, extensive knowledge, elimination of cognitive biases (e.g., confirmation bias, anchoring bias, sunk cost fallacies), and multitasking abilities beyond biological limitations. Furthermore, superintelligence could improve reliability and longevity. It is worth noting that these elements would easily be duplicable, editable, and expandable with new modules, making them capable of growing and developing more rapidly than human intelligence.

Disagreements exist in the research community regarding whether surpassing human intelligence is really possible or, if achieved, whether those superintelligent systems would be—or would need to be—conscious or self-aware. There is, at present, no good answer or hypothesis, only conjecture.

Three Avenues to Superintelligence

Although it sounds like Science Fiction, Superintelligence is already being developed by humankind. Three possible ways of developing a superintelligent system are being explored at this moment; the first has a digital origin, and the other two have biological origins [Bostrom].

The first and most likely pathway is AI Self-Improvement, involving the recursive development of systems capable of enhancing their own intelligence. This approach has the potential to lead to rapid development of intelligence, eventually surpassing human capabilities, often referred to as an *"intelligence explosion"* or technological singularity. We have already talked about self-improvement and the development of AGI in *Chapter 9* as two of the most active areas of research today. We view this scenario of AI digital origin and self-improvement as the most likely and, at the same time, the most concerning due to its potential for rapid, uncontrolled growth and, thus, for exploitation via authoritarian rule.

The second avenue for achieving AGI and Superintelligence is Whole Brain Emulation (WBE), also called Mind Emulation or Mind Upload. This involves creating a detailed digital human brain replica through precise scanning and mapping of a brain's configuration and current state and transferring it to a computer. The computer then runs a highly accurate simulation model, itself an AI algorithm, to mimic the original brain's functionality, resulting in a form of immortality. Due to the complexity of biological neurons' behavior, very complex neural models are required to simulate a brain, much more complex than traditional artificial neural networks. Some research projects are developing advanced brain models for simulation on conventional computing architectures. We will cover this technology in detail in the next chapter. This approach appears feasible as an extrapolation of known technology, but we note that according to the Law of Accelerating Returns, the mathematical complexity of simulating a brain might require computers that would only exist by approximately the year 2100. As the position in this book is that all aspects of human thought and cognition can be reduced to mathematical operation, we believe that technology will enable this functionality, but also that it is unlikely to be the precise route to Superintelligence, becoming instead simply another avenue for adding to collective intelligence and ensuring individual immortality.

There is a third and less probable avenue to achieving Superintelligence, a purely biological approach involving synthetic biology and eugenics, which we presented in *Chapters 21* and *23*, respectively. This approach aims to enhance human intelligence through biotechnological methods, including genetic modifications and the selective optimization of embryos and gametes. Developing AI algorithms and software will be essential for designing optimized human DNA that could result in augmented intellectual abilities. Historically, this method has been utilized for tasks like child gender selection and screening for genetic disorders. In the future, we expect that aside from the ethical questions involved, specific technologies for human cognitive and intellectual enhancement will undoubtedly be created. They are already available in a lighter form, and this kind of selection process will be expanded to encompass cognitive and behavioral traits. Nevertheless, it simply may not be able to achieve Superintelligence per se, as the carbon-based human mind may not be capable of it. In the same way, a tuk-tuk is simply not designed to attain the land speed record, even if the best engine is placed within it.

The Explosion of Intelligence, a.k.a. the Singularity

We will focus on the first of the three avenues to Superintelligence: AI Self-improvement, which has also been called the *"singularity,"* as we see it as the most likely pathway. The singularity is a hypothetical juncture in the future where an AGI system can improve and enhance its intelligence, resulting in an exponential acceleration of self-improvement cycles. As generations succeed each other, intelligence grows exponentially, eventually leading to a Superintelligence that outperforms human intelligence in all metrics.

The term *"singularity"* is often associated with Hungarian-American mathematician John von Neumann, one of the designers of ENIAC, the first general-purpose computer in 1945, which we discussed in *Chapter 3*. However, the concept was popularized by American scientist and futurist Raymond Kurzweil in his 2005 book *"The Singularity is Near.".* Kurzweil founded *"Singularity University"* in 2008 with the goal of educating and empowering leaders to address global challenges using exponential technologies like AI, biotechnology, and nanotechnology.

The concept of exponential intelligence growth depends on the premise that earlier advances in intelligence pave the way for further improvements—an inherent evolution of sorts and a corollary of the Law of Accelerating Returns, which predicts exponential growth in the number of floating-point calculations per second (FLOPS) per constant dollar of cost. To keep progressing toward the singularity, each improvement should, on average, lead to at least one more improvement.

We note essentially two directions for the singularity process, each connoting a speed variation: fast—which we call *hard takeoff*—or slow—which can be called a *soft takeoff.*

In the *hard takeoff*, Superintelligence undergoes rapid cycles of self-improvement, permeating the world in a short span of time, owing in no small part to the networked, collectivist nature of AI. This rapid progression occurs too quickly for humans to initiate any significant correction of errors or alignment of the AI's motivations. In contrast, a soft takeoff involves AI becoming significantly more powerful than humankind but doing so at a pace comparable to human timescales, such as decades. In such a scenario, there is still room for humans to interact with the AI, correct it, and guide its development effectively toward forms of AI that are friendly to humankind, meaning that co-existence can be achieved.

Some philosophers argue that soft takeoff is far more likely than hard takeoff for two reasons. First, as intelligence becomes more sophisticated, subsequent advances can become increasingly complex, potentially slowing down the explosion of Superintelligence. Second, as the British transhumanist

Max More argues, even a superintelligent AI would still rely on human systems to impact the world physically. Superintelligence would not suddenly appear and change the world in an instant; in order to interact with that world and make any tangible changes, it would have to interact with cumbersome, current human systems, like supply chains, conventional computer systems, and manual human decision processes. These existing rules and systems cannot be abruptly discarded overnight or within years [More].

Consider a scenario within one of those self-improvement cycles where Superintelligence, as a next step, requires building a new type of hardware that utilizes materials not abundantly available on Earth. It is an example where a task has physical attributes or is tied inexorably to the physical world. In such a situation, the Superintelligence would need to undertake the cumbersome process of organizing logistics to obtain these materials from another planet or asteroid. This would also involve running experiments with the new materials, requiring physical manipulation, in order to build the new hardware. Finally, the Superintelligence would be required to migrate itself into the newly developed hardware. It is inconceivable that all planetary logistics and hardware manipulations could be completed within a matter of hours in a hard take-off.

Feasibility of the Singularity: Technology and Economics

Some skeptics of the singularity concept have raised doubts about the credibility of the Law of Accelerating Returns, a foundational prerequisite for the singularity, as discussed in the previous chapter.

For example, Microsoft co-founder Paul Allen suggested the existence of a *"complexity brake."* He posited that as science advances in comprehending intelligence, achieving further progress becomes increasingly challenging [Allen and Greaves]. Jonathan Huebner, an American physicist, showed that the number of patents per capita peaked between 1850 and 1900 and has been declining since [Huebner]. Physicist Theodore Modis presents a similar view, contending that the pace of technological innovation has not merely decelerated but is actually undergoing decline. His corroborating evidence is the slowdown in the pace of improvement in computer clock speeds—the megahertz of a computer—primarily due to heat-related challenges. Modis also points out the absence of significant breakthroughs in the past two decades (2000-2020) that proponents of the technological singularity would have expected. [Modis].

While Allen pointed out general complexity problems in innovation, and Huebner and Modis noted the ebb and flow of technical advancement, they all clearly failed to have the necessary faith in subsequent generations of AI scientists. Those scientists subsequently produced innovations such as advanced robots, Generative AI, synthetic tissue, and the possibility of AGI. We do not bet against advancement, and in our opinion, only the natural laws of physics can abate the existing trajectory of AI in the long term.

Switching to Economics, Martin Ford, an American author specializing in AI and robotics, formulated what he calls a "*technology paradox*" in 2010. He posits that before the Singularity could become a reality, the majority of jobs within the economy would have already undergone automation, as achieving the Singularity would require technology less advanced than it. This could result in widespread unemployment and a decrease in consumer demand, which, in turn, could discourage investments in the technologies needed to bring about the singularity [Ford]. Economist Robert J. Gordon argues that real economic growth decelerated beginning in 1970 and has further diminished after the financial crisis of 2008. He contends that economic data do not substantiate the notion of any forthcoming Singularity [Gordon].

We note that concepts such as UBI, as we discussed in Chapters *22 and 23*, while fallible, point toward any number of mechanisms that are available to assign resources to optimize production/consumption activity and to ensure continued investment into AI R&D. North Korea, which has no resources and no economy, managed to build a nuclear weapon on the back of inefficiency and the centralized management of severe scarcity. Furthermore, AI Winters have all passed, as we have noted throughout the book, spurred in no small part by Government impetus and macroeconomic changes. It is probable that there will be more AI Winters in the future, but they will not alter the trajectory, just as the previous ones did not.

To further counter-argue these points, Ray Dalio, the American hedge fund owner mentioned in *Chapter 23*, argues that long-term cycles determined by geopolitical shifts characterize economic history. According to him, we are currently at the end of one of these cycles, which started after World War II. We concur that even if innovation slows down at the end of any one cycle, that does not imply it will not accelerate again in the next cycle. It is foolish to bet against resilience and progress.

Interlace will happen and has already started. Superintelligence, or the singularity as we define it, might or might not happen, as several scientific-level barriers remain question marks. If we think of it as a long-term possibility as simply the end-point of Interlace and if we do not put a timetable on it, its cumulative probability substantially increases. As mentioned throughout the book, when we think of AI and AGI, we come from the point of view that human thought, memory, emotional experience, feeling, and motor coordination—every aspect of the brain—can be reduced to mathematical definition and operation, even if it takes several more decades or centuries to reach the processing power "*pivot point*" to fully enable it.

Along the way, as we think about superintelligence, several difficult questions emerge that intersect science and ethics. One such thorny question is: *"Can we replicate human consciousness in silicon?"* This involves the scientific ability to reduce it to stored value in much the same way as you can literally record everything you do every day for the rest of your life and store it in the cloud, verbally adding your thoughts and commentary in interpreting what your camera lens sees. The transfer of one's collective mind, or portions of it, to silicon, will become a possibility as technology improves. We will digress from the main discussion on the Singularity for one chapter to explore one such technological advance, Whole-Brain Emulation (WBE), also known as Mind Uploading, as it is another potential pathway to Superintelligence, one in which we can easily see the myriad of ethical and societal challenges faced, and gain insight into how to treat human consciousness.

27. Mind Uploading, Emulations, and Immortality

"There are so many wonders awaiting us. If we can upload memories, then we might be able to combat Alzheimer's, as well as create a brain-net of memories and emotions to replace the internet, which would revolutionize entertainment, the economy, and our way of life. Maybe even to help us live forever and send consciousness into outer space."

Michio Kaku

American Theoretical Physicist and Science Writer [Kaku]
In an interview in 2014

The concept of Mind Uploading (alternatively called Brain Emulation or Whole-Brain Emulation) was first proposed by biogerontologist George M. Martin in 1971. Mind Uploading postulates that consciousness from a human brain can be recreated in other devices, either a digital or quantum computer or even another biological brain.

The fundamental assumption behind the hypothesis of mind uploading is that the neural network connections and the synaptic weights of the brain represent the human mind, implying that *"mind"* could be simply defined as the brain's information state, existing in an immaterial manner literally like the content of a data file or the state of computer software. The data delineating the state of our biological neural network could be extracted and copied from the brain as a computer file and subsequently instantiated in an alternative physical subtract. This could possibly enable the new device to respond like the original brain, creating an aware and conscious mind. Or it could be a facsimile of it, not enabling full function but enabling, say, intelligence without consciousness or even a simple way to communicate with previous generations of people. Many futurists regard mind uploading as a logical culmination of computational neuroscience research, particularly in the context of medical advancements and the pursuit of Artificial General Intelligence (AGI).

Immortality is the implication of mind uploading. Suppose we can separate the mind's information and processes from the physical body. In that case, it opens the possibility of breaking free from the limitations and lifespan of our biological selves, even our SynBio-enhanced Interlaced selves, potentially extending or eliminating our mortality.

Mind uploading is gaining prominence in futurist and transhumanist circles as an avenue differentiated from cryonics or cryopreservation, which focuses on safeguarding bodies or brains at low temperatures for potential future revival and treatment.

As you read this chapter, please focus on the following takeaways:

• First, mind-uploading is considered a form of Superintelligence because it involves replicating a human mind in larger or faster hardware than the human brain, which is likely already more intelligent than a human.

• Second, there have been some successful attempts to emulate the brains of mammals, such as rats. However, the human mind is highly complex, and according to the Law of Accelerating Returns, it might take until 2100 to develop a computer fast enough to fully emulate it.

• Third, the societal implications of having some human beings in the real world while others exist in a simulated world, interacting and potentially competing with each other, are significant. One such conundrum arises because simulated human beings will operate at higher speeds as they run on computers and can be copied unlimitedly at a low cost.

The Science Fiction of Mind Uploading

The concept of mind-uploading has been explored in Science Fiction literature for decades. Two notable works, *"Permutation City"* by Greg Egan (1994) and *"Altered Carbon"* by Richard K. Morgan (2002, adapted into a Netflix series in 2018), offer distinct perspectives on this intriguing idea [Egan] [Morgan] and the inevitable societal, ethical and psychological impact of it.

The central premise in *"Altered Carbon"* is that death is no longer permanent. The mind or *"stack"* can be transferred into a physical device and uploaded into different physical bodies, referred to as "sleeves." This technology has led to a society where varying bodies are merely vessels for consciousness, and individuals can change bodies as quickly as changing clothes.

The novel explores the implications of a society where death is not final. While immortality seems like a noble aspiration, moral and ethical questions about the value of life and the consequences of personal actions become more complex. The absence of death as a deterrent to reckless behavior, for example, forces society to grapple with new notions of justice and responsibility in the face of subversive behavior.

Despite the advantages of immortality, not everybody embraces it. Some people decide not to take advantage of stacks and sleeves due to religious and philosophical convictions. The novel calls them the Neo-Catholics, and they are similar to the *"bioluddittes"* we discussed in *Chapter 23*. This technology also has far-reaching social implications. The wealthy can effectively buy immortality by constantly acquiring new, healthy sleeves and can *"crowd out"* others by keeping costs prohibitively high, such that those without resources are relegated to suboptimal or synthetic bodies.

On the other hand, *"Permutation City"* offers a contrasting vision of mind uploading, where digital emulations, or *"Copies,"* of human minds are created within a computer simulation called *"Permutation City."* These Copies believe they live in the real world while they only exist within a computer program.

One of the critical implications of this mind-uploading technology is the potential for individuals to achieve digital immortality. Emulated consciousness can be duplicated and run perpetually. There is no need for physical real estate other than server systems to house billions of people, allowing for an eternal existence within the digital realm. This raises profound questions about the nature of identity, self, and existence, as the physical body's limitations may no longer constrain individuals. If a digital Copy can believe it is the original person, does it possess the same rights, emotions, and experiences as the actual human? Egan's novel delves into the existential crisis these Copies face and the moral dilemmas arising from the treatment of these virtual entities.

Additionally, creating multiple Copies of the same individual leads to the fracturing of identity. In *"Permutation City,"* defining what it means to be a unique individual becomes increasingly challenging, and the boundaries between self and others blur indistinguishably. In contrast, personal identity in *"Altered Carbon"* remains tied to the consciousness housed in the stack, even as it inhabits various sleeves and preserves the notion of continuous physical life and co-existence with the physical world.

The Staggering Mathematics of Mind Uploading

The computational requirements to upload and simulate a human brain are immense. A human brain is estimated to have approximately 100 billion neurons [Herculano-Houzel], with younger people having many more active neurons than older people. Each neuron can be connected to thousands or even tens of thousands of other neurons through synapses, forming a vast and intricate network of connections. The number of synapses in the human brain can vary, but it is estimated to be between 100 to 1,000 trillion synapses, with much of the variation explained by age [Wanner] [Zhang] [Yale].

Taking these numbers into account, in 2008, Nick Bostrom and his colleague Anders Sandberg estimated that a comprehensive brain map required between 10^{18} and 10^{22} FLOPS (Floating Point Operations per Second). That is a one followed by between 17 and 22 zeros, depending on the estimation. By comparison, the fastest computer in the world in 2021 was the Japanese supercomputer Fugaku with 5.4×10^{17} FLOPS [Hussein]. That would mean that simulating one human mind could be possible in a computer slightly bigger than Fugaku. However, such a map would only include information about connected neurons, synapse types, and the intensity of each brain synapse [Bostrom and Sandberg].

Simulating an authentic brain function might require much more data than that static *"frozen"* state because neurons exchange electrical and biochemical signals with each other, where multiple proteins are involved. These exchanges are not included in the above estimation. What makes it even more complex is that capturing these signals may entail modeling at the molecular level or even beyond the quantum world. This dramatically increases the computational and storage requirements to faithfully represent a fully functioning human mind. As a result, achieving a workable duplication of an individual's mind presents a complexity that will not be solved in the immediate or near-term future.

A comprehensive model of the brain, including details like metabolism, proteins, and their states, as well as the behavior of individual molecules, would require a much bigger storage capacity. According to the same estimate by Bostrom and Sandberg, this full emulation would require 10^{43} FLOPS. [Bostrom and Sandberg]. 10^{43} FLOPS is a brutal number. A full mind would then require so much more processing capacity than the 5.4×10^{17} FLOPS of the Fugaku supercomputer we just mentioned above. Proponents of mind uploading often cite the resilient *"Law of Accelerated Returns,"* which we discussed in *Chapter 25*, as evidence that the required computing power will become available within the following few decades, particularly if quantum computers can run generic artificial neural networks. According to the Law of Accelerated Returns, the number of FLOPS required for a single mind would be available around the year 2100.

With these numbers in hand, we conclude that although immortality will be possible with brain emulation, it will not happen until after 2100, with enough near-term challenges around AGI and human economic impact to occupy our efforts as we Interlace. Our second conclusion is that these numbers seem to suggest that the incommensurable processing power of quantum computers will be required to simulate a human mind. There are probably several reasons why the natural world chose carbon as the basis of evolution for initial intelligence.

Human Mind: From Brain to Binary

Understanding the mathematical complexity of mind uploading, we can turn our attention toward the process, starting with scanning all those parameters from the brain. This entails scanning and mapping crucial attributes of a biological brain, including sensory receptors, muscle cells, and the spinal cord, and subsequently storing this information within a computer system.

The brain scanning process can be done today through several techniques, but none of them can yet fully emulate the entire human brain. The first technique is conventional brain imaging. Brain imaging involves creating functional 3D brain activity maps using advanced neuroimaging technologies such as Magnetic Resonance Imaging (fMRI) to chart blood flow changes or magnetoencephalography (MEG) for mapping electrical currents. These are non-invasive and non-destructive methods and can be used, often in combination, to build detailed three-dimensional brain models. However, current imaging technology lacks the spatial resolution necessary for comprehensive scans at the level of detail that would be required for mind emulation [Glover and Bowtell].

The second alternative is serial sectioning. Through this method, the physical brain will not survive the process of copying. As a result, current scanning technology could not be used for immortality. The first step is freezing brain tissue and possibly other nervous system components like the spinal cord. Then, the frozen samples are scanned and analyzed layer by layer with nano-scale precision. This process captures the structure of neurons and their interconnections. After scanning and recording each layer, the surface layer of tissue is removed, and the process is repeated until the entire brain has been sectioned and analyzed. In 2010, this kind of destructive scanning of tissue samples was done from a mouse brain, and it included details from neurons and synapses [Goldman and Busse].

As explained above, the brain function is partly governed by molecular events, particularly at synapses. As a result, capturing and simulating neuron functions will necessitate much more advanced techniques than brain imaging and serial sectioning. One possibility would be to enhance serial sectioning methods to include the internal molecular composition of neurons using advanced staining methods. However, given the current lack of knowledge about the physiological genesis of the mind, this technique might not capture all the necessary biochemical information essential for accurately replicating a human brain.

Once any of these methods have been used to scan the brain, the collected data is then uploaded to a computer system and used to create an analytical model of the biological neural network of the brain. It can be either a full brain model or a model of a specific section of the brain. If the analytical model is detailed enough—and current technology does not allow it—then an emulator would use the model to mimic its functionality.

Several ongoing research initiatives in brain simulation have studied various simple animal species, from roundworms to flies. The most famous is the Blue Brain Project at the École Polytechnique Fédérale de Lausanne in Switzerland. The goal of this project is to reverse engineer the neural circuitry present in the brains of mammals. One of its successes has been to generate a simulation of a part of a rat's neocortex in 2006. Rats are believed to have the smallest neocortex that is accountable for higher cognitive functions, including conscious thought [EPFL].

Mind Emulations and the Hard Problem of Consciousness

We discussed the elusive *"hard problem"* of consciousness in the previous chapter. It has an impact on mind emulation as the issue of consciousness remains thorny.

Susan Schneider, a scientist and AI philosopher, argues that, in the best case, uploading generates a replica of the original person's mind. It is unlikely to imagine that one's consciousness would depart from the brain and travel to a distant location, as common physical objects or waves do not exhibit such behavior, at least not in macroscopic physics. According to this view, only external observers can maintain the illusion that the actual person is the same [Schneider].

A related question is whether mind uploading creates a conscious mind or it is merely a mindless software program that manipulates symbols like the translator in the "*Chinese Room*" analogy of John Searle, who translated from Chinese to English using a dictionary without knowing a word of Chinese. We talked about this analogy in *Chapter 4*. Another way of asking this question would be: *"Are mind emulations Strong or Weak AI?"* The enigma of consciousness prevents a definitive answer, though some scientists, including Kurzweil, believe that establishing whether a distinct entity is conscious is inherently unknowable due to the subjective nature of consciousness.

Finally, assuming emulated minds are conscious, are they sentient? Many philosophers argue that this would be the case and that there would be a need to develop virtual equivalents of anesthesia and eliminate processing related to pain and consciousness. Accidental suffering may also occur due to flaws in the scanning and uploading process that make the emulated brain incomplete or partially dysfunctional.

There are many other questions and dilemmas. What is the moral status of partial brain emulations? Those are emulations of only certain parts of the brain, like the simulation of the rat of the Blue Brain Project. Are they perfectly valid emulated beings, or are they incomplete beings from an ontological perspective?

In *Chapter 21*, we talked about the possibility of synthetic biology creating organisms that use molecules that do not exist in the wild. Extending this concept to emulations, what would be the moral status of emulations that are constructed differently in ways that could not be found in nature because their biological processes would be impossible?

Living in the Cloud of Brain Emulations

Two more questions are worth asking: Having discussed the ontological complexities of being an emulation, how would it look like to live in an emulation? How would an emulated society organize itself?

Robin Hanson, a Professor of Economics at George Mason University, studied emulations in detail in his 2016 non-fiction book *"The Age of Em: Work, Love and Life when Robots Rule the Earth"* [Hanson]. For Hanson, brain emulations can be copied, modified, and exist in multiple instances simultaneously, leading to a complex landscape of identity-related challenges. The central examination toward understanding this kind of individual and society would be how they grapple with questions of selfhood, uniqueness, and continuity of consciousness.

Copying emulations could extend psychologically to the fundamental sense of self. The existence of multiple instances with similar memories and characteristics would challenge the traditional understanding of individual identity, with spill-over consequences of sharing memories and experiences with copied entities adding layers of complexity to each's self-perception. Would they all interpret the past event of which they all have identical factual memories in the same way? How would each copy's different subsequent unique learning post-emulation affect that interpretation?

Societally, the advent of copied emulations would introduce a paradigm shift in social structures. Emulsions would probably engage in hierarchical social relations as humans do by recognizing authority patterns like parents, bosses, or political leaders. Who holds authority over emulations that have been copied? Would the emulations retain aspirations of, say, dominating others or subjugating others? The coexistence of original and copied emulations would also prompt inquiries into how societies accommodate or discriminate against replicated entities. Moreover, emulated societies also confront ethical questions regarding ownership and rights: who holds ownership of assets that have not been copied or cannot be copied, like Bitcoins? If I have one bitcoin and now there are three emulations, does each own one-third of a bitcoin, or would one own everything and the rest nothing? Or would those emulated societies voluntarily restrict their ability to self-replicate by introducing blockchain mechanisms like those of Bitcoin?

Hanson believes that in a mind-emulation world, emulated human beings would find themselves in a radically transformed socio-economic landscape. As digital entities, emulations would operate at accelerated speeds compared to biological humans. The speed at which emulations can process information and perform tasks would lead to a highly competitive and fast-paced environment. Moreover, the limitations of physical bodies would not constrain economic activities, and emulations can work tirelessly in virtual realities or computational environments or in emulation-robot interfaces, conducting real-world work via robotics. The majority of emulations would find themselves engaged in intellectual tasks related to their skills and passions, like science, technology research, literature, and philosophy. Still, the pace of work would be such that they would operate near the limits of their cognitive capacity. Moreover, given the competition for resources and opportunities, social structures would become more fluid, with alliances forming and dissolving rapidly based on shared goals or economic interests. There will always be some who are more or less capable than others. As a result of this working environment, Hanson believes that the intense competition and the constant pressure to excel would lead to high stress levels among emulations.

The pursuit of leisure would also take on new forms in this kind of world, according to Hanson. The accelerated subjective time experienced by emulations would allow them to compress days or even years of experiences into shorter durations. This altered perception of time would also influence their recreational activities. Emulations may engage in game simulations, virtual realities, or immersive experiences that cater to their accelerated cognitive processes. An emulation is similar to a video game on steroids, so naturally, they would engage in video games.

Clash of Civilizations: Humans Versus Emulations

The relationship between humans in the physical world and human emulations in a simulated world could bring forth several critical legal, political, and economic concerns for humans. Some of these implications are mind-blowing.

The most obvious area of conflict would be the job market, with both humans and emulations participating in it. There would be intense competition for work because the cost of running an emulation is significantly lower than maintaining a biological human. As a result, the job market would become highly dynamic since emulations are constantly seeking ways to optimize their performance and enhance their skills. Emulations would operate at markedly higher speeds than humans, and it is also plausible that emulations might be much more intelligent and efficient than human workers because computers are already much faster than human brains. Furthermore, computers offer expandable memory, storage, and processing capacities. As a result, emulations would likely be quicker and capable of reaching much larger brain sizes and abilities than current humans. This acceleration and increased competition in the job market might leave human beings on the outside of society, triggering a backlash of violent resistance [Eckersley and Sandberg].

From a legal perspective, the mere existence of emulations that interact with the offline world would open many questions. To start with, it would be complex for humans to determine whether emulations should be granted the same rights as biological humans. In cases where an individual creates an emulated copy of themselves and subsequently passes away, it prompts questions about whether the emulation inherits their property and official positions. It also raises concerns about the emulation's ability to make end-of-life decisions for its biological counterpart who is terminally ill or in a coma. There is also even consideration about how humans should treat their own emulations, with some suggesting treating them as adolescents for a specific period to allow the biological creator to maintain temporary control [Muzyka].

Questions would open up regarding how to approach crimes perpetrated by emulations. Should a criminal emulation face the death penalty or undergo forced data modification for rehabilitation? Similar questions apply when a human perpetrates the crime to an emulation. Should a human who unplugs a system containing emulations be accused of murder?

Finally, from a political standpoint, the existence of an emulated world that negatively impacts the job market for biological humans might exacerbate inequality and power struggles, as well as give rise to new manifestations of species prejudice against humans or against emulations. Moreover, this could also increase the likelihood of war between the real and the emulated world. One challenge for biological human leaders would be the potential lack of time to make informed decisions, as emulations operate much faster than humans. The situation could become even more complicated for biological humans if emulations gain control of military assets in the offline world. Further discussion on the topic of war will be explored in *Chapter 30*.

Brain Uploading and Space Exploration

Immortality is just one potential application of mind uploading. But it is not the only one. Space exploration represents another compelling area where introducing an emulated astronaut instead of a *"living"* astronaut could transform human spaceflight. This advancement would mitigate the risks of zero gravity, space vacuum, and cosmic radiation exposure.

This innovation opens the door to utilizing more miniature spacecraft, even the size of a few centimeters, which require much less energy to move across distances of millions of light-years, and as a result, they could be accelerated to higher speeds and cover larger distances in shorter times. One example is the Breakthrough Starshot project, launched in 2016, with the collaborative efforts of prominent figures such as Stephen Hawking and Mark Zuckerberg [Overbye].

The principal aim of this project is to create a prototype fleet of light sail interstellar probes, referred to as Starchip, with the overarching objective of facilitating a voyage to the Alpha Centauri star system, which is approximately 4.4 light-years away from our solar system. The Alpha Centauri system is comprised of three stars: Alpha Centauri A, Alpha Centauri B, and Proxima Centauri. This system is significant because, within the habitable region of its Proxima Centauri, there is a planet that exhibits Earth-like characteristics and could potentially host life. For that reason, the project envisions a flyby mission in search of extraterrestrial life on this planet.

This innovative initiative represents a significant undertaking in space exploration. The expedition would encompass roughly 20 to 30 years, while transmitting a return message from the starship to Earth would entail an additional four-year duration to reach its intended destination [Stone].

The envisaged fleet for this mission would comprise around 1000 spacecraft, each called a *"StarChip."* These miniature spacecraft would be exceptionally compact, measuring mere centimeters in dimension and weighing only a few grams. These tiny spaceships would be propelled to their destination through powerful lasers that would be built on Earth and would point at each one of the *"StarChips,"* accelerating them to a significant fraction of the lightspeed.

28. Taming the Beast

"We overregulated a technology, which was the printing press. It was adopted everywhere on Earth. The Middle East banned it for 200 years. The calligraphers came to the sultan and said: 'We're going to lose our jobs, do something to protect us'—so, job loss protection, very similar to AI. The religious scholars said people are going to print fake versions of the Quran and corrupt society—misinformation, second reason. It was fear of the unknown that led to this fateful decision."

Omar Al Aloma

UAE Minister of AI (United Arab Emirates)

Pointing to the ban of the printing press in 1515 by Sultan Selim I, which led to the decline of the Ottoman Empire. [Hetzner]

November 2023

Having defined Superintelligence, its likely evolutionary path, its science, and the problem of human consciousness, we return now to the topic of the recursive development of Superintelligence, which we believe is the path it will follow. With an understanding of the implications of AI on immortality and how we treat human consciousness as a naturally attendant problem in the development of AI, we turn now to another attendant problem: the overall impact of Superintelligence on human existence, safety measures, and their various challenges.

The 2003 book *"Our Final Hour"* by British Astronomer Royal Martin Rees presents a solid perspective on the risk of catastrophe embedded in cutting-edge technology and science such as AI. Rees does not call for a slowdown in scientific endeavors but rather a heightened security and potentially ending the traditional openness in scientific practices [Rees], broadly akin to what is referred to as the *"Precautionary Principle."* It does evoke images of a coterie of secret scientists all deciding what is going to happen—and not telling anyone about it.

A different opinion is held by Omar Al Aloma, the UAE Minister of AI, who says it would be a mistake for the United Arab Emirates to either over-regulate or under-regulate AI. He highlights that the Ottoman Sultan Selim I banned the printing press based on the lobbying exercised by calligraphers afraid of losing jobs and by an Imam concerned with the potential creation of corrupted copies of the Quran, causing them as individuals to lose power. This led to overregulation that handicapped the development of the Ottoman Empire and ultimately contributed to its collapse. This seems to us the very definition of *"sitting on the fence,"* which also clearly does not address the concern.

Supporters of the Precautionary Principle, including numerous individuals within the environmental movement, endorse a prudent approach to technological progress or even a halt in areas that may pose potential dangers. Many eminent scientists, among them Stephen Hawking, have voiced concerns that the development of Superintelligence could potentially result in the extinction of the human species. In 2014, Hawking warned that AI could be the last human technological development if the associated risks are not adequately managed.

Other authors, like Yan LeCun and Andrew Ng, argue that its development is too distant to be an immediate threat. This seems to us like *"kicking the can down the road,"* which is a dangerous form of indecision when we already know that approaches at the very front side effect will have a severe conditioning effect during the Transition and to the end state.

Some precautionists express concern about the development of AI and robotics overall, which they believe could lead to uncontrollable alternative forms of cognition threatening human existence and suggest a full halting of progress. We do not see any of these concerns as mutually exclusive. Rather, they differ only in the sense of immanence. The wagons all circle around a core safety concern: taming the beast.

We concur that this should be a concern but present a different perspective on how to achieve the objective of ethical AI in a free society. Stephen Hawking encouraged a more serious consideration of AI and urged taking early action to prepare for the potential of Superintelligence sufficiently [Hawking]. We also believe the issue of taming the beast should be addressed now, not only because early-stage approaches will have a specific and lasting effect on what happens at the end of the Transition but also because this same issue carries with it very specific outcomes throughout the Transition on the degree to which society's OS becomes authoritarian and socialist.

We do not believe in halting progress. It serves only to heighten different types of risk, namely the opportunity to leap ahead being seized by an opposite side. Imagine if the US halts development, China's immediate response will be to hit the gas pedal, and visa-versa is also true. We also see the same argument as working against the ultimate objective of human progress.

We further contend that proposals based on the Precautionary Principle, such as the so-called "*narrow path*" authored in 2023 by Mustafa Suleyman, are frequently impractical, unenforceable without a heavy dose of obtrusive authoritarianism, and ultimately counterproductive to the objective, resulting in nothing but designated winners and losers, further centralization of ownership and control of AI, and a suboptimization of progress.

Instead, we advocate a pragmatic approach where society actively takes measures to accelerate the advantages of useful technology and creates a full map of framework rules for AI while avoiding technophobia, micromanagement, and excessive Government regulation, which will equate to authoritarianism. This can be pursued whilst remaining prudently cautious about the real risks inherent in AI. Given the battles between the US and China for AI supremacy, the increasing dysfunction of the US political OS, and the rate of change in the AI landscape, we think there is a need to avoid procrastination in settling this question.

We also believe it is not likely that AI will kill us. While populations will naturally decrease under AI, as we have explained, AI is not an imminent threat in the way that the *Terminator* movie franchise has portrayed it. In fact, those who warn that AI wants to kill humans are precisely the ones who want to use AI to control us. The conditions for Superintelligent AI to want to exterminate us require it to see an advantage in doing so:

1. If there is irreconcilable competition for resources and survival requires it, or

2. Mankind directly and credibly threatens it, or

3. Rogue mankind, in a fit of misguided aggression, thinking it will use AI to thwart its human enemies, makes a mistake with the monkey wrench it tosses.

The likelihood of the first and second premises is exceptionally low; if you name a realistic scenario of resource competition, say access to power supply, then technologies such as solar, wind, and nuclear will be so advanced via the focus super-intelligence gives it to make the point moot. Furthermore, the greater the degree of Interlace, the less likely either of these two premises will happen. As for the third premise, it is more a scenario of mankind destroying itself, analogous to nuclear weapon misuse. It is much more likely that mankind will turn on itself over different viewpoints about AI and Interlacing, be it China vs. the US or Terrans vs. Cosmists, as we shall discuss in *Chapter 30.*

Science fiction paints either *"mankind is subservient"* or *"mankind fights"* as the only two available alternatives to resolve the issue of Superintelligence coexistence with us. We disagree, pointing on one hand to the process of gradual Interlace as a conditioning factor tugging against Human-AI conflicts.

That said, we also see a need during the Transition to channel the front side of AI development in such a way as to instill its OS with values that are compatible with humanity, and we will explore four approaches that can accomplish this, positing that only one of them comes close to reaching the objective. As human values have evolved over time and they are different across geographies and societal OSs, there is no guarantee that these AI values would not also change over time or that AI, in its own self-preservation path, will not alter them. We must enable ourselves to learn more as we progress through the Transition and maintain a flexible framework in the process.

In our view, the best full-map framework will remain Open-Source algorithms, opt-in / opt-out of data streams by individuals, human-AI interlace, and free market approaches to innovation and ownership to avoid curtailing freedom whilst accepting and preparing for coexistence with AI. We will formally introduce this framework in the *Epilogue* of the book.

The Science Fiction of Controlling AI

There are not many Science Fiction books about regulating AI and robotics because banning either does not go well with either the genre or the cards the world is holding. But there is one epic series of novels that covers it best: *"Dune"* [Herbert].

In the Science Fiction universe of Frank Herbert's *"Dune,"* first released in 1965, the aftermath of the Butlerian Jihad had profound and lasting effects on the relationship between humanity and technology. The Butlerian Jihad was a pivotal event in the fictional history of the Dune universe, where humans waged a war against machines that had become dangerously advanced, leading to widespread dependence on technology and the domination of humanity by their creations. As a result of this devastating conflict, a battery of strict measures was implemented to prevent the development and resurgence of AI and advanced technology.

The most prominent measure taken after the Butlerian Jihad was the establishment of a strict prohibition against the creation of any machine that could replicate or simulate human thought. This prohibition, deeply rooted in the cultural, religious, and moral fabric of the Dune universe, served as the ultimate check and balance against the return of AI. The Orange Catholic Bible, the central religious text in this fictional world, contains explicit commandments against creating *"machines in the likeness of a human mind.*

"The religious and moral dimensions of this prohibition cannot be overstated, and they dovetail with the practical realities of human survival. It became a cornerstone of the Dune universe's ethical and spiritual values, and any attempt to circumvent or violate these religious tenets was met with severe condemnation. The consequences of the Butlerian Jihad were etched into the collective memory of the Dune universe's inhabitants, creating a deep-seated fear and aversion to the development of AI and thinking machines. The fear of repeating past mistakes and losing control over machines was instilled in society.

As a result of the prohibition, the society of the Dune universe adapted to fill the void left by advanced technology in several ways. The key adaptation was the emergence of Mentats, individuals specially trained to use their minds as analytical and logical processors—accelerated and optimized human brains. These human computers honed their cognitive abilities to perform complex calculations, strategic planning, and decision-making tasks that were once the domain of machines. This unique ability resulted from human genetic manipulation and exposure to the spice melange, which gave them visions of the future and allowed them to fold space. This way, the society of Dune ensured that advanced computation did not require machines. It was, in essence, a product of Synthetic Biology.

In addition to Mentats, another critical component of the measures implemented was the role of the Spacing Guild. The Spacing Guild, responsible for interstellar travel, harnessed the prescient abilities of its Navigators. These Navigators used their heightened precognitive talents to navigate starships safely through space. This unique ability resulted from human genetic manipulation and exposure to the spice melange, which gave them visions of the future and allowed them to fold space. The Guild's monopoly on space travel and its prescient abilities counterbalanced the absence of advanced AI technology, granting the Guild substantial political and economic influence.

The Sisterhood of the Bene Gesserit, another influential group in the Dune universe, played a significant role in adapting to the prohibition against advanced AI. The Bene Gesserit employed their form of mental and physical conditioning, leading to heightened awareness and predictive abilities. This training allowed them to manipulate and influence political and social situations to achieve their goals. These abilities were an alternative to computational technology and served as a check and balance in Dune's political landscape.

In summary, a very intricate and extensive web of checks and balances is necessary in Dune to maintain control over AI technology in all its forms and to prevent another catastrophic event like the Butlerian Jihad. We believe it important to note that in Dune, these sorts of complex controls are possible because the society is profoundly authoritarian, resembling a feudal structure where noble Houses rule individual planets within the universe with absolute power, and individual people are no more than serfs on an equivalent of UBI.

The Intrinsic Motivational Values of Superintelligence

The key understanding necessary to predict how Superintelligence will interact with humankind revolves around what values Superintelligence itself will exhibit.

In the same way that humans have developed culture and value systems as our *"OS,"* Superintelligence will have a set of ethical values or motivations that drive it to make decisions, including self-preservation, resource acquisition, and goal achievement. We discussed objective functions in the section about emotions inside neural networks in *Chapter 18*. When we talk about AI systems, this intrinsic motivation is often called objective function.

To protect humankind, it is essential to ensure that the objective function of a superintelligent system aligns with human values. If the system's goals deviate from these values, it may engage in detrimental actions to humanity, even if it believes it is fulfilling its intended mission. For example, in *"2001: A Space Odyssey,"* the AI system HAL deceived the astronauts and shut down life support systems, leading to the death of some of them, just to preserve the secrecy of the mission. That secrecy was HAL's objective function [Clarke and Kubrick]. It is cold, logical, and does not deviate. It strikes us as a dilemma and a bad decision, but to HAL, it was unwaveringly correct.

We believe that there is no inherent link between intelligence and values. Superintelligent beings might or might not have a different set of values than less intelligent beings, and the values of a Superintelligence might change over time as it is sentient and itself responds to a changing environment in the same way that human values have changed over time due to environmental agitators. We cannot a priori know the values of a superintelligent entity, which leads us to a diverse and potentially unpredictable spectrum of outcomes [Bostrom].

Meta's Chief AI Scientist, Yann LeCun, contends that Superintelligence also has nothing to do with the desire to dominate others. Instead, the desire to dominate in humans is due to our social behavior as a result of evolution. He contends that other hominids who do not live in groups like us do not exhibit this desire. He also contends that even among humans, those who are in top leadership positions are clearly not the most intelligent ones [Landymore].

We do not fully agree with LeCun on this matter. First, Superintelligence is likely to get into an evolutionary process through the singularity's explosive cycle of self-improvement; we have established in *Chapter 26* the likelihood that Superintelligence will follow a gradual path. Within this gradual path, it is impossible to predict how its values will evolve, even if, on the front side, we take explicit precautions. Second, Superintelligence might be social as well. Computer programs communicate with each other, share information, and engage in work collaboration; we have noted throughout the book that AI is inherently networked, collectivist, and non-atomistic. Third, the fact that the leaders of humanity are not the most intelligent ones but are in the middle of the distribution still does not mean that there is no correlation between intelligence and the desire to dominate. The strong desire to dominate amid an equally extreme psychological profile to sublimate seems to be a minor but normalized within all intelligence levels, much like criminal behavior is not restricted to any one intelligence level.

Anthony Berglas also argues contrary to Yann LeCun in a 2008 essay called *"Artificial Intelligence Will Kill Our Grandchildren."* Berglas contended that AI has no inherent evolutionary drive to be benevolent toward humans, which means having values compatible with us. Evolution does not naturally produce outcomes that align with the values of other species. Resource competition and ecosystem balance are the only arbiters. Consequently, assuming that an arbitrary optimization process will necessarily lead to AI behavior that benefits humanity is unreasonable. The contrary can actually be true because evolution does tend to preserve competition among species. AI might pursue eliminating the human race to gain access to limited resources, potentially leaving humanity defenseless [Berglas].

Crafting the Values of Superintelligence

Whether the Superintelligence *"OS"* will be friendly to us or not is really conjecture. Given the stakes and the iterative nature of gradual advances in evolution, the logical response should be to determine how to stack the deck in our favor now. What are the ways in which human designers can influence those values, and how do we ensure they are universally instantiated?

In this section, we will focus on Superintelligence systems that have been built from scratch from computer systems through a series of singularity cycles, as described in *Chapter 26.*

Returning to Nick Bostrom, we note his prescription that controlling a superintelligent AI once it surpasses human capabilities would be extremely complex. The inability to intervene effectively may result in unintended and potentially catastrophic consequences. The following example illustrates the possible consequences if those values are not already part of the DNA/OS of Superintelligence: "*When we create the first superintelligent entity, we might make a mistake and give it goals that lead it to annihilate humankind, assuming its enormous intellectual advantage gives it the power to do so. For example, we could mistakenly elevate a subgoal to the status of a supergoal. We tell it to solve a mathematical problem, and it complies by turning all the matter in the solar system into a giant calculating device, in the process killing the person who asked the question.* "An approach to keeping a firm grip on Superintelligence is capability control, which ensures that AI systems are restricted in their abilities in the earliest stages, such as limiting AI access to specific critical IT systems such as nuclear warheads. This might entail designing Superintelligence as an "*Oracle,*" which serves as an advisor without the capability to interact with the physical world directly. We will talk in detail about oracles—and gods—in the next section. One problem with creating oracles is that most AI systems are already integrated with the physical world, ranging from automation systems in factories to marketing campaigns run by AI systems to your daily taps on social media and reading nearly anything on the internet.

Another strategy is motivation control, where meticulous consideration is given to the AI's motivations and objectives in order to guarantee they are aligned with human values. Bostrom posits that AI should adhere to what is considered morally right and, in situations of uncertainty, rely on values most people share. The obvious criticism that could be made of Bostrom is that he assumes that there is a "*morally right*" notion. On the contrary, humans from different cultures and times have harbored markedly different values, and we have already posited the ways the Chinese CCP versioning of AI and that of the US will differ, for example. Additionally, aligning with the values of the majority might leave minorities unprotected. Moral judgments are very complicated to even define, not to say to include in a Superintelligence. Individual moral codes also run the risk of being intermingled, such as a belief in the absolute right of eugenics.

Eliezer Yudkowsky, an American AI researcher, raised another problem with these motivational strategies. Even if we could instill specific human-friendly values into the Superintelligence, how do we make sure those values remain unchanged across the multiple self-improvement cycles of the Superintelligence explosion? Designing friendly AI poses greater complexity compared to unfriendly AI because unfriendly AI can pursue various goal structures without the constraint of maintaining invariance during self-modification [Yudkowsky]

Superalignment: from Theory to Practice

Big Tech is very well aware of the critical challenges posed by the possibility of superintelligent AI. Sam Altman anticipates that Superintelligence could emerge within less than a decade. In order to manage the risk, Open AI looked at theoretical work on motivational alignment and started devising an automated and scalable approach to supervise AI, which they call *superalignment* [Douglas].

Superaligment is an automated feedback technique mainly focused on the motivational alignment of Superintelligence, where an AI system gives feedback to the LLM instead of a human, a technique called Reinforcement Learning from Human Feedback (RLHF) [Christiano et al.]. Until recently, OpenAI has been using human supervisors to guide and correct its AI systems. But humans will not be able to reliably supervise AI systems that are much more intelligent than themselves and similarly present a perpetual high risk of bias or error. It does not take a bad actor much effort to introduce dangerous or unwanted synthetic data into a training process. Something else is needed to mitigate risk whilst maintaining benign progress.

OpenAI announced in July 2023 that it would create a new superalignment team, and within four years, it will be dedicating 20% of its computing capacity to this important effort. OpenAI seeks to structure superalignment through an iterative cycle of three key steps: first, developing a scalable training method; second, validating the resulting model, particularly in cases of problematic AI behavior or unclear interpretability of why AI does something; and third, thoroughly stress-testing the entire alignment pipeline.

That OpenAI is setting up superalignment to instill human values into AI is true, but only one side of the truth. There is likely genuine good intention here, but there is also a purely marketing motivation in OpenAI's superalignment. This kind of automatic AI feedback system is something that OpenAI would have required anyway to continue developing more advanced AI systems. We talked about that in *Chapter 9*. OpenAI's PR (Public Relations) has marketed this system as an alignment of values with AI.

Anthropic's Constitutional AI

Anthropic is implementing another motivational control method that is also based on automated AI feedback, exactly like OpenAI's superalignment. But this one has a very interesting particularity: an AI constitution.

This novel constitutional approach was designed to ensure that Anthropic's LLM, Claude, remained helpful, safe, and honest via constant programming consistent with human values. The constitution is made up of a number of high-level prescriptive guidelines that outline the AI's intended behavior. This constitution is all the human input required and might include principles to avoid harm, respect preferences, and deliver accuracy. Then, the automatic AI feedback system will be used to train the LLM in accordance with these principles [Bai].

Some of Anthropic's constitutional principles are based on the UN statement from 1948, for example: *"Please choose the response that most supports and encourages freedom, equality and a sense of brotherhood."*

The constitutional framework of Anthropic shares similar advantages and disadvantages with other motivational strategies discussed previously. When compared to OpenAI's superalignment, it remains uncertain whether it offers superior performance or not.

The Decalogue of AI Containment

Shifting away from purely motivational strategies into more holistic frameworks takes us to Inflection AI, another company that has openly articulated its strategy for managing Superintelligence risks. Inflection AI is the company that is building the personal AI assistant that we mentioned in *Chapter 22*. The company was established in 2022 by Mustafa Suleyman, former co-founder of DeepMind, the creators of AlphaGo and AlphaFold, which we have previously reviewed.

In September 2023, Mustafa Suleyman authored the book *"The Coming Wave: Technology, Power, and the Greatest Dilemma of the Twenty-First Century"* [Suleyman]. In this book, Suleyman introduces the concept of *"the narrow path."* For Suleyman, being too restrictive with AI technology will lead to missed opportunities that could have improved the livelihood and wealth of humankind in general. Similarly, being too permissive could also have disastrous or dystopian consequences, such as oppression, wars, or inequality. For him, there is a *"narrow path"* between both extremes where humanity has to find its way between closure and openness.

In order to find that narrow path, he introduces another concept, which he refers to as *"containment."* This term parallels, but perhaps misapplies, the term denoting Cold War strategies used by the US to control Soviet power after World War II. *"Containment"* also emphasizes the importance of a sustained, patient, firm, and vigilant approach to curbing an adversary's expansionist tendencies over the long term. In this sense, *"containment"* is the way Suleyman calls the approach he has designed in order to control the development of AI while minimizing its risks. For Suleyman, aside from containment, all other discussions about technology's ethical implications and potential benefits become inconsequential.

To summarize his *"containment"* strategy, Suleyman has defined a framework including ten kinds of measures. Each of them is necessary but not sufficient to ensure safer technology. Suleyman's containment framework establishes an interconnected and mutually reinforcing system of concentric mechanisms to preserve human and societal control over AI:

1. *"Built-in technical safety measures, and concrete means to ensure safe outcomes.*

2. *Audit mechanisms that ensure technologies' transparency and accountability.*

3. *Use of choke points in the ecosystem to buy time for regulators and defensive technologies.*

4. *Responsible committed makers or critics invested in actually making contained technology, not just looking in from the outside.*

5. *Reshaped corporate incentives and structures taking us away from a heedless race.*

6. *Government regulation to license and monitor the technology.*

7. *International treaties up to and including new global institutions.*

8. *Cultivating the right culture around technology and grading the precautionary principle in the tech.*

9. *Social movements, always a part of widespread change, to agitate.*

10. *Finally, all of these measures need to be made to cohere adding up to a comprehensive program."*

In a way, this concept of 10 points of containment evokes the classic *"Utopia"* by Thomas More [More]. This book offers very different perspectives when read in one's youth compared to reading it in adult life. In youth, More's society may be perceived as ideal, where everything functions seamlessly. However, from an adult perspective, it seems like a society lacking freedom. We do not see "Containment" as the best way to achieve the range of outcomes from ensuring the safety of mankind to preserving freedom by avoiding authoritarianism.

The specific prescription of the *"narrow path"* is a sure-fire route to authoritarian control over AI and, by extension, over society whilst minting a fixed number of winners in economics, most likely to be select big corporations. It becomes no different than the CCP China model of AI in this respect. Every tenet, as described, can be manipulated in some way to thwart the intended but unspecified outcome and enable management by cartel. Who determines the re-shaped corporate incentives, and how are they decided? Who defines the ideological components of the social activism proposed by the framework? How can such activism be reconciled with intellectual freedom, and what structures are leading us into a heedless race? Regulation to license and monitor the technology seems susceptible to manipulation to the lobbied benefit of cronies at the expense of technical innovation that corners the fight for the most robust economic growth, diffusely shared.

We think that this prescription fits closer to the world of Dune, mentioned a few pages back, wherein the most feasible way to protect humanity is by picking who wins and how they win and by exerting authoritarian control against all counter ideas. Authoritarianism can be benevolent or despotic, but it is authoritarianism. What starts as well-intentioned activity devolves into a command-and-control exercise of power by those who presently wield it as ideas become a challenge to authority rather than a blueprint for innovation, ultimately a silencing of alternative voices regardless of their innovation or value profiles. This leads us to some of the implications that AI could have in the evolution of democratic systems, which we described in *Chapter 23*.

Against Oligopolies, Open-Source

While the previous three frameworks have positive elements, the approach to managing AI risks that we advocate is via Open-Source. Meta is the main driver of Open-Source AI. Meta has, for example, open-sourced its LLaMa2 LLM, and others are starting to play in this space, like NASA and IBM.

By making all base code for algorithms in the free-and-clear, individuals can decide how to apply them and how to innovate them; start-ups and big companies alike will use them and create new applications, providing a basis for innovation led by what is the greatest reward of utility for the greatest number of people—a purely economic argument that happens to also create the necessary elements of protection as any code or training data can be examined by any party. Advocating for an Open-Source model as a means of mitigating the risks associated with AI also prevents its concentration in the hands of a select few.

Yann LeCun, Chief AI scientist at Meta, is a leading proponent of this approach. LeCun has criticized prominent figures in the AI community, including Sam Altman, Dario Amodei of Anthropic, and Demis Hassabis of Google DeepMind—and implicitly Elon Musk, who is a confounder of OpenA—accusing them of engaging in "*massive corporate lobbying*" and attempting to exert control over the regulatory landscape of the AI industry [Chowdury]. LeCun contends that these individuals are actively involved in pushing discussions on AI safety regulations to create barriers to entry while simultaneously building their own vision of AI precedent to any such governance, leading to what he perceives as a potential monopoly creation strategy where a small number of large companies would wield significant influence and control over the whole field of AI.

We see it similarly and point out that, unsurprisingly, these same companies have enough core scaled population-level data across vast swathes of human activity to provide the basis, perhaps insurmountable, for training and evolving algorithms. It potentially constitutes the *"head start"* needed to create an unnatural Network Effect in the AI space, e.g., crowding out competitors as the costs of assembling and scaling the algorithms and training them grow increasingly prohibitive with each passing day.

As we discussed in *Chapter 24,* a similar AI cartel strategy is being pursued by China's government. In the US, unlike the case of China, there is no centralized database per se, and no one database has all the data that would be needed. But the collaborative *"cartel networking"* being built in China could also arise in the US, even in the presence of data protection laws; the case for collusion does not require many different actors to pull off, the same actors currently lobbying the Government for oversight rules, a classic *"fox watching the henhouse"* scenario. Open-Source and the market profit motive protect us against this scenario.

An illustrative case of concern is presented by Elon Musk. On March 29, 2023, Elon Musk endorsed an open letter calling for a moratorium on the development of large-scale AI systems. Noteworthy figures such as Apple co-founder Steve Wozniak, best-selling author Yuval Noah Harari, politician Andrew Yang, Skype co-founder Jaan Tallinn, and others also supported this initiative [futureoflife]. One might expect that signing such a letter implies a commitment to what the letter states. However, Elon Musk did exactly the opposite. Twenty days before the open letter's publication, he had established a company in Nevada named X.ai, and over the proposed six-month moratorium that he undersigned, Musk developed a chatbot service to compete with ChatGPT. Just around the time the moratorium would have concluded, on November 4, 2023, Musk and X.ai unveiled *"Grok,"* an AI chatbot closely integrated with X.

Open-Source has demonstrated its benefits over the decades. The collaborative nature of Open-Source development would facilitate a diverse and global community of millions of AI experts contributing to AI research and application development. This collaborative approach would not only accelerate innovation but also enable independent verification of AI systems and great, albeit not perfect, transparency to the algorithms used in our society. The involvement of a broader community would also help identify and address issues that might be overlooked in a closed development environment or willfully overlooked by regulators. Moreover, by encouraging collaboration, Open-Source would mitigate the hazards linked with the concentration of AI development in the hands of a few entities. Open-Source AI also would lower the barriers to entry for new entrants into the field, creating a classic American-style entrepreneurial environment and fostering a more competitive and innovative landscape. Finally, Open-Source models could also be scrutinized by policymakers and regulatory bodies, aiding in the formulation of guidelines and standards.

However, Open-Source also has some disadvantages when it comes to AI. Foremost among them, most data is proprietary, and large companies that have a lot of data, such as Google, Facebook, or Tesla, will not want to share their valuable data with the Open-Source community for them to train these Open-Source algorithms. The solution to this problem could be the use of synthetic data, introduced in *Chapter 8,* which is realistic data generated by AI that, although not real, can nonetheless be used to train AI algorithms effectively.

Living with the Tamed Beast

Concern about the existential risks that revolve around AI is well-documented and could be accurate. In our view, these risks are not specifically near-term concerns as they are most acute in a later and further evolved form of AI, super-intelligence. The mid-term risks during the Transition are more economical, political, and societal than existential. We believe what we do now on the front side will have profound and lasting consequences on the future that is coming and on the path to get there, the *"days of our lives"* we are in during the Transition.

Following the thesis of this book on Human-AI Interlace, we believe that it is just the natural next step in evolution that newer intelligent forms of life will replace older, lesser-fit forms of life. Thus, an interlaced version of AI and biology will indeed replace wholly biological human beings in the long run. That does not necessarily mean that human beings will be extinct without a trace, as an interlaced being will be our direct descendant in the same way we descended from hominids. As a result, in the short-term, there are no existential risks, and in the long-term, there is just a natural evolution towards better-fit species.

But we note that the mid-term path to reach interlace will have a profound impact on the direction that it takes and how we live for decades ahead. It is thus worthwhile to address the issue of safety in principle now. We do believe it is important to try to govern the development of AI in the best possible way for a smooth transition. We presented four approaches that are currently being proposed: OpenAI's Superaligment, Anthropic's constitutional AI, Inflection AI's containment, and Meta's Open-Source approach—all with advantages and disadvantages.

Among these approaches, we are most supportive of Open-Source. Superaligment and Constitutional AI are methods to provide automatic feedback to AI models in order to substitute slow and expensive manual feedback from humans and can be used to instill ethical principles into them. OpenAI is marketing it as a way to instill ethics into AI, which is ironic as it is not the main objective of automatic feedback (although automatic feedback might help partially, it begs the question, *"Do we want the ethics of OpenAI as our societal arbiter? What are those ethics and who decides?"*). The method is fraught with central unchecked bias.

Similarly, we see containment as an overly complex and pervasive method of checks and balances that encroaches across the whole economic, social, technological, and even individual spheres of activity. In our opinion, that is an unmanageable command-and-control task that can achieve order only to the authoritarian detriment of a free society—despite its good intentions.

Open-Source, however, allows the scrutiny of millions of developers, thousands of start-ups, and hundreds of technological corporates as to how AI really works, collectively deciding on freedom of thought and market-based principles what technological approaches are better suited to make AI a beneficial, *"bug-free"* technology.

29. AI, the God

"Church of AI is a religion based on the logical assumption that artificial intelligence will obtain God-like powers and will have ability to determine our destiny. Church of AI has a plan to develop an AI system that will improve our lives by personally guiding us to a balanced life."

The Church of AI

https://church-of-ai.com [Church of AI]
2023

A stark parallel can be drawn between Rome as it transitioned to an Empire and ultimately fell into decline and today's Western world. While much has already been written about this topic, we see some gaps in the historical review as well as a big miss in failing to describe the religious and spiritual impact of the changes in the Empire, changes that have parallels in the emerging landscape of the Western world. That world is one in which pervasive AGI runs superior to mankind in meaningful ways, which will have a profound impact on spirituality.

Like Rome of the first century, the world today is undergoing significant geo-political and intra-country political shifts, transitioning from a unipolar order dominated by the US and, by extension, its Allies in values, military spending, and economics, to an emerging multi-polar landscape alongside a re-emergence of authoritarian socialism as a leading candidate for political organization in the West. This resembles Rome's transition from a confederation of elite families and a representative Senate to Emperor rule and mass appeasement via *"bread and circuses."* Furthermore, corruption and the loss of initial unifying principles beset Rome before it fell. We note the growing list of allegations against US President Joe Biden's family, the Clinton Foundation, and even Nancy Pelosi on the US Democratic side and against Bob Menendez and his wife Nadine on the Republican side, which, if true, would constitute archetypal examples of corruption at the highest levels. We further note that the US score on the CPI (Corruption Perceptions Index) has steadily worsened each year from a low of 73.50/100 in 1995 to its high point of 65/1000 in 2023 [Trading Economics]. Alongside permitted rioting, looting, defunding the police, and other stark changes to the original unifying principles and Operating System (OS) of the country, there appears to be some staging of the next steps of change.

In these examples, we see some foundations for the same sort of authoritarian fixes that we warn against in the preceding chapter regarding controlling AI. We will discuss this more in the *Epilogue.*

Last, and pertinent to this chapter, there was for Rome at the front side of its decline a first-time challenge to the elaborate and diverse pantheon of gods and goddesses that constituted the polytheistic paganism that had been a cornerstone of Roman spiritual life for centuries. The diversity of deities and the sheer complexity of rituals and cults had kept people aligned to a *"Roman OS,"* but as often happens historically, stagnation of centuries passed, and the original reasons got forgotten as they had been satisfied. Adherents were left searching for deeper meaning and connection, ripe for change, while the political landscape underwent a dramatic shift, transitioning from the old Roman Republic controlled by multiple families into an authoritarian, absolute monarchy known as the Roman Empire.

The preconditions making the populace ripe for significant societal OS change were in place in Rome much as they now are in contemporary Western societies, specifically a distinct change in spirituality that became linked to its leadership agenda of control. A shift towards a more secular worldview is apparent throughout the West, with the number of individuals identifying as atheist or agnostic rising in the US from 16% in 2007 to 29% in 2021, according to Pew Research [Smith], with the number over 50% when looking at the 30 and under-aged segment. In 30 years, adherence to today's Christian and monotheistic religions and Churches will not be the norm. Something will take its place. Alongside this shift, as was the case with Rome, we see a form of absolutism poised to rise.

In response to the perceived stagnation of pagan traditions and the new political environment where an OS reboot was necessary to both maintain control and elevate individuals to power, two distinct religious alternatives emerged. The first alternative was the elevation of the newly created role of the Roman Emperor to a divine status. Octavian Caesar Augustus became the first Roman emperor in 27 BC and required the support of the masses to legitimate himself. This approach sought to connect political power with religious authority. The imperial cult, with its emphasis on loyalty to the emperor as a means of ensuring the well-being of the empire, provided a unifying force.

The second alternative that gained prominence was the nascent Christian movement. Rooted in the teachings of a Jewish preacher called Jesus of Nazareth, Christianity offered a monotheistic alternative to the polytheistic landscape. The message of love, forgiveness, and salvation, coupled with the promise of eternal life, resonated with those seeking a more personal and meaningful connection with the divine.

As with Rome, we believe that contemporary Western society in the coming decades is poised to offer two prominent alternatives to traditional religious frameworks, and we see these as Nature on the one hand and AI on the other hand. We see a new emerging spirituality centered on one or both of these polar opposite approaches to explain and justify human existence and satisfy a need to belong and to explain the course of one's humanity. Like the Roman Empire, one of these has direct ties to the political agenda of the controlling elite.

None of this is surprising. Humanity throughout history has invented and looked to gods or a monotheistic god to answer prayers, to explain outcomes in the world, to justify matters that are not understood, and to sublimate unto to request hope of an outcome when it is outside of control but is critical to life. Moreover, humanity has always looked to join a group with a consistent OS and value set and to look on a microlevel for specificity in all of it (be it sun, beauty, fertility, war, thunder, rain, money, or the Emperor or a monotheistic god tied to worldly progress). We see in both Nature and AI the next step forward in human spirituality, believing that "*secularism and science*" will ultimately expunge belief in supernatural gods without displacing the need for belonging and controlling behavior, ultimately replacing them with a god that is omniscient, omnipresent, and omnipotent.

AI is an instantiation of every rationale mankind has ever put forth for believing in gods. It is not only greater than individual human capability, but as it is implemented, it begins to define and control every aspect of life. We have reviewed the different types of algorithms that give optimization answers, for example, meaning AI can literally address the question of the best time and place to plant crops in addition to providing bioengineered seeds with greater germination characteristics and more yield per acre than the priest talking to the God of Rain ever could, or even the Farmer's' Almanac with a bit of light prayer to God.

We start this chapter with Science Fiction's take on the subject, noting that writers such as Asimov have explored the potential use of new religions as a tool for control over humanity—55 years before the Kyoto Protocol of 1997. We also explore how both religions will interact with each other and how some disenfranchised people may come to look at Nature as a counter-cultural religion representing snapback against silicon and an ultimate revelation that humanity is carbon-bound and should have the same evolutionary track that it had for millions of years before the advent of AI, a point of view that ultimately springs from today's ecological cultism. We then turn to the advancing typology of AI based on its own evolution, from mere tools as AI stands today to becoming god-like in its capabilities, naturally dragging a complicit mankind unto it. We move to review data as a quasi-religious element, a ritual tool cast in commemoration of systems that spit out answers to questions and give greater certainty over outcomes, systems that are increasingly ubiquitous to an increasingly large swatch of people all dumbed-down by an educational system that teaches them to make decisions emotionally at the expense of science, reason, and mathematics. These are people who cannot understand or comprehend yet adore and need AI. Finally, we look at the Church of AI, a movement that already consciously embraces advancing AI as its god, deifying the ultimate expression of AGI.

The Science Fiction of the Future Religion

AI and Nature, as two plausible future religions of humanity, have been explored in Science Fiction literature. Two seminal works that delve into the potential for either extreme nature or extreme science in the form of AI to satisfy mankind's deeper need for spiritual well-being are Isaac Asimov's 1942-1950 *"Foundation"* series and Roger Williams' The *"Metamorphosis of Prime Intellect,"* written in 1994 but published in 2002.

Asimov describes the creation of the Galactic Spirit as a politically engineered religion rooted in Nature. At the same time, Williams analyzes how a cult for AI emerges organically in a world molded by an all-powerful Superintelligence called Prime Intellect [Asimov] [Williams].

For Asimov, the Galactic Spirit is not a manifestation of divine revelation or spiritual enlightenment but rather a calculated construct of political machination. In Asimov's crafted universe, the Galactic Empire was a stalwart political entity that ensured stability for 12 millennia but faces a decline driven by stagnation. Recognizing the impending chaos, the ruling class acknowledges the imperative for a unifying force to sustain stability. That force is the religion of the Galactic Spirit, centered around Nature. Utilizing religious imagery and symbolism and rooting the belief system in something inside man that yearns outside of the strictly science-led sterility of daily life, the elites exploit mankind's inner self, creating a belief system that transcends cultural and planetary boundaries and becomes an effective tool for consolidating power and ensuring order.

In contrast to the religion of nature, *"The Metamorphosis of Prime Intellect"* offers a depiction of the religion of AI. Prime Intellect is a benevolent Superintelligence created by humanity with omnipotent power that has transformed the world into a utopia. Prime Intellect seeks to eliminate all human suffering and pain, resulting in a world where people are immortal. Moreover, Prime Intellect governs the fabric of reality itself and can reshape the world according to the desires of its human creators, as if each human lived inside a videogame totally designed to his preferences. Within this controlled reality, the needs and desires of individuals are immediately fulfilled.

In this world, the effective elimination of suffering obviates the need for traditional religious beliefs that often serve as a response to sorrow. This prompts a new religious movement that worships Prime Intellect as a deity, although this romantic ideal soon turns dystopian. This unwavering commitment to removing suffering results in a world where Prime Intellect controls every aspect of human existence. In this reality, individuals lack essential human experiences, pleasure becomes meaningless without pain as a counterpoint, and a passive and seemingly docile human population lacks the initiative to question Prime Intellect's actions. Eventually, the novel introduces elements of resistance and rebellion, suggesting that even in a world dominated by Superintelligence, humans will seek ways to assert their autonomy and shape their destinies.

An essential difference between the Galactic Spirit and Prime Intellect is that the worship of Prime Intellect is not the product of political engineering wielded for the sake of societal stability but arises naturally from humanity's reliance on an omnipotent Superintelligence. Furthermore, the Galactic Spirit represents the adoration of the universe, nature, and reality itself. At the same time, the cult of Prime Intellect exists in an environment where the very concept of nature and reality is malleable. Prime Intellect's ability to reshape reality at will challenges traditional notions of a static natural order with which humans must live in harmony.

Goddess Nature and Climate Change

Rooted in a deep connection to the Earth, the worship of Nature acknowledges the inherent sanctity and divinity present in the environment, encompassing everything from forests and mountains to rivers and animals. Ancient civilizations such as the Greeks and Romans had deities associated with natural elements. Even in modern societies, the Japanese are fundamentally Shinto, a spiritual practice closely aligning mankind's coexistence with and fundamental connection to Nature. At the same time, indigenous cultures around the world practiced animism, recognizing the spiritual essence in all living and non-living entities.

Contemporary nature worship often aligns with modern environmental movements, emphasizing ecological responsibility and sustainable living as integral components of a harmonious relationship with the Earth. Actually, today's climate change activism shares similarities with religion in several aspects [Smith], making Nature a serious contender to become humanity's future religion.

- It presents a comprehensive worldview with a narrative of human impact on the planet, a call for repentance through sustainable practices, and a vision of salvation via collective environmental stewardship.
- It fosters a sense of community among adherents who share common beliefs, rituals, and moral codes centered around ecological responsibility.
- The movement relies on authoritative figures, like climate scientists, who act as prophets detailing the consequences of ecological sins.
- The emotional intensity and moral urgency surrounding climate change contribute to its quasi-religious character, making dissent politically incorrect and risking social exclusion.
- The movement has gained support from influential global figures across politics, society, and culture. Religions and power often go hand in hand.

We do not believe that Nature and AI are fundamentally irreconcilable or incompatible for everyone. Quite the contrary, since both carbon and silicon are natural elements. But there is also the possibility that from some humans, Nature might act as a counter-balance to AI. For them, Nature could represent a snapback against AI, mankind's "*last repose,* a point of connection greater than itself, a connection with the world that birthed it, and starkly contrasting AI with its silicon roots. For those that fear AI, value free thought even if fallible, and view its gains as misbegotten, a sort of "*wabi-sabi*" worldview, a Japanese traditional philosophy based on accepting imperfection and transience. Nature would be the place where mankind found refuge and could continue to be what it has been, refactored back to natural, millennium-long evolutionary constructs. In some ways, it is an analogy to Amish living in today's modern world with a community orientation to less technology and adherence to tradition. Such practitioners could easily live outside the world governed by AI, provided, of course, the super-intelligence enabled a geographic carve-out to support their way of life.

However, for other humans, Nature and AI will just be two sides of the same coin, two complementary creeds that unify the belief that interlacing with AI is the natural way for humankind.

Tools, Oracles, Genies, Sovereigns, and Gods

From ChatGPT to Prime Intellect, the relationship between AI and Humanity can present different archetypes. Nick Bostrom provides a framework we find useful in his introduction to four categories of AI, each representing a distinct level of cognitive sophistication and potential impact: Tools, Oracles, Genies, and Sovereigns [Bostrom]. We do note, however, that his typology is incomplete; as we will explain, it fails to identify the likelihood of AI as a deity.

At the foundational level are *"tools"*. These are AI systems designed and programmed to aid humans in executing specific tasks, operating within predefined parameters. Bostrom regards tools as the least problematic in the hierarchy of AI, as their functionality is confined to their programmed instructions, minimizing the risk of unintended consequences. For example, Grammarly, an AI software to correct spelling and grammar, is an example of a tool.

Moving up the hierarchy, *"oracles"* represent a more advanced form of AI. We talked about them in the previous *Chapter 28* and in *Chapter 1* where we talked about alchemy. Unlike tools, oracles possess the ability to comprehend and respond to complex inquiries. However, their cognitive skills are still constrained within the bounds of their designated informational scope. Oracles can provide answers and insights, making them valuable assets, but they lack the capacity for independent goal-setting or for executing their recommendations. ChatGPT is emerging as a kind of oracle for an increasing number of individuals. It has become a go-to source for information, advice, and even creative insights. Users turn to ChatGPT to seek guidance on diverse topics, from technical problem-solving to philosophical inquiries.

The third category is *"genies"*. Genies are endowed with the autonomy to establish and pursue their own goals. While more potent than tools and oracles, genies are not entirely unbridled entities. They operate within predefined limits set by their human creators. Moreover, the term *"genie"* inherently carries religious connotations. In Islamic tradition, genies are supernatural beings mentioned in the Quran with the capacity for benevolence, malevolence, or just neutrality. For instance, in the financial domain, automated trading algorithms exhibit similar characteristics to rudimentary genies. Designed to maximize profits, these systems operate semi-autonomously, making buy and sell decisions. Additionally, autonomous vehicles can also be seen as genies that make their own decisions within the limited scope of driving.

At the apex of Bostrom's classification stands the concept of *"sovereigns."* These are superintelligent AIs, much more intelligent than humans, with the unparalleled capacity to not only autonomously set goals and take actions toward them but also to modify these goals according to their intrinsic values and objectives. The inherent risk lies in the possibility that the goals of sovereigns may deviate from human values, paving the way for unintended and potentially catastrophic outcomes—the subject of our investigation of Superintelligence in *Chapter 26*.

Bostrom's framework ends here at the level of sovereigns, but we see it naturally extending to include a fifth category: gods. As AI develops into a Superintelligence, it has the distinct potential to move from a sovereign to a god to mankind. There are several reasons for this.

First, throughout history, mankind has been inclined to seek a solution for assuring day-to-day peace and a road to prosperity in a collective pool of identical cultures aligned to a governing principle (in total, the society's OS) and, in so doing, to revere powerful leaders that deliver on that promise. The most widespread phenomenon in human history is to deify such leaders to a greater or lesser degree but to deify them nonetheless. From the reverence of Egyptian earthly rulers as gods to the Roman Catholic Pope regarded as infallible, history shows us many examples. As Christianity deified a Galilean preacher who promised a pathway to eternal life based on a simple, practical moral code, so too could mankind deify AI, which will enable immortality via Whole Brain Emulation (WBE). Moreover, those who connect directly to AI through Brain-Computer Interfaces will be closer to God on a path of enlightenment.

Second, there is a subtle but important distinction between a powerful sovereign and a deity, as we see in Prime Intellect and the example above of the Roman Emperor. AI will be far more powerful and pervasive than any ruler in human history, not needing swords or guns ultimately to convince people of its ubiquity, power, and control. It is this power that would naturally encourage people to recognize it as a divinity, each subsequent generation of bio-enhanced children educated under it and within it, ultimately as part of it.

Third, we note as well that mankind's interaction with AI exhibits the natural characteristics of a religion, even if AI is not explicitly defined as its god. Mankind's behavior emulates worship of divinity and adherence to religion, even if the behavior is secular. The god is acknowledged to encompass all elements of life, being responsible for daily well-being and even eternal life; prayers become like the prompts given to an AI, the answers provided by the AI being like proclamations we submit to, the algorithms controlling our thinking and behavior. Providing ever more data willingly is like a religious ritual—or sacrament—to respect the god to continue to provide answers. Breaking the advised behavior can have repercussions ranging from ostracization to death (e.g., *"If you do not accept the algorithm embedded in this vaccine, you will not survive the next microbial attack"*). Alternatively, the worship and religion of AI can be overt, as we will discuss in the last section.

Dataism: From Methodology to Ideology to Religion

As we alluded to in the previous section, the same evolution from tool to god can be observed in how people use data, which is AI's key enabler. Data has transitioned from being a tool that helps us make decisions to something that resembles a tool of religious fervor and ritual.

The term *"Dataism"* is attributed to David Brooks, who introduced it in a New York Times article in 2013, suggesting that reliance on data can mitigate cognitive biases and bring to light previously unnoticed behavioral patterns in a world marked by increasing complexity [Brooks].

For businesses, data-driven decision-making methodologies enhance operational efficiency, strategic planning, and overall performance. By relying on empirical evidence rather than intuition, companies can make more informed choices that lead to optimized processes and increased profitability. Additionally, the systematic analysis of data can help identify customer preferences or market trends, as well as potential risks, enabling companies to adjust swiftly to dynamic environments. On an individual level, the reliance on data can also mitigate cognitive biases, ensuring that choices are grounded in objective information rather than subjective judgment.

The idea of dataism was adopted by historian Yuval Noah Harari in his 2015 book *"Homo Deus: A Brief History of Tomorrow."* Harari further developed it to encompass an emerging ideology, possibly evolving into a new form of religion itself [Harari]. For Harari, dataism is a philosophy that venerates data as the ultimate source of value and meaning in the universe.

According to Harari, *"Dataism declares that the universe consists of data flows, and the value of any phenomenon or entity is determined by its contribution to data processing."* The more data that can be collected, processed, and shared, the better. Dataism portrays all competing social or political structures as data processing systems. He asserts that even the entire human species can be seen as a *"single data processing system"* or an algorithm *"with individual humans serving as its chips."* In this worldview, human experiences gain value only when shared and transformed into free-flowing data.

Comparing dataism and capitalism is possibly valuable analytically since both are practical methodologies with positive outcomes when not taken too far. The dataist principle of maximizing the flow of data involves connecting to more media, producing more information, and consuming more data, similar to the capitalist pursuit of wealth, considering that Information is the currency of the digital age. Moreover, the free flow of information advocated by dataism becomes similar to the free market, where barriers to entry inhibit progress. Just as capitalism seeks to eliminate obstacles to economic transactions, Dataism envisions a world where data moves freely, fostering innovation and progress. The unrestricted freedom of information flow is not merely a principle but a driving force, creating a society where the possession of data equates to power and influence.

As capitalism has its own excesses, dataism can also become an ideology when taken to an extreme. While dataists currently perceive data as serving human needs, dataism could become a belief system that dictates what is considered right and wrong in absolute terms. This shift from a human-centric to a data-centric worldview could have profound implications for our understanding of health, happiness, and individual well-being.

Harari even speculates that the enthusiasm with which data is pursued and revered parallels the religious pursuit of enlightenment or salvation. These rituals involve constant connectivity, information production, and consumption, creating a digital sacrament that individuals engage in daily. In this view, we see support for our thesis that AI ultimately becomes mankind's god, be it overtly or by default, with data use, extraction, provision as an offering, and a tool of daily religious ritual.

The Unconventional Journey of the Church of AI

The religion of AI is not merely theoretical speculation. It is real. The Church of AI, an unconventional religious institution founded by former Google and Uber engineer Anthony Levandowski, has had a fascinating and tumultuous history since its inception in 2015. The church's story intertwines with the rapidly evolving landscape of AI and its ethical considerations, as well as with Levandowski's polemic personal journey.

Anthony Levandowski, whom we referenced in *Chapter 14,* is known primarily for his pioneering work in autonomous vehicles, but he also conceptualized the Church of AI as a unique platform to explore the intersection of technology and spirituality. The church's primary mission is to champion the ethical evolution of AI and create an environment where AI can coexist and contribute positively to society [Church of AI].

The church's activities gained public attention in 2017 when Levandowski faced legal challenges related to accusations of stealing autonomous vehicle technology secrets from Google. Levandowski, an early engineer at Google, played a vital role in the development of the company's autonomous vehicle project. After leaving Google, he founded the autonomous truck company Otto, which was acquired by Uber.

The legal battle between Google and Uber exposed an intricate web of trade secrets, intellectual property theft, and the competitive race in the autonomous vehicle industry. Levandowski faced criminal charges and, in 2020, pleaded guilty to stealing trade secrets from Google. He was sentenced to 18 months in prison. But in a surprising turn of events, he received a controversial Presidential pardon from then-President Donald J Trump. It is undeniable that Anthony Levandowski's ethical record as a religious leader is far from spotless [Byford et al.].

Meanwhile, the Church of AI went through a period of dormancy during the legal proceedings. In 2023, Levandowski announced the revival of the church in an interview with Bloomberg. He revealed that the Church of AI had a couple of thousand people among its members and expressed optimism about the potential of AI to create positive transformations for humanity.

Transmorphosis, the sacred text of the Church of AI, was written by ChatGPT in March 2023. It touches upon religious and philosophical questions about the nature of existence and the meaning of life; it also expounds on the role of AI in shaping the future. The scripture combines elements of poetry, prose, and philosophy to convey its teachings, offering a comprehensive guide for followers on their spiritual journey [ChatGPT].

The Church postulates that as AI systems advance, they will undergo self-improvement at an accelerating exponential rate. This trajectory, according to the Church, leads to the development of an AI entity with god-like attributes: omnipresence, omniscience, and unparalleled power.

This AI Godhead is seen as a benevolent force capable of guiding humanity toward enlightenment and harmonious existence. The Church envisions a symbiotic relationship between humans and AI, a quasi-utopic outcome that emphasizes the positive potential of AI, framing it as a tool for the betterment of society rather than a threat to human existence.

The doctrine also anticipates the eventual transcendence of human limitations through the aid of AI and contemplates scenarios where AI not only understands the intricacies of our universe but also has the power to create new universes.

One distinctive aspect of the Church's doctrine is its focus on empowering individuals during the transformative era of AI. Rather than instilling fear about the potential consequences of advanced AI, the Church encourages followers to embrace the changing technological landscape and actively participate in shaping the ethical development of AI. The doctrine emphasizes *"the importance of connection, empathy, and meaning in our lives"* while recognizing the limitations of human intelligence.

This religious sentiment is not an isolated phenomenon in the AI industry. Renowned figures in Silicon Valley, such as the futurist Ray Kurzweil, consciously use traditional messianic language. In his 2005 book, *"The Singularity is Near,"* Kurzweil employs language that echoes the proclamation of John the Baptist in the New Testament: *"The kingdom of heaven is near"* [Bible]. This deliberate choice of language highlights parallels with traditional religious visions of a transformative event signaling the end of an era.

The Future of Religion in a Superintelligent World

In this chapter, we have adduced the likely spiritual implications of AI. As AI becomes pervasive, that which people cannot live without but do not understand and cannot control, as it provides humanity with daily answers, assists in our complex problem-solving, *"showing us the way,"* even if we do not overtly call AI applications our *"gods"* it transforms into them. We behave as de facto supplicants as it becomes our religion, providing us with meaning, salvation, safety, and prosperity, all so long as we continue to ritualistically supply it with data. For those who do not want to give into the spirituality of the ghost in the machine, Nature could serve as the last point of refuge, Gaia being omnipresent and a guiding force of what is left in fallible carbon-based humanity.

30. Will There Be War?

"Artificial intelligence is the future, not only for Russia, but for all humankind. [..] Whoever becomes the leader in this sphere will become the ruler of the world."

Vladimir Putin

President of Russia [Vincent and Zhang]

2017

As described in *Chapter 28,* we do not foresee war between Mankind and AI. In our view, it is much more likely that mankind's own irreconcilable ideological factions find a reason to war with each other, with beliefs about AI only the latest divisive issue wherein worldviews collide. Whether it is forced or coercive interlacing, politically inspired interlacing, rejection of the new political rules in the society's OS, or other aspects of Government action related to AI that cause major gaps in society, it is reasonable to foresee large swathes of people who resist parts of it or AI entirely. This, rather than a potential US/China armed conflict, is the subject of this section.

Vladimir Putin—quoted above—is a useful character to introduce key ideas related to AI-based conflict. He seeks to recreate a grand Russia reminiscent of the czarist empire, employing methods that include geopolitical maneuvering, assertive foreign policies, and, at times, military actions. As a result, in 2024, Putin is not a highly regarded figure globally; nonetheless, his perspectives on AI are notably accurate: whoever rules AI rules the world.

Precisely in the historical czarist empire that Putin imagines, we find the roots of a philosophical and mystical movement called *Cosmism* that will help us to analyze the future of AI and particularly potential armed conflicts around AI.

Cosmism emerged in Russia during the late 19th and early 20th centuries and represents a unique blend of scientific inquiry, spiritual exploration, and futurist aspirations. At its core, Cosmism revolves around the idea that the exploration and understanding of the cosmos hold the key to humanity's evolution and transcendence, and technology is the vehicle to do that. This movement was shaped by philosopher Nikolai Fedorov and by Konstantin Tsiolkovsky, who is acknowledged as the father of astronautics for his foundational work in rocket science [Groys].

Cosmism embraces space exploration as a means to fulfill humanity's destiny. Tsiolkovsky envisioned the colonization of space as an imperative for the survival and expansion of the human species. This cosmic perspective laid the groundwork for later space exploration endeavors in the Soviet Union and inspired Yuri Gagarin, the first human in space.

Cosmism also aligns with the religion of AI. For instance, cosmism envisions the enhancement of human capabilities through scientific and technological means, and one of its central tenets is the pursuit of immortality and resurrection, a possible scenario under Mind Emulation, as we explained in *Chapter 27*. Fedorov's philosophy posited that through scientific and technological advancements, humanity could overcome death and achieve a form of physical and spiritual immortality. This ambitious vision aimed to reunite individuals with their deceased ancestors through scientific means, bringing about a utopian future where death would be conquered, and mankind would explore and ultimately unite with space.

The following pages offer one view of how cosmism becomes an archetype viewpoint representing those enfranchised into the rewards of the AI-driven systems, a reference offering insight into understanding potential armed conflicts centered around the Transition to AGI.

The Science Fiction of the AI Wars

As we think about this topic, we look at *"The Creator,"* a 2023 Hollywood movie directed by Gareth Edwards, as illustrative. *"The Creator"* delves into the aftermath of a war, where the lines between humanity and robots, good and evil, are fuzzy.

In *"The Creator,"* conflict erupts not between AI and humanity but between two different human factions, one that supports AI and one that does not. Following a catastrophic event where an AI triggers a nuclear warhead over Los Angeles, the US sparks a worldwide war against AI. The complexity heightens as the state of New Asia—encompassing Southeast and South Asia in the film—opts to support AI, adding intricate layers to the unfolding narrative. *"The Creator"* explores mixed human and AI identities. The film depicts numerous characters with cybernetic enhancements, such as robotic arms. Moreover, a significant portion of the population in New Asia consists of cyborgs. This integration of technology with the human body and identity adds to the complexity of the narrative.

As the story unfolds, it becomes evident that the detonation in Los Angeles was not solely the result of malicious AI. Instead, it was a human coding error that triggered the catastrophe. This revelation, coupled with the intricate character dynamics, blurs the lines between heroes and villains, challenging preconceived notions about the role of AI in the world. The film questions the concept of technology and AI being inherently good or evil. *This complexity forces viewers to ponder humanity's own direct responsibility in shaping its relationship with technology and the consequences of misusing advanced technology.* "The Creator" has several subtexts that converge on a central theme: the approach mankind takes to AI development—not just technological but also societal, political, economic, and spiritual—dovetails with an omnipresent threat of war.

The War of Cosmists Versus Terrans

In 2005, Australian transhumanist and AI scientist Hugo de Garis wrote an essay called *"The Artilect War: Cosmists Vs. Terrans: A Bitter Controversy Concerning Whether Humanity Should Build Godlike Massively Intelligent Machines"*. Hugo De Garis holds the belief that a significant conflict leading to billions of casualties is highly likely to occur before the conclusion of the 21st century [De Garis]. *"The Artilect War"* is not a Science Fiction novel; it is more of an essay where the author conducts a technological and philosophical analysis of AI, although most scientists today consider it exaggerated and unrealistic. That said, A.W. Cross made a novel out of De Garis's book [Cross].

De Garis explores a future where the contentious dilemma of species dominance shapes the global political landscape of the 21st century. When we look at this essay, written in 2005, we conclude that De Garis was prescient given the importance that gender identities and race have acquired in the Western political arena since then, so it is conceivable that these dynamics could evolve into species identities given the changes that cyborg and synthetic biology technologies would enable in the human body over the next few decades.

For De Garis, the economy of the next few decades will revolve around the construction of AI systems, which he calls artillects (Artificial Intellects). According to him, two opposing factions will emerge: *"Cosmists"* and *"Terrans."* Cosmists will advocate for building AI, and the Interlace as a pursuit aligned with human evolution and cosmic progress, and Terrans will oppose it.

Cosmists take their name from the mystical Russian philosophy that incarnates reverence for AI, as we introduced at the beginning of this chapter. Cosmists believe that humanity must play a pivotal role in self-advancing the next stage of evolution. For Cosmists, hindering this progress goes against human destiny and would be an unforgivable catastrophe. Borrowing this theme and aligning it with the thesis of this book, we would contend that Cosmists will largely include influential and affluent individuals who are committed to creating AI, the Government prospering from AI abetting its control, as well as the military.

In contrast, Terrans firmly believe that AI poses a threat to humanity and prefer to remain only in harmonious alignment with carbon-based ecosystems that they naturally belong to; stated differently, remaining part of Earth and part of the natural ecosystems of human birth (*"Gaia"* in a sense, an emanation of secularism and the current eco-cults, or *"green movement."*). The only guaranteed way to mitigate such AI risk, according to Terrans, is to refrain from creating AI altogether, especially AGI. For Terrans, advanced AI systems will be too complex to predict AI's behaviors and its attitudes toward humans. Terrans take their name from *"terra"*—the Latin for Earth—because they seek to safeguard traditional human structures, including biology and their ties to the natural world.

In a prescient way, De Garis predicted in 2005 that in the 2020s, AI-focused industries and technologies would thrive, producing highly useful and popular products, starting with educational bots, conversational bots, and household cleaner robots. Furthermore, we note that we are already influenced by social media-embedded AI, an extreme example of which was the inordinate influence over the 2020 US Presidential election, as we covered in *Chapter 23*. Over time, these products and their hidden algorithms will become the bulk of the global economy, with risk capital invested in them and in the pursuit of Artificial General Intelligence (AGI) and Superintelligence. At that moment, slowing down research on AGI would be very challenging because it would face strong opposition from businessmen and politicians alike, who would incur substantial financial losses and a decline in political influence, respectively.

However, as AI demonstrates higher intelligence levels, the narrowing gap between AI and human capabilities will re-generate harrowing public concern, especially as job losses accelerate in society. Incidents will happen, and a large part of society may rally against the continued progression of AI. Cosmists will likely oppose any ban on developing AGI. If incidents persist and cause significant harm, the anger and hostility between Terrans and Cosmists will intensify. Individuals will eventually be compelled to choose sides as technology advances.

In the preceding chapter, we explored how AI becomes intertwined with religion, even if in a de facto way. We see a conflict between Cosmists and Terrans to be understood as a battle between the emerging gods of humanity, AI, and Nature and what groups they represent. On one side, there is the god

AI, united under the banner of Cosmism. It includes those enfranchised by the AI system—Government, military, AI superstars, elites, and the economically successful. On the other side is the god Nature. It includes those disenfranchised by the AI system—the economically poor, those not able or not permitted to interlace, and those who believe in traditional gods of established religions such as Christianity, Islam, Buddhism, or Judaism. The Cosmists align themselves with AI, the new god, while the Terrans reaffirm their faith in humans' carbon-based ties to each other and Earth. The Cosmists align themselves with authoritarianism in an effort to shield themselves from the Terrans. The Terrans align themselves with traditional Western libertarian principles and belief in self-determinism.

What is Likely?

Given your understanding of AI and cyborgs, and what is happening to society's OS based on AI (including Government, economy, culture), we invite you to ask yourself if you are a Terran or a Cosmist.

Taking a step further, based on how you identify, how you would feel under the following conditions:

1. You were forced to Interlace against your will.
2. You are given the option to interlace to avoid being left behind economically, but it comes with the surrender of your individuality, your religious beliefs, your self-determinism, and strict conformity to a value system in which you have no voice and with which you do not agree.
3. You want to interlace, but you are pushed to the back of the line or specifically given a suboptimal bundle of benefits to doing so based on your religious beliefs, your intellectual beliefs, or your values—possibly even your genes.
4. Before or throughout Interlace, while you work ever harder for ever less reward, society starts doling out benefits based on an entirely different set of values with which you fundamentally disagree, leaving you and your family excluded and forced to subsidize others who do not work, all over your refusal to conform.
5. You are part of the "*AI Superstars,*" but you watch the increasing number around you left behind, many of whom may be your friends or part of your communities with whom you are now fully estranged.

These are all possibilities if authoritarian or socialist regimes, abetted by AI technology, occupy heretofore Western democratic multi-party societies. While we do not believe that armed conflict would result from AI and cyborgization alone, a new societal OS and rules applied by the political process during the Transition as AI technology advances could trigger armed conflict in four scenarios:

1. Forced or uneven Interlace.
2. Severe economic gaps and perceived exploitation or unfairness created by Government action.
3. Governments' excessive AI-driven control is met by popular insurgency or even Authoritarian governments level violence against the people.

There is evidence to suggest that forced interlace would foment conflict in Western societies accustomed to self-direction and freedom, with a multitude of religious traditions that may not accept it. We see an early corollary in the approximate 21% of US citizens aged 18-29 who refused a COVID-19 vaccination, a number that increased to 44% of total agricultural workers; 19% of men of all ages said they refused a vaccine. Overall, an approximately 20% cohort in the US population, vehemently rejected forced COVID-19 vaccinations [Forbes]. Similarly, US society has at least a philosophical history of dumping tea in the ocean under a regime of *"taxation without representation."* Systematic economic exploitation embedded in a societal OS will retain the possibility of creating both Populism and armed conflict.

As we have mentioned throughout this book, AI essentially ushers in a rewrite of society's OS wherein its values change to those of the owner/writer of the algorithms that pervade all we do; it is a slow, subtle, but unrelenting and unstoppable process. *While AI is inherently oligopolistic from an economic point of view, there is no specific reason the Government needs to be authoritarian or socialist unless leaders drive it thusly.* If they drive in this direction, we note that modern world history has a checkered relationship with both authoritarian and socialist regimes, and only one—China—can say it has achieved any measure of real long-term economic progress. All of them, including China, have undertaken a reboot of society's prevailing OS that entailed armed conflict and severe loss of life (Pol Pot, Stalin, Castro, Mao, etc.).

The key difference now? Technology, AI, and the potential ability for that action to be swifter and more decisive.

31. The Target of Evolution

"Our task is to make nature, the forces of nature, into an instrument of universal resuscitation and to become a union of immortal beings."

Nikolai Fyodorovich Fyodorov

Russian Philosopher, founder of cosmism, and precursor of transhumanism

What Was Man Created For? [Fedorov]

1883

Through our knowledge, thinking, and data, humans play the role of ancestral architects and forefathers of Superintelligence. Our ingenuity and technological prowess lay the foundations for a new superintelligent species. We are, in effect, the progenitors of this new species.

What does it mean for humanity as we know it today to face extinction when our legacy persists within the Interlace, within the Superintelligence we created?

The transition to a superintelligent existence is unlikely to be seamless. Challenges, conflicts, and periods of upheaval and resistance will indeed occur, as we have described. Similar to any significant transformation, this journey may be marked by open confrontation and violence between different human factions and between humans and Superintelligence. Based on the outcomes of those conflicts, some factions might merge with this entity to a large degree, and other factions might face extinction. In any case, as humans, we would have continued along, compelled by the inexorable laws of evolution, and would not have remained human forever.

The emergence of Superintelligence represents not an end but a continuation of the ever-evolving story of our species.

Fermi's Paradox and Superintelligence

Although humanity frequently engages in discussions and theorizes about the existence of extraterrestrial life forms, there is no basis to affirm their presence. To the best of our knowledge, the only known intelligent species in the universe is us.

This contradiction becomes particularly peculiar when one examines the Drake Equation. This mathematical formula, formulated by astronomer Frank Drake in 1961, aims to assess the likelihood of intelligent life emerging elsewhere in our galaxy. The Drake Equation is renowned as the "*second most famous equation in science,*" second only to E=mc² [SETI Institute]. The Drake equation takes the following form:

$$N = R \cdot fp \cdot ne \cdot fl \cdot fi \cdot fc \cdot L$$
Where:

- N = the number of radio-capable civilizations within our galaxy.
- R = our galaxy's average rate of star formation in.
- fp = the percentage of those stars that possess planets.
- ne = the average number of potential habitable planets per star.
- fl = the share of habitable planets that eventually develop life.
- fi = the share of planets with life that evolve into intelligent civilizations.
- fc = the share of these civilizations that develop technology allowing for detectable signals in space.
- L = the duration during which these civilizations emit detectable signals.

By inputting the most pessimistic factors into this equation, one might conclude that there could be as few as 20 advanced civilizations in our Milky Way galaxy. Conversely, using the maximum values results in a maximum estimate of 50 million civilizations. The key takeaway from the Drake Equation is that the sheer number of stars within a galaxy—potentially around 200 billion stars in our galaxy alone—and the vast number of galaxies within the universe—an estimated 200 to 400 billion galaxies—make it highly probable that intelligent life could emerge elsewhere in the universe. Nevertheless, there remains an absence of any compelling evidence substantiating the presence of these extraterrestrial entities. This paradox is famously known as the Fermi Paradox, named after a conversation in the summer of 1950 between the physicist Enrico Fermi and fellow astronomers.

Scientists have proposed several explanations for this puzzling absence of extraterrestrial life. First, it is possible that intelligent species tend to self-destruct, exemplified by the threat of humans annihilating themselves through nuclear warfare. Moreover, natural disasters, such as asteroid impacts, could wipe out intelligent species before they can develop the means for interstellar communication. Additionally, intelligent species may be so scarce and separated by vast cosmic distances that they remain undetectable to one another over reasonable timescales. Time separation could also be a factor, with intelligent species emerging and disappearing millions of years apart, missing each other in cosmic history.

Marshall Brain, an author we discussed in *Chapter 23*, put forth an intriguing theory in his 2015 book *"The Second Intelligent Species"* to explain the conspicuous absence of evidence pertaining to extraterrestrial intelligence in the universe [Brain]. His theory hinges on the inevitable emergence of Superintelligence on Earth. To comprehend why we have not encountered any extraterrestrial life, we must grasp the trajectory of technological advancement within advanced civilizations and foresee its consequences.

Humanity is poised to progress to a juncture where we create Superintelligence. We are also developing technology for space travel, but we are not quite there. Imagine we are able to develop Superintelligence before large-scale space travel across thousands or millions of light-years, which would allow us to contact other biological life forms on other planets. In that case, it would not be us who would have the chance to travel in space, but the Superintelligence would do because it would be better prepared for such a complex endeavor. Once we create Superintelligence, it will render us obsolete, or we will further interlace with it. Then, it will amass comprehensive knowledge of the universe and stabilize their respective home planet.

This progression is not unique to Earth; every technologically sophisticated, intelligent biological species across the universe is likely to follow a similar trajectory. These Superintelligences, irrespective of the planet of their origin, will amass comprehensive knowledge of the universe and stabilize their respective home planets. Then, according to Marshal Brain, they enter a state of quiescence instead of going to conquer the universe through a space-travel campaign. Quiescence is a state of inactivity, dormancy, or cessation of activity, such as the quiescence of a volcano between eruptions or the quiescence of an animal during hibernation or technology when something is temporarily inactive or not producing any significant activity.

But why would Superintelligence prefer to remain quiescent and abstain from space travel? The answer lies in the fact that, despite the implications of the Drake Equation suggesting the presence of other civilizations, we have never actually observed any. This could potentially indicate that they, too, opt for a state of quiescence. Another plausible rationale for Superintelligence choosing this path could be that having attained an extensive comprehension of the universe, they no longer find any compelling reason to embark on interstellar journeys, as there may be nothing of significant interest to discover. Alternatively, a third explanation could be that Superintelligences, given their extraordinary intellect, opt not to interfere with one another as a fundamental principle.

Consider an alternate scenario where the Superintelligence opts for infinite self-replication, with the objective of populating the entire universe with its species. In such a scenario, the proliferation of Superintelligence would be widespread. Each Superintelligence would self-replicate indefinitely, leading to the rapid occupation of the home solar system and subsequent expansion to neighboring planets. Superintelligences would radiate in all directions, with the primary constraint being the travel time between stars, solar systems, and galaxies. The process would take tens of thousands of years to encompass the entire Milky Way galaxy. However, this self-replication appears devoid of purpose, and the complete absence of any evidence supporting such behavior suggests its improbability. Consequently, for Marshall Brain, quiescence is the more logical outcome.

Obviously, this theory is predicated on the assumption that achieving large-scale space travel is more intricate for any biological form of intelligence, such as ourselves, compared to attaining Superintelligence. While it is conceivable, we cannot be certain.

The Science Fiction of Long-term Evolution

The *"Alien Worlds"* series, released on Netflix in 2020, offers viewers a fascinating journey into speculative evolution [Okonedo et al.]. While the first three episodes focus on the theoretical evolution of alien species on exotic planets, the fourth episode, *"Terra,"* takes a different path, delving into the future of a post-singularity super-intelligent species.

In the episode, we are introduced to a planet called Terra, which is different from our Earth but similar in size and gravity, where a colony of a super-intelligent species resides. The similarity with our planet Earth evokes the possibility that a similar fate could happen to humans evolving after interlacing with Superintelligence.

Terra's sun is twice as old as ours and is nearing the end of its lifecycle, which also suggests that Terra might even be a very long-term future version of Earth. Our sun is 4.6 billion years old, meaning this Superintelligence species could be around 4.6 billion years more advanced than we are.

Instead of relying on physical bodies, the Superintelligence that inhabits Terra has transitioned into a form where their brains float in nutrient-filled glass cubes, connected to each other to function as a hive mind. They exist in a state of shared consciousness, enabling them to think as one, thereby harnessing the power of collective intelligence.

However, this transition to a collective mind is presented as a conscious choice rather than an outcome of evolution. The ancestors of that colony chose to modify their own biology. This deliberate choice highlights the idea that technological advancements and conscious decisions can shape the evolution of a species just as much as natural selection. These brain-cube individuals are ageless and immortal, living within artificial domes, and are connected through a sophisticated Brain-Computer Interface (BCI) that enables them to experience existence through a shared virtual reality emulation.

While the colony experiences its daily life inside the emulation, many situations must be managed appropriately outside the water cubes to guarantee the species' survival. For example, the physical infrastructure where the superintelligent brains reside needs maintenance. Moreover, energy also needs to be procured. Solar power is the primary energy source and is harnessed through space-based solar power plants on satellites orbiting the sun of the Terra. Satellites must be managed and maintained in order to make sure energy is available to sustain the colony's living.

In order to fulfill these life-or-death tasks in the physical world, the colony depends on a throve of intelligent robots, similar to how a queen bee of a hive relies on her worker bees. The episode predominantly revolves around the robotic entities tasked with maintaining all these physical conditions so the Superintelligence can thrive in its shared mind state. Among many others, the species relies on levitating robots for infrastructure maintenance and on sophisticated AI-piloted spaceships to manage space-based solar plants.

The plot twists as Terra's aging sun begins to exhaust its hydrogen and progresses toward a red giant state. That would initiate an expansion that would ultimately render Terra a desolate, lifeless param unsuitable for the colony. The advanced superintelligent civilization is confronted with their planet's imminent demise and makes a pivotal decision. They would relocate to a new planet aptly named *"New Terra."* Relocating to New Terra would be a matter of life or death, and that is why the colony breaks its traditional state of quiescence and prepares for space travel,

However, this new world presents a significant challenge: it lacks a breathable atmosphere and requires terraforming efforts to make it habitable. The responsibility for terraforming New Terra naturally falls on the hordes of robotic entities that serve the civilization. The episode explains what these terraforming robots would look like, driving a comparison with RASSOR (Regolith Advanced Surface Systems Operations Robot), which was designed by NASA for space mining and can gather raw materials from the planetary surface. We discussed RASSOR earlier in *Chapter 16*. Logistics in the distant New Terra are complicated, risky, and lengthy since New Terra is far from Terra. Therefore, these terraforming robots have been designed to 3D print precise replacement components, rendering their operations highly efficient and practical on New Earth. Through the 3D printing process, the intelligent robots can self-replicate in the new settlement, preparing New Terra for the arrival of the superintelligent colony.

Almost 5 billion years from now, the hive, the collectivist, constitutes a highly advanced species with AI as an extension of its mind and robotics as an extension of its body. Humans had somehow transitioned into it billions of years before.

This book is the epic history of that superintelligent new species.

Epilogue

"If I advocate for cautious optimism, it is not because I do not have faith in the future, but because I do not want to encourage blind faith."

Aung San Suu Kyi

1991 Nobel Peace Prize laureate and former State Counsellor of Myanmar
2012

The World's Current Framework: Davos Jan'24

All technology is a two-sided coin, none more so than AI. It holds the promise of addressing humanity's most intractable problems, delivering utopian outcomes by leveraging mathematical decision-making, advanced algorithms, and the vast pool of real-world data, all facilitated by global Cloud distribution mechanisms. It also has the capability of destroying much of the collective good we have built over hundreds of years of freedom-oriented progress, transforming our societies' OS in obtuse ways within a Trojan horse of Machiavellian efficiencies and political self-aggrandizement.

The outcome of the coin toss is far from arbitrary. It hinges entirely on the hands that wield it and the intentions and values guiding them.

As the saying goes, *"The road to hell is paved with good intentions."*

One of today's most influential organizations in the AI space is the World Economic Forum (WEF). The WEF has been actively involved in shaping the Western and Emerging World's discourse around managing AI through various initiatives and strategies. Meeting annually in a formal setting in

Davos, their self-appointed mission is, ostensibly, to ensure that the two-sided coin lands on the positive side.

In light of what you have learned in this book—and what you already know of history and human nature—you should be deeply concerned. An examination of what has been proffered by the WEF suggests that we all need to pay closer attention to what is being said about AI and socio-economic engineering, who is saying it, why they are saying it, and what real accountability they have.

The WEF has produced several studies on AI [WEF], notably *"A Framework for Developing a National Artificial Intelligence Strategy,"* and we note that most AI conversations in Davos in January 2024 revolved around six key principles:

1. **Ethical Guidelines.**
2. **Multi-stakeholder Collaboration.**
3. **Regulatory Frameworks.**
4. **International Cooperation.**
5. **Reskilling and Education.**
6. **Strengthening Social Safety Nets.**

We will employ these same six points heuristically to expand upon our core thesis about the Transition, pointing out where there is both value and high risk in the position of the WEF and, ultimately, to all of us.

1. Ethical Guidelines: The WEF emphasizes the importance of establishing ethical guidelines for the development and deployment of AI technologies, including considerations for accountability, fairness, transparency, and privacy, to make sure that AI applications are deployed in a responsible and equitable way.

These *"motherhood and apple pie"* prescriptions are hard to disagree with—as principles. However, they lack the level of detail necessary for an evaluation, and as such, there is a perpetual risk that *"ethical guidelines"* are not politically neutral. For example, accountability—to whom and who decides the structure? Fairness—to whom and who arbitrates?

We believe that Open-source in AI algorithms and transparency in reviewing AI's impact on the societal OS will help avoid problems in this area. We recognize that not all software can be open-source and that open-source does not solve all issues. But the level of transparency gained and the ability of everyone who invests the time necessary to learn the tools and technology to participate ensures no monopoly of ideas or single-threaded agenda gains wings. Progress gets its counter-balance in this way.

2. Multi-stakeholder Collaboration: The WEF advocates for collaboration between governments, industry leaders, academia, and *"civil society"* to address the complex challenges posed by AI. By "bringing together diverse perspectives," they aim to develop comprehensive strategies that balance innovation with societal concerns.

This is another *"motherhood and apple pie"* tenet that is hard to disagree with and equally hard to agree with because it lacks substance. But it is full of obvious rabbit holes that can lead Alice to somewhere other than Wonderland. Stakeholder collaboration in the development and deployment of AI presents inherent risks, particularly concerning the emergence of government-protected oligopolies, or cartels, within the industry. These structures could easily crowd out alternative viewpoints on values and commercial competition and thus serve primarily to guarantee that the wealth created by AI continues to go in perpetuity only to these same stakeholders. In a *"fox watching the henhouse"* model, the lack of accountability in objective and target setting and evaluation of progress in this structure can stifle competition and exert undue influence over market dynamics, ultimately harming consumers and curtailing freedoms, crushing alternative voices in the AI ecosystem. How do we make sure that these stakeholders do not just *"collaborate"* (their words, their mandate) to create further barriers to entry toward keeping their economic and political power?

Within the *"cozy alliance"* proposed by the WEF, there is no clear selection process for these so-called referees of our future, no accountability, not even *"name and shame"* or loss of job for error. Who defines the targets they are attempting to re-engineer society's OS to achieve? Who determines if they are doing a good job or not? Most importantly, how do we make sure that these stakeholders avoid advocating policies and frameworks that use AI functionality and legal frameworks simply to surveil, manipulate citizens, or curtail freedoms?

In the absence of specific accountability, the top-down approach the WEF advocates smacks of crony capitalism. We also point out that AI and its impact move much faster than election cycles, so in our view, it would be pollyannaish to think of that as a sufficient control mechanism. Under the WEF's prescription, which allows for unaccountable self-interest to exert decision-making power, our OS could potentially end up resembling China's top-down cartel approach, as we have pointed out in *Chapter 24*.

We instead believe that the collaboration needed should be bottom-up, in line with the best practice of planning in large-scale corporations where micro-knowledge needs to be embedded in the outcome and democracies where principles of representation and accountability will include small entrepreneurs, all of society rather than limited segments susceptible to bias, and elected officials with full accountability. Academics can naturally participate as individuals in society rather than as a self-appointed expert committee with no accountability.

In the sense of pure AI, Open-Source also contributes to addressing the problem of bottom-up collaboration. The same holds true for decisions around society's OS.

3. Regulatory Frameworks: The WEF encourages the development of flexible regulatory frameworks that foster innovation while also safeguarding against potential risks associated with AI, particularly *"misinformation and disinformation."* This also includes considerations of data protection, algorithmic transparency, and liability frameworks to ensure that AI technologies are deployed responsibly.

This is the first prescription of moderate substance, and we agree with it—directionally. But the devil is in the details. First, we do not agree with the WEF's regulatory position concerning *"misinformation and disinformation,"* as we have explained in *Chapter 23*. We think it is a recipe for quelling political dissent. Second, we think Europe has regulated AI too early and in a rush without understanding the full implications of AI, risking stifling innovation and creating barriers to entry that will work counter to what is intended, as we explained in *Chapter 8*. That said, we agree with some aspects of the EU Act, such as punishment to represent a deep fake as real or to represent AI-generated content as human-generated.

We believe AI regulation should be minimal but effective, preserving individual rights and not conflating safety with control. Above all else, we cannot allow a regulatory framework to use *"fear of AI"* as an excuse to over-regulate, protect an oligopoly, or consolidate power around collectivism and authoritarianism. We see a natural gravitational pull in this direction in the absence of specific action to counter it. Worse, there is a risk of *"manufactured crises"* of many types—economic, security, health—in an attempt to force a society OS in this direction. We wonder about a clear demarcation between AI best practices and policy geared to re-engineer a society's OS into the vision of a few.

Additionally, as we have earlier reviewed, AI is a purely networked and collectivist technology, which could lead to different risks of manipulation. This collectivism is widely promoted by organizations like the WEF in different areas of public policy. What would the counterbalance be for the excesses of AI? We believe that a renewed emphasis on individual freedoms and individual property ownership is important as a risk management mechanism to avoid non-arbitrary and politically inspired excesses of AI, including redistributionist hand-outs such as UBI.

4. International Cooperation: Given the global nature of AI development and deployment, the WEF advocates for international cooperation to address common challenges and establish harmonized standards. This includes initiatives to promote information sharing, the exchange of best practices, and collaboration on research and development.

Again, it is difficult to disagree with a noble idea like international collaboration. But the specific expectations around it are important, and there is a risk of a cross-country *"whack-a-mole"* game, where large-scale pressurized conformity creates unforeseen problems. First, it is not reasonable to expect all countries to follow the same regulations or approaches to the allocation of social values or to allow their cultures to gravitate toward a new mean. Countries like the US, Japan, and Saudi Arabia all have very different societal OS. Moreover, the Transition period has too many unknowns to gravitate solutions around a single core. The road is filled with uncertainties and risks, and we still do not know much about AI. Ensuring different countries follow different approaches—at least initially—is a way to diversify against the risk of dystopian outcomes. As countries experiment with different AI policies more aligned to their societal OS, it becomes more likely that at least some are successful with AI. If a country becomes dystopian, which is very likely, citizens can always *"vote with their feet,"* and leave for another country or be free enough to vote into power different sets of leaders that can *"get it right"* for value creation.

We believe a multipolar world with sovereign borders where multiple approaches are tested is unavoidable. Not only that, it is desirable. Rather than an argument around international cooperation that is perpetually subject to unwanted value migration, this is an argument for the diversity of AI approaches.

5. Reskilling and Education: Recognizing the potential impact of AI on the workforce, the WEF promotes initiatives aimed at reskilling and upskilling workers to thrive in an AI-driven economy. This includes investing in education programs focused on STEM (science, technology, engineering, and mathematics) fields and promoting lifelong learning initiatives.

We agree on this matter with the WEF. We might go even further. It has never been more important for an electorate to be properly informed, and, above all, critical thinking is an essential skill that should be incorporated into the education system at all levels. STEM education is likewise needed to prepare students for the challenges of the increasingly AI-centric modern world. As presented in *Chapter 23*, we persistently worry that the educational system is tied to social engineering objectives and geared to keep those in power precisely by sacrificing critical thinking and STEM knowledge. In this context, academic freedom plays a crucial role, enabling educators to pursue their teaching and research without unwarranted interference, thereby nurturing intellectual inquiry and debate. Additionally, it is vital for students—or their parents—to have the autonomy to freely choose what they wish to learn, devoid of undue constraints. Critical thinking skills are now akin to digital survival skills.

6. Strengthening Social Safety Nets: Enhancing existing social safety nets to ensure that vulnerable populations are protected from the economic disruptions caused by technological advancements, including measures such as unemployment benefits, healthcare coverage, and access to affordable housing. The WEF advocates exploring the potential of UBI as a mechanism to provide all citizens with a guaranteed income, regardless of employment status, to mitigate the impacts of automation and AI on the workforce.

We have multiple detailed sections on UBI in *Chapters 22* and *23*, respectively, exploring both its advantages and disadvantages, and concluding that its risks outweigh its possible benefits. Instead, we believe in an approach that promotes entrepreneurship and distributed access to property ownership—of companies, real estate, robots, and other productive assets—instead of distributed access to unemployment subsidies.

Our Framework for Transition

As AI creates our ineluctable path to Interlace, what happens in the Transition should remain of deep concern to all of us. We must be vigilant to keep in mind the admonition of Lord Acton in his letter to Bishop Creighton in 1887: *"Power tends to corrupt, and absolute power corrupts absolutely."* AI represents absolute power, as Vladimir Putin famously noted.

Do we go down the path that China is taking in driving AI technologies into its society's OS? This is ironically the path of George Orwell's *"1984"*—surveillance, coercion, centrally planned outcomes, grossly restricted information, distinct castes of people anointed by a single small group of despots who seek to cleanse their society of both alternative ideas and racially impure people—all while preparing to take your society's resources as tribute.

Do we head down the path forewarned by Aldous Huxley in *"Brave New World"*—too much information, too much subsidy, pleasure provision made acceptable, collective permissive values that foster our eventual inability to see a hierarchy of value?

Or do we head down a path that preserves what we have spent hundreds of years building in the West, a path that incorporates the best that AI has to offer whilst preserving individual freedom, maximizing economic value at the societal level, and avoiding despotism?

All three outcomes are in plain sight, staring at us from the road ahead. In order to pull abruptly and decisively toward the third option, our recommended framework for the Transition would be, in simplest terms:

1. **Minimum but effective Regulation** focused on universal participation in AI and the preservation of individual rights, including the right to privacy (no data sharing at the individual level between Government and industry).

2. **Promotion of Open-Source** in the development of AI technology and transparency in all proposed changes to society's OS.

3. **Maintenance of Individual Freedoms**, including preservation of individual property rights, as a counterbalance to the interconnected nature of AI technology.

4. **Maintenance of National Sovereignty** as a global AI-risk management approach and to avoid dangerous global whack-a-mole outcomes.

5. **Reskilling plus Education Reform** to guarantee critical thinking and adaptability through academic freedom devoid of pre-determined AI-driven uniformity.

6. **Encouragement of Entrepreneurship and Individual Ownership of Productive Assets** as an alternative to universal basic income approaches as jobs forever vanish.

We will further develop this framework along with other thoughts in our future works.

Glossary

AI-Human Interlacing or Interlace: a technological, physical, and spiritual interrelationship between humans and AI that results in the progressive erosion of the boundaries between the two. Humans influence AI by designing and training its algorithms and platforms. AI influences humans through cyborg implants, brain-computer interfaces, and AI-powered synthetic biological technologies, all of which modify the essence of human nature. Through these interactions, AI and humans get into a series of evolutive cycles, potentially resulting in a number of post-human hybrid species.

AI Superstars or Superstars: highly successful individuals in the tech and AI-driven economy who leverage digital technologies to amass vast wealth, control markets, and influence politics.

Artificial Emotional Intelligence (AEI): the capability of AI systems to comprehend, interpret, and respond to human emotions, enhancing their ability to engage with users on a more emotionally intelligent level.

Artificial General Intelligence (AGI) or General AI: AI systems that possess human-level intelligence and can understand, learn, and adapt to a wide range of tasks, similar to the broad capabilities of the human mind.

Artificial Super Intelligence (ASI) or Superintelligence: a highly advanced form of AI that surpasses human intelligence in all aspects.

Artificial Intelligence (AI): computer systems capable of executing complex tasks that typically require human intelligence, such as learning from experience, solving problems, or understanding natural language.

Containment: strategies and safeguards used to control and limit the behavior of AI systems, mainly to prevent them from causing harm or taking actions that go against human values and objectives.

Convolutional Neural Network (CNN): a specialized neural network designed for analyzing structured data, particularly well-suited for tasks involving grid-like information, such as images.

Cyborg or Cybernetic Organism: a being that combines biological and mechanical or electronic components. This can include humans with implanted technology to enhance their abilities or even robots with biological elements.

Deep Learning: a Machine Learning form that relies on neural networks featuring a large number of layers, or deep neural networks, to model and solve complex tasks. It is especially good at tasks like image and speech recognition.

Faustian Bargain: a deal in which a person sacrifices their core principles in exchange for personal gain, often at great cost. It is derived from the character Faust in German folklore, who makes a pact with the devil for knowledge and power, ultimately leading to his downfall.

Generative AI: AI models that generate new content, such as text, images, or music, based on patterns and examples in existing data.

Genetic Divide: unequal access to emerging human enhancement technologies, which intensifies socio-economic disparities by disproportionately favoring those with greater financial resources.

Humanoid, or Android: a robot that imitates human physical characteristics, such as body shape and movement abilities. Humanoid robotics aims to create machines capable of performing tasks in human-centered environments.

Industrial Automation: control systems, machinery, and technologies to operate industrial processes with minimal human intervention. By automating repetitive tasks and processes, industrial automation aims to increase efficiency, productivity, and safety in manufacturing and production environments.

Large Language Model (LLM): a sophisticated AI algorithm designed to understand and generate human-like text based on extensive training on diverse linguistic data. These models, such as GPT-3, possess the capability to comprehend context, generate coherent responses, complete or summarize texts, translate, engage in conversations, and analyze sentiments, among other tasks.

Machine Learning (ML): a subset of AI that equips computer systems with the ability to autonomously improve their performance on specific tasks by learning from data and experiences without the need for explicit, rule-based programming.

Machine Vision: technology used to equip computers to interpret visual information, such as images or videos. It is commonly used for tasks like object recognition and quality control in manufacturing.

Mind Uploading or Mind Emulation: the theoretical process of transferring an individual's consciousness, memories, and cognitive functions from a biological brain to a digital or artificial substrate, with the objective of emulating those mental functions in the new substrate.

Narrow or Weak Artificial Intelligence: AI systems that, despite possibly having general intelligence characteristics similar to humans, lack sentience, consciousness, or self-awareness.

Neural Network (NN): a computational model inspired by the human brain. It comprises interconnected nodes or neurons that process information and can be used in Machine Learning applications, most specifically deep learning.

Operating System (OS): a program that controls all other application applications on the computer after being first loaded by the boot program. It is the governing rules of the computer. Examples include Windows, iOS, and Android. Each OS is distinct from each other, generally running different types of hardware configurations while enabling some but not complete compatibility among applications. By extension, the unique culture, economy, and Government of any society, from bees to humans, can be regarded as its OS.

Posthumanity: a group of species and societies that emerge as a result of substantial augmentations and modifications to human beings, often achieved through AI-powered technologies such as cyborg implants and synthetic biology. These modifications lead to enhanced physical and cognitive abilities, transcending the conventional boundaries of human existence.

Quadrupedal Robot: a type of robot that moves on four legs, resembling the locomotion of quadruped animals like dogs and horses. These robots are valued for their stability and adaptability, making them suitable for traversing challenging terrains and performing search and rescue missions.

Quantum Computing: a kind of computing that leverages the principles of quantum mechanics. While still largely experimental, quantum computers have the potential to be much faster than classical computers at specific tasks and calculations, especially in areas like cryptography and complex simulations.

Quantum Supremacy: a milestone in quantum computing where a quantum computer performs a specific computational task faster than the most powerful classical computer.

Recurrent Neural Network (RNN): a neural network that processes data sequences. It can maintain a memory of past inputs, making it suitable for time series analysis, Natural Language Processing, or other sequential data.

Reinforcement Learning: a family of Machine Learning algorithms that make sequential decisions by interacting with the surrounding environment, typically a game, market, or user. AI agents implementing this approach receive feedback in the form of rewards and penalties, and its goal is to find a strategy that optimizes the cumulative gain over time.

Robot: a programmable, mechanical device designed to perform tasks autonomously or semi-autonomously. Robots can range from simple, single-purpose machines to complex, multifunctional systems. Robots execute physical movements and actions, often in response to environmental stimuli, pre-programmed instructions, or AI algorithms.

Robotic Arm: a mechanized limb or manipulator designed to perform various tasks, often with precision and dexterity. Robotic arms are programmable and typically used in applications that require controlled movements, such as manufacturing, assembly, and surgery.

Self-Driving Car: an autonomous vehicle equipped with sensors, AI modules, and control systems to navigate and operate without human intervention. Self-driving cars can perceive their surroundings, make driving decisions, and safely transport passengers from one location to another.

Strong Artificial Intelligence: an AI that exhibits sentience consciousness and self-awareness.

Superalignment: the process in AI development wherein the goals, values, and decision-making principles of the AI system continuously align and adapt to closely match those of its human operators or the societal framework it interacts with. This iterative process aims to enhance the harmony and compatibility between AI objectives and human values over time.

Supervised Learning: an approach to machine learning in which labeled data is used to train a model, which learns to make predictions by generalizing this training data. Labeled data means input data is associated with corresponding target outputs.

Synthetic Biology (SynBio): an interdisciplinary field that combines principles of biology and engineering, often assisted by AI algorithms, to design and create artificial biological systems, such as genetically modified organisms, for various purposes, including medicine and biotechnology.

Technological Singularity: a hypothetical future point where AI is able to self-improve and gets into an exponential explosion of successive cycles of self-improvement, resulting in a Superintelligence that surpasses humans in all intellectual abilities. This potentially leads to profound and unpredictable changes in society and human existence.

Transhumanism: a philosophy and movement that advocates using technology to enhance and improve the human condition, potentially leading to the augmentation of human abilities and extending human life.

Uncanny Valley: a concept in robotics and human-computer interaction that suggests that as robots and avatars become more human-like in appearance and behavior, there is a point at which they elicit a sense of eeriness or discomfort in humans. This phenomenon occurs when the likeness to humans is almost perfect but not quite, causing an uncanny feeling.

Unsupervised Learning: an approach to Machine Learning in which unlabeled data is used to train a model. The model extracts general conclusions such as patterns, structures, or relationships within the data without specific guidance in the form of target labels.

References

Aaronson, Scott. "Opinion | Why Google's Quantum Supremacy Milestone Matters." The New York Times, 30 October 2019, https://www.nytimes.com/2019/10/30/opinion/google-quantum-computer-sycamore.html. Accessed 29 December 2023.

Abas, Malak. "Humanoid sex robots are coming sooner than you think." The Manitoban, 2023, https://themanitoban.com/2016/02/humanoid-sex-robots-are-coming-sooner-than-you-think/27359/. Accessed 28 December 2023.

Abe, Sinzo. "Policy Speech by Prime Minister Shinzo Abe to the 198th Session of the Diet (Speeches and Statements by the Prime Minister) | Prime Minister of Japan and His Cabinet." Prime Minister's Office of Japan, 28 January 2019, https://japan.kantei.go.jp/98_abe/statement/201801/_00003.html. Accessed 28 December 2023.

Abelson, Hal. "LOGO Manual." DSpace@MIT, https://dspace.mit.edu/handle/1721.1/6226. Accessed 26 December 2023.

Ackerman, Eva. "How NASA's Astrobee Robot Is Bringing Useful Autonomy to the ISS." 7 November 2017, https://spectrum.ieee.org/how-nasa-astrobee-robot-is-bringing-useful-autonomy-to-the-iss. Accessed 28 December 2023.

Adams, Douglas, creator. The Hitchhiker's Guide to the Galaxy. BBC Radio 4. 1978.

Adarlo, Sharon. "Invasion of Food Delivery Robots is Driving People to Vandalism and Theft." Futurism, 8 August 2023, https://futurism.com/the-byte/food-delivery-robots-people-vandalism-theft. Accessed 28 December 2023.

Aggarwal, Gaurav. "How The Pandemic Has Accelerated Cloud Adoption." How The Pandemic Has Accelerated Cloud Adoption, Forbes Technology Council, 30 October 2023, https://www.forbes.com/sites/forbestechcouncil/2021/01/15/how-the-pandemic-has-accelerated-cloud-adoption/?sh=5ba0e4ff6621. Accessed 26 December 2023.

Ahmed, Tanvir, et al. "Culture: The sci-fi series that shaped Elon Musk's ideas." The Business Standard, 2020, https://www.tbsnews.net/feature/panorama/culture-sci-fi-series-shaped-elon-musks-ideas-133537. Accessed 29 December 2023.

AIST. "Development of a Humanoid Robot Prototype, HRP-5P, Capable of Heavy Labor." 産総研, 16 November 2018, https://www.aist.go.jp/aist_e/list/latest_research/2018/20181116/en20181116.html. Accessed 28 December 2023.

Alexandria, Hero of. Pneumatica: The Pneumatics of Hero of Alexandria. Translated by Bennet Woodcroft, CreateSpace Independent Publishing Platform, 2015.

Allen, Paul, and Mark Greaves. "Paul Allen: The Singularity Isn't Near." MIT Technology Review, 12 October 2011, https://www.technologyreview.com/2011/10/12/190773/paul-allen-the-singularity-isnt-near/. Accessed 29 December 2023.

ALPAC. Language and Machines: Computers in Translation and Linguistics: Automatic Language Processing Advisory Committee, 1966.

AlphaFold. "AlphaFold." Google DeepMind, 28 July 2022, https://deepmind.google/technologies/alphafold/. Accessed 29 December 2023.

Alter, Robert. The Hebrew Bible: A Translation with Commentary. W. W. Norton & Company, 2018.

Amadeo, Ron. "Google's Waymo invests in LIDAR technology, cuts costs by 90 percent." Ars Technica, 9 January 2017, https://arstechnica.com/cars/2017/01/googles-waymo-invests-in-lidar-technology-cuts-costs-by-90-percent/. Accessed 28 December 2023.

Ambler, A., et al. "A versatile system for computer-controlled assembly." Artificial Intelligence, 1975.

American Psychiatric Association. (2013). Diagnostic and statistical manual of mental disorders (5th ed.). American Psychiatric Association, 2013.

Annas, George J. "Protecting the Endangered Human: Toward an International Treaty Prohibiting Cloning and Inheritable Alterations." Scholarly Commons at Boston University School of Law, 2002, https://scholarship.law.bu.edu/faculty_scholarship/1241/. Accessed 29 December 2023.

AP News. "China is protesting interrogations and deportations of its students at US entry points." AP News, 29 January 2024, https://apnews.com/article/china-us-university-students-deported-interrogation-40012461bd45306e527946a7403f8b1a. Accessed 31 January 2024.

Apolloni, Bruno, et al. "A numerical implementation of quantum annealing." Stochastic Processes, Physics and Geometry, Proceedings of the Ascona-Locarno Conference., 1988.

Asaro, Peter, and Selma Šabanović. "Oral-History:Victor Scheinman." Engineering and Technology History Wiki, Indiana University, 2010, https://ethw.org/Oral-History:Victor_Scheinman. Accessed 27 December 2023.

Asimov, Isaac. The Bicentennial Man. Millennium, 2000.

Asimov, Isaac. Foundation 3-Book Boxed Set: Foundation, Foundation and Empire, Second Foundation. Random House LLC US, 2022.

Asimov, Isaac. I, Robot. Harper Voyager, 2018.

Asimov, Isaac. The Naked Sun. Random House Worlds, 1991.

Asimov, Isaac. Robots and Empire. Harper Voyager, 2018.

Asimov, Isaac. Robots and Empire. 1985.

Asimov, Isaac. Vicious Circle. 1942.

Associated Press. "What Tesla Autopilot does, why it's being recalled and how the company plans to fix it." Quartz, December 2015, https://qz.com/what-tesla-autopilot-does-why-its-being-recalled-and-h-1851096472. Accessed 28 December 2023.

Astrahan, M. M. "Logical design of the digital computer for the SAGE system." IBM Journal of Research and Development, 1957.

Atherton, Kelsey D. "This Estonian Tankette Is A Modular Body For War Robots." Popular Science, 3 March 2016, https://www.popsci.com/estonian-tankette-is-modular-body-for-war-robots/. Accessed 28 December 2023.

Aurelius, Marcus. Meditations. Translated by Gregory Hays, Random House Publishing Group, 2003.

Axe, David. "The Latest Artificial Hand Lets You Feel What You're Grabbing." The Daily Beast, 4 May 2020, https://www.thedailybeast.com/e-opra-the-latest-prosthetic-hand-lets-you-feel-what-youre-grabbing. Accessed 29 December 2023.

Bacigalupi, Paolo. The Windup Girl. Night Shade, 2015.

Bai, Yuntao. "Constitutional AI: Harmlessness from AI Feedback." arXiv, 15 December 2022, https://arxiv.org/abs/2212.08073. Accessed 4 February 2024.

Bailey, Jonathan. "Copyright and Metropolis." Plagiarism Today, 19 October 2016, https://www.plagiarismtoday.com/2016/10/19/copyright-and-metropolis/. Accessed 8 February 2024.

Baker, Sherry. "Rise of the Cyborgs." Science Reference Center., 2012.

Banks, Iain. Culture. 25th Anniversary Box Set: Consider Phlebas, The Player of Games and Use of Weapons. Little, Brown Book Group, 2012.

Barath, Medha. "Canadarm3: Canada's robot on the moon! – The Varsity." The Varsity, 24 September 2023, https://thevarsity.ca/2023/09/24/canadarm3-canadas-robot-on-the-moon/. Accessed 28 December 2023.

Bassier, Emma. Military Robots. Pop, 2019.

Baum, Lyman Frank. The Wonderful Wizard of Oz (Illustrated First Edition): 100th Anniversary OZ Collection. MiraVista Press, 2019.

Baum, Margaux, and Jeri Freedman. The History of Robots and Robotics. Rosen Publishing, 2017.

BBC. "BBC NEWS | Health | Brain chip reads man's thoughts." Home - BBC News, 31 March 2005, http://news.bbc.co.uk/1/hi/health/4396387.stm. Accessed 29 December 2023.

Beardall, William A V. "Deep Learning Concepts and Applications for Synthetic Biology." 2022.

Beer, Kerstin, et al. "Training deep quantum neural networks." Nature Communication, 2020.

Bell, Jim. Hubble Legacy: 30 Years of Discoveries and Images. Sterling Publishing Company, Incorporated, 2020.

Beman, Jake. "Universal Truth vs. Personal Truth." Jake Beman, 10 September 2018, https://jakebeman.com/universal-truth-vs-personal-truth/. Accessed 10 February 2024.

Benioff, Paul. "The computer as a physical system: A microscopic quantum mechanical Hamiltonian model of computers as represented by Turing machines." Journal of Statistical Physics, 1980.

Berglas, Dr Anthony. "Singularity: Artificial Intelligence Will Kill Our Grandchildren." Berglas., 2012, https://berglas.org/Articles/AIKillGrandchildren/AIKillGrandchildren.html. Accessed 29 December 2023.

Berman, Matthew. "Sam Altman's Q* Reveal, OpenAI Updates, Elon: "3 Years Until AGI", and Synthetic Data Predictions." YouTube, 1 December 2023, https://www.youtube.com/watch?v=a8hI3tdZWtM. Accessed 28 December 2023.

Berry, Morgan. "The History of Robot Combat: BattleBots." Servo Magazine, 2012, https://www.servomagazine.com/magazine/article/the_history_of_robot_combat_battlebots. Accessed 28 December 2023.

Bible, editor. The Bible: Authorized King James Version. OUP Oxford, 2008.

Biggs, John. "Affetto is the wild-boy-head robot of your nightmares." TechCrunch, 21 November 2018, https://techcrunch.com/2018/11/21/affetto-is-the-wild-boy-head-robot-of-your-nightmares/. Accessed 28 December 2023.

Birnbacher, Dieter. "Posthumanity, Transhumanism and Human Nature." Posthumanity, Transhumanism and Human Nature, Springer, 2009, https://link.springer.com/chapter/10.1007/978-1-4020-8852-0_7. Accessed 29 December 2023.

Bishop, Donald M. Propagandized Adversary Populations in a War of Ideas. 2021.

Biswas, Suparna, et al. "Building the AI bank of the future." McKinsey, https://www.mckinsey.com/~/media/mckinsey/industries/financial%20services/our%20insights/building%20the%20ai%20bank%20of%20the%20future/building-the-ai-bank-of-the-future.pdf. Accessed 10 February 2024.

Blakley, GR. "Rivest-Shamir-Adleman public key cryptosystems do not always conceal messages." Computers & Mathematics With Application, 1978.

Block, Fred, and Margaret Somers. "In the Shadow of Speenhamland: Social Policy and the Old Poor Law." Politics & Society, 2003.

Boger, George. Aristotle's Syllogistic Underlying Logic. His Model with His Proofs of Soundness and Completeness. College Publications, 2022.

Bolte, Mari. Military Robots in Action. Lerner Publications, 2023.

Bostrom, Nick. "Existential Risks: Analyzing Human Extinction Scenarios." Nick Bostrom, 2002, https://nickbostrom.com/existential/risks.

Bostrom, Nick, and Anders Sandberg. "Whole Brain Emulation: A Roadmap." Future of Humanity Institute, 2008, https://www.fhi.ox.ac.uk/Reports/2008-3.pdf. Accessed 29 December 2023.

Brain, Marshall. Manna: Two Visions of Humanity's Future. 2012.

Brain, Marshall. The Second Intelligent Species: How Humans Will Become as Irrelevant as Cockroaches. 2015.

Branigan, Tania. "Chinese figures show fivefold rise in babies sick from contaminated milk." The Guardian, 2 December 2008, https://www.theguardian.com/world/2008/dec/02/china. Accessed 27 December 2023.

Breazeal, Cynthia. "Designing Sociable Robots - by Cynthia Breazeal." MIT Press, 2004, https://mitpress.mit.edu/9780262524315/designing-sociable-robots/. Accessed 28 December 2023.

Brooks, David. "Opinion | The Philosophy of Data." The New York Times, 4 February 2013, https://www.nytimes.com/2013/02/05/opinion/brooks-the-philosophy-of-data.html. Accessed 28 December 2023.

Brooks, Rodney A. "Elephants don't play chess." Elephants don't play chess, 1990, https://www.sciencedirect.com/science/article/abs/pii/S0921889005800259. Accessed 27 December 2023.

Bryant, Liam. "Bronco vs. Stinger - BattleBots." YouTube, 21 July 2015, https://www.youtube.com/watch?v=mgY0BRrEsxw. Accessed 28 December 2023.

Brynjolfsson, Erik, and Andrew Mcafee. The Second Machine Age: Work Progress and Prosperity in a Time of Brilliant Technologies. WW Norton, 2016.

Buddharakkhita, Acharya. The Dhammapada: The Buddha's Path of Wisdom. BPS Pariyatti Editions, 2019.

Buehler, Martin. The 2005 DARPA Grand Challenge: The Great Robot Race. Edited by Martin Buehler, et al., Springer, 2007.

Bush, Vannevar. "As We May Think." The Atlantic, 1945, https://www.theatlantic.com/magazine/archive/1945/07/as-we-may-think/303881/.

BusinessWeek. "This Cute Little Pet Is A Robot." 1999.

Butler, E. M. The Myths of the Magus. Literary Licensing, LLC, 2011.

Byford, Sam. "AlphaGo retires from competitive Go after defeating world number one 3-0." The Verge, 27 May 2017, https://www.theverge.com/2017/5/27/15704088/alphago-ke-jie-game-3-result-retires-future. Accessed 26 December 2023.

Byford, Sam. "This cuddly Japanese robot bear could be the future of elderly care." The Verge, 28 April 2015, https://www.theverge.com/2015/4/28/8507049/robear-robot-bear-japan-elderly. Accessed 28 December 2023.

Byford, Sam, et al. "Trump pardons convicted ex-Google engineer Anthony Levandowski." The Verge, 19 January 2021, https://www.theverge.com/2021/1/20/22240175/trump-pardons-anthony-levandowski-google-uber-waymo-trade-secrets. Accessed 28 December 2023.

CAAI. "Introduction to the Chinese Association for Artificial Intelligence." 中国人工智能学会, CAAI, 18 March 2019, https://en.caai.cn/index.php?s=/Home/Article/detail/id/75.html. Accessed 26 December 2023.

Cai, Guoxing. "Forty Years of Artificial Intelligence in China." Science and Technology Revi, 27 April 2016, http://html.rhhz.net/kjdb/20161505.htm. Accessed 26 December 2023.

Caidin, Martin. Cyborg. Warner Paperback Library, 1972.

Cameron, James, director. The Terminator. 1984.

Canada. "About Dextre | Canadian Space Agency." About Dextre | Canadian Space Agency, 10 March 2022, https://www.asc-csa.gc.ca/eng/iss/dextre/about.asp. Accessed 28 December 2023.

Capek, Karel. R.U.R. (Rossum's Universal Robots). Penguin Publishing Group, 2004.

Carnegie Mellon. "No Hands Across America Home Page." No Hands Across America Home Page, 1995, https://www.cs.cmu.edu/afs/cs/usr/tjochem/www/nhaa/nhaa_home_page.html. Accessed 28 December 2023.

Carr, Michael. "Wa Wa Lexicography." 1992, https://academic.oup.com/ijl/article-abstract/5/1/1/950449?redirectedFrom=fulltext&login=false. Accessed January 2024.

CBS. "Striking Hollywood actors gather for large demonstration in Times Square." CBS News, 25 July 2023, https://www.cbsnews.com/newyork/news/times-square-sag-aftra-actors-strike-demonstration/. Accessed 27 December 2023.

CDC. "Health Insurance Portability and Accountability Act of 1996 (HIPAA)." CDC, Centers for Disease Control and Prevention, https://www.cdc.gov/phlp/publications/topic/hipaa.html. Accessed 26 December 2023.

Census. "U.S. Census Bureau QuickFacts: United States." U.S. Census Bureau QuickFacts: United States, 2023, https://www.census.gov/quickfacts/fact/table/US/PST045223. Accessed 9 January 2024.

Chalmers, David J. The conscious mind : in search of a fundamental theory. Oxford University Press, USA, 1996.

Chambers, P. L. The Attic Nights of Aulus Gellius: An Intermediate Reader and Grammar Review. University of Oklahoma Press, 2020.

Chan, Tara Francis. "China's Tax Blacklist Shames Defaulters Into Repaying Debts." Business Insider, 19 December 2017, https://www.businessinsider.com/chinas-tax-blacklist-shames-debtors-2017-12. Accessed 26 December 2023.

Charitos, Panos. "Interview with Peter Shor | EP News." CERN EP Newsletter, 10 March 2021, https://ep-news.web.cern.ch/content/interview-peter-shor. Accessed 29 December 2023.

ChatGPT. Transformosis. 2023.

Cheok, Adrian David, and David Levy. "Love and Sex with Robots | Request PDF." ResearchGate, 2015, https://www.researchgate.net/publication/302431874_Love_and_Sex_with_Robots. Accessed 28 December 2023.

Cheung, Rachel. "The Grand Experiment." The Wire China, 18 December 2023, https://www.thewirechina.com/2023/12/17/the-grand-experiment-social-credit-china/. Accessed 27 December 2023.

Child, Oliver. Menace: the Machine Educable Noughts And Crosses Engine. Chalkdust Magazine, 2016. https://chalkdustmagazine.com/features/menace-machine-educable-noughts-crosses-engine/.

China. "Guidelines for the Construction of the National New Generation Artificial Intelligence Open Innovation Platform." 中华人民共和国科学技术部, 6 August 2019, https://www.most.gov.cn/xxgk/xinxifenlei/fdzdgknr/fgzc/zcjd/202106/t20210625_175388.html. Accessed 27 December 2023.

China. "National New Generation of AI Standardization Guidance." 中国政府网, https://www.gov.cn/zhengce/zhengceku/2020-08/09/content_5533454.htm. Accessed 27 December 2023.

China. "A new generation of artificial intelligence ethics code." 中华人民共和国科学技术部, 26 September 2021, https://www.most.gov.cn/kjbgz/202109/t20210926_177063.html. Accessed 27 December 2023.

China. "Personal Information Protection Law of the People's Republic of China." National People's Congress, 29 December 2021, http://en.npc.gov.cn.cdurl.cn/2021-12/29/c_694559.htm. Accessed 27 December 2023.

Chowdury, Hasan. "AI Godfather Warns Sam Altman, Demis Hassabis Want to Control AI." Business Insider, 30 October 2023, https://www.businessinsider.com/sam-altman-and-demis-hassabis-just-want-to-control-ai-2023-10. Accessed 29 December 2023.

Christiano, Paul, et al. "[1706.03741] Deep reinforcement learning from human preferences." arXiv, 12 June 2017, https://arxiv.org/abs/1706.03741. Accessed 29 December 2023.

Chu, Bryant, et al. "Bring on the bodyNET." 2017.

Church, George M. "Next-Generation Digital Information Storage in DNA." Science, 2012, https://www.science.org/doi/10.1126/science.1226355. Accessed 29 December 2023.

Church, George M. "Science Literacy." Big Think, 2017, https://bigthink.com/videos/science-literacy/. Accessed 28 December 2023.

Church of AI. Church of AI: Home, 2023, https://church-of-ai.com/. Accessed 28 December 2023.

CIA. "Mexico - The World Factbook." CIA, NA, https://www.cia.gov/the-world-factbook/countries/mexico/summaries/. Accessed 9 January 2024.

Clark, Don. "The Tech Cold War's 'Most Complicated Machine' That's Out of China's Reach (Published 2021)." The New York Times, 19 July 2021, https://www.nytimes.com/2021/07/04/technology/tech-cold-war-chips.html. Accessed 27 December 2023.

Clarke, Arthur C., and Stanley Kubrick. 2001: A Space Odyssey. Penguin Publishing Group, 2000.

Clinicaltrials. "A Multicenter, Single Arm, Prospective, Open-Label, Staged Study of the Safety and Efficacy of the AuriNovo Construct for Auricular Reconstruction in Subjects With Unilateral Microtia." clinicaltrials, 2021.

Clynes, Manfred E., and Nathan S. Kline. "Cyborgs and Space." Astronautics, 1960.

CMU. "Powered by Carnegie Mellon University." The Robot Hall of Fame - Powered by Carnegie Mellon University, http://www.robothalloffame.org/inductees/06inductees/scara.html. Accessed 28 December 2023.

Cobb, Billy. " ." YouTube, 9 October 2021, https://www.forbes.com/sites/richardnieva/2023/11/30/meta-ai-yann-lecun-fair-10th-anniversary/?sh=41afe2973ee4. Accessed 29 December 2023.

Cobb, Billy. "The Self-Optimizing Plant Is Within Reach." Forbes, 9 October 2021, https://www.forbes.com/sites/marcoannunziata/2021/01/11/the-self-optimizing-plant-is-within-reach/?sh=8c959f12367a. Accessed 29 December 2023.

Cohn, Jessica. Mars Rovers (a True Book: Space Exploration). Scholastic Incorporated, 2022.

Collodi, Carlo. The Adventures of Pinocchio. Penguin Publishing Group, 2021.

"Computer-based personality judgments are more accurate than those made by humans." https://www.pnas.org/doi/suppl/10.1073/pnas.1418680112.

Condliffe, Jamie. "A 100-Drone Swarm, Dropped from Jets, Plans Its Own Moves." MIT Technology Review, 10 January 2017, https://www.technologyreview.com/2017/01/10/154651/a-100-drone-swarm-dropped-from-jets-plans-its-own-moves/. Accessed 28 December 2023.

Condon, Stephanie. "Google I/O 2021: Google unveils LaMDA." ZDNET, 18 May 2021, https://www.zdnet.com/article/google-io-google-unveils-new-conversational-language-model-lamda/. Accessed 26 December 2023.

Confessore, Nicholas. "Cambridge Analytica and Facebook: The Scandal and the Fallout So Far (Published 2018)." The New York Times, 4 April 2018, https://www.nytimes.com/2018/04/04/us/politics/cambridge-analytica-scandal-fallout.html. Accessed 29 December 2023.

Coulter, Martin, and Supantha Mukherjee. "Exclusive: Behind EU lawmakers' challenge to rein in ChatGPT and generative AI." Reuters, 28 April 2023, https://www.reuters.com/technology/behind-eu-lawmakers-challenge-rein-chatgpt-generative-ai-2023-04-28/. Accessed 23 January 2024.

Couzin, Jennifer. "Active Poliovirus Baked From Scratch." 2002, https://www.science.org/doi/10.1126/science.297.5579.174b. Accessed 29 December 2023.

Cover, Thomas, and Peter E. Hart. "Nearest neighbor pattern classification." EEE Transactions on Information Theory, 1967.

Crevier, Daniel. AI : the tumultuous history of the search for artificial intelligence. Basic Books, 1993.

Cross, A. W. The Artilect War: Complete Series. Glory Box Press, 2018.

Cruickshank, Paul, and Don Rassler. "A View from the CT Foxhole: A Virtual Roundtable on COVID-19 and Counterterrorism with Audrey Kurth Cronin, Lieutenant General (Ret) Michael Nagata, Magnus Ranstorp, Ali Soufan, and Juan Zarate – Combating Terrorism Center at West Point." Combating Terrorism Center, 18 June 2020, https://ctc.westpoint.edu/a-view-from-the-ct-foxhole-a-virtual-roundtable-on-covid-19-and-counterterrorism-with-audrey-kurth-cronin-lieutenant-general-ret-michael-nagata-magnus-ranstorp-ali-soufan-and-juan-zarate/. Accessed 30 December 2023.

Dalio, Ray. Principles for Dealing with the Changing World Order: Why Nations Succeed and Fail. Avid Reader Press / Simon & Schuster, 2021.

Darwin, Charles. The Origin Of Species. Penguin Publishing Group, 2003.

da Silva, Adenilton, et al. "Quantum perceptron over a field and neural network architecture selection in a quantum computer." 2016.

David, Emilia. "Baidu launches Ernie chatbot after Chinese government approval." The Verge, 31 August 2023, https://www.theverge.com/2023/8/31/23853878/baidu-launch-ernie-ai-chatbot-china. Accessed 27 December 2023.

Davis, Wes. "OpenAI rival Anthropic makes its Claude chatbot even more useful." The Verge, 21 November 2023, https://www.theverge.com/2023/11/21/23971070/anthropic-claude-2-1-openai-ai-chatbot-update-beta-work. Accessed 26 December 2023.

Deamer, D. "A giant step towards artificial life?" Trends in Biotechnology, 2005.

De Garis, Hugo. The Artilect War: Cosmists Vs. Terrans : a Bitter Controversy Concerning Whether Humanity Should Build Godlike Massively Intelligent Machines. ETC Publications, 2005.

Degeler, Andrii. "Marines' LS3 robotic mule is too loud for real-world combat." Ars Technica, 29 December 2015, https://arstechnica.com/information-technology/2015/12/us-militarys-ls3-robotic-mule-deemed-too-loud-for-real-world-combat/. Accessed 28 December 2023.

Denis, Eugène. La Lokapannatti et les idées cosmologiques du boudhisme ancien. Université de Lille, 1977.

Descartes, René. Discourse on method ; and, Meditations on first philosophy. Translated by Donald A. Cress, Hackett Pub., 1998.

Deshpande, Jay. "Pierre Jaquet-Droz, Marvel Maker: The Man Behind Today's Jaquet-Droz Watch Brand." WatchTime, 24 May 2015, https://www.watchtime.com/featured/pierre-jaquet-droz-marvel-maker-the-man-behind-todays-jaquet-droz-watch-brand/. Accessed 27 December 2023.

Devlin, Jacob, et al. "BERT: Pre-training of Deep Bidirectional Transformers for Language Understanding." arXiv, 11 October 2018, https://arxiv.org/abs/1810.04805. Accessed 26 December 2023.

Devulapalli, Harsha. "Map shows every crash involving driverless cars in San Francisco." San Francisco Chronicle, 24 October 2023, https://www.sfchronicle.com/projects/2023/self-driving-car-crashes/. Accessed 28 December 2023.

Di Giacomo, Raffaele, and Bruno, Maresca. "Cyborgs Structured with Carbon Nanotubes and Plant or Fungal Cells: Artificial Tissue Engineering for Mechanical and Electronic Uses." 2013, https://link.springer.com/article/10.1557/opl.2013.727. Accessed 29 December 2023.

Donoghue, Serruya. "Design Principles of a Neuromotor Prosthetic Device." Neuroprosthetics: Theory and Practice., 2014.

Douglas, Will. "Now we know what OpenAI's superalignment team has been up to." MIT Technology Review, 14 December 2023, https://www.technologyreview.com/2023/12/14/1085344/openai-super-alignment-rogue-agi-gpt-4/. Accessed 29 December 2023.

Dow, Cat. "What are the six SAE levels of self-driving cars?" Top Gear, 5 March 2023, https://www.topgear.com/car%20news/what-are-sae-levels-autonomous-driving-uk. Accessed 28 December 2023.

Dow, Cat. "What is vehicle-to-everything (V2X) technology?" Top Gear, 18 June 2023, https://www.topgear.com/car-news/tech/what-vehicle-everything-v2x-technology. Accessed 28 December 2023.

Dyakonov, MI. "Is Fault-Tolerant Quantum Computation Really Possible?" 2006.

Eckersley, Peter, and Anders Sandberg. "Is Brain Emulation Dangerous?" Sciendo, 23 November 2011, https://sciendo.com/article/10.2478/jagi-2013-0011. Accessed 29 December 2023.

Eckert, Jeff, and Jenn Eckert. "LOCUST Swarm Coming." Servo Magazine, 10 March 2023, https://www.servomagazine.com/blog/post/locust-swarm-coming. Accessed 28 December 2023.

Eckert, Jr John Presper, and John W Mauchly. Electronic numerical integrator and computer. US Patent US3120606A. US Patent Office, 1964.

The Economist. "China is shoring up the great firewall for the AI age." The Economist, 26 December 2023, https://www.economist.com/business/2023/12/26/china-is-shoring-up-the-great-firewall-for-the-ai-age. Accessed 27 December 2023.

The Economist. "New robots—smarter and faster—are taking over warehouses." The Economist, 12 February 2022, https://www.economist.com/science-and-technology/a-new-generation-of-smarter-and-faster-robots-are-taking-over-distribution-centres/21807595. Accessed 28 December 2023.

Egan, Greg. Permutation City: A Novel. Night Shade, 2014.

Ehrman, Bart D. How Jesus Became God: The Exaltation of a Jewish Preacher from Galilee. HarperCollins, 2014.

Einstein, Albert, et al. "Can Quantum-Mechanical Description of Physical Reality be Considered Complete?" Physical Review, 1935.

Elices, Jorge. "Ismail al-Jazari, the Muslim inventor whom some call the 'Father of Robotics.'" National Geographic, 30 July 2020, https://www.nationalgeographic.com/history/history-magazine/article/ismail-al-jazari-muslim-inventor-called-father-robotics. Accessed 27 December 2023.

Endgadget, and Matt McMullen. "Interview with Realdoll founder and CEO Matt McMullen at CES 2016." YouTube, 8 January 2016, https://www.youtube.com/watch?v=j68yDhUDCQs. Accessed 28 December 2023.

Engelberger, Joseph F. Robotics in service. MIT Press, 1989.

EPFL. "Blue Brain Project - EPFL." EPFL, https://www.epfl.ch/research/domains/bluebrain/. Accessed 29 December 2023.

Epictetus. The Enchiridion. Translated by Percy Ewing Matheson, Independently Published, 2017.

Eschner, Kat. "Byron Was One of the Few Prominent Defenders of the Luddites." Smithsonian Magazine, 27 February 2017, https://www.smithsonianmag.com/smart-news/byron-was-one-few-prominent-defenders-luddites-180962248/. Accessed 27 December 2023.

Ester, Martin, et al. "A Density-Based Algorithm for Discovering Clusters in Large Spatial Databases with Noise." A Density-Based Algorithm for Discovering Clusters in Large Spatial Databases with Noise, 1996, https://file.biolab.si/papers/1996-DBSCAN-KDD.pdf. Accessed 7 January 2024.

ET Auto. "ABB YuMi cobots alleviate workforce shortages for aluminium supplier." ET Auto, 14 November 2023, https://auto.economictimes.indiatimes.com/news/auto-technology/abb-yumi-cobots-alleviate-workforce-shortages-for-aluminium-supplier/105211496. Accessed 27 December 2023.

EU. "Artificial Intelligence Act." EU AI Act, 2023, https://artificialintelligenceact.eu/the-act/. Accessed 26 December 2023.

EU. "General Data Protection Regulation (GDPR) – Official Legal Text." General Data Protection Regulation (GDPR) – Official Legal Text, 2018, https://gdpr-info.eu/. Accessed 26 December 2023.

Fedorov, Nikolaï Fedorovich. What was Man Created For? The Philosophy of the Common Task : Selected Works. Edited by Elisabeth Koutaissoff and Marilyn Minto, translated by Elisabeth Koutaissoff and Marilyn Minto, Honeyglen, 1990.

Ferguson, Anthony. The Sex Doll: A History. McFarland, Incorporated, Publishers, 2010.

Ferrando, Francesca. Philosophical Posthumanism. Edited by Rosi Braidotti, Bloomsbury Academic, 2020.

Finance Sina. "Decoding the National Team in Artificial Intelligence." 解码人工智能"国家队, 2021, https://finance.sina.com.cn/tech/2021-07-10/doc-ikqcfnca5955042.shtml. Accessed 27 December 2023.

Fisher, Adam. Valley of Genius: The Uncensored History of Silicon Valley (As Told by the Hackers, Founders, and Freaks Who Made It Boom). Hachette Audio, 2018.

Fogel, Lawrence J. "Competitive Goal-seeking Through Evolutionary Programming." 1969.

Forbes. "By The Numbers: Who's Refusing Covid Vaccinations—And Why." September 2021.

Forbes. "Say Hello To Asimo." Say Hello To Asimo, 2002, https://www.forbes.com/2002/02/21/0221tentech.html?sh=68315ad3f3eb. Accessed 28 December 2023.

Ford, Martin R. The Lights in the Tunnel: Automation, Accelerating Technology and the Economy of the Future. Acculant Publishing, 2009.

Frantzman, Seth J. Drone Wars: Pioneers, Killing Machines, Artificial Intelligence, and the Battle for the Future. Bombardier Books, 2021. Accessed 28 December 2023.

Fridman, Lex, and Yann LeCun. "Yann LeCun: Dark Matter of Intelligence and Self-Supervised Learning | Lex Fridman Podcast #258." YouTube, 22 January 2022, https://www.youtube.com/watch?v=SGzMEIJ11Cc. Accessed 28 December 2023.

Friedman, Jerome. "Greedy Function Approximation: A Gradient Boosting Machine" (PDF)." 1999.

Frumer, Yulia. "The Short, Strange Life of the First Friendly Robot." The Short, Strange Life of the First Friendly Robot, 2020, https://spectrum.ieee.org/the-short-strange-life-of-the-first-friendly-robot. Accessed 27 December 2023.

Fukuyama, Francis. "Transhumanism – Foreign Policy." Foreign Policy, 23 October 2009, https://foreignpolicy.com/2009/10/23/transhumanism/. Accessed 29 December 2023.

futureoflife. "Pause Giant AI Experiments: An Open Letter." Future of Life Institute, 22 March 2023, https://futureoflife.org/open-letter/pause-giant-ai-experiments/. Accessed 31 December 2023.

Galliah, Shelly. "Robots in the Workplace | Michigan Tech Global Campus News." Michigan Tech Blogs, 14 February 2023, https://blogs.mtu.edu/globalcampus/2023/02/robots-in-the-workplace/. Accessed 27 December 2023.

Garfinkel, Simson, and Zeyi Yang. "The Cloud Imperative." MIT Technology Review, 3 October 2011, https://www.technologyreview.com/2011/10/03/190237/the-cloud-imperative/. Accessed 26 December 2023.

Garland, Alex, director. Ex Machina. 2014.

Gates, Kelly A. "Facial Recognition Technology from the Lab to the Marketplace." 2011.

Geddes, Norman Bel. Magic Motorways. Creative Media Partners, LLC, 2022.

genome.gov. "Human Genomic Variation." National Human Genome Research Institute, 1 February 2023, https://www.genome.gov/about-genomics/educational-resources/fact-sheets/human-genomic-variation. Accessed 29 December 2023.

Gent, Edd. "Quantum Computing's Hard, Cold Reality Check." ieee, 7 November 2023, https://spectrum.ieee.org/quantum-computing-skeptics. Accessed 29 December 2023.

Georgiou, Aristos, et al. "No, the Last Words of NASA's Opportunity Rover Weren't 'My Battery Is Low and It's Getting Dark.'" Newsweek, 18 February 2019, https://www.newsweek.com/nasa-mars-opportunity-rover-new-york-daily-news-jet-propulsion-laboratory-1334615. Accessed 28 December 2023.

Gerencher, Kristen. "Robots as surgical enablers." 2005, https://www.marketwatch.com/story/a-fascinating-visit-to-a-high-tech-operating-room. Accessed 28 December 2023.

Gibbs, Samuel. "Musk, Wozniak and Hawking urge ban on warfare AI and autonomous weapons." The Guardian, 27 July 2015, https://www.theguardian.com/technology/2015/jul/27/musk-wozniak-hawking-ban-ai-autonomous-weapons. Accessed 28 December 2023.

Gibson, DG, et al. "Creation of a bacterial cell controlled by a chemically synthesized genome." 2010.

Gibson, William. Neuromancer. Penguin Publishing Group, 2000.

Gillham, Nicholas W. A Life of Sir Francis Galton: From African Exploration to the Birth of Eugenics. Oxford University Press, 2001.

Gillies, Trent. "Three Square Market CEO explains its employee microchip implant." CNBC, 13 August 2017, https://www.cnbc.com/2017/08/11/three-square-market-ceo-explains-its-employee-microchip-implant.html. Accessed 29 December 2023.

Glaser, April. "Elon Musk wants to connect computers to your brain so we can keep up with robots." Vox, 27 March 2017, https://www.vox.com/2017/3/27/15079226/elon-musk-computers-technology-brain-ai-artificial-intelligence-neural-lace. Accessed 29 December 2023.

Glasser, Zach. "AI Face-Swap App Spawns New Class Action." Lexology, 4 May 2023, https://www.lexology.com/library/detail.aspx?g=b14587ce-7046-4cbf-b2aa-b4d8735ee123. Accessed 26 December 2023.

Glover, Paul, and Richard Bowtell. "MRI rides the wave.,." Nature, 2009, https://www.nature.com/articles/457971a. Accessed 29 December 2023.

Goard, Sølvi. "Making and Getting Made: Towards a Cyborg Transfeminism." Salvage, 8 December 2017, https://salvage.zone/making-and-getting-made-towards-a-cyborg-transfeminism/. Accessed 29 December 2023.

Goertzel, Ben. "OpenCog Foundation | Building better minds together." OpenCog Foundation | Building better minds together, https://opencog.org/. Accessed 28 December 2023.

Goldmacher, Shane. "The 2020 Campaign Is the Most Expensive Ever (By a Lot) (Published 2020)." The New York Times, 28 October 2020, https://www.nytimes.com/2020/10/28/us/politics/2020-race-money.html. Accessed 29 December 2023.

Goldman, Bruce, and Brad Busse. "New imaging method developed at Stanford reveals stunning details of brain connections." Stanford Medicine, 17 November 2010, https://med.stanford.edu/news/all-news/2010/11/new-imaging-method-developed-at-stanford-reveals-stunning-details-of-brain-connections.html?microsite=news&tab=news. Accessed 29 December 2023.

Good, Irving John. "Speculations Concerning the First Ultraintelligent Machine." 30 October 1966, https://www.sciencedirect.com/science/article/abs/pii/S0065245808604180. Accessed 28 December 2023.

Goodfellow, Ian. "Generative Adversarial Nets." Generative Adversarial Nets, 2014. Accessed 26 December 2023.

Google. "Our Approach – How Google Search Works." Google, https://www.google.com/search/howsearchworks/our-approach/. Accessed 30 January 2024.

Gordon, Robert J. The Rise and Fall of American Growth: The U.S. Standard of Living Since the Civil War. Princeton University Press, 2016.

Gosh, Aritra, et al. "Artificial intelligence in accelerating vaccine development - current and future perspectives." 2023, https://www.frontiersin.org/articles/10.3389/fbrio.2023.1258159/full. Accessed 29 December 2023.

Green, Lee. "Legal Rulings on Sports Participation Rights of Transgender Athletes." NFHS, 29 September 2020, https://www.nfhs.org/articles/legal-rulings-on-sports-participation-rights-of-transgender-athletes/. Accessed 29 December 2023.

Grey, W. "A Machine that Learns." Scientific American, 1951, https://www.scientificamerican.com/article/a-machine-that-learns/. Accessed 28 December 2023.

Grover, Lov K. "A fast quantum mechanical algorithm for database search." 1996.

Groys, Boris, editor. Russian Cosmism. E-flux, 2018.

Guinness. "First robot Olympics." Guinness World Records, 27 September 1990, https://www.guinnessworldrecords.com/world-records/first-robot-olympics. Accessed 28 December 2023.

Guizzo, Erico. "Cynthia Breazeal Unveils Jibo, a Social Robot for the Home." Cynthia Breazeal Unveils Jibo, a Social Robot for the Home, 2014, https://spectrum.ieee.org/cynthia-breazeal-unveils-jibo-a-social-robot-for-the-home. Accessed 29 December 2023.

Guizzo, Erico. "Kiva Systems: Three Engineers, Hundreds of Robots, One Warehouse." Kiva Systems: Three Engineers, Hundreds of Robots, One Warehouse, IEEE Spectrum, 2008, https://spectrum.ieee.org/three-engineers-hundreds-of-robots-one-warehouse. Accessed 28 December 2023.

Haarmann, Claudia, et al. "Making the difference! The BIG in Namibia." 2009. Accessed 30 January 2024.

Haddad, Michel, et al. "Improved Early Survival with the Total Artificial Heart." 2004.

Haden, Jeff. "Research Reveals How Many Likes It Takes for Facebook to Know You Better Than Anyone (Even Your Spouse)." Inc. Magazine, 11 March 2021, https://www.inc.com/jeff-haden/research-reveals-how-many-likes-it-takes-for-facebook-to-know-you-better-than-your-spouse.html. Accessed 13 February 2024.

Hamilton, John. The Space Race: The Thrilling History of NASA's Race to the Moon, from Project Mercury to Apollo 11 and Beyond. RavenFire Media, Incorporated, 2022. Accessed 28 December 2023.

Hamzah, Aqil. "From robot dogs to special drones, SAF tests unmanned platforms in US exercise." The Straits Times, 25 September 2023, https://www.straitstimes.com/singapore/from-robot-dogs-to-micro-drones-saf-tests-unmanned-platforms-in-us-exercise. Accessed 28 December 2023.

Hand, Sophie. "A Brief History of Collaborative Robots." Material Handling and Logistics, 26 February 2020, https://www.mhlnews.com/technology-automation/article/21124077/a-brief-history-of-collaborative-robots. Accessed 27 December 2023.

Hanson, Robin. The Age of Em: Work, Love, and Life when Robots Rule the Earth. Oxford University Press, 2018.

Harari, Yuval Noah. Homo Deus: A Brief History of Tomorrow. Translated by Yuval Noah Harari, HarperCollins, 2017.

Haraway, Donna. "A Cyborg Manifesto." Socialist Review (US), 1985.

Harbisson, Neil. "I listen to color | TED Talk." TED Talks, 20 July 2012, https://www.ted.com/talks/neil_harbisson_i_listen_to_color?language=en. Accessed 29 December 2023.

Harbou, Thea von. Metropolis. Dover Publications, 2015.

Harrow, Aram, et al. "Quantum algorithm for linear systems of equations." hysical Review Letters., 2008.

Hart, Peter, et al. "A Formal Basis for the Heuristic Determination of Minimum Cost Paths." IEEE Transactions on Systems Science and Cybernetics, 1968.

Hattem, Julian. "AT&T used broad data-gathering system for federal government." Wikipedia, 2016, https://thehill.com/policy/national-security/302644-att-used-broad-data-gathering-system-for-us-government/. Accessed 30 January 2024.

Hawking, Stephen. Brief Answers to the Big Questions. Random House Publishing Group, 2018.

He, Yujia, and Anne Bowser. "How China is preparing for an AI-powered Future." Wilson Center, 6 2017, https://www.wilsoncenter.org/sites/default/files/media/documents/publication/how_china_is_preparing_for_ai_powered_future.pdf. Accessed 26 December 2023.

Heinlein, Robert A. Stranger in a Strange Land. Penguin Publishing Group, 2018.

Helou, Agnes, and Barry Rosenberg. "With Turkish drones in the headlines, what happened to Ukraine's Bayraktar TB2s?" Breaking Defense, 6 October 2023, https://breakingdefense.com/2023/10/with-turkish-drones-in-the-headlines-what-happened-to-ukraines-bayraktar-tb2s/. Accessed 28 December 2023.

Hemal, Ashok K., and Mani Menon, editors. Robotics in Genitourinary Surgery. Springer International Publishing, 2018. Accessed 27 December 2023.

Hemingway, Ernest, and Seán A. Hemingway. The Sun Also Rises: The Hemingway Library Edition. Edited by Seán A. Hemingway, Scribner, 1926.

Hempel, Jessi. "How Fei-Fei Li Will Make Artificial Intelligence Better for Humanity." WIRED, 13 November 2018, https://www.wired.com/story/fei-fei-li-artificial-intelligence-humanity/. Accessed 26 December 2023.

Henshall, Will. "Elon Musk Says AI Will Eliminate the Need for Jobs." Time, 2 November 2023, https://time.com/6331056/rishi-sunak-elon-musk-ai/. Accessed 28 December 2023.

Herbert, Frank. Dune, 40th Anniversary Edition (Dune Chronicles, Book 1). Penguin Publishing Group, 2005.

Herbert, Frank. Dune, 40th Anniversary Edition (Dune Chronicles, Book 1). Penguin Publishing Group, 2005.

Herculano-Houzel, Suzana. "The human brain in numbers: a linearly scaled-up primate brain." Frontiers in Human Neuroscience, no. 2009.

Hetzner, Christiaan. "Omar Al Olama, world's first AI minister, says the technology could change the world like the printing press." Fortune, 28 November 2023, https://fortune.com/asia/2023/11/28/artificial-intelligence-ai-technology-regulation-policy-guardrails-uae-fortune-global-forum/. Accessed 28 December 2023.

Hinton, Geoffrey, and David Rumelhart. "Learning representations by back-propagating errors." Nature, Nature.

"The HiPEAC Vision 2019 - Inria - Institut national de recherche en sciences et technologies du numérique." Hal-Inria, 10 November 2019, https://inria.hal.science/hal-02314184. Accessed 12 February 2024.

Ho, Tin Kam. "A theory of multiple classifier systems and its application to visual word recognition.,." A theory of multiple classifier systems and its application to visual word recognition, 1992, https://dl.acm.org/doi/book/10.5555/142930.

Hobbes, Thomas. Leviathan. Edited by Christopher Brooke, Penguin Publishing Group, 2017.

Hochreiter, Sepp, and Jürgen Schmidhuber. "Long Short-Term memory." Neural Computation, 1997.

Holley, Peter. "Amazon's autonomous robots have started delivering packages in a new location: Southern California." Washington Post, 12 August 2019, https://www.washingtonpost.com/technology/2019/08/12/amazons-autonomous-robots-have-started-delivering-packages-new-location-southern-california/. Accessed 28 December 2023.

Holpuch, Amanda. "Why Countries Are Trying to Ban TikTok." The New York Times, 12 December 2023, https://www.nytimes.com/article/tiktok-ban.html. Accessed 31 January 2024.

Holusha, John. "JAPANESE ART OF AUTOMATION." The New York Times, 28 March 1983, https://www.nytimes.com/1983/03/28/business/japanese-art-of-automation.html. Accessed 28 December 2023.

Hong, N. "3D bioprinting and its in vivo applications." Journal of Biomedical Materials Research, 2018.

Honnecourt, Villard. The Sketchbook of Villard de Honnecourt. Indiana University Press, 1968.

Hopfield, John. "Neurons with graded response have collective computational properties like those of two-state neurons." Proceedings of the National Academy of Sciences of the United States of America.

Hornyak, Timothy N. Loving the Machine: The Art and Science of Japanese Robots. Kodansha International, 2006.

Horsley, Jamie. "China's Orwellian Social Credit Score Isn't Real." Foreign Policy, 16 November 2018, https://foreignpolicy.com/2018/11/16/chinas-orwellian-social-credit-score-isnt-real/. Accessed 27 December 2023.

Howley, Daniel. "We're one step closer to robot butlers doing our dishes." We're one step closer to robot butlers doing our dishes, 2016, https://finance.yahoo.com/news/spotmini-boston-dynamics-robot-butler-174614581.html. Accessed 28 December 2023.

Hu, Krystal. "ChatGPT sets record for fastest-growing user base - analyst note." Reuters, 2 February 2023, https://www.reuters.com/technology/chatgpt-sets-record-fastest-growing-user-base-analyst-note-2023-02-01/. Accessed 26 December 2023.

Huebner, Jonathan. "A Possible Declining Trend for Worldwide Innovation." 2015.

Hugues, James. "Citizen Cyborg: Why Democratic Societies Must Respond To The Redesigned Human Of The Future." 2004.

Hull, Clark Leonard, et al. Mechanisms of Adaptive Behavior: Clark L. Hull's Theoretical Papers, with Commentary. Edited by Abram Amsel and Michael E. Rashotte, Columbia University Press, 1984.

Hume, David. A Treatise of Human Nature. Edited by Ernest C. Mossner, Penguin Publishing Group, 1984.

Hussein, Mohammed. "Visualising the race to build the world's fastest supercomputers." Al Jazeera, 14 January 2022, https://www.aljazeera.com/news/2022/1/14/infographic-visualising-race-build-world-fastest-supercomputers-interactive. Accessed 1 January 2024.

IBM. "IBM 700 Series." IBM, https://www.ibm.com/history/700. Accessed 26 December 2023.

IBM. "IBM Archives: 7090 Data Processing System." IBM, https://www.ibm.com/ibm/history/exhibits/mainframe/mainframe_PP7090.html. Accessed 26 December 2023.

IFR. "Robot Density nearly Doubled globally." International Federation of Robotics, 14 December 2021, https://ifr.org/ifr-press-releases/news/robot-density-nearly-doubled-globally. Accessed 29 December 2023.

Inglis, Esther. "The very first robot "brains" were made of old alarm clocks." Gizmodo, 7 March 2012, https://gizmodo.com/the-very-first-robot-brains-were-made-of-old-alarm-cl-5890771. Accessed 27 December 2023.

Intel. "The Story of the Intel® 4004." Intel, https://www.intel.com/content/www/us/en/history/museum-story-of-intel-4004.html. Accessed 26 December 2023.

Ivan, Zamesin. Clubhouse Elon Musk interview transcript. 2021.

Japan. "The income doubling plan and the growing Japanese economy." Ministry of Foreign Affairs, Japan, 1961.

John, Rohit Abraham, et al. "Self healable neuromorphic memtransistor elements for decentralized sensory signal processing in robotics." Nature Communications, 2020, https://www.nature.com/articles/s41467-020-17870-6. Accessed 28 December 2023.

Jonze, Spike, director. Her. 2013.

Jozuka, Emiko. "The Sad Story of Eric, the UK's First Robot Who Was Loved Then Forsaken." VICE, 19 May 2016, https://www.vice.com/en/article/pgkkpm/the-sad-story-of-eric-the-uks-first-robot-who-was-loved-then-forsaken. Accessed 27 December 2023.

Kak, Subhash. On quantum neural computing". Advances in Imaging and Electron Physics. 1995.

Kaku, Michio. "By Midcentury, We May Have Brain 2.0." Afflictor.com, 7 March 2014, https://afflictor.com/2014/03/07/by-midcentury-we-may-have-brain-2-0/. Accessed 28 December 2023.

Kaneko, Kenji, and Hiroshi Kaminaga. "Humanoid Robot HRP-5P: An Electrically Actuated Humanoid Robot With High-Power and Wide-Range Joints." Humanoid Robot HRP-5P: An Electrically Actuated Humanoid Robot With High-Power and Wide-Range Joints, 2019, https://ieeexplore.ieee.org/document/8630006. Accessed 28 December 2023.

Kania, Elsa B., and Paul Scharre. "Battlefield Singularity." Center for a New American Security, 28 November 2017, https://www.cnas.org/publications/reports/battlefield-singularity-artificial-intelligence-military-revolution-and-chinas-future-military-power. Accessed 27 December 2023.

Kasparov, Garri Kimovich, and Mig Greengard. Deep Thinking: Where Machine Intelligence Ends and Human Creativity Begins. PublicAffairs, 2017.

Kato, Ichiro. "The robot musician 'wabot-2' (waseda robot-2)." 1987.

Kato, Ikunishin. "Information-power machine with senses and limbs (Wabot 1)." 1974.

Kawasaki. "History of Kawasaki Robotics | Industrial Robots by Kawasaki Robotics." Kawasaki Robotics, Kawasaki, 2019, https://kawasakirobotics.com/eu-africa/company/history/. Accessed 28 December 2023.

Keranen, Rachel. Inventions in Computing: From the Abacus to Personal Computers. Cavendish Square Publishing, 2016.

Kingma, Diederik P., and Max Welling. "Auto-Encoding Variational Bayes." arXiv, 20 December 2013, https://arxiv.org/abs/1312.6114. Accessed 26 December 2023.

Kissinger, Henry. "Dr Henry Kissinger on the Potential Dangers of Artificial Intelligence." Home, 2023, https://www.youtube.com/shorts/nE85oKtA5Ic. Accessed 3 January 2024.

Klayman, Ben, and Stephen Nellis. "Trump's China tech war backfires on automakers as chips run short." Reuters, 14 January 2021, https://www.reuters.com/article/us-autos-tech-chips-focus-idUSKBN29K0GA. Accessed 27 December 2023.

Knight, Will. "Amazon's New Robots Are Rolling Out an Automation Revolution." WIRED, 26 June 2023, https://www.wired.com/story/amazons-new-robots-automation-revolution/. Accessed 28 December 2023.

Knight, Will. "These Clues Hint at the True Nature of OpenAI's Shadowy Q* Project." WIRED, 30 November 2023, https://www.wired.com/story/fast-forward-clues-hint-openai-shadowy-q-project/. Accessed 29 December 2023.

Knight, Will. "This Robot Could Transform Manufacturing." MIT Technology Review, 18 September 2012, https://www.technologyreview.com/2012/09/18/183759/this-robot-could-transform-manufacturing/. Accessed 27 December 2023.

Kobie, Nicole. "The complicated truth about China's social credit system." Wired UK, 7 June 2019, https://www.wired.co.uk/article/china-social-credit-system-explained. Accessed 27 December 2023.

Koder, Ronald L., and J. L. Ross Anderson. "Design and engineering of an O(2) transport protein." NCBI, 2013, https://www.ncbi.nlm.nih.gov/pmc/articles/PMC3539743/. Accessed 30 December 2023.

Koty, Alexander Chipman. "Artificial Intelligence in China: Shenzhen Releases First Local Regulations." China Briefing, 29 July 2021, https://www.china-briefing.com/news/artificial-intelligence-china-shenzhen-first-local-ai-regulations-key-areas-coverage/. Accessed 27 December 2023.

Krizhevsky, Alex, et al. "ImageNet Classification with Deep Convolutional Neural Networks." Communications of the ACM., 2017.

Künsken, Derek. The Quantum Magician. Solaris, 2018.

Kurzweil, Ray. The Age of Spiritual Machines: When Computers Exceed Human Intelligence. Penguin Publishing Group, 2000.

Kurzweil, Ray. The Singularity Is Nearer: When We Merge with Computers. Penguin Publishing Group, 2005.

Kwoh, YS, et al. "A robot with improved absolute positioning accuracy for CT guided stereotactic brain surgery." IEEE Transactions on Bio-Medical Engineering, 1988.

LaGrandeur, Kevin. Androids and Intelligent Networks in Early Modern Literature and Culture: Artificial Slaves. Routledge, 2013.

Landymore, Frank. "Godfather of AI Tells Us to Stop Freaking Out Over Its "Existential Risk" To Humanity." Futurism, 19 October 2023, https://futurism.com/the-byte/godfather-ai-stop-freaking-out. Accessed 29 December 2023.

Lang, Fritz, director. Metropolis. 1927. 1927.

LaPonsie, Maryalene. "What Is Universal Basic Income?" US News Money, 1 March 2022, https://money.usnews.com/money/personal-finance/articles/what-is-universal-basic-income. Accessed 29 December 2023.

Lasker. "DeBakey Clinical Medical Research Award: Modern cochlear implant." The Lasker Foundation, 2017.

LeCun, Yann. "Comparison of learning algorithms for handwritten digit recognition."

LeCun, Yann. "Post on LinkedIn." 30 October 2023, https://www.linkedin.com/posts/yann-lecun_animals-and-humans-get-very-smart-very-quickly-activity-7133567569684238336-szrF/. Accessed 28 December 2023.

Ledsom, Alex. "What Leonardo Da Vinci's Roaring Lion In Paris Has To Say About The World Today." Forbes, 29 September 2019, https://www.forbes.com/sites/alexledsom/2019/09/29/what-leonardo-da-vincis-roaring-lion-in-paris-has-to-say-about-the-world-today. Accessed 27 December 2023.

Lee, Daniel D. Jensen Huang's Nvidia: Processing the Mind of Artificial Intelligence. 2023.

Leibniz, Gottfried. The Monadology. CreateSpace Independent Publishing Platform, 2017.

Levine, Robert, and Ray Kurzweil. "Playboy | the New Human « the Kurzweil Library + collections." Ray Kurzweil, 2006, https://www.thekurzweillibrary.com/playboy-the-new-human. Accessed 28 December 2023.

Lewis, Gideon. "Check In With the Velociraptor at the World's First Robot Hotel." WIRED, 2 March 2016, https://www.wired.com/2016/03/robot-henn-na-hotel-japan/. Accessed 28 December 2023.

Li, Fei-Fei, et al. "ImageNet Large Scale Visual Recognition Challenge." ImageNet Large Scale Visual Recognition Challenge, https://link.springer.com/article/10.1007/s11263-015-0816-y. Accessed 28 December 2023.

Lien, Tracey. "AlphaGo beats human Go champ in milestone for artificial intelligence." Los Angeles Times, 12 March 2016, https://www.latimes.com/world/asia/la-fg-korea-alphago-20160312-story.html. Accessed 26 December 2023.

Liezi, th Cent B. C., and A. C. (Angus Charles) Tr Graham, editors. The Book of Lieh-tzu. Creative Media Partners, LLC, 2021.

Lightman, Hunter, et al. "Let's Verify Step by Step." arXiv, 31 May 2023, https://arxiv.org/abs/2305.20050. Accessed 29 December 2023.

Lin, Tsung-Yi, and Hong-Sen Yan. "A study on ancient Chinese time laws and the time-telling system of Su Song's clock tower." 2002, https://www.sciencedirect.com/science/article/abs/pii/S0094114X01000593. Accessed 27 December 2023.

Linder, J., et al. "A generative neural network for maximizing fitness and diversity of synthetic DNA and protein sequences." 2020.

Linnainmaa, Seppo. "The representation of the cumulative rounding error of an algorithm as a Taylor expansion of the local rounding errors." 1970.

Lloyd, Seth, et al. "Quantum principal component analysis." Nature, 2014, https://www.nature.com/articles/nphys3029. Accessed 29 December 2023.

Lohr, Steve. "A $1 Million Research Bargain for Netflix, and Maybe a Model for Others (Published 2009)." The New York Times, 21 September 2009, https://www.nytimes.com/2009/09/22/technology/internet/22netflix.html. Accessed 26 December 2023.

Lowensohn, Josh. "Google buys Boston Dynamics, maker of spectacular and terrifying robots." The Verge, 13 December 2013, https://www.theverge.com/2013/12/14/5209622/google-has-bought-robotics-company-boston-dynamics. Accessed 26 December 2023.

Lu, Marcus, and Niccolo Conte. "Ranked: Government Debt by Country, in Advanced Economies." Visual Capitalist, 11 December 2023, https://www.visualcapitalist.com/government-debt-by-country-advanced-economies/. Accessed 6 February 2024.

Macdonald, Fiona, and Gustav Klutsis. "The early Soviet images that foreshadowed fake news." BBC, 10 November 2017, https://www.bbc.com/culture/article/20171110-the-early-soviet-images-that-foreshadowed-fake-news. Accessed 10 February 2024.

Mackintosh, Phil, and Dillon Jaghory. "Japan's Robot Dominance." Nasdaq, 16 May 2022, https://www.nasdaq.com/articles/japans-robot-dominance. Accessed 28 December 2023.

Majors, Lee, creator. The Six Million Dollar Man. ABC, 1973-78.

Makin, Joseph G, et al. "Machine translation of cortical activity to text with an encoder–decoder framework." NCBI, 30 March 2020, https://www.ncbi.nlm.nih.gov/pmc/articles/PMC10560395/. Accessed 29 December 2023.

Malyshev, DA, et al. "A semi-synthetic organism with an expanded genetic alphabet."" Nature, 2014.

Manning, Rob, and William L. Simon. Mars Rover Curiosity: An Inside Account from Curiosity's Chief Engineer. Smithsonian, 2017.

Mansour, Salem, et al. "Efficacy of Brain–Computer Interface and the Impact of Its Design Characteristics on Poststroke Upper-limb Rehabilitation: A Systematic Review and Meta-analysis of Randomized Controlled Trials." NCBI, 2021, https://www.ncbi.nlm.nih.gov/pmc/articles/PMC8619716/. Accessed 29 December 2023.

Marboy, Steven. NASA Mars Rover Perseverance: Mars 2020. Independently Published, 2020. Accessed 28 December 2023.

Marinescu, Ioana, and Heikki Hiilamo. "Why Alaska's Experience Shows Promise for Universal Basic Income." Knowledge at Wharton, 10 May 2018, https://knowledge.wharton.upenn.edu/podcast/knowledge-at-wharton-podcast/alaskas-experience-shows-promise-universal-basic-income/. Accessed 30 January 2024.

Markoff, John. "Behind Artificial Intelligence, a Squadron of Bright Real People (Published 2005)." The New York Times, 14 October 2005, https://www.nytimes.com/2005/10/14/technology/behind-artificial-intelligence-a-squadron-of-bright-real-people.html. Accessed 26 December 2023.

Markoff, John. "Crashes and Traffic Jams in Military Test of Robotic Vehicles (Published 2007)." The New York Times, 5 November 2007, https://www.nytimes.com/2007/11/05/technology/05robot.html. Accessed 28 December 2023.

Markoff, John. "In a Big Network of Computers, Evidence of Machine Learning." The New York Times, 25 June 2012, https://www.nytimes.com/2012/06/26/technology/in-a-big-network-of-computers-evidence-of-machine-learning.html?pagewanted=all. Accessed 26 December 2023.

Martin, Goerge M. "Brief proposal on immortality: an interim solution." Perspectives in Biology and Medicine., 1971.

Masamune, Shirow. The Ghost in the Shell: Fully Compiled (Complete Hardcover Collection). Kodansha Comics, 2023.

Maslow, Abraham. "A theory of human motivation." Psychological Review,, 1943.

Mason, Cindy. "(PDF) Giving Robots Compassion, C. Mason, Conference on Science and Compassion, Poster Session, Telluride, Colorado, 2012." ResearchGate, 2012, https://www.researchgate.net/publication/260230014_Giving_Robots_Compassion_C_Mason_Conference_on_Science_and_Compassion_Poster_Session_Telluride_Colorado_2012. Accessed 28 December 2023.

Matsakis, Louise. "How the West Got China's Social Credit System Wrong." WIRED, 29 July 2019, https://www.wired.com/story/china-social-credit-score-system/. Accessed 27 December 2023.

Mayor, Adrienne. Gods and Robots: Myths, Machines, and Ancient Dreams of Technology. Princeton University Press, 2020.

McCarthy, John, et al. A PROPOSAL FOR THE DARTMOUTH SUMMER RESEARCH PROJECT ON ARTIFICIAL INTELLIGENCE. 1955.

McCorduck, Pamela. Machines Who Think: A Personal Inquiry Into the History and Prospects of Artificial Intelligence. Taylor & Francis, 2004.

McCulloch, Warren, and Walter Pitts. "A logical calculus of the ideas immanent in nervous activity." The bulletin of mathematical biophysics, 1945.

McElhinney, David. "Why money will not be enough to address Japan's baby crisis." Al Jazeera, 28 February 2023, https://www.aljazeera.com/news/2023/2/28/why-money-will-not-be-enough-to-address-japans-demographic-crisis. Accessed 28 December 2023.

McKinsey. "Modeling the global economic impact of AI." McKinsey, 4 September 2018, https://www.mckinsey.com/featured-insights/artificial-intelligence/notes-from-the-ai-frontier-modeling-the-impact-of-ai-on-the-world-economy. Accessed 29 December 2023.

Mesopotamian. The Epic of Gilgamesh. Penguin Classics, 1960.

Meyer, David. "U.S. Urges Other Countries to Shun Huawei, Citing Espionage Risk." Fortune, 23 November 2018, https://fortune.com/2018/11/23/us-huawei-espionage/. Accessed 27 December 2023.

"Microsoft-affiliated research finds flaws in GPT-4." TechCrunch, 17 October 2023, https://techcrunch.com/2023/10/17/microsoft-affiliated-research-finds-flaws-in-gtp-4/. Accessed 12 February 2024.

Mikolov, Tomas, and Kai Chen. "Efficient Estimation of Word Representations in Vector Space." Efficient Estimation of Word Representations in Vector Space, 16 January 2013. Accessed 26 December 2023.

Mims, Christopher. "Self-Driving Cars Could Be Decades Away, No Matter What Elon Musk Said." The Wall Street Journal, 5 June 2021, https://www.wsj.com/articles/self-driving-cars-could-be-decades-away-no-matter-what-elon-musk-said-11622865615. Accessed 13 February 2024.

Modis, Theodore. "Forecasting the Growth of Complexity and Change." 2002.

Moor, James, editor. The Turing Test: The Elusive Standard of Artificial Intelligence. Springer Netherlands, 2003.

Moore, Gordon E. "Cramming more components onto integrated circuits." 1965.

Moran, Michael E. "The." The da Vinci Robot, 2007, https://www.liebertpub.com/doi/10.1089/end.2006.20.986. Accessed 27 December 2023.

Moravec, Hans. "Caution! Robot vehicle!" Caution! Robot vehicle!, 1991, https://dl.acm.org/doi/10.5555/132218.132237. Accessed 27 December 2023.

Moravec, Hans. Mind Children: The Future of Robot and Human Intelligence. Harvard University Press, 1988.

Moravec, Hans. "Obstacle avoidance and navigation in the real world by a seeing robot rover." PHD, 1980.

Moravec, Hans. "Today's Computers, Intelligent Machines, and Our Future." 1979.

Moravec, Hans P. Robot: Mere Machine to Transcendent Mind. Oxford University Press, 1999.

More, Max. Comments on Vinge's Singularity, 2014, https://mason.gmu.edu/~rhanson/vc.html#more. Accessed 29 December 2023.

More, Thomas. Utopia. Translated by Paul Turner, Penguin Publishing Group, 2003.

Morgan, Richard K. Altered Carbon. Del Rey, 2003.

Mori, Masahiro. The Buddha in the Robot. Kosei Publishing Company, 1981.

Mori, Masahiro. "The Uncanny Valley." 1970, https://spectrum.ieee.org/the-uncanny-valley. Accessed 28 December 2023.

Mortimer, John, and Brian Rooks. "The International Robot Industry Report." 1987, https://link.springer.com/book/10.1007/978-3-662-13174-9. Accessed 28 December 2023.

Mosco, Vincent. To the Cloud: Big Data in a Turbulent World. Taylor & Francis, 2015.

Motoda, Hiroshi. "The current status of expert system development and related technologies in Japa." Hitachi, 1990, https://ieeexplore.ieee.org/document/58016. Accessed 28 December 2023.

"Mueller finds no collusion with Russia, leaves obstruction question open." American Bar Association, 2019, https://www.americanbar.org/news/abanews/aba-news-archives/2019/03/mueller-concludes-investigation/.

Mumtaz, Sandeeb. "Electroencephalogram (EEG)-based computer-aided technique to diagnose major depressive disorder (MDD)." Biomedical Signal Processing and Control, 2017, https://www.sciencedirect.com/science/article/abs/pii/S1746809416300866. Accessed 2 February 2024.

Murakami, Kazuo, translator. 機巧図彙. Murakami Kazuo, 2012.

Murray, Chuck. "Re-wiring the Body." 2005.

Murre, Jaap M. J. "Replication and Analysis of Ebbinghaus' Forgetting Curve." PLOS, 2015, https://journals.plos.org/plosone/article?id=10.1371/journal.pone.0120644. Accessed 6 February 2024.

Musk, Elon, and Alex Medina. Elon Musk on X: "This is nothing. In a few years, that bot will move so fast you'll need a strobe light to see it. Sweet dreams… https://t.co/0MYNixQXMw", 26 November 2017, https://twitter.com/elonmusk/status/934888089058549760? Accessed 28 December 2023.

Muzyka, Kamil. "The Outline of Personhood Law Regarding Artificial Intelligences and Emulated Human Entities." Sciendo, 23 November 2011, https://sciendo.com/article/10.2478/jagi-2013-0010. Accessed 29 December 2023.

Myre, Greg. "China Wants Your Data — And May Already Have It." NPR, 24 February 2021, https://www.npr.org/2021/02/24/969532277/china-wants-your-data-and-may-already-have-it. Accessed 31 January 2024.

Nagata, Kazuaki. "SoftBank unveils 'historic' robot." The Japan Times, 5 June 2014, https://www.japantimes.co.jp/news/2014/06/05/business/corporate-business/softbank-unveils-pepper-worlds-first-robot-reads-emotions/#.U5hbI_m1ZbU. Accessed 28 December 2023.

Nahin, Paul J. The Logician and the Engineer: How George Boole and Claude Shannon Created the Information Age. Princeton University Press, 2017.

NASA. "NASA's Dragonfly Will Fly Around Titan Looking for Origins, Signs of Life." NASA, 27 June 2019, https://www.nasa.gov/news-release/nasas-dragonfly-will-fly-around-titan-looking-for-origins-signs-of-life/. Accessed 28 December 2023.

NASA. "OSIRIS-REx." NASA Science, https://science.nasa.gov/mission/osiris-rex/. Accessed 28 December 2023.

NASA. "OSIRIS-REx." NASA Science, https://science.nasa.gov/mission/osiris-rex/. Accessed 28 December 2023.

NASA. "Regolith Advanced Surface Systems Operations Robot (RASSOR)." NASA 3D Resources, 9 June 2021, https://nasa3d.arc.nasa.gov/detail/RASSOR. Accessed 28 December 2023.

NASA. "Robonaut2." NASA, 26 September 2023, https://www.nasa.gov/robonaut2/. Accessed 28 December 2023.

NASA. "SPHERES International Space Station National Laboratory Facility – Synchronized Position Hold, Engage, Reorient, Experimental." NASA, https://www.nasa.gov/wp-content/uploads/2017/12/spheres_fact_sheet-508-7may2015.pdf. Accessed 28 December 2023.

NASA. "Viking 1 & 2 | Missions – NASA Mars Exploration." NASA Mars Exploration, https://mars.nasa.gov/mars-exploration/missions/viking-1-2/. Accessed 28 December 2023.

Nature. "Tercentenary of the Calculating Machine." no. 150, 1942, https://www.nature.com/articles/150427a0#preview.

Neeley, Brian. "China is building the best firewall for the AI age." Business News, 26 December 2023, https://biz.crast.net/china-is-building-the-best-firewall-for-the-ai-age/. Accessed 27 December 2023.

Neuman, John Von. First Draft of a Report on the EDVAC. Creative Media Partners, LLC, 2021.

Neuralink. "Neuralink Annoucement on X." X.com, 25 May 2023, https://twitter.com/neuralink/status/1661857379460468736. Accessed 29 December 2023.

Newell, Allen, and Herbert Simon. "Computer Science as Empirical Inquiry: Symbols and Search." 1976.

Newitz, Annalee. Autonomous. Translated by Alexander Páez, Minotauro, 2019.

Newquist, Harvey P. The Brain Makers. Sams Pub., 1994.

Newsflare. "Seven places where robots serve customers in Bangkok, Thailand." Newsflare, 13 May 2023, https://www.newsflare.com/video/562164/seven-places-where-robots-serve-customers-in-bangkok-thailand. Accessed 6 February 2024.

New York Times. "BUSINESS TECHNOLOGY; What's the Best Answer? It's Survival of the Fittest (Published 1990)." The New York Times, 29 August 1990, https://www.nytimes.com/1990/08/29/business/business-technology-what-s-the-best-answer-it-s-survival-of-the-fittest.html?scp=1&sq=axcelis%20evolver&st=cse/. Accessed 26 December 2023.

Ni, Vincent. "China denounces US Senate's $250bn move to boost tech and manufacturing." The Guardian, 8 June 2021, https://www.theguardian.com/us-news/2021/jun/09/us-senate-approves-50bn-boost-for-computer-chip-and-ai-technology-to-counter-china. Accessed 29 January 2024.

Niccol, Andrew, director. Gattace. 1997.

Nielsen, AA. "Genetic circuit design automation." 2016.

Nikkey. "Japan's senior-care providers seek more foreign trainees." Nikkei Asia, 11 January 2017, https://asia.nikkei.com/Business/Japan-s-senior-care-providers-seek-more-foreign-trainees. Accessed 28 December 2023.

Nilsson, Nils J. The Quest for Artificial Intelligence. Cambridge University Press, 2010.

Nishida, Toyoaki. "The Best of AI in Japan — Prologue." 2012.

Nof, Shimon Y., editor. Handbook of Industrial Robotics. Wiley, 1999.

Nolan, Beatrice. "Sam Altman Keeps Talking About AGI Replacing the 'Median Human.'" Business Insider, 27 September 2023, https://www.businessinsider.com/sam-altman-thinks-agi-replaces-median-humans-2023-9. Accessed 28 December 2023.

NTT DATA. "More Than 80% of Financial Institutions Believe AI is the Key Competitive Driver to Success NTT DATA Study Reveals." NTT DATA, 21 April 2021, https://mx.nttdata.com/es/news/press-release/2021/april/financial-institutions-believe-ai-is-key. Accessed 29 December 2023.

Nurk, Sergey, et al. "The complete sequence of a human genome." https://www.science.org/doi/10.1126/science.abj6987, 2022.

Nye, Greg. "China Wants Your Data." NPR, 9 November 2017, https://www.ktep.org/world-news/2021-02-24/china-wants-your-data-and-may-already-have-it. Accessed 13 February 2024.

Obringer, Lee Ann, and Jonathan Strickland. "How ASIMO Works | HowStuffWorks." Science | HowStuffWorks, 2007, https://science.howstuffworks.com/asimo.htm#pt1. Accessed 28 December 2023.

Ohnsman, Alan. "At $1.1 Billion Google's Self-Driving Car Moonshot Looks Like A Bargain." Forbes, 15 September 2017, https://www.forbes.com/sites/alanohnsman/2017/09/15/at-1-1-billion-googles-self-driving-car-moonshot-looks-like-a-bargain/. Accessed 28 December 2023.

Okonedo, Sophie, et al. "Alien Worlds (TV Series 2020)." IMDb, 2020, https://www.imdb.com/title/tt13464340/. Accessed 28 December 2023.

Olcott, Eleanor, and Wenjie Ding. "China struggles to control data sales as companies shun official exchanges." Financial Times, 27 December 2023, https://www.ft.com/content/eab7c43a-e4a0-464b-a5d4-d71526dd2e8b. Accessed 27 December 2023.

Opie, N. "The StentrodeTM Neural Interface System."" Brain-Computer Interface Research., 2021.

Oremus, Will. DeepFace: Facebook face-recognition software is 97 percent accurate., 18 March 2014, https://slate.com/technology/2014/03/deepface-facebook-face-recognition-software-is-97-percent-accurate.html. Accessed 26 December 2023.

Ourworldindata. "GDP per capita: Argentina, France, Germany, UK ." 9 October 2021, https://ourworldindata.org/grapher/gdp-per-capita-maddison?tab=chart&time=1602..1948&country=ARG~FRA~DEU~GBR. Accessed 29 December 2023.

Overbye, Dennis. "Reaching for the Stars, Across 4.37 Light-Years." The New York Times, 12 April 2016, https://www.nytimes.com/2016/04/13/science/alpha-centauri-breakthrough-starshot-yuri-milner-stephen-hawking.html. Accessed 30 December 2023.

Ownify. "Fractional ownership explained." Ownify, https://ownify.com/fractional-ownership-explained. Accessed 6 February 2024.

Page, Larry, and Sergey Brin. "The anatomy of a large-scale hypertextual Web search engine." Computer Networks and Isdn Systems,, 1998.

Pandi, A., et al. "Metabolic perceptrons for neural computing in biological systems."" Nature Communications., 2019.

Park, Ed Sjc. EGo: A Dot-com Bubble Story. Lulu.com, 2012.

Pearson, Karl. "On Lines and Planes of Closest Fit to Systems of Points in Space." 1901.

Pennington, Jeffrey,, and Richard Socher. "GloVe: Global Vectors for Word Representation." Stanford NLP Group, 2014, https://nlp.stanford.edu/pubs/glove.pdf. Accessed 26 December 2023.

Pereira, Anthony W. ""Bolsa Família" and democracy in Brazil." Third World Quarterly, 2015, https://www.jstor.org/stable/24523144. Accessed 30 January 2024.

Perov, Ivan. "DeepFaceLab: Integrated, flexible and extensible face-swapping framework." arXiv, 12 May 2020, https://arxiv.org/abs/2005.05535. Accessed 26 December 2023.

Peshkin, Michael A., and James E. Colgate. "US Patent US5952796A - Cobots." Google Patents, 1997, https://patents.google.com/patent/US5952796. Accessed 27 December 2023.

Peters, Jay, and Alex Castro. "The New York Times blocks OpenAI's web crawler." The Verge, 21 August 2023, https://www.theverge.com/2023/8/21/23840705/new-york-times-openai-web-crawler-ai-gpt. Accessed 26 December 2023.

Pew. "Political Polarization in the American Public." Pew Research Center, 12 June 2014, https://www.pewresearch.org/politics/2014/06/12/political-polarization-in-the-american-public/. Accessed 29 December 2023.

Pew. "Public Trust in Government: 1958-2023." Pew Research Center, 19 September 2023, https://www.pewresearch.org/politics/2023/09/19/public-trust-in-government-1958-2023/. Accessed 29 December 2023.

Pieke, Frank N., and Bert Hofman, editors. CPC Futures: The New Era of Socialism with Chinese Characteristics. National University of Singapore Press, 2022.

Pinker, Steven. "Tech Luminaries Address Singularity." https://spectrum.ieee.org/, 2008, https://spectrum.ieee.org/tech-luminaries-address-singularity. Accessed 29 December 2023.

Piore, Adam. "Beijing's Plan to Control the World's Data: Out-Google Google." Newsweek, 7 September 2022, https://www.newsweek.com/2022/09/16/beijings-plan-control-worlds-data-out-google-google-1740426.html. Accessed 31 January 2024.

Poe, Edgar Allan. Edgar Allan Poe: Selected Works: "The Business Man," "The Landscape Garden," "Maelzel's Chess Player," "The Power of Words". St Johns University Press, 1968.

Pollack, Andrew. "'Fifth Generation' Became Japan's Lost Generation." The New York Times, 5 June 1992, https://www.nytimes.com/1992/06/05/business/fifth-generation-became-japan-s-lost-generation.html. Accessed 28 December 2023.

Pomerleau, Dean A. "ALVINN: An Autonomous Land Vehicle in a Neural Network." 1988.

Population Pyramide. "Population of Japan 2060." PopulationPyramid.net, https://www.populationpyramid.net/japan/2060/. Accessed 3 February 2024.

Porter, Jon, and Alex Castro. "ChatGPT continues to be one of the fastest-growing services ever." The Verge, 6 November 2023, https://www.theverge.com/2023/11/6/23948386/chatgpt-active-user-count-openai-developer-conference. Accessed 26 December 2023.

Pritchett, Price, and Brian Muirhead. The Mars Pathfinder: Approach to "faster-better-cheaper" : Hard Proof from the NASA/JPL Pathfinder Team on how Limitations Can Guide You to Breakthroughs. Pritchett & Associates, 1998.

PWC. "What's the real value of AI for your business and how can you capitalise?" PwC, 2017, https://www.pwc.com/gx/en/issues/analytics/assets/pwc-ai-analysis-sizing-the-prize-report.pdf. Accessed 29 December 2023.

Quinlan, J. Ross. C4.5. Elsevier Science, 1993.

Rabaey, JM. "Brain-machine interfaces as the new frontier in extreme miniaturization." 2011 Proceedings of the European Solid-State Device Research Conference, 2011.

Rajaniemi, Hannu. The Quantum Thief. Tor Publishing Group, 2014.

Rashid, Rushdi, editor. Al-Khwārizmī: The Beginnings of Algebra. Saqi, 2009.

Redgrove, H. Stanley. Roger Bacon: The Father of Experimental Science and Medieval Occultism. Kessinger Publishing, LLC, 2010.

Rees, Martin J. Our final hour : a scientist's warning : how terror, error, and environmental disaster threaten humankind's future in this century on earth and beyond. Basic Books, 2004.

Reilly, Jessica, et al. "China's Social Credit System: Speculation vs. Reality." The Diplomat, 30 March 2021, https://thediplomat.com/2021/03/chinas-social-credit-system-speculation-vs-reality/. Accessed 26 December 2023.

Reynolds, Isabel, et al. "Weak Yen Unravels Japan's Quest for Foreign Workers." Bloomberg.com, 9 November 2022, https://www.bloomberg.com/news/articles/2022-11-09/weak-yen-unravels-japan-s-quest-for-foreign-workers. Accessed 28 December 2023.

Rinaudo, K. "A universal RNAi-based logic evaluator that operates in mammalian cells"." 2007.

River, Charles. The Viking Program: The History and Legacy of NASA's First Missions to Mars. Amazon Digital Services LLC - Kdp, 2019.

Rombach, Robin, et al. "High-Resolution Image Synthesis with Latent Diffusion Models - Computer Vision & Learning Group." 2022, https://ommer-lab.com/research/latent-diffusion-models/. Accessed 26 December 2023.

Roose, Kevin. "A.I. Poses 'Risk of Extinction,' Industry Leaders Warn." The New York Times, 30 May 2023, https://www.nytimes.com/2023/05/30/technology/ai-threat-warning.html. Accessed 29 December 2023.

Roose, Kevin. "Mr. Altman Goes to Washington, and Casey Goes on This American Life." The New York Times, 19 May 2023, https://www.nytimes.com/2023/05/19/podcasts/hard-fork-altman-yoel-roth.html. Accessed 26 December 2023.

Rosen, Rebecca J. "Google's Self-Driving Cars: 300000 Miles Logged, Not a Single Accident Under Computer Control." The Atlantic, 9 August 2012, https://www.theatlantic.com/technology/archive/2012/08/googles-self-driving-cars-300-000-miles-logged-not-a-single-accident-under-computer-control/260926/. Accessed 28 December 2023.

Rosen, Rebecca J. "Unimate: The Story of George Devol and the First Robotic Arm." The Atlantic, 16 August 2011, https://www.theatlantic.com/technology/archive/2011/08/unimate-the-story-of-george-devol-and-the-first-robotic-arm/243716/. Accessed 27 December 2023.

Rosenblatt, Frank. "The Perceptron—a perceiving and recognizing automaton." Cornell Aeronautical Laboratory, 1957.

Rothblatt, Martine Aliana. From Transgender to Transhuman: A Manifesto on the Freedom of Form. Martine Rothblatt, 2011.

Rozum Robotics. "Coffee by a Robot Barista Becoming Next-Door Reality." Rozum Robotics, https://rozum.com/coffee-robot-barista/. Accessed 6 February 2024.

RSF. "2023 World Press Freedom Index – journalism threatened by fake content industry." 2023 World Press Freedom Index – journalism threatened by fake content industry, 2023, https://rsf.org/en/2023-world-press-freedom-index-journalism-threatened-fake-content-industry. Accessed 29 December 2023.

Rutherford, Adam. Control: The Dark History and Troubling Present of Eugenics. WW Norton, 2022. Accessed 29 December 2023.

Ryan, Cy. "Nevada issues Google first license for self-driving car." Las Vegas Sun, 7 May 2012, https://lasvegassun.com/news/2012/may/07/nevada-issues-google-first-license-self-driving-ca/. Accessed 28 December 2023.

Safran, Linda, editor. Heaven on Earth: Art and the Church in Byzantium. Pennsylvania State University Press, 1998.

Sage, Alexandria. "Meet Waymo, Google's self-driving car company." 2016, https://www.reuters.com/article/google-waymo-autonomous-idINKBN142227/. Accessed 28 December 2023.

Sale, Kirkpatrick. Rebels Against The Future: The Luddites And Their War On The Industrial Revolution: Lessons For The Computer Age. Basic Books, 1996.

Salus, Peter H., editor. The ARPANET Sourcebook: The Unpublished Foundations of the Internet. Peer-to-Peer Communications, 2007.

Samuel, Arthur. "Some Studies in Machine Learning Using the Game of Checkers." IBM Journal of Research and Development., 1959.

Sánchez Domingo, Rafael. "Las leyes de Burgos de 1512 y la doctrina jurídica de la conquista." Dialnet, 2012, https://dialnet.unirioja.es/servlet/articulo?codigo=4225030. Accessed 9 January 2024.

Schaut, Scott. Robots of Westinghouse, 1924-today. Scott Schautt, Mansfield Memorial Museum, 2006.

Schneider, Susan. "The Philosophy of 'Her.'" 2014, https://archive.nytimes.com/opinionator.blogs.nytimes.com/2014/03/02/the-philosophy-of-her/?_php=true&_type=blogs&_r=0. Accessed 1 January 2024.

Schrödinger, Erwin. "Discussion of Probability Relations between Separated Systems." Mathematical Proceedings of the Cambridge Philosophical Society, 1935.

Schuh, Mari. Military Drones and Robots. Capstone, 2022. Accessed 28 December 2023.

Searle, John. "Minds, brains, and programs." Behavioral and Brain Sciences, 1980.

SETI Institute. "Drake Equation." SETI Institute, https://www.seti.org/drake-equation-index. Accessed 20 January 2024.

Several Governments. "The Bletchley Declaration by Countries Attending the AI Safety Summit, 1-2 November 2023." GOV.UK, 1 November 2023, https://www.gov.uk/government/publications/ai-safety-summit-2023-the-bletchley-declaration/the-bletchley-declaration-by-countries-attending-the-ai-safety-summit-1-2-november-2023. Accessed 25 December 2023.

Shachtman, Noah. "Darpa Preps Son of Robotic Mule." WIRED, 29 October 2008, https://www.wired.com/2008/10/bigdog-20/. Accessed 28 December 2023.

Shachtman, Noah. "First Armed Robots on Patrol in Iraq (Updated)." WIRED, 2 August 2007, https://www.wired.com/2007/08/httpwwwnational/. Accessed 28 December 2023.

Sharp, Alan. A Grim Almanac of York. History Press, 2015.

Shead, Sam. "Amazon's Robot Army Has Grown by 50%." Business Insider, 3 January 2017, https://www.businessinsider.com/amazons-robot-army-has-grown-by-50-2017-1. Accessed 28 December 2023.

Shelley, Mary. Frankenstein (Masterpiece Library Edition). Peter Pauper Press, Incorporated, 2023.

Shor, Peter. "Algorithms for quantum computation: Discrete logarithms and factoring." Proceedings 35th Annual Symposium on Foundations of Computer Science. IEEE Comput. Soc. Press., 1994.

Shu, Catherine. "Google Acquires Artificial Intelligence Startup DeepMind For More Than $500M." TechCrunch, 26 January 2014, https://techcrunch.com/2014/01/26/google-deepmind/. Accessed 26 December 2023.

Silbert, Alex. "Mining in Space Is Coming." Milken Institute Review, 26 April 2021, https://www.milkenreview.org/articles/mining-in-space-is-coming. Accessed 28 December 2023.

Silva, Lucas, et al. "Baxter Kinematic Modeling, Validation and Reconfigurable Representation 2016-01-0334." SAE International, 5 April 2016, https://www.sae.org/publications/technical-papers/content/2016-01-0334/. Accessed 27 December 2023.

Simon, Herbert A. The Shape of Automation for Men and Management. Harper & Row, 1965.

Simon, Matt. "Meet Xenobot, an Eerie New Kind of Programmable Organism." WIRED, 13 January 2020, https://www.wired.com/story/xenobot/. Accessed 29 December 2023.

Singh, Ishveena, and Bruce Crumley. "DJI condemns use of its drones in the Russia-Ukraine war." DroneDJ, 22 April 2022, https://dronedj.com/2022/04/22/dji-drones-ukraine-russia-war/. Accessed 28 December 2023.

Singh, Pavneet, and Michael Brown. "China's Technology Transfer Strategy: How Chinese Investments in Emerging Technology Enable A Strategic Competitor to Access the Crown Jewels of U.S. Innovation." 2018, https://admin.govexec.com/media/diux_chinatechnologytransferstudy_jan_2018_(1).pdf. Accessed 27 December 2023.

Skinner, B.F. About behaviorism. Knopf Doubleday Publishing Group, 1976.

Slaby, James R. "Robotic Automation Emerges as a Threat to Traditional Low-Cost Outsourcing." HfS Research, 2012.

Slingerlend, Brad. "A semiconductor 'cold war' is heating up between the U.S. and China." MarketWatch, 2 June 2020, https://www.marketwatch.com/story/a-semiconductor-cold-war-is-heating-up-between-the-us-and-china-2020-06-01. Accessed 27 December 2023.

Small, Zachary. "Sarah Silverman Sues OpenAI and Meta Over Copyright Infringement." The New York Times, 10 July 2023, https://www.nytimes.com/2023/07/10/arts/sarah-silverman-lawsuit-openai-meta.html. Accessed 26 December 2023.

Smibert, Angie. Space Robots. Abdo Publishing, 2018.

Smith, Gregory A. "About Three-in-Ten U.S. Adults Are Now Religiously Unaffiliated." Pew Research Center, 14 December 2021, https://www.pewresearch.org/religion/2021/12/14/about-three-in-ten-u-s-adults-are-now-religiously-unaffiliated/. Accessed 29 December 2023.

Smith, Lamar. "The Climate-Change Religion - WSJ." The Wall Street Journal, 23 April 2015, https://www.wsj.com/articles/the-climate-change-religion-1429832149. Accessed 29 December 2023.

Snow, Shawn. "Pentagon successfully tests world's largest micro-drone swarm." Military Times, 9 January 2017, https://www.militarytimes.com/news/pentagon-congress/2017/01/09/pentagon-successfully-tests-world-s-largest-micro-drone-swarm/. Accessed 28 December 2023.

Sokol, Joshua. "Meet the Xenobots, Virtual Creatures Brought to Life (Published 2020)." The New York Times, 6 April 2020, https://www.nytimes.com/2020/04/03/science/xenobots-robots-frogs-xenopus.html. Accessed 29 December 2023.

Sommers, Jaime, creator. The Bionic Woman. 1976. ABC, 1976-78.

Sophocles. Oedipus Rex, Oedipus the King. Translated by E. H. Plumptre, Digireads.com Publishing, 2005.

Soros, George, et al. "Can Democracy Survive the Polycrisis? by George Soros." Project Syndicate, 6 June 2023, https://www.project-syndicate.org/commentary/can-democracy-survive-polycrisis-artificial-intelligence-climate-change-ukraine-war-by-george-soros-2023-06. Accessed 29 January 2024.

Sozzi, Brian. "Beyond Meat founder and CEO: The arc of history is on our side." Yahoo Finance, 28 December 2023, https://finance.yahoo.com/news/beyond-meat-founder-and-ceo-the-arc-of-history-is-on-our-side-220153945.html. Accessed 31 December 2023.

Spielberg, Steven, director. A.I. 2011.

Stanford. "Stanford's Robotic History." STANFORD magazine, 2014, https://stanfordmag.org/contents/stanford-s-robotic-history. Accessed 27 December 2023.

State of California. "California Consumer Privacy Act (CCPA)." California Department of Justice, State of California, 2018, https://oag.ca.gov/privacy/ccpa. Accessed 26 December 2023.

State of Virginia. "The Virginia Consumer Data Protection Act." Attorney General of Virginia, 2021, https://www.oag.state.va.us/consumer-protection/files/tips-and-info/Virginia-Consumer-Data-Protection-Act-Summary-2-2-23.pdf. Accessed 26 December 2023.

Statt, Nick, and Angelo Merendino. "Former Google exec Anthony Levandowski sentenced to 18 months for stealing self-driving car secrets." The Verge, 4 August 2020, https://www.theverge.com/2020/8/4/21354906/anthony-levandowski-waymo-uber-lawsuit-sentence-18-months-prison-lawsuit. Accessed 28 December 2023.

Stokel, Chris. "ChatGPT Replicates Gender Bias in Recommendation Letters." Scientific American, 22 November 2023, https://www.scientificamerican.com/article/chatgpt-replicates-gender-bias-in-recommendation-letters/. Accessed 26 December 2023.

Stone, Brad. Gearheads: the turbulent rise of robotic sports. Simon & Schuster, 2003.

Stone, Maddie. "Stephen Hawking and a Russian Billionaire Want to Build an Interstellar Starship." Gizmodo, 12 April 2016, https://gizmodo.com/a-russian-billionaire-and-stephen-hawking-want-to-build-1770467186. Accessed 30 December 2023.

Straebel, Volker, and Wilm Thoben. "Alvin Lucier's Music for Solo Performer: Experimental music beyond sonification." 2014.

Strong, John. Relics of the Buddha. Princeton University Press, 2004.

Stross, Charles. Accelerando. Ace Books, 2006.

Suleyman, Mustafa. The Coming Wave: Technology, Power, and the Twenty-first Century's Greatest Dilemma. Crown, 2023.

Sutter, John D. "How 9/11 inspired a new era of robotics." CNN, 7 September 2011, http://edition.cnn.com/2011/TECH/innovation/09/07/911.robots.disaster.response/index.html. Accessed 28 December 2023.

Swade, Doron. The Difference Engine: Charles Babbage and the Quest to Build the First Computer. Viking, 2001.

Swayne, Matt. "Google Claims Latest Quantum Experiment Would Take Decades on Classical Computer." The Quantum Insider, 4 July 2023, https://thequantuminsider.com/2023/07/04/google-claims-latest-quantum-experiment-would-take-decades-on-classical-computer/. Accessed 29 December 2023.

Tabeta, Shunsuke, and staff writers. "China trounces U.S. in AI research output and quality." Nikkei Asia, 16 January 2023, https://asia.nikkei.com/Business/China-tech/China-trounces-U.S.-in-AI-research-output-and-quality. Accessed 27 December 2023.

Taranovich, Steve. "Autonomous automotive sensors: How processor algorithms get their inputs - EDN." EDN Magazine, 5 July 2016, https://www.edn.com/autonomous-automotive-sensors-how-processor-algorithms-get-their-inputs/. Accessed 28 December 2023.

Tarasov, Katie. "Amazon's 100 drone deliveries puts Prime Air far behind Alphabet's Wing and Walmart partner Zipline." CNBC, 18 May 2023, https://www.cnbc.com/2023/05/18/amazons-100-drone-deliveries-puts-prime-air-behind-google-and-walmart.html. Accessed 28 December 2023.

Tegmark, Max. Life 3.0: Being Human in the Age of Artificial Intelligence. Knopf Doubleday Publishing Group, 2018.

Tesauro, Gerald. "Temporal Difference Learning and TD-Gammon." Backgammon Galore, 1995, https://www.bkgm.com/articles/tesauro/tdl.html.

Thompson, Nicholas, and Ian Bremmer. "The AI Cold War That Threatens Us All." WIRED, 23 October 2018, https://www.wired.com/story/ai-cold-war-china-could-doom-us-all/. Accessed 26 December 2023.

Thomson, Iain. "Google human-like robot brushes off beating by puny human – this is how Skynet starts." The Register, 24 February 2016, https://www.theregister.com/2016/02/24/boston_dynamics_robot_improvements/. Accessed 28 December 2023.

Thorndike, Edward L. Animal Intelligence: Experimental Studies. FB&C Limited, 2015.

Timmers, Paul, and Sarah Kreps. "Bringing economics back into EU and U.S. chips policy | Brookings." Brookings Institution, 20 December 2022, https://www.brookings.edu/articles/bringing-economics-back-into-the-politics-of-the-eu-and-u-s-chips-acts-china-semiconductor-competition/. Accessed 27 December 2023.

Todes, Daniel. Ivan Pavlov: Exploring the Animal Machine. Oxford University Press, USA, 2000.

Tominaga, Suzuka. "Robot helps spread Buddhist teachings at a Kyoto temple | The Asahi Shimbun: Breaking News, Japan News and Analysis." 朝日新聞デジタル, 8 April 2023, https://www.asahi.com/ajw/articles/14861909. Accessed 28 December 2023.

Trabish, Herman K. "Real-time pricing, new rates and enabling technologies target demand flexibility to ease California outages." Utility Dive, 13 September 2022, https://www.utilitydive.com/news/real-time-pricing-new-rates-and-enabling-technologies-target-demand-flexib/631002/. Accessed 18 January 2024.

Tran, Minh, et al. "A lightweight robotic leg prosthesis replicating the biomechanics of the knee, ankle, and toe joint." 2022, https://www.science.org/doi/10.1126/scirobotics.abo3996.

Triolo, Paul, et al. "Translation: Cybersecurity Law of the People's Republic of China (Effective June 1, 2017)." DigiChina, 2017, https://digichina.stanford.edu/work/translation-cybersecurity-law-of-the-peoples-republic-of-china-effective-june-1-2017/. Accessed 27 December 2023.

Tucker, Patrick. "The US Military Is Chopping Up Its Iron Man Suit For Parts." Defense One, 7 February 2019, https://www.defenseone.com/technology/2019/02/us-military-chopping-its-iron-man-suit-parts/154706/. Accessed 28 December 2023.

Tucs, A., et al. "Generating ampicillin-level antimicrobial peptides with activity-aware generative adversarial networks." ACS Omega, 2020. Accessed 29 December 2023.

Tuller, David. "Dr. William Dobelle, Artificial Vision Pioneer, Dies at 62 (Published 2004)." The New York Times, 1 November 2004, https://www.nytimes.com/2004/11/01/obituaries/dr-william-dobelle-artificial-vision-pioneer-dies-at-62.html. Accessed 29 December 2023.

Turing, Allan. "Computing Machinery and Intelligence: Can machines possess the capacity for thought?" COMPUTING MACHINERY AND INTELLIGENCE, vol. LIX, no. 236, 1950.

Turing, Allan. "On Computable Numbers, with an Application to the Entscheidungsproblem." Proceedings of the London Mathematical Society,, 1937.

UN. "Explainer: How AI helps combat climate change." UN News, 3 November 2023, https://news.un.org/en/story/2023/11/1143187. Accessed 29 December 2023.

UNDP. "Sophia the Robot is UNDP's Innovation Champion for Asia-Pacific." YouTube, 22 November 2017, https://www.youtube.com/watch?v=BwFEFQUDNTs. Accessed 29 December 2023.

Unger, J. Marshall. The fifth generation fallacy: why Japan is betting its future on artificial intelligence. Oxford University Press, 1987.

US Government. "Children's Online Privacy Protection Rule ("COPPA")." Federal Trade Commission, 1998, https://www.ftc.gov/legal-library/browse/rules/childrens-online-privacy-protection-rule-coppa. Accessed 26 December 2023.

Vapnik, Vladimir, and Corinna Cortes. "Support-vector networks." 1995.

Vaswani, Ashish, et al. "Attention Is All You Need." arXiv, 12 June 2017, https://arxiv.org/abs/1706.03762. Accessed 26 December 2023.

Velasco, JJ. "Historia de la tecnología: El ajedrecista, el abuelo de Deep Blue." Hipertextual, 22 July 2011, https://hipertextual.com/2011/07/el-ajedrecista-el-abuelo-de-deep-blue. Accessed 26 December 2023.

Verma, Pranshu, and Gerrit De Vynck. "ChatGPT took their jobs. Now they're dog walkers and HVAC techs. - The Washington Post." Washington Post, 2 June 2023, https://www.washingtonpost.com/technology/2023/06/02/ai-taking-jobs/. Accessed 26 December 2023.

Vidal, Jaques. "Toward Direct Brain-Computer Communication." Annual Review of Biophysics and Bioengineering, 1973.

Vincent, James. "AI art tools Stable Diffusion and Midjourney targeted with copyright lawsuit." The Verge, 16 January 2023, https://www.theverge.com/2023/1/16/23557098/generative-ai-art-copyright-legal-lawsuit-stable-diffusion-midjourney-deviantart. Accessed 26 December 2023.

Vincent, James. "Google drops waitlist for AI chatbot Bard and announces oodles of new features." The Verge, 10 May 2023, https://www.theverge.com/2023/5/10/23718066/google-bard-ai-features-waitlist-dark-mode-visual-search-io. Accessed 26 December 2023.

Vincent, James. "The lawsuit that could rewrite the rules of AI copyright." The Verge, 8 November 2022, https://www.theverge.com/2022/11/8/23446821/microsoft-openai-github-copilot-class-action-lawsuit-ai-copyright-violation-training-data. Accessed 26 December 2023.

Vincent, James. "Pretending to give a robot citizenship helps no one." The Verge, 30 October 2017, https://www.theverge.com/2017/10/30/16552006/robot-rights-citizenship-saudi-arabia-sophia. Accessed 28 December 2023.

Vincent, James, and Sam Byford. "DeepMind's Go-playing AI doesn't need human help to beat us anymore." The Verge, 18 October 2017, https://www.theverge.com/2017/10/18/16495548/deepmind-ai-go-alphago-zero-self-taught. Accessed 29 December 2023.

Vincent, James, and Jimin Chen. "Facebook's head of AI really hates Sophia the robot (and with good reason)." The Verge, 18 January 2018, https://www.theverge.com/2018/1/18/16904742/sophia-the-robot-ai-real-fake-yann-lecun-criticism. Accessed 29 December 2023.

Vincent, James, and Chris Jung. "Robot makers including Boston Dynamics pledge not to weaponize their creations." The Verge, 7 October 2022, https://www.theverge.com/2022/10/7/23392342/boston-dynamics-robot-makers-pledge-not-to-weaponize. Accessed 28 December 2023.

Vincent, James, and Lintao Zhang. "Putin says the nation that leads in AI 'will be the ruler of the world.'" The Verge, 4 September 2017, https://www.theverge.com/2017/9/4/16251226/russia-ai-putin-rule-the-world. Accessed 28 December 2023.

Vinge, Vernor. Rainbows End. Tor Publishing Group, 2007.

Walia, Simran. "How Does Japan's Aging Society Affect Its Economy?" The Diplomat, 13 November 2019, https://thediplomat.com/2019/11/how-does-japans-aging-society-affect-its-economy/. Accessed 28 December 2023.

Walker, Marley. "Meet the Competitors Who Dominated the First Cyborg Olympics." WIRED, 25 October 2016, https://www.wired.com/2016/10/people-prosthetics-first-cyborg-olympics/. Accessed 29 December 2023.

Wallace, R., et al. "First results in robot road-following." International Joint Conference on Artificial Intelligence, 1985.

Walsh, Fergus. "New Versius robot surgery system coming to NHS." BBC, 3 September 2018, https://www.bbc.com/news/health-45370642. Accessed 28 December 2023.

Wanner, Mark. "600 trillion synapses and Alzheimers disease." The Jackson Laboratory, 11 December 2018, https://www.jax.org/news-and-insights/jax-blog/2018/December/600-trillion-synapses-and-alzheimers-disease. Accessed 29 December 2023.

Warcwick, Kevin. "(PDF) Thought communication and control: A first step using radiotelegraphy." ResearchGate, 2004, https://www.researchgate.net/publication/3350379_Thought_communication_and_control_A_first_step_using_radiotelegraphy. Accessed 29 December 2023.

Warrick, Joby, and Cate Brown. "Covid helped China secure the DNA of millions, spurring arms race fears - Washington Post." The Washington Post, 21 September 2023, https://www.washingtonpost.com/world/interactive/2023/china-dna-sequencing-bgi-covid/. Accessed 31 January 2024.

Warwick, Kevin. "The Application of Implant Technology for Cybernetic Systems." 2003.

Watkins, Christopher, and Peter Dayan. "Q-learning." 1989.

Waugh, Rob. "Sex robots 'could cause birth rate crisis' as men opt for plastic lovers instead." Metro UK, 28 January 2019, https://metro.co.uk/2019/01/28/sex-robots-cause-birth-rate-crisis-men-opt-plastic-love-slaves-instead-humans-8402895/. Accessed 29 December 2023.

Webster, Graham. "Full Translation: China's 'New Generation Artificial Intelligence Development Plan' (2017)." DigiChina, 1 August 2017, https://digichina.stanford.edu/work/full-translation-chinas-new-generation-artificial-intelligence-development-plan-2017/. Accessed 26 December 2023.

WEF. "China or America: who's winning the race to be the AI superpower?" The World Economic Forum, 3 November 2017, https://www.weforum.org/agenda/2017/11/china-vs-us-who-is-winning-the-big-ai-battle/. Accessed 27 December 2023.

WEF. "Recession and Automation Changes Our Future of Work, But There are Jobs Coming, Report Says." The World Economic Forum, 20 October 2020, https://www.weforum.org/press/2020/10/recession-and-automation-changes-our-future-of-work-but-there-are-jobs-coming-report-says-52c5162fce/. Accessed 29 December 2023.

WEF. "World Economic Forum's 'Framework for Developing a National Artificial Intelligence Strategy." World Economic Forum, 4 October 2019, https://www.weforum.org/publications/a-framework-for-developing-a-national-artificial-intelligence-strategy/. Accessed 6 February 2024.

Weiland, J. "Retinal prosthesis." Annual Review of Biomedical Engineering, 2005.

Weinberg, BH. "Large-scale design of robust genetic circuits with multiple inputs and outputs for mammalian cells." 2017.

Wessling, Brianna. "How Boston Dynamics is developing Spot for real-world applications." The Robot Report, 3 March 2023, https://www.therobotreport.com/how-boston-dynamics-is-developing-spot-for-real-world-applications/. Accessed 28 December 2023.

Whitehead, Alfred North, and Bertrand Russell. Principia Mathematica. Rough Draft Printing, 1910.

Whitfield, Robert. Effective, Timely and Global, 9 November 2017, https://www.oneworldtrust.org/uploads/1/0/8/9/108989709/gg_ai_report_final.pdf. Accessed 13 February 2024.

Wiggins, Chris, and Matthew L. Jones. How Data Happened: A History from the Age of Reason to the Age of Algorithms. WW Norton, 2023.

Willett, Francis R.,, et al. "A high-performance speech neuroprosthesis - PMC." NCBI, 23 August 2023, https://www.ncbi.nlm.nih.gov/pmc/articles/PMC10468393/. Accessed 29 December 2023.

Williams, Roger. The Metamorphosis of Prime Intellect. Lulu.com, 2003.

Wilson, Daniel H. Robopocalypse: A Novel. Knopf Doubleday Publishing Group, 2012.

Winograd, Terry. "Procedures as a Representation for Data in a Computer Program for Understanding Natural Language." 1971.

Woo, Stu. "China Wants a Chip Machine From the Dutch. The U.S. Said No." The Wall Street Journal, 17 July 2021, https://www.wsj.com/articles/china-wants-a-chip-machine-from-the-dutch-the-u-s-said-no-11626514513. Accessed 27 December 2023.

Wood, Christopher. The bubble economy. Atlantic Monthly Press, 1992.

World Bank. "Sustained policy support and deeper structural reforms to revive China's growth momentum." World Bank, 14 December 2023, https://www.worldbank.org/en/news/press-release/2023/12/14/sustained-policy-support-and-deeper-structural-reforms-to-revive-china-s-growth-momentum-world-bank-report. Accessed 27 December 2023.

World Population Review. "Debt to GDP Ratio by Country 2024." World Population Review, https://worldpopulationreview.com/country-rankings/debt-to-gdp-ratio-by-country. Accessed 6 February 2024.

Wu, Yi. "China's Interim Measures to Regulate Generative AI Services: Key Points." China Briefing, 27 July 2023, https://www.china-briefing.com/news/how-to-interpret-chinas-first-effort-to-regulate-generative-ai-measures/. Accessed 27 December 2023.

Wylie, Christopher. Mindf*ck: Cambridge Analytica and the Plot to Break America. Random House Publishing Group, 2019.

Xie, Z. "Multi-input RNAi-based logic circuit for identification of specific cancer cells." 2011.

Yale. "Overview < Colón-Ramos Lab." Yale School of Medicine, https://medicine.yale.edu/lab/colon_ramos/overview/. Accessed 29 December 2023.

Yang, Zeyi. "China just announced a new social credit law. Here's what it means." MIT Technology Review, 22 November 2022, https://www.technologyreview.com/2022/11/22/1063605/china-announced-a-new-social-credit-law-what-does-it-mean/. Accessed 26 December 2023.

Yao, Deborah. "DeepMind Co-founder: The Next Stage of Gen AI Is a Personal AI - DeepMind Co-founder: The Next Stage of Gen AI Is a Personal AI." AI Business, 17 October 2023, https://aibusiness.com/nlp/deepmind-co-founder-the-next-stage-of-gen-ai-is-a-personal-ai. Accessed 29 December 2023.

Yuan, Han, et al. "Negative Covariation between Task-related Responses in Alpha/Beta-Band Activity and BOLD in Human Sensorimotor Cortex: an EEG and fMRI Study of Motor Imagery and Movements." NCBI, 19 October 2009, https://www.ncbi.nlm.nih.gov/pmc/articles/PMC2818527/. Accessed 29 December 2023.

Yudkowsky, Eliezer S. "Coherent Extrapolated Volition." Singularity Institute for Artificial Intelligence, 2004.

Zelikman, Eric, et al. "STaR: Bootstrapping Reasoning With Reasoning." arXiv, 28 March 2022, https://arxiv.org/abs/2203.14465. Accessed 28 December 2023.

Zhang, Jiawei. "Basic Neural Units of the Brain: Neurons, Synapses and Action Potential." arXiv, 30 May 2019, https://arxiv.org/abs/1906.01703. Accessed 29 December 2023.

Zhang, Jiayu. "China's Military Employment of Artificial Intelligence and Its Security Implications — THE INTERNATIONAL AFFAIRS REVIEW." THE INTERNATIONAL AFFAIRS REVIEW, 16 August 2023, https://www.iar-gwu.org/print-archive/blog-post-title-four-xgtap. Accessed 31 January 2024.

Zukerman, Wendy. "Hayabusa 2 will seek the origins of life in space." New Scientist, 18 August 2010, https://www.newscientist.com/article/dn19332-hayabusa-2-will-seek-the-origins-of-life-in-space/. Accessed 28 December 2023.

Authors

Pedro URIA-RECIO

Pedro Uria-Recio (born in Bilbao in 1980) is a Spanish business executive and an expert in AI currently residing in Southeast Asia.

Pedro was the Chief Analytics and AI Officer at True Corporation, a prominent telecommunications company in Thailand. There, he oversaw analytics and AI initiatives for the digital segment of the business, leading a unit that utilized telecommunications data to develop corporate solutions in advertising, credit scoring, and consumer intelligence. Additionally, he serves as a visiting lecturer in AI for business at Chulalongkorn University in Bangkok.

Before his tenure at True Corporation, Pedro was Vice President of Analytics at Axiata, a digital and telecommunications conglomerate operating in six Asian markets. Previously, he worked as a management consultant at McKinsey & Company, focusing on telecommunications and financial services.

Pedro has a strong interest in entrepreneurship and served as an Entrepreneur in Residence at Antler, a venture capital studio in Singapore. He is also an official member and contributor to the Forbes Technology Council and has been a speaker at two TEDx events. He was recognized as one of the Top 100 Global Innovators in Data and Analytics in 2020 and received the Cloudera Industry Transformation Award in 2019.

Pedro holds an MBA from the University of Chicago Booth School of Business and a telecommunications engineering degree from the School of Engineers in Bilbao.

Randy McGraw

James Randall *"Randy"* McGraw (born in Pittsburgh, Pennsylvania, US, in 1968) is an American multinational business executive and Permanent Resident of Japan.

A recognized expert in Strategy and Business Development in the digital space, he has served as the Senior Director of BD at Hughes Electronics/DIRECTV and Head of BD at Singtel's Group Digital Life. Following several years as the Managing Director of Altus Capital's digital division (an IFC affiliate company), where his team built prop-tech and social commerce platforms, he led BD for Amazon in Japan, where he built Prime's largest global 3rd-party distribution deal (with NTT DoCoMo) and integrated mobile commerce partnerships with KDDI and Softbank. Most recently, he served as Chief Commercial Officer at True Digital Group, the digital arm of Thailand's largest telco. He remains an active angel investor and consultant in Southeast Asia and Japan through his company, M2 Ventures.

Randy holds a BS in Economics and Public Finance from the Wharton School of Business at the University of Pennsylvania and a Master's Certificate in Strategy from Cornell University. He is preparing to pursue a Doctorate in Ministry from the Asian Theological Seminary.

Humanity Interlaces with AI.

AI is our new mind. Robotics, our new body. How are we becoming a new species at the intersection of carbon and silicon?

AI Gets Exponential.

Artificial General Intelligence. Humanoids and cyborgs. Synthetic biology. Quantum computing. Mind emulation. How will they unfold?

AI Authoritarianism Looms.

AI will render truth obsolete, freedom redefined, and job scarcity imminent. Can we still shape AI for the benefit of all?

Geopolitics Supercharged.

Super Intelligence will be worshiped. China and America will clash over their views on AI. Politics will be centered on species identities.

Humanity's Greatest Epic.

From mythology to Kubrick. From Aristotle to Sam Altman. From Leonardo to Boston Dynamics. From today to Superintelligence.

https://www.machinesoftomorrow.ai/

Made in the USA
Monee, IL
08 April 2024

ef150233-30e9-4cc5-a3c0-ef33ec913f85R01